Adorno:
A Critical Reader

BLACKWELL CRITICAL READERS

The *Blackwell Critical Readers* series presents a collection of linked perspectives on continental philosophers, and social and cultural theorists. Edited and introduced by acknowledged experts and written by representatives of different schools and positions, the series embodies debate, dissent, and a committed heterodoxy. From Foucault to Derrida, from Heidegger to Nietzsche, *Blackwell Critical Readers* address figures whose work requires elucidation by a variety of perspectives. Volumes in the series include both primary and secondary bibliographies.

Adorno:
A Critical Reader

Edited by
Nigel Gibson and Andrew Rubin

BLACKWELL
Publishers

Copyright © Blackwell Publishers Ltd 2002

First published 2002

2 4 6 8 10 9 7 5 3 1

Blackwell Publishers Inc.
350 Main Street
Malden, Massachusetts 02148
USA

Blackwell Publishers Ltd
108 Cowley Road
Oxford OX4 1JF
UK

Library of Congress Cataloging-in-Publication Data

Adorno : a critical reader / edited by Nigel C. Gibson and Andrew Rubin.
p. cm.—(Critical readers)
Includes bibliographical references and index.
ISBN 0-631-21248-5—ISBN 0-631-21249-3 (pbk.: alk. paper)
1. Adorno, Theodor W., 1903–1969. I. Gibson, Nigel C. II. Rubin, Andrew.
III. Series.
B3199.A34 A34 2001
193—dc21

00-065804

British Library Cataloguing in Publication Data
A CIP catalogue record for this book is available from the British Library.

Typeset in $10\frac{1}{2}$ on $12\frac{1}{2}$ pt Bembo
by Best-set Typesetter Ltd., Hong Kong
Printed in Great Britain by Antony Rowe Ltd, Chippenham, Wiltshire

This book is printed on acid-free paper

Contents

Contributors

Russell Berman is a Professor and Chair of German Studies at Stanford University. He is the author of several books, including *Cultural Studies of Modern Germany: History, Representation and Nationhood* (1993) and *Enlightenment or Empire: Colonial Discourse in German Culture* (1998).

Mauro Bozzetti is a research fellow in the Department of Philosophy and Education at the University of Urbino, Italy. He is the author of *Hegel and Adorno: die kritische Funktion des philosophische Systems* (1996) and has also written on Plato, Kafka, and Karl Kraus in the *Rivista di Filosofia Neoscholastica*, the *Rivista di Esthetica*, and *Humanities*.

Nigel Gibson is Assistant Professor at the Institute of Liberal Arts and Interdisciplinary Studies at Emerson College in Boston, where he teaches philosophy and postcolonial studies, and a research associate at Harvard University and at Brown University. He is editor of *Rethinking Fanon* (1999) and co-editor of *Contested Terrains and Constructed Categories: Africa in Focus* (2001).

Miriam Hansen is the Ferdinand Schevill Distinguished Service Professor in the Humanities in the Department of English and a member of the Committee on Cinema Studies at the University of Chicago.

Andreas Huyssen is the Villard Professor of Germanic Languages at Columbia University. He is the author of several books, including *After the Great Divide* (1986) and *Twilight Memories* (1995).

Douglas Kellner is George F. Kneller Professor of Philosophy of Education at the University of California, Los Angeles. He is the author or editor of numerous books, including *The Postmodern Turn* (1997) and *Articulating the Global and the Local* (1997).

Max Paddison is Professor of Music at the University of Durham, England. He is the author of *Adorno's Aesthetics of Music* (1993) and *Adorno, Modernism and Mass Culture: Essays on Critical Theory and Music* (1996).

Henry W. Pickford is the translator and editor of Theodor Adorno's *Critical Models: Interventions and Catchwords*. He has also published essays on Benjamin, Adorno, Mandelshtam, and Celan.

Anson Rabinbach is Professor of History and Director of the Program in European Cultural Studies at Princeton University. His most recent book is *In the Shadow of Catastrophe: German Intellectuals Between Apocalypse and Enlightenment* (1997). Since 1973 he has been an editor of *New German Critique*.

Andrew Rubin is a doctoral candidate in the Department of English and Comparative Literature at Columbia University. He is the co-editor of *The Edward Said Reader* (2000).

Jennifer Rycenga is Associate Professor of Comparative Religious Studies at San José State University. She is co-editor, with Marguerite Waller, of *Frontline Feminisms: Women, War, and Resistance* (2000).

Edward W. Said is University Professor of English and Comparative Literature at Columbia University. He is the author of nineteen books, including *Orientalism*, which was nominated for the National Book Critics' Circle Award, *Culture and Imperialism*, and *Representations of the Intellectual*.

Rose Rosengard Subotnik is Professor of Music at Brown University, and has written extensively on music in relation to Adorno's writings and other critical theory. The author of *Deconstructive Variations* (1997), Subotnik is generally credited with having initiated the study of Adorno in American musicology.

Lou Turner teaches urban studies and social theory at North Central College, Illinois. He is the author of a number of articles on philosophy and social theory and is the author of *The Marxist Humanist Statement on the Black Dimension* (2002).

Samuel Weber is Professor of English and Comparative Literature at UCLA. He is the author of numerous books, including, most recently, *The Return to Freud*.

Krzysztof Ziarek is Associate Professor of English at the University of Notre Dame. He is the author of *Inflected Language: Toward a Hermeneutics of Nearness. Heidegger, Levinas, Stevens, Celan* (1994) and *The Historicity of Experience: Modernity, the Avant-Garde, and the Event* (2000).

Acknowledgments

The idea of collecting a series of critical essays on the writings of Theodor Adorno owes its origins to the stimulation and the encouragement of Edward W. Said, Andreas Huyssen, and Russell Berman whose lectures and seminars on Adorno were memorable moments for both of us at Columbia University. We wish to thank all who have given of their time to read portions of the manuscript and have engaged with us over the issues at stake. Particular thanks to Gil Anidjar, Moustafa Bayoumi, Nicole Barrett, Patrick Deer, Kate Josephson, Teodros Kiros, John Lawhead, Joseph Massad, Diana Reese, Inez and Johnny Rogers, Lecia Rosenthal, Matthew Specter, and, above all, the late Eloise Segal. Indiana University Press kindly gave us their permission to reprint Andreas Huyssen's "Adorno in Reverse" from *After the Great Divide: Modernism, Mass Culture, Postmodernism* (1986); as did the editors and publishers of *New German Critique* to reprint Miriam Hansen's "Mass Culture as Hieroglyphic Writing: Adorno, Derrida, Kracauer" (*New German Critique* 56 [Spring-Summer 1992]: 43–73). In the final stages, the book benefited enormously from the meticulous attention of Mary Traveras and the patience of Simon Eckley and Beth Remmes. Most of all, we would like to thank all of our contributors whose reflections on Adorno made this book imaginable in the first place.

Introduction: Adorno and the Autonomous Intellectual

Nigel Gibson and
Andrew Rubin

Few other intellectuals have captured so much critical attention in the late twentieth century as Theodor W. Adorno. As more of Adorno's writings, lectures, letters, and radio addresses have become available in English in recent years, both Adorno and his work have become the subject of reconsideration. The German publication of Adorno's complete works, as well as a three-volume collection that documents the Frankfurt School's relationship to the student movement, has ignited a discussion about the roles and responsibilities of the public intellectual.[1]

Prominent critics ranging from Edward Said to Judith Butler have looked to Adorno as a model of the independent, critical thinker. In his 1993 Reith Lectures for the BBC, Edward Said declared that "Adorno was a quintessential intellectual hating *all* systems, whether on our side or theirs, with equal distaste" (1994a: 55). For Judith Butler, a professor of rhetoric at the University of California at Berkeley, Adorno represented a mode of criticism, which, at a time when the alternatives of resistance have become less visible, was the source of legitimacy. Citing Adorno as an example of the intellectual who provides "the intellectual resources we must preserve as we make our way toward the politically new," Butler argued that Adorno's often dense and labyrinthine prose forces readers to reflect on the power of language to shape the world (*New York Times* March 20, 1999: A15).

Yet in spite of Adorno's renewed appeal, his own work has become, as Slavoj Žižek argues, part of an industry. Adorno studies have experienced somewhat of a boom. According to the MLA bibliography, since 1995 there have been over 100 articles published on his work. For a thinker who is mostly quoted in the popular press for his remark "to write poetry after Auschwitz is barbaric," his fragmentary and aphoristic writings in *Minima Moralia* and elsewhere have rendered Adorno perhaps among the more quoted intellectuals of the twentieth century. Simple declarative sentences such as his statement that "man is the ideology of dehumanization" have become the fetishized marks of political commitment.

Adorno's status as a figure of the lonely, intransigent, and fiercely independent intellectual is in many ways symptomatic of a conjuncture of forces that confront scholars and critics in America and Europe after the collapse of communism in Eastern Europe and the former Soviet Union in 1989. Indeed, in spite of the hopes that the revolutions of 1989 would engender a free and open "civil society," the imposition of free-market capitalism has simply narrowed the terms of intellectual and public debate on a global scale. With the corporatization of universities, the ascendancy of think-tanks and institutes, the often coercive contingencies of government and nongovernmental funding, in addition to the global flow of the academic commodity circuit, the space of the critic has narrowed considerably. Legislation such as the University–Small Business Patent Act has in effect contributed to the industrialization of the university. While Masao Miyoshi and others have decried this process, Adorno, much like his aesthetic, holds out irreconcilably against the reifications of capitalist society.

Independent critics have in recent years turned to Adorno's writings as a model and an unexhausted alternative to the encroaching powers of the market. In many respects, Adorno's position as an autonomous thinker who refuses both the dictates of the party and the market has kept alive the often embattled space of the intellectual in the late twentieth century. As Fredric Jameson remarked in 1990, Adorno "may turn out to have been the analyst of our own period" (1990: 5).

Theodor Weisengrund Adorno was born on September 11, 1903, in Frankfurt am Main to a bourgeois family. His father was a proudly assimilated German Jew and a successful wine merchant. Theodor's mother, née Maria Cavelli, was the daughter of a German Catholic singer and a French army officer. The Frankfurt of Adorno's youth was a relatively tolerant metropolis with a vibrant cultural life and little overt antisemitism.

As a boy, Theodor devoted a great deal of his energies to the study and appreciation of music. Both his mother and his aunt were accomplished musicians, and together they sang and played the piano, imparting to Adorno an unshakeable passion for Western classical music. At the Hoch Conservatory, Theodor studied under Bernhard Sekles, renowned for his instruction of Paul

Hindemith, and developed into a rather competent pianist impressing Thomas Mann with his performance of Beethoven's difficult Opus 111 (Jay, 1984: 25). As Susan Buck-Morss observed, Adorno's immersion in music at a young age "proved far more influential than any social or religious orientation" (1977: 2).

When Adorno was not practicing the piano or listening to his mother and aunt perform, he focused his attention on the study of modern philosophy. Through his family contacts, he had met Sigfried Kracauer, one of Weimar's leading cultural and film critics, who took a personal interest in Adorno's education. Although Kracauer was fourteen years older, together they spent their evenings reading Goethe's *Elective Affinities* and Kant's *Critique of Pure Reason*. Kracauer's approach to Kant was unconventional. They read Kant not only as a work of epistemology, but also as a work of history that revealed the conditions of thought and knowledge in late eighteenth-century Germany (Wiggershaus, 1994: 67). "Under Kracauer's guidance," Adorno recalled, "I experienced [Kant's *Critique of Pure Reason*] . . . as a kind of coded text from which the historical spirit could be read, with the vague expectation that in doing so one could acquire something of truth itself" (*Notes to Literature* I 58–9).

By the time Adorno graduated from Kaiser Wilhelm Gymnasium in 1921, his writing career had already begun. He had published two articles, one on Expressionism and the other on an opera written by his teacher Bernhard Sekles. After graduating from the Gymnasium, he then enrolled at Johann Wolfgang Goethe University, where he took courses on music, philosophy, sociology, and psychology. His interests were primarily philosophical and influenced by the seminars of Hans Cornelius, an eccentric leftist and neo-Kantian, whose readings straddled religion and philosophy. Cornelius imparted to Adorno a passion for Husserl whose phenomenological writings were then in vogue. It was during one of Cornelius' seminars on Husserl in 1922 that Adorno was introduced for first time to Max Horkheimer. Together the two took courses on Gestalt psychology with Adhemar Gelb, and they began one of the most productive intellectual friendships of the century (Jay, 1984: 27).

Adorno experienced the crisis of Weimar Germany in purely philosophical and musical terms. He read and absorbed Ernest Bloch's *Utopia Spirit*, Rosenzweig's *The Star of Redemption*, Georg Lukács' *Theory of the Novel* and *History and Class Consciousness*. He displayed little concern for the revolutionary politics of the KPD (Communist Party) or even the SPD (Social Democratic Party), and did not share Lukács' belief that the proletariat was the agent of social change. For Adorno, politics was an abstraction connected with a certain kind of Western, polyphonic music embodied in the operas of Arnold Schönberg and Alban Berg, whom he first met at the Frankfurt

Festival of the Universal German Music Society in 1924. When Adorno heard Berg's opera *Wozzeck*, he was deeply gripped by it and followed Berg to Vienna in January 1925.

Adorno held a lasting fascination for Arnold Schönberg whose new music had, in Adorno's view, revolutionized the technique of musical composition. In Vienna, he sought out Schönberg's circle and took up the study of musical composition with Alban Berg. He studied piano under Eduard Steuermann and had every intention of becoming either a musician or a music critic. Beginning in 1925, he wrote a number of articles in avant-garde music journals such as *Musikblätter des Anbruch* and *Pult und Takstock* where he defended the new Viennese music and the compositions of Schönberg, Anton Webern, Alban Berg, and Hanns Eisler. Yet Vienna did not live up to his expectations. Schönberg had grown increasingly aloof, and when the circle of musicians and writers who frequented the composer's salons gradually dissolved, Adorno returned to Frankfurt.

In Frankfurt, Adorno revisited his academic work with the intention of lecturing at the University. By the end of 1927, he completed his *Habilitationsschrift*. Entitled "The Concept of the Unconscious and the Transcendental Theory of the Mind," the work was a study of Freud, whose increasingly popular writings Adorno had discovered in Vienna. The work was a Marxist reading of Freud and Kant that explained Freud's concept of the unconscious as the ideological expression of economic conditions in post-Hapsburg Austria. His professor, Hans Cornelius, was unimpressed. Cornelius felt that Adorno's deference to Marxism was complacent and unoriginal. Cornelius wrote that Adorno had "simply repeated what . . . he knows from my own lectures and books, although it is embellished with a great many words" (Wiggershaus, 1994: 82).

Cornelius' rejection encouraged Adorno to reconsider his lasting ambition to become a music critic, the prospects for which were better in Berlin than in Frankfurt. With a generous stipend from his father, he traveled frequently to Berlin, where he enjoyed the company of Walter Benjamin, Ernst Bloch, Bertolt Brecht, and his lover Gretel Karpus. He immersed himself in his music criticism, writing essays like "The Curves of the Needle" which addressed the ways the emerging recording industry and the gramophone had transformed the experience of listening to music ("the diffuse and atmospheric comfort of the small but bright gramophone sound corresponds to the humming gaslight and is not entirely foreign to the whistling teakettle of bygone literature," he wrote ["Curves" 605]). He reviewed Berg's opera *Wozzeck*, his first piece of "Marxian" music criticism ("the suffering of every individual has entered into the class struggle and turned itself against the continuance of the bourgeois order" [Buck-Morss, 1977: 211 n231]). He emphasized what he saw as Schönberg's revolutionary technique in articles like "On the Twelve-Tone Technique" (1929) and "Reaction and Progress" (1930). But despite his concerted efforts to gain full-time work as a music critic, his hopes were repeatedly dashed. The *Berliner Zeitung* had no need for him. In 1929, however, the editors of *Musikblätter des Anbruch* invited him to join its editorial board, which he gladly did.

Adorno's musical writings challenged both academic and journalistic conventions. They combined an interest in philosophy, Marxism, and his one political passion: atonal music. But Adorno's chances of becoming a lecturer in Frankfurt quickly improved when Cornelius resigned his post in 1929. The theologian Paul Tillich had replaced him, and with Tillich as chair of philosophy, Adorno shifted his focus to another subject that arguably was geared more toward Tillich's interests. His second *Habilitationsschrift*, entitled *Kierkegaard: Construction of the Aesthetic*, was an academic success. Both his readers – Tillich and Max Horkheimer – saw the work on the fashionably rediscovered Danish existentialist philosopher as promising. Though Horkheimer gave it a mixed review, the work was enough to give Adorno the opportunity to present his first lecture as a *Privatdozent* in philosophy at the University of Frankfurt and the Institute for Social Research in May 1931.

The Institute for Social Research had been founded nearly a decade earlier to establish an independent forum that connected Marxism to the scholarly investigation of the material conditions of society. The Institute, which was started by Felix Weil and Kurt Gerlach, explored the Marxist study of political economy. Under Horkheimer, who had assumed what was half-jokingly referred to as the "dictatorship of the directorship" in January 1931, the institute's Marxist emphasis shifted to the field of culture. For the Institute, socialism still remained an "unredeemable promissory note, of little more practical value than that held by Weimar's worthless currency in the year of the Institute's founding," Michael Sprinker later observed (1999: 120–1). Among Horkheimer's first actions as head was to invite Adorno to deliver his inaugural lecture on the subject of "The Actuality of Philosophy." Dedicated to Walter Benjamin, whom he had known since 1923, Adorno's talk was a critique of epistemology and Lukácsian totality in Benjaminian terms: "Whoever chooses philosophy as a profession today must first reject the illusion that earlier philosophical enterprises began with: that the power of thought is sufficient to grasp the totality of the real. No justifying reason could rediscover itself in a reality whose order and form suppresses every claim to reason; only polemically does reason present itself to the knower as total reality, while only in traces and ruins is it prepared to hope that it will ever come across correct and just reality" (120).

On January 30, 1933, on the very day Adorno's Kierkegaard book was published, Hitler's National Socialist Party seized control of the Reichstag. Two months later, the German authorities shut down the Institute on the grounds that it expressed "tendencies hostile to the state" (Jay, 1973: 29). The police confiscated the Institute's extensive library, and on April 13, Horkheimer, Tillich, and Karl Mannheim were dismissed from their teaching posts in Frankfurt. On September 11, his thirtieth birthday, Adorno was stripped of academic credentials as well. Within the year, almost all of the Institute's members had gone into exile. At first, Adorno was extremely reluctant to leave Germany, thinking that he faced little danger if he remained. As his friend Leo Löwenthal recalled, "we had to drag him almost physically [out of Germany] . . . [H]e just could not believe anything would happen to the son of Oskar Wiesengrund" (1984: 159).

By the spring of 1934, Adorno eventually did go into exile, but he did not follow the majority of the Institute's affiliates to Geneva where Horkheimer had regrouped. Instead, Adorno decided to go to Oxford, where he became an advanced student at Merton College, a setting he found asphyxiating and archaic. In a letter to Walter Benjamin, he compared his Oxford experience to the "life of a mediaeval scholar 'in Cap and Gown'" (*Correspondence* 55). Yet England was good to Adorno. He completed a book on Husserl, he wrote a number of articles for the Institute's journal *Zeitschrift für Sozialforschung*, and began what is perhaps among his most politically and culturally significant work, *In Search of Wagner*.

In Search of Wagner was Adorno's political and cultural response to the Nazis' appropriation of Richard Wagner's operas. Wagner was symbolically of central importance to the Third Reich's expression of national identity. "Of all of Wagner's musical dramas the *Meistersinger* stands out as the most German," Joseph Goebbels declared on German radio during an intermission of its performance. "It is simply the incarnation of our national identity. In it is contained everything that conditions and inspires the German cultural soul" (Hanisch, 1992: 201). Selections of *Die Meistersinger* were broadcast nationally on Hitler's forty-fourth and fiftieth birthdays, and occasionally played at party meetings. Hitler is even reported to have removed the mayor of Leipzig because he was unfamiliar with Wagner's work (Hanisch, 1992: 201). Adorno's *In Search of Wagner* was an attempt to grasp the origins and brute appropriation of Wagner's opera by fascism. Adorno also explored how Wagner's technique was the reified expression of the culture industry. *In Search of Wagner* was "not only . . . an account of the birth of fascism out of the spirit of the *Gesamtkunstwerke*, but also . . . an account of the birth of the culture industry *in* the most ambitious high art of the nineteenth century" (Huyssen, 1975: 35).

In spite of Adorno's critique of the totalitarian elements of Wagner's opera, Adorno's anti-fascism was never translated into a real or even an entertained engagement with the popular fronts of the 1930s. At Oxford, Adorno showed little interest in efforts to aid Republican forces in the Spanish Civil War. He remained aloof and his ties with the Oxford community did not reach beyond the Oxford Philosophical Society. Instead, he immersed himself in his writings and exerted a great deal of his intellectual energies in his correspondence with his friend Walter Benjamin.

Both Benjamin and Adorno were prolific letter-writers, and their correspondence to one another expressed a spirited attempt to grasp the relationship between art and politics. For Benjamin, the technological advances in printing and film-making had meant that the work of art was rapidly losing its aura and could become a source of both artistic and political expression. "For the first time in world history," Benjamin wrote, "mechanical reproduction emancipates the work of art from the parasitical dependency on ritual . . . and begins to be based on another practice: politics" (1973: 218). Gripped by Benjamin's discussion, Adorno refuted his claims. The aura of works of art was not disappearing because of their reproduction, Adorno maintained, but because they fulfilled their own formal and technical laws. For example, Adorno argued, the gramophone did not necessarily entail the end of music's aesthetics, it simply altered the experience of listening to it. Art's autonomy was not necessarily compromised by its reproduction. "[You] neglect a fundamental experience which daily becomes increasingly evident to me in my musical work," Adorno wrote Benjamin, "that precisely the uttermost consistency in the pursuit of technical laws of autonomous art actually transforms this art itself, and instead of turning it into a fetish or a taboo, brings it that much closer to a state of freedom" (*Correspondence* 129). For Adorno, works of art possessed a hope that he was unwilling to ever give up.

Just as the work of art struggled against the pressures of society, so too did Adorno resist the idea of joining Horkheimer's Institute, which had relocated to New York in 1934. All along, Adorno had harbored the illusion that his exile was a temporary phase in which he could complete his work. For him, moving to America signified the end of his political wish to return to Germany. He had little fondness for the United States; he didn't care for its jazz, and thought that America was a barren wasteland. As he later wrote in *Minima Moralia* "the shortcoming of the American landscape is not so much as romantic illusion would have it, the absence of historical memories, as that it bears no traces of the human hand. This applies not only to the lack of arable land, the uncultivated woods often no higher than scrub, but above all to the roads" (48). Furthermore, Adorno perceived academic life in the US as dangerously specialized, conducive to a corporate mindset that he vigorously wished to avoid throughout his years of exile. In a letter to Leo Löwenthal, Adorno warned of the risks entailed by narrowing his intellectual pursuits to his long-standing passion for music: "Specialization . . . has its dangers, particularly in the isolated situation we find ourselves" (quoted in Löwenthal, 1984: 161).

On a visit to New York in 1937, Horkheimer managed to persuade Adorno to work at the Princeton Radio Project, a position that he had procured for him from Paul Lazarsfeld. From its outset, the Princeton experience disconcerted Adorno. The project, whose mandate was to examine the "essential value of radio to all types of listeners" (Wiggershaus, 1994: 239), was housed in an abandoned brewery in Newark, New Jersey, which Adorno likened to a "Kafka Nature Theatre in Oklahoma" (*Critical Models* 218). Directed by Hadley Cantril, a psychologist at Princeton, and Frank Stanton, who was a former research director for Columbia Broadcasting Systems (CBS), the Project's goal was, in Cantril's words, "to try to determine eventually the role of radio in the lives of different types of listeners, the value of radio to people psychologically, and the various reasons why they like it" (Wiggershaus, 1994: 239).

Adorno found the social-scientific and empirical methods anathematic and confining. He complained bitterly about polling listening habits and saw little value in its method. Adorno's wariness with the project turned out to be well-founded. The data collected in Newark would indirectly go on to have commercial applications and contribute to the very standardization of life that he and Horkheimer would later inveigh against in the *Dialectic of Enlightenment*.[2] Adorno was not entirely complacent toward the American social-scientific research methods. Largely as a result of Adorno's intransigence and unwillingness to acquiesce in the project's assumptions, the Rockefellers discontinued their funding in the summer of 1940.

In 1940, Theodor and Gretel Adorno had expected Walter Benjamin to join them in New York, where the latter had been given a position at the Institute for Social Research. "I am quite silly with happiness and constantly wonder in what order we should show you New York's attractions, so that you will also like it here among the barbarians," Gretel Adorno wrote Benjamin (quoted in Habermas, 1997: 120). Yet Benjamin never made it. With the manuscript of *The Arcades Project* bundled under his arm and wheezing from the grueling ascent up the mountain trail across the Pyrenees, Benjamin was told that his visa was invalid. He returned to the small Spanish village of Port Bou and swallowed a handful of cyanide tablets after telling a friend: "I would like you to pass on my thoughts to my friend Adorno and to explain to him the situation in which I have now found myself. I no longer have enough time to write all those letters I would dearly have written"

(*Correspondence* 342). Benjamin's suicide devastated Adorno; it was a tragic shock that remained with him throughout his life.

With the Princeton Project defunct and Benjamin buried, the Adornos left New York and moved to Pacific Palisades, a suburb of Hollywood popular with other German exiles like Horkheimer, Thomas Mann, Hans Eisler, and Bertolt Brecht. Adorno's California years were a productive period replete with the rewards of intellectual collaboration. He worked with the composer Hans Eisler on a study called *Composing for Films* (1947). He consulted with Thomas Mann who was then writing *Doctor Faustus* (1947), a novel that put Adorno's ideas about Schönberg into literary form. He contributed to *The Authoritarian Personality*, an empirical study of the psychology of authoritarianism and antisemitism. Moreover, he began to work more intensively with Max Horkheimer on their major book, the *Dialectic of Enlightenment*.

The *Dialectic of Enlightenment* was a somber, wan account of how Enlightenment reason had lost its liberating potential in the age of monopoly capitalism. "The program of Enlightenment was the disenchantment of the world," Adorno and Horkeimer wrote. Tracing the Enlightenment concept of reason to Homer's *Odysseus*, Horkheimer and Adorno saw Odysseus' cunning as the emergence of an instrumental, administrative, and dominating form of reason that was expressed in the ideology of the cultural industry. The terms of instrumental reason – exchange and equivalence – were, in their opinion, the groundwork for reification. But whereas Georg Lukács had held on to the promise that the proletariat was the agent of change, Adorno and Horkheimer offered no political alternative. Against the backdrop of Stalinism, fascism, the culture industry, Adorno and Horkheimer held out little hope that reason – *ratio* – could serve as an emancipatory force. As Jürgen Habermas later wrote, "it becomes intelligible how the impression could . . . get established in the darkest years of the Second World War that the last sparks of reason were being extinguished from this reality and had left the ruins of a civilization in collapse without any hope" (1987: 117).

Horkheimer and Adorno's excoriation of mass culture was not entirely novel. The New York intellectuals had issued similar lamentations before. In 1944, for example, Dwight McDonald wrote "Theory of Mass Culture" in which he bemoaned the way in which "the Lords of kitsch . . . exploit the cultural needs of the masses in order to make a profit and . . . maintain class rule" (quoted in Wald, 1987: 223). The sociologist C. Wright Mills had also arrived at equally critical conclusions about the masses. Adorno and Horkheimer had no monopoly on their grim diagnosis of mass culture. The question was how the dictates of the market were to be resisted. For Adorno, the struggle was not to be found in wild-cat strikes or mass demonstrations; his political commitment remained to music.

Adorno considered *The Philosophy of New Music* (1949) an extension of his work with Horkheimer. A study of Schönberg and Stravinsky, the book expressed Adorno's contention that music, or a certain kind of music – atonal music – negated society. Schönberg's demonic twelve-tone compositions, Adorno argued, had freed the musical work from the hand of the composer, yet tragically enslaved it to the bleak constructivist rigors of its form. Schönberg's use of the twelve-tone system, Adorno observed, thus articulated and resisted the predicament of the work of art in face of its reification. In *The Philosophy of New Music* he wrote, "The basis of the isolation of radical modern music is not its asocial, but precisely its social substance. It expresses its concern through its pure quality, doing so all the more emphatically, the more purely this quality is revealed; it points out the ills of society, rather than sublimating those ills into a deceptive humanitarianism that had already been achieved in the present. This music is no longer an ideology" (131).

If Schönberg's atonal row compositions resisted the techniques of mass art, the fate of the exile had embodied the fractured experience of the individual. In *Minima Moralia: Reflections from Damaged Life* (1951), Adorno's second major work of his California period, he offered an aphoristic, almost cryptic account of the philosophy of exile. Written on the occasion of Horkheimer's fiftieth birthday, *Minima Moralia* expressed Adorno's homelessness in a fragmentary form that itself suggested how deeply exile had ruined his experience. For Adorno, the essay form could not capture the complexities of the life of exile.

The fate of the exile was not without its ironies. When the war ended in 1945, Adorno had mixed feelings about returning to West Germany. He confessed to Horkheimer that he was more immersed with his own concerns "than with the course of world history, which those concerns are supposed to be resisting" (Wiggershaus, 1994: 381). Accustomed to life in the United States, he and Gretel became US citizens in 1948. Nevertheless, Adorno's reservations about ending his years of exile proved short-lived. Miffed by an American publisher's decision to reject *The Philosophy of New Music*, Adorno felt that the US did not appreciate the value of his work. In 1949 he returned to West Germany, after deciding that his energies were most effectively spent teaching and rebuilding postwar German culture under the aegis of the Institute.

By the 1950s the Institute had relocated to Frankfurt, after Horkheimer had made arrangements ironically with the same German officials who had presided over its shut-down in the 1930s (Wiggershaus 399). The political tone of the postwar Institute of Social Research was substantially different from its predecessor. "As early as 1951, members of the Institute who remained in America noted a subtle change in its orientation," writes Martin

Jay (1984: 47). Adorno and the Institute devoted many of their energies to developing the sociological study of postwar German society and culture. Adorno's political engagement thus assumed the form of a sociological activism that relied on empirical methods. His major collaborative project of those years grew out of *The Authoritarian Personality* (1950). Entitled *Group Experiment*, the study was a sociological examination of the attitudes of the German population toward the US government, the Third Reich, democracy, and the Holocaust. He saw his sociological research as a continuous critique of fascist cultural politics. His concern was how to build and sustain the democratic institutions of the postwar Republic of Germany. As he later wrote, he found "the survival of National Socialism *within* democracy to be potentially more menacing than the survival of fascist tendencies *against* democracy (*Critical Models* 90). According to the results of the *Group Experiment*, which attempted to gauge subjects' predilections for authoritarianism along what was called the "A–Scale," Adorno's fears were well-founded. Antisemitism remained a widespread phenomenon after the war. Many in Konrad Adenauer's West Germany displayed a disturbing ignorance of the realities of the Holocaust, and a sizable minority continued to express positive opinions for Nazism.

Psychoanalysis bridged Adorno's interest in philosophy and sociology. Erich Fromm and Herbert Marcuse's writings on Freud – about whom Adorno had written in his first *Habilitationsschrift* – offered Adorno a way to stress the importance of the German past as well as to raise awareness about it. Adorno's prescription for the latent political expression of fascism and antisemitism was mass psychotherapy. Short of that, he thought "education must transform itself into sociology . . . It must teach about the societal forces that operate beneath the surface of political forms" (*Critical Models* 203).

In July 1957, Adorno at last achieved the academic recognition that had been denied him over the years. The news was a great relief for a scholar who had undergone so much dislocation throughout his life. He was promoted to full professor with a chair in both philosophy and sociology at the University of Frankfurt and became head of the Institute for Social Research. After his promotion, he finally and officially broke ranks with positivist and empirical research. In several essays – "Sociology and Empirical Research" (1957), "Teamwork in Social Research" (1957), and "Opinion Delusion Society" (1961) – he systemically articulated what he clearly always thought problematic about empiricism. He declared "culture is precisely the very condition that excludes a mentality that would wish to measure it." His critique of positivism instituted a major split within German sociology, which achieved its fullest expression in his debate with Karl Popper in Tübingen in 1961.

The repudiation of positivism and empirical research owed as much to Adorno's academic success as to his growing sense of his own importance as a public intellectual no longer having to rely on the authority of "empirical" evidence to articulate his critique of society and culture. By the late 1950s, Adorno had become increasingly visible and was gradually emerging from behind Horkheimer's eclipse. Adorno frequently delivered radio talks, and on a few occasions he even appeared on television – a medium that he took on in essays like "Prologue to Television" and "Television as Ideology." His reputation grew in direct proportion to the publication of his works. *Prisms: Cultural Criticism and Society*, which contained essays on the importance of dialectic criticism, appeared in 1955; *Dissonances* in 1956, *Notes on Literature* in 1958, *Tone Configurations* in 1959, *Mahler* in 1960, *Introduction to the Sociology of Music, Interventions, The Loyal Music Coach, Quasi una Fantasia* all in 1963.

He also remained deeply involved in the avant-garde music scene, which enjoyed the support of a number of institutes in West Germany, such as the Darmstadt International Vacation Courses on New Music, which he attended regularly during the summers. There he heard the Stockhausen's *Zeitmasse, Gruppen, Kontackte*, as well as Boulez's *Marteau san maître*. He developed and expanded his analysis of music and returned to the importance of the question of Wagner and Schönberg's music, which, in the aftermath of war, took on an entirely different meaning as Schönberg's twelve-tone technique had been superseded by Anton Webern's serial music and the Viennese School. In "Vers une musique sociale" (1961) Adorno argued for the development of a *musique informelle* in which "deformation of rationalism that exits today would be abolished and converted into a true rationality. Only what is fully articulated in art provides the image of an undeformed and hence free humanity" (318–19).

No longer confined to the empirical restraints of positivism and the constructions of typologies that had characterized much of his pragmatic work for the Institute in the 1950s, by the early 1960s Adorno began to extend his analysis of music to other mediums of cultural production like film. In a number of essays such as his "Résumé on the Culture Industry" (1963) as well as "Transparencies on Film" (1966), Adorno reconsidered his earlier thesis on universal manipulation.[3] He saw new possibilities and gravitated closer to some of the claims that Benjamin had made about the surrealists.

Ironically, just as Adorno was reevaluating the possibilities offered by a cultural avant-garde, the emerging student movement was demanding that he lend his support to student actions against the war in Vietnam. Yet Adorno was unwilling to provide the analysis that students insisted on. Unlike other members of the Frankfurt School, Adorno spoke only infrequently of the student teach-ins, sit-ins, and strikes that had shaken German universities after 1966, disagreeing with his friends Herbert Marcuse and Jürgen Habermas about the importance of student actions. He expressed even less sympathy for antiwar protesters and the struggle for national liberation in Vietnam. And to the dismay of their readers, he and Horkheimer at first refused to reprint *Dialectic of Enlightenment*, doing so only after student leaders distributed it in mimeograph. Georg Lukács charged that Adorno had checked into the "'Grand Hotel Abyss' . . . equipped with every comfort" (1971: 3).

Adorno viewed the events of the 1960s through his experience of the 1930s and 1940s. Most of his critical declarations denounced authoritarianism, which had become for him associated with antisemitism. As a public figure Adorno defined his relation to society as an opposition to what he saw as the authoritarian elements in culture and politics. In April 1968, for example, Adorno attacked the Bundestag's proposal to grant itself emergency powers and suspend basic civil liberties. That same month he delivered a lecture in Berlin on "Late Capitalism or Industrial Society?" which many of his followers had expected would make sense of the incendiary political realities of the day. He spoke briefly and approvingly of the students' "resistance to blind conformism," but offered them only the enigmatic observation that the triumph of "society's growing urge to destroy itself . . . remains to be seen." To the leaders of the student movement these remarks were frustratingly opaque. The League of German Socialist Students attacked him for political quietism and declared that he was guilty of "sophisticated despair." His own doctoral student Hans-Jürgen Krahl charged that "Adorno was not able to translate his private compassion for the wretched of this earth into a . . . theory for liberation of the oppressed." Activists repeatedly disrupted his lectures and often ridiculed him for his failure of nerve. After a talk on Goethe's *Iphigenia*, students mocked his commitment to Marxism by presenting him with a red, inflatable-rubber teddy bear (his friends called him "Teddy") (Wiggershaus, 1994: 621). "At one point in the 1960s he claimed that he couldn't take part in a political demonstration because he was too fat" (Gauss, 1999: 103). On January 31, 1969, Krahl and seventy-six other students occupied his Institute for Social Research, only to be arrested by the police, whom Adorno had summoned. Three months later, during a lecture on "An Introduction to Dialectical Thinking," three shirtless women members of the Socialist Students disrupted his talk, presenting him with a bouquet of lilies (Wiggershaus, 1994: 635).

Adorno cancelled his lectures on "Dialectical Thinking" and accused the students of self-interest and narcissism. He criticized their blind faith in collective struggle. "The question 'what is to be done?' as an automatic reflex to every critical thought before it is fully expressed . . . recalls the gesture of someone demanding your papers," he wrote in "Marginalia to Theory and Practice." He questioned the limits of their political solidarity with the Vietcong and argued that their bourgeois self-interest would in the end prevail. He wrote: "It would be difficult to believe that Vietnam is robbing anyone of sleep, especially since every opponent of colonial wars must know that the Vietcong . . . use Chinese methods of torture. Whoever imagines that as a product of this society he is free of the bourgeois coldness harbors illusions about himself as much as about the world; without such coldness one could not live" (274).

But the crux of Adorno's argument was that the students had confused practice with theory. He lamented that criticism had become identified with activism for its own sake. "One continually finds the word critique, if it is tolerated at all, accompanied by the word constructive," he wrote. "The insinuation is that only someone can practice critique who can propose something better than what is being criticized" ("Critique" 287). In "Resignation," Adorno wrote that "the uncompromisingly critical thinker, who neither signs over his consciousness nor lets himself be terrorized into action, is in truth the one who does not give in" (292).

Since his death in 1969, Adorno's writings have had a remarkably widespread influence on late twentieth-century Anglo-American intellectual culture. His work has affected nearly every field in the humanities. In many respects, Adorno's persistent appeal is bewildering. In the current intellectual atmosphere, Adorno does not necessarily speak directly to many of the preoccupations and predicaments of the late twentieth century. He was deeply Eurocentric and possessed no real knowledge of a world outside of Austria and Germany, let alone Europe. He wrote little about sexual difference. He rarely mentioned race. He possessed no theory of imperialism or colonialism. He admired a dissonant music that is today rarely performed. In spite of his difficulty, Adorno has appealed to precisely those fields that are motivated by a fundamental attention to the glaring absences in Adorno's body of work. Postcolonial theorists have located in *Minima Moralia* a theory of exilic thought and agency. Feminists have considered the implication of Adorno's negative dialectic for theories of sexual difference. While the canonization of Adorno clearly owes some debt to the exacting labor of translators who have continued to improve his English for non-German readers, there is obviously more to Adorno's reputation than the financial impetus of the academic publishing industry to corner the market in difficult dialectical Marxist criticism.

Adorno's writing arises out of a conjuncture of historical, cultural, and political circumstances in the late twentieth century. It intervenes at a site where Marxism, poststructuralism, and cultural studies collide. Placed at the core of twentieth-century dialectical Marxism, Adorno was seen to enact the contradictions that his writings denounced. More than any other Frankfurt School theorist, Adorno concentrated on the secret of commodity fetishism in the commodity form.

In spite of the ground swell of interest in Adorno's writings in the 1970s and after, he did not enjoy unmitigated praise. His writing presented a paralyzing aporia that posed an insurmountable opposition between theory and practice. He remained one of the most consistent and rigorous critical thinkers, yet any claim to social critique is at once undermined as the macabre dance of "praxis." Not only was praxis always equated with reification and commodification (Adorno, 1978: 166), but reason itself becomes instrumental. In contrast to Marcuse's *Reason and Revolution*, for example, *Dialectic of Enlightenment* charted the development of reason toward instrumentality. Reason was not only identified with capitalist techniques, but also subsumed by the irrational. Jürgen Habermas questioned the assumption of his former professor and attacked the political limitations of the *Dialectic of Enlightenment*. Habermas argued that Adorno's conception of enlightened reason was limiting. Adorno and Horkheimer expressed, Habermas wrote, an "uninhibited skepticism regarding reason, instead of weighing the grounds that cast doubt on this skepticism itself" (1987: 129).

Habermas's critique had consequences that went well beyond his own theory of communicative action. By establishing an interest in the epistemological foundations of critical theory, Habermas's critique helped open the way for poststructuralist readings of Adorno. Michael Ryan and Rainer Nägele, for example, attempted to trace a continuity between poststructuralism and critical theory. Works such as Adorno's *Negative Dialectics* were seen to affirm Jacques Derrida's concern with challenging the metaphysical foundations of Western logocentricism. Moreover, Adorno's work on Heidegger, *The Jargon of Authenticity*, placed Adorno within the poststructuralist canon and even seems to have attracted Derrida's interest (1992: 273). Yet Adorno was never fully integrated into French poststructuralist and postmodernist thought, though Lyotard did in fact write a short article on Adorno and Doctor Faustus. In the end, his French reception was uneventful. In an interview, Michel Foucault once lamented that he discovered the Frankfurt School's critique of Enlightenment reason too late to be incorporated into his own work on the organization of Western reason, *The Order of Things*.

Against the tide of French theory, however, the rise of cultural studies in the United States in the 1980s challenged Adorno's theory of mass culture. American cultural studies dismissed him as an elitist and a mandarin who had held little regard for popular culture and subcultural practices. The Gramscian thrust of cultural studies, which placed an emphasis on the role

played by counter-hegemonic forces, recapitulated Habermas's epistemological charges in terms of cultural resistance. Against this wave of criticism,
however, there arose an attempt to read Adorno against the grain.

It is out of this intellectual constellation of a renewed interest in Adorno
that the essays that make up *Adorno: A Critical Reader* emerged. As one of
the most important thinkers and intellectuals of mid-twentieth-century
Europe, Adorno is both one of the profoundest dialectical thinkers and one
of the deepest critics of dialectics. His dense, often difficult prose approaches
if not embodies a dialectical style that in all of its manifestations demands a
knowledge of the highest achievements of Western European philosophy and
art. His prose is the stuff of an intransigent intellectual. Throughout most of
his life and throughout his immense collection of writings, Adorno refused
to subordinate his theoretical project to immediate political or social action.

Adorno: A Critical Reader attempts to explore the continuing relevance and
force of Adorno's work through a consideration of his writings on aesthetics, music, philosophy, sociology, and politics. All of the essays in this volume
examine Adorno's writing against the dominant and traditional readings of
Adorno. If critical theory was initially developed to analyze political disappointments at the absence of revolutions in the Western Europe, the emergence of Stalinism in the East, and the victory of Nazism in Germany, the
difficulty that remains is to consider the continued relevance of Adorno's
work when many of the conditions to which his writings responded have
assumed different political, cultural, and economic forms. "How a rigorously
historicized Adorno might still strike sparks in literary, visual, and aesthetic
analysis at a time when print is losing its power as dominant medium, the
nation state is waning as guarantor of traditional high culture, and globalization creates ever more diverse and hybrid cultural formations remains a task
to be further explored," observes Andreas Huyssen in his new postscript to
"Adorno in Reverse" (see p. 51).

"Adorno in Reverse" is a reading of Adorno against the grain – that is to
say, from *Dialectic of Enlightenment* backward to the Wagner essay of 1937/8,
from Nazism back to Imperial Germany. Adorno's *In Search of Wagner* can be
read not only as an account of the birth of Nazism out of the spirit of the
Gesamtkunstwerk, but also as an account of the birth of the culture industry
in the most ambitious high art of the nineteenth century. Yet Huyssen adds
that this dialectic can be turned also toward postmodernity. Large parts of *In
Search of Wagner*, therefore, can be read as a modernist polemic against
postmodernism.

In this vein, Miriam Hansen reads Adorno against the grain of poststructuralist and cultural studies repudiations of Adorno. Adorno's conception
of spectatorship, Hansen argues in "Mass Culture as Hieroglyphic Writing,"

is deeply connected to the decoding of what Adorno, echoing Marx, calls the hieroglyphic script. For Hansen, the viewers of mass culture are not simply manipulated as passive consumers, but duped as "active readers." Mass culture prevents human beings from distinguishing their own wishes and needs from those imposed upon them. Hansen argues for a more dialectical approach that emphasizes the different valences of hieroglyphics in Adorno in the context of the development of different forms of cinema and video, thereby suggesting how cultural practices are not necessarily stable administrations of the culture.

While challenging many of Hansen's conclusions, Douglas Kellner questions whether Adorno's now classical critical theory continues to be useful for cultural studies and criticism today. In "Theodor W. Adorno and the Dialectics of Mass Culture," Kellner believes that we need a much more multidimensional approach to media culture, seeing in it more than an expression of ruling-class hegemony. Just as popular art might have progressive effects and provide a culture of political mobilization, art films do not necessarily provide artists with an element of autonomy. Because Adorno's aesthetic is undialectical we need to move beyond his intransigent oppositional stance, Kellner concludes. We are back to the old chestnut of Adorno and political praxis, but now in the context of new forms of struggle against globalized capitalism.

Adorno rejected judging art by its political message. It didn't much matter whether Schönberg was narrowly bourgeois or Webern was soft on the Nazis. Indeed, even the politics of the artist, and here we could include Adorno himself, were unimportant to the objectivity of the work of art. Whether this disconnection between theory and practice represents a dialectic for our postmodern age or not, doesn't the artwork's objectivity have to manifest itself politically at some stage?

Adorno's politics has always been a contested terrain. The right wing views him as a Marxist critic of capitalism; the Old Left finds him too close to American foreign policy; and the New Left is split between finding inspiration in his critique of capitalist culture and being disenchanted by his dismissal of practice. Adorno's preeminence after 1989 in many ways may be connected to the theoretical impotence of the North American Left to offer any fundamental challenge to US capitalist hegemony. Yet whether Adorno's Marxism is "dogmatic," as Peter Hohendahl argues (1995: 16), or "just what we need" as Fredric Jameson insists (1990: 5), Adorno's own attitude to Marx remains problematic. His equation of Marxism with a theory of production means that Marx's critique of political economy is seen in instrumental rather than revolutionary humanist terms. For Adorno there is a connection between Marx and Stalin which makes his "retreat from Marx" compelling.

Yet while Adorno can be considered among the first post-Marxists, his "retreat" from Marx can also be read as a retreat from a dialectical critique of capitalism.

Despite the "new world order" and postmodernity, on one hand, and the recent scholarly emphasis on location of the source of Adorno's method in the authentically autonomous artwork, on the other, the statement from Adorno's student, Hans-Jürgen Krahl, who had led some of the protests against Adorno in 1968, still concerns those looking for an engaged or activist scholarship. Ironically, the assertion also helps highlight the lure of Adorno today: "Adorno was incapable of transforming his private compassion toward the 'damned of the earth' into an organized partisanship of theory engaged in the liberation of the oppressed." Without such a theory it should be no surprise that Adorno called the police against the students who had taken over the Institute for Social Research building. He found the student's "actionism" akin to Nazi anti-intellectualism. For him the student's "praxis" was an unreflective, regressive, collective, knee-jerk activity that sacrificed independent thinking for immediate goals. Whatever the truth of Adorno's anti-authoritarian perspective against the left, the fact that he was "incapable" of articulating a theory of liberation is very much related to his negative dialectics. The notion of autonomy was the closest he got to "liberation." Given the importance that Adorno put on holding on to the last vestiges of autonomy in the age of state capitalism, it is not surprising that, as Russell Berman puts it in "Adorno's Politics," the priority of private life over the manipulated public sphere corresponded to "the project of maintaining a personal autonomy."

How, nonetheless, are we to understand Adorno's politics? Berman argues for a twofold approach, through art and criticism and through a directly political investigation. Disagreeing with Krahl and other activist critics, who argued that Adorno's politics are mired in the memory of defeat and the apparent futility of resistance to Hitler, Berman claims that resistance was a constant theme throughout his writings. While the discussion of Adorno's politics has often been "taboo," politics always lies behind those who shout their apoliticalism the loudest. After Adorno's return to Germany, his postwar writings reveal a more complex and concrete grasp of politics, argues Berman, as he addresses contemporary matters, especially coming to terms with Germany's antisemitic past. His explicit anti-Communism places him much closer to mainstream social democracy, even though he remains critical of its underlying state capitalist structure which threatens individual autonomy. The political conclusions are limited, notes Berman, to "'a democratic pedagogy' which could break the German repression of the past." Such self-limiting conceptions are a result of Adorno's almost Manichaean division between a (false or forced) "collectivism" and an (authentic and free) individual autonomy. "After Auschwitz" there can be no radical restructuring, only an aspiration that human beings become less brutal.

What is often overlooked is Adorno's involvement in the postwar politics of the German Democratic Republic, and his special concern with the resilience of Nazism and antisemitism. One of the most important aspects of his politics "after Auschwitz" is his concern that it should never happen again. In his postwar essays and radio broadcasts he questions denazification and wonders about the culture of National Socialism in the body politic of democracy. For Adorno, the social structure that created Nazism and the Nazi personality persists in the postwar West German democracy, making "Education after Auschwitz" not only a lecture but a political program and an expression of his fear. It was a fear that preoccupied him in 1968, as students were demonstrating on the streets. When Benno Ohnesorg was killed by a policeman, Adorno interpreted the event in terms of the legacy of Nazism. Watching Ohnesorg's killer on a television interview, Adorno reported that the tone and language reminded him of the Nazis. The policeman's statement that "a student lost his life . . . frighteningly similar to one heard in the trials against torturers in the concentration camps . . . victims are treated as examples of species."

Perhaps there is no better entrée into a reevaluation of Adorno's conception of political agency than through a reconsideration of his approach to the antisemitism. Anson Rabinbach and Lou Turner provide contrasting views. Rabinbach attempts to rethink the *Dialectic of Enlightenment* from the standpoint of the victims of antisemitism; Lou Turner argues that *The Authoritarian Personality* not only lacks social critique but its psychological rather than phenomenological approach strips the Jews of their historical agency.

In 1940 Adorno expressed a shift in perspective from the proletariat to the Jews, "All that we were used to seeing in terms of the proletariat has today shifted with terrible intensity to the Jews . . . who represent the counterpoint to power." For Adorno the Jew becomes the paradigmatic figure of the dialectic of enlightenment. Judaism prohibits mimesis, even banning the name G–d. Fascism is the mirror opposite. To protect the Jews became a symbol of humanity. The survival of the Jews, wrote Max Horkheimer in 1944, is "inseparable from the survival of culture." Antisemitism, Adorno argues, is not a result of modern racial thinking but emerges at the threshold of human evolution: it is "the desire for mimicry," rooted in fear. Modern antisemitism, therefore, is the last social refuge of the desire to return to the "mimetic practice of sacrifice."

After the Holocaust it is impossible to speak of a progressive secularization of dialectical reason as totality, progress, or an "immanence as endowed with a meaning radiated by an affirmative positive transcendence" (Adorno, 1973: 361). For Adorno, the Jews embody both the process of civilization and a refusal to accommodate to civilizing maxims, and thus antisemitism reveals the essential truth of the philosophy of non-difference. Though others have found Adorno's equation of Hegel's absolute negativity with the Nazi Holocaust a "vulgar reductionism" (Dunayevskaya, 1980: 173), Adorno fore-shadows the postmodernist debate about the representation of genocide and the production of the past after a holocaust.

While Lou Turner argues that the positivist methods apparent in Adorno's collaborative project, *The Authoritarian Personality*, necessarily entail a retreat from Marxism, Adorno's role as intellectual emerged out of his particular experience with some of the more staid and prosaic techniques of empirical sociological research in the United States. In "The Adorno Files" Andrew Rubin situates Adorno's experience of exile in terms of the Federal Bureau of Investigation's efforts to monitor the activities of the Frankfurt School. Drawing on evidence obtained under the Freedom of Information Act, Rubin shows how Adorno and other members of the Institute of Social Research were systematically observed by Federal agents during their exile in the United States. Against the trend to read Adorno in response to the human tragedies and political disasters of the mid-twentieth century, Rubin traces the emergence of Adorno as an "antipositivist intellectual" to the polit-ical pressure of anticommunist surveillance.

If irreconcilability represents Adorno's Leibnizian pedigree, there are two other philosophic tendencies in Adorno's theorization of art, one associated with Kant and the other with Hegel (see Geuss, 1998: 297). The Kantian emphasizes the autonomy of aesthetic judgments and the "irreducibility" of the aesthetic to other kinds of judgment (a point articulated in Edward Said's "Late Style"). The Hegelian viewed art as an aspect of Absolute Spirit which was the richest form of dialectic and the highest achievement of civilization. Art expresses something about truth and something about the world (sug-gested by Paddison).

Though Hegel saw philosophy itself, rather than an art whose time had past, as the highest expression of the Absolute, the great divide between Hegel and Adorno concerned the question of dialectical affirmation. For Adorno a truly radical work of art in our reified society is negative; that is to say, rather than giving us a positive or pleasurable identity with the world, the task of art is not to entertain but to make us uncomfortable. In religious terms, the world is evil and sinful and thus "any art that would make us comfortable in our fallen world . . . would be a quasi-moral failing" (Geuss, 1998: 300). This moral failing, expressed as a negative dialectic, can thus only be expressed in Kantian terms, as autonomy and formalism. The intelligibility of the late modern work of art depends on its inescapable formalism. The form expresses both fragmentation and autonomy.

The logics of disintegration are thereby expressed in the form of the work of art. The late modernist art work is condemned to be a fragment, and therefore, ironically, does not have what the immanence of its form claims it has. It is always by definition growing old. Its form also expresses autonomy; art's meaning is immanent in itself. It is its own end. Its authority is immanent and not found in an external source: "The truth content of artworks, as the negation of their existence, is mediated by them though they do not in any way communicate it" (Adorno, 1997: 133).

It is precisely the restlessness of *irreconcilable* opposites in Adorno's theory of "late style" that appeals to Edward Said. In "Adorno as Lateness Itself," Said argues that Adorno's writings, in particular his musical criticism, place an emphasis on the fragmented qualities and forms of late works. Despite Adorno's resistance to any scheme of assimilation, "he oddly reflects the predicament of ending without illusory hope or manufactured resignation," notes Said. Though late style conjures up an image of the death of the dialectic itself, Said considers Adorno's aesthetic inherently constitutive of an antithetical and oppositional theory as praxis.

Whereas for Said Adorno's theory of late style is preoccupied with resisting resolution, Max Paddison explores Adorno's theory of immanent criticism in terms of the role played by the mediating forces of society. Setting Adorno's aesthetic writing in the context of his polemics against empiricism and positivism, Paddison shows how the concept of mediation is central to the problem of the form in two respects: in relation to the individual musical work, and second, in terms of the material and technical developments which are mediated by society and culture. In contrast to Paddison's approach, Rose Subotnik proposes an alternative reading of Adorno indebted more to semiotics than to dialectics. By doing this she expresses another tendency, namely that Adorno can be reread, not simply against the grain, but against his own method. Adorno is not simply a source of dialectics or a critique of dialectics, but for Subotnik, Adorno's concept of mediation is best disclosed by understanding the relationship between music and society in terms of semiology. Although linguistics plays no role in Adorno's theory, the new musicology has set out on a path toward a poststructuralist conception of a "floating signifier"; ironically it was Adorno, more than anyone else, she thinks, who helped launch the problematic. Adorno entered new musicology bearing strong affinities to deconstruction.

The theoretical similarities with, say, deconstruction are premised on the idea that in the intellectual's reading of a work as autonomous there is a presupposition of a distinction between the critical activity of reading as a repetition, for a critical reading that necessitates reading a text more than once, and the reified reading as entertainment. Above all, Adorno's aesthetic theory is about the *reason* of art, its material logic and the claim of that logic. The late modern artwork is of necessity short with impending ending.

If a focus on late modernism brings to mind the highbrow context of Adorno's emphasis on autonomy, Adorno's modernist aesthetic fails to provide an adequate account of autonomy in the age of art's global reproducibility. Yet a focus on the political and economic forces that place the work of art at the service of government and corporate funding had been intimated by Adorno's colleague Frederic Pollock in his thesis on state capitalism. Centered on a critique of politics rather than a critique of political economy, on the market rather than alienated labor, Pollock saw power not profit as the motive force of the system. The regime that emerges looks quite a bit like an Orwellian *1984* where the proletariat are happy that the beer is cheap. Thus rather than intensifying contradictions, bringing new elements forward, state capitalism is able to assimilate them. Pollock's theory served as a basis for *Dialectic of Enlightenment*, and though it did not rule out autonomy, it clearly compromised it. Rooted in Marx's discussion of the commodity, Adorno went beyond Pollock, argues Nigel Gibson in "Rethinking an Old Saw." Adorno emphasized Marx's analysis of capital is the quest for identity, for sameness, not only in its indifference to the differentials of human labor and what it produces but in thought itself.

If Adorno saw art as providing an alternative to thought, it was his vision of philosophy that most closely approximated his theory of aesthetic. While Adorno never succumbed to an aesthetic view of philosophy, he did place a notable emphasis on the particularity of the object, which, as in the artwork, revealed not the totality of the concept but rather the structure of its truth content. Adorno's aesthetics thus cannot be understood outside of the legacy of his vision of dialectical criticism from which philosophy derives. In Adorno's "Cultural Criticism and Society," for example, it is dialectical criticism that is juxtaposed to the immanent and transcendental interpretations of culture. That Adorno is a dialectical critic is unquestioned. The very movement of his prose, the logical development within his essays, the progression of the terms of his critique are themselves relics of a dialectics held at a standstill on the printed page. The question remains, however, what model of dialectics does Adorno propose?

In contrast to this monadic structure, Mauro Bozzetti views Adorno's critique of Hegel within a Hegelian structure. Though Adorno might not have sufficiently emphasized how the Absolute grounds thinking rather than how thinking grounds the Absolute, in "Hegel on Trial" Bozzetti views Adorno's project as fundamentally a Hegelian one and notes the positive references to Hegel scattered throughout Adorno's writings, such as his declaration to Scholem that he remains "true to *The Phenomenology of Spirit.*" Though Adorno agrees with Hegel's idea of what philosophy should do, he could propose no philosophical solution because to do so would lead him back into the Hegelian identity of concept and reality that he resisted.

Despite Gibson's critique that, speculative moments to the contrary, Adorno flattens Hegel's dialectic, perhaps Adorno is better labeled a left Hegelian. Adorno agreed with aspects of Marx's critique that decried Hegel's transcendence as only conceptual. But where Marx wanted to stand Hegel on his feet and realize transcendence in reality, Adorno's negative dialectics implies that to sublate contradictions only results in a reified positive dialectic. In other words, as Gibson assesses in "Rethinking an Old Saw," Adorno reintroduces the division between understanding and change, between philosophy and praxis, that Marx tried to overcome.

While Adorno's theoretical emphasis on the "logics of disintegration" anticipated many poststructuralist critiques of agency and subjectivity, Adorno's work clashes with the orthodox poststructuralist genealogies of Nietzsche, Heidegger, and Derrida. Adorno gestures toward deconstruction, but as far as he does not want to abolish mediation and remains a critic of capitalism, he avoids poststructuralist affirmations which collapse the concepts of subject into object. In spite of the inherent resistance of Adorno's dialectics to deconstruction, Adorno's philosophical writings are often raised as an affirmation of dialectically-inflected poststructuralism. Thus, while Krzysztof Ziarek's essay "Radical Art" reintroduces political resistance as a "political otherwise," neither poststructuralism nor its detractors have solved the problem of Adorno's politics. For some, Adorno offered conceptual tools to get beyond poststructualism; others, emboldened by Michel Foucault's own admonition about the importance of the Frankfurt School, created an affinity between Foucault and Adorno; Nietzsche displaced Hegel. When it came to questions of the "subject" and agency, both were caught in the webs of power and reification. Across the disciplines, Adorno's resistance to the concept of a transformative human subject resonated with an intellectual pessimism. In contrast to Marcuse, Adorno had been skeptical of the new social movements and had emerged untarnished. In an appropriately Adornian twist, a thinker who had nothing to say about sexism, about racism, about imperialism and anticolonialist revolts, was taken up as an important critic of identity politics in the theorizations of gender, race, and postcoloniality from the 1980s on.

Despite Adorno's ambivalent attitude to Hegelian dialectics, he still considered the goal of Hegel's philosophy, which he projected as an intersubjective recognition without recourse to domination, an attractive one. Adorno's claim that this type of reciprocity would not "be the philosophical imperialism of annexing the alien. Instead, its happiness would lie in the fact that the alien in the proximity it is granted, remains what is distant and different" (1973: 191), has been attractive to postcolonial and gender theorists. While some have interpreted Adorno's metaphor of a "Philosophical imperialism" that annuls the Other as a literal critique of European imperialism and all dialectics, others have found Adorno's aspiration to a nonviolent relationship to the Other and to otherness refreshing.

Though Adorno seems at times to sunder Subject and subjectivity, he does so to attempt to distinguish a spontaneous subjectivity from a transcendental Subject which he identifies with the Hegelian system. What Adorno craves through determinate content is limited by its specificity and often becomes a fixed particular caricatured in postmodernism's celebration of "resistance" without determinate content, the type of action that Adorno found appalling. It is this separation of subjectivity from transcendence that can result in the exhaustion of dialectic in "resistance" which motivates Jennifer Rycenga's "Queerly Amiss."

Rycenga moves beyond a vision of identity and difference, and resistance and agency that has limited discussions about subjectivity and politics. Reading the dialectic of Subject and subjectivity differently, Rycenga argues that Adorno does have something to say about homosexuality, even if most of what he writes is at times homophobic. Rycenga observes that Adorno's privatization of the concept of sexuality results from his rejection of the category of the Subject as it emerges from the realm of sexuality and sexual politics. For Rycenga, that problem is a result of a general problem of the dialectic in Adorno: "He abandons the transformation of reality because, quite literally, there is no one to carry out such a project in the absence of the subject." Adorno's politics, therefore, are reduced to a categorical imperative, a form of moralism that includes the reduction of "passion" to old-fashioned structures of heterosexual romance. Despite all its apparent fissures, Adorno's dialectic is always already closed to new subjective impulses.

In " 'As though the end of the world had come and gone,' " Sam Weber identifies the central aporia present in Adorno's thought. If, as Weber writes, "a systematization of the System of the Culture Industry necessarily falls prey to the same tendencies it claims to criticize: the subsumptive tendency of the system," then what role does critique play in Adorno's writing? Not only is praxis always equated with reification and commodification (Adorno, 1978: 166), but reason itself becomes instrumental. In *Dialectic of Enlightenment* the development of reason is contradictory yet it moves toward instrumentality. This in itself would not be controversial as one gets an intimation of such a development of Marx's critique of the Hegelian dialectic when Marx writes that with Hegel "Reason is at home with unreason." Yet with Adorno, one gets not only the identity of reason with capitalist techniques, but the subsumption of reason by the irrational. Foucault saw in the latter a move toward his own project; Habermas also saw in *Dialectic of Enlightenment* the shadow of Nietzsche but lamented the end of reason as the collapse of a communicative and moral standpoint. Other readers have defended Adorno, claiming that reason is in fact immanent in Adorno's critique of reason. Additionally, while Adorno gibes with the postmodern celebration of media culture, the cult of performance, attacks on modernism as obsolete and elitist, and its more affirmative attitude toward contemporary culture, he also challenges the rigid conceptual division between late modernity and postmodernity. The modernity/postmodernity problem is seen less in Adorno's critique of mass culture than in the idea of intellectual autonomy.

Whatever side one falls on the modernism/postmodernism and rationalism/irrationalism debates depends on a number of factors. Yet the underlining problematics run like a red thread throughout the essays collected here. For example, Adorno's notion of identity and subjectivity in the negative dialectics, disputed in Rycenga's "Queerly Amiss," finds its counter in Anson Rabinbach's claim that the Jew is the "last" subject in *Dialectic of Enlightenment*. The notion of Adorno's "Retreat from Marx" (Turner) can be contrasted to Adorno's escape from Marxism (Berman). The return to a historicized Adorno (Huyssen) can be contrasted to left cultural studies criticisms (Kellner). Finally, even in terms of attitudes to dialectics and Hegel we find that Adorno is not Hegelian enough (Gibson) or is too Hegelian (Bozzetti).

A number of tendencies can thus be deduced in approaches to Adorno. His own ambivalent attitude to Hegelian dialectics expresses one: the problematic of the autonomy of the artwork and of the critical thinker another. In the 1990s and early twenty-first century, the figure of the lonely intellectual struggling against the increasingly reified corporate world is emblematic of the academic whose own life is less and less autonomous and more and more subsumed in a marketplace dominated by the pressures of standardization and conformity and professionalization.

Since Adorno's death, and especially over the past two decades, Adorno's work has been subject to shifting intellectual trends within the academy, often reflecting larger social and political events and trends. At once a poststructuralist *avant la lettre* and a proto-deconstructionist, Adorno's writings and theories have significantly contributed to a number of emergent theories. Even when these appropriations are at odds with his own project, Adorno's negative dialectic has been suggestively employed in fields such as cultural studies and postcolonial studies. On the other hand, Adorno's unwillingness to take a more openly political stand remains deeply problematical to the status of dialectical criticism.

Notes

1   See, for example, Wolfgang Kraushaar's *Frankfurter Schule und Studentenbewegung. Von der Flaschenpost zum Molotowcocktail 1946 bis 1995*; Michael Sprinker, "The Grand Hotel Abyss," *New Left Review* 237 (Sept.–Oct. 1999); Noah Isenberg, "Critical Theory at the Barricades," *Lingua Franca* 8 (November 1998): 19–22; and Russell Berman, "Adorno's Politics," in this volume, pp. 110–31.

2   *Critical Models*, 222. Cf. Christopher Simpson, *Science of Coercion: Communication Research and Psychological Warfare* (New York: Oxford University Press, 1994): 20.

3   See, for example, Andreas Huyssen, "Introduction to Adorno," *New German Critique* 6 (Fall 1975): 3–11; Miriam Hansen, "Introduction to Adorno 'Transparencies on Film,'" *New German Critique* 24–25 (Fall–Winter 1981): 186–98; and Thomas Y. Levin, "For the Record: Adorno on Music in the Age of Its Technical Reproducibility," *October* 55 (Winter 1990): 23–47.

Part I
Politics and Culture

Part I

Politics and Culture

1

Adorno in Reverse: From Hollywood to Richard Wagner

Andreas Huyssen

Ever since the failure of the 1848 revolution, the culture of modernity has been characterized by the contentious relationship between high art and mass culture. The conflict first emerged in its typical modern form in the Second Empire under Napoleon III and in Bismarck's new German Reich. More often than not it has appeared in the guise of an irreconcilable opposition. At the same time, however, there has been a succession of attempts launched from either side to bridge the gap or at least to appropriate elements of the other. From Courbet's appropriation of popular iconography to Brecht's immersion in the vernacular of popular culture, from Madison Avenue's conscious exploitation of avant-gardist pictorial strategies to postmodernism's uninhibited learning from Las Vegas there has been a plethora of strategic moves tending to destabilize the high/low opposition from within. Yet this opposition – usually described in terms of modernism vs. mass culture or avant-garde vs. culture industry – has proven to be amazingly resilient. Such resilience may lead one to conclude that perhaps neither of the two combatants can do without the other, that their much heralded mutual exclusiveness is really a sign of their secret interdependence. Seen in this light, mass culture indeed seems to be the repressed other of modernism, the family ghost rumbling in the cellar. Modernism, on the other hand, often chided by the left as the elitist, arrogant, and mystifying master-code of bourgeois culture while demonized by the right as the Agent Orange of natural social cohesion, is the straw man desperately needed by the system to provide an aura of popular legitimation for the blessings of the culture industry. Or, to put it differently, as modernism hides its envy for the broad appeal of mass culture behind a screen of condescension and contempt, mass culture, saddled as it is with pangs of guilt, yearns for the dignity of serious culture which forever eludes it.

Of course, questions raised by this persistent complicity of modernism and mass culture cannot be solved by textual analysis alone or by recourse to categories such as taste or quality. A broader framework is needed. Social scientists in the Marx–Weber tradition such as Jürgen Habermas have argued that with the emergence of civil society the sphere of culture came uncoupled from the political and economic systems. Such a differentiation of spheres (*Ausdifferenzierung*) may have lost some of its explanatory power for contemporary developments, but it is certainly characteristic of an earlier stage of capitalist modernization. It was actually the historical prerequisite for the twin establishment of a sphere of high autonomous art and a sphere of mass culture, both considered to lie outside the economic and political spheres. The irony, of course, is that art's aspirations to autonomy, its uncoupling from church and state, became possible only when literature, painting and music were first organized according to the principles of a market economy. From its beginnings the autonomy of art has been related dialectically to the commodity form. The rapid growth of the reading public and the increasing capitalization of the book market in the later eighteenth century, the commercialization of music culture and the development of a modern art market mark the beginnings of the high/low dichotomy in its specifically modern form. This dichotomy then became politically charged in decisive ways when new class conflicts erupted in the mid-nineteenth century and the quickening pace of the industrial revolution required new cultural orientations for a mass populace. Habermas himself has analyzed this process in his *Strukturwandel der Öffentlichkeit* where he argues convincingly that the period of the Second Reich occupies a central place in the emergence of a modern mass culture and in the disintegration of an older bourgeois public sphere.[1] What Habermas has attempted to do, of course, is to insert a historical dimension into what Adorno and Horkheimer, some twenty years earlier, had postulated as the closed and seemingly timeless system of the culture industry. The force of Habermas' account was not lost on John Brenkman who, in an important article, fully agrees with Habermas' periodization: "This public sphere, like all the institutions and ideologies of the bourgeoisie in the nineteenth century, underwent extreme contortions as soon as its repressive functions showed through its initial transforming effects. The ethical-political principle of the public sphere – freedom of discussion, the sovereignty of the public will, etc. – proved to be a mask for its economic-political reality, namely, that the private interest of the capitalist class determines all social and institutional authority."[2] Indeed there can be little doubt that – just as the beginnings of modernism – the origins of modern mass culture date back to the decades around 1848, when, as Brenkman sums up, "The European bourgeoisie, still fighting to secure its triumph over aristocracy and monarchy, suddenly faced the counterrevolutionary task of suppressing the workers and preventing them from openly articulating *their* interests."[3]

While the emphasis on revolution and counterrevolution in the mid-nineteenth century is important to a discussion of the origins of mass culture, it certainly does not tell the whole story. The salient fact is that with the universalization of commodity production mass culture begins to cut across classes in heretofore unknown ways. Many of its forms attract cross-class audiences, others remain class-bound. Traditional popular culture enters into a fierce struggle with commodified culture producing a variety of hybrid forms. Such resistances to the reign of the commodity were often recognized by the modernists who eagerly incorporated themes and forms of popular culture into the modernist vocabulary.[4] When we locate the origins of modern mass culture in the mid-nineteenth century, the point is therefore not to claim that the culture of late capitalism "began" in 1848. But the *commodification of culture* did indeed emerge in the mid-nineteenth century as a powerful force, and we need to ask what its specific forms were at that time and how precisely they were related to the industrialization of the human body and to the commodification of labor power. A lot of recent work in social history, history of technology, urban history, and philosophy of time has converged on what Anthony Giddens calls the "commodification of time-space" during the formative decades of industrial capitalism.[5] We only need to think of the well-documented changes in the perception and articulation of time and space brought about by railroad travelling,[6] the expansion of the visual field by news photography, the restructuring of city space with the Haussmannization of Paris, and last but not least the increasing imposition of industrial time and space on the human body in schools, factories, and the family. We may take the periodic spectacles of the World Expositions, those major mass-cultural phenomena of the times, as well as the elaborate staging of the commodity in the first giant department stores as salient symptoms of a changing relationship between the human body and the object world that surrounds it and of which it is itself a major part. What, then, are the traces of this commodification of time and space, of objects and the human body, in the arts? Of course, Baudelaire's poetry, Manet's and Monet's painting, Zola's or Fontane's novels, and Schnitzler's plays, to name but a few examples, provide us with powerful visions of modern life, as it used to be called, and critics have focused on a number of social types symptomatic for the age, such as the prostitute and the dandy, the *flâneur*, the bohemian, and the collector. But while the triumph of the modern in "high art" has been amply documented, we are only beginning to explore the place of mass culture vis-à-vis the modernization of the life-world in the nineteenth century.[7]

Clearly, Adorno and Horkheimer's concept of the culture industry does not yield much with regard to specific historical and textual analyses of nineteenth-century mass culture. Politically, adherence today to the classical culture industry thesis can only lead to resignation or moralizing about universal manipulation and domination. Blaming the culture industry for capitalism's longevity, however, is metaphysics, not politics. Theoretically, adherence to Adorno's aesthetics may blind us to the ways in which contemporary art, since the demise of classical modernism and the historical avant-garde, represents a new conjuncture which can no longer be grasped in Adornean or other modernist categories. Just as we would want to avoid elevating Adorno's *Aesthetic Theory* to the status of dogma, the last thing we want to start with is a simple projection of the culture industry theory back into the nineteenth century.

Yet, a discussion of Adorno in the context of the early stage of the mass culture/modernism dichotomy may still make sense for a number of simple reasons. First, Adorno is one of a very few critics guided by the conviction that a theory of modern culture must address both mass culture and high art. The same cannot be said for most literary and art criticism in this country. Nor can it be said of mass communication research which takes place totally apart from literary and art historical studies. Adorno actually undermines this very separation. The fact that he himself insists on fundamental separation between the culture industry and modernist art is to be understood not as a normative proposition but rather as a reflection of a series of historical experiences and theoretical assumptions which are open to debate.

Secondly, the theory of the culture industry has exerted a tremendous influence on mass culture research in Germany and, to a somewhat lesser extent, also in the United States.[8] Recalling the ways in which Adorno theorized about modern mass culture may not be the worst place to start. After all, a critical, yet sympathetic discussion may be quite fruitful in countering two current trends: one toward a theoretically decapitated and mostly affirmative description of "popular" culture, the other toward a moralizing condemnation of imperial mind management by a media apparatus allegedly totally in the grip of capital and profit interests.

Any discussion of Adorno, however, will have to begin by pointing out the theoretical limitations inherent in his thought which, contrary to what one often hears, cannot be reduced simply to a notion of brainwashing or manipulation. Adorno's blindnesses have to be interpreted as simultaneously theoretical and historical ones. Indeed, his theory may appear to us today as a ruin of history, mutilated and damaged by the very conditions of its articulation and genesis: defeat of the German working class, triumph and subsequent exile of modernism from central Europe, fascism, Stalinism, and the Cold War. I do not feel the need to either resurrect or bury Adorno, as the saying goes. Both gestures ultimately fail to place Adorno in the ever-shifting context of our attempts to understand the culture of modernity. Both attitudes tend to sap the energy from a body of texts which maintain their provocation for us precisely because they recede from a present which increasingly seems to indulge in a self-defeating narcissism of theory or in the hopeless return of jolly good old humanism.

I will begin, then, by briefly recapitulating some of the basic propositions of the culture industry concept and by pointing to some of the problems inherent in it. In a second section, I will show that Adorno can be read against the grain, that his theory is by no means as closed as it may appear at first sight. The task of this reading is precisely to open Adorno's account to its own hesitations and resistances and to allow it to function in slightly different frames. In the two final sections I will discuss how both Adorno's theory of modernism and the theory of the culture industry are shaped not only by fascism, exile, and Hollywood, but also quite significantly by cultural phenomena of the late nineteenth century, phenomena in which modernism and culture industry seem to converge in curious ways rather than being diametrically opposed to each other. Locating elements of the culture industry, with Adorno, in *l'art pour l'art*, Jugendstil, and Richard Wagner may serve two purposes. It may help sustain the claim that Adorno's view of the culture industry and modernism is not quite as binary and closed as it appears. And, on a much broader level, it may point us – in a reversal of Adorno's strategy – toward a desirable and overdue exploration of how modernism itself appropriates and transforms elements of popular culture, trying like Antaeus to gain strength and vitality from such contacts.[9] . . .

Marginal Revisions: Reading Adorno against the Grain

No account of the culture industry theory can be considered adequate unless it also locates Adorno's hesitations, resistances, and displacements within the texts themselves. In a close reading of Adorno's "Transparencies on Film" Miriam Hansen has recently made a convincing case for reading Adorno against the grain.[10] Such a reading can indeed show that Adorno himself frequently cast doubt in the positions taken in *Dialectic of Enlightenment*. One of

the most salient examples, quoted by Hansen, can be found in the posthumously published draft "Schema der Massenkultur," which was originally
meant to be part of the culture industry chapter in *Dialectic of Enlightenment*.
In capsule form Adorno and Horkheimer give the central thesis of the work:
"Human beings, as they conform to the technological forces of production
which are imposed on them in the name of progress, are transformed into
objects which willingly allow themselves to be manipulated and thus fall
behind the actual potential of these productive forces."[11] But then, in a dialectical move, the authors place their hope in the very repetitiveness of reification: "Because human beings, as subjects, still constitute the limit of
reification, mass culture has to renew its hold over them in an endless series
of repetitions; the hopeless effort of repetition is the only trace of hope that
the repetition may be futile, that human beings cannot be totally controlled."[12] Examples such as this one could easily be multiplied. But while
reading the classical texts on the culture industry against the grain may testify
to Adorno's insight into the potential limitations of his theory, I doubt
whether such insights should compel us to fundamentally revise our interpretation of these texts. The difficulty may only have been displaced to
another area. The same move in which the monolithic closure of the culture
industry theory comes undone in the margins seems to reaffirm another
closure at the level of the subject. In the quoted passage any potential resistance to the culture industry is ascribed to the subject, however contingent
and hollowed out it may be, rather than, say, to intersubjectivity, social action,
and the collective organization of cultural experience in what Negt and
Kluge have called counter-public spheres (*Gegenöffentlichkeiten*). It is not
enough to reproach Adorno for holding on to a monadic or "bourgeois"
notion of the subject. Isolation and privatization of the subject are after all
the very real effects of much of capitalist mass culture, and the resulting subjectivity is, in Adorno's own terms, quite different from that of the ascendant
earlier bourgeois class. The question rather has to be how Adorno defines
that subjectivity which would elude manipulation and control.

Jochen Schulte-Sasse has recently argued that Adorno relies on an ahistorical hypostatization of the subject as a self-identical ego equipped with
analytical power.[13] If this reading is correct, the subject resisting reification
through mass culture is none other than the critical theorist's younger
brother, less stable perhaps and less forceful in his resistance, but the hope for
resistance would indeed have to place its trust in the residues of that ego-
formation which the culture industry tends to destroy. But here, too, one can
read Adorno against the grain and point to passages in his work in which
the stable and armored ego is seen as the problem rather than the solution.
In his critique of Kant's subject of epistemology Adorno attacks the notion

of the self-identical subject as a historically produced construct bound up with social experiences of objectification and reification: "It is obvious that the hardness of the epistemological subject, the identity of self-consciousness mimics the unreflected experience of the consistent, identical object."[14] Adorno's critique of the deeply problematic nature of such fortifications of the subject, which is reminiscent of the Jena romantics, is summed up poignantly when he writes: "The subject is all the more a subject the less it is so; and the more it imagines itself to *be* and to be an objective entity for itself, the less it is a subject."[15]

Similarly, in a critical discussion of Freud and the bourgeois privileging of genital sexuality, Adorno recognized the principle of ego-identity as socially constituted: "Not to be oneself is a piece of sexual utopia . . . negation of the ego principle. It shakes up that invariant of bourgeois society understood in its broadest sense: the demand of identity. First identity had to be constructed, ultimately it will have to be overcome (*aufzuheben*). That which is only identical with itself is without happiness."[16] Such passages point to Adorno's fragile utopian vision of a reconciliation with nature which, as always in Adorno and Horkheimer, is understood as both outer and inner nature in a way that calls their very separation into question: "The dawning sense of freedom feeds upon the memory of the archaic impulse not yet steered by any solid I. The more the I curbs that impulse, the more chaotic and thus questionable will it find that prehistoric freedom. Without an anamnesis of the untamed impulse that precedes the ego – an impulse later banished to the zone of unfree bondage to nature – it would be impossible to derive the idea of freedom, although that idea in turn ends up in reinforcing the ego."[17] As against the previous quote from *Eingriffe* where the *Aufhebung* of bourgeois ego-formation seemed to hold out a promise, here the dialectic ends in aporia. Surely, one problem is that Adorno, like Freud in *Civilization and Its Discontents*, metaphorically collapses the phylogenetic with the ontogenetic level. He permits his historical and philosophical speculations about the dialectic of self-preservation and enlightenment to get in the way of pursuing the question, in relation to mass culture, to what extent and for what purposes the products of the culture industry might precisely speak to and activate such pre-ego impulses in a non-regressive way. His focus on how the commodification of culture dissolves ego-formation and produces mere regression blinds him to that possibility. He founders on the aporia that in his philosophy of civilization these impulses preceding the ego simultaneously contain a sign of freedom and the hope for a reconciliation with nature on the one hand while on the other hand they represent the archaic domination of nature over man which had to be fought in the interest of self-preservation.

Any further discussion of such pre-ego impulses (e.g., partial instincts) in relation to mass culture would lead to the central question of identification, that ultimate bogeyman of Adorno's – and not only Adorno's – modernist aesthetic. Adorno never took that step. The suspension of critical distance which is at stake in any identification with the particular leads inexorably to a legitimation of the false totality. While Adorno recognized that there were limitations to the reification of human subjects through the culture industry which made resistance thinkable at the level of the subject, he never asked himself whether perhaps such limitations could be located in the mass cultural commodities themselves. Such limits do indeed become evident when one begins to analyze in detail the signifying strategies of specific cultural commodities and the mesh of gratification, displacement, and production of desires which are invariably put in play in their production and consumption. How precisely identification works in the reception of mass culture, what spaces it opens and what possibilities it closes off, how it can be differentiated according to gender, class, and race – these are questions to which the theory of the culture industry might have led had it not been conceived, in the spirit of the negative dialectic, as the threatening other of modernism. And yet, reading Adorno against the grain opens up precisely some of these spaces inside his texts where we might want to begin rewriting his account for a postmodern age.

Prehistory and Culture Industry

To write a prehistory of the modern was the stated goal of Benjamin's never completed arcades project on nineteenth-century Paris. The dispute between Benjamin and Adorno revolving around their different readings of cultural commodification and of the relationship between prehistory and modernity is well-documented and researched. Given Adorno's trenchant critique of Benjamin's 1935 exposé of the arcades project it is somewhat baffling to find that he never wrote about mass culture in the nineteenth century. Doing so would have allowed him to refute Benjamin on his own ground, but the closest he ever came to such an undertaking is probably the book on Wagner written in London and New York in 1937 and 1938. Instead he chose to battle Benjamin, especially the Benjamin of "The Work of Art in the Age of Mechanical Reproduction," in his analysis of the twentieth-century culture industry. Politically, this choice made perfect sense in the late 1930s and early 1940s, but the price he paid for it was great. Drawing on the experience of mass culture in fascism and developed consumer capitalism, the theory of the culture industry was itself affected by the reification it decried since it left no room for historical development. Culture industry represented for Adorno the completed return to prehistory under the sign of the eternal recurrence of the same. While Adorno seemed to deny mass culture its own history, his critique of Benjamin's arcades exposé shows clearly that he saw the later nineteenth century as prefiguring that cultural commodification which reached its fully organized state in the culture industry of the twentieth century. If the late nineteenth century, then, already lives under the threat of cultural barbarism and regression, one might want to take Adorno another step further back. After all, throughout his work he interpreted the culture of modernity with its twin formation of modernism and culture industry as tied to high or monopoly capitalism which in turn is distinguished from the preceding phase of liberal capitalism. The decline of the culture of liberal capitalism, never very strong in Germany in the first place, was by and large complete with the foundation of the Second Reich, most certainly by the 1890s. The history of that crucial transition from the culture of liberal capitalism to that of monopoly capitalism never receives much explicit attention in Adorno's writing, certainly not as much as the artistic developments in the later nineteenth century which led to the emergence of Adorno's modernism. But even here Adorno writes about the major artists of the period only (the late Wagner, Hofmannsthal, George) while ignoring the popular literature of the times (Karl May, Ganghofer, Marlitt) as well as working-class culture. For naturalism he only reserves some flippant remarks, and the early developments of technological media such as photography and film are all but absent from his accounts of the late nineteenth century. Only with Wagner does Adorno reach back to that earlier stage; and it is no coincidence that Wagner is indeed the pivotal figure in Adorno's prehistory of the modern.

Another point needs to be raised pertaining to this curious absence of nineteenth-century mass culture in Adorno's writing. Already in the 1930s Adorno must have been aware of historical research on mass culture. He only had to look at the work of one of his fellow researchers at the Institute, Leo Löwenthal, who did much of his work on eighteenth- and nineteenth-century German culture, high and low, and who never tired of drawing the connections that existed between twentieth-century critiques of mass culture and earlier discussions of the problem in the work of Schiller and Goethe, Tocqueville, Marx, and Nietzsche, to name only the most salient figures. Again the question presses itself upon us: why does Adorno ignore the mass culture of the Second Reich? He could have made much of the observation that many of the late nineteenth-century popular classics were still common fare in the Third Reich. Interpreting such continuities could have contributed significantly to the understanding of the prehistory of fascist culture[18] and the rise of authoritarianism, the process George Mosse has described as the

nationalization of the masses. But that was just not Adorno's primary interest. His first and foremost goal was to establish a theory of *die Kunst der
Moderne*, not as a historian, but as a participant and critic reflecting upon a
specific stage in the development of capitalist culture and privileging certain
trends within that stage. Adorno's prime example for the emergence of a genuinely modernist art was the turn to atonality in the music of Arnold Schönberg rather than, as for Benjamin and many historians of modernism, the
poetry of Baudelaire. For my argument here the difference in choice of examples is less important than the difference in treatment. Where Benjamin juxtaposes Baudelaire's poetry with the texture and experience of modern life,
showing how modern life invades the poetic text, Adorno focuses more narrowly on the development of the musical material itself, which he nevertheless interprets as *fait social*, as an aesthetic texturing and constructing of
the experience of modernity, however mediated and removed from *subjective*
experience that construction may ultimately turn out to be. Given Adorno's
belief that the late nineteenth-century commodification of culture prefigures
that of the culture industry and sets the stage for the successful modernist
resistance to commodification in the works of Schönberg, Kafka, and Kandin-
sky, it seems only logical that Adorno should attempt to locate the germs of
the culture industry in the high art of the late nineteenth century which
precedes modernism – in Wagner, Jugendstil, and *l'art pour l'art*. We are faced,
then, with the paradox of having to read Adorno on the high art of the times
if we want to find traces of the mass culture problematic in his writings on
nineteenth-century culture. Here I anticipate the habitual battlecry of
"elitism" which usually serves to end all discussion. Certainly, the bias is there
in Adorno. But it is not as if the questions he raises had ever been convincingly answered. If modernism is a response to the long march of the commodity through culture, then the effects of cultural commodification and all
it entails *also* need to be located *in* the development of the artistic material
itself rather than only in the department store or in the dictates of fashion.
Adorno may be wrong in his answers – and his rigorously atrophied account
of modernism simply leaves too much out – but he is most certainly right
in his questions. Which, again, is not to say that his questions are the only
ones we should ask.

How, then, does Adorno deal with the late nineteenth century? On the
face of it his history of modernism seems to coincide with that of Anglo-
American criticism which sees modernism evolving continuously from the
mid-nineteenth century to the 1950s, if not to the present. Despite occasional shifts in the evaluation of certain authors (e.g., George and Hofmannsthal) Adorno privileges a certain trend of modernist literature – to take
but one medium – from Baudelaire and Flaubert via Mallarmé, Hof-

mannsthal, and George to Valéry and Proust, Kafka and Joyce, Celan and Beckett. The notion of a politically committed art and literature is anathema for Adorno as it is for the dominant account of modernism in Anglo-American critcism. Major movements of the historical avant-garde such as Italian futurism, Dada, Russian constructivism, and productivism, as well as surrealism, are blatantly absent from the canon, an absence which is highly significant and which bears directly on Adorno's account of the late nineteenth century.

A closer look at Adorno's aesthetic theory will indeed dispel the notion of unilinear evolutionary development of modernism since the mid-nineteenth century. It will show on the contrary that Adorno locates a major rupture in the development of modern art after the turn of the century, i.e., with the emergence of the historical avant-garde movements. Of course, Adorno has often been described as a theorist of the avant-garde, a use of terminology based on the problematic collapsing of the notion of the avant-garde with that of modernism. Since Peter Bürger's *Theory of the Avant-Garde*, however, it seems no longer permissible to use the terms interchangeably, even though Bürger himself, at least in his earlier work, still talks about Adorno as a theorist of the avant-garde.[19] But if it is true, as Bürger argues, that the main goal of the historical avant-garde was the reintegration of art into life, a heroic attempt that failed, then Adorno is not a theorist of the avant-garde, but a theorist of modernism. More than that, he is a theorist of a construct "modernism" which has already digested the failure of the historical avant-garde. It has not gone unnoticed that Adorno frequently scorned avant-garde movements such as futurism, Dada, and surrealism, and that he acidly rejected the avant-garde's various attempts to reintegrate art and life as a dangerous regression from the aesthetic to the barbaric. This insight, however, has often prevented critics from appreciating the fact that Adorno's theory of modernism owes as much to the historical avant-garde's onslaught against notions of the work of art as organism *or* as artificial paradise as it owes to late nineteenth-century aestheticism and to the autonomy aesthetic. Only if one understands this double heritage will statements such as the following in the *Philosophy of Modern Music* be fully comprehensible: "Today the only works which really count are those which are no longer works at all."[20] As far as I can see, only Peter Bürger has located this historical core of Adorno's aesthetic theory when he wrote in a more recent essay:

> Both the radical separation of art from life completed by aestheticism *and* the reintegration of art and life intended by the historical avant-garde movements are premises for a view which sees art in total opposition to any rationally organized life-praxis and which at the same time attributes to art a revolu-

tionary force challenging the basic organization of society. The hopes which
the most radical members of the avantgarde movements, especially the dadaists
and early surrealists, invested in this possibility of changing society through art,
these hopes live on residually in Adorno's aesthetic theory, even though in a
resigned and mutilated form. Art is that "other" which cannot be realized in
the world.[21]

Adorno indeed holds in charged tension two diverging tendencies: on the
one hand aestheticism's insistence on the autonomy of the artwork and its
double-layered separateness from everyday life (separate *as* work of art *and*
separate in its refusal of realistic representation) and, on the other, the avant-
garde's radical break with precisely that tradition of art's autonomy. In doing
so he delivers the work's autonomy to the social while preserving it at the
same time: "Art's double character, its being autonomous and fait social,
relentlessly pervades the zone of its autonomy."[22] Simultaneously he radicalizes modernity's break with the past and with tradition in the spirit of avant-
gardism: "Contrary to past styles, it [the concept of modernity] does not
negate earlier art forms; it negates tradition per se."[23] We need to remember
here that the radical break with tradition, first articulated by artists such as
Baudelaire and Manet, becomes dominant in German culture much later than
in France: in Schönberg rather than Wagner, Kafka rather than George, i.e.,
after the turn of the century. From the perspective of German developments
Baudelaire could then be seen as Adorno sees Poe in relation to Baudelaire:
as a lighthouse of modernity.[24]

Adorno's fundamental indebtedness to the project of the post-1900 historical avant-garde can be gleaned from the ways in which he discusses *l'art
pour l'art*, Jugendstil, and the music of Richard Wagner. In each case, the emergence of "genuine" modernism is seen as resulting from a deterioration *within*
forms of high art, a deterioration which bears witness to the increasing commodification of culture.

Adorno's work bristles with critiques of aestheticism and the *l'art pour l'art*
movements of the nineteenth century. In his essay "Standort des Erzählers im
zeitgenössischen Roman" (1954) we read: "The products [of modernist art]
art above the controversy between politically committed art and *l'art
pour l'art*. They stand beyond the alternative which pits the philistinism of
Tendenzkunst against the philistinism of art as pleasure."[25] In *Dialectic of Enlightenment* Adorno relates *l'art pour l'art* polemically to political advertising:
"Advertising becomes art and nothing else, just as Goebbels – with foresight
– combines them: *l'art pour l'art*, advertising for its own sake, a pure representation of social power."[26] *L'art pour l'art*, advertising, and the fascist aes-
thetization of politics can only be thought together under the sign of that

false universal of modernity which is the commodity. In a more historical vein, to give a third example, Adorno writes in *Ästhetische Theorie*: "*L'art pour l'art*'s concept of beauty is strangely hollow, and yet it is obsessed with matter. It resembles an art nouveau event as revealed in Ibsen's charms of hair entwined with vine leaves and of a beautiful death. Beauty seems paralyzed, incapable of determining itself which it could only do by relating to its 'other.' It is like a root in the air and becomes entangled with the destiny of the invented ornament."[27] And somewhat later: "In their innermost constitution the products of *l'art pour l'art* stand condemned by their latent commodity form which makes them live on as Kitsch, subject to ridicule."[28] Adorno's critique here is actually reminiscent of Nietzsche's, that most trenchant and yet dubious critic of mass culture in Imperial Germany, whose influence on Critical Theory has recently been the subject of much debate. But while Nietzsche criticizes *l'art pour l'art*, for instance, in *Beyond Good and Evil*, as a form of decadence and relates it metaphorically to the culture of deluded scientific objectivity and of positivism, Adorno succeeds in grounding the critique systematically with the help of Marx's notion of the commodity form. It is this emphasis on the commodity form (to which Nietzsche was totally oblivious) which permits Critical Theory to articulate a consistent critique of the objectivistic social sciences and of a reified aestheticism. And it furthermore connects Adorno's critique of *l'art pour l'art* with his discussion of Jugendstil, a style which in a certain sense aimed at reversing *l'art pour l'art*'s separation from life.

The Jugendstil of the turn of the century is indeed pivotal to Adorno's historical account of the emergence of modernist art. Although he highly values certain individual works that were part of Jugendstil culture (e.g., works by the early Stefan George and the young Schönberg), he argues that the commodity character of art which had been an integral, though somewhat hidden part of all emancipated bourgeois art becomes external in Jugendstil, tumbling, as it were, out of the artworks for all to see. A longer quote from *Ästhetische Theorie* is appropriate here:

> Jugendstil has contributed greatly to this development, with its ideology of sending art back into life as well as with the sensations created by Wilde, d'Annunzio, and Maeterlinck, all of them preludes to the culture industry. Increasing subjective differentiation and the heightened dissemination of the realm of aesthetic stimuli made these stimuli manipulable. They could now be produced for the cultural market. The tuning of art to the most fleeting individual reactions allied itself with art's reification. Art's increasing likeness to a subjectively perceived physical world made all art abandon its objectivity thus recommending it to the public. The slogan *l'art pour l'art* was but the veil of its opposite. This much is true about the hysterical attacks on decadence:

subjective differentiation reveals an element of ego weakness which corresponds
to the spiritual make-up of the clients of the culture industry. The culture
industry learned how to profit from it.[29]

Three brief observations: Adorno's aversion against later avant-gardist
attempts to reintegrate art and life may have been as strong as it was because
he held those attempts, however one-sidedly, to be similar to that of Jugendstil. Secondly, the avant-garde's attempts to dissolve the boundaries between
art and life – whether those of Dada and surrealism or those of Russian productivism and constructivism – had ended in failure by the 1930s, a fact
which makes Adorno's skepticism toward sending art back into life quite
understandable. In a sense never intended by the avant-garde, life had indeed
become art – in the fascist aestheticization of politics as mass spectacle as well
as in the fictionalizations of reality dictated by the socialist realism of Zhdanov
and by the dream world of capitalist realism promoted by Hollywood. Most
importantly, however, Adorno criticizes Jugendstil as a prelude to the culture
industry because it was the first style of high art to fully reveal the commodification and reification of art in capitalist culture. And it would not be
Adorno if this account of Jugendstil did not precisely thrive on the paradox
that the culture industry's antecedents are traced to a style and an art which
is highly individualistic and which was never meant for mass reproduction.
Jugendstil, nevertheless, marks that moment of history in which the commodity form has pervaded high art to the extent that – as in Schopenhauer's
famous example of the bird hypnotized by the snake – it throws itself blissfully into the abyss and is swallowed up. That stage, however, is the prerequisite for Adorno's negative aesthetic of modernism that first took shape in
the work of Schönberg. Schönberg's turn to atonality is interpreted as the
crucial strategy to evade commodification and reification while articulating
it in its very technique of composition.

Richard Wagner: Phantasmagoria and Modern Myth

Schönberg's "precursor" in the medium of music of course is Richard
Wagner. Adorno argues that the turn toward atonality, that supreme achievement of musical modernism, is already latent in certain composition techniques of Richard Wagner. Wagner's use of dissonance and chromatic
movement, his multiple subversions of classical harmony, the emergence of
tonal indeterminacy and his innovations in color and orchestration are seen
as setting the stage for Schönberg and the Vienna School. And yet, Schönberg's relation to Wagner, which is central to Adorno's account of the birth

of modernism in the arts, is described as one of continuation *and* resistance, most succinctly perhaps in the "Selbstanzeige des Essaybuches 'Versuch über Wagner'": "All of modern music has developed in resistance to his [Wagner's] predominance – and yet, all of its elements are latently present in him."[30] The purpose of Adorno's long essay on Wagner, written in 1937/8, was not to write music history or to glorify the modernist breakthrough. Its purpose was rather to analyze the social and cultural roots of German fascism in the nineteenth century. Given the pressures of the times – Hitler's affiliation with Bayreuth and the incorporation of Wagner into the fascist culture machine – Wagner's work turned out to be the logical place for such an investigation. We need to remember here that whenever Adorno says fascism, he is also saying culture industry. The book on Wagner can therefore be read not only as an account of the birth of fascism out of the spirit of the *Gesamtkunstwerk*, but also as an account of the birth of the culture industry *in* the most ambitious high art of the nineteenth century. On the face of it such an account would seem patently absurd since it appears to ignore the existence of a well-developed industrial mass culture in Wagner's own time. But then Adorno's essay does not claim to give us a comprehensive historical description of the origins of mass culture as such, nor does he suggest that the place to develop a theory of the culture industry is high art alone. What he does suggest, however, is something largely lost in the dominant accounts of modernism which emphasize the triumphal march of abstraction and surface in painting, textual self-referentiality in literature, atonality in music, and irreconcilable hostility to mass culture and Kitsch in all forms of modernist art. Adorno suggests that the social processes that give shape to mass culture cannot be kept out of artworks of the highest ambition and that any analysis of modernist or, for that matter, premodernist art, will have to trace these processes in the trajectory of the aesthetic materials themselves. The ideology of the artwork's autonomy is thus undermined by the claim that no work of art is ever untouched by the social. But Adorno makes the even stronger claim that in capitalist society high art is always already permeated by the textures of that mass culture from which it seeks autonomy. As a model analysis of the entanglements of high art with mass cultural commodification the Wagner essay is actually more stimulating than, say, the *Philosophy of Modern Music* which in many ways represents the negative version of modernist triumphalism. Preceding Jugendstil and *l'art pour l'art*, which are blamed for simply capitulating to the commodity, it is the body of Wagner's *oeuvre*, towering as it does at the threshold of modernity, which becomes the privileged locus of that fierce struggle between tradition and modernity, autonomy and commodity, revolution and reaction, and, ultimately, myth and enlightenment.

As I cannot possibly do justice here to Adorno's various writings on Wagner, I will only outline those elements which connect Wagner's aesthetic innovations to features of the modern culture industry. The other half of Adorno's Wagner – Wagner as premodernist – will have to remain underexposed.

To begin with, Adorno concedes throughout his essay that in his time Wagner represented the most advanced stage in the development of music and opera. However, he consistently emphasizes both progressive *and* reactionary elements in Wagner's music, making the point that the one cannot be had without the other. He credits Wagner for heroically attempting to elude the market demands for "easy" opera and for trying to avoid its banality. But this flight, according to Adorno, leads Wagner even more deeply into the commodity. In his later essay "Wagner's Aktualität" (1965) Adorno finds a powerful image for this dilemma: "Everything in Wagner has its historical core. Like a spider his spirit sits in the gigantic web of nineteenth-century exchange relations."[31] No matter how far Wagner would spin out his music, spider and web will always remain one. How, then, do these exchange relations manifest themselves in Wagner's music? How does the music get caught in the web of cultural commodification? After a discussion of Wagner as social character, which I will skip here, Adorno turns to an analysis of Wagner's role as composer-conductor. He argues that Wagner disguises the growing estrangement of the composer from the audience by conceiving his music "in terms of the gesture of striking a blow" and by incorporating the audience into the work through calculated "effects": "As the striker of blows . . . the composer-conductor gives the claims of the public a terrorist emphasis. Democratic considerateness towards the listener is transformed into connivance with the powers of discipline: in the name of the listener, anyone whose feelings accord with any measure other than the beat of the music is silenced."[32] In this interpretation of Wagner's "gesture" Adorno shows how the audience becomes "the reified object of calculation by the artist."[33] And it is here that the parallels with the culture industry emerge. The composer-conductor's attempt to beat his audience into submission is structurally isomorphic to the way in which the culture industry treats the consumer. But the terms of the isomorphism are reversed. In Wagner's theater the composer-conductor is still visible and present as an individual – a residue of the liberal age, as it were – and the spectators are assembled as a public in the dark behind the conductor's baton. The industrial organization of culture, however, replaces the individual conductor with an invisible corporate management and it dissolves the public into the shapeless mass of isolated consumers. The culture industry thus reverses the relations typical of the liberal age by de-individualizing cultural production and privatizing reception. Given Adorno's description of Wagner's audience as the reified object of aesthetic calculations, it comes as no surprise that he would claim that Wagner's music is already predicated on that ego-weakness which would later become the operational basis of the culture industry: "The audience of these giant works lasting many hours is thought of as unable to concentrate – something not unconnected with the fatigue of the citizen in his leisure time. And while he allows himself to drift with the current, the music, acting as its own impresario, thunders at him in endless repetitions to hammer its message home."[34] Such endless repetitions manifest themselves most obviously in Wagner's leitmotiv technique which Adorno relates to Berlioz's *idée fixe* and to the Baudelairian spleen. Adorno interprets the leitmotiv's double character as allegory and advertising. As allegory the leitmotiv articulates a progressive critique of traditional totalizing musical forms and of the "symbolic" tradition of German idealism. At the same time, however, it functions like advertising in that it is designed to be easily remembered by the forgetful. This advertising aspect of the leitmotiv is not something projected back onto it from hindsight. Adorno already locates it in the reactions of Wagner's contemporaries who tended to make crude links between leitmotivs and the persons they characterized. The commercial decay of the leitmotiv, latent in Wagner, becomes full-blown in Hollywood film music "where the sole function of the leitmotiv is to announce heroes or situations so as to help the audience to orientate itself more easily."[35]

Reification emerges as the conceptual core of Adorno's account. "Allegorical rigidity" has not only infected the motiv like a disease, it has infected Wagner's *oeuvre* as a whole – its music and its characters, its images and myths, and last but not least its institutionalization in Bayreuth as one of the major spectacles of the times. Adorno goes on to discuss reification, which can be regarded as the effect of commodification *in* the musical material, on the levels of melody, color, and orchestration. The overriding concern here is the question of what happens to musical time in Wagner's *oeuvre*. Adorno argues that time becomes abstract and as such defies musical and dramatic development on the level of melody as well as on that of character. The musical material is pulverized, characters are frozen and static. The construction of motiv as temporal sequence is replaced by impressionistic association: "For the composer the use of the beat is a fallacious method of mastering the empty time with which he begins, since the measure to which he subjects time does not derive from the musical content, but from the reified order of time itself."[36] The predominance of "sound" in Wagner also dissolves the temporal pressures of harmony. It spatializes musical time, depriving it, as it were, of its historical determinations.[37]

These observations about the leitmotiv, the reified order of time, and the atomization of musical material lead Adorno to a central point where he affiliates Wagner's composition technique with the mode of production: "It is difficult to avoid the parallel with the quantification of the industrial labor process, its fragmentation into the smallest possible units . . . Broken down into the smallest units, the totality is supposed to become controllable, and it must submit to the will of the subject who has liberated himself from all pre-existing forms."[38] The parallel with the culture industry becomes fully obvious when we read a little further on: "In Wagner's case what predominates is already the totalitarian and seigneurial aspect of atomization; that devaluation of the individual vis-à-vis the totality, which excludes all authentic dialectical interaction."[39]

What Adorno describes here, of course, is the reflection of the nineteenth-century industrialization of time and space in Wagner's *oeuvre*. The devaluation of the individual vis-à-vis the totality appears in Wagner's orchestration as the tendency to drown out the voice of the individual instrument in favor of a continuum of timbres and large-scale melodic complexes. The "progress" of such orchestration techniques is as suspect to Adorno as the progress of the industrial upsurge of the Bismarck era to which it is compared.

If reification of musical and dramatic time is one major element of Adorno's account, then subjectivistic association and ambiguity of musical meaning is the other side of the same coin. What is at stake here is that which Wagner's contemporaries described as nervousness and hypersensitivity, what Nietzsche called decadence, and what we might call Wagner's modernity. It is interesting to take notice of Adorno's scattered references to the relationship of Wagner's modernity to that of Baudelaire and Monet: "Like Baudelaire's, his reading of bourgeois high capitalism discerned an anti-bourgeois, heroic message in the destruction of *Biedermeier*."[40] In the essay "Wagner's Aktualität" the discussion of the composer's handling of color unmistakably conjures up the art of Monet: "Wagner's achievement of a differentiation of color by dissolution into minute detail is supplemented by his technique of combining the most minute elements constructively in such a way that something like integral color emerges."[41] Yet Wagner only approaches that threshold which Baudelaire and Monet had already crossed: "No comparison of Wagner with the impressionists will be adequate unless it is remembered that the credo of universal symbolism to which all his technical achievements subscribe is that of Puvis de Chavannes and not Monet's."[42] Therefore Adorno calls Wagner an "impressionist *malgré lui*" and relates his backwardness to the backwardness of economic and aesthetic developments in mid-nineteenth-century Germany. The key point that emerges from this comparison is the paradox that Wagner's anticipation of the culture industry is proportionate to his aesthetic backwardness in his own time. His music conjures up a distant future because it has not yet succeeded in shedding a past rendered obsolete by modern life. To put it differently, the modernity of allegory and dissonance in Wagner's work is consistently compromised by that "universal symbolism" which simulates a false totality and forges an equally false monumentality, that of the *Gesamtkunstwerk*.

Wagner's affinity to the culture industry is worked out most explicitly by Adorno in the chapters on phantasmagoria, *Gesamtkunstwerk*, and myth. Adorno's characterization of Wagner's opera as phantasmagoria is an attempt to analyze what happens to aesthetic appearance (*ästhetischer Schein*) in the age of the commodity and as such it is the attempt to come to terms with the pressure commodity fetishism puts on works of art. As phantasmagorias Wagner's operas have veiled all traces of the labor that went into their production. Blocking out traces of production in the work of art is of course one of the major tenets of an earlier idealist aesthetic and as such nothing new in Wagner. But that is precisely the problem. As the commodity form begins to invade all aspects of modern life, all aesthetic appearance is in danger of being transformed into phantasmagoria, into the "illusion of the absolute reality of the unreal."[43] According to Adorno, Wagner yields to the pressures of the commodity form. With some minor changes, the following passage taken from the chapter on phantasmagoria could easily be imagined as part of the mass culture chapter in *Dialectic of Enlightenment*:

> It [the illusion of the absolute reality of the unreal] sums up the unromantic side of the phantasmagoria: phantasmagoria as the point at which aesthetic appearance becomes a function of the character of the commodity. As a commodity it purveys illusions. The absolute reality of the unreal is nothing but the reality of a phenomenon that not only strives unceasingly to spirit away its own origins in human labor, but also, inseparably from this process and in thrall to exchange value, assiduously emphasizes its use value, stressing that this is its authentic reality, that it is "no imitation" – and all this in order to further the cause of exchange value. In Wagner's day the consumer goods on display turned their phenomenal side seductively towards the mass of consumers while diverting attention from their merely phenomenal character, from the fact that they were beyond reach. Similarly, in the phantasmagoria, Wagner's operas tend to become commodities. Their tableaux assume the character of wares on display (*Ausstellungscharakter*).[44]

At this point myth enters the stage as the embodiment of illusion and as regression to prehistory: "Phantasmagoria comes into being when, under the constraints of its own limitations, modernity's latest products come close to the archaic. Every step forward is at the same time a step into the remote past. As bourgeois society advances it finds that it needs its own camouflage of illusion simply in order to subsist."[45] As phantasmagoria Wagner's opera reproduces the dream world of the commodity in the form of myth: "He

[Wagner] belongs to the first generation to realize that in a world that has been socialized through and through it is not possible for an individual to alter something that is determined over the heads of men. Nevertheless, it was not given to him to call the overarching totality by its real name. In consequence it is transformed for him into myth."[46] Myth becomes the problematic solution to Wagner's struggle against the genre music of the Biedermeier period, and his gods and heroes are to guarantee the success of his simultaneous flight from the banality of the commodity age. But as the present and the mythical merge in the *Gesamtkunstwerk*, Wagner's divine realm of ideas, gods, and heroes is nothing but a deluded transcription of the banal world of the present. In a number of scattered observations Adorno juxtaposes, in a quite Benjaminean way, moments of Wagner's *oeuvre* to the culture of everyday life in late nineteenth-century Germany. Thus the *Mastersingers* are said to conjure up – like the images on the box containing the famous *Nürnberger Lebkuchen* – the bliss of an unsullied, premodern German past, which later fed seamlessly into *völkisch* ideology. Elsa's relationship to Lohengrin ("My lord, never shall this question come from me") celebrates the subjugation of women in marriage. Wotan is interpreted as the phantasmagoria of the buried revolution, Siegfried as the "natural" rebel who accelerates rather than prevents the catastrophic destruction of civilization. The thunder motiv from the *Ring* becomes the signal sounded by the horn of the Emperor's motor car. Adorno gets to the historical core of Wagner's modern mythology when he writes:

> It is impossible to overlook the relationship between Wagnerian mythology and the iconic world of the Empire, with its eclectic architecture, fake Gothic castles, and the aggressive dream symbols of the New-German boom, ranging from the Bavarian castles of Ludwig to the Berlin restaurant that called itself "Rheingold". But the question of authenticity is as fruitless here as elsewhere. Just as the overwhelming power of high capitalism forms myths that tower above the collective conscious, in the same way the mythic region in which the modern consciousness seeks refuge bears the marks of that capitalism: what subjectively was the dream of dreams is objectively a nightmare.[47]

Thus the drama of the future, as Wagner called his *Gesamtkunstwerk*, prefigures that nightmarish regression into an archaic past which completes its trajectory in fascism. The *Gesamtkunstwerk* is intended as a powerful protest against the fragmentation and atomization of art and life in capitalist society. But since it chooses the wrong means it can only end in failure: "Like Nietzsche and subsequently Art Nouveau, which he [Wagner] anticipates in many respects, he would like, single-handed, to will an aesthetic totality into being, casting a magic spell and with defiant unconcern about the absence of the social conditions necessary for its survival."[48] While the mythic dimension of

Wagner's opera conjures up fascism, its homogenization of music, word, and image is said to anticipate the essential features of Hollywood film: "Thus we see that the evolution of the opera, and in particular the emergence of the autonomous sovereignty of the artist, is intertwined with the origins of the culture industry. Nietzsche, in his youthful enthusiasm, failed to recognize the artwork of the future in which we witness the birth of film out of the spirit of music."[49] The totality of Wagner's music drama, however, is a false totality subject to disintegration from within: "Even in Wagner's lifetime, and in flagrant contradiction to his programme, star numbers like the Fire Music and Wotan's farewell, the Ride of the Valkyries, the Liebestod and the Good Friday music had been torn out of their context, rearranged and become popular. This fact is not irrelevant to the music dramas, which had cleverly calculated the place of these passages within the economy of the whole. The disintegration of the fragments sheds light on the fragmentariness of the whole."[50] The logic of this disintegration leads to Schönberg's modernism on the one hand and to the Best of Wagner album on the other. Where high art itself is sucked into the maelstrom of commodification, modernism is born as a reaction and a defense. The point is made bluntly in *Philosophy of Modern Music*: "The liberation of modern painting from representation (*Gegenständlichkeit*), which was to art the break that atonality was to music, was determined by the defensive against the mechanized art commodity – above all photography. Radical music, from its inception, reacted similarly to the commercial depravity of the traditional idiom. It formulated an antithesis against the extension of the culture industry into its own domain."[51] While this statement seems quite schematic, especially in its mechanical derivation of abstraction in painting, it serves to remind us again that modernism itself is held hostage by the culture industry and that theories of modernism neglecting this conjuncture are seriously deficient. Adorno's bleak description of modern mass culture as dream turned nightmare has perhaps outlived its usefulness and can now take its place as a historically contingent and theoretically powerful reflection on fascism. What has not outlived its usefulness, however, is Adorno's suggestion that mass culture was not imposed on art only from the "outside," but that art was transformed into its opposite thanks precisely to its emancipation from traditional forms of bourgeois art. In the vortex of commodification there was never an outside. Wagner is the case in point.

Coda

Reading Adorno in reverse, from *Dialectic of Enlightenment* backward to the Wagner essay of 1937/8, from fascism and the capitalist culture industry back to Imperial Germany, leads to the conclusion that the framework for his theory of the culture industry was already in place *before* his encounter with American mass culture in the United States. In the Wagner book the pivotal categories of fetishism and reification, ego weakness, regression, and myth are already fully developed, waiting, as it were, to be articulated in terms of the American culture industry. At the same time, reading Adorno's brilliant tour de force on Wagner – and a tour de force it is – produces a strange sense of *déjà vu* in which the temporal terms are once more displaced. It is as if accompanying Adorno on his travels into the nineteenth century we were simultaneously travelling into yet another time-space Adorno himself did not live to experience: that of the postmodern. Large segments of the book on Wagner could be read as a modernist polemic against postmodernism. It is indeed easy to imagine how Adorno would have panned those facile citations of the historical idiom in postmodern architecture and music, how he would have poured scorn over the decay of allegory into the "anything goes" of the art "scene," how he would have resisted the new mythology of aesthetic experience, the cult of performance, of self-help, and of other forms of narcissistic indulgence. Adorno would not have hesitated one moment to see the disintegration of modernism as a return to its prehistory and to collapse the prehistory of the modern with its posthistory.

After all, the artwork is still in the grip of the commodity form, more so, if anything, than in the nineteenth century. The giant spider web of exchange relations Adorno spoke of has certainly expanded since that time. The late nineteenth century still had resistant popular cultures and it left more uncolonized spaces for possible evasions and challenges than today's thoroughly administered culture. If such a reading is by and large correct we will have to ask what the chances are for a genuine contemporary art after the demise of classical modernism. One conclusion would be to see the only possibility for contemporary art in a further elaboration of the modernist project. Possibly, Adorno would have advocated this route even though he was perfectly aware of the dangers of Alexandrian sterility, of a dogmatic ossification of modernism itself. Another conclusion, however, would be to try and relocate contemporary artistic production and practices in the interstices between modernism and mass culture. Commodification invaded Wagner's *oeuvre* without completely debilitating it. On the contrary, it actually gave rise to great works of art. But then one must be permitted to ask why it should not be possible today to produce ambitious and successful works of art which would draw both on the tradition of modernism and on mass culture, including various subcultures. Some of the most interesting art of our time seems to pursue precisely this project. Of course Adorno would argue that the conjuncture that produced Wagner's *oeuvre* is irretrievably past. True enough, but

I am not suggesting simply to revive Wagner's art as a model for the present. Where something like that is being done, e.g., in the films of Syberberg, the results are often less than convincing. The point is rather to take heart from Adorno's account of Wagner's contradictions and dilemmas and to abandon that set of purist stances which would either lock all art in the laboratory of ever more involuted modernist experimentation or reject, uncompromisingly, any attempt to create a contemporary art precisely out of the tensions between modernism and mass culture. Who, after all, would want to be the Lukács of the postmodern . . . ?

Postscript 2000

When this essay was written almost twenty years ago in the midst of a broad revival of interest in Frankfurt School theories of modern culture and society, Adorno's fate on the American intellectual scene was clouded whereas Benjamin's star was rising fast. Increasingly, Adorno served as a straw man in the high/low debate that then energized the emerging field of postmodern studies and their attacks on high modernism. Adorno's rigorous insistence on the autonomy of modernist art was mistakenly equated with a conservative defense of the high cultural canon. People would inveigh *ad nauseam* against Adorno's negative take on jazz and film, two phenomena that signified Americanness in need of defense from European attacks. Adorno served as a welcome target in this post-1960s counterattack on Eurocentric mandarin elitism and postmodern triumphalism. His detractors, rarely familiar with the complexities of his writings, many of which were not available in English or, if so, in exceedingly poor translations, could thus bask in the glow of breaking a lance for American popular culture and racial correctness, as if there had not been a comparable lack of understanding of jazz and mass media among American academic critics and much of the public in the US at the time when Adorno formulated these critiques in the 1940s.

My point in the essay was twofold. I tried to show that Adorno's critique of American mass culture was already prefigured in his work on Richard Wagner, an icon of international high culture, in work which actually preceded Adorno's exile in the US. At stake then and in the exile writings was a dialectic between high and low which the pop culture celebrations of our times mostly choose to ignore. Secondly, the essay was part of an attempt by *New German Critique*, most consistently argued in the brilliant work of Miriam Hansen, to read Adorno against the grain of his stark condemnations of the culture industry. There were indeed indications both in his later essays from the 1960s such as "The Culture Industry Reconsidered" (*NGC* 6) and

"Transparencies of Film" (*NGC* 24–25) as well as in originally unpublished sections of the *Dialectic of Enlightenment*, entitled "Schema der Massenkultur," and in *Composition for the Films* (co-authored with Hanns Eisler) that lowered the polemic several notches and allowed for a more differentiated analysis of mass culture and its reception. At the same time, Adorno never relented in his overriding critique of the commodity and fetishization, tied as they were to his historical analysis of the shift from liberal to monopoly capitalism. Acknowledging such nuances of argument did not radically change the received overall reading of Adorno's critique of the culture industry, but it permitted us to shift the ground from a moralizing leftist argument against elitism and Eurocentrism to a focus on structural categories such as commodification, fetishization, repetition, and ideology, which remain important for any post-Adornean critique of contemporary culture high or low.

Our attempt to complicate the US reception of Adorno, however, fell mostly on deaf ears. The stage was set for the arrival of cultural studies, and cultural studies began to read mass culture as the realm of transgression and subversion while at the same time losing all interest in high culture, traditional or modernist. The image of Adorno as high-cult elitist was so established that an attack on the German philosopher routinely accompanied celebrations of the radical aspirations of the new cultural studies approach. To be sure, this line was not argued by the Birmingham school of cultural studies itself, but by Birmingham's disciples and progeny in the US. Adorno's European high, already chided by some US critics in the 1950s, was yet once again knocked off its imaginary pedestal, and up went low with the establishment of cultural studies programs in this country. In the process, the old hierarchy was simply reversed. Forgotten was the fact that Adorno never thought about high art in terms of pedestals, which was always one of the first things he critiqued (cf. his radical critique of the role of Bach and baroque music in the German post-1945 restoration). Forgotten also was the fact that Adorno's 1940s critique of American mass culture was shared by most of the left New York intellectuals at the time. Ignored finally was the fact that postmodernism in its most ambitious manifestations generated new and exciting hybrid forms that could no longer be captured by the old high/low binary model. The possibility Adorno's work offered, namely to explore the dialectic between high and low in a new historical constellation, went by the wayside, and the old conservative binary model triumphed in its now populist version.

It is worth noting that this basic move of the cultstud left displayed a disturbing similarity to the attack of the canonstud right on another set of European interlopers in the American paradise – Nietzsche, Heidegger, Derrida. Except that the right, in its antimodernist zeal, of course defended high canons and the classics, lamented the closing of the American mind, and demonized cultural studies together with poststructuralism, feminism, and postcolonialism. Where one cohort screamed "elitism," the other attacked relativism, nihilism, and narcissism. Both views are the diametrically opposed after-effects of the 1960s; both are based on shoddy readings, and neither one seems very helpful at a time when the whole high/low dichotomy has itself become rather tired and historically obsolete.

There was thus an all but total failure to acknowledge that for Adorno the high/low binary of capitalist culture was never a strict hierarchical opposition, but rather something like a mirror relationship. The mirror of mass culture demonstrated how all culture under capitalism had become contaminated by structures of profit, power, and class. Surely Adorno's project, ever more difficult to sustain over the decades, was to secure a realm of high modernist culture which to him provided the one and only form of resistance to an immutable status quo. In a famous formulation in a letter to Benjamin, he argued that both modernist art and mass culture bear the scars of capitalism, and that both are torn halves of an integral freedom to which, however, they do not add up. In *After the Great Divide*, I spoke of a compulsive *pas de deux* which still strikes me as a good metaphor for the high/low relationship in the age of modernism. How to think about the high/low dialectic in the age of the new media and the Internet would require fuller treatment which, however, could still draw substantially on Adorno's thought precisely because it refuses to be locked into a reductive dichotomous pattern.

Indeed, there may now be a reversal in Adorno's fate in this country. The 1990s have seen a plethora of new critical treatments of Adorno from a variety of different theoretical and disciplinary angles. More of his work, especially his literary and music criticism, has been translated into English, thus making a more complex understanding possible. His reputation will not match the cult image Benjamin has achieved in the US, but increasingly the two are being read together rather than played off against each other. The recent resurgence of interest in questions of aesthetics, literature, and media issues in the broadest sense make Adorno more pertinent than Habermas, whose work has always neglected these areas central to an earlier Critical Theory. In the realm of studies of mass culture, finally, it seems that an Adorno resurgence is called for at a time when the increasing vertical integration of the culture industry by megamergers and global expansion proceeds apace, and when the cultstud myth of the rebel consumer and her transgressions has run aground.

At a time when so many other positions on media culture fall on the side of either apocalypticism or triumphalism, Adorno's work on high modernism and on the mass culture of a different epoch still provides a good starting point for current discussions. Neither the American populist ethnography of cultural reception, nor sociologies of taste and distinction, whether of the American (Herbert Gans) or French (Pierre Bourdieu) brand, suffice to analyze the constellation of high art and popular culture and their various intersections after postmodernism. How a rigorously historicized Adorno might still strike sparks in literary, visual, and aesthetic analysis at a time when print is losing its power as a dominant medium, the nation state is waning as garantor of traditional high culture, and globalization creates ever more diverse and hybrid cultural formations, remains a task to be further explored.

Notes

1 Jürgen Habermas, *Strukturwandel der Öffentlichkeit* (Neuwied/Berlin: Luchterhand, 1962). See also Habermas, "The Public Sphere," *New German Critique*, 3 (Fall, 1974), 49–55.

2 John Brenkman, "Mass Media: From Collective Experience to the Culture of Privatization," *Social Text*, 1 (Winter 1979), 101.

3 Ibid.

4 For a recent discussion of the interface between modernism and popular culture in Germany see Peter Jelavich, "Popular Dimensions of Modernist Elite Culture: The Case of Theatre in Fin-de-Siècle Munich," in Dominick LaCapra and Steven L. Kaplan (eds.), *Modern European Intellectual History* (Ithaca and London: Cornell University Press, 1982), pp. 220–50.

5 Anthony Giddens, "Modernism and Postmodernism," *New German Critique*, 22 (Winter, 1981), 15. For a different approach to the problem of changes in perception in the 19th century see Anson G. Rabinbach, "The Body without Fatigue: A 19th-Century Utopia," in Seymour Drescher, David Sabean, and Allan Sharlin (eds.), *Political Symbolism in Modern Europe* (New Brunswick, NJ: Transaction Books, 1982), pp. 42–62.

6 Wolfgang Schivelbusch, *Geschichte der Eisenbahnreise. Zur Industrialisierung von Raum und Zeit im 19. Jahrhundert* (Munich and Vienna: Hanser, 1977). Translated into English as *The Railway Journey* (New York: Urizen, 1979).

7 At the same time it should be noted that the major accounts of modernism in literature and art rarely if ever try to discuss the relationship of the modernist work of art to the social and cultural process of modernization at large.

8 I do not know of any specific study which traces the pervasive impact of the culture industry thesis on mass culture research in Germany. For the impact of Adorno and Horkheimer in the United States see Douglas Kellner, "Kulturindustrie und Massenkommunikation. Die kritische Theorie und ihre Folgen," in *Sozialforschung als Kritik*, ed. Wolfgang Bonss and Axel Honneth (Frankfurt am Main: Suhrkamp, 1982), pp. 482–515.

9 For an excellent discussion of the theoretical and historical issues involved in an analysis of the modernism/mass culture/popular culture nexus see Thomas Crow, "Modernism and Mass Culture in the Visual Arts," in S. Guilbaut and D. Solkin (eds.), *Modernism and Modernity* (Halifax, Nova Scotia: The Press of the Nova Scotia College of Art and Design, 1983).

10 Miriam Hansen, "Introduction to Adorno's 'Transparencies on Film'," *New German Critique*, 24–25 (Fall/Winter 1981–2), 186–98.

11 Horkheimer and Adorno, "Das Schema der Massenkultur," in Adorno, *Gesammelte Schriften*, 3 (Frankfurt am Main: Suhrkamp, 1981), p. 331.

12 Ibid.

13 Jochen Schulte-Sasse, "Gebrauchswerte der Literatur," in Christa Bürger, Peter Bürger, and Jochen Schulte-Sasse (eds.), *Zur Dichotomisierung von hoker und niederer Literatur* (Frankfurt am Main: Suhrkamp, 1982), pp. 62–107.

14 Adorno, "Zu Subjekt und Objekt," in *Stichworte* (Frankfurt am Main: Suhrkamp, 1969), p. 165.

15 Ibid. On Adorno's relationship to early German romanticism see Jochen Hörisch, "Herrscherwort, Geld und geltende Sätze: Adornos Aktualisierung der Frühromantik und ihre Affinität zur poststrukturalistischen Kritik des Subjekts," in B. Lindner and W. M. Lüdke, *Materialien zur ästhetischen Theorie Th. W. Adornos* (Frankfurt am Main: Suhrkamp, 1980), pp. 397–414.

16 Adorno, "Sexualtabus und Rechte heute," in *Eingriffe* (Frankfurt am Main: Suhrkamp, 1963), p. 104f.

17 Adorno, *Negative Dialectics*, trans. E. B. Ashton (London: Seabury Press, 1973), p. 212f. (trans. modified).

18 See for instance Bertold Hinz, *Die Malerei im deutschen Faschismus* (Munich: Hanser, 1974).

19 Peter Bürger, *Theory of the Avant-Garde* (Minneapolis: University of Minnesota Press, 1984).

20 Adorno, *Philosophy of Modern Music* (New York: Seabury Press, 1973), p. 30.

21 Peter Bürger, *Vermittlung-Rezeption-Funktion* (Frankfurt am Main: Suhrkamp, 1979), p. 130f. Eugene Lunn, in his valuable study *Marxism and Modernism* (Berkeley, Los Angeles, and London: University of California, 1982), has emphasized Adorno's indebtedness to the "aesthetic of objectified expression" prevalent in Trakl, Heym, Barlach, Kafka, and Schönberg.

22 Adorno, *Ästhetische Theorie* (Frankfurt am Main: Suhrkamp, 1970), p. 16.

23 Ibid., p. 38.

24 Ibid. – The problem here is a historical one, namely that of non-simultaneous developments in different countries and different art forms. Explaining such *Ungleichzeitigkeiten* is no easy task, but it certainly requires a theory of modernism able to relate artistic developments more cogently to social, political, and economic contexts than Adorno's (theoretically grounded) *Berührungsangst* would permit him to do. This is not to say that Adorno misunderstood the genuine modernity of Baudelaire or Manet. On the contrary, it is precisely in the way in which Adorno distinguishes Wagner from the early French modernists that we can glimpse his recognition of such *Ungleichzeitigkeiten*.

25 Adorno, *Noten zur Literatur*, I (Frankfurt am Main: Suhrkamp, 1958), p. 72.
26 Horkheimer and Adorno, *Dialectic of Enlightenment*, p. 163.
27 Adorno, *Ästhetische Theorie*, p. 352.
28 Ibid.
29 Ibid., p. 355.
30 Adorno, *Gesammelte Schriften*, 13 (Frankfurt am Main: Suhrkamp, 1971), p. 504. For a good discussion of Adorno's Schönberg interpretation see Lunn, *Marxism and Modernism*, pp. 256–66. The question of whether Adorno is right about Wagner from a musicological standpoint cannot be addressed here. For a musicological critique of Adorno's Wagner see Carl Dahlhaus, "Soziologische Dechiffrierung von Musik: Zu Theodor W. Adornos Wagner Kritik." *International Review of the Aesthetics and Sociology of Music*, 1:2 (1970), 137–46.
31 Adorno, *Gesammelte Schriften*, 16 (Frankfurt am Main: Suhrkamp, 1978), p. 562.
32 Adorno, *In Search of Wagner*, trans. Rodney Livingstone (London: New Left Books, 1981), p. 31 (trans. modified).
33 Ibid. Cf. also Michael Hays, "Theater and Mass Culture: The Case of the Director," *New German Critique*, 29 (Spring/Summer, 1983), 133–46.
34 Ibid., p. 32.
35 Ibid., p. 46.
36 Ibid., p. 33.
37 Adorno, *Gesammelte Schriften*, 13, p. 499.
38 Adorno, *In Search of Wagner*, p. 49.
39 Ibid., p. 50.
40 Ibid., p. 101.
41 Adorno, "Wagners Aktualität," in *Gesammelte Schriften*, 16, p. 555.
42 Adorno, *In Search of Wagner*, p. 50.
43 Ibid., p. 90.
44 Ibid.
45 Ibid., p. 95.
46 Ibid., p. 119.
47 Ibid., p. 123.
48 Ibid., p. 101.
49 Ibid., p. 107.
50 Ibid., p. 106.
51 Adorno, *Philosophy of Modern Music*, p. 5 (trans. modified).

2

Mass Culture as Hieroglyphic Writing: Adorno, Derrida, Kracauer

Miriam Hansen

The vicissitudes of Adorno's reception in English-language cinema and media studies make a well-known and tedious saga. In its latest chapter, marked by the dissemination of British Cultural Studies in American academic institutions and publishing, the invocation of Adorno's writings on film and mass culture amounts to little more than a ritualistic gesture, reiterating the familiar charges of elitism, pessimism, and high-modernist myopia.[1] The trouble with such accounts is not that they are critical of Adorno – there is much to be critical about – nor even that they use him as a foil against which to assert the identity of a new paradigm or to defend the legitimacy of a field of study which Adorno himself, at his darkest, considered as little more than an appendix of political economy. The trouble is that such accounts effectively preclude critical engagement with the body of thought in question. They do so, for one thing, because they limit themselves to a rather well-trod and narrow basis of texts (narrower even than the amount of writings available in English, whatever problems there may be with the translations). More importantly, they evade the challenge posed by any historical theory of film and mass culture: how to discuss the theoretical claims made in these earlier texts without neutralizing their historical distance and contingency; and, by the same token, how to enlist their very historicity in theorizing the break, as well as the links, between earlier forms of mass culture and our own.

The more interesting critics of Adorno's writings on film and mass culture all, in one way or another, tend to take up this challenge. They try to engage his writings as "a living thought" by historicizing them, by tracing their concerns in relation to ours, by mobilizing disjunctions and contradictions in the texts themselves.[2] Whether reading "Adorno in reverse," "against the grain," or in the spirit of "redemptive critique," such revisionist approaches seek to defamiliarize the well-known arguments, both about him and his own, and to make the texts articulate problems for which they themselves may not have an answer. (Admittedly, this is more difficult in the case of Adorno than it seems for Benjamin. The latter's ostensible endorsement of cinematic technology's inherent political potential has earned him the status of good object in the same canon that dismisses Adorno – the status of a bourgeois theorist who could nonetheless envision a democratic, class-conscious appropriation of mass and consumer culture. Yet, if we wish to learn more from Benjamin than what merely confirms our intellectual-political desire, there is no question that this account needs to be defamiliarized as well.)

One strategy of redeeming Adorno's position on mass culture, in particular film, has been to highlight tropes of "writing" – the graphic, the scriptural – in those texts in which he attempts to conceptualize an aesthetics of film, irrespective of its industrial-technological context of exploitation.[3] To recall the familiar argument, Adorno's reservations against film are rooted in the photographic basis of cinematic representation which subtends its seemingly unmediated doubling of empirical reality; in semiotic terms, its indexically grounded iconic character, that is, a form of signification based in the perceptual likeness between sign and referent. In the context of Adorno and Horkheimer's chapter on the "Culture Industry" in *Dialectic of Enlightenment*, this iconicity is seen as a major source of the cinema's ideological complicity, because it allows the filmic image to function as an advertisement for the world "as is." But even where Adorno begins to think about film in terms of an alternative artistic practice, as in *Composing for the Films* (1947) or "Transparencies on Film" (1966), the philosophical problem remains: that, in its very specificity, (live-action) film conflicts with the Biblical ban on graven images (*Bilderverbot*) which, as Gertrud Koch and other scholars have emphasized, constitutes a regulative idea in Adorno's aesthetic theory.[4] For film to become art, in Adorno's view, it would have to inhibit the photographic iconicity of the image flow by means of cinematic techniques that make it "resemble the phenomenon of writing," that would fracture the illusionist self-identity of the moving image and make it an object of immanent construction, figuration, and deciphering. As Koch points out, the search for a specifically cinematic form of "determinate negation" finds one answer in the principle of montage which, according to Adorno, "arranges [things] in a constellation akin to writing"[5] – that is, discontinuous editing in the widest sense (which for Adorno and Eisler includes sound/image relations).

In a similar vein, Tom Levin defends Adorno against the charge of a Luddite and mandarin hostility toward the mass media by shifting the discussion to Adorno's writings on the gramophone record. Adorno could display a remarkably open, even enthusiastic attitude toward this particular medium of technical reproduction, Levin argues, because he saw in it an indexical, that is, materially motivated, form of inscription (acoustic waves etched into a vinyl plate) that was not hitched, as in film, to an iconically asserted surface resemblance and hence to false immediacy and facile intelligibility. Adorno goes so far as to justify the reification of the live performance by means of the phonograph record on the grounds that it reestablishes "an age-old, submerged and yet warranted relationship: that between music and *writing.*" For the phonograph record replaces the arbitrary conventions of musical notation with a form of non-subjective writing that is at once motivated and unintelligible, a language of "determined yet encrypted expressions." Adorno links this kind of writing to Benjamin's early speculations on language, in particular the *Trauerspiel* book's vision of a "last remaining universal language since the construction of the tower," and Levin in turn links both to the Romantic tradition of a "hieroglyphics of nature."[6]

Whether in the context of film aesthetics or the ontology of record grooves, "writing" for Adorno (as for Benjamin or, for that matter, Derrida) clearly means something different from the notation systems of phonetic languages. In both media, it refers to a form of inscription that is fixed and motivated in its discrete signs, yet is not immediately accessible and requires deciphering. For both film and the phonograph, the emphasis on "writing" implies a form of reception closer to the activity of "reading" than to the automatic consumption excoriated by Adorno in "The Fetish Character of Music and the Regression of Listening" and elsewhere. If this were indeed the case, we should be able to extrapolate from Adorno's writings on film aesthetics and the phonograph not only an alternative practice of filmmaking and composition, but also a different vision of collective reception.

To emphasize Adorno's investment in the scriptural character of the technological media is, I think, a valid and necessary argument. It occludes, however, the negative valence that the terms "writing" and "reading" have for Adorno in the context of mass culture, nowhere as strongly as in his notion of film and other media as hieroglyphics. Focusing on the latter, I will ask what kinds of writing and reading, what processes of signification and reception are involved in that comparison. Among other things, this raises the question of the subject(s) and situations of reading, in particular the relationship of the critical theorist to both the mass-cultural hieroglyph and its "ordinary" consumers. Moreover, if we find that Adorno may have captured something about processes of mass-cultural identification for the period in which he was writing – that is, Hollywood at its most classical, American mass culture at its most Fordist – what does this analysis tell us about post-modern, post-Fordist media culture and its seemingly obverse strategies of diversification? Finally, Adorno's untimely negativity may encourage us to rethink the possibility and necessity of critique, even if today we are likely to invest greater confidence in the ability of mass-cultural publics to reappropriate industrially manufactured meanings in diverse, oppositional and collective ways: the stakes and methods of manipulation may have changed, but postmodern media culture is still a far cry from any utopian, radically democratic notion of the "popular."

In his 1953 essay, "Prolog zum Fernsehen" (Prologue to Television), Adorno speaks of mass culture as a "language of images" (*Bildersprache*), "pictographic writing" (*Bilderschrift*), or "hieroglyphic writing" (*Hieroglyphenschrift*). This language of images lends itself to the "will of those in charge," all the more so as it attempts "to pass itself off as the language of those whom it supplies":

> By giving visual representation to what slumbers in the preconceptual layers of their minds, [this language of images] simultaneously shows them how to behave. While the images of film and television strive to conjure up those that are buried in the viewer and indeed resemble them, they also, in the manner of their flashing up and gliding past, approach the effect of writing: they are grasped but not contemplated. The eye is pulled along by the shot as it is by the printed line and in the gentle jolt of the cut a page is turned. As image, this pictographic language is the medium of regression in which producer and consumer collude; as writing, it displays the archaic images of modernity.[7]

The analogy between mass-cultural images and hieroglyphic writing is grounded, at first sight, on the level of psychoanalysis, in the affinity of filmic/televisual discourse with pre- and unconscious modes of thought. Accordingly, Adorno footnotes an article by two Italian psychoanalysts who belabor that affinity drawing mainly on Freud's *Interpretation of Dreams*.[8] But where these authors celebrate the pictographic and prelogical quality of filmic images as the ideal of "pure cinema," Adorno discerns a powerful mechanism of ideology, reminiscent of Leo Löwenthal's quip about the culture industry as "psychoanalysis in reverse." By mimicking the figurations of unconscious or preconscious phantasy, Adorno argues, mass-cultural hieroglyphics actually spell out a behavioral script; by disguising the very fact that they were written, and with it their heteronomous origin, they create the regressive illusion of a common discourse. Similar to film theorists of the 1970s such as

Metz and Baudry, Adorno ascribes this ideological effect to the configuration of the apparatus, the psychotechnical conditions of film reception, rather than a particular mode of film practice.[9]

The regression that Adorno sees facilitated by the hieroglyphics of mass culture, however, is not just a matter of individual or even social psychology. The statement that, "as writing," they display "the archaic images of modernity" points to another context – the historico-philosophical framework of the *Dialectic of Enlightenment*. In the note citing the psychoanalytic article, Adorno primarily refers the reader to his (and Horkheimer's) use of the term hieroglyphic writing in the long-time apocryphal sequel to the chapter on the culture industry, entitled "Das Schema der Massenkultur" (not published until 1981). In that context, the notion of mass culture as hieroglyphics ties in with the familiar themes of the *Dialectic of Enlightenment*: the reversion of Enlightenment into myth and the resurfacing of the archaic in modern forms of domination; the dissociation of image and sign, and the concomitant instrumentalization of language and reification of aesthetic expression; the double character of mimesis; and the false identity of individual and social totality under monopoly capitalism, advanced by a cultural economy of commodity fetishism, repetition, and regression.

In "The Schema of Mass Culture," the interpretation of mass culture as hieroglyphics seems to confirm the most problematic aspect of Horkheimer and Adorno's indictment of the culture industry, the thesis of total manipulation and delusion, compounded with the system's timeless, perennial quality. Like the fascist resurrection of archetypes, the ostensibly consumer-engendered dream production of Hollywood is seen as a manufacturing of archaic symbols on an industrial scale; like the former, these function as allegories of domination: "In the rulers' dream of the mummification of the world, mass culture serves as the priestly hieroglyphic script which addresses its images to those subjugated, not to be relished but to be read." Predicated on repetition and effect, such pictographic language culminates the historical "transition from image to writing" or "script" (*Übergang von Bild in Schrift*), the absorption of mimetic capabilities by monopolistic practice.[10]

The term "priestly hieroglyphics" refers back to the opening chapter of *Dialectic of Enlightenment* in which Horkheimer and Adorno elaborate the imbrication of myth and enlightenment in terms of a genealogy of language. Here hieroglyphics is introduced as a "symbolic" language, mediated by "the doctrine of the priests," but one in which the functions of word and image still converged. The core of the symbolic is the mythical conception of nature as cyclical, endlessly renewable and permanent. The historical process of disenchantment, in Horkheimer and Adorno's account, inevitably entails a dissociation of verbal and pictorial functions. In the division of labor between science and the arts, language degenerates, on the one hand, into a "mere system of signs," into an instrument of recognizing nature by renouncing any similarity with it; as image (*Bild*), on the other, language is made to resign itself to the function of copy, imitation, or reflection (*Abbild*), to become all nature but renounce any claims to recognize it.[11] Implied in this historico-philosophical construction, however, is another genealogy, which traces the fall of language as a movement from an originary *written* language to a demythologized language described in *phonological*, Saussurian terms. This implies further that the mimetic capability of language is conceived as belonging to its originary form as (hieroglyphic) writing, rather than the spoken word. With the shift to a phonocentric concept of language, mimetic capability recedes into the realm of the image, the preverbal layers of aesthetic expression. But inasmuch as that realm too, in monopolistic culture, is increasingly subject to reification, it reverts to a state of writing, in the sense of allegorical mortification. Thus, in the universal idiom of modern mass culture, the ancient hieroglyphs return to consummate mimetic desire with a vengeance. With the technologically enhanced "transition from image to writing" the reversal of enlightenment into myth has come full circle.

As an instance of the progressive reification of aesthetic expression, the notion of mass-cultural hieroglyphics merely elaborates for film and television what Adorno had stressed earlier in his critique of popular music, in particular his writings on jazz and his essay on Wagner. There he traced the reification of musical expression into formulaic fragments that could be end-lessly replicated, corresponding to the reduction of listening to hearing only what one has heard before. Instead of exposing or refiguring the effects of reification, alienation, and fragmentation, popular music, following Wagner, works to cover them up, to rehumanize and provide an affective "glue" for irrevocably sundered social relations.

By a similar logic, aggravated by the iconicity of the visual media, the hieroglyphics of mass culture exert a regressive appeal, in Horkheimer and Adorno's account, not because they would reflect the general state of reification ("the mummification of the world") but, on the contrary, because they mask that state, disguising script as pure image, as natural, humanized presence. In the emphasis on false concreteness, the notion of mass-cultural hieroglyphics echoes Marx's troping of the commodity as a "social hieroglyph," his attempt to locate the "magic" of the commodity in its simultaneously sensual and hypersensual quality.[12] If the commodity beckons the consumer as a real thing, its value, its "real" meaning, is determined by its abstraction of labor and its position within a total system of exchange. Similarly, the "secret doctrine" communicated by the hieroglyphics of mass culture is not the historical truth of reification, but the "message of capital." Its secrecy, its encryptment, however, has nothing to do with the enigma of the non-intentional, transsubjective language of aesthetic images; rather, it is a ploy of total domination to keep itself invisible: "no shepherd and a herd."

Simulating immediacy, individuality, and intimacy, the "characters" of mass culture spell out norms of social behavior – ways of being, smiling, and mating. Regardless of the explicit messages touted via dialogue and plot, the viewer is ceaselessly asked to translate image into script, to read the individual appearance of a star as an imperative of identity – "to be like her" – and to articulate the most subtle nuances in terms of the binary logic of "do and don't" (*GS* 3: 333; *CI* 81). While we might expect this to happen to a supposedly passive viewer under the spell of diegetic absorption, Adorno and Horkheimer rather impugn mass culture's specific forms of hermeneutic pleasure, that is, narrative and generic conventions that encourage the viewer to second-guess the apparent mysteries of plot or construction. It is in the shift of the viewer's attention to the "how" by which the trivial resolution is achieved, "the rebus-like detail," that the "hieroglyphic meaning flashes up in him or her." In other words, Horkheimer and Adorno ascribe the effectivity of mass-cultural scripts of identity not simply to the viewers' manipulation as passive consumers, but rather to their very solicitation as experts, as active readers.[13] The identification *with* the stereotype is advanced by the appeal to a particular type of knowledge or skill predicated on repetition: the identification *of* a familiar face, gesture, or narrative convention takes the place of genuine cognition.

In "Prologue to Television," Adorno gives the hieroglyphic imperative of identity a somewhat subtler twist by qualifying it as the culture industry's cynical recommendation, "become what you are."

> Its lie consists in the repeated affirmation and rigidification of mere being, of that which the course of the world has made of human beings. . . . Instead of paying tribute to the unconscious by elevating it to consciousness so as to fulfill its urge and at the same time pacify its destructive force, the culture industry . . . reduces human beings to their unconscious behavior even more than the conditions of their existence do all along. [*GS* 10.2: 514]

The ideological effect of mass-cultural hieroglyphics is not so much a matter of administering positive (or negative) models but, rather, of preventing human beings from changing, from being different, from distinguishing their own wishes and needs from those imposed upon them by distribution from above. As Adorno says in a later text, analyzing the myth of "consumer-oriented art": "By reproducing [the reified consciousness of the audience] with hypocritical subservience, the culture industry in effect changes this consciousness all the more, that is, for its own purposes: it actually prevents that consciousness from changing on its own, as it deep down, unadmittedly desires. The consumers are made to remain what they are: consumers" ("TF" 205).

In "Schema," Horkheimer and Adorno see the identificatory spell of the mass-cultural hieroglyph linked to the return of mimesis, as I suggested earlier, coupled with the resurfacing of archaic writing. "Mimesis," they propose, "explains the mysteriously empty ecstasy of the fans of mass culture." If this is clearly a perverted form of mimesis, it still feeds on its utopian opposite, the possibility of reconciliation. What "drives human beings into the movie theaters," Adorno and Horkheimer observe, as it were, in the same breath, may be "the deeply buried hope" that one day the hieroglyphic "spell may be broken" (GS 3: 334; CI 82).

"Mimesis" notably is a central category in Adorno's thought and a notoriously difficult one at that.[14] Like many of his key categories, mimesis has a number of different, possibly conflicting meanings depending on the constellation in which it is used – meanings to which I can only allude here in a rather reductive manner. In the anthropological-philosophical context of *Dialectic of Enlightenment*, the concept of mimesis is derived from magic and shamanistic practices as well as zoological forms of mimicry. It involves making oneself similar to the environment; a relation of adaptation, affinity, and reciprocity, a non-objectifying interchange with the Other; and a fluid, pre-individual form of subjectivity. In this sense, the concept of mimesis assumes a critical and corrective function vis-à-vis instrumental rationality and the identifying logic of conceptual language which distances subject from object and represses the non-identity of the latter. Since, however, the historical subjugation of nature has irrevocably transformed nature and sundered its relations with society, mimetic practice can be thought of only in a utopian mode. As a utopian category, mimesis prefigures the possibility of a reconciliation with nature, which includes the inner nature of human beings, the body, and the unconscious.

By the twentieth century, mimetic experience in the utopian sense is conceivable only in the realm of art, specifically art that inscribes the historical disfigurement of human, social relations with nature. In the context of Adorno's *Aesthetic Theory*, mimesis marks a form of aesthetic expression that inverts traditional (Platonic) notions of mimesis as imitation, in particular Marxist theories of reflection.[15] Mimesis for Adorno does not pertain to the relation between sign and referent; it is not a category of representation. Rather, it aims at a mode of subjective experience, a preverbal form of cognition, which is rendered objective in works of art, summoned up by the density of their construction. Such moments of transsubjective expression constitute art's *promesse de bonheur*, the unfulfilled promise of reconciliation. At the same time, throughout modern art history, the mimetic impulse has also objectified itself in the bent toward imitation, in the futile attempt to close the gap with the object by doubling it.[16]

To the extent that it is patterned on zoological forms of "mimicry," Adorno's concept of mimesis involves the slippage between life and death, the assimilation to lifeless material (as in the case of the chameleon) or feigning death for the sake of survival. This paradox, indebted to Freud's theory of the death drive, structures the dichotomies of the mimesis concept in significant ways. In an unreflected form, mimesis as mimicry converges with the regime of instrumental reason, its reduction of life to self-preservation and the reproduction of domination by the very means designed to abolish it. In that sense, mimesis entails what Michael Cahn calls "a deadly reification compulsion" that perpetuates the state for which Adorno likes to cite Kürnberger's apothegm, "Das Leben lebt nicht" (life is not alive). In the context of aesthetic theory, however, this mimesis onto the reified and alienated ("Mimesis ans Verhärtete und Entfremdete"), the world of living death, is a crucial means of negation available to modern art – as an "admixture of poison," a pharmakon that allegorizes the symptoms though it necessarily fails as a therapy.[17]

In the context of the culture industry, the concept of mimesis is obviously dominated by the negative connotations of both an unreflected mimicry onto reified and alienated conditions and the misguided aesthetic investment in imitation. But it is important to remember that even at this low point of its dialectics, mimesis does not concern a semiotic relation between sign and referent, but the social relations between subjects and commodities. These are determined by a reification compulsion that enjoins economic and psychoanalytic senses of fetishism in the "I-know-quite-well-but-all-the-same" of enlightened consumption. The "triumph of advertising in the culture industry," the chapter on the culture industry concludes, is made possible by "the compulsive mimesis of the consumers onto the cultural commodities, even as they see through them."[18]

In "Schema of Mass Culture," Horkheimer and Adorno elaborate on this remark in terms of the hieroglyphic analogy. As hieroglyphic signs, the characters of film and television rehearse the compulsive assimilation of human beings to the commodity. In the very assertion of individuality, every face, every smile congeals into a mask, a grimace: "The face becomes a letter by freezing that which brings it to life – laughter." The secret of the "keep smiling" is that it transforms the horror over the possibility of such fixation "into obedience before the mortified face." In the economy of perverted mimesis, reification is not just a metaphor: mass culture "literally makes the human beings it reproduces resemble things, even where their teeth do not signify toothpaste, even where the lines of grief in their faces do not conjure up a laxative."[19] By identifying with such images, the viewers surrender their mimetic desire to the universe of death, accepting a false social identity in place of the genuine collectivity and reciprocity they secretly hope for in the experience of mass culture.

This expectation is not entirely a matter of (self-)deception. Horkheimer and Adorno grant at least the potential for true mimetic experience to silent film as a medium and apparatus. For the tendency toward hieroglyphics, they argue, reached its full force only with the transition to sound: the masks of mass culture are all the more terrifying once they begin to talk, once they are naturalized by synchronized dialogue. In silent film, the alternation between written titles and images, as antithetical materials, allowed the images to retain some of their imagistic, mimetic quality. This dialectic, however, was incompatible with the culture industry's bent toward amalgamation and homogeneity. It altogether collapsed with the advent of sound, when written language was "expelled from film as an alien presence [*Fremdkörper*], but only to transform the images themselves into the writing which they in turn absorbed" (*GS* 3: 333; *CI* 81). The material heterogeneity of silent film thus harbors a moment of resistance which, once eliminated, makes technological progress all the more a catalyst of regression.

In a similar movement, Adorno's "Prologue to Television" affirms his case against the bad present by highlighting the critical difference of similar conventions in the past. There he contrasts the stereotypes of the mass-cultural hieroglyphic with stereotypical figures in earlier forms of popular art which, "in the spirit of allegory," registered and hyperbolized objective developments. Unlike the character masks of the modern mass media, "the highly stylized types of the Commedia dell'arte," for instance, "were so removed from the everyday existence of the audience that it would not have occurred to anyone to model their own experience after the mask-like clowns" (*GS* 10.2: 515).

But is this objectifying "spirit of allegory," a notion clearly indebted to Benjamin, not to some extent still present in the hieroglyphics of mass culture, in the very metaphor of hieroglyphics? The reified idiom of mass-cultural products is, after all, also the condition of their critical readability; only as figurations of writing can the naturalized images of mass culture be deciphered, can their "secret code" be cracked. As Adorno and Horkheimer assert in the introduction of *Dialectic of Enlightenment*, echoing Benjamin's programmatic transformation of myth into allegory: "Dialectical thought interprets every image as writing. It teaches how to read in its own features the admission of its falsity so as to deprive it of its power and appropriate it for truth" (*GS* 3: 41; *DE* 24). The same double vision seems to inform Adorno's approach to mass-cultural hieroglyphics, specifically in the phrase quoted earlier: "As image, this pictographic language is the medium of regression in which producer and consumer collude; as writing, it displays the archaic images of modernity."

Alas, not quite. It is easy to misread this phrase in light of the poststructuralist aura of "writing" and "reading," and I have done so myself by mistranslating the verb, "*zur Verfügung stellen*," as "display" instead of "supply" or "make available." A more adequate translation would therefore be: "as writing, [this pictographic language] supplies the archaic images of modernity," or alternatively, if we read "*der Moderne*" as the dative case, "supplies archaic images to modernity."[20]

There are actually, at least, two kinds of writing, and two kinds of reading, involved in Adorno's notion of mass-cultural hieroglyphics. Indeed, his argument hinges upon the distinction between a literal and a figurative, between a complicit and a critical form of reading.[21] Himself a critical reader, Adorno discerns the emergence of a different type of reading, a mode of enlightened viewer response which amounts to little more than predetermined picture-puzzle solving, based on a short circuit between mass-cultural conventions and the consumer's disfigured unconscious.

Adorno's concept of writing is just as ambivalent, and relative to constellations, as his concept of mimesis, to which it is intimately linked. In the context of the culture industry, writing apparently means script in the sense of *Vorschrift* or prescription, a discourse that masks itself in iconic images and familiar sounds. In the context of aesthetic theory, however, writing becomes *écriture*, the non-subjective, indirect language of modern music and abstract painting. In its renunciation of traditional imitational and even expressive elements, this *écriture* is profoundly historical. Adorno links the scriptural character of modern art to a "seismographic" capacity, the "breaking through of early mimetic behavior" comparable to physical irritations, by which such art registers the tremors of distant, even future, catastrophes.[22] More generally, Adorno joins writing, and tropes of graphicity such as "cipher" and "hieroglyph," with the character of art as enigma (*Rätsel*). "All works of art are scripts [*Schriften*] . . . that is, hieroglyphic ones whose code has been lost and whose gravity [*Gehalt*] not least depends on the fact that their code is missing" (*GS* 3: 189). The enigmatic character of artworks is constitutive and unsolvable; the secret of mass-cultural hieroglyphs, by contrast, translates into a singular meaning – which in turn can be decoded only by the critical reader.

The ambivalence of Adorno's notion of writing may be yet another symptom of the split between his aesthetic theory and the analysis of culture as commodity and industry in the *Dialectic of Enlightenment*.[23] It would therefore make sense that the section on the mass-cultural hieroglyphic does not follow the rhetorical strategy of the culture industry chapter, that is, the pairing of particular aspects of mass-cultural practice with particular concepts of bourgeois aesthetics (such as "Gesamtkunstwerk," "catharsis," or the Kantian "purposefulness without purpose") which the culture industry at once mocks and consummates. The opposition between "script" and "*écriture*," between "secret code" and "enigma" has to remain implicit, because the absent counterpart belongs to a different register (as well as to a later phase of Adorno's work).

By the same token, however, it could be argued that, especially in Adorno's postwar texts, the distinction between writing as *écriture* and writing as script all too often coincides with the institutional divisions between high art and popular culture. The problem with this linkage is not so much the insistence on an aesthetic dimension (to which I will return), but the way it circumscribes the position of the critical theorist toward mass-cultural phenomena, in particular his relation to the "ordinary" consumers. Notwithstanding the principle of immanent critique, Adorno's attitude toward mass culture involved a notorious gap, if not an unreflected hierarchy between the critical intellectual and the subjects of consumption, the "slow-witted" or "batrachians" (*Lurche*). While it would be foolish to deny Adorno's "mandarin" sensibility, the issue is more complicated. For it raises the question as to the possibility of an alternative discourse on mass culture that is simultaneously receptive and critical, non-elitist and yet not simply "popular." Bound up with this question is the larger one of whether and how mimetic-aesthetic experience can be generalized, that is, democratized, even under the conditions of late capitalist, electronic media publics. I will return to these questions via a detour through other concepts of film and mass culture as hieroglyphic, with a focus on Derrida and Kracauer.

The comparison between cinema and hieroglyphics appears rather early and frequently in discourse on film throughout the silent era; with the transition to sound, the analogy became less obvious and less opportune. In France, commentators like Victor Perrot celebrated film for its restoration of "humanity's first writing system" (1919) and film-makers like Abel Gance claimed that the cinema would save the cultural heritage for the future by returning to the ancient Egyptian language of images.[24] In the United States, the poet Vachel Lindsay advertised film as a new "American hieroglyphics" as early as 1915, resuming the fascination with the Egyptian hieroglyph in the writings of Whitman, Emerson, Poe, and Thoreau, as well as a popular undercurrent ranging from hieroglyphic Bibles to children's books like *Mother Goose in Hieroglyphics*. D. W. Griffith, at home in the tradition of the American Renaissance, was certainly familiar with Lindsay's slogan when he made *Intolerance* (1916), a film that put the hieroglyphic analogy into practice and thus aimed to affiliate itself with this particular tradition in American culture.[25]

In most commentaries during the silent era, the comparison between cinema and hieroglyphics is celebratory, if not apologetic; the underlying concept of hieroglyphics is one of a language of mystical correspondence and visual self-evidence, reincarnated in the new universal language of film. Yet there is another direction of conceptualizing film as hieroglyphic, or ideographic writing in a wider sense. In a famous essay of 1929, Sergei Eisenstein illustrates his argument for "intellectual montage" (the signification of an abstract meaning by juxtaposing two separate visual representations) with reference to the Chinese ideogram and its composition from pictographic elements (which he calls "hieroglyphics"). During the 1930s, he abandoned this basically constructivist model in favor of a more complex notion of film as ideographic writing based on the psycholinguistic concept of "inner speech," a topic explored by the Bakhtin circle at the time.[26] The analogy between filmic writing and the process of association and figuration in the human mind, a process that mixes images, words, and symbols, entailed an emphasis on the composite character of the cinematic sign, its mixing of figural, graphic, and phonic matters of expression. If the filmic hieroglyph is thus conceived as fundamentally heterogeneous, however, its mode of signification is anything but self-evident, self-identical, and universal.

It is in this sense that the hieroglyphic analogy has been revived, in the more recent past, by Derridean film theory.[27] The key text for this endeavor is notably *Of Grammatology*, where Derrida traces the suppression of writing in the name of speech through the vicissitudes of the hieroglyph. In particular, he elaborates on the epistemological shift in the concept of the hieroglyphic sign, from the long-standing Western idealization of the hieroglyph as a form of mystical correspondence between sign and referent to the eighteenth-century discovery of the hieroglyph's simultaneously phonetic and non-phonetic mode of signification which enabled the deciphering of the Rosetta Stone. For Derrida, the conceptualization of "the organized cohabitation, within the same graphic code, of figurative, symbolic, abstract, and phonetic elements" emblematizes the moment at which "a systematic reflection upon the correspondence between writing and speech could be born."[28] The hieroglyph assumes a further paradigmatic function for Derrida in his reading of Freud, especially with regard to the pictographic writing of dreams which "exceeds phonetic writing and puts speech back in its place."[29]

Derrida's notion of hieroglyphics is no doubt more complex than Adorno's because, ironically one might say, Derrida historicizes the very concept of the hieroglyph which Adorno assumes as a given. While they converge in the critique of hieroglyphics as a "natural language," Derrida draws more radical conclusions from the irreducible heterogeneity of the hieroglyphic sign. Granting it an indeterminacy and indirection that Adorno reserves only for works of autonomous art, Derrida shifts the question of meaning from the sign to the reader: the hieroglyphic is ultimately not a property of the text but a method and metaphor of interpretation.

As a struggle of interpretations, the history of the hieroglyph exemplifies the indissociable relationship between writing and power. In his reading of Bishop Warburton's 1744 essay on Egyptian hieroglyphs, Derrida focuses on Warburton's contention that hieroglyphics were not originally a sacral, esoteric script but a natural medium for preserving knowledge and civil organization, and that its deflection from common usage came about by a historical and political act of encryptment which rendered writing a secret and reserved knowledge in the hands of the priests. While Derrida predictably questions the naturalist origin of the hieroglyph posited by Warburton, he stresses the latter's insistence that the hieroglyph's encryptment came about as a political event or strategy (rather than a divine mystery as earlier accounts would have it). Spinning out the dual figure of priest and hieroglyph, Derrida traces the net that binds writing to the production, circulation, and contestation of meaning and knowledge, and both to a "caste" of intellectuals and institutions that ensure "hegemony, whether [their] own or that of special interests."[30] Unlike Warburton, Derrida sees the "crypto-politics of writing" as a necessary and inevitable process, inseparable from the effort to undo the "discriminating reservation." "Whenever a code is inverted, disencrypted, made public, the mechanism of power produces another one, secret and sacred, 'profound.'" Thus writing is never outside or independent of power, just as power cannot be grasped, or indicted, as a unitary and general principle; rather, it is a matter of "struggles and contending forces" that set up and permeate "writings and counter-writings." Nor is any form of writing or power originary. The cryptographic maneuver of intellectuals and politicians "*does not consist in inventing new religions but in making use of the remanence,*" Derrida concludes, quoting Warburton, "*in 'taking advantage of those that they find already established.'*"[31]

Such reasoning places Derrida in surprising vicinity with cultural theories indebted to Gramscian notions of hegemony or, closer to the Frankfurt School, with conceptions of the public sphere as multiple, hybrid and antagonistic such as we find in Negt and Kluge. This strand of Derrida's thinking on the gnoseo-politics of writing, however, seems to have had little impact on Derridean approaches to film and the electronic media. Marie-Claire Ropars-Wuilleumier, for instance, the most eminent Derridean film critic in France, limits her elaboration of "filmic writing" (*cinécriture*) to certain "hieroglyphic texts" – Eisenstein's *October*, films by Resnais, Duras, and Godard – and thus to a canon inspired by literary modernism. On the other end of the spectrum we have Gregory Ulmer's attempt to popularize Derrida in *Applied Grammatology*, a book that celebrates the electronic media in McLuhanesque fashion as the last nail on the coffin of the metaphysics of the "Book": "The pedagogy of grammatology is, finally, an educational discourse for an age of video."[32] In either case, there is hardly any reflection on the institutional parameters of film/video writing (and the hegemonic valorization of image over writing), its contestation within particular public spheres, its imbrication with networks of profit and power. By privileging "graphicity" as such, these adaptations perpetuate, to paraphrase Derrida, the "mystification" of the "singular abstraction," of Writing as much as of Power, "fostering the belief that one can do otherwise than to oppose powers to powers and writings to other writings."[33]

Moreover, Derridean film theory lacks a historical perspective that would relate the emergence of the mass media, as a rather specific form of writing, to the cultural, economic, and political transformations associated with modernity or, for that matter, postmodernity – to the emergence of new forms of subjectivity and knowledge, domination and resistance. One could argue that Adorno's indictment of mass-cultural hieroglyphics is just as ahistorical, unspecific, and abstract as the Derridean valorization of Writing, and therefore just as inadequate to the tasks of critical media theory and practice. If the object of critique is the culture industry as "system" and totality, there is no space for concepts of cultural difference and contestation and hence no way to conceptualize historical change.

In each paradigm, the hieroglyph functions as an allegory of signification itself: in one case demonstrating the irreducible heterogeneity internal to the sign which undermines fictions of identity, unity, linearity, priority; in the other, rehearsing the script of reification that veils itself in moving images. These tropological structures inform the very styles of reading and reasoning. If catachresis is the master trope of deconstruction, Adorno reasons in figures of paradox and contradiction. For instance: "Every peal of laughter resonates with the blackmailer's threat and the comic types are written characters [*Schriftzeichen*] for the disfigured bodies of the revolutionaries."[34] Or: "The photographic assertion that the trees are green, the sky is blue and that the clouds are moving already turns these images [of nature] into cryptograms of factory chimneys and gas stations" – cryptograms, that is, of a double violation of nature, the industrial one as well as the cultural denial of such disfigurement in the industrial imaging of nature as pure (*GS* 3: 171; *DE* 149).

From a deconstructionist point of view, such statements flaunt a moral pathos that impairs their analytic claims. But they also illustrate a crucial difference of cognitive interest, not just between Derrida and Adorno but between deconstruction and Critical Theory in a wider sense. If the former seeks to demonstrate the epistemic primacy of language over history, the latter is concerned with the historical inscription of the present, as the juncture of economic, social, political forces that are not outside or before language yet also cannot be explained solely in terms of the problematic of language.[35] The dissociation of language and experience, like the dialectic of writing and mimesis, itself becomes a mark of historicity, linked to the advent of modernity, even if – as in Adorno and Benjamin – modernity is seen as entering into peculiar constellations with prehistory.

The question of the historical place of modernity leads me to my last example, an alternative concept of mass culture as hieroglyphic in the context of Critical Theory. In his articles and reviews of the 1920s and early 1930s, Siegfried Kracauer reads the ephemeral, unnoticed, and culturally marginalized phenomena of everyday life as configurations of writing, resorting to scriptural figures such as "hieroglyph," "ornament," "rebus," or "arabesque." With his turn to the quotidian and neglected, Kracauer belongs to a larger tradition, related in turn to the philosophical program of "the readability of the world."[36] In the crisis perceived as modernity, this program finds a particular inflection in the work of Jewish intellectuals – Simmel, Benjamin, Bloch, Franz Hessel, to mention only a few – who direct reading skills developed in the interpretation of sacred and canonical texts to the spaces and artifacts of modern urban life, trying to decipher a hidden subtext that is referred to redemption. Like Adorno, Kracauer realized the importance of Benjamin's study on the *Baroque* Trauerspiel for the contemporary situation, particularly the latter's redefinition of allegory in the framework of *Naturgeschichte*. But Kracauer also insisted that Benjamin's own allegorical method, "the dissociation of immediately experienced unities," would not reach its "detonating" force unless actually applied to the present.[37]

Kracauer's recourse to scriptural metaphors, like his entire emblematic mode of reading, seems initially motivated by an apocalyptic sense of withdrawal of meaning from the world, which blends contemporary theories of alienation and reification (Weber, Lukács) with the imagery of Jewish Messianism and Gnosticism.[38] Adorno, reared on the same discourse, was wont to imagine the social reality of reification in images of mortification, rigidification, and death by freezing (*Kältetod*) – the most negative form of mimesis. Kracauer, using similar imagery, visualized the effects of reification simultaneously as a process of dissociation, as a "disintegration of the world" (*Weltzerfall*). Once he moved beyond a history of decline, Kracauer saw the fracturing of all familiar relations and shapes increasingly (that is, before 1933) as a chance – to point up the "*preliminary* character of all given configurations,"[39] to watch the fragments reconfigure themselves, perhaps into something new.

The crystallization of the social environment into scriptural figures is no more the "authorless script" of a metaphysical History than it is an invitation to random readings. From the mid-twenties on, Kracauer conceives of this process quite concretely in terms of the effects of capitalist rationalization, specifically, the abstraction of human labor and bodies; the progressive detemporalization and discontinuity of perception and experience; and a turn to the "surface," the tendency toward "pure externality" he discerned in the emerging mass culture of entertainment and consumption.[40] Like many Weimar intellectuals, Kracauer welcomed mass culture as a practical critique of the remnants of bourgeois high culture and philosophical attempts to patch up the actual state of disintegration and disorder. The figuration of the "mass as ornament," for instance, which Kracauer observed in musical revues and sports displays, objectivates the "exodus of the human figure from sumptuous organic splendor and individual shape into anonymity" and thus promotes the demise of concepts such as personality and the self-identical subject.[41]

Above and beyond this iconoclastic, allegorizing function, the mass ornament remains profoundly ambiguous – as ambiguous as the historical process which it congeals into legibility. On the one hand, the anti-organic tendency of such figurations has a utopian dimension for Kracauer in prefiguring a state in which only those remnants of nature prevail that do not resist reason. On the other, the mass ornament encapsulates the dialectic of capitalist rationality (which points in the direction of the *Dialectic of Enlightenment*): instead of emancipating humanity from the forces of nature, capitalist rationality perpetuates society as mere nature and thus reverts into myth; reproducing forms of economic and social organization that do not include the human being, the process of disenchantment stops half-way, arresting thought in empty abstraction and false concreteness.[42] While the mass ornament achieves a measure of (aesthetic) abstraction and succeeds in inspiring in the spectating mass a measure of spontaneous recognition (of their own reality), its patterns ultimately remain "mute," renaturalized, unpermeated by reason. Kracauer's distress seems to be far less over the parallel between chorus line and assembly line, as is often claimed, than over the "muteness" of the mass ornament, its lack of (self-)consciousness, as it were, its inability to read itself. But the answer, as Kracauer asserts here as in other contexts, is not evasion or critical rejection: "the process leads right through the middle of the mass ornament, not back from it."[43]

Not all of Kracauer's scriptural tropes are that clearly defined or decoded in historico-philosophical terms. More often, the figures he traces are writerly attempts to register a multiplicity of phenomena that are as yet unnamed; the very image of the "turn to the surface" is an effort to trope them into legibility. What these phenomena share is an increased focus of perception on the visual, a "primacy of the optical" that Adorno found characteristic – and problematic – in Kracauer's own mode of thinking.[44] It is no coincidence that so many of Kracauer's essays traverse sites and media of visual fascination: photography, film and movie theaters, hotel lobbies, bars, streets, squares, arcades, department stores, city maps, neon lighting, amusement parks, circus and variety shows. Visuality itself becomes a cipher that Kracauer explores from a number of different and conflicting angles, often within one and the same text. While the paradigm of reification and disintegration and their opposite, the ideological masking of such developments in the "flight of images," remains an important code for Kracauer throughout, these emblems of visuality also occasion reflections on the historically changed relation between image and reality, epitomized by the relation of photography and history.[45] On whichever side he comes down in the particular case, his readings at their best describe new forms of subjectivity, fantasy, and pleasure that we now associate with the psychosexual dynamics of consumption – new forms of ideology but also new possibilities of collective experience and expression.

But the historical process not only brings forth emblems of glamor or excesses of so-called information. What Kracauer understood like hardly any of his contemporaries is how a society that "externalizes" itself in terms of visuality and visibility defines what remains repressed, hidden from public view. In his 1930 essay on Berlin unemployment agencies, he rejects the official debates and interpretations of statistics in favor of a reading of unemployment as an arrangement of social space, as a spatial hieroglyph:

> Every typical space is produced by typical social relations which it expresses without the distorting intervention of consciousness. Everything denied by consciousness, everything studiously ignored participates in the construction of such a space. The images of space [*Raumbilder*] are the dreams of society. Wherever the hieroglyph of a spatial image is deciphered, it displays the foundation of social reality.[46]

Notwithstanding the epistemological optimism, this hieroglyph is anything but unitary. Kracauer maps the dreams of society in terms of the nightmares of those who have been ejected from it. What makes his account so poignant is not only his description of the misery, psychic as well as physical, that congregates in these spaces; it is his tracing of the ways in which society administers that misery, through signs, directions, and instructions that speak the ideology of property and propriety. "This is, after all, the genius of language: that it fulfills orders which it was not given and that it erects bastions in the unconscious" (5.2: 189).

As one might imagine, Adorno was rather disturbed by this text and accused Kracauer of having accepted "Benjamin's formula of buildings as the dreams of the collective – just without using the word collective which I can't stand either."[47] Kracauer was quick to distance himself from Benjamin's "romantic" notion of the city as "a dream of collectivity": he was using the word "dream" merely in the sense of uncensored manifestations, as opposed to an "epoch's judgments about itself."[48] And yet, if one reads Kracauer's essays side by side with Benjamin's, one cannot help feeling that Adorno's critique of Benjamin's concept of the "dialectical image" to some extent also aired his misgivings about Kracauer's hieroglyphic readings; the epistemological shortcut he observes in the one could as well be held against the other:

> The notion of collective consciousness was invented to divert attention from true objectivity and its correlate, alienated subjectivity. It is up to us to polarize and dissolve this "consciousness" into a dialectical relationship of society and individual, rather than galvanize it as an imagistic correlate of the commodity character.[49]

One can see how Adorno himself came to use the metaphor of the mass-cultural hieroglyph – as "an imagistic correlate of the commodity character" – in such a singularly condemnatory sense, all the more so since he was increasingly convinced that any existing collectivity could only be false. In the systematic analysis of the culture industry, the hieroglyph epitomized modes of reception and identification assumed to manipulate people other than oneself; its particular meanings, accordingly, were predetermined by a critique of ideology.

Like Benjamin, Kracauer was not primarily interested in a critique of ideology (though he considered that too his task, especially in his work as daily reviewer for the *Frankfurter Zeitung*); his impulse was the work of critical redemption. Nor was he primarily concerned with the relation of individual and society or, for that matter, the question of collectivity, at least not from the mid-twenties on. The more pressing issue for Kracauer, I believe, was the increasingly repressive, conflictual, volatile make-up of the public sphere, and the place of the intellectual within that public sphere. For much as he maintained a critical perspective, he would rather have considered himself a member of the spectating mass – and, as an employee, potentially one of the unemployed – than a consciousness apart from, or above, the battleground of publics and counterpublics.

What is at stake, then, in reading the scriptural figurations of modernity is a question of, to borrow Derrida's term, the "gnoseo-politics" of the public sphere. Kracauer's distress over the "muteness" of the mass ornament has to do with the blockage of its rationalizing force: it fails to include the mass it abstracts in the process of cognition. Just as Kracauer, as I have argued elsewhere, knows himself to be vulnerable to the lure of mass-cultural fascination, he proceeds on the assumption that, in principle, the capacity for critical reading is available to others as well, including those who are the target of – and in practice often complicit with – capitalist manipulation.

The possibility that consumers could relate to the scriptural condensations of modern life in a simultaneously receptive and critical manner distinguishes Kracauer's reading politics from Horkheimer and Adorno's analysis of mass-cultural hieroglyphs and their single-minded customers. For Adorno, the dialectic of mimetic experience and critical reflection that characterizes Kracauer's – and Benjamin's – approach to mass culture is reserved only for works of autonomous art, and only insofar as these works acknowledge their precarious status, the price of their autonomy. To the extent that aesthetic experience becomes the refuge of an individuality alone capable of critique, it runs the risk of functioning as a "discriminating reservation." The problem is not just that this aesthetic double standard led Adorno to hypostasize the opposition between the subject of mass manipulation and critical subjectivity, but that it also prevented him from imagining alternative – and unpredictable – engagements with the hieroglyphics of mass culture; in other words, that he denied the mass-cultural hieroglyph even the potential of indeterminacy and ambiguity that he assumes for the hieroglyphic *écriture* of modern art.

Or did he? Earlier in this essay, I referred to efforts to revise Adorno's position on film and mass culture with recourse to moments in his *oeuvre* in which he himself crosses the dividing line between aesthetic theory and the critique of the culture industry. Among those moments (which are far more numerous than generally assumed) his 1966 essay "Transparencies on Film" has been singled out as his most systematic attempt to redeem film as an aesthetic medium. In a key passage of that text, Adorno recommends that an aesthetics of film should base itself on a subjective form of experience which it resembles: "A person who, after a year in the city, spends a few weeks in the mountains abstaining from all work, may unexpectedly experience colorful images of landscape coming over or though him in dreams or daydreams." Elaborating on this type of experience, Adorno resumes his earlier comparison of film as writing and film viewing as reading. In its discontinuous movement, he observes, the flow of these involuntary mental images resembles the phenomenon of writing, "similarly moving before our eyes while fixed in its discrete signs." "As the objectifying recreation of this type of experience," he concludes, "film may yet become art. The technological medium *par excellence* is thus intimately related to the beauty of nature [*dem Naturschönen*]" ("TF" 201).

As Gertrud Koch has shown, the imbrication of mimetic experience with writing permits Adorno to envision techniques of immanent aesthetic construction that would permit film to negate its technologically grounded violation of the *Bilderverbot*; to achieve mimetic expression by filmic means of "enscriptment" (*Verschriftung*) such as montage.[50] However, in light of the problematic of writing I have tried to unfold, this aesthetic redemption leaves crucial questions untouched. While it is an important contribution to theorizing avant-garde and feminist film practice (as Koch suggests), it also reproduces the split between modernist *écriture* and mass-cultural script on another level, by making the possibility of critical difference in cinema a matter of whether and how film can "yet become art."[51]

To make the imbrication of mimesis and writing productive for a theory of cinema and mass culture we need to complicate both terms, writing and mimesis, with the negative connotations they have in the critique of the culture industry. For a film aesthetics that brackets the institutional conditions of production and reception remains an aesthetics of film rather than one of cinema or mass culture. By the same token, however, a cinema and media theory that jettisons the question of aesthetic difference ultimately resigns itself to rationalizing existing practices in the name of reception studies.[52]

To theorize the nature of the aesthetic experience that, to echo Benjamin, people have a right to expect from film, the concept of mimesis needs to be expanded beyond the individualistic bent that characterizes Adorno's notion of experience in relation to art, as in the passage from "Transparencies" cited above. To recall an earlier point, mimesis in its perverted form animates the mass-cultural script not only by the reduction of the image to iconic doubling, but also in the consumers' adaptation to the false image, the reification compulsion operating in the hieroglyphic spell. This form of mimesis, however baleful, is a collective one, grounded in the institution of cinema, its economic origins as much as its public mode of reception. Under the conditions of the culture industry, the collectivity enacted is a mirage, enhancing the false identification of individual and social totality. Yet in "Transparencies," Adorno himself attributes an intrinsic collectivity to film, mediated by the "mimetic impulse" of its movements, which gives it an affinity with music. He even goes so far as to speak of "the constitutive subject of film as a 'we,'" albeit a rather vague collective id/it that lends itself to ideological misuse. "The liberated film would have to wrest its *a priori* collectivity from the mechanisms of unconscious and irrational influence and enlist this collectivity in the service of emancipatory intentions" (203–4). If this entails the possibility of a filmic *écriture* that would give expression to collective experience, then one would also have to conceive of this collective as a plural, heterogeneous term, capable of diverging readings and interpretations. Such pluralization would shift the potential for resistance, which Adorno occasionally grants the isolated, damaged subject, to an intersubjective agency of readings and counter-readings, publics and counterpublics.[53]

It is not surprising that Adorno's concept of mimesis has been claimed, within the tradition of the Frankfurt School, for a theory of communicative reason, notable by Habermas in his *Theory of Communicative Action* (1982). This adaptation involves removing the category from the language philosophy underpinning the *Dialectic of Enlightenment* – which, in Albrecht Wellmer's words, places mimesis in a position "extraterritorial to the sphere of discursive reason" – and conceptualizing it instead as "a mimetic-communicative dimension *internal* to discursive reason."[54] It also means turning Adorno's utopia of a reconciliation with nature (which pertains to relations within the subject, between subject and object, and among objects) into a regulative principle for the communication *between* or *among subjects*, that is, intersubjective action and the organization of the public sphere. But, as Josef Früchtl and others have cautioned, such adaptation of Adorno's mimesis concept cannot be accomplished without a paradigm shift. Not only was Adorno adamantly opposed to a subjective, let alone intersubjective grounding of reason but, to the extent that he could think of mimesis as an intersubjective relation at all, it was mediated by objective forms of communication, such as the non-communicative language of art.[55]

From the perspective of a theory of cinema and mass culture, I share these reservations, not necessarily to preserve the purity of Adorno's legacy, but because the communicative inflection of his mimesis concept tends to occlude the relation between mimesis and writing, which I consider one of Adorno's key insights into film. This is not to collapse the two terms: on the contrary, the tension between expressive and constructive elements in filmic *écriture* is essential to preventing their bad convergence in the mass-cultural hieroglyphic. Yet, while the preverbal or, rather, nonverbal qualities of the mimetic may or may not be diametrically opposed to language as speech, they are definitively not outside or other to writing, but part of it. This is important with regard to film and the mass media for two reasons.

One, film and other forms of mass culture have given rise to more and more mediated, deterritorialized forms of *Öffentlichkeit*: publics that crystallize around texts which are always already written, fixed by means of their – indexical and often iconic – technology, and whose dissemination, as commodities, increasingly exceeds the boundaries of local and even national space. These publics can no longer be theorized in terms of an ideal of communication modelled on face-to-face relations, but require a concept of the public that accounts for the profoundly changed organization of social experience.[56] Two, to think of the mimetic as an element of filmic writing implies conceiving of the filmic sign as irreducibly heterogeneous, whether in a Derridean sense or that of "inner speech," a heterogeneity Adorno himself stressed when reflecting on the critical potential of silent film versus the practice of synchronized sound. On the level of the public sphere, this corresponds to an irreducibly composite, hybrid make-up of twentieth-century "publicity," its mixing of industrial-commercial, bourgeois and popular, global and local, technologically generated and live elements. According to Negt and Kluge, such a volatile mixture makes for unexpected fissures, conjunctures, and alliances – and thus provides the conditions for the formation of counterpublics.

This argument returns us to a question raised earlier, concerning the historicity of Adorno's observations. If his analysis of the hieroglyphic mechanisms of identity captures something about cinema and mass culture during the 1940s and '50s, how does it help us understand analogous processes in the present? Postmodern culture has not only obviated the divisions between high and popular art, but also replaced the Fordist principles of standardization and homogenization with new strategies of differentiation on a global scale. Whether the diversity of this new culture of consumption will set into play the conditions of a "new cultural politics of difference" (Cornel West),[57] or whether it represents just another, more subtly disguised form of subjection and stabilization remains to be seen. If we "relativize" Adorno's critique of mass culture as hieroglyphic (in the spirit of Wellmer's proposal for a relativization – not moderation – of his critique of reason),[58] it could help us formulate critical perspectives that would keep both these possibilities in view. Thus the split between mass-cultural script and modernist *écriture* could be mobilized into a stereoscopic vision that spans the extremes of contemporary media culture: on the one hand, an instrument for the ever more effective simulation of presence and relentless reinscription of difference and identity; on the other, a matrix for a postmodern culture of difference, for new, syncretistic forms of experience and unpredictable formations of public life.

Finally, if the split between script and *écriture* today acquires a different meaning, it is not in the name of the foolish assertion that postmodernism has abolished aesthetic distinctions. This shift is indicated, rather, by developments within mass-cultural practices, in particular with the proliferation of video and its impact on cinema – developments that have decisively weakened the reality or doubling effect, film's insistence on its iconic character, that Adorno abhorred. In "Prologue to Television," Adorno himself observed how television deviated from cinematic standards of verisimilitude, speculating that "the public" must be unconsciously aware of the discrepancies: "The suspicion will grow that the reality that is being served up is not what it pretends to be" (GS 10.2: 510). Contemporary film and television practice abounds with examples of such "discrepancies," with highly stylized, ironic, hyperbolic forms of representation, from camp to overt parody and excentric fantasy. To modify Adorno's point about the allegorical quality of the Commedia dell'arte: even if, unlike the latter, television programs purport to relate to the everyday existence of the audience, it is questionable whether viewers would *model* their experience after the mast-like characters of soap operas, although they are likely to use them to *interpret* their own lives. However problematic the nexus of media and corporate power remains, the institutional weakening of iconicity would permit mass-cultural hieroglyphics to become *écriture*, to generalize the possibility of mimetic experience and memory within and against the very institutions that promote their reification. This *écriture* may not look like the modernist one theorized by Adorno; it may have many different faces and styles. Its distinction from the mass-cultural script can only be relative, impure, and conjunctural; its difference will remain, at any rate, a matter of readings and counter-readings.

Notes

1   For a recent example of such rhetoric, see Jim Collins, *Uncommon Cultures: Popular Culture and Post-Modernism* (New York, London: Routledge, 1989). The following essay is part of a larger research project that has been generously supported by the Alexander von Humboldt-Stiftung. Unless otherwise indicated, translations are my own.

2   See, for instance, Andreas Huyssen, "Adorno in Reverse: From Hollywood to Richard Wagner" (1983), repr. in *After the Great Divide: Modernism, Mass Culture, Postmodernism* (Bloomington: Indiana UP, 1986) and on pp. 29–56 of this book; Bernard Gendron, "Theodor Adorno Meets the Cadillacs," *Studies in Entertainment*, ed. Tania Modleski (Bloomington: Indiana UP, 1986); Richard Allen, "The

Aesthetic Experience of Modernity: Benjamin, Adorno, and Contemporary Film Theory," *New German Critique*, 40 (Winter 1987): 225–40; Gertrud Koch, "Mimesis und Bilderverbot in Adornos ästhetik: ästhetische Dauer als Revolte gegen den Tod," *Babylon*, 6 (1989): 36–45; Thomas Y. Levin "For the Record: Adorno on Music in the Age of Technological Reproducibility," *October*, 55 (1990): 23–47; the quotation is from Fredric Jameson, *Late Marxism: Adorno, or, The Persistence of the Dialectic* (London, New York: Verso, 1990), 7.

3 See Koch and Levin, as well as my introduction to Adorno's "Transparencies on Film," *New German Critique*, 24–25 (Fall/Winter 1981–2): 186–98.

4 Koch 39ff.; Adorno, *Ästhetische Theorie, Gesammelte Schriften* (in the following abbreviated as *ÄT* and *GS*), ed. Rolf Tiedemann (Frankfurt/Main: Suhrkamp, 1970) 7: 106, 416 and passim. This is the place to reiterate Kluge's paraphrase of Adorno's iconophobia: "I love to go to the movies: the only thing that bothers me is the image on the screen." Klaus Eder and Alexander Kluge, *Ulmer Dramaturgien: Reibungsverluste* (Munich: Hanser, 1981), 48.

5 Adorno, "Transparencies on Film" (1966), trans. Thomas Y. Levin, *NGC* 24–25 (1981–2): 199–205; 201 (in the following abbreviated as "TF").

6 Levin, "For the Record," 35–41; Adorno, "The Form of the Phonograph Record" (1934), trans. Thomas Y. Levin, *October*, 55 (1990): 56–61.

7 Adorno, "Prolog zum Fernsehen" (1953), *GS* (Frankfurt/Main: Suhrkamp, 1977), 10.2: 513–14.

8 Angelo Montani and Giulio Pietranera, "First Contribution to the Psycho-Analysis and Aesthetics of Motion-Picture," *Psychoanalytic Review*, 33 (1946): 177–96.

9 Cf. Jean-Louis Baudry, "Ideological Effects of the Basic Cinematic Apparatus," and "The Apparatus," repr. in Theresa Hak Kyung Cha (ed.), *Apparatus* (New York: Tanam, 1980); Christian Metz, *The Imaginary Signifier* (Bloomington: Indiana UP, 1982); Teresa de Lauretis and Stephen Heath (eds.), *The Cinematic Apparatus* (London: Macmillan, 1980).

10 "Das Schema der Massenkultur," *GS* 3: 332; for a recent (not entirely reliable) translation by Nicholas Walker, see Adorno, *The Culture Industry: Selected Essays on Mass Culture*, ed. J. M. Bernstein (London: Routledge, 1991), 53–84; 80 (in the following abbreviated as *CI*).

11 *GS* 3: 33–4, 41; *Dialectic of Enlightenment*, trans. John Cumming (New York: Seabury, 1972), 17–18 (in the following abbreviated as *DE*). The sentence containing the distinction between language and "a mere system of signs" is missing in the translation, *DE* 41.

12 Karl Marx, *Capital* (New York: International, 1975), 1: 74–5; on the structure of this Marxian trope see also W. J. T. Mitchell, *Iconology: Image, Text, Ideology* (Chicago, London: U of Chicago P, 1986), ch. 6.

13 This observation ties in with Horkheimer and Adorno's analysis of the peculiar fetishism of enlightened consumption which I discuss below. The critique of this kind of active reading has implications for attempts, such as David Bordwell's, to counter psychoanalytic views of the spectator as passive and manipulated with a conception of the spectator as an active participant "in creating the illusion,"

patterned on the "hypothesis-checking" unitary subject of cognitive psychology. Bordwell, Janet Staiger, and Kristin Thompson, *The Classical Hollywood Cinema* (New York: Columbia UP, 1975), 7, 9; Bordwell, *Narration in the Fiction Film* (Madison: U of Wisconsin P, 1985), 30. Horkheimer and Adorno's skepticism regarding consumerist expertise should also make us think twice about the *type* of knowledge generated by studio and fan publicity, as well as the vexed issue of Hollywood's "self-reflexivity."

14 Josef Früchtl, *Mimesis: Konstellation eines Zentralbegriffs bei Adorno* (Würzburg: Königshausen und Neumann, 1986); Michael Cahn, "Subversive Mimesis: T. W. Adorno and the Modern Impasse of Critique," in *Mimesis in Contemporary Theory*, ed. Mihai Spariosu (Philadelphia, Amsterdam: John Benjamins, 1984), 27–64; see also Susan Buck-Morss, *The Origin of Negative Dialectics* (New York: Free Press, 1977), 87f.

15 In its opposition to contemporary advocates of realism or naturalism, Adorno's concept of mimesis converges with Benjamin's, specifically as developed in "The Doctrine of Similarity" (1933), trans. Knut Tarnowski, *New German Critique*, 17 (Spring 1979): 65–9, and the second version of this essay, "On the Mimetic Faculty" (1935), trans. Edmund Jephcott, in *Reflections* (New York: Harcourt Brace Jovanovich, 1978). Like the latter, though with significant distinctions, Adorno opposes any surface resemblance of representation in favor of what Benjamin called a "non-sensual similarity," a mimetic "affinity" achieved only through materially specific techniques of determinate negation; like Adorno, Benjamin associated this non-sensual similarity with the phenomenon of writing.

16 *ÄT*, *GS* 7: 169ff., 424–5 and passim.

17 Cahn 32–3; Adorno, *GS* 7: 39, 201f and passim.

18 "Das ist der Triumph der Reklame in der Kulturindustrie: die zwangshafte Mimesis der Konsumenten an die zugleich durchschauten Kulturwaren." *GS* 3: 191; in the translation, *DE* 167, the word "mimesis" is dropped from the text.

19 *GS* 3: 333–4; in the English version, *CI* 82, the word "Laxativ" is translated as "cosmetics."

20 The subsequent sentence further eliminates any possible ambiguity in the word "writing" here: "As magic that has lost its enchantment, they [the archaic images of modernity] no longer convey any secret but are models of a behavior that corresponds as much to the gravitation of the total system as to the will of those in control" (*GS* 10.2: 514).

21 There is a third notion of reading in Adorno, on which he comments in conjunction with Hegel's writings, a "kind of gestic or curve-like writing" that makes the signifying function withdraw in favor of a mimetic one which compels the reader to retrace the thoughts with a "speculative ear as if they were musical notations." "Skoteinus oder Wie zu lesen sei," *GS* 5: 353f.

22 "Über einige Relationen zwischen Musik und Malerei," *GS* 16: 628–42; 635–6, 633. Adorno explicitly adopts the term *écriture* from Daniel-Henry Kahnweiler to whom the essay is dedicated.

23 This is what Jameson argues, quite convincingly, in *Late Marxism* (107–8, 145), although I think he underrates the complex and problematic ways in which the concept of mimesis brackets both projects. See Albrecht Wellmer, *Zur Dialektik von Moderne und Postmoderne: Vernunftkritik nach Adorno* (Frankfurt/Main: Suhrkamp, 1985); in Wellmer, *The Persistence of Modernity*, trans. David Midgley (Cambridge: MIT, 1990).

24 Abel Gance, "Le temps de l'image est venu" (1927), cited in Christian Metz, *Language and Cinema*, trans. Donna Jean Umiker-Sebeok (The Hague: Mouton, 1974), ch. 11.

25 Vachel Lindsay, *The Art of the Moving Picture*, 2nd edn. (New York: Liveright, 1970); John T. Irwin, *American Hieroglyphics: The Symbol of Egyptian Hieroglyphics in the American Renaissance* (Baltimore: Johns Hopkins UP, 1983); Miriam Hansen, *Babel and Babylon: Spectatorship in American Silent Film* (Cambridge: Harvard UP, 1991), ch. 8.

26 Sergei Eisenstein, "Beyond the Shot," *Writings 1922–34*, ed. and trans. Richard Taylor (London: BFI; Bloomington: Indiana UP, 1988), 140f.; on the concept of "inner speech" see essays by Stephen Heath and Paul Willemen in *Cinema and Language*, ed. S. Heath and Patricia Mellencamp, American Film Institute Monograph Series, I (Frederick, Md.: University Publications of America, 1983).

27 Marie-Claire Ropars-Wuilleumier, *Le texte divisé* (Paris: Presses Universitaires de France, 1981); "The Graphic in Filmic Writing: *A bout de souffle*, or the Erratic Alphabet," *Enclitic*, 5.2/6.1 (1981–2): 147–61; Gregory Ulmer, *Applied Grammatology* (Baltimore: Johns Hopkins UP, 1985); and, more recently, Tom Conley, *Film Hieroglyphs: Ruptures in Classical Cinema* (Minneapolis, Oxford: U of Minnesota P, 1991). Also see D. N. Rodowick, "The Figure and the Text," *Diacritics*, 15.1 (1985): 34–50; Peter Brunette and David Wills, *Screen/Play: Derrida and Film Theory* (Princeton, NJ: Princeton UP, 1989), ch. 4.

28 Jacques Derrida, *Of Grammatology*, trans. Gayatri Chakravorty Spivak (Baltimore: Johns Hopkins UP, 1976), 81.

29 Derrida, "Freud and the Scene of Writing," in *Writing and Difference*, trans. Alan Bass (Chicago: U of Chicago P, 1978), 218. For Freud's own use of the term, see *The Interpretation of Dreams, Standard Edition*, 4: 277–8; 5: 341; and "The Claim of Psychoanalysis to Scientific Interest," *Standard Edition*, 13: 177.

30 Derrida, "Scribble (writing-power)," trans. Cary Plotkin, *Yale French Studies*, 58 (1979): 117–47; 124. Warburton's essay is the French translation of a part of the second edition of *The Divine Legation of Moses Demonstrated* (London, 1742).

31 "Scribble," 140; 138; 117f.; 147.

32 Ulmer, *Applied Grammatology*, 265. I am aware that this is a caricature of Derridean film theory, highlighting an idealistic tendency in the adaptation of the hieroglyphic analogy; for a critique of Ulmer, see Brunette and Wills 125.

33 "Scribble," 117, 144.

34 "Schema," *GS* 3: 335; *CI* 82. This statement is part of Adorno's desperate argument with Benjamin who valorized the collective laughter inspired by slapstick comedy and Disney cartoons as an "antidote," a "therapeutic detonation" of tech-

nologically created mass psychoses and violent tensions; see earlier versions of the Artwork essay, Benjamin, *Gesammelte Schriften*, ed. Rolf Tiedemann and Hermann Schweppenhäuser (Frankfurt/Main: Suhrkamp, 1972–), I.2: 462; VII.1: 376f.; Adorno, letter to Benjamin, 18 Mar. 1936, trans. Harry Zohn, in Fredric Jameson (ed.), *Aesthetics and Politics* (London: New Left, 1977), 123f.

35   This is a particular problem with DeManian readings of Benjamin that tend to reduce the promiscuous and contradictory quality of Benjamin's texts to a single, doctrinal core – a tendency rehearsed in de Man's own ingenious reading of "The Task of the Translator," *Yale French Studies*, 69 (1985), 25–46.

36   The phrase is from Hans Blumenberg, *Die Lesbarkeit der Welt* (Frankfurt/Main: Suhrkamp, 1986). Also see Benjamin's programmatic invocation of Hofmannsthal's phrase: "to read what was never written." *GS* 1.3: 1238.

37   Siegfried Kracauer, "Zu den Schriften Walter Benjamins" (1928), *Schriften* 5.2, ed. Inka Mülder-Bach (Frankfurt/Main: Suhrkamp, 1990): 123 and passim. On the tension between violence and redemption that characterizes this secularized Jewish reading program, see Anson Rabinbach, "Between Enlightenment and the Apocalypse: Benjamin, Bloch and Modern German Jewish Messianism," *New German Critique*, 34 (Winter 1985): 78–124.

38   Miriam Hansen, "Decentric Perspectives: Kracauer's Early Writings on Film and Mass Culture," *New German Critique*, 54 (Fall 1991): 47–76; 50–9; also see Inka Mülder, *Siegfried Kracauer – Grenzgänger zwischen Theorie und Literatur: Seine frühen Schriften 1913–1933* (Stuttgart: J. B. Metzler, 1985), 19ff.

39   "Die Photographie" (1927), *Schriften*, 5.2: 97.

40   "Cult of Distraction" (1926), trans. Thomas Y. Levin, *New German Critique*, 40 (Winter 1987): 91–6; 94. On Kracauer's own "turn to the surface," see Inka Mülder-Bach, "Der Umschlag der Negativität: Zur Verschränkung von Phänomenologie, Geschichtsphilosophie und Filmästhetik in Siegfried Kracauers Metaphorik der 'Oberfläche,'" *Deutsche Vierteljahresschrift*, 61.2 (1987): 359–73.

41   "Das Ornament der Masse" (1927), *Schriften*, 5.2: 64; "The Mass Ornament," trans. Barbara Correll and Jack Zipes, *New German Critique*, 5 (Spring 1975): 67–76.

42   Obviously, Kracauer had a slightly more optimistic view of the Enlightenment than Horkheimer and Adorno, as he did of the emancipatory possibilities of capitalism. Thus, against romantic anti-capitalists who seek to overcome alienation by restoring a *Gemeinschaft*, he insists that the problem with capitalism is not that "it rationalizes too much but *too little*" (*Schriften*, 5.2: 62).

43   *Schriften*, 5.2: 67.

44   Adorno, "The Curious Realist: On Siegfried Kracauer" (1964), trans. Shierry Weber Nicholsen, *New German Critique*, 54 (Fall 1991): 163.

45   See, in particular, his 1927 essay on Photography; on Kracauer's affinity with postmodern reflections on image-reality relations, see Hansen, "Decentric Perspectives," 63ff.

46   "Über Arbeitsnachweise: Konstruktion eines Raumes" (1930), *Schriften*, 5.2: 186.

47   Adorno, letter to Kracauer, 25 July 1930; quoted in Mülder, *Kracauer*, 181, n. 17.

48 Kracauer, letter to Adorno, 1 Aug. 1930; quoted in Mülder, *Kracauer*, 181, n. 17; "Ornament," *Schriften*, 5.2: 55; "Mass Ornament," 67.

49 Adorno, letter to Benjamin, 2 Aug. 1935; trans. Harry Zohn, in Jameson (ed.), *Aesthetics and Politics*, 113 (trans. modified).

50 Koch 44. It should be added here that, notwithstanding his own endorsement of montage in *Composing for the Films*, Adorno remained skeptical as to the aesthetic scope of the procedure; see "TF" 203 and *ÄT, GS* 7: 90, 231–34.

51 In a lecture on "Art and the Arts," delivered the same year as "Transparencies," Adorno himself calls the "question as to whether or not film is art," a "helpless" question, inasmuch as film (and here Adorno invokes Benjamin's Artwork essay) has paradigmatically challenged that distinction. Yet, unlike Benjamin, Adorno concludes: "Whereas, by its immanent laws, film tries to rid itself from any resemblance to art – as if that contradicted its own aesthetics – by its very rebellion it becomes and expands art. This contradiction, which film is prevented from acting out in a pure form by its dependency on profit, is the vital element of all truly modern art" ("Die Kunst und die Künste" (1967), *GS* 10.1 [Frankfurt/Main: Suhrkamp, 1977]: 451–2). That the reservation is phrased in economic rather than technological terms may make it less absolute: if film cannot act out the contradiction "purely," it could just as well do so in an impure form.

52 To the extent that Cultural Studies approaches have privileged the area of mainstream reception to the exclusion of alternative practices and a critique of production they could be said to repeat, on the level of analysis, the negative-mimetic adaptation to reified conditions that Adorno observed in the consumers themselves.

53 Huyssen, 26.

54 Wellmer, *Zur Dialektik*, 97.

55 Früchtl, 190ff., 235–40.

56 See my introduction to Oskar Negt and Alexander Kluge, *Public Sphere and Experience* (Minneapolis: U of Minnesota P, 1993).

57 Cornel West, "The New Cultural Politics of Difference," Russell Ferguson, Martha Gever, Trinh T. Minh-ha, Cornel West (eds.), *Out There: Marginalization and Contemporary Cultures* (New York: New Museum of Contemporary Art; Cambridge, London: MIT, 1990), 19–36.

58 Wellmer, *Zur Dialektik*, 99.

3

Theodor W. Adorno and the Dialectics of Mass Culture

Douglas Kellner

While Theodor W. Adorno is a lively figure on the contemporary cultural scene, his thought in many ways cuts across the grain of emerging postmodern orthodoxies. Although Adorno anticipated many poststructuralist critiques of the subject, philosophy, and intellectual practice, his work clashes with the postmodern celebration of media culture, attacks on modernism as obsolete and elitist, and the more affirmative attitude toward contemporary culture and society found in many, but not all, postmodern circles. Adorno is thus a highly contradictory figure in the present constellation, anticipating some advanced tendencies of contemporary thought, while standing firmly against other regnant intellectual attitudes and positions.

In this article, I argue that Adorno's analyses of the functions of mass culture and communications in contemporary societies constitute valuable, albeit controversial, legacies. Adorno excelled both as a critic of so-called "high culture" and "mass culture," while producing many important texts in these areas. His work is distinguished by the close connection between social theory and cultural critique, and by his ability to contextualize culture within social developments, while providing sharp critical analysis. Accordingly, I discuss Adorno's analysis of the dialectics of mass culture, focusing on his critique of popular music, the culture industry, and consumer culture. I argue that Adorno's critique of mass culture is best read and understood in the context of his work with the Institute for Social Research. In conclusion, I offer alternative perspectives on mass communication and culture, and some criticisms of Adorno's position. The focus will be on the extent to which

Adorno's now classical critical theory does or does not continue to be valid and useful for cultural studies and criticism today.

Adorno, Benjamin, and the Cultural Contradictions of Radical Cultural Theory

Adorno's theory of culture was bound up with his analysis with Max Horkheimer of the "dialectic of enlightenment" (1972). For Horkheimer and Adorno, in the contemporary era of World War II, fascist death camps, and the threat of the triumph of fascist barbarism, Enlightenment had turned into its opposite – democracy had produced fascism, reason had generated unreason as instrumental rationality created military machines and death camps, and the culture industries were transforming culture from an instrument of *Bildung* and enlightenment into an instrument of manipulation and domination.[1] Culture – once a refuge of beauty and truth – was falling prey, they believed, to tendencies toward rationalization, standardization, and conformity which they interpreted as a consequence of the triumph of the instrumental rationality that was coming to pervade and structure ever more aspects of life. Thus, while culture once cultivated individuality, it was now promoting conformity, and was a crucial part of "the totally administered society" that was producing "the end of the individual."

This pessimistic analysis of the fate of culture in modernity was part and parcel of Institute pessimism concerning the rise of the totally administered society in its fascist, democratic state capitalist, and state communist forms. Yet Adorno and his colleagues continued to privilege culture as an important, and often overlooked, source of social knowledge, as well as a potential form of social criticism and opposition. As Adorno once wrote:

> the task of [cultural] criticism must be not so much to search for the particular interest-groups to which cultural phenomena are to be assigned, but rather to decipher the general social tendencies which are expressed in these phenomena and through which the most powerful interests realize themselves. Cultural criticism must become social physiognomy. The more the whole divests itself of all spontaneous elements, is socially mediated and filtered, is "consciousness," the more it becomes "culture."[2]

This passage points both to Adorno's position that administered culture was coming to play ever more fundamental roles in social production and reproduction, and to the belief that analysis of culture can provide crucial insights into social processes. Adorno ascribed a central role to cultural criticism and ideology critique precisely because of the key functions of culture and ideology within contemporary capitalist societies. This focus on culture – which corresponded to some of his deepest interests – took the form of a systematic inquiry into the different types, forms, and effects of culture and ideology in contemporary capitalist societies. These ranged from theoretical reflections on the dialectics of culture (i.e., the ways in which culture could be both a force of social conformity and opposition) to critiques of mass culture and aesthetic reflections on the emancipatory potential of high art – themes at which Adorno excelled and which were central to his thought.

In this section, I will first disclose the origins of Adorno's critique of mass culture in his writings on popular music in the 1930s and argue that he radicalizes his critique as a response to Walter Benjamin's defense of art in the age of mechanical reproduction. From this optic, Horkheimer and Adorno's theory of the culture industry emerges from intense focus and debates over mass culture in Institute of Social Research discussions and publications, and can thus be read as a classic articulation of the Institute critique of mass culture – as I argue in the following section.

In the first issue of the *Zeitschrift fur Sozialforschung*, articles appeared by Leo Löwenthal and T. W. Adorno which set forth respectively a program for a sociology of literature and for a theory and critique of mass culture.[3] In addition to pioneering attempts to develop a sociology of literature, the Institute was among the first to apply the Marxian method of ideology critique to the products of mass culture. Whereas critical theorists like Horkheimer and Marcuse rarely analyzed artifacts of mass culture, others like Adorno and Löwenthal developed both global theories and critiques, while carrying out detailed studies of what they came to call the "culture industries." Adorno began the Institute critique of mass culture in his 1932 article, "On the Social Situation of Music," and continued it in a series of studies of popular music and other forms of mass culture over the next decades.[4] Adorno initially criticized popular music production for its commodification, rationalization, fetishism, and reification of musical materials – thus applying the key neo-Marxist social categories to culture – while criticizing as well the "regression" in hearing produced by popular music. The framework for his critique was thus the Institute theory of the spread of rationalization and reification into every aspect of social life and the resultant decline of the individual.

A remarkable individual on the margins of the Institute, Walter Benjamin, contested the tendency to sharply separate "authentic art" from mass culture and to valorize one at the expense of the other (Benjamin 1969).[5] For Benjamin, mechanical reproduction (his term for the processes of social rationalization described by Adorno and others in the Institute) robbed high art of its "aura," of the aesthetic power of the work of art related to its earlier functions in magic, religious cults, and as a spiritual object in the religions of art celebrated in movements like romanticism or "art for art's sake." In these cases, the "aura" of the work derived from its supposed authenticity, its uniqueness and individuality. In an era of mechanical reproduction, however, art appeared as commodities like other mass-produced items, and lost its special power as a transcendent object – especially in mass-produced objects like photography and film with their photo negatives and techniques of mass reproduction. Benjamin experienced this process – which he believed to be irreversible – ambivalently:

> For the first time in world history, mechanical reproduction emancipates the work of art from its parasitical dependence on ritual. To an even greater degree the work of art reproduced becomes the work of art designed for repro-ducibility. From a photographic negative, for example, one can make any number of prints; to ask for the "authentic" print makes no sense. But the instant the criterion of authenticity ceases to be applicable to artistic produc-tion, the total function of art is reversed. Instead of being based on ritual, it begins to be based on another practice – politics. (Benjamin 1969: 224)

While Adorno tended to criticize precisely the most mechanically medi-ated works of mass culture for their standardization and loss of aesthetic quality – while celebrating those works that most steadfastly resisted com-modification and mechanical reproduction – Benjamin saw progressive fea-tures in high art's loss of its auratic quality and its becoming more politicized. Such art, he claimed, assumed more of an "exhibition value" than a cultic or religious value, and thus demystified its reception. Furthermore, he believed that proliferation of mass art – especially through film – would bring images of the contemporary world to the masses and would help raise political consciousness by encouraging scrutiny of the world, as well as by bringing socially revelatory images to millions of spectators:

> By close-ups of the things around us, by focusing on hidden details of famil-iar objects, by exploring commonplace milieus under the ingenious guidance of the camera, the film, on the one hand, extends our comprehension of the necessities which rule our lives; on the other hand, it manages to assure us of an immense and unexpected field of action. Our taverns and our metropoli-tan streets, our offices and furnished rooms, our railroad stations and our fac-tories appeared to have us locked up hopelessly. Then came the film and burst this prison-world asunder by the dynamite of the tenth of a second, so that now, in the midst of its far-flung ruins and debris, we calmly and adventur-ously go traveling. (Benjamin 1969: 236)

Benjamin claimed that the mode of viewing film broke with the reverential mode of aesthetic perception and awe encouraged by the bourgeois cultural elite who promoted the religion of art. Montage in film, its "shock effects," the conditions of mass spectatorship, the discussion of issues which film viewing encouraged, and other features of the cinematic experience, produced, in his view, a new sort of social and political experience of art which eroded the private, solitary, and contemplative aesthetic experience encouraged by high culture and its priests. Against the contemplation of high art, the "shock effects" of film produce a mode of "distraction" which Benjamin believed makes possible a "heightened presence of mind" and cultivation of "expert" audiences able to examine and criticize film and society (Benjamin 1969: 237–41).

In some essays on popular music and in his studies of the culture industries, Adorno attempted to provide a critical response to Benjamin's optimistic appraisal of the oppositional potential of popular art. In a 1938 essay, "On the Fetish-Character in Music and the Regression of Listening," Adorno analyzed in detail the various ways that music performers, conductors, instruments, technical performance, and arrangement of works were fetishized, and how this signified the ways that exchange-value was predominating over use-value in musical production and reception – thus pointing again to how capitalism was able to control aspects of life once resistant to commercial concerns. In Adorno's words:

> The works which are the basis of the fetishization and become cultural goods experience constitutional changes as a result. They become vulgarized. Irrelevant consumption destroys them. Not merely do the few things played again and again wear out, like the Sistine Madonna in the bedroom, but reification affects their internal structure. They are transformed into a conglomeration of irruptions which are impressed on the listeners by climax and repetition, while the organization of the whole makes no impression whatsoever. (FSR: 281)

In this situation, musical listening regresses to mere reaction to familiar and standardized formulas which increase social conformity and domination (FSR: 285ff.). Regression closes off

> the possibility of a different and oppositional music. Regressive, too, is the role which contemporary mass music plays in the psychological household of its victims. They are not merely turned away from more important music, but they are confirmed in their neurotic stupidity, quite irrespective of how their musical capacities are related to the specific musical culture of earlier social phases. The assent to hit songs and debased cultural goods belongs to the same complex of symptoms as do those faces of which one no longer knows whether the

film has alienated them from reality or reality has alienated them from the film, as they wrench open a great formless mouth with shining teeth in a voracious smile, while the tired eyes are wretched and lost above. Together with sport and film, mass music and the new listening help to make escape from the whole infantile milieu impossible. The sickness has a preservative function. (FSR: 287)

Adorno's infamous attack on jazz should be read in the context of his theory of musical fetishism and regression.[6] For Adorno, the often faddish taste for jazz also exhibited features of fetishism, reification, and regression that he observed in other forms of popular music. Contrary to popular belief, Adorno argued that jazz was as standardized, commercialized, and formulaic as other kinds of popular music and encouraged cultural conformity (to dominant models, tastes, etc.) in its devotees as much as other forms of mass culture. Its seeming spontaneity and improvisation are themselves calculated in advance and the range of what is permissible is as circumscribed as in clothes or other realms of fashion.

Adorno and Horkheimer argued that film and the other instruments of mass culture functioned in similar ways to popular music in Adorno's critique. In particular, they attempted to counter Benjamin's optimistic appraisal of the progressive elements of film through critique of Hollywood film production. They argued that film in the culture industries was organized like industrial production and utilized standardized formulas and conventional production techniques to mass-produce films for purely commercial – rather than cultural – purposes. Films reproduced reality as it was and thus helped individuals to adjust and conform to the new conditions of industrial and mass society: "they hammer into every brain the old lesson that continuous friction, the breaking down of all individual resistance, is the condition of life in this society. Donald Duck in the cartoons and the unfortunate in real life get their thrashing so that the audience can learn to take their own punishment" (Horkheimer and Adorno 1972: 138). Finally, films

are so designed that quickness, powers of observation, and experience are undeniably needed to apprehend them at all; yet sustained thought is out of the question if the spectator is not to miss the relentless rush of facts. Even though the effort required for his response is semi-automatic, no scope is left for the imagination. Those who are so absorbed by the world of the movie – by its images, gestures, and words – that they are unable to supply what really makes it a world, do not have to dwell on particular points of its mechanics during a screening. All the other films and products of the entertainment industry which they have seen have taught them what to expect; they react automatically. (Horkheimer and Adorno 1972: 126–7)

During the late 1930s and the 1940s, when Adorno was developing his critique of popular music (and culture), he was working with Paul Lazarsfeld on some of the first academic studies of the communications industry, and thus was being exposed to some of the more debased and commercialized forms of popular music.[7] Obviously, Adorno was criticizing these musical forms from the standpoint of his conception of "authentic" music which he found instantiated in high modernism. "Authentic art," for Adorno, is a preserve of both individuality and happiness, as well as a source of critical knowledge. Further, an element of resistance is inherent in the most aloof art. Mass culture for Adorno merely reproduced the status quo and thus helped to reproduce personality structures which would accept the world as it is.

High culture, by contrast, is conceptualized as at least a potential force of enlightenment and emancipation. For Adorno, however, only the most radically avant-garde works could provide genuine aesthetic experience. Against the false harmonies of kitsch and affirmative art, Adorno defended the "de-aestheticization" (*Entkunstung*) of art, its throwing off false veils of harmony and beauty in favor of ugliness, dissonance, fragmentation, and negation which he believed provided a more truthful vision of contemporary society, and a more emancipatory stance for socially critical art. In Adorno's view, art had become increasingly problematical in a society ruled by culture industries and art markets, and to remain "authentic," art must therefore radically resist commodification and integration. This required avant-garde techniques which would enhance art's shock-value, and its critical, emancipatory effects.

In his volumes of critical writings, Adorno always championed precisely those most negative and dissonant artists: Kafka and Beckett in literature, Schönberg and Berg in music, Giacometti in sculpture, and Celan in poetry. Through de-aestheticization, autonomous art would undermine specious harmonization and reconciliation with the existing world which could not legitimately take place, Adorno believed, until the world was radically changed.[8] For example, in his well-known critique of "politically committed art," "Commitment," Adorno writes:

> It is not the office of art to spotlight alternatives, but to resist by its form alone the course of the world, which permanently puts a pistol to men's heads . . . Kafka's prose and Beckett's plays, or the truly monstrous novel *The Unnameable*, have an effect by comparison with which officially committed works look like pantomimes. Kafka and Beckett arouse the fear which existentialism merely talks about. By dismantling appearance, they explode from within the art which committed proclamation subjugates from without, and hence only in appearance. The inescapability of their work compels the change of attitude which committed works merely demand. (Adorno 1977: 180, 191).[9]

Thus, for Adorno "authentic art" provided insight into existing reality, expressing human suffering and the need for social transformation, and provided as well an aesthetic experience which helped to produce critical consciousness and the need for individual and social transformation. Art for Adorno was thus a privileged vehicle for emancipation. Aesthetic experience alone, he came to believe, provided the refuge for truth and a sphere of individual freedom and resistance. In addition, authentic art substantiates the claims of sensuous particularities and pure experience, providing bodily experiences of pleasure and validating sense experience devoid from ends. Art is thus an end in itself: it liberates one from the cares of the world, it provides access to another dimension at the same time that it illuminates sociohistorical reality, and is a repository of historical truth.

Adorno's problem was that from his perspective only authentic art could provide genuine aesthetic experience, and it was precisely authentic art which was disappearing in the administered society. It is impossible here to go into the complexities of Adorno's theory of art, or to discuss the full range of his contributions to the sociology of culture, to ideology critique, and to aesthetic theory and political aesthetics. Instead, I turn to his and Max Horkheimer's critique of the culture industry and the ways that the Institute model influenced debates over mass culture and society from the 1950s to the present.

Adorno and Horkheimer on the Culture Industry

While the origins of the Institute for Social Research approach to mass culture and communication are visible in Adorno's early writings on music, Horkheimer and Adorno did not really develop the theory of the culture industries until their emigration to the United States in the 1930s.[10] During their exile period from the mid-1930s through the 1940s, members of the Institute witnessed the proliferation of mass communications and culture and the rise of the consumer society, experiencing at first hand the advent to cultural power of the commercial broadcasting systems, President Roosevelt's remarkable use of radio for political persuasion, and the ever-growing popularity of cinema during a period in which from 85,000,000 to 110,000,000 Americans paid to see "the movies" each week.[11] And they experienced as well the widespread popularity of magazines, comic books, cheap fiction, and the other flora and fauna of the new mass-produced culture.

The culture industry theory was developed in the United States during the heyday of the press, radio, and cinema as dominant cultural forms; it was published just before the first wave of the introduction of television, whose importance Adorno and Horkheimer anticipated, and whose forms and effects were analyzed by Adorno in a classic article originally entitled "How to Look at Television."[12] Interest in the new communications media was growing, and a new discipline was emerging to study its social effects and functions. Research into media communications in the United States was largely inaugurated by the Institute for Social Research, then located at Columbia University, and by Paul Lazarsfeld and his associates in the "Radio Research Project" and later the "Bureau of Applied Social Research" at Princeton and then Columbia University. Lazarsfeld was connected with the Institute for Social Research in various ways, and for several years the groups interacted and undertook common projects.[13]

From their vantage point in California during the 1940s, where many of their exiled compatriots from Germany worked for the film industry, Adorno and Horkheimer were able to experience how business interests dominated mass culture, and they could scrutinize the fascination that the entertainment industries exerted within the emerging media and consumer society. Marcuse, Lowenthal, and others, who worked in Washington during this period for the Office of War Information and the US intelligence services, were able to observe government use of mass communications as instruments of political propaganda. The critical theorists thus came to see what they called the "culture industries" as a central part of a new configuration of capitalist modernity which used culture, advertising, mass communications, and new forms of social control to induce consent to and reproduce the new forms of capitalist society. The production and transmission of media spectacles which transmit ideology and consumerism through the means of allegedly "popular entertainment" and information were, they believed, a central mechanism through which contemporary society came to dominate the individual.

Adorno and Horkheimer adopted the term "culture industry," as opposed to concepts like "popular culture" or "mass culture," because they wanted to resist notions that products of the culture industry emanated from the masses or from the people (see Adorno 1975, 11). For they saw the culture industry as being administered culture, imposed from above, as instruments of indoctrination and social control. The term "culture industry" thus contains a dialectical irony typical of the style of critical theory: culture, as traditionally valorized, is supposed to be opposed to industry and expressive of individual creativity while providing a repository of humanizing values. In the culture industries, however, culture has come to function as a mode of ideological domination rather than of humanization or emancipation.

The culture industry was perceived as the culmination of a historical process in which technology and scientific organization and administration came to dominate thought and experience. Although Adorno and Horkheimer carry out a radical questioning of Marxism and the development of an alternative philosophy of history and theory of society in *Dialectic of Enlightenment*, their theory of the culture industry provides a neo-Marxian account of the mass media and culture which helps explain both the ways in which the culture industries reproduce capitalist societies and why socialist revolutions failed to take place in these societies. In this sense, the Institute theory of "culture industry as mass deception" provides a rebuttal both to Lukács' theory of revolution and "class consciousness," and to Brecht's and Benjamin's belief that the new forces of mass communications – especially radio and film – could function as instruments of technological progress and social enlightenment which could be turned against the capitalist relations of production and used as instruments of political mobilization and struggle.[14]

For Adorno and Horkheimer, by contrast, these new technologies were used as instruments of ideological mystification and class domination. Against Lukács and others who argued that capitalist society necessarily radicalized the working class and produced class consciousness, Adorno and Horkheimer suggested that the culture industries inhibit the development of class consciousness by providing the ruling political and economic forces with a powerful instrument of social control. The conception of the culture industry therefore provides a model of a technically advanced capitalist society which mobilizes support for its institutions, practices, and values *from below*, making class-consciousness more difficult to attain than before. Using Gramsci's terminology, the culture industries reproduce capitalist hegemony over the working class by engineering *consent* to the existing society, and thus establishing a socio-psychological basis for social integration.[15] Whereas fascism destroyed civil society (or the "public sphere") through politicizing mediating institutions, or utilizing force to suppress all dissent, the culture industries coax individuals into the privacy of their home, or movie theater, while producing consumers-spectators of media events and escapist entertainment who are being subtly indoctrinated into dominant ideologies and conformist behavior.

The analysis of the culture industry stands, therefore, in an ambivalent relationship to classical Marxism. On one hand, the theory is part of the foundation for the critical theory of society, replacing the critique of political economy which had been the foundation for social theories previously in the Marxian tradition. And it served as an important part of the explanation of why the critical theorists no longer placed faith in the revolutionary vocation of the proletariat. Yet in other ways, the analysis of the culture industry employs Marxian arguments through stressing capitalist control of culture, the commodification and reification of culture, its ideological functions, and the ways that it integrates individuals into capitalist society.

For example, Adorno and Horkheimer utilize a model that pits the individual against its "adversary – the absolute power of capitalism" (1972: 120), and describe the tendencies toward conformity, standardization, and deception in the culture industry by means of its control by monopoly corporations which themselves are central to the capitalist system (pp. 120ff.). The very processes of production in the culture industry are modelled on factory production where everything is standardized, streamlined, coordinated, and planned down to the last detail. Indeed, Adorno and Horkheimer use their analysis of the culture industry to call attention to what they perceive as the fundamental traits of the administered society, and to carry out a radical critique of capitalism. They suggest that reflection on the culture industries illuminates the processes toward standardization, homogenization, and conformity that characterize social life under what they call "totalitarian capitalism." The tendencies toward manipulation and domination in the culture industry illuminate similar trends throughout capitalist society.

In a key passage, they indicate how technological and material forces of progress can be used to foster domination and regression:

> The fallen nature of modern man cannot be separated from social progress. On the one hand the growth of economic productivity furnishes the conditions for a world of greater justice; on the other hand it allows the technical apparatus and the social groups which administer it a disproportionate superiority to the rest of the population. The individual is wholly devaluated in relation to the economic powers, which at the same time press the control of society over nature to hitherto unsuspected heights. Even though the individual disappears before the apparatus which he serves, that apparatus provides for him as never before. In an unjust state of life, the impotence and pliability of the masses grow with the quantitative increase in commodities allowed them. (1972: pp. xiv–xv)

Adorno and Horkheimer point to similarities between industrial and cultural production, and a growing social unification based on increasing homogenization and control:

> The ruthless unity in the culture industry is evidence of what will happen in politics. Marked differentiations such as those of A and B films, or of stories in magazines in different price ranges, depend not so much on subject matter as on classifying, organizing, and labelling consumers. Something is provided for all so that none may escape; the distinctions are emphasized and extended. The public is catered for with a hierarchical range of mass-produced products

of varying quality, thus advancing the rule of complete quantification. Everybody must behave (as if spontaneously) in accordance with his previously determined and indexed level, and choose the category of mass product turned out for his type. Consumers appear as statistics on research organization charts, and are divided by income groups into red, green, and blue areas; the technique is that used for any type of propaganda. (1972: 123)

Later in the chapter, Adorno and Horkheimer describe the blend between mass culture, advertising, and consumption in the consumer society (Horkheimer and Adorno 1972: 156ff.). They argue:

The assembly-line character of the culture industry, the synthetic, planned method of turning out its products (factory-like not only in the studio but, more or less, in the compilation of cheap biographies, pseudodocumentary novels, and hit songs) is very suited to advertising: the important individual points, by becoming detachable, interchangeable, and even technically alienated from any connected meaning, lend themselves to ends external to the work. The effect, the trick, the isolated repeatable device, have always been used to exhibit goods for advertising purposes, and today every monster close-up of a star is an advertisement for her name, and every hit song a plug for its tune. Advertising and the culture industry merge technically as well as economically. In both cases the same thing can be seen in innumerable places, and the mechanical repetition of the same cultural product has come to be the same as that of the propaganda slogan. In both cases the insistent demand for effectiveness makes technology into psycho-technology, into a procedure for manipulating men. In both cases the standards are the striking yet familiar, the easy yet catchy, the skillful yet simple; the object is to overpower the customer, who is conceived as absent-minded or resistant. (1972: 163)

The mass deception present in the culture industries is similar to the deception, false promises, and manipulation in the economic, political, and social spheres. In this conception, one of the main trends of contemporary capitalist societies is the synthesis of advertising, culture, information, politics, and manipulation that characterizes the culture industries. This dialectical focus on the relationships between the culture industry and capitalism points to a basic methodological position within critical theory that in turn marks its affinity to Marxian dialectics. For critical theory every social phenomenon must be interpreted in terms of a theory of society which itself is part of a theory of capitalism. The analysis of the relationships between society and the economy illuminate phenomena like the culture industry, and its analysis in turn sheds light on the economy and society. Consequently, critical theory operates with a dialectic between its topics of analysis (the culture industry, or antisemitism, or whatever other topic is addressed) and its theory of society. In this dialectic, the theory of society illuminates the topic under investigation – which in turn illuminates the fundamental social trends (i.e., commodification, reification, etc.) described in the social theory.

After describing the style of culture industry products and the formulas, conventions, and stereotypes that constitute it, Adorno and Horkheimer analyze several of the strategies used to indoctrinate its consumers into acceptance of the existing society. "Entertainment," they claim, accustoms the audiences to accept existing society as natural by endlessly repeating and reproducing similar views of the world which present the existing way of life as the way of the world. The eternal recurrence of the same in the culture industry changes, they suggest, the very nature of ideology:

> Accordingly, ideology has been made vague and noncommittal, and thus neither clearer nor weaker. Its very vagueness, its almost scientific aversion from committing itself to anything which cannot be verified, acts as an instrument of domination. It becomes a vigorous and prearranged promulgation of the status quo. The culture industry tends to make itself the embodiment of authoritative pronouncements, and thus the irrefutable prophet of the prevailing order. It skillfully steers a winding course between the cliffs of demonstrable misinformation and manifest truth, faithfully reproducing the phenomenon whose opaqueness blocks any insight and installs the ubiquitous and intact phenomenon as ideal. Ideology is split into the photograph of stubborn life and the naked lie about its meaning – which is not expressed but suggested and yet drummed in. To demonstrate its divine nature, reality is always repeated in a purely cynical way. Such a photological proof is of course not stringent, but it is overpowering . . . The new ideology has as its objects the world as such. It makes use of the worship of facts by no more than elevating a disagreeable existence into the world of facts in representing it meticulously. (1972: 147–8)

The culture industry thus tries to induce the individual to identify with society's typical figures and models: "Pseudo-individuality is rife: from the standardized jazz improvisation to the exceptional film star whose hair curls over her eye to demonstrate her originality. What is individual is no more than the generality's power to stamp the accidental detail so firmly that it is accepted as such. The defiant reserve or elegant appearance of the individual on show is mass-produced like Yale locks, whose only difference can be measured in fractions of millimeters" (1972: 154). The culture industry thus serves as a powerful instrument of social control that induces individuals to accept their fate and conform to existing society. Advertising progressively fuses in style and technique with the entertainment of the culture industry (1972: 156–67) which in turn can be read as advertisements for the existing society and established way of life.

Like every theoretical conception, the notion of the culture industries was a product of its historical period and its insights and limitations result primarily from the fact that it theorized features of a past historical conjuncture. The Institute conception of the role of mass culture and communication was first shaped in the period of Nazi Germany, where they witnessed Hitler's extraordinary use of mass communications and fascist spectacles. Obviously, the experience of fascism shaped the critical theorists' views of the rise of a behemoth state and cultural apparatus combined with an eclipse of democracy, individuality, and what they saw as authentic art. And in exile in the United States, they observed Roosevelt's impressive use of the media and the propagandistic uses of the mass media during World War II. Consequently, political use and control of the media during conditions of warfare, with an enlarged wartime state and subordinate wartime economy, coupled with capitalist control of the entertainment industries, provided the historical roots of the Institute model of the culture industries as instruments of social control. Indeed, the media under this type of militarized social system and war conditions – whether liberal-democratic, fascist, or state socialist – will be rather one-dimensional and propagandistic. Moreover, the critical theory model of the media and society also rather accurately described certain dominant trends and effects during the post-World War II Cold War period when the media were enlisted in the anticommunist crusade and when media content was subject to tight control and censorship – a situation signalled by Adorno and Horkheimer's allusions to "purges" (1972: 123).[16]

Adorno and Cultural Studies: Contributions and Limitations

The critique of the culture industries was one of the most influential aspects of critical theory, and its impact on social theory and on theories and critiques of mass communication and culture was significant. While there are many limitations to Adorno's analyses of mass culture, it provides models of radical critique of the artifacts of media culture, situates culture and communication within the capitalist political economy and historical context of its day, and anticipates British cultural studies in taking seriously artifacts of media culture, conceptualizing the interaction between text and audience, and relating culture and politics.[17]

Thus, despite its limitations, which I shall outline in this section, Adorno's analyses of the culture industries make many important contributions to the study of media culture. Adorno and his colleagues conceptualize culture and communications as part of society and focus on how socio-economic imperatives helped constitute their nature, function, and effects. By conceiving of these important cultural forces as part of socio-economic processes, critical theory integrates study of culture and communication with study of the economy and society. And by adopting a critical approach to the study of all social phenomena, Adorno and critical theory are able to conceptualize how the culture industries function as instruments of social control and thus serve the interests of social domination. Adorno and his Institute colleagues were thus among the first social theorists to see the importance of mass culture and communication in the reproduction of contemporary societies and developed a critical approach, whereas more mainstream approaches were either "administrative" (Lazarsfeld's term), serving the interests of media industries and the status quo, or were "empirical," following the model of positivist science at the time.[18] Moreover, whereas studies of mass culture and communications tended to divide into social-science-based empirical studies of mass communication and humanities and text-based cultural studies, Adorno's model focused – at least in principle – on production and political economy, text, and audience reception, thus providing a more integral model for cultural and communications studies than were developing during the epoch that he wrote and lived.[19]

Yet in contrast to the mode of condemnatory criticism associated with Adorno and critical theory, radical cultural criticism today should develop more complex strategies and should attempt to develop a more multidimensional approach to media culture. Rather than seeing its artifacts simply as expressions of hegemonic ideology and ruling class interests, it is more useful to see popular entertainment as complex products that contain contradictory moments of desire and its displacement, articulations of hopes and their repression. In this view, media culture provides access to a society's dreams and nightmares, and contains both ideological celebrations of the status quo and utopian moments of transcendence, moments of opposition and rebellion, and its attempted containment (see Jameson 1979; Kellner 1995). In reading the texts of media culture, we should also perceive how social struggles and conflicts enter into works of popular entertainment, and see culture as a contested terrain rather than a field of one-dimensional manipulation and illusion (cf. Biskind 1983; Kellner and Ryan 1988; Kellner 1995).

Post-Adornoesque critical theories of culture and communication must therefore be able to develop more complex methods of cultural interpretation and criticism that pay attention to and conceptualize the contradictions, articulation of social conflicts, oppositional moments, subversive tendencies, and projection of utopian images and scenes of happiness and freedom that appear within media culture. In his study "On the Fetish Character in Music," Adorno wrote: "The familiarity of the piece is a surrogate for the quality ascribed to it. To like it is almost the same thing as to recognize it. An approach in terms of value judgements has become a fiction for the person who finds himself hemmed in by standardized musical goods. He can neither escape impotence nor decide between the offerings where everything is so completely identical that preference in fact depends merely on bio-graphical details or on the situation in which things are heard" (Adorno 1995: 26).

Arguing that all popular music is "so completely identical" might have some validity in the analysis of the radio-based popular music of the day, although on the whole it violates Adorno's own defense of particularity and critique of identity-thinking which subsumes heterogeneous particulars to abstract categories. The classical critical theory approach, especially Adorno's work, generally limits itself to attacking the ideology and purely retrogressive effects of radio, popular music, films, television, and so on. In this sense, the model of cultural interpretation and criticism is remarkably similar to crude Marxian critique of ideology which restricts cultural analysis to denunciation of ideological content and social functions. Part of the problem is that for Adorno the artifacts of the culture industry are simply beneath contempt. In *Minima Moralia*, Adorno writes: "Every visit to the cinema leaves me, against all my vigilance, stupider and worse" (Adorno 1974: MM★ 25). Such an arro-gant and grandiose gesture of absolute disdain, however, precludes under-standing what gratifications popular culture actually provide and what needs it serves, in however distorted a fashion. This attitude also leads critical the-orists to neglect, with some exceptions, analyzing specific films, television programs, or artifacts of popular culture, since they presume in advance that such artifacts are simply a debased form of culture and vehicle of ideology which are not worthy of detailed study or critique. Thus, when Adorno does analyze examples of popular music and television, he generally limits himself to attacking their ideologies and "retrogressive" effects on consciousness without analyzing the work's contradictions, critical or oppositional moments, or potential to provide insight into social conditions or to elicit a critical response.[20]

But while popular music may, as Adorno argued, exhibit features of com-modification, reification, and standardization, which may in turn have retro-gressive effects on consciousness, such a theoretical optic cannot adequately account for the genesis and popularity of many forms of popular music such as the blues, jazz, rock and roll, reggae, punk, and other forms of music connected with oppositional subcultures. Since music is the most non-representational of all arts, it provides vehicles for the expression of pain, rage, joy, rebellion, sexuality, and other basic human experiences which might have progressive effects. Historically, the production of certain types of popular music was often carried out by oppressed groups, like blacks or hispanics, or by working-class whites or marginalized youth. Much popular music thus articulates rebellion against the standardization, conformity, submission, and other features that Adorno criticized.

Moreover, the forms of reception of popular music have frequently been dances and festivities in a context of transgression of propriety through drinking, wildly dancing, communally singing, making love, and other socio-erotic activities. Ragtime, jazz, bop, swing, and rock have been more at home in the brothel, dance-hall, or bedroom than within His Master's Voice in the living room. Though contemporary forms of punk and hard rock can provide background for young fascists and conservatives, it can also provide the social cement for a culture of political mobilization and struggle – as the Rock Against Racism and *Rock gegen Rechts* concerts in England and Germany indicated in the 1980s and various Internet and other concerts did in the 1990s.

Indeed, popular music can mobilize youth and help to cultivate oppositional subcultures, as well as provide opportunities for the commodification of culture and harmless catharsis – although, as Adorno argued, all forms of media culture can be absorbed and coopted by the existing system. But Adorno's model of the culture industry does not allow for the heterogeneity of popular culture and contradictory effects, instead straitjacketing media culture in the form of reification and commodification as signs of the total triumph of capital and the total reification of experience. To be sure, much popular culture lends itself precisely to Adorno's categories and critique, though as suggested, other examples resist his categories and require a more complex approach to cultural interpretation and critique. Yet occasionally, Adorno did qualify his one-dimensional condemnation of popular culture, and also allowed for the possibility of audience resistance to media manipulation. In "Transparencies on Film," Adorno uncharacteristically indicated that a certain sort of film might contain socially critical potential and that mass culture itself reproduces existing conflicts and antagonisms: "In its attempts to manipulate the masses, the ideology of the culture industry itself becomes as internally antagonistic as the very society which it aims to control. The ideology of the culture industry contains the antidote to its own lie" (p. 202). In particular, Adorno believed that the technique of montage (the juxtaposition of images to create multiple effects of meaning and socially critical associations) developed by Sergei Eisenstein and the revolutionary Soviet cinema provides models for a socially progressive cinema: "Film is faced with the dilemma of finding a procedure which neither lapses into arts-and-crafts nor slips into a more documentary mode. The obvious answer today, as forty years ago, is that of montage which does not interfere with things but rather arranges them in a constellation akin to that of writing" (p. 203).

Yet Adorno believed that pure montage and cinematic shock effects (such as were celebrated by Benjamin) "without the addition of intentionality in its details, refuses to accept intentions merely from the principle itself" (p. 203). Progressive film would thus have to combine montage in image construction with other effects, like advanced music (and progressive political intentions and insights?), to turn the images of film into a socially critical direction for Adorno: "The liberated film would have to wrest its *a priori* collectivity from the mechanisms of unconscious and irrational influence and enlist this collectivity in the service of emancipatory intentions" (pp. 203–4).

In another late article, "Leisure," Adorno pointed to limitations of the ability of the culture industry to manipulate spectator consciousness. Reflecting on a study conducted of the media's presentation of the marriage of a Dutch Princess to an upper-class German, Adorno stressed that the audience saw through the media hype of this event, and realistically perceived its insignificance. He thus concluded: "The integration of consciousness and leisure is obviously not yet entirely successful. The real interests of the individuals are still strong enough, at the margins, to resist total control" (Adorno cited in Huyssen 1975: 10).[21] Yet, as Jay Bernstein suggests in an introduction to Adorno's writings on the culture industry, Adorno also emphasized a dialectics of "seeing through and obeying," whereby audiences saw through the façade of astrology, advertising, and propaganda, while continuing to submit to the reign of mass culture, capital, and the existing social system (Bernstein in Adorno 1995: 10ff.).

Hence, critical approaches to media culture today should not simply limit themselves to denouncing bourgeois ideologies and escapist functions. Even conservative media culture often provides insights into forms of dominant ideologies and sometimes unwittingly provides images of social conflict and opposition. Studies of Hollywood films, for instance, reveal that this form of commercial culture exhibits a conflict of representations between competing social ideologies over the last several decades. Particularly, in the period from around 1967 to the present, a variety of competing ideological standpoints have appeared in mainstream Hollywood film (cf. Kellner and Ryan 1988 and Kellner 1995). Consequently, there is no one monolithic, dominant ideology which the culture industries promote, and indeed the conflicting ideologies in contemporary culture industry artifacts point to continuing and intensifying social conflict within capitalist societies.

Yet in the Institute critique of mass culture, there are no theories of oppositional and emancipatory uses of the media and cultural practices. There is neither a strategy for cultural revolution as is found in Brecht, Benjamin, and Enzensberger, nor is there a media politics to overcome the harmful effects that Adorno and Horkheimer describe.[22] In an era of media saturation, however, such asceticism would only further marginalize already marginalized critical intellectuals and oppositional groups. Consequently, a radical media politics should replace the pessimistic denunciation found in classical critical theory – a point even more salient in the Age of the Internet.

Part of the problem is that Adorno and his followers rigidly juxtapose their concepts of "authentic art" – modelled on masters of the avant-garde like Schönberg, Kafka, and Beckett – against mass culture, which they denounce for failing to have the qualities that they find in their preferred aesthetic models. It's true that Adorno writes, in an often-cited letter to Walter Benjamin:

> 'Les extrêmes me touches' [Gide], just as they touch you – but only if the dialectic of the lowest has the same value as the dialectic of the higher, rather than the latter simply decaying. Both bear the stigmata of capitalism, both contain elements of change (but never, of course, the middle-term between Schönberg and the American film). Both are torn halves of an integral freedom to which, however, they do not add up. It would be romantic to sacrifice one to the other, either as the bourgeois romanticism of the conservation of personality and all that stuff, or as the anarchistic romanticism of blind confidence in the spontaneous power of the proletariat in the historical process – a proletariat which is itself a product of bourgeois society. (Adorno to Benjamin in Jameson 1983: 123)

This citation is significant as it suggests that Adorno recognizes that high art* and popular culture are both socially mediated by capitalism and that Adorno does not attack popular culture per se, but the forms it takes under capitalism. Indeed, there are plenty of positive references to popular forms of entertainment like the circus, the music hall, and the carnival in Adorno, as well as positive references to Betty Boop films, even in the infamous essay on the culture industry written with Max Horkheimer. Rather than rejecting the popular *tout court*, Adorno is critical of a form of standardized mass culture that is part of the industrial processes of mass production and consumption within contemporary capitalism which in turn contributes to processes of homogenization and massification of both culture and audiences.

Usually, however, Adorno makes a rather rigid distinction between "high culture" and "mass culture," a dualism that has not only come under critical attack, but which is undermined by the very tendencies of postmodern culture to implode cultural boundaries and collapse hierarchies. Adorno, no doubt, would see this as an example of cultural barbarism, but it seems perverse to demand that products of the culture industries have the qualities of works of previous "high culture" or the avant-garde. Yet by limiting his model of authentic art to those few avant-garde examples of highly negative art, Adorno's model of emancipatory aesthetics is intolerably ascetic and narrow, limited only to those avant-garde productions which resist assimilation and co-optation.

In a sense, Adorno's aesthetics are undialectical. He operates with a binary contrast between "authentic" art and mass culture in which the latter is primarily debased and emancipatory effects are limited to the former. This stance reproduces the German religion of high art and its inevitable elitism, and completely excludes the "popular" from the domain of "the authentic," thus regressing behind the critiques of Brecht and Benjamin – and Adorno's own critique of "the authentic" in his book *Jargon of Authenticity*. Indeed, Adorno's own esoteric aesthetic theory itself becomes a jargon motivated by a dual fear of co-optation and regression.[23] Yet his uncompromising radicalism provides a healthy antidote to all affirmative and idealist aesthetics, and his obstinate obsession with art provides a wealth of insights into the mediations between art and society which might become productive for materialist social theory and cultural criticism of the future.

It is, admittedly exceedingly difficult to read and critique Adorno. An incomparable stylist, he defies summary. The Adorno adventure involves entering into his language, letting his writing and style carry you into a new way of seeing. Adorno's *bon mot* concerning Kafka – "He over whom Kafka's wheels have passed, has lost for ever both any peace with the world and any chance of consoling himself with the judgement that the way of the world is bad" (P: p. x) – holds as well for him: once one has genuinely appropriated Adorno's insights one cannot see the media and society in quite the same way. Once one has appropriated Adorno's vision, one finds his ideas instantiated and confirmed over and over, day after day. One has lost one's innocence, one finds one's self distanced from media culture, detects its standardization, pseudo-individualism, stereotypes and schemata, and the baleful effects of cultural commodification and reification. In a postmodern scene that celebrates the active audience, that finds resistance everywhere, that ritualistically acclaims the popular, Adorno is thus a salutary counterforce.

In fact, while there is no question but that Adorno has overly one-sided and excessively negative and critical views of both the texts and the audiences of media culture, occasionally I have a nightmare that in some sense Adorno is right, that media culture by and large keeps individuals gratified and subservient to the logic and practices of market capitalism, that the culture industry has become thoroughly commodified and absorbs and deflects all oppositional culture to subservient ends. At times, web-surfing, channel-shifting on cable systems, or scanning commercial radio can provide the impression that Adorno is correct, that most media culture is reified rubbish and blatant ideology, that culture has been fundamentally commercialized, homogenized, and banalized in contemporary capitalism. Yet when such nightmare thoughts dissolve, one sees a society in conflict with competing groups struggling to control the direction of society, with progressive and regressive forces in contention, and with a variety of cultural artifacts offering diverse pleasures and oppositional form and content. In this situation, to have a dialectical and adversarial cultural criticism that intervenes in the struggles of the present moment, it is clear that we must move beyond Adorno while assimilating his intransigent oppositional stance and critical insights.

Notes

1   See Horkheimer and Adorno 1972 and the discussion in Kellner 1989, ch. 4. On Adorno and the Frankfurt School, see the articles collected in Arato and Gebhardt (1982) and Bronner and Kellner (1989) (hereafter CTR); the discussions of the history of the Frankfurt school in Jay 1971 and Wiggershaus 1996; and the discussion of the Frankfurt school combination of social theory and cultural criticism in Kellner 1989.

2   T. W. Adorno, "Cultural Criticism and Society" (1967: 30). Adorno was influenced by the view that social reality was articulated within works of art which required hermeneutical deciphering held by his friend and mentor Siegfried Kracauer. See his article "The Mass Ornament" in CTR. On Adorno's cultural criticism, see Susan Buck-Morss (1977), Gillian Rose (1978), and Deborah Cook (1996).

3   See the translations in Adorno (1978: 130) and Leo Löwenthal (1984). Later Adorno would become increasingly critical of what he saw as the superficiality of Löwenthal's sociology of culture and his own efforts would be much more sophisticated.

4   See, for example, Adorno 1978. "On the Fetish Character of Music and the Regression of Hearing," in Andrew Arato and Eike Gebhardt (eds.), *The Essential Frankfurt School Reader* (hereafter FSR); and "On Popular Music," *Studies in Philosophy and Social Science*, IX, no. 1. (1941). See also the collection of Adorno's writings on mass culture edited by J. M. Bernstein, T. W. Adorno, *The Culture Industry*, and *The Stars Down to Earth and Other Essays on the Irrational in Culture*, edited by Stephen Crook.

5   On Adorno and Benjamin's shared aesthetic interests and debates, see Buck-Morss (1977).

6   Adorno, "Jazz: Perennial Fashion," in Adorno (1967: 119–32). It should be noted that Adorno developed his conception of jazz while researching popular music

for CBS on a grant obtained by Paul Lazarsfeld. Thus his sample of jazz music was mostly mediocre radio performances or popular records; there is no evidence that Adorno ever heard live jazz performances or was aware of the wealth of different types of jazz circulating at the time; thus, while his critique might describe aspects of the sort of jazz broadcast on network radio, it obviously misses the richness of the jazz tradition and is probably the most harshly criticized of any of Adorno's work.

7   On the relationship between Lazarsfeld, Adorno, and the Institute, see the memoirs by Lazarsfeld (1969) and David E. Morrison (1978). Lazarsfeld published over 50 books and many articles that helped to found the new discipline of communications research.

8   For Adorno's various analyses of high art, see Adorno 1973, 1984, and 1991.

9   The notion of authentic art as negation runs throughout Adorno's writings on art, which generally formulate the notion in paradoxical terms: "Art records negatively just that possibility of happiness which the only partially positive anticipation of happiness ruinously confronts today. All 'light' and pleasant art has become illusory and mendacious. What makes its appearance aesthetically in the pleasure categories can no longer give pleasure, and the promise of happiness, once the definition of art, can no longer be found except where the mask has been torn from the countenance of false happiness" (FSR: 274).

10 While Adorno began the Institute critique of mass culture in his analyses of the standardization, pseudo-individuality, and manipulative effects of popular music (discussed above), Max Horkheimer spoke of the "entertainment industry" in several 1930s articles, and analyzed the differences between "authentic art" and "mass culture" in "Art and Mass Culture," now collected in *Critical Theory* (New York: Seabury Press, 1972). Leo Löwenthal, who earlier had carried out a study of popular magazine biographies in Germany, analyzed images of success in American magazines, noting a shift from "heroes of production" to "heroes of consumption," in which the "stars" of the culture industry played a major role (in LPCS). A 1941 issue, in English, of *Studies in Philosophy and Social Science* (IX, no. 1) was devoted to mass communications and advanced the notion of "critical research" which combined "theoretical thinking with empirical analysis." Thus the famous study of the "culture industry" in *Dialectic of Enlightenment* built on earlier work and highlighted a theme that had become central to the work of Adorno and the Institute for Social Research.

11 See William Dieterle, "Hollywood and the European Crisis" in *Studies* 1971: 96ff.

12 Interestingly, Adorno and Horkheimer also anticipated in the early 1940s that television would become the most powerful part of the culture industry: "Television aims at a synthesis of radio and film, and is held up only because the interested parties have not yet reached agreement, but its consequences will be quite enormous and promise to intensify the impoverishment of aesthetic matter so drastically, that by tomorrow the thinly veiled identity of all industrial culture products can come triumphantly out into the open, derisively fulfilling the

Wagnerian dream of the *Gesamtkunstwerk* – the fusion of all the arts in one work" (1972: 124). They foresaw a condition in which television would be the apotheosis of the commercialization of culture to an extent that the movies would be perceived as a cultural form relatively uncluttered with commercial messages: "if technology had its way – the film would be delivered to people's homes as happens with the radio. It is moving toward the commercial system. Television points the way to a development which might easily enough force the Warner Brothers into what would certainly be the unwelcome position of serious musicians and cultural conservatives" (1972: 161).

13 For a further discussion of the relation between the Institute and Lazarsfeld and the impact of Critical Theory on media theory and research in the United States, see Douglas Kellner, "Critical Theory, Mass Communications and Popular Culture," *Telos*, 62 (Winter 1984/5): 196–206. For a provocative critique of Lazarsfeld's paradigm, see Todd Gitlin, "Media Sociology: The Dominant Paradigm," *Theory and Society*, 6 (1978): 205–53. Although Gitlin presents an excellent critique of Lazarsfeld's paradigm, especially as set forth in *Personal Influence*, he tends to neglect the critical elements of Lazarsfeld's work and also fails to point out that an alternative critical paradigm was present alongside Lazarsfeld's in the work of the Institute. Many essays in the issue of the *Journal of Communication*, "Ferment in the Field," 33, no. 3 (Summer 1983) contain appraisals of Lazarsfeld's influence on communications research; other articles mention the impact of Institute critical theory on communications research in the United States, though none of these studies systematically demonstrates how the Institute for Social Research influenced theories of communications, culture, and social theory.

14 Lukács (1971), Brecht (1979), Benjamin (1969). On the other hand, the culture industry theory can also be seen as an application of Lukács' theory of the commodity fetishism and the reification of culture and consciousness in capitalist society to artifacts of mass communications and culture, which is then turned against Lukács' political theory by claiming that these phenomena prevent the development of class consciousness, upon which Lukács' theory of revolution depends.

15 On Gramsci's theory of hegemony, see Gramsci (1971) and Boggs (1984).

16 On the culture industries and the blacklist, see Navasky (1980).

17 On the Frankfurt School anticipation of British cultural studies, similarities and differences, see Kellner (1997).

18 For discussion of the contributions of Adorno and critical theory to the study of culture and communications, see Douglas Kellner (1982, 1984, and 1989, chs. 5 and 6).

19 For discussion of how Adorno and the Frankfurt School overcome the divide between communications and cultural studies, see Kellner (1997a).

20 I'll cite some qualifications below which are seized upon by Adorno's defenders to pose alternative readings of his denunciation of the culture industry.

Alternative readings are always possible and are sometimes fruitful, but the over-whelming force of Adorno's writing on mass culture is purely negative and, I believe, provides obstacles to more incisive radical approaches to mass-mediated culture.

21 T. W. Adorno, "Freizeit," *Stickworte* (Frankfurt: Suhrkamp, 1969) translated as "Free Time" in Adorno 1995.

22 See Hans Magnus Enzensberger, "Constituents Toward a Theory of the Media" in *The Consciousness Industry* (New York: Seabury, 1974) and Douglas Kellner, "TV, Ideology, and Emancipatory Popular Culture," *Socialist Review*, 45 (Nov.–Dec.) and "Public Access Television: *Alternative Views*," in *Making Waves*, *Radical Science* 16 (London: 1975). For Brecht's radio theory and Benjamin's analysis of the radicalizing potential of film, see the material cited in note 4. Brecht's radio plays are found in *Gesammelte Schriften*, vol. 2), and Benjamin's are collected in *Gesammelte Schriften*, Band IV, 2, or the *Werkausgabe*, Band 11 (Frankfurt, 1980). For my more recent studies of oppositional Internet politics, see Douglas Kellner, "Intellectuals, the New Public Spheres, and Technopolitics," *New Political Science*, 41–42 (1997): 169–88 and "Toward a Radical Democratic Technopolitics," *Angelaki*, 4:2 (1999): 101–13

23 Most Adorno critics have noted his almost paranoic fear of co-optation, and Peter Bürger makes a salient argument that fear of regression motivated Adorno's aesthetic theory in "The Decline of the Modern Age," *Telos*, 62 (Winter 1984–5): 117–30.

4

Adorno's Politics

Russell Berman

To understand Adorno's politics requires making one's way through a fog of accusations and ressentiments. During the mid-seventies, the violent political actions of the Red Army Faction occupied the public life of the Federal Republic of Germany (FRG), and conservative politicians were quick to point a finger to blame Adorno's Critical Theory for spawning a generation of terrorists and revolutionaries. For the ideologues of the right, at least, Adorno's politics appeared to lead directly from theory to practice. It is, however, the quite contrary judgment on the left that has come to dominate the reception of his work and the estimation of his political significance. Adorno is generally taken to stand for a quietism, fundamentally hostile to politics, and given to such an infinitely pessimistic account of capitalist development that no possible praxis, let alone a revolution, could turn humanity away from its sorry conclusion in a thoroughly administered society.

While it is true that Adorno doubted the efficacy of direct political action, these standard misrepresentations have been repeated so often that they obscure the genuine moments of political substance in his work. The condemnation that Adorno fails to provide political leadership, that his theory is not an immediate guide to action, is based on various arguments: by an extrapolation from the negative teleology implicit in *Dialectic of Enlightenment*, or by suggesting that his aestheticist predilections were inimal to political action, or with reference to his disputes with the German student movement, especially during 1967–9. The suggestion that Adorno lacks politics typically assumes that someone else has them, i.e., Adorno's failings represent the opposite of Marcuse's revolutionism, or Habermas' theory of communicative action, or even orthodox Marxists of some stripe or other. In other words, there is extensive agreement among Adorno's critics that he was not adequately political, and this agreement masks the lack of unanimity on what an adequate politics would entail. Ultimately the persistent complaint regarding Adorno's political failure amounts to a ritual accusation that reveals more about the aspirations of the critics than it does about Adorno himself.

The irritation that the notion of "Adorno's politics" unleashes across a wide spectrum of the left indicates that something of a taboo surrounds the issue. By labelling Adorno politically impossible, his critics provide themselves an illusory security in their own political self-understanding. Meanwhile, Adorno's posthumous conviction as a failed political thinker resembles the fate of renegades within the socialist movement: the more he is repressed for allegedly betraying "the movement," the more he looms larger as a potential critic of "left politics," but because he remains a critic from within the left, the scandal is all the greater (cf. Rohrwasser 1991). His consistent assertion of the autonomy of theory from practice, within a dialectical interdependence, as well as that leitmotif of Critical Theory since the thirties, the need for reason to reflect upon itself, amount to admonitions to caution which could only irritate a left which, since the student movement, has spiralled through dogmatism, sectarianism, and conformism, only to land in today's more moderate but no less reified political correctness. In other words, the image of Adorno, the unpolitical aesthete, is little more than a phantom that haunts a left that cultivates its own self-deceptions about an immediacy of political practice. Because it is convinced that progressive politics must be easy, it demonizes Adorno for pointing out the difficulties.

Leaving Germany

Given the reputation that precedes Adorno, it is quite striking to hear how Max Horkheimer eulogized him at the burial in the Central Cemetery of Frankfurt on August 13, 1969. Recalling how he came to Adorno to persuade him to leave Germany in 1933, after Hitler's accession to power, he reports Adorno's reply: "No Max, we have to stay here; we have to fight" (Kraushaar I: 457). This evocation of a pugnacious Adorno stands at odds with the routinized image of the antipolitical aesthete. Horkheimer's account contrasted sharply with the obituary written by Adorno's student, Hans-Jürgen Krahl, which had appeared that same day in the *Frankfurter Rundschau* and which repeated the by then common complaint about Adorno's distance from practice. Nothing is more unexpected than Horkheimer's image of Adorno as an antifascist resistance fighter. Yet Horkheimer's account of a forgotten political Adorno willing to take up a battle with the Nazi regime is

corroborated by evidence from an unexpected source. In an exchange published in *Diskus*, the student newspaper in Frankfurt, in January 1963, Adorno,
who was by then well known as a critic of authoritarian and antisemitic
potential in West Germany, was confronted with an article which he had
himself published in 1934 in *Die Musik*, which at that point had been taken
over as an official organ of the Nazi youth organization. In it, Adorno praised
a cycle of songs for a male chorus composed by Herbert Müntzel, which
drew its texts from poems by the Nazi leader, Baldur von Schirach. The discovery of the material was presented to *Diskus* in order to suggest opportunism on Adorno's part in the early thirties and to undermine the integrity
of his criticism of latent fascist tendencies in the FRG.

In his reply, Adorno immediately concedes having written the review and
expressly regrets particular aspects of it, above all the embarrassment that von
Schirach was the author of the songs' lyrics. Yet he also provides contextual-
ization that sheds important light on his own political personality across
several decades:

> Whoever reads my essay without prejudice is able to see my intention: to
> defend modern music; to help it survive the Third Reich; as I recall, Müntzel's
> very talented work was a good place to start. My emphasis alone on internal
> compositional legitimacy in contrast to the pressure "to be comprehensible and
> immediate" leaves no doubt about my goal. I wrote this at a time when any-
> thing like this was denounced as cultural bolshevism; they gave me special treat-
> ment in the exhibit on "Degenerate Music." If anyone wants to suspect me of
> trying to appease the new powers, my reply is that I would not have come to
> the public defense of the denounced music. (Kraushaar 1998 II: 168)

During the twenties Adorno had been a regular contributor to *Die Musik*,
and he continued to contribute reviews during 1933 and into the summer
of 1934 (Wiggershaus 87). The review in question falls into this period,
between Hitler's appointment as Chancellor and Adorno's decision to leave,
and his retrospective account of his stance is consonant with Horkheimer's
report of Adorno's insistence on the urgency of resistance. This resistance, to
be sure, takes place in the mediated sphere of music criticism and does not
have any of the romance of illegal, underground conspiracies. However, in
order to evaluate this instance of Adorno's politics, or later ones as well, it is
important to reflect on the comparison set, the plausible political alternatives.
The dearth of resistance activity in Nazi Germany is well known (and its
extent elsewhere in Western Europe has surely been exaggerated); what did
take place testifies to the honor of the individual participants, but there is no
evidence that direct political action, for example, in the form of assassination
conspiracies, had a greater impact on the stability of the regime than efforts

to maintain a free space in the cultural sphere. Indeed, if the Nazi *Gleich-schaltung*, the purging of the public sphere and the world of art, was an important part of the exercise of dictatorial power, then it was certainly not implausible for Adorno in 1934 to imagine that a strategically masked defense of modern music represented a possible mode of political practice.

This early brush with politics in 1934, as interpreted from the vantage point of 1963, provides a complex entry into Adorno's strategy. On the one hand, politics takes place through art and criticism: he defends modern music, while exploring its internal complexities, precisely because the contemporary state opposes it. On the other hand, his reluctance to leave Germany depended on a political miscalculation, the notion that the Hitler regime might come to a quick conclusion. He was not alone in this mixture of political naiveté and wishful thinking, a rare moment of exaggerated optimism for Adorno:

> The genuine error lay in my incorrect evaluation of the situation, or, if you will, in the foolishness of someone for whom the decision to emigrate was very difficult. I believed that the Third Reich could not last long, and that one should stay in order to save whatever was possible. This and this alone led me to my naively tactical phrases. Against these phrases stands everything that I have written during my life, before and after Hitler, including my book on Kierkegaard, which appeared on the day that Hitler took power. Anyone who reviews the continuity of my work cannot compare me with Heidegger, whose philosophy is fascist into its innermost cells. (Wiggershaus 1986: 87)

Adorno's "incorrect evaluation of the situation," the illusion that Hitler would quickly be removed from power, could have cost him his life, had his friends not succeeded in convincing him to leave. One can speculate that this one instance in which Adorno succumbed to unwarranted expectations of imminent progress may have left him in his later life with a predisposition to minimize the likelihood of political change and precisely therefore to remain distant from aspirations to political action. Krahl argues this point in the obituary by claiming that "Adorno's intellectual biography, including its aesthetic abstractions, is marked by the experience of fascism" (Kraushaar 1998 II: 673). Yet to conclude that the memory of the apparent futility of individual resistance to Hitler entails a disability which undermines Adorno's subsequent work is not convincing. The lesson to draw from the *Musik* review is more complex and involves the simultaneity of a stance of resistance, an orientation toward a redefinition of theoretical and aesthetic fields as an appropriate terrain for political reflection, and an empirical political judgment of questionable character. Adorno's later reluctance to advocate direct political action may reflect the internalization of his error of judgment in

1933, but it also draws on multiple other intellectual-historical legacies: the tenuous status of a political sphere within Marxism itself, given the predisposition to place much greater emphasis on developmental laws of capitalist economics; the model of aesthetic education, inherited from Kant and Schiller, which located opportunities for social progress in the aesthetic rather than in the political sphere; and the epochal disappointment with the legacies of 1917, the failure of revolution in the West, and the emergence of Stalinism in the East. Against this background, the strategy of maintaining an autonomous theoretical discourse about the possibility of resistance, while focusing on emancipatory moments in philosophy and art, appears less as a political failing than as a much more plausible stance than the direct political action of the student movement and the terrorism into which it quickly collapsed.

While Adorno did express deep reservations regarding the feasibility of direct political action, politics were hardly absent from his work. On the contrary, the one theme that pervades his writing is the possibility of resistance, figured in the complex tensions between particular subjectivity and objective social forces. To be sure, this discussion generally takes place in a highly abstract philosophical register, and the specific political references are sometimes – but hardly always – disguised in the specialized language of Critical Theory. Understanding Adorno's politics means bracketing the chorus of critics in order to trace the array of political positions and themes which Adorno addressed across several decades. Adorno explores the complexity of the dialectic most extensively in his philosophical and aesthetic writings, but there is a layer in his *oeuvre* in which he grapples with political questions in a relatively direct fashion. This expressly political stratum is in fact quite substantial and yields compelling evidence regarding the nature of his evaluation of several eminently political themes: the character of the state in twentieth-century capitalism, potentials for democracy after 1945, particularly in the FRG, and an array of topics around the student movement. Reviewing Adorno's engagement with these issues, one discovers a thinker deeply concerned with the political structure of domination and the urgency of resistance to it, although unwilling to transform theory into a mere alibi for an activist praxis with no prospect for success.

The United States and/as Nazi Germany

The development of Adorno's political thought between his arrival in the United States in 1938 and the completion of *Dialectic of Enlightenment* in 1944 takes place above all with reference to Germany – the overriding issue is the evaluation of National Socialism – but within a double framework: on the one hand, the debates among the exiled intellectuals associated with the Institute for Social Research concerning the nature of the Nazi regime, on the other hand the larger vicissitudes of the American left in the era of the New Deal. The controversial political judgment at the core *Dialectic of Enlightenment* conjoins these two perspectives, while integrating into them some of Adorno's specific intellectual legacies from Europe: the theory of reification developed by the young Lukács, Kracauer's observations of standardization in capitalism, Benjamin's admixture of theology and Marxism, and Adorno's own aesthetic bias toward the role of the work of art in social formations.

The Institute debates were driven by concerns with the stability of the Nazi regime, as evidenced in Horkheimer's essay on "the Authoritarian State," Friedrich Pollock's account of "State Capitalism," both in 1940, and Franz Neumann's *Behemoth* in 1941 (cf. Wiggershaus 1986: 314–27). In this period, the likelihood of a German defeat (evident in the later *Dialectic of Enlightenment*) was by no means given. On the contrary, extrapolating from the Marxist theorization of different economic formations within the history of capitalism, National Socialism is treated as a new stage of state capitalism, in contrast both to the early twentieth-century model of a monopoly capitalism and to a previous stage of liberal capitalism associated with the laissez faire of the nineteenth century. This historiography lent an air of inevitability to the extensive interpenetration of state and economy, just as it provided a basis for a potential comparison between Nazi Germany and other cases of state capitalism. Meanwhile, within the American left at large, important shifts were taking place (cf. Hohendahl 1995: 23–30). The emphatically socialist programs of the twenties and early thirties dwindled in the course of the decade, particularly in the light of the news of the Moscow Trials, the institutionalization of the New Deal (as a specifically nonsocialist response to the economic crisis), and the rise of Hitler, which led to an allegiance with the Roosevelt regime. Instead of a revolutionary opposition outside the political system, left intellectuals and leaders of the working-class movement alike advocated integration into the system, and they did so precisely with progressive rationales: to overcome the depression and to defeat Hitler. American critics of this capacity of the New Deal to integrate the erstwhile opposition were few and far between, and there was consequently no obvious example of a self-evidently oppositional political practice. What remained was the New Deal and the Popular Front, which was the option which Herbert Marcuse, for example, was prepared to choose, working for American intelligence during the war. In this sense, Marcuse was more engaged than Adorno as early as the 1940s; there is no little irony in the fact that the very same distinction between the allegedly unpolitical Adorno and the explicitly activist Marcuse became central to the student movement's interpretation of the Frankfurt School more than two decades later.

Dialectic of Enlightenment poses as a civilizational-historical statement, a summary judgment on millennia of Western culture: from its anthropological reflections on animism, sacrifice, and myth; through its critical reading of the *Odyssey*, as both the original and most symptomatic epic; continuing into the philosophical treatment of classical texts by Sade and Nietzsche and concluding with the treatise on the "culture industry," the industrial production of film and music, juxtaposed with reflections on antisemitism, a topic of inordinate urgency in the era of the Holocaust. The structure of the trajectory relies on an assumption regarding the teleology of culture, and the volume appears to invite the reader to consider the issues within a *longue durée* of history. Yet the book also attempts a precise and controversial evaluation of the current political moment. Horkheimer and Adorno modify the state-capitalist analysis of Nazi Germany, emphasize the distinction between an earlier "liberal" era and the current stage of intertwined state and economy, but then displace the interpretation from Germany and onto the United States, where the expansive state and the culture industry appeared to have absorbed all significant opposition into a totally administered society. To suggest a similarity between Nazi Germany and the United States of the New Deal era was an extraordinary provocation (modified only by the limited circulation of the manuscript and the arcane and coded phrasing). As Jameson comments,

> it was the originality of Adorno and Horkheimer first to have linked [American mass democracy and the Nazi interregnum] culturally, and to have insisted, with an implacability that must surely be counted as a form of political commitment, on the indissociability of the Culture Industry and fascism; and to have mingled their American and their German examples and illustrations throughout their exposition in a provocative fashion that could not fail to scandalize. (Jameson 1990: 140)

The radical political claim of the comparability of Nazi Germany and the United States in terms of state capitalism underlies the central argument regarding the history of enlightenment. For in contemporary political discourse, Germany was usually cast as the representation of mythic irrationalism, while the United States stood for reason and democracy as the teleology of Western civilization. Horkheimer and Adorno destabilize this binary opposition through the equation of myth and enlightenment. The first of their double theses, the claim that myth was always enlightenment, subverts the fascist aesthetic and its fascination with myth as an alternative to reason by insisting that myth was itself an attempt, albeit an early one, to explain nature and thereby to control it, anticipating the project of the natural sciences. The twin claim is that enlightenment reverts to myth: the same reason which pursued emancipation from natural violence reproduces that violence through its eradication of particularity through a relentless identity logic. While the first point is directed against the standard understanding of fascism as irrational, the second challenges the presumed rationality of the progressive camp, the New Deal and the Popular Front. It is not the case that Horkheimer and Adorno fully equate the opposing political models, but they do present them as variants of a single state capitalism; the provocation is the skepticism it directs toward the standard political judgment of the absolute difference between the two.

The ostensible topics of the essays in *Dialectic of Enlightenment* are philosophical, aesthetic, and civilization-historical. The political scandal is inserted into the interstices of argument, through asides or passing references, the implications of which are enormously grave. For example, an extended passage treating the structural characteristics of commercial film and other products of the culture industry focuses first on standardization and then, in a line of thought reminiscent of Nietzsche's critique of Wagner, on the revised relationship between part and whole in the work. In place of mediation, components collide abruptly, without reason. The description of the interior composition of the aesthetic material conveys an allegory of social organization:

> The whole inevitably bears no relation to the details – just like the career of a successful man into which everything is made to fit as an illustration or a proof, whereas it is nothing more than the sum of all those idiotic events. The so-called dominant idea is like a file which ensures order but not coherence. The whole and the parts are alike; there is no antithesis and no connection. Their prearranged harmony is a mockery of what had to be striven after in the great bourgeois works of art. (Horkheimer and Adorno 1972: 126)

The critical account of the incoherence of commercial art is one of the central tenets of the argument concerning the culture industry, and the contrast with the foil, the adequately dialectical art of the liberal era, "the great bourgeois works," confirms the historical trajectory familiar from the developmental account of capitalism.

Yet suddenly, in the final sentence of the paragraph, the description of the film industry, be it Hollywood or Weimar, takes on an ominous dimension: "In Germany the graveyard stillness of the dictatorship already hung over the gayest films of the democratic era." The specific thesis regarding the history of the cinema was developed in *From Caligari to Hitler* by Adorno's mentor

Kracauer. In this context, however, the salient issue is the dissolution of the otherwise sacrosanct border between democracy and dictatorship, between Weimar and Nazi Germany. While standard political opinion could speak of Weimar's collapse as a failure of democracy in Germany, Horkheimer and Adorno abrasively suggest that the much touted democracy of Weimar culture already displayed significant fascist characteristics. Consequently their critique of the culture industry, which may have sounded uncomfortably close to a cultural conservative complaint of aesthetic decline and a nostalgia for the great art of the past, suddenly turns into an accusation that democratic culture – Weimar film and, by extension, the commercial film industry in general, and therefore especially Hollywood – promulgates precisely those structures of meaning which are constitutive of National Socialism. The authors have reserved their political conclusion for this unexpected punchline; and they pass by it quickly. Instead of lingering on the political implications, they move quickly on to treat other aspects of the culture industry.

A second example: a discrete reference posits the liberal era as past and designates "industrialized and fascist [völkisch] culture" as co-equal subsequent forms, sharing the same repressive relationship toward individual desire (Horkheimer and Adorno 1972: 141, translation modified). Elsewhere Horkheimer and Adorno posit the social-structural similarity between Germany and the United States; here the similarity involves the psychoanalytic economy:

> In contrast to the liberal era, both industrialized and fascist culture can permit themselves outrage over capitalism, but neither can refuse the threat of castration. This is at their core. It outlasts the organized loosening of morals for soldiers in the cheerful films produced for them as well as in reality. Puritanism is no longer decisive, although it is still influential through the women's organizations; what is decisive is the systemic necessity never to let go of the consumer, never to let him catch a glimpse of the possibility of resistance. (Horkheimer and Adorno 1972: 141, translation modified)

Popular cultural representations of Americans and Germans typically caricature the authoritarian personalities of the Germans in contrast to the more supple Americans. For Horkheimer and Adorno, by way of contrast, the respective cultural structures ("industrialized and fascist") pursue the same goal, the interpellation of a recipient without the possibility of resistance, who is tied to the products of cultural representation through an economy of desire, but who is simultaneously bound to accept perpetual disappointment as the only imaginable result: anything else is rendered explicitly unimaginable. The cultural structures of the two regimes, despite differences, are treated as comparable variants within a single contemporary formation, while the genuine alternative is not to be found in some socialism (which has fully disappeared from sight in the wake of the Moscow Trials) but at best, nostalgically, in the "liberal" era, before the thorough interpenetration of state and economy and which was alone capable of the "great bourgeois works" mentioned earlier.

Dialectic of Enlightenment is replete with these elisions between the United States and Nazi Germany. The political substance of the analogy is a profound critique of the transformation in the United States regarding the expansion of the state administration, standardization of life practices, the proliferation of the commercial culture industry, and a transformation of individual personality type increasingly incapable of maintaining an autonomy, an individual integrity, in the face of overarching structures of power. Within this framework, Nazi antisemitism tends to lose any specific reference to Jews or for that matter to Germans; unlike subsequent interpretations that present the Holocaust as a defining experience for a Jewish ethnicity or as evidence of the specific character of a German cultural will, Horkheimer and Adorno treat it as the extension of the identity logic or "ticket thinking" with its inimical hostility to any difference (cf. Goldhagen 1996, and Horkheimer and Adorno 1972: 200). Their suggestion that the same logic of abstraction applies from "the battlefield to the studio" inculpates Hollywood in the crimes of war because the very structure of its representations disseminates a force of homogenization that is cut from the same cloth as Nazi hostility to difference. Hence their boldly dismissive judgment on film at its most antifascist: "The ears of corn blowing in the wind at the end of Chaplin's *The Great Dictator* give the lie to the anti-Fascist plea for freedom. The are like the blond hair of the German girl whose camp life is photographed by the Nazi film company in the summer breeze" (Horkheimer and Adorno 1972: 149). Antifascism as fascism: not until the collapse of the Soviet empire in 1989 and the rethinking of the ideological role played by "antifascism" in the East could this political judgment begin to appear credible (cf. Grünenberg 1993).

The identity of the aesthetic artifacts from the two warring camps points toward a shared conception of a healthy nature, precisely the standpoint from which a persecution of the putatively degenerate outsiders could start. Hence the exceptionally stark and frank judgment that the imminent defeat of fascism may not rid Europe of fascist predispositions. "In Germany, Fascism won the day with a crassly xenophobic, collectivist ideology which was hostile to culture. Now that it is laying the whole world waste, the nations must fight against it; there is no other way out. But when all is over there is nothing to prove that a spirit of freedom will spread across Europe; its nations may become just as xenophobic, pseudocollectivistic, and hostile to culture as

Fascism once was when they had to fight against it" (Horkheimer and Adorno 1972: 221). If the social structures are the same, if the nature of contemporary capitalism is the same, then surely a predisposition toward the same cultural attitudes may arise. The passage clarifies the status of the equation between the United States and Germany. There is no doubt that for Horkheimer and Adorno "the nations must fight against" Nazi Germany; this is a clear endorsement of a practical action. Yet at the same time, they refrain from censoring their own doubts. The fact that a political praxis might be posited, in this case, the war against Nazi Germany, is not taken as grounds to level the distinction between theory and practice or to turn theory into a retrospective alibi for a given practice. This relative autonomy of theory vis-à-vis the *vita activa* of political practice would become the bone of contention with the student movement two decades later. Yet it was the speculation concerning the afterlife of a fascist potential within postwar Europe that first defined much of Adorno's political agenda when he followed Horkheimer back to Germany.

Anticommunism and Psychoanalysis in West Germany

Adorno's politics take on a greater complexity after his return to Europe, where he appears to have been more prepared to address contemporary matters directly, in contrast to the cryptic formulations of *Dialectic of Enlightenment*, where political judgments were submerged in the larger cultural-critical narrative. In place of the stringent logic of the theory of state capitalism and the concomitant equation of the United States and Nazi Germany, two separate lines of political reflection, only loosely connected, emerge and interweave. One line concerns Communism; the explicit anticommunist turn in Adorno's thinking moved him, as Peter Uwe Hohendahl (1995: 44) has argued, much closer to the mainstream of political opinion in the FRG than he had been in Weimar, at least with regard to the estimation of the Soviet Union. The reflection on Communism and on orthodox Marxism includes writings on international politics as well as the seminal literary critical essays on Lukács, "Extorted Reconciliation," of 1958, and on Sartre and Brecht, "Engagement," of 1962. Meanwhile a second strand of political thinking focused on the FRG and, to some extent, postwar Western democracies more generally, in which, so Adorno argued, authoritarian, fascist, and antisemitic potentials for violence may lie just below a deceptively placid surface. Pursuing this topic, Adorno engaged in empirical social-scientific research on aspects of public opinion, but he drew the political consequences in public addresses that pointed toward educational programs as well as to psychoanalytic diagnoses for the carriers of prejudice: "What is 'Coming to Terms with the Past?'" (1959) and "Education after Auschwitz" (1966). Despite the different focal points, the critique of Communism and the critique of Western democracies share the paradigm of an underlying sociopolitical structure (derived from the earlier model of state capitalism) that threatens, in different ways, the viability of autonomous thought.

By 1950 Germany was formally divided into two states, the Cold War was in full swing, and Russian initiatives to steer West Germany toward a neutral course were under way. An unpublished document, "the USSR and the Peace," by both Adorno and Horkheimer and dated August 1950, sheds important light on the critical theorists' estimation of Soviet Communism. The short essay represents a draft of a response to an appeal from a peace organization to support an absolute ban on atomic weapons; it is therefore particularly interesting as evidence of a very early encounter between Critical Theory and the German peace movement, an encounter that would continue to be contentious decades later (cf. Berman 1983). While the urgency of peace, particularly in the nuclear age, is self-evident, Adorno and Horkheimer take the Soviet manipulation of an indisputably legitimate goal as symptomatic of the dialectical transformation of politics.

> It is an expression of the intractable and blind situation, heading toward absolute horror, that it can turn the truth into a lie, when it is put to the service of a lie. The peace appeal and the condemnation of atomic weapons are a piece of Soviet propaganda with the intention to misuse humane sentiments in order to break the resistance against the violence that comes from the Soviet Union. It would not refrain from unleashing a war if the violent rulers in Moscow thought they could win it. The yearning for peace, shared by all peoples, is being used to gain time for the new totalitarian enterprise. (Kraushaar 1998 II: 51)

The political estimation of the peace movement as a front for Soviet politics represents a standard position on the western side in the Cold War. Yet the essay goes beyond this straightforward condemnation. Instead the authors convey considerable skepticism toward public politics in general, very much in line with the sort of cultural criticism familiar from the *Dialectic of Enlightenment*, but now shifted out of the cultural and into the political sphere. "What propaganda has done to the concept of peace is symptomatic of the changes which the concept of politics is undergoing. In the past, politics meant the conscious, independent, and critical effort, in thought and deed, to replace bad social conditions with better ones. Today politics is generally merely a façade. It no longer means the realization of humanity but only inter-state power struggles" (Kraushaar 1998 II: 52). Propaganda has degraded politics in much the same way that the culture industry has degraded art. Critical Theory, in contrast, has tried to maintain its independence "through which alone we hope to be able to prevent the disaster." Critique cannot spare Stalinist Russia, nor can it spare Marxism itself. "No thought can avoid becoming a delusion if it loses contact with lived experience and becomes an idol. This is the fate of the Marxist conception today. The meaning of every one of its claims is turned all the more into its opposite, the more it is rigidly parroted. If Marx is turned into a positive system or a world formula, an unspeakable impoverishment of all cognition and all praxis follow, and ultimately a total hallucination." Given Adorno's project of integrating a Freudian component into his analysis of personality structure in contemporary capitalism, the attack on the exclusivity of Marxism in the Stalinist world was, of course, urgent. The conclusion they draw foreshadows later debates. The alternative to official Communism is certainly not to be found in one or other splinter group which, for Critical Theory, is largely committed to the same authoritarian paradigms which characterize the orthodox position. On the contrary, "in times like these, more truth is found in private life, that avoids the intoxicating imagery of collective power, than in the machinery of grand politics." The passage echoes Weber's "Science as Vocation" of 1918, when he insisted that truth was to be found in "the smallest and most intimate circles" rather than in a "monumental style" (Weber 1958: 155). For Adorno the priority of private life over the manipulated public sphere corresponds to the project of maintaining a personal autonomy and resisting the pressure toward a false collectivization: on this point, the Freudian critique of conformism and the political critique of Stalinism converge.

Adorno's response to the orthodox Marxism of the Communist movement also unfolded in the two essays on Lukács and on Sartre and Brecht. Included in the collection *Notes on Literature*, they are best understood within the framework of Adorno's literary criticism and the essayistic studies preparatory to the *Aesthetic Theory*. Nevertheless aspects of this writing do shed some additional light on Adorno's political thinking. "Extorted Reconciliation" is a review of Lukács' volume *Against Misunderstood Realism*. Adorno had met Lukács in 1925 in Vienna and had borrowed extensively from his pre-Marxist writings as well as his theory of reification from *History and Class Consciousness* (1923). Yet their political paths had diverged, and Lukács had become the foremost spokesmen for the doctrines of socialist realism, antithetical to all of Adorno's aesthetics; Adorno's disappointment with an erstwhile mentor fuels the polemical animus he directs at the volume.

To be sure, Lukács' goals included resisting the worst tendencies toward propagandistic writing in the Soviet Union, precisely by invoking models of nineteenth-century "bourgeois realism." Moreover, within the Soviet world,

Lukács represented a relatively liberal voice, and he had therefore become the focal point of political interest in the Hungarian uprising of 1956. Nevertheless, despite these rudimentary dissident credentials, Adorno attacks Lukács for the latter's ongoing rejection of modernist literature, a consequence of an inability to ascribe to art even a relative autonomy, and it is this threatening loss of autonomy which Adorno finds most dangerous. Lukács imputes a fundamental unity to social existence, a reconciliation of subject and object, and he expects the work of art to repeat this unity; Adorno does not only object to the reflection theory itself, the conception of the work of art as a mirror of nature, but, more profoundly, to Lukács' harmonizing view of the real, a concession to the power of the Soviet regime, and hence an "extorted reconciliation." Autonomy of both art and theory disappear into the prescribed orderliness of social repression. Adorno's political agenda, in contrast, insists on maintaining that autonomy: of art, of theory, and the individual, for only the autonomous subject has the capacity to resist the violent collective of the authoritarian state.

Quite removed from Lukács' realism, Sartre and Brecht represent variants of a Marxist modernism: innovative playwrights, both (publicly at least) supportive of Soviet politics, and advocates of an "engaged" literature. In their case, Adorno's political target is therefore no longer the orthodox Marxism of Lukács but rather a left radicalism, indebted to a Marxist idiom, and dismissive of aesthetic autonomy. Aside from his specific readings of the works of the two opponents (themselves revealing examples of the literary critic Adorno at work) the essay is important for an evaluation of Adorno's political thinking precisely because of the judgment on "engagement." Adorno's criticism of engaged art is clearly not a refusal of the political but rather a complaint that the self-appointed political literature undercuts its own political strength precisely because of its refusal of aesthetic autonomy. Sartre's dramas, for example, intended as exemplary demonstrations of human freedom as elaborated in existentialism, in fact reveal the opposite: the compulsive and constrictive nature of the social conditions in which freedom is precisely not to be had. The abstract freedom of existentialism depends on a refusal to recognize the administered society and its mechanisms of manipulation and heteronomy; the drama of abstract choices is therefore sorely inadequate, at best a simulation of freedom in a state of unfreedom. In contrast, Adorno, precisely as a consequence of his social theory, insists on aesthetic autonomy as the potential vehicle for a criticism of the political situation, even if it is not a tendentious or an engaged literature. "Art does not mean pointing out alternatives, but rather, through nothing more than form, resisting the way of the world that is always pointing a pistol to the breast of humanity" (Weber 1958: 155). The critique of Brecht is similar: the more political the literature, the less adequate the political analysis, despite the loss of aesthetic autonomy. Fully consistent with the spirit of resistance identified in Horkheimer's eulogy, as well as with the propensity to displace the organ of political criticism into the hermetic work of art, he concludes that "Political works of art are not appropriate for out time; but politics has immigrated into autonomous work, and there most of all where they play dead, as far as politics is concerned" ("Erpresste Versöhnung" in *Gesammelte Schriften*, XI, 430).

The political Adorno is therefore the literary Adorno, or at least, the literary critic Adorno defines the work of art as the location of politics when it is most hermetic. Yet simultaneously with these essays, during the late fifties and early sixties, Adorno grappled with the nature of political culture in the FRG in a very different register as well. If political resistance had migrated into the work of art, art was not its only location. Adorno directed his attention to the quite explicitly political question of the viability of German democracy. The *Wirtschaftswunder* lent the new democracy a semblance of stability that had been denied the Weimar Republic, but doubts persisted that the FRG would withstand an economic downturn. Moreover Germany faced several dramatic waves of antisemitic vandalism at synagogues and Jewish cemeteries during the fifties; even the university committee meeting at which Adorno was appointed to a professorship in 1957 was reportedly marred by an antisemitic outburst against Adorno from a faculty member (Kraushaar 1998 I: 117). In a 1959 address to the Coordinating Board for Christian–Jewish Cooperation, Adorno turned to the question "What is 'Coming to Terms with the Past'?" Was Germany's public concern with its past a vehicle to repress and deny it by declaring it concluded or could it, alternatively, entail a genuine working through of memory? Instead of focusing on the phenomenon of neo-Nazis, the marginal extremists who captured headlines, Adorno raised a topic regarding the very center of West German culture. "I consider the continuity of National Socialism *within* democracy as potentially more dangerous than the continuity of fascist tendencies *against* democracy" ("Was bedeutet Aufarbeitung der Vergangenheit" in *GS* X/2: 556). As bad as the outright opponents of democracy may be, the greater concern is the authoritarian potential within democratic culture. The political move is a familiar one: destabilizing the established binary of extremists and democrats, Adorno calls into question the complacent self-understanding of the FRG: the problem is less what happened before 1945 than the potential that it might happen again.

Adorno's argument links a Marxist with a Freudian claim: the social structures persist that produced the personality type that participated in fascism. Hence the conclusion: "We will have come to terms with the past only when we remove the causes of what came to pass. Its spell has still not been broken because its causes continue" (GS X/2: 557). In contrast to contemporary cultural studies' interest in regimes of discourse, Adorno gestures repeatedly to social structure as a source of political behavior. In addition, the essay interweaves critical comments regarding aspects of German political opinion that reflect a blindness to the German past, e.g., the version of anticommunism that refuses to admit that it was Hitler's foreign policy that brought the Soviet empire into Central Europe (GS 560–1). Still Adorno's provocation is that a social structure continues that has not changed since fascism. It is an assertion reminiscent of the comparison of the United States and Nazi Germany in 1944, since Adorno again comes close to equating Nazi Germany and the postwar democracy, with all of its American traits. It should be noted that significant factors are absent in this analysis of the FRG: the democratic political system, the disappearance of the Junkers, the reduced scope of the military, the independence of unions and professional associations, etc. Still, Germany remained a relatively centralized economy, dominated by a small number of established corporations with not inconsiderable predemocratic aspects in its political culture, and this social structure provides, according to Adorno, the basis for the potential recurrence of fascism because it militates against the development of autonomous subjectivity: "The economic order and, accordingly, the economic organization as well condemn the majority to a dependency on factors over which they have no control and therefore to a lack of independence. If they want to live, they have no choice but to conform to the given situation and to adapt; they must give up that autonomous subjectivity" (GS 567). The conclusion he draws, the praxis that could emerge from the analysis, is limited: a "democratic pedagogy" which could break the German repression of the past and spread an awareness of the violence, past and potential. The underlying calculation is that a knowledge of the horrors of the past could counteract the tendency to repeat them, even though, ultimately, a transformation of the social conditions would be necessary.

In *Dialectic of Enlightenment*, Horkheimer and Adorno registered their political and economic claims without elaborating on them, hiding them instead within the larger cultural critical text. In these later essays as well, Adorno gestures toward social change but refrains from moving toward a clear program. The allusion to the urgency of changing the social conditions might be read as a code for radical restructuring, for some version of socialism, or alternatively as a return to the "liberal" era. The anticentralist implications have led subsequent critical theory toward models of federalism and populism (cf. Piccone 1994). Adorno does not clarify a specific political program in any explicit way. In "Education after Auschwitz," he repeats the assertion that the social conditions responsible for fascism have not changed, but then notes that the likelihood of influencing the objective conditions is minimal; therefore he turns to the "subjective" side to raise questions of education and psychology. Recognizing the continued potential for political violence, he proposes developing an educational program designed to make individuals less likely to participate in a future genocide. This in turn depends on elaborating an understanding of the psychic predisposition to organized brutality. Adorno's account amounts to a psychoanalytic foundation for a possible political education, which would have to address several components: the claustrophobia in administered society which leads to a sense of rage against civilization; the lack of autonomy and attractions of collective identity formation; masochism and sadism; a fetishism of technical means without regard to ends; and, especially, coldness as a preponderant characteristic. Without "coldness," Auschwitz would not have been possible, but this basic disinterest in the well-being of others, a diminished capacity to identify with the other, Adorno goes on to claim, is a determining feature of society for millennia. The potential praxis which Adorno can prescribe is typical: reflection on the social conditions of coldness – this is consistent with the older proposal from *Dialectic of Enlightenment* that the enlightenment reflect upon itself – and efforts to overcome coldness, but limited to a private sphere (as in the statement on the peace movement): "If anything can help against coldness as a condition of catastrophe, it is the insight into its own conditions and the anticipatory attempt to work against these conditions in the private sphere" ("Erziehung nach Auschwitz," in *Kulturkritik und Gesellschaft II*: 688).

The Student Movement

As early as 1952, during Horkheimer's rectorship at the University of Frankfurt, a positive relationship between Critical Theory and the German student movement began to develop. The initial issues involved student initiatives to improve relations betweens Germans and Jews as well as protests against a new film by Veit Harlan, notorious as the director of the antisemitic *Jud Süss* for the Nazi cinema (Kraushaar 1998 I: 78). During the subsequent decade, there was much in Adorno's political thinking that the students could share: the critique of conservative West Germany, the rejection of the Nazi past and its legacies in contemporary culture, the skepticism toward a solely instrumental concept of enlightenment. At the same time, however, Adorno's anticommunism would eventually elicit opposition from parts of the student movement closer to an orthodox Marxism. More importantly, however, his judgment that change in objective structures is less feasible than in the subjective realm of education and psychology would run foul of a movement increasingly oriented toward immediate political action in the realm of bona fide policy. The two sides addressed different levels of politics: while Adorno's education after Auschwitz aspired to changing individuals to become less prone to brutality, the student movement's goals included toppling the Shah or stopping the war in Vietnam. By the end of the sixties, Adorno's initial sympathy toward the students as victims of an authoritarian society turned into an anxiety that the students had themselves succumbed to a regressive temptation to collective identification, losing the same autonomy of thought which was always at the center of his political program.

Despite the ultimate rupture between Adorno and parts of the student movement, understanding Adorno's politics requires recognizing the extent of his sympathy for student radicalism. He saw the students as targets of the same hostility once directed against Jews, and therefore the violence they incurred only confirmed his own doubts regarding the depth of democratic institutions in Germany. On June 2, 1967, during a demonstration against the Shah visiting Berlin, a literature student, Benno Ohnesorg, was shot in the back and killed by a police officer. Adorno's comments in his lecture on June 6 invoke the relationship to the Holocaust – particularly in light of the simultaneous war in the Middle East – and place the killing in the context of his critique of the authoritarian society:

> It is impossible for me to begin my lecture today without saying a word about the situation in Berlin, no matter how much it is overshadowed by the terrible threat to Israel, the home of so many Jews who fled the terror. I understand how difficult it is to form a just and responsible opinion of even the simplest facts, since all news that reach us are already manipulated. But that cannot prevent me from expressing my sympathy for the student whose fate, no matter what is reported, stands in no relation to his participation in a political demonstration. Regardless of which of the contradictory reports of the terrible events is correct, one can in any case observe that Germany is still ruled by the official habit of higher powers, incompatible with the spirit of democracy, to cover up the actions of (in the double sense of the word) subordinate organs. . . . Not only the urge to gain justice for the victims but also the concern that the nascent democratic spirit in Germany not be strangled by hierarchic practices make it necessary to demand that the investigation in Berlin be conducted by officials who are not organizationally linked to those who shot and swung their batons, and who cannot be suspected of having any interest whatsoever in the outcome of the investigation. That the investigation proceed in full freedom, expeditiously, and without authoritarian tampering, in accordance with the spirit of democracy is not my private wish but one that is rooted in the objective situation. I suspect you share it. (Kraushaar 1998 II: 123)

The statement integrates several parameters of Adorno's political thinking: the reference to the Holocaust, the concern with authoritarian structures in Germany, the advocacy of democratic process, and, perhaps most strikingly, the concluding reflection on the relationship between the private and public. Elsewhere we have seen him argue that objective social change is unlikely and that consequently it is important to focus on subjectivity – education, psychoanalysis, the private sphere – rather than engage in public politics. At this point, however, with reference to Ohnesorg's killing, he crosses that line, making a public statement with an explicit political content: the call for an impartial investigation. The suggestion that his proposal is not merely private but objective, and that his addressees, the students in his lecture on aesthetics, share it, demonstrates the degree of solidarity that underlay the relationship between Adorno and the student movement as late as 1967.

In November, Karl-Heinz Kurras, the officer who had shot Ohnesorg, was acquitted, and Adorno's comments are revealing. He concedes a lack of expertise in legal matters, just as he describes his own fundamental doubts regarding the social need for punishment in general, and hence an ambivalence regarding punishment in this case as well. Yet he is quite emphatic in his judgment on the political process, in a way fully compatible with his earlier treatments of authoritarian tendencies in democracies: "If the police officer could not be convicted because guilt in the sense of the law could not be proven, then the guilt of his superiors is all the greater. That the police carry weapons during student demonstrations is itself the temptation to carry out those acts which the officer described as his orders." He goes on to compare Frankfurt, where police were not armed at demonstrations, with Berlin, and demands that an investigation into this policy be carried out. All this constitutes a direct intervention into current political debate; characteristically, however, Adorno moves dialectically from this objective aspect to the subjective side, without in any way reducing the political substance. He comments on his impression of Kurras in a television interview:

> I heard him say something like, "Unfortunately a student lost his life." His tone was unmistakably reluctant, as if Mr. Kurras had to try hard to squeeze out those meager words and was not at all seriously aware of what he had done. The emotional poverty of that "unfortunately" condemns him as much as the impersonal "a student lost his life." That sounds as if on June 2 some objective, higher power had appeared and that it was not Mr. Kurras, whether he aimed or not, who had pulled the trigger. This language is frighteningly similar to the one heard in the trials against the torturers in the concentration camps. Mr. Kurras did not even manage to say, "I am unhappy that I killed an innocent man." The expression "a student" in his remark is reminiscent of the usage

of the word "Jew" still today in the trials and the press that reports on them. Victims are treated as examples of a species. (Kraushaar 1998 II: 324)

The radicalism of the earlier psychoanalytic reflections in "Education after Auschwitz" comes to the fore in the criticism of the Berlin police, a stand-in for sadistic potential, and Adorno concludes this digression into the subjective sphere, with a return to a specific political demand: "An answer is urgently needed to the question of how someone in Berlin could hire a man with the mentality of Mr. Kurras and put him in a situation that would encourage him to act the way he did."

Adorno made comparable public comments in a lecture on May 9, 1968, after the attack on the SDS leader Rudi Dutschke, describing the mood in Berlin and, in particular, the shrill right-wing journalism of the Springer newspapers (a target of student demonstrations) as a "pogrom." On May 28 he spoke at a demonstration against the "Emergency Laws," proposed legislation widely perceived as undermining the substance of German democracy, and in early December a flyer was distributed in Frankfurt, signed by Adorno, Habermas, and their colleague Ludwig von Friedeburg, announcing that they "support the student protests against the dangers of a technocratic university reform" (cf. Kraushaar 1998 II: 375–7, 392, 502–3). Throughout the period, Adorno also remained engaged in less formal discussions with members of the SDS (cf. Kraushaar 1998 II: 233, 263–5, 271, 325–9). None of this is in any way compatible with the image of the unpolitical Adorno. Nevertheless differences with the students emerged, not only in spectacular disruptions of some of Adorno's lectures but also in Adorno's criticism, both private and public, of aspects of the protest movement, including the turn toward violence (arson attacks on department stores) and its redirection of political protest toward the university itself (Adorno and Marcuse 1999).

Adorno's defense of the students against anti-intellectualism also implied a defense of the university which, Adorno anticipated, could easily become the target of similarly motivated attacks (Kraushaar 1998 II: 309). This strategic consideration, the urgency of protecting the relative autonomy of the university, correlated to the theoretical position, the importance of the autonomy of theory. Of course Adorno doubted the rationality of aspects of the student protest, described as "actionism" or "decisionism," i.e., action for the sake of action: a praxis with little hope of success served no useful purpose. Yet separate from the nature of the judgment on particular actions, Adorno remained insistent on the independence of theory, i.e., theory genuinely committed to the project of enlightenment could not be reduced to a mere vehicle for given strategic intentions. Hence the substantive and, ultimately, political urgency of defending the autonomy of theory even when the student movement turned against it. On January 31, 1969, striking students occupied the building of the Institute for Social Research, and Adorno called the police to remove them. Among those arrested was Adorno's student, Krahl (cf. Kraushaar 1998 I: 395–6).

The trauma of that event, compounded by Adorno's fatal heart attack in August and Krahl's death in a car accident the following February, has blocked the discussion of Adorno's politics: he has been taken to stand for resignation in the face of student activism, despite the strong evidence of his political thinking since the forties and, especially, his outspoken statements on events since the killing of Ohnesorg. The record points to a vibrant participation in political life, albeit in the medium of theory. The summation of his position, a radio address in February 1969 entitled "Resignation," turns the accusation around. The urgency of independent thought, particularly in the face of the potential violence of the political structure, makes the hostility to theory or the effort to reduce it to practice all the more dangerous. To the activists' call for an immediate sublation of theory and practice, Adorno replies, "The trouble with this view is that it results in the prohibition of thinking. Very little is needed to turn the resistance against repression repressively against those who – little as they might wish to glorify their state of being – do not desert the standpoint that they have come to occupy. The often-evoked unity of theory and praxis has a tendency to give way to the predominance of praxis" (Adorno 1978: 165–6). The fetishization of action turns into a crude "do-it-yourself" attitude, the same fascination with technical means which, as discussed in "Education after Auschwitz," becomes blind to the ends. Meanwhile, unreflected activity allows for a mode of collective regression, a participation in a group activity that responds to the individual's feelings of isolation: "The feeling of new security is purchased with the sacrifice of autonomous thinking" (Adorno 1978: 68). Yet succumbing to the temptation to belong merely in order to overcome the isolation of the thinker, opting just "to do it," without any prospect of success, is nothing else than resignation, as Adorno turns his critics' complaints back at them.

The gap that separated Adorno from the student movement at its most activist cannot be bridged, but the posthumous distortion of Adorno as bleakly devoid of political thought can be corrected. His criticism is replete with political references, from the criticism of the New Deal, through the analysis of orthodox Marxism, the diagnosis of West German conservatism, and the complex interventions both for and critical of the student movement. From a contemporary perspective, aspects of his political vision seem dated; above all, the explicitly (in current terminology) Fordist model of capitalism that underlies the *Dialectic of Enlightenment* is not appropriate for the post-Fordist, deregulated economies that have emerged since the eighties. Arguably, however, Adorno's implicit criticism of centralized authority would be quite compatible with contemporary discussions of regionalism and federalism. In retrospect, his criticism of Soviet Communism cannot be faulted; thanks to this theoretical disposition, he was far ahead of the more practical New Left on that point, nor is there considerable evidence that the intellectual left, at least in the United States, has fully thought through the failures of the Soviet regime in even an initial manner. Most striking, however, is the accuracy of Adorno's concern with the possibility of the repetition of the horror of Auschwitz: Rwanda, Bosnia, Kosovo – none is exactly the same, of course, as comforting critics are wont to point out, but the human capacity for mass murder is evidently part of continued social and psychic predispositions, rather than a singular event. Reflection on the origins of that violence and on the unwillingness of individuals to resist it is the point where Adorno's politics might commence today.

5

"Why Were the Jews Sacrificed?" The Place of Antisemitism in Adorno and Horkheimer's *Dialectic of Enlightenment*

Anson Rabinbach

Like many German-Jewish exiles, the Frankfurt School theorists first con-fronted the phenomenon of antisemitism and their fate as Jews once they had been forced out of Germany and once the Nazi regime unleashed its antisemitic violence on November 9, 1938. During the early years in exile the studies produced by the members of the Institute for Social Research touched on the question of antisemitism only peripherally, as part of studies on propaganda, character structure, and authoritarianism. Only in his 1939 essay, "Die Juden in Europa," did Horkheimer broach the subject and attempt a substantive explanation. At that time, Horkheimer's account was very much in keeping with his Marxist understanding of the social origins of fascism: liberalism had reached its apogee and the individual, whose psychological and social autonomy was a product of liberal economic institutions, was destined to be supplanted by the collective, just as fascist corporatism proved more efficient than liberal political and economic structures. The Jews, whose iden-tity and social character was tied to the fate of liberalism and the free market, were singled out for elimination from society because their distinctiveness was deemed atavistic in the face of the new, totally administered society.

Unsatisfactory as Horkheimer's rendering of the situation may have been, it was an important step toward acknowledgment of the centrality of antisemitism in the worldview of National Socialism for the Frankfurt School theorists. In the same year Horkheimer proposed that the Institute undertake a major study of antisemitism from a variety of perspectives – economic, social, anthropological, and psychological – and two years later the Institute's journal, *Studies in Philosophy and Social Science*, announced the new project.[1] Despite these best intentions, no study of antisemitism was ever produced by the Frankfurt School in exile. Instead, a number of theses entitled "Elements of Antisemitism" were composed and published separately as the penultimate section of *Dialectic of Enlightenment*, published in 1944.

Not initially intended for the volume that appeared under the title *Philosphische Fragmente* in 1944, the "Elements of Antisemitism" is usually described as a set of theoretical elaborations destined for the "antisemitism project" and not integrally related to the volume that eventually became *Dialectic of Enlightenment*. The "Elements" was composed in the summer of 1943, four years after work on the book had begun, and after all the other sections were completed. As was the case with only the first chapter, the "Elements" was a collaborative enterprise, since Leo Löwenthal contributed to the first three theses, and it is likely that the remaining three, and certainly the fifth and most original thesis on "idiosyncrasy" and "mimesis," were jointly dictated by Horkheimer and Adorno in July 1943.[2] The seventh thesis, added in 1947, was solely the work of Horkheimer.

The decision to publish the "Elements" separately is intimately connected to the disappointments that accompanied the progress of the "antisemitism project" during 1944. In mid-1943 the "antisemitism project" took on renewed importance when the institute was trusted by the Jewish Labor Committee to conduct a massive study of American labor's attitudes toward Jews. The following year, the American Jewish Committee selected Horkheimer as its Director of Scientific Research and launched an ambitious program culminating in the five-part *Studies in Prejudice* series published in 1949 and 1950.[3] By 1944, when it was clear to Horkheimer and Adorno that publication of the results of these ongoing research projects would not soon be forthcoming, and especially when publication plans for the labor research collapsed, the theses were included in the mimeographed edition presented to Friedrich Pollock on his fiftieth birthday.[4]

Twenty-five years later Adorno recalled that the "Elements" ultimately found its "literary impact" in *The Authoritarian Personality*. But he also emphasized that it was a counterpoint to the exclusively psychoanalytic and empirical character of that work. Its more explicitly philosophical and "objective" character led Adorno to regret *Dialectic of Enlightenment*'s unavailability (in 1969) in English translation because, he thought, the "Elements" might have prevented the "misunderstanding" that usually accompanied *The Authoritarian*

Personality (and of which it was not entirely innocent), namely "that the authors had attempted to explain anti-Semitism, and even fascism in general, from a solely subjective perspective."[5] Adorno recalled that "the 'Elements of anti-Semitism' situated racial prejudice in the context of an objectively oriented critical theory of society. However, in so doing, and in contrast to a certain economic orthodoxy, we did not rigidly oppose psychology, but accorded it its place as a moment of explanation in our draft. We never allowed any doubt about the primacy of objective factors over the psychological."[6] In retrospect, the "misunderstanding" was not merely occasioned by the relative inaccessibility of a book first produced in a mimeographed edition, and subsequently by an obscure Dutch exile press. The discrepancy between the attempt to discover the roots of antisemitism in an anthropological and philosophical account of the archaic roots of the origins of civilization in *Dialectic of Enlightenment*, and the interdisciplinary sociological and psychological theory that dominates *The Authoritarian Personality*, and the Institute's *Studies in Prejudice* series has been the subject of considerable discussion. While some critics prefer to see the disjuncture as evidence of the differences between Adorno's proclivity to a philosophy of history and Horkheimer's interdisciplinary program, as Jay points out, the Frankfurt theorists aimed their American studies at the broader question of the propensity to antisemitism and racism, focusing on the rather more banal theme that "the weaker the personality, the stronger becomes the influence of the social field."[7] Yet another, perhaps more important rationale emerges from Horkheimer's correspondence. The psychologism of the institute's empirical studies was to no small extent the product of two other factors: Horkheimer and Adorno's frustration with the magnitude of the problem of providing an adequate explanation of antisemitism; and the immediate demand for "a thesis simple enough to be understood an appreciated by those who are trying to fight the giant fire with means which are by definition inadequate."[8] As an internal Institute memorandum revealed,

> When we drafted our first plan of study of anti-Semitism, we had in mind a comprehensive work covering all the aspects of the problem, showing the development and the functions of anti-Semitism in various countries and periods of history, describing its interconnection with other social phenomena, analyzing the economic and cultural forces behind it. However, when we started our work in the spring of 1943, we became aware that the hour was too late for such a general historical and international survey. We decided to devote our efforts immediately to the drafting of methods which might lead to a better grasp of the social and psychological mechanisms underlying anti-Semitism.[9]

Horkheimer also later confirmed that he believed antisemitism in America differed fundamentally from European antisemitism, where it was more deeply rooted in tradition: "It is my conviction that the role which a firmly established antisemitic tradition plays in Europe is assumed here largely by the psychological phenomenon of mass imitation – that is, political anti-Semitism in America has rather the character of a contagion, of an epidemic, than of a deep seated and slowly developing illness."[10]

Adorno did not elaborate further on the place of the "Elements" in *Dialectic of Enlightenment*, but his remarks underscored its departure from the arguments first put forward in Horkheimer's "The Jews and Europe" in 1939. Horkheimer had reduced antisemitism to an epiphenomenon of a larger historical process: because of the putative extinction of the sphere of circulation in the transition from liberal society to the authoritarian or totalitarian state (not merely the fascist version) the Jews had been rendered superfluous; as representatives of individualism and exchange their very existence threatened the new mechanisms of administrative power. "The result is bad for the Jews," he wrote. "They are being run over. Others are the most capable today: the leaders of the new order in the economy and the state."[11]

Those insights, shared by many other European Marxists at the time, turned out to be extremely short-sighted, a limitation which *Dialectic of Enlightenment* explicitly rectified in its refusal to attribute a primacy of economics in the genesis of antisemitism. During the most intense phase of work on the "Elements" Horkheimer explained to Herbert Marcuse that "the problem of anti-Semitism is much more complicated than I thought in the beginning. On the one hand we have to differentiate radically between the economic-political factors which cause and use it, and the anthropological elements in the present type of man which respond to antisemitic propaganda as they would respond to other oppressive incentives; on the other hand we must show these factors in their constant interconnection and describe how they permeate each other."[12] This dual (actually triple) purpose accounts for the unsystematic juxtaposition and intertwining of anthropological, sociological, psychological, and economic perspectives in the "Elements." The economic dimension is still paramount in the assertion that the ultimate purpose of bourgeois antisemitism is to "disguise domination in production" and the Jews are scapegoats, "inasmuch as the economic injustice of the whole class is attributed to them."[13] But the emphasis here is no longer on the *presence* of the Jews in the sphere of circulation, but on the Jews in the mental "imagery" of Nazism which metaphorically substitutes the Jews as the "hated mirror image of capitalism." However, as the argument deepens, antisemitism appears in more fundamental terms as "a deeply imprinted schema, a ritual of civilization" (*DE*: 171). The Jews still occasionally appear in the "Elements" as the "colonizers for progress"(*DE*: 174) and as the victims of a massive shift in the tectonic plates of capitalism, a theme not entirely compatible with the assertion that antisemitism belongs to the "primitive instincts negated by civilization."[14] Horkheimer conceded as much when he remarked to Marcuse that "the Jews seem to be the aliens under all circumstances."[15]

Jay and others have shown that Horkheimer and Adorno's views on anti-semitism had begun to change during the early 1940s.[16] The new orientation is marked by the sentence "Whereas there is no longer any need for economic domination, the Jews are marked out as the absolute object of domination pure and simple" (*DE*: 175). As early as 1941 Horkheimer wrote to the British political philosopher Harold Laski: "As true as it is that one can understand anti-Semitism only from our society, as true it appears to me to become that by now society itself can be properly understood only through anti-Semitism."[17] By November 1944, when the first confirmed reports of the extermination camps began to be circulated in the US, Horkheimer acknowledged to the editor of the magazine, *The Jewish Forum*, that "wittingly or unwittingly, the Jews have become the martyrs of civilization. To protect them is no longer an issue involving any particular group interests. To protect the Jews has come to be a symbol of everything mankind stands for. Anti-Semitic persecution is the stigma of the present world whose injustice enters all its weight upon the Jews. Thus, the Jews have been made what the Nazis always pretended that they were, the focal point of world history. Their survival is inseparable from the survival of culture itself."[18] But, if this is indeed the case, we might ask, does this not affect the argument of *Dialectic of Enlightenment* as a whole? Was Adorno's later recollection that the "Elements" was merely a bridge to *The Authoritarian Personality* a misremembering of its status at the time? Does the "Elements" contain, as Wiggershaus suggests, the "hidden center" of the book?

At first glance this seems to be historically implausible, since there was little attention to antisemitism during the first few months of work on what they then called the "dialectic book." Nor was antisemitism mentioned in the internal Institute memoranda at the time. "It appeared," Wiggershaus comments, "as if Horkheimer and Adorno were still afraid of this theme."[19] No doubt a decision to shift the focus of critical theory from the traditional Marxist questions of monopoly capitalism or class conflict to the fate of the Jews would have produced skepticism among some of the Institute's more orthodox Marxist contributors, like Franz Neumann, for example, who wrote Adorno in 1940 that "I can imagine, and I have done this in my book, that one can represent National Socialism without attributing to the Jewish problem a central role."[20]

Yet, even if the "Elements" was composed after the other sections were complete, and even if it was never preordained to be part of *Dialectic of Enlightenment*, Horkheimer had in fact proposed to Adorno much earlier that the fate of the Jews and not the fate of the "bourgeois subject" could indeed be the focal point of their joint enterprise:

> How would it be, he wrote in October 1941, if we allowed our book to crystallize around anti-Semitism? That would mean the concretizing and limiting which we have been searching for. It would also permit us to activate a large part of the co-workers of the institute. Whereas, if we were to write something like a critique of the present measured by the category of the individual, I can already imagine the nightmare that Marcuse would then demonstrate that since the early bourgeois era the category of the individual contained progressive and reactionary tendencies. Also, anti-Semitism today really marks the focal point of injustice, and our physiognomy must turn to the world where it shows its most horrible face. Finally, the question of anti-Semitism is the one that best fits into the effective complex that we are writing about, without our having revealed anything about it [*ohne dass wir darüber etwas verrieten*].[21]

The death of Benjamin and the arrival of his philosophical testament provided Horkheimer and Adorno, as Wiggershaus notes, with a kind of "guiding star" around which the constellation of themes – the fate of the exile, the fate of the Jews, and catastrophe of civilization – that ultimately make up *Dialectic of Enlightenment* could be organized. For Adorno especially the legacy of Benjamin weighed heavily on his willingness to accept the fact that the Jews – and not the working class – were the prime objects of Nazi terror. Like most German-Jewish intellectuals from the upper ranks of the bourgeoisie, Adorno had grown up in a highly assimilated milieu, taking his Christian mother's name as opposed to his Jewish father's Wiesengrund. The famous episode in which he tried to "pass" in the first year of the Nazi regime, by publishing a positive review of an operatic work by the Nazi composer Herbert Müntzels, whose libretto was based on the poetry of the youth leader Baldur von Schirach, was not insignificant in this regard. Adorno's praise for the work as an example of "romantic Realism" could of course be read ironically, and certainly the review was a masquerade, but a telling one nonetheless.[22] Yet, at the same time, there are innumerable indications of Adorno's interest in Jewish theological motifs in his writings during the 1930s, many of which self-consciously suggest Benjamin's notion of redemption through a radicalized heterogeneity or non-identity functioning as a kind of secret code to be encrypted by only those initiated into the subtleties of esoteric thought. As Hullot-Kentor has pointed out, "theology is always moving right under the surface of all of Adorno's writings."[23] Adorno mirrored his sympathetic reading of Kierkegaard's notion of the text or "Schrift" as a cipher, whose origin is always historical but whose core remains theological. Fundamentally, the text remains indecipherable, however open to interpretation it might be, just as the "fullness of divine truth is hidden from the creature" (*K*: 25).

In his "Notes on Kafka," Adorno equated Kafka's "Schrift" with an act of redemption "tied to the salvation of things, of those which are no longer enmeshed in the network of guilt, those which are non-exchangeable."[24] Though it would be presumptuous to read Adorno's theological motifs as a disguised way of preserving the hidden possibilities of German-Jewish otherness within the framework of a critique of idealist metaphysics, Adorno leaves numerous clues to support such an interpretation. Most striking is a letter to Benjamin, written in December 1934, where Adorno elaborated on his affinities to Benjamin's own thinking, referring to "our agreement in the philosophical center."[25] In Benjamin's 1934 essay on Kafka, which he had just read in draft, Adorno recognized an "inverse theology," which, as he wrote to Benjamin, "I would gladly see both thoughts disappear." The "Schrift," as elaborated by Benjamin is for Adorno "the essence of our theology as cipher."[26]

Even more dramatically, Adorno explicitly referred to "the Jewish tradition" as one of the key sources – along with Hegel's *Philosophy of Right* and Hermann Cohen's interpretation of guilt – of his own conception of myth. Only many years later, in *Negative Dialectics*, did Adorno give a name and a place to the philosophical conviction that "the mutual indifference of temporality and eternal ideas is no longer tenable by virtue of the destruction inherent in its concept" – Auschwitz. In other words, the theme of the destructive power of totality and identity is explicitly associated, in his later work, with the fate of the Jews. Their sacrifice becomes precisely that "cipher" through which the secularization of dialectical reason as totality, progress, or destiny could be challenged and confronted. Those events, he wrote, "make a mockery of the construction of immanence as endowed with a meaning radiated by an affirmatively positive transcendence."[27] In other words, the "inverse theology" of non-identity, elaborated in *Dialectic of Enlightenment* and almost all of Adorno's essays, underwent an important change with the discovery of antisemitism as revealing the essential truth of the philosophy of non-difference or homogeneity. By reflecting on antisemitism, the importance of non-identity, or "difference" as we would say today, is given concrete form and substance as a social and philosophical challenge to homogeneity and domination. The Jews, by virtue of their suffering, had revealed the truth of social and psychological domination. Even language revealed a similar structure of power, as Adorno remarked acerbically in *Minima Moralia*: "German words of foreign derivation are the Jews of language."[28] This process, as I will elaborate, first occurred during the drafting of *Dialectic of Enlightenment* in the early 1940s.

In August 1940 Adorno wrote to Horkheimer: "It often seems to me, as if all that, which we were used to seeing in terms of the proletariat, has today shifted with terrible intensity to the Jews. I ask myself, though it is not completely consistent with the project, if the things, which we actually want to say should not be said in connection with the Jews, who represent the counterpoint to power."[29] At the same time, Horkheimer also emphasized the implicit connection between the story of Odysseus as the first modern individual and the theme of the overcoming of sacrifice in the first chapter, which he said: "will probably play a dominant role in the psychology of anti-Semitism."[30] The Odysseus chapter of *Dialectic of Enlightenment*, written by Adorno, provides the allegorical foundation for the book as a whole and an implicit link to the "Elements." As Odysseus resists regression into the boundaryless world of magic and matriarchy, the modern epic of the homelessness, exile, and diaspora of reason is self-consciously counterpoised to the fascist glorification of rootedness and the mythology of *Heimat*. In his adventure, modern subjectivity is constituted in the epic narrative by the figure who "by his cunning and reason escapes prehistory."[31] Yet, the price of this "escape" is to initiate the ritual of sacrifice, the subordination of the instincts that occurs in the *imitatio* of the power of the gods over nature, the "introversion of sacrifice." Reason outwits myth only when it sacrifices itself. However complex, "the sacrifice of consciousness is carried out according to its own categories, rationally" (*K*: 114). As Adorno explained in his Habilitation dissertation on Kierkegaard, "all sacrifice in the domain of consciousness assumes the form of the paradoxical" (*K*: 119).

The first chapter of *Dialectic of Enlightenment* is an attempt to reconstruct the genealogy of sacrifice through an analysis of the concept of mimesis: first, in the order of animistic identification, then in magic, subsequently in myth, and finally in reason. At each of these stages the concept of mimesis is not understood as mere imitation, but as a form of mimicry or semblance that appropriates rather than replicates its object in a non-identical similitude.

Following Freud's *Totem and Taboo* (1912), Horkheimer and Adorno regarded mimesis as directly connected to the substitution that occurs in ritual sacrifice, the appeasement of the gods with an animal that is both represen-

tative and surrogate; the "non-specificity of the example," already marks a
step toward discursive logic" (*DE*: 10). Freud placed great emphasis on how
"identification with the totem is carried into effect" by various forms of
mimicry, "dressing in the skin of the animal, by incising a picture of the totem
upon his own body, and so on."[32] In Freud's conception, the "fetish" enacts
the dialectic of non-identity by "splitting the ego" while preserving both
symbolic and real components, knowing and not-knowing.[33] In the ascent
from *mana*, the originary mysterious power of the taboo, to the "ancient
covenant with the totem, and the elevation of the father to a God, imitation
plays an ambiguous role, simultaneously symbolic and real, as Freud admon-
ishes us, no matter how "impious" it may appear "to us moderns." Mimesis
is not the suppression of difference but an act of substitution that intervenes
between the helpless subject and the overpowering object: it appears in the
frozen terror with which all living creatures react to fear, in the magician's
impersonation of demons, in his gestures of appeasement to the gods, or in
the wearing of masks which guarantee that the identity of self "cannot disappear through identification with another" (*DE*: 10). Semblance preserves
the possibility of freedom, of a resistance to the assimilation of the concept
in much the same way that in Kierkegaard's theology "enciphered images
oppose the existential sacrifice" (*K*: 133). In *Dialectic of Enlightenment* the
modern principle of calculability and equivalence is already prefigured by a
growing abstraction and distance from nature that occurs first in the "specific" duplication of anthropomorphism, in the "non-specific" sacrifice, and
ultimately in the unification of myth as the sovereignty of the human subject
over nature. Yet, at the same time, mimesis is a step away from discursive logic
in its preservation of the concrete, sensual, and thing-like substance which is
the very opposite of the liquidation of subjectivity in the symbol or concept
that Adorno saw in his analysis of intellectual sacrifice.

Mimesis therefore represents both the prefiguration of and the "other" of
reason. But mimesis itself undergoes repression in the act of subjugating
nature to instrumental reason: The *ratio*, which represses mimesis, is not simply
its opposite. It too is mimesis: mimesis of death. As the "Elements" notes,
antisemitism is "the counterpart of true mimesis and fundamentally related
to the repressed form; in fact it is probably the morbid expression of repressed
mimesis. Mimesis imitates the environment, but false projection makes the
environment like itself" (*DE*: 187).

These quotations demonstrate how deeply connected is the passage from
mimesis to reason, and from reason to that kind of mimesis (not simply its
opposite) that infuses modernity with the compulsion to subjugate, imitate,
and annihilate. Yet, at the same time, there is a theological (and aesthetic)
residue in the concept of mimesis that holds out the possibility for a differ-

ent kind of appropriation, one which does not do violence to its object, which retains the recognition of its distinctiveness through the activation of inauthenticity, in play, in irony, or in the cunning that Adorno and Horkheimer identified with the figure of Odysseus.

Like Freud, Horkheimer and Adorno identified the *Bildverbot*, the taboo on pictoriality in Jewish monotheism, as the event that inaugurates modernity. By proscribing the direct personification of the Gods, ritual substitution and sacrifice is converted into law. For Freud the monotheistic prohibition on images transformed Judaism into a religion of instinctual renunciation "for it signified subordinating sense perception to an abstract idea; it was a triumph of *Geistigkeit* over sensuality."[34] The Jews, Horkheimer and Adorno continued, crossed the threshold from mythology to rationality by converting the image into a series of duties in the form of ritual: The Jews "transformed taboos into civilizing maxims when others still clung to magic" (*DE*: 186). Following *Moses and Monotheism*, they argued that Christianity failed to sustain the purity that Judaism had achieved, that it descended into polytheism and mother-god worship: "the Jews seemed to have succeeded where Christianity failed: they defused magic by its own power − turned against itself as ritual service of God. They have retained the aspect of expiation but have avoided the reversion to mythology which symbolism implies" (*DE*: 186).[35] However, even in the "disenchanted world of Judaism," Horkheimer and Adorno wrote, the power of mimesis was still expressed in the "bond between name and being" that is recognized in "the ban on pronouncing the name of God" (*DE*: 23). The next passage succinctly states their central argument:

> The disenchanted world of Judaism is reconciled with magical thought through its negation in the idea of God. The Jewish religion does not tolerate any word that offers solace to despair in the face of mortality. It associates hope only with the prohibition against calling what is false God, against invoking the finite as the infinite, lies as truth. The guarantee of redemption lies in the rejection of any belief that would subscribe to this; it is knowledge obtained in the denunciation of madness . . . The legitimacy [*Recht*] of the image is salvaged [*gerettet*] in the faithful carrying out of th s prohibition.

To sum up: the Jewish proscription on images, the *Bildverbot*, is at the origin of enlightenment, and at the same time, contains its redemptive moment. Redemption can only be salvaged by thinking that radically refuses any compromise with magical practices, myth, or the transposition of worldly events into symbols. Fascism is the mirror opposite of the prohibition on mimesis, an archaic world of inauthenticity and terror masquerading as authenticity, heroism, and "being-in-the-world." For Adorno and Horkheimer there is no "outside" of enlightenment once image and knowledge are completely severed. No "authentic experience" can artificially restore the world of mimesis, but in a radically disenchanted world, mimesis is not *imitatio* but self-conscious "inauthenticity." Inauthenticity is a ruse, an act of "cunning," for example, in the ritual sacrifice, in the amalgamation of sacrifice and totemism that dispenses with the need for actual murder: the "stupidity of the ritual" serves "the cleverness of the weaker." In the same way, works of art both preserve the utopian remembrance of the world before the prohibition and enact the illusion of its overcoming: "the capacity of representation is the vehicle of progress and regression at one and the same time" (*DE*: 35).

During their initial conversations during the winter of 1939, it was Oedipus and not Odysseus who came to mind as the figure who fuses the identity of selfhood with property and power. But the story of Odysseus took center stage since Oedipus' defenseless blindness to his fate could not compete with the Homeric hero's successful evasion of the presymbolic and premythical world of identity through cunning and deception.

If, as Adorno asserted in *Minima Moralia*, all that is human is "indissolubly linked to imitation," any claim to genuineness is ultimately disingenuous. Theology adopts the "likeness" of self to God, but never assumes its identity. As opposed to the idea of genuineness and authenticity, the "self should not be spoken of as the ontological ground, but at most theologically, in the name of its likeness to God."[36] The mimetic world of fascism – with its alluring images, rituals, symbols – points to the destructive and deceptive potential of mimetic identification with nature.

That side of mimesis was suggested to Adorno by a curious text which played an important if peripheral role in the discussions out of which *Dialectic of Enlightenment* emerged, *La Mante religieuse. Recherche sur la nature et la signification du mythe*, by the French anthropologist Roger Caillois. Caillois was a leading figure of the Collège de Sociologie (with which Benjamin was briefly associated). Adorno was drawn to this book because of its emphasis on the mimetic impulse in nature, an impulse that was all the more uncanny because Caillois demonstrated that the female mantis actually devours the male during intercourse. It is this negative dimension of mimesis, the eradication of the vital difference between life and matter, or the organic and inorganic in the sexual act, that suggested the theme of annihilation (and not insignificantly, the gendering of fascist identification as matriarchal in origin). Caillois's account of mimesis, Adorno remarks, does not distinguish between "playing" and being dead. But in a letter to Benjamin, he explained that he admired the fact that Caillois did not operate at the level of myth, but instead focused on the residues of a kind of primal biological "memory" of "psy-

chasthenia" in human behavior, which Caillois derived from the "materialism that he has in common with Jung and certainly with Klages," and from
a "cryptofascist belief in nature. Adorno was fascinated by the ways in which
mimesis could lead to a "fatal attraction" that literally annihilates the object
of its of desire, which was not unlike the analysis of theological sacrifice we
have already discussed. Adorno's analysis of antisemitism in *Dialectic of Enlightenment*, as we shall see, adopts the same strategy, locating in modern Jew-hatred
the return of the archaic impulse to mimesis, however, in its "repressed form"
(*Verdrängte Mimesis*), which in its paranoid fear, imitates and liquidates the Jew,
all the more consequentially. Unlike mimesis, whose illusion is self-conscious,
repressed mimesis always contains a principle of self-deception and destruction: "this form of repressed mimesis and the destructive are the same – the
no-longer-self-hood."[37]

In September 1940 Adorno sent Horkheimer "a couple of – completely
unformulated – thoughts on the theory of anti-Semitism . . . We have arrived
at a really important place," Adorno wrote, "namely, at a unified and non-
rationalistic explanation for anti-Semitism." Adorno's analysis is something of
an imaginary prehistory of the Jews, with its emphasis on their persistence
in a nomadic existence long after the world consisted of permanent settle-
ments. As "the secret gypsies of history," the Jews are a "prematriarchal"
people whose lack of ties to the earth and to a fixed locale always threatened to subvert the ideals of civilized life: home, family, labor. From the standpoint of other peoples "the image of the Jew represented a stage of humanity
which did not yet know labor, and all later attacks on the parasitic, thieving
character of the Jews were mere rationalizations." Here the Jews represent, in
an argument that eventually finds its way into the "Elements," not the "colonizers of progress," nor the purveyors of a universal enlightenment, but the
very refusal to be "civilized" and submit to the primacy of labor. The Jews'
collective remembrance of a "land of milk and honey" is the "Jewish utopia."
The taboo on that image – which, presumably the *Bildverbot* initiates – is
simultaneously the taboo on the recalling of a nomadic existence and is,
according to Adorno, "the origin of anti-Semitism."[38]

In the Odysseus essay, written just one year later, we find further clues to
the suspicion that the nomadic Odysseus is not merely the primordial
"subject," the bourgeois *in nuce*, but also the Hellenic prototype of Ahasuerus,
the wandering Jew. Odysseus reveals "the fate that the language of the
cunning man, the middleman brings down on himself." He is described in
terms that suggest the stereotype of the Jewish tradesman: he is a rootless
wanderer, physically weak, deceitful, and babbles incessantly. In his excessive
attachment to speech, to language, Homer embodies in his hero, as does the
eternal Jew, "the disaster that the enlightened word brings down on itself"

(*O*: 132). The "Semitic element" of the Odyssey is also suggested in a foot-note which echoes the theme that Odysseus, "the feudal lord, bears the trace of the oriental merchant" (*O*: 125). Not incidentally, the "Elements" describes the Jews as "die ersten Bürger"(*DA*: 216).

As Horkheimer and Adorno point out, it is of little consequence whether the Jews really do have the "mimetic features" attributed to them: "when all the horror of prehistory which has been overlaid with civilization is reha-bilitated as rational interest by projection onto the Jews, there is no restric-tion" (*DE*: 186). This suggests a connection to Adorno's provisional 1940 theses: that the Jews are sacrificed as the ultimate victims of the taboo on mimesis for having inflicted the taboo on civilization. Civilization, they argue, replaces "mimetic behavior proper, by organized control of mimesis" and ulti-mately by prescribing rational practice, by work. "Uncontrolled mimesis is expunged first in the religious prohibition on idolatry, on images of god, sub-sequently in the general contempt for all image-bound wanderers: nomads, actors, gypsies, and finally in rationalization which consigns to oblivion the indelible mimetic heritage of all practical experience" (*DE*: 181). The murder of the Jews is a form of revenge for civilization's triumph over nature; those who first turned ritual sacrifice into rationality by carrying out the prohibi-tion are themselves sacrificed as the expression of "repressed mimesis" (*DE*: 187). The Jews represent, not only the carriers of the taboo on mimesis, but also those who have not entirely succumbed to its logic.

This analysis should also make us uneasy for two reasons. First, the passages on "idiosyncrasy and mimesis" betray a strong trace of Caillois's theories of the natural substratum of these motifs, which seem to locate anti-semitism in what Horkheimer and Adorno called "biological *Urgeschichte*"(*DE*: 180). Antisemitism is not, as the conventional arguments go, either the result of Christian Jew-hatred or modern scientific racial thinking, but emerges at the very threshold of human evolution. As Adorno remarked during their discussions, antisemitism is a form of "idiosyncratic behavior" (idiosyncrasy) which evokes the "desire for that situation, in which such reac-tions as being paralyzed with fear still existed, that is the desire for mimicry."[39] Freud once referred to this approach, very like his own, as a "phylogentic fantasy" of a set of inherited mechanisms which primeval humanity devel-oped in its confrontation with the terrors of nature. As if in flight from exces-sively time-bound Marxist and psychoanalytic theories of antisemitism, they embraced a theory of the origins of antisemitism in a timeless reaction to the terror of the overpowering force of nature. Mimicry is rooted in fear, in the impulse to become like nature by hardening oneself against it. It is an "archaic stigmata of the urge to survive" (*DE*: 1880).

Antisemitism is ultimately the last social refuge of the mimetic impulse: "The mental energy harnessed by political anti-Semitism is this rationalized idiosyncrasy" (*DE*: 183). In antisemitism the "aboriginal" desire to return to the "mimetic practice of sacrifice finds its ultimate fulfillment"(*DE*: 186). It is ultimately not clear whether in this version of primal antisemitism can usefully distinguish modern racism, Christian Jew-hatred, ancient or primordial anti-Judaism, or whether – in the end – it has anything to do with the Jews at all. Nor is it possible to distinguish totalitarian antisemitism from "bourgeois" antisemitism or American racial prejudice. Horkheimer himself later admitted "it is not mere accident that the great explosion of anti-Semitism occurred in Germany," yet this fact plays no role whatsoever in the "Elements," which underscores Horkheimer's assertion that "the basic features of destructive hatred are the same everywhere."[40]

More seriously, the "Elements of Antisemitism," it might be argued, ultimately holds the Jews accountable for their own fate. In contrast to the image of the Jews in the first chapter, where, in Freud's words, they secure "a triumph of *Geistigkeit* over sensuality," the Jews appear in the "Elements" in a more ambivalent light, as those who impose the taboo on mimesis and as the carriers of a "premythological," "prematriarchal" residue. Adorno's thesis that antisemitism preserves the image of Jews as "nomadic" explicitly identified them, not merely with the perpetration of the taboo, but with the refusal to adapt to it. The Jews embody both the process of civilization and the sins of capitalism, and with the refusal to accommodate to civilizing maxims. Totalitarian domination is hostile to the Jews because "no matter what the Jews as such may be like," since they represent "happiness without power, wages without work, a home without frontiers, religion without myth" (*DE*: 199). That idea, which is the very opposite of Freud's conviction that Christianity was in fact a regression from Judaism, can be found, as Josef Yerushalmi has shown, in Carl Gustav Jung's infamous 1934 attack on Freud's "soulless rationalism." There we find Jung's ruminations on the creative energies of the "Aryan unconscious" and his claim that the Jew, "who is something of a nomad, has never yet created a cultural form of his own."[41] Horkheimer, of course, did not share Jung's ennobling of the Aryan spirit, but rather drew parallels between the Jewish and German prehistory: "Both peoples were originally nomads, e.g., pastoral tribes, and both are intensely patriotic, though in very different ways: However, if both Germans and Jews show a militant sort of patriotism, the patriotism of the Jews is characterized by a longing for the soil which was lost, while the Germans want to possess soil they never possessed."[42]

Although Horkheimer and Adorno emphasized in an Institute memorandum that "antisemitic feelings are not aroused by Jewish behavior, but by prejudice pure and simple," their correspondence indicates that they were not entirely convinced that this was the case. Horkheimer was in fact preoccupied with the opposite possibility, that at a much deeper level the Jews were not merely an arbitrary target of economically or psychoanalytically rooted "scapegoatism." As he wrote to Löwenthal about the "Thesen" in March 1944: "I am particularly eager to know my answer to your question as to why the Jews are such an appropriate object of projection. I think I referred to mimesis, but there was something else too."[43] Recall that Horkheimer had remarked that "wittingly or unwittingly," the Jews had become the martyrs of civilization. His remark sheds light on the persistent theme that it is in fact the very success of the Jews in perpetrating the "civilizatory virtues" that is the ultimate reason for their sacrifice."[44] The Jews have been the pioneers of civilization. Their recent history is deeply interconnected with the progress of industry, commerce, and science. Their existence is a constant challenge to those who want to be lazy. The Jews are the competitors par excellence.[45] As the war drew to an end, Horkheimer asserted that "objective" factors were at work, and that antisemitism was elicited by the Jews, for example, when he says that though he is speaking of the "partly involuntary role of the Jews," it "is good to remember that the slight lack of assimilation in our assimilated Jewish individuals consists exactly of the unflinching readiness and impatience to outdo all bystanders in just that society which has no pity for the dumb."[46] The "Elements" also reiterates Freud's thesis that it is ultimately "the special character" of the Jewish religion that has made the Jews and the antisemites what they are, and that it is ultimately Christian self-hatred, the displacement of Christian resentment at the constraints of monotheism and the desire to overturn the ban on images and return to paganism, that accounts for the persistence of hatred and the belief in a Jewish conspiracy. "The reflective aspect of Christianity, the intellectualization of magic, is the root of evil" (DE: 177). Jewish self-confidence, optimism, and what Freud called the "secret treasure" of the Jewish people, that they regard themselves as superior to other peoples, turns into the antisemitic belief in a secret Jewish power. "They are branded absolute evil by those who are absolutely evil, and are now, in fact the chosen people" (DE: 168; DA: 197).

For the theorists of the Frankfurt School the catastrophe of the Jews was inextricably bound up with the prohibition on mimesis and its return in the form of antisemitism and "false" politicized mimicry. The fascist return to what they called "mimetic modes of existence" was the ultimate price of civilization. But dark as their tale may have been, it was still not the last chapter. As Odysseus replaced Oedipus because his wit permitted him to evade the fate to which Oedipus blindly succumbed, Horkheimer and Adorno's *Dialectic of Enlightenment* was an effort to philosophically outwit myth, and to create "the possibility of escape" through enlightenment sensitized to the power of mimesis. This conclusion, that only the end of the dialectic of enlightenment can make antisemitism disappear, makes explicit the connection between the first chapter and the "Elements": "if thought is liberated from domination and if violence is abolished, the long absent idea is liable to develop that Jews too are human beings. This development would represent the step out of an anti-Semitic society which drives Jews and others to madness, and into the human society. This step would also fulfill the Fascist lie, but in contradicting it: the Jewish question would prove in fact to be the turning point of history"(*DE*: 199–200). In this respect Horkheimer and Adorno may have succeeded despite the multiple sins of their analysis of antisemitism. As Hermann Broch wrote after he read one of the first copies of *Philosophische Fragmente*: "The fact that a book like the *Philosophical Fragments* can exist at all attests to the powers of self-reflection of the intellect [*Ratio*], about which it might at first glance be asked, whether it doesn't penetrate far more deeply than it might think, and whether it might not itself be counted as a signpost of the reawakening of the impulse to life and civilization. It is still not decided whether the death drive has won the definitive upper hand over the drive to life."[47]

Notes

1   *Studies in Philosophy and Social Science*, IX:1 (1941). For a discussion of the "antisemitism project" see Rolf Wiggershaus, *Die Frankfurter Schule: Geschichte, Theoretische Entwicklung, Politische Bedeutung* (Munich, Vienna: Hanser Verlag, 1986): 346, 347 (hereafter cited as *FS*).

2   Alfred Schmidt and Gunzelin Schmid Noerr (eds.), Max Horkheimer, *Gesammelte Schriften*, Bd. 12 "Nachgelassene Schriften 1931–1949" (Frankfurt am Main: Fischer Verlag, 1985): 586–92 (hereafter cited as *GS* 12).

3   On the Jewish Labor Committee, the American Jewish Committee, and the Institute, see Martin Jay, *The Dialectical Imagination: A History of the Frankfurt School and the Institute of Social Research* (Boston: Little Brown, 1973): 224, 225.

4   See Wiggershaus, *FS*: 363.

5   T.W. Adorno, "Wissenschaftliche Erfahrung in Amerika," *Stichworte* (Frankfurt am Main: Suhrkamp, 1969): 132.

6   Adorno, "Wissenschaftliche Erfahrungen in Amerika," 132, 133.

7   Jay, *Dialectial Imagination*, 227.

8   Letter, Max Horkheimer to Herbert Marcuse, July 17, 1943, Max Horkheimer, *Gesammelte Schriften* 17, *Briefwechsel 1941–1948* (Frankfurt am Main: Fischer Taschenbuch, 1996): 463 (hereafter GS17).

9   Institute Memorandum, December 30, 1943, GS17: 522.

10 Max Horkheimer to Philip Klein, July 24, 1944, GS17: 572.

11 Max Horkheimer, *Die Juden und Europa*, Max Horkheimer, *Gesammelte Schriften* 4 (Frankfurt am Main: Fischer Verlag, 1988): 325.

12 Max Horkheimer to Herbert Marcuse, July 17, 1943, GS17: 463.

13 Max Horkheimer and Theodor W. Adorno, *Dialectic of Enlightenment*, trans., John Cumming (New York: Seabury Press, 1972): 173 (hereafter cited in parentheses as *DE*).

14 See Dan Diner, "Reason and the 'Other': Horkheimer's Reflection on Anti-Semitism and Mass Annihilation," in *On Max Horkheimer*, ed. Seyla Benhabib, Wolfgang Bonß, and John McCole (Cambridge, MA, London: MIT Press, 1993): 356.

15 Max Horkheimer to Herbert Marcuse, September 11, 1943, GS17: 471.

16 Martin Jay, "The Jews and the Frankfurt School: Critical Theory's Analysis of Anti-Semitism," *Permanent Exiles: Essays on the Intellectual Migration from Germany to America* (New York: Columbia University Press, 1986): 90–100.

17 Wiggershaus, *FS*: 347.

18 Max Horkheimer to Isaac Rosengarten, September 12, 1944, GS17: 599.

19 Wiggershaus, *FS*: 396.

20 Franz Neumann to Theodor W. Adorno, 14 August 1940, Max Horkheimer Correspondence. Max Horkheimer-Archiv, Stadt und Universitätsbibliothek, Frankfurt am Main (hereafter cited as MHA).

21 Max Horkheimer to Theodor W. Adorno, cited in Wiggershaus, *FS*: 346.

22 Wiggershaus, *FS*: 180.

23 Theodor W. Adorno, *Kierkegaard: Construction of the Aesthetic*, trans. Robert Hullot-Kentor (Minneapolis: University of Minnesota Press, 1989): xxi (hereafter cited in parentheses as *K*).

24 Theodor W. Adorno, *Prisms*, trans. Samuel and Shierry Weber (London: Neville Spearman, 1967): 271.

25 *Theodor Adorno–Walter Benjamin: Briefwechsel 1928–1940*, ed. Henri Lonitz (Frankfurt am Main: Suhrkamp, 1994): 90.

26 Ibid.

27 Theodor W. Adorno, *Negative Dialectics*, trans. E. B. Ashton (New York: Seabury Press, 1973): 361.

28 Theodor W. Adorno, *Minima Moralia: Reflections from a Damaged Life*, trans. E. F. N. Jephcott (London: Verso, 1974): 110.

29 Theodor Adorno to Max Horkheimer, August 5, 1940, GS16: 764.

30 Max Horkheimer to Friedrich Pollock, March 20, 1943, in Wiggershaus, *FS*: 362.

31 Theodor Adorno and Max Horkheimer, "Odysseus or Myth and Enlightenment," *New German Critique*, 56 (Spring–Summer 1992): 139 (hereafter cited in the text as *O*). Robert Hulott-Kentor's translation is often superior to Cummings', but both have been consulted for this essay.

32 Sigmund Freud, *Totem and Taboo*, trans. James Strachey (New York: W. W. Norton, 1950): 145.

33 See the illuminating psychoanalytic discussion of this problem in Thomas H. Ogden, *The Matrix of the Mind: Object Relations and the Psychoanalytic Dialogue* (Northvale, NJ: Jason Aronson, 1986): 222.

34 Sigmund Freud, *Moses and Monotheism*, trans. James Strachey (Standard Edition, London: Hogarth Press, 1939): 113. See the discussion of this theme in Yosef Hayim Yerushalmi, *Freud's Moses: Judaism Terminable and Interminable* (New Haven: Yale University Press: 1991): 51.

35 Ibid., 88.

36 Adorno, *Minima Moralia*, 154.

37 GS12: 591.

38 Adorno to Horkheimer, 18 September 1940, MHA. The theses comprise four typescript pages.

39 GS12: 590.

40 See the argument in Max Horkheimer, "Sociological Background of the Psychoanalytic Approach," in Ernst Simmel (ed.), *Anti-Semitism: A Social Disease* (New York: International Universities Press, 1946): 6.

41 Cited in Yerushalmi, *Freud's Moses*, 49.

42 Max Horkheimer to Leo Löwenthal, July 24, 1944, GS17: 566.

43 Max Horkheimer to Leo Löwenthal, March 17, 1944, GS17: 549.

44 Max Horkheimer to Theodor W. Adorno, December 27, 1944, GS17: 614.

45 Max Horkheimer to Theodor W. Adorno, October 11, 1945, GS17: 658–9.

46 Max Horkheimer to Theodor W. Adorno, October 11, 1945, GS17: 657.

47 Hermann Broch to Max Horkheimer, October 2, 1945, GS17: 654.

6

Demythologizing the Authoritarian Personality: Reconnoitering Adorno's Retreat from Marx

Lou Turner

I

In *The Eclipse of Reason*, Max Horkheimer suggests that the "'repressed mimetic impulse' returns as a destructive force manipulated by fascism and other systems of social domination" (Kellner 1989: 102). His and Theodor Adorno's notion of the mimetic impulse was formulated as an argument concerning the psychosemantics of "late capitalism" in *Dialectic of Enlightenment*. The mimetic impulse to be like nature contra the identificatory impulse to classify, rationalize, and subsume nature is supposed to be a fetish against the fetishism of commodities (Jarvis 1998: 117).

Douglas Kellner credits the World War II émigré experience of Horkheimer and Adorno for their retreat from proletarian and political involvement. Their presumed shift toward more philosophical and literary forms of intellectual engagement, according to Raya Dunayevskaya's evaluation of Adorno's *Negative Dialectics*, represented nothing less than a shift from permanent revolution to permanent critique (Dunayevskaya 1980: 183). Adorno's "Reflections on Class Theory" announced his contention that the proletariat was no longer the revolutionary subject (Kellner 1989: 106; Jarvis 1998: 55–61). In Kellner's view,

> Adorno and Horkheimer were rapidly abandoning . . . orthodox Marxism perspectives . . . Indeed, they, along with [Leo] Lowenthal and [Friedrich] Pollock,

were becoming increasingly involved in a study of anti-Semitism, funded by the, at best, liberal American Jewish Committee. Moreover, they would never again return to the sort of revolutionary Marxian perspectives which, it can be argued, characterized their earlier work and would continue to characterize [Herbert] Marcuse's work. (Kellner 1989: 109)

Notwithstanding this critical assessment of Adorno's move away from Marxism, it's fair to say that Kellner uncritically attributes *The Authoritarian Personality* with important insights into the potentially fascist personality of "New Right" conservatism in the US of the last two decades. "I believe that the variables which constituted the basic content of the F [Fascism] scale and which were thus the defining characteristics of the authoritarian personality provide an analytical framework particularly suitable for describing and criticizing contemporary conservatism" (Kellner 1989: 115–16).

Like Kellner, Franz Samelson too traces the Frankfurt School retreat from Marxian theory in its analysis of fascism, particularly by the time of the Berkeley project on the authoritarian personality (Samelson 1986). Given his analysis of Horkheimer's and Adorno's retreat from Marxism during the war years, and there being no dispute with Samelson's assessment of the non-Marxian character of *The Authoritarian Personality*, it's difficult to fathom Kellner's uncritical enthusiasm for that work. From a somewhat different direction, Stephen Bronner argues for a break between *The Authoritarian Personality* and *Negative Dialectics* with the latter's bold assertions against Hegelian–Marxian dialectic for its alleged positivism. The "death of the dialectic" in the devastating rise of fascism and the plunge into barbarism with the Holocaust signified more a continuity between Adorno's two works than a discontinuity.

The Russian linguist V. N. Volosinov identifies the psychosemantics of authoritarianism with a "linear, impersonal, monumental style" (Volosinov 1986: 120) of rhetoric dating back to the Middle Ages. Marx too discovered this identity between disparate epochal forms, e.g., modern capitalist and archaic. A stubborn problematic attends this identity involving the perception and understanding of the nature of one's own age. Marx, for instance, found that "the civilized horrors of over-work are grafted onto the barbaric horrors of slavery, serfdom etc." wherever the latter earlier forms of labor "are drawn into a world market dominated by the capitalist mode of production" (Marx 1977: 345). Grafting historically distinct forms of labor onto each other is indicated in an extensive note on Black slavery in the Southern United States, in volume 1 of *Capital*: "In the slave states bordering on the Gulf of Mexico, down to the date of the Civil War, the only ploughs to be found were those constructed on the old Chinese model, which turned up the earth like a pig or a mole, instead of making furrows" (Marx 1977: 304, n18).

The problematic contained in Marx's concept of historical identity (grafting) takes two distinct but inseparable forms. The first revolves around the ongoing subjective revolt of the slave which impelled the slave-owning class to resort to the implementation of the most cumbersome, least versatile, and archaic instruments of production. The second problem concerns the laws of historical development, particularly the law of combined and uneven development. Knowing when one is dealing with the historical development of a single country as a type, and when the historical phenomenon involves the law of motion of universal socioeconomic structures, e.g., slavery, feudalism, capitalism, is itself a condition of whether one comprehends the self-activity of subjects of revolution as the dialectical nodal points of revolutionary theory (cf. Dunayevskaya 1991: 170–2).

The identity or grafting in the sphere of material (re)production gets reflected in the sphere of ideological manipulation. Volosinov insists that we "define the degree of authoritarian reception of an utterance and the degree of its ideological assurance – its dogmatism. The more dogmatic an utterance, the less leeway permitted between truth and falsehood or good and bad in its reception by those who comprehend and evaluate, the greater will be the depersonalization that the forms of reported speech will undergo" (Volosinov 1986: 120).

The ideological assurances of authoritarian speech and language presuppose a social-historical environment in which not only the labor-power of human beings is materialized in things (commodities) whose value form gives them an independent social life of their own, but one in which speech and language assume the materialized form of power relations between political communicators and audiences. The transmission of speech and language in such an environment becomes more linear and impersonal with the development of capitalist relations of production and transformations in the division of labor. Ideological assurances become more, not less, authoritarian with capitalist futurism. Similarly, the requirement of a Marxian critique becomes more, not less, imperative.

Samelson is less than sanguine about the prognosis that *The Authoritarian Personality* held out regarding the authoritarianism of a capitalist society like the US; whereas Kellner is over-committed to "an analytical framework" whose liberal character found it the better part of valor to discreetly distance itself from Marx. Several years ahead of the publication of *The Authoritarian Personality*, Gunnar Myrdal had observed of the most authoritarian region of the US, the South, that "The region is exceptional in Western non-fascist civilization since the Enlightenment in that *it lacks every trace of radical thought*. In the South all progressive thinking going further than mild liberalism has been practically non-existent for a century."[1] Adorno too found that "widespread ignorance and confusion in political matters," general anti-intellectualism and absence of critical thinking, made the United States susceptible to fascist ideology (Kellner 1989: 117).

And yet, "civilization" and a kind of anti-intellectual intellectualism is at the heart of the authoritarian personality. Hannah Arendt observed the same impulse in the European colonial mentality that Frantz Fanon highlights in the course of his critique of Octave Mannoni's so-called dependency complex of the colonized, namely Arendt's notion that "The world of native savages [sic] was a perfect setting for men who had escaped the reality of civilization" (Arendt 1958: 190). These were the same men(tality) at the center of Arendt's judgment in *Eichmann in Jerusalem*, that sheer "thoughtlessness" motivates the "banality of evil." This is less an expression of the ignorance of the masses than a characterization of the suspension of moral reason by the petty bourgeoisie.

As T. Denean Sharpley-Whiting uncovers in her study of the role of Black female sexuality in early nineteenth-century European science and popular culture, however, science and culture also function as perfect settings (museums) to display the "world of native savages [sic]." The classificatory impulse and mimetic impulse achieve a perfect identity in the liberal bourgeois setting of the museum of natural history of the colored world. "Under the ever so watchful eyes and the pen of the naturalist [Georges Cuvier], the master text on the Black female body [the "Hottentot Venus," Sarah Bartmann] is created; the light of white maleness illuminates this dark continent" (Sharpley-Whiting 1986: 120). Sharpley-Whiting's examination of the Eurocentric text of Cuvier's reading of the Black female body indicates the identity between "objective scientific inquiry" (the identificatory or classificatory impulse) and "cultural aestheticism and biases" (the mimetic impulse) (Sharpley-Whiting 1986: 124).

II

In the introductory remarks to his summary essays for the 1950 American Jewish Committee/Frankfurt School project *The Authoritarian Personality* (*AP*), Theodor Adorno makes a point of delimiting the role of "external factors, such as economic status" to get at the "nature of the ideological data" of authoritarianism, inasmuch as the "evidence point[s] unmistakably to the role played by motivational forces in the personality" (*AP*: 603). The Adorno 1950 project had as its focus not only the relationship of ideology to personality but the quantitative measurement of degrees of prejudice on psychodynamic scales, the most prominent being the so-called F scale (Fascist scale). Data for the study were gathered from interviews and respondent questionnaires administered by the Department of Scientific Research of the American Jewish Committee, the Berkeley Public Opinion Study, and the Frankfurt School Institute of Social Research. The data were analyzed by a research team, which included Adorno, at the University of California at Berkeley.

Material for the Adorno 1950 project was gathered in Los Angeles and Berkeley field surveys. Adorno's team of social psychologists found that antisemitic opinions were subscribed to without much differentiation of the stereotypes held, due, it was hypothesized, to the pre-established "'inner consistency' of anti-Semitic ideology, or . . . the mental rigidity" of high-scoring respondents (Adorno 1950: 607). The extraordinary relevance/revelation of the Adorno 1950 study is that with the World War II Holocaust, that is, the near extermination of European Jewry, still fresh in the world's mind, Americans were nevertheless responsive to extreme antisemitic ideology and stereotypes, "as if they were no longer disreputable but rather something which can be sensibly discussed" (Adorno 1950: 609). Adorno believed that the reputability of antisemitism worked "as a kind of antidote for the superego and may stimulate imitation even in cases where the individual's 'own' reactions would be less violent" (Adorno 1950: 607). The continuity and consistency of antisemitic ideology in modern civil societies is the ambient terrain in which fascist violence becomes systematic. It is doubtful that individual Germans held views more antisemitic than the American respondents in the Adorno 1950 study. That Americans still believed that there is a "'Jewish problem,' after the European genocide, suggests, however subtly, that there might have been some justification for what the Nazis did" (Adorno 1950: 607).

The Adorno 1950 study took as its "subject" the antisemite rather than the "object" of antisemitism, the Jew, since "anti-Semitic prejudice has little to do with the qualities of those against whom it is directed" (Adorno 1950: 607). The psychosocial function of antisemitism is postulated by Adorno as largely manifesting unconscious hostility as a result of frustration and repression which get

> socially diverted from its true object, [and] *needs* a substitute object through which it may obtain a realistic aspect and thus dodge, as it were, more radical manifestations of a blocking of the subject's relationship to reality, e.g., psychosis. This "object" of unconscious destructiveness, far from being a superficial "scapegoat," must have certain characteristics in order to fulfill its role. It

must be tangible enough; and yet not *too* tangible, lest it be exploded by its own realism. It must have a sufficient historical backing and appear as an indisputable element of tradition. It must be defined in rigid and well-known stereotypes. Finally, the object must possess features, or at least be capable of being perceived and interpreted in terms of features which harmonize with the destructive tendencies of the prejudiced subject. (Adorno 1950: 607–8)

Adorno believes that while Jews "*can* perform this function in the psychological households of many people" (Adorno 1950: 608), the hostility of antisemites is easily transferred to non-Jewish minorities. "It was my philosophy professor, a native of the Antilles," Frantz Fanon writes in *Black Skin, White Masks*, published two years after *The Authoritarian Personality*, "who recalled the fact to me one day: 'Whenever you hear anyone abuse the Jews, pay attention, because he is talking about you.' And I found that he was universally right – by which I meant that I was answerable in my body and in my heart for what was done to my brother. Later I realized that he meant, quite simply, an anti-Semite is inevitably anti-Negro" (Fanon 1967: 122).

The relative independence of the phenomenon of antisemitism from its object allows it to function "as a device for effortless 'orientation' in a cold, alienated, and largely ununderstandable world" (Adorno 1950: 608); this is achieved through the instrumentality of stereotyping. The conflict which arises between stereotyping, real existence, and the "still-accepted standards of democracy" gets resolved by "the underlying anti-Semitism of our cultural climate, keyed to the prejudiced person's own unconscious or preconscious wishes, [that prove] . . . to be stronger than either conscience or official democratic values" (Adorno 1950: 608). In other words, antisemitism is not dependent on the nature of its object, which is in any event stereotyped, but on the prejudiced subject's "psychological wants and needs" (Adorno 1950: 609). The structure of the feeling of prejudice functions to satisfy unmet needs and cognitive fantasies. Adorno explains that racism's structure of feeling operates through "The transference of unconscious fear to the particular object[;] however, the latter being of a secondary nature only, always maintains an aspect of accidentalness. Thus, as soon as other factors interfere, the aggression may be deflected, at least in part, from the Jews and to another group, preferably one of still greater social distance" (Adorno 1950: 609).

Hence, it was not merely for ethical reasons that Fanon insisted on not relativizing forms or degrees of racism. The psychodynamics of the phenomenon follows a logic in which racism gets deflected from one "object" to another. The accidentality that Adorno maintains as a salient feature of the psychodynamics of racism, however, gets sublated once it is recognized that the interference of so-called "other factors," which deflect prejudice from Jews to another group "of still greater social distance," points to historical material conditions. In the absence of a Marxian critique of these "other factors" and the imperative to change them, Adorno falls back on a Myrdalian moral framework whose imperative is merely to bring American racial attitudes into conformity with the American democratic creed.

The glorification of in-group personality and culture is not only a function of antisemitism, it is the context in which one minority more than another is chosen as the object of racism. This process in which the racist "picks" his enemy is an instance, Adorno observes, of negatively falling in love (Adorno 1950: 611). As he experiences the fears and frustrations of modernity, the bigot constructs, or as Fanon would have it, enters into a pseudo-reality that was always already there, waiting for him, wherein he channels "his otherwise free-floating aggressiveness and then leave[s] alone other potential objects of persecution" (Adorno 1950: 611). As we will see later, there is a solipsistic aestheticism at work – Adorno's mimetic impulse – which fell out of his perspective.

One other functionalist characteristic of antisemitism must be mentioned here. Strong conformist tendencies among minority groups also find expression in the authoritarian personality. Inter-ethnic solidarities among minority groups are thwarted by " 'shifting the onus' of defamation of other groups in order to put one's own social status in a better light" (Adorno 1950: 611). The pressures of minority group conformity have been the object of ethnic and race relations studies for much of the twentieth century, primarily as a consequence of European immigrant experience, as well as the failure of the conformity/melting-pot perspective to explain the persistent foreclosure to African-American integration. Antisemitism and anti-Black racism do not simply satisfy the psychopathological needs of racists; they may also fulfill the conformity demands of minorities.

The psychosocial fantasies of antisemitism and other forms of racism are said to "run wild" when they "make themselves completely independent from interaction with reality" (Adorno 1950: 613). When forced back into a relationship with reality such wild fantasies manifest "blatant distortions" of reality, e.g., attributing inordinate power to a hated group. The self-contradiction between a stereotype that characterizes the weakness of a minority group, while at the same time attributing omnipotent power to it, represents the projective psychopathology of racism. Recognition of suffering and persecution gets easily perverted into delusional fantasies of minority group ubiquity ("they're everywhere"), omnipresence ("they're behind powerful institutions or dangerous organizations"), and omnipotence ("they're out to rule over us"). Ironically, among other things, these fears of intrusion and being overrun are fueled by the migratory escape of oppressed minorities from persecution and genocide. Fear of domination by a minority group is ameliorated by the totalitarian countermeasures that antisemites and racists have in mind, and which may easily be elicited by racist demagogues and ideologues. Racist demagogues and "subjects" will strategically displace omnipotence with omnipresence in the face of no actual evidence of minority power or domination.

In a given society whose moral imperatives are steeped in its power relations, fantasies of power get channeled into contradictory "ideas of dangerous, mysterious ubiquity" (Adorno 1950: 614). This gets counterposed to the "totality of presence" that the racist and the antisemite makes his exclusive right against any "intruder" not of his group. This too gets projected on the Jew in one form and on the Black in another. The persistent crises in the socio-economic condition of modernity give rise to this totality of presence that the racist or nativist feels, and which, in Fanon's view, drives the European with a latent superiority complex to seek a "world without men," that is, the world of the dark other. This colonial impulse and personality is descriptive of a kind of detotalizing presence. Where the totality of presence that adheres to the strict exclusion of minority groups or individuals may lead to genocidal extermination, or "ethnic cleansing," or apartheid segregation, the detotalization of presence motivating the colonial personality seeks a "heart of darkness" as an escape from civilization.

III

Simon Jarvis narrates the epistemics of Adorno's "immanent critique" as, among other things, "a critique of concepts to get to a critique of the real experience which is already sedimented in those concepts" (Jarvis 1998: 6). "Permanent critique" in lieu of permanent revolution and interventions into conceptual disciplines are not removed from Adorno's own understanding of his method of "critically interpreting conceptual contradictions [as] a way of critically interpreting our real social experience" (Jarvis 1998: 6). The social psychology of *The Authoritarian Personality* makes this even more reflexive, insofar as racist stereotyping and ideology are subjected to critical examination for the bodily fears, frustrations, and satisfactions contained in them. The subjectivity of the authoritarian personality is therefore deconstructed in its own terms, while the terms of the world, whose material contradictions produced this subjectivity, get read as nothing more than background for the cognitive drama (trauma). The non-identity of subject and object found easy political acceptance in the liberal agenda of the American Jewish Committee and the American academic world in which Adorno moved in the 1940s.

The Authoritarian Personality was a psychosocial examination of the damaged life of "modern man" subjected to an immanent critique whose liberal utopian demand was to bring the "subject" into conformity with democratic principles.[2] The liberal utopianism that Karl Mannheim discusses extends no further than the demand to reform the irrational remnants of earlier social formations in order to bring them into conformity with the ideals of bourgeois democracy. There is, however, a certain disingenuousness in Jarvis' assertion that a liberal utopianism inheres in Adorno's thought *contra* Georg Lukács' "idea that the proletariat were a cognitively privileged collective subject of history." Neither Lukács nor Adorno posited such a view of the historical role of the proletariat. Each instead, in his own way, made the false consciousness to which the proletariat is susceptible in bourgeois society a critical dimension of his social theory. When it comes to the question of Adorno's method of immanent critique developing along the lines of a utopian negativity Jarvis is on more creditable ground; although the opportunity to apply Adorno's method to his own theory in order to discern its historical materialistic basis in modern society remains a missed moment.[3]

Though Jarvis explains the positivist duality on which social theory runs aground as a problem of classifying instead of interpreting experience, it is not self-evident that *The Authoritarian Personality* founders on such a dualism, that is, that it succeeds more in classifying experience (indeed, in the most positivist manner possible through quantitative measures) than in interpreting experience. Jarvis' judgment that the efficacy of Adorno's method of immanent critique lies in its self-explanatory power – a self-reflexive approach to which Adorno gives credence – is more evident in Raya Dunayevskaya's approach to Hegel:

> If, as Hegel expresses it, "nothing is either conceived or known in its truth, except insofar as it is completely subject to method," why not subject Hegel's Absolutes to that method? . . . It is high time to encounter Hegel on his own ground – the Absolute Method – which is supposed simultaneously to be in constant motion and so "adamant" as to refuse to bow to any Absolute Substance. This is because, precisely because, it is the dialectic of the subject, the continuous process of becoming, the self-moving, self-active, self-transcending method of "absolute negativity." (Dunayevskaya 1989: 6–7)

This is the immanent critique Adorno wishes to undertake in relation to the Hegelian dialectic, but does not, instead relinquishing his hold on Hegel's negative dialectic wherein absolute negativity and subject are synonymous.

Dunayevskaya cautioned against the positivist pitfall that the Frankfurt School so critically distanced itself from but whose greatest dialectician, Adorno, so tragically fell into.

Adorno himself makes the self-critical claim in *Critical Models* that while "*The Authoritarian Personality* made a contribution . . . it is not to be found in the absolute conclusiveness of its positive insights, let alone in its measurements, but above all in the conception of the problem, which is marked by an essential interest in society and is related to a theory that had not previously been translated into quantitative investigations of this kind" (Adorno 1998: 235).

The Authoritarian Personality was one of a five-volume series edited by Horkheimer and titled *Studies in Prejudice*. The original research project on antisemitism had been outlined in 1939 at Columbia University by Horkheimer with other Frankfurt School theorists at the International Institute for Social Research. In order to secure funding, however, the project had to be reformulated to appeal to the quantitative approach of American social scientists. Work began in Los Angeles and subsequently developed in Berkeley when Horkheimer met Nevitt Sanford "who had been interested in the problems of personality structure and ideology for some time, and was then in the process of constructing the anti-Semitism scale" (Samelson 1986: 199).

According to Sanford, "Adorno's function was to teach the American academics some critical and Marxist theory" (Samelson 1986: 199). Samelson assesses Adorno's effectiveness in this area to have been negligible, whereas Susan Buck-Morss judges otherwise (though most of the weight for her contention lies on the chapter "Elements of Antisemitism" in the earlier *Dialectics of Enlightenment*), while Kellner, as we saw, falls somewhere in between. Jarvis offers the most intriguing argument for a Marxian *philosophic* underpinning to *The Authoritarian Personality* when he notes that "Adorno takes concepts which are meaningful only in the context of individual case histories and turns them into a negative anthropology. Adorno's defense is that it is not he who has abstracted from the individuals, but the unceasing conversion of concrete into abstract labor. The psychoanalytic categories are to help us understand the negativity of this process of abstraction itself" (Jarvis 1998: 85–6). In observing Adorno's retreat from Marxism, Samelson maintains that

the historic social forces determining character and ideology had been reduced to amorphous "antecedent sociological and economic factors," passed over quickly in the introduction [to *The Authoritarian Personality*]; class and class consciousness had in effect disappeared; and ideology had become anybody's "organization of opinions, attitudes and values." . . . [Wilhelm] Reich's original problem [postulated in his 1933 Marxian analysis of *The Mass Psychology of Fascism*] had been transformed to fit a liberal, empiricist, individual-psychology framework. (Samelson 1986: 199–200)

Buck-Morss' more nuanced evaluation of the epistemological duality of *The Authoritarian Personality* contends that it "was perhaps less a sublation than a sublimation of his [Adorno's] Benjaminian epistemological method, allowing qualitative, philosophical speculation to get past the quantitative, positivistic censorship of the social science establishment" (Buck-Morss 1977: 178). One already finds, however, in the *Dialectics of Enlightenment* essay, "Elements of Antisemitism" (written with the collaboration of Leo Löwenthal), elements of a theory of retrogressionism regarding the proletariat. In the so-called incompatibility of Marx and Freud, the Marxian framework gets sublated. The socialist proletariat in Germany, who had attempted revolution three times in the aftermath of the 1917 Russian Revolution (1919, 1921, and 1923) only to be suppressed by the Prussian state with the help of the proto-fascist Freikorp, still had power enough to challenge Hitler's Nazis a decade later. The proletariat in the Spanish Civil War achieved international solidarity in its fight against Franco's fascist military. The American proletariat in the same period discovered its own unique form of revolutionary organization at the point of capitalist production relations with the sit-down strike and in-plant committees, even to the extent of transcending the anti-Black racism that has historically been the Achilles' heel of the American working class.

In Buck-Morss' estimation Adorno's and Horkheimer's thesis in "Elements of Antisemitism" argues that the

> [r]eal experience of [the worker's] condition was blocked by the necessity of conforming to the given social system in order to survive. The result was suppressed aggression: "the hatred felt by the led, who can never be satisfied economically or sexually, knows no bounds." The deflection of this aggression onto the Jews was the psychological dynamics which fascism used to its advantage, "in that it seeks to make the rebellion of suppressed nature against domination directly useful to domination." Instead of criticizing society, the workers mimicked its reification and authoritarianism, masochistically consenting to be led, while falsely projecting upon the Jews as "outsiders" their own socially unacceptable (hence potentially revolutionary) traits and desires. (Buck-Morss 1977: 179)

Not only does this strip the proletariat of its historical agency, but Jews of theirs. Fanon will have none of it! "Racism, to come back to America, haunts and vitiates American culture," declares Fanon. "And this dialectical gangrene is exacerbated by the coming to awareness and the determination of millions of Negroes and Jews to fight this racism by which they are victimized" (Fanon 1968: 36). Fanon, the practicing psychotherapist, boldly confronted the limitations of the discipline, that is, of a merely psychological comprehension of racism:

> The perfecting of the means of production inevitably brings about the camouflage of the techniques by which man is exploited, hence of the forms of racism. It is therefore not as a result of the evolution of people's minds that racism loses its virulence. No inner revolution can explain this necessity for racism to seek more subtle forms, to evolve. On all sides men become free, putting an end to the lethargy to which oppression and racism had condemned them.
>
> In the very heart of the "civilized nations" the workers finally discover that the exploitation of man, at the root of a system, assumes different faces. At this stage racism no longer dares appear without disguise. (Fanon 1968: 35–6)

Where Adorno's epistemology does touch on, if not go to the heart of, today's concerns over ethnic cleansing, "identity politics," religious fundamentalism, and narrow nationalism is in his speculations "on fear of the non-identical" (Buck-Morss 1977: 180). Ethnic pluralism, which is supposed to be constitutive of liberal tolerance ("That all men are alike is exactly what society would like to hear") is also an instrumentality Adorno discovers in "[t]he technique of the concentration camp . . . to make the prisoners like their guards, the murdered, murderers" (cited in Buck-Morss 1977: 180). An emancipated society, in Adorno's terms, is not a unitary state, but is instead "the realization of universality in the reconciliation of differences" (Buck-Morss 1977: 180). *The Authoritarian Personality* elaborated the fear of the non-identical thesis, that is, the authoritarian subject's incapacity to experience non-identity, or the new (Buck-Morss 1977: 181). Non-identity makes the ethnic minority into the "outsider," a theme that one sees in Fanon's work and that of Richard Wright, whose novel *The Outsider* explores right and left totalitarian personalities for whom the "Black" is in different ways an "Outsider."

As against the weight of this *Weltanschauung* of the retrogressive character of the post-World War II age, a worldview that found philosophic utterance in existentialism and which exercised considerable pull on Black writers and intellectuals, Raya Dunayevskaya articulated a philosophy of Marxist-Humanism postulated on what she called "the maturity of the age." This maturity in social consciousness and philosophic cognition was manifested in workers battling the first signs of automation in capitalist production in the

US and the 1953 East German workers' revolt against "Communist" work norms. It showed itself as early as 1952 in the Bolivian revolution and other Third World struggles against Western imperialism, e.g., Prime Minister Mohammed Mossadiq's 1953 nationalization of Iran's oil reserves. In the US, the beginnings of the Civil Rights Movement with the Montgomery Bus Boycott disclosed new grassroots forms of organization and Black leadership that put "American civilization on trial," while the 1956 Hungarian Revolution against Communist totalitarianism saw the Petofi Circle bring Marx's 1844 humanist essays out of the archives onto the world historic stage.

This maturity of the age had neither the ear nor the mind of Adorno and the Frankfurt School, who instead pressed their World War II critical social theory of retrogression to its logical conclusion. The "culture industry" of Western democracies was susceptible to neofascist appeals and manipulation. Adorno perceived the fetishization of ideology as both propaganda and cultural products to be nothing more than the natural outcome of these mass-media societies. What is more, capitalist globalism first reached non-Western societies in the form of a mass-media culture. Fanon wrote perspicaciously about the duality the Western radio evoked in the emerging national consciousness of revolutionary Algeria (see Fanon 1967 and Gibson 1996). Today, in such disparate societies as Bosnia-Herzegovina and Rwanda, mass communications, if only in the low-tech form of the radio, have provided neofascists the instrumentality for mobilizing civil society's ethnic self-cleansing. Through this instrumentality a disturbing coalescence of government, paramilitary, and academic agencies have conspired to manufacture neofascist popular consent in Western and non-Western civil societies.

IV

Adorno's early view of antisemitism, which he perceived as a fear of mediation, complexity, and those minorities whose mediational ("middleman") position in the capitalist world personified that complexity, retains its explanatory cogency whether the group in question is Jewish, or the Chinese in Indonesia, or East Indians in East Africa, or Arabs and Koreans in urban America. According to Simon Jarvis, "the fear and hatred aroused by the non-transparency of social relations is revenged on mediators, on those (the Jews) who are taken to epitomize the sphere of circulation itself, as though their mediation were itself the reason for society's lack of transparency" (Jarvis 1998: 63).

Adorno was aware of the dangers of making a legalistic critique of formal freedoms and rights under capitalism, since it leaves the sphere of capitalist production unscrutinized and makes opaque antisemitism's personification of capitalist market or exchange relations which are calculable and administered by legal norms. Settling for merely "preserving freedom" (Jarvis 1998: 64) while retreating from directly confronting the conservative retrenchments on social freedoms and human rights, on the assumption that such confrontations are "ultra-leftist" politically and risk accelerating civil society's rightward drift toward authoritarianism, was incredibly myopic. Though widely misunderstood, Marx's theses *Zur Judenfrage*, against Bruno Bauer's opposition to extending civil rights to Germany's Jewish minority, nonetheless refused to subsume the particularity of Jewish rights under an abstraction like the "universal rights of man" (see Turner 1995). "Throughout *Negative Dialectics*," writes Jarvis *sans* Adorno's more radical awareness,

> Adorno is aware that left-wing criticisms of liberal concepts of freedom may participate in the demise of the very concepts of freedom without in anyway hastening the arrival of the "substantive" freedom for which they hope. The jurist [Franz] Neumann already regarded some of the left critics of the Weimar constitutions – themselves influenced by the National Socialist philosopher of law Carl Schmitt – as a case in point. Adorno's willingness to present the demise of the rule of law in Germany as less significant than the supposedly common advance of monopoly capitalism in Germany and the West alike is provocative; it is nevertheless a significant weakness of his early account not only of fascism, but also of capitalism. (Jarvis 1998: 64)

Max Horkheimer, as did Adorno, kept his distance from the student radicalism of the 1960s, expressing the same self-limiting critical theory to which he retreated in the 1930s and 1940s: "To protect, preserve, and, where possible, extend the limited and ephemeral freedom of the individual in the face of the growing threat to this freedom, is far more urgent a task than the abstract negation of it, or the endangering of this freedom by actions that have no hope of success" (quoted in Slater 1977: 88).

Here, of course, it would be quite facile to dismiss Phil Slater's judgment that this amounts to a "repudiation of the notion of 'social fascism'" as no more than hyperbole. However, some support for this conclusion comes from so seemingly distant a quarter as Soledad political prisoner George Jackson, writing in the same period. In *Blood In My Eye*, his posthumously published letters and essays on class struggle, war, revolution, and fascism, George Jackson debates the Communist Party position on fascism that Angela Davis espoused in much the same terms we've identified in Horkheimer and Adorno. Jackson rejected Davis' view of fascism, criticizing its basis as "tied into several old left notions that are at least open to some question now" (Jackson 1990: 129).[4] Jackson explains that out of the economic crisis of the last great depression fascism-corporativism did indeed emerge, develop and consolidate itself into its most advanced form here in Amerika. In the process, socialist consciousness suffered some very severe setbacks. Unlike Angela, I do not believe that this realization leads to a defeatist view of history ... To contend that corporativism has emerged and advanced is not to say that it has triumphed. We are not defeated. Pure fascism, absolute totalitarianism, is not possible. (Jackson 1990: 128–30)

George Jackson at this point critically cites the "early Frankfurt School" work of Wilhelm Reich, *The Mass Psychology of Fascism,* as "overanalyzed to the point of idealism," and Franz Neumann's *Behemoth: The Structure and Practice of National Socialism,* as not having "truly sensed the importance of the anti-socialist movement" (Jackson 1990: 130). In Jackson's view the great economic crisis of depression and world war reached its culmination and most "advanced form . . . here in Amerika" (Jackson 1990: 128). He concludes that "the forces of reaction and counterrevolution were allowed to localize themselves and radiate their energy here in the US. The process has created the economic, political and cultural vortex of capitalism's last *re*-form" (Jackson 1990: 131).

Finally, in a descriptive aphorism which utterly radicalizes Adorno's and Horkheimer's theory of authoritarian manipulation through the "culture industry," George Jackson writes:

The . . . notion that stands in the way of our understanding of fascist-corporativism is a semantic problem. When I am being interviewed [in San Quentin prison] by a member of the old guard and point to the concrete and steel, the tiny electronic listening device concealed in the vent, the phalanx of goons peeping in at us, his barely functional plastic tape-recorder that cost him a weeks labor, and point out that these are all manifestations of fascism, he will invariably attempt to refute me by defining fascism simply as an economic geo-political affair where only one political party is allowed to exist and no opposition political party is allowed. (Jackson 1990: 132)

George Jackson recognized that fascism could not be adequately accounted for merely by an economic analysis; he was aware that the psychosocial dynamics of fascism were complex, involving even certain strata of the working class itself manipulated by the "empty, cheap, spectacular leisure of sports[,] parades," empty consumerism, and "ritualistic, ultra-nationalistic events" (Jackson 1990: 157). According to the theoretical presupposition of Jackson's view of fascism, Freud's location of the repressive superego in the family, in order to render the former the critical measure of the latter, is translated into a theory of ideology and the psychosocial origins of authoritarianism by Erich Fromm (1941).

Slavoj Žižek, however, interrogates Adorno's and the Frankfurt School's concept of the authoritarian personality for its hidden ambiguities and inversions. The theory's assumptions regarding normality and a Weberian ideal type are subjected to what Žižek calls the "instead of" logic of the young Marx ("instead of recognizing in the product of my work the actualization of my essential forces, this product appears to me as an independent power oppressing me" [Žižek 1994: 13]). In a retrospective look at *The Authoritarian Personality*, Adorno recollects that "Our intention, similar to that of psychoanalysis, was to determine present opinions, and dispositions. We were interested in the fascist *potential*. In order to be able to work against that potential, we also incorporated into the investigation, as far as was possible, the *genetic* dimension, that is, the emerging of the authoritarian personality" (Adorno 1998: 235).

Adorno's ideal type of authoritarianism is arrived at, according to Martin Jay, "by simply inverting the features that define the (ideological) image of the liberal bourgeois individual" (Žižek 1994: 14). Žižek's preoccupation with a Lacanian double reflection dialectic takes only as its first moment the liberal bourgeois who may be viewed as an opposite whose "essential possibility" is *realized* in the authoritarian personality, along the lines of a "Fascist 'regression.'" In this instance, the "instead of" logic operates according to the hypothesis: "instead of critically examining every authority, the subject uncritically obeys those in power" (Žižek 1994: 14). In the second reflection, the authoritarian personality is symptomatic of "the 'repressed truth' of the liberal, 'open' personality . . . that is, the liberal personality is confronted with its 'totalitarian' foundation" (Žižek 1994: 14).

The problem with this is that it succumbs to its own "instead of" logic. That's to say that the so-called "Fascist 'regression'" is relegated to an ancillary background position or circumstance of the authoritarian personality, as if the process of realization or the repression analysis of symptomatic authoritarianism could be forwarded as ahistorical essences. Ahistoricism need not only assume the form of an abstract universalism that does not differentiate between historical epochs. It may just as well involve universalizing a particular epoch or period in history. We have witnessed both forms in the Bosnia and Kosovo conflicts. The ahistoricism involved in describing the conflicts as the irruption of "ancient ethnic feuds" is accompanied by universalizing descriptions of today's ethnic cleansing as identical to the period of Hitlerian Nazism.

The "Fascist 'regression'" is more historically assessed in Simon Kuznets' attribution of the barbaric deformation of Nazism to the "transient difficulties" of capitalist accumulation. It may be that all Žižek means is what he later articulates more clearly, namely that "Fascism, to take a worn-out example, is not an external opposite to democracy but has its roots in liberal democracy's own inner antagonisms" (Žižek 1994: 180).

Contemporary phenomena of neofascism, complete with ethnic cleansing of subjugated communities in places like Bosnia, Rwanda, Kosovo, East Timor, and the Sudan, implicating the authoritarian personality of intellectual elites, surely involves more than an aversion to complexity. That is to say, fascism involves more than the "ignorance of the masses" who reject the complexities of modern society, and who "are always 'populist' and maliciously anti-intellectual" (Adorno 1950: 658–9). Robert Bernasconi argues in the case of Heidegger's "political involvement with Nazism and . . . his postwar silence on the Holocaust" that "It is not only Heidegger, both the man and his thought, who is diminished . . . but also, and perhaps primarily, philosophy itself" (Bernasconi 1993: 57). Surely the role of a "socialist humanist" philosopher like Mikhailo Markovic as "state philosopher" in the service of the neofascist policies of Serbian President Slobodan Milosevic in Bosnia and Kosovo raises questions about the pursuit of philosophical knowledge if its praxis can be made susceptible to such "moral error." The name the Greeks gave to the problem of philosophy and moral evil, Bernasconi reminds us, is *akrasia* (Bernaconi 1993: 57). Rwandese Hutu university professors assumed the role of public ideologues, broadcasting and writing diatribes against the Tutsi minority and Hutus suspected of holding pluralistic sentiments for a multi-ethnic civil society.

We ought not to pass too quickly over the importance of *akrasia* for comprehending the truth of philosophy and the moral/political failure of the philosopher. *Akrasia* is rooted in a critical failure to unite theory and practice. Of the critical aspects of this crisis of reason, the professionalization of philosophy as an academic vocation whose distance from the political and moral concerns of the real world impairs the capacity of the intellectual to recognize the situation around him. Seemingly, this comes close to Adorno's profile of the authoritarian personality as an ego-type disdainful of complexity. However, more is at stake here. The moral reason of tolerance presupposes the identity and equality of individuals; yet, the formalism of the philosopher-teacher as the ideal-type of individual makes of him an *absolute subject*. But whereas Adorno's "authoritarian personality" purports to be a psychodynamic measure grounded on moral reason, racism relies equally on aesthetic judgments of difference as a reactionary revolt against modernity (cf. Michel 1998).

In a section of *The Authoritarian Personality* called "The Anti-Semite's Dilemma," Adorno identifies the psychological "symptom" with an "'economic' function": "If anti-Semitism is a 'symptom' which fulfills an 'economic' function with the subject's psychology, one is led to postulate that this symptom is not simply 'there,' as a mere expression of what the subject happens to be, but that it is the outcome of a conflict. It owes its very irrationality to psychological dynamics which force the individual, at least in certain areas, to abandon the reality principle" (Adorno 1950: 627). He notes that the conflict is between the superego which is identified as the psychological agency of society imbued in the individual versus the individual's own drives and wishes for instinctual gratification. The universality of the former expresses itself as ethical laws in conflict with the so-called expressive uniqueness of the latter. The personal terms in which prejudice expresses itself is inversely proportional to the abstract character of the universal obligation of tolerance. Tolerance, after all, is a liberal construction thought not to have abolished prejudice, or the historical condition of it, but instead to have come to a contractual compromise with it.

V

At the heart of Adorno's awareness of the dangers of uncoupling the critique of legal and cultural superstructure from the need for a thoroughgoing critique of the contradictory development of capitalist accumulation was the problematic the Frankfurt School faced in relating the recently discovered *1844 Economic-Philosophic Manuscripts* of the young Marx, the so-called humanist essays, to the dialectic of *Capital* of the later Marx. How, for instance, was Marx's philosophic treatment of the forms of social alienation to be related to the empirical laws of capitalist accumulation? Alfred Sohn-Rethel's *Intellectual and Manual Labor: A Critique of Epistemology* was an exception to this (though he remained on the margin of the Frankfurt School), and Marcuse's 1932 "Foundations of Historical Materialism" was one of the first examinations of the *1844 Manuscripts* (cf. Sohn-Rethel 1983 and Marcuse 1973). To be sure, the relation of alienation to value was studied by Adorno, particularly the significance of *surplus* value, but only insofar as it impinged on such questions as ideology and culture.

Economic laws describe humanity's economic behavior, whereas philosophic laws describe the behavior of cognition. Hegel's concept of law, as it was formulated at different stages of development in his *Phenomenology* and *Science of Logic*, contends Dunayevskaya, "has degrees of validity which corresponds to degrees of economic development and the forms it takes in our concepts or ideological development" (Dunayevskaya 1981: 9223).[5] The "kingdom of laws" that Hegel treats in the *Phenomenology* appears at an early stage in the development of social consciousness, one which Dunayevskaya also understood to correspond to the state of ideological development under Russian "Communism." The "Law of development, on the other hand, is an opposite concept, and gives us the motion of development of society irrespective of the consciousness of man" (Dunayevskaya 1981: 9223). The uneven development of objective historical laws and subjective cognitive/ideological laws becomes transparent when the material laws of society's development are mechanically transposed to the epistemological realm of cognition and ideology. So "innocent of the contradictions in life" is this mode of thought, Dunayevskaya argues, that it reverts back "to so primitive a stage that it can be compared with nothing higher than mythology, or the invention of gods for every element incomprehensible to [society], i.e., that it has not mastered" (Dunayevskaya 1981: 9223). This seems a more consistently Hegelian–Marxian formulation of a dialectic of enlightenment, in my view, than Adorno's and Horkheimer's Freudian approach, if only for the fact that Dunayevskaya sees in money and its fetishism "the *connection* between the *value form* and [the] *social order*" (Dunayevskaya 1981: 9229).

Money, or the money-form of value, represents a primitive form of law, one whose historical materialistic origins were derived from the utility to which African and Amerindian peoples put their religious fetishes, both domestic and communal, in regulating their exchange relations with Europeans. Money represents the "height of self-estrangement," an integral part of which is the level of abstraction to which "freedom" is driven as a concept. The bourgeoisie, and the mode of thought corresponding to its class rule, see in *freedom* only the

> *reduction* of all kinds of labor to uniform, *simple, average* labor, under which the individual, private labor, was completely *subsumed* . . . The *equality* of labors of *different* individuals achieved through alienation of their private persons could have been mistaken for freedom only by him who had so abstract a conception of it, that he failed to see that he himself [is] the victim of *a process of production that had the mastery over men*, and thus missed all the links that the *form of value* had to *the form of social production*. (Dunayevskaya 1981: 9229)

What Adorno identifies as domination and its entanglements with reason, Dunayevskaya grasps conceptually as arising from the authoritarian *plan* of capitalist production relations (Dunayevskaya 1981: 9244). The inseparability of politics and economics guarantee not only that "*exchange is the politics* of the economics of the labor process," but that the *plan*, far from being the equivalent of socialism, is actually representative of the bureaucratic domination of humanity's social labor. Classical political economy's failure to see that freedom, i.e., marketplace "equality," represented a reduction of various kinds of concrete living labor to abstract uniformity, i.e., to abstract labor, was in fact a failure to understand that labor assumed its *social* form through "the mediation of an *outside, not human, force*," namely, the market (Dunayevskaya 1981: 9230). It is that species of socioeconomic alienation, which is by no means limited to the working class, that resorts to the antisemitic personification of this moment of exchange mediation. The social form that labor assumes through the barbarous reduction of its life-process to an abstraction, that is, to a *spectre* of itself, and which gets further abstracted as "freedom" and "equality," is an open secret to the worker. It is a dirty little secret that gets reified in the monstrous form of antisemitism in the course of capitalism's transient, but unresolved, crises.[6]

The outside, nonhuman force of the market that works this magic is itself magically given a perverse human effacement through antisemitism. Like the omnipotence and omnipresence of the market, the perverse stereotyping of antisemitism stigmatizes "the Jew." The racist import of this logic also operates in another direction: anti-Black racism stems from the fear and revulsion associated with the reduction of different kinds of living laborers into one abstract mass. The process of alienation of the individuality and personality of an ethnically diverse civil society is mistakenly taken for freedom and social equality. This happens as a result of the uncritical attitude taken toward the process of violent abstraction that arises from the marketplace, which in turn results in identifying with so abstract a concept of freedom and equality that one fails to see oneself as a victim of the same process that dominates and exploits humanity. It means missing the connection between the form of value and of social production that gives rise to forms of social domination.

It is Dunayevskaya's contention that in the law of value, Marx discerned the law of motion of society as a whole, inasmuch as he began with the *reduction* of private labor, that is, the individual laborer, to a social form brought about not by a social relation but by a material relation, by the mediation of exchange.

That . . . the logical end of capitalism is its own self-destruction is made clear for it in manifold forms, whether it be in the decline of the rate of profit and insufficient capital for world development along value lines, or in the single discovery of atom splitting which is embodied in a bomb . . . Counter-revolution as an outside force, the lumpen proletariat and petty-bourgeoisie organized by Hitler, has failed. But counter-revolution as a *internal* force, through the proletariat elite, administrators, organizers [expresses itself as:] my plan is succeeding "better." At this stage dialectics can no longer be a personal matter for it is not merely that one thing can be "transformed" into its opposite; it is that it *and* its opposite having become enmeshed must be *resolved* and only proletarian socialist revolution can do that. (Dunayevskaya 1981: 9242)

Petty-bourgeois planning, with the aim of organizing exchange, results in a plan to organize the whole of human life and labor. The capitalistic authoritarian plan is the external counterpart and perverse determination of the authoritarian personality. Fordism-Taylorism meant the necessity of imposing a fascistic order in the factory. Gangsterism becomes part of the intelligentsia as an ideological form of social control so long as the masses themselves are not in control. The Berkeley Authoritarian Personality project interviewed and surveyed prisoners, students, the petty bourgeoisie, and proletarian elites – the very social strata from which the fascists drew their storm troopers against the proletariat and minority groups.

It may be said that the implicit promise in Adorno's thought to articulate a metaphysics of fascism went largely unfulfilled, at least on the grounds that *The Authoritarian Personality* would logically have tendered such a promise. Ironically, it is the undialectical skepticism of enlightenment thinking, that is, instrumental reason, which fixes the phenomena of fascism in the form of an authoritarian personality. Instead of Adorno's phenomenological approach (cf. Hannush 1973) comprehending the fact of fascism as a changing/changeable object, it is fixed, measured, and classified in its particularity. Adorno, like his satirized medieval theologian who has read Dante's *Inferno*, elaborates, in the psychoanalytic vocabulary of a modern alchemy, the interior scaling of the souls of antisemites. The problem with this lies in fascism being a psychosocial phenomenon that is already a demythologized myth inasmuch as it partakes in the concept of race.

The *philosophes* of the Enlightenment constructed and partook of the "science" of this demythologized myth, using it instrumentally to animate their philosophies of history and natural histories of religion – both of which were foundational for Enlightenment and post-Enlightenment philosophies of mind. "Race," in other words, was constitutive of the concept of the "science of man." Race did not only function at the level of the "lived experience" of the masses and popular culture but as a scientific myth of so-called rational discourse. It was instrumental to demythologizing biblical accounts and superstitious fears and fantasies. It was, in short, a more rational myth. The metaphysics of race in Enlightenment thought, of which the phenomenology of fascism partakes, eluded Adorno's skepticism and critical theory.

Notes

1　Cited in *American Civilization on Trial: Black Masses as Vanguard* (Detroit: News & Letters, 1983), 5. Myrdal's attack on the Marxian framework that Black intellectuals like Ralph Bunche relied on in their research memoranda for the American Dilemma project is, if nothing else, an ideological spectre that haunted academia in the war and immediate postwar years. Cf. Raya Dunayevskaya, "Negro Intellectuals in Dilemma," in Dunayevskaya 1981: 271–4.

2　I'm using the expression "liberal utopian" in Karl Mannheim's sense of that mentality which never goes beyond a certain progressive critique and reform of the status quo. The liberal utopian mentality is a "battle cry against that stratum of society whose power comes from its inherited position in the existing order, and which is able to master the here and now at first unconsciously and later through rational calculation" (cf. Karl Mannheim 1960: 226).

3　Dunayevskaya suggests such an immanent critique through the agency of her method of "absolute negativity as new beginning." Her reappropriation of the Hegelian concept of absolute negativity (negation of the negation) is comprehended, following Marx's 1844 "Critique of the Hegelian Dialectic," as the dialectic's "moving and creative principle" (cf. Dunayevskaya 1980).

4　Angela Davis, it should be recalled, was not only the prominent icon of the Communist Party USA, but had been a student of Herbert Marcuse at Brandeis University.

5　Dunayevskaya's philosophic correspondence from 1949–51 with C. L. R. James and Grace Lee-Boggs is found in Dunayevskaya 1981.

6　Along these lines Dunayevskaya quotes Simon Kuznets on the relationship between crises in capitalist accumulation and the monstrous political/ideological distortions that attach to them: "[The] emergence of the violent Nazi regime in one of the most economically developed countries of the world raises grave questions about the institutional basis of modern economic growth – if it is susceptible to such a barbaric deformation as a result of transient difficulties" (cited in Dunayevskaya 1989: 228).

7

The Adorno Files

Andrew Rubin

Although Adorno's writings have had a pronounced influence on late twentieth-century intellectual culture, the sustained interest in Adorno is, in many respects, curious. In the current atmosphere, Adorno does not necessarily address many of the preoccupations and predicaments of the late twentieth century. He was deeply Eurocentric and possessed no real knowledge of a world outside of Europe. He wrote little about sexual difference; he rarely mentioned race. He possessed no theory of imperialism or colonialism; he admired a dissonant music that is even today rarely performed. Yet in spite of all this, Adorno has appealed to precisely those fields that are motivated by a fundamental attention to the absences in Adorno's vast body of writing. Intellectuals like Edward Said, for example, have located in *Minima Moralia* a theory of exilic thought and agency.[1] Feminists and postcolonial critics have considered the importance of Adorno's negative dialectic for theories of subjectivity.[2] While the renewed interest in Adorno clearly owes some debt to the exacting labor of translators who have continued to improve his English for non-German readers, there is obviously much at stake in the resurgent interest in Adorno's writing.

Over the past decade, a significant body of Adorno criticism has focused on the exilic dimensions of Adorno's writing. Peter Hohendahl, for example, argues that "Adorno's complex and ambiguous attitude toward America was rooted in his European and German *Weltanschauung* and his critical humanism, which motivated him to reject modern America: its political order, its economic system, and particularly its culture."[3] Martin Jay has claimed that Adorno's writings on exile convey "the crisis of European culture and society that forced him into exile in the first place."[4] In one of the few close readings of Adorno's *Minima Moralia*, Nico Israel has shown how the geography and spatiality of Los Angeles informs Adorno's construction of a "critical" and even dialectical identity.[5] Yet for all of the attention devoted to Adorno's exile, what often is overlooked is the fact that his writing was both articulated and elaborated in a persistent relation to the specific institutional, political, and even national pressures with which he was engaged as both a critic and an exile. Indeed, Adorno's theory of critique and aesthetics, which many critics have decried for its apparent elitism and its distrust of political activism, can be understood to have emerged not only out of the conditions of exile and emigration, but also in opposition to the very institutional forces that attempted to delimit and constrain his criticism.

According to documents released under the Freedom of Information Act, as early as 1935 the Institute for Social Research (or the Frankfurt School as it has come to be known) was the object of a widespread surveillance operation by the Federal Bureau of Investigation. Almost without exception nearly every member of the Frankfurt School in exile – Theodor Adorno, Max Horkheimer, Herbert Marcuse, Henryk Grossmann, Leo Löwenthal, Karl Wittfogel, Frederick Pollock, Franz Neumann, and several others – were policed and investigated; their mail and telegrams were opened and read; their telephones were wiretapped, their apartments burgled; their private affairs scrutinized; their income taxes audited, all for the slightest sign of any radical left-wing political activity.

As Alexander Stephan has shown in his powerfully documented and argued book, *Communazis: FBI Surveillance of German Émigré Writers*, beginning in 1934 the Federal Bureau of Investigation began to monitor the activities of many German exiles who had come to the United States under the duress of Nazism.[6] "Few exiles suspected that their telephone conversations were being recorded and their mail not only open and read but translated, summarized, cataloged, photographed, and passed to other government bureaus," Stephan writes.[7] Mobilized by a confluence of anxieties about Germany, Communism, and other fears that contributed to the consolidation of American national culture, these exiles, all of whom lived, taught, and wrote in New York and Los Angeles, were branded "communazis" by the FBI director J. Edgar Hoover.[8] Their German identity and their fate as exiles were produced as a double threat. Figures including Thomas Mann, Heinrich Mann, Leon Feuchtwanger, and others were also the object of censorship, harassment, and interrogation. Anti-nazi organizations, like the Free Germany Movement and the Council for a Democratic Germany, were systemically observed to such an extent that the FBI could "justly be called the head of the world's first center for German exile research."[9] Henryk Grossmann, for example, was interrogated while vacationing in Cape Cod. "[Grossmann] has all kinds of data regarding the location of harbors," a police official wrote Hoover. "It is believed that part of his identification is phony and he is being checked with Fifth Column activities."[10] As part of its investigation of the composer Hanns Eisler, with whom Adorno collaborated and who was eventually deported, Adorno's movements in Los Angeles were closely scrutinized by the bureau. According to one FBI memo, Adorno owned a green 1936 Plymouth with license plates 5E5507.[11]

As far as Adorno and Horkheimer's writings were concerned, the FBI's surveillance had visible effects on the content of their work. Responding to the pressures of anti-communism, Adorno and Horkheimer completely rewrote several of passages of *Dialectic of Enlightenment* in order to conceal any rhetorical sign of Marxism. In its first published edition (1947), the mention of "capitalism" was changed to the infinitely vaguer and euphemistic expression "existing conditions."[12] "Class society" was substituted by metaphors of "domination" and "order."[13] "Capital" was abstracted and became "economic system."[14] Insinuations of vampirism were erased; "capitalist bloodsuckers" was replaced with the more dignified expression "knights of industry."[15] Gone was the mention of "ruling class"; they were simply, in the 1947 edition, "rulers."[16] Even the utterance "classless society" was suppressed.[17]

Far from being part of the Frankfurt School's long-standing "tradition" to censor itself, as Rolf Wiggershaus has asserted,[18] the new metaphors and euphemisms were clearly the result of political pressures in the United States. In fact the new metaphors did elude their censors. To the literal-minded analysts of the FBI, the Institute for Social Research evinced little sign of "communistic" thought. "It is to be noted," an FBI agent wrote with obvious regret to the FBI director J. Edgar Hoover, "that nowhere ... have the authors themselves mentioned Communism or indicated their attitude toward Communism. Furthermore, no explanation was offered as to the reasons for this omission, in spite of the fact that the ideas expounded ... appear to coincide in many respects with what is being practiced in Russia today."[19]

Indeed, the FBI had enormous difficulty in grasping exactly what kind of intellectual labor it was examining. Memoranda and telegrams that were sent from Horkheimer to Adorno discussing the philosophy of Nietzsche were redirected to confounded cryptographers on the grounds that the two critics were writing to one another in a secret language. The FBI director J. Edgar Hoover thought the mention of "Nietzsche" and the "[German] Expressionism" could "possibly be code."[20] What exactly "Nietzsche" and German "expressionism" was code for, Hoover did not say. Nevertheless, the very names signified the national, ethnic, and political fears that were mobilized to harass and monitor the activities of German exiles in the United

States. Max Horkheimer, for example, signed his telegrams "Alright," an apparent parody of American complacency; yet in the inventive minds of the FBI, the name suddenly became both a pseudonym and thus a sign of possible subversion.[21] Indeed, the agency at first thought that the Frankfurt School was a group of Nazis tracking the movements of Jewish refugees, when they were merely trying to assist Walter Benjamin's safe passage from France to the United States.[22]

That Adorno was monitored and investigated was only part of the experience of exile. For Adorno, exile also entailed a confrontation with other specific institutional practices that he struggled throughout his writings to resist. Beginning in 1938, during his first year in exile in the United States, Adorno was hired by the Rockefeller Foundation's Princeton Radio Research Project to analyze the effect that classical music broadcasts had on its audience. Working in an abandoned brewery in Newark, New Jersey, Adorno devoted his critical attention to study of the "improvement of the standard of listening attitudes."[23] He argued that the popularity of a piece of music was not something that could be measured; rather, he contended that what was popular was "a functional term" that necessarily "depended on the structure of the object of art that is supposed to be popular as much as on the structure of the people with whom it is supposed to be popular."[24]

From the very start of his research, Adorno's method challenged the assumptions of the Princeton Project. Paul Lazarsfeld, the sociologist who oversaw Adorno's research, expressed strong reservations about how Adorno conducted his research. He wrote that Adorno showed a "disregard for evidence and systematic empirical research." He charged that Adorno had "confused ethical and esthetic judgments and questions of scientific fact." He even claimed that Adorno's writing possessed a "dishonest tinge" and displayed a "lack of candidness." Overall, Lazarsfeld implied, Adorno was reluctant to submit to the dictates of American empiricism and positivism.[25]

Nevertheless, Adorno's intransigence was well-founded. Not only was the data collected in Newark of a commercial nature,[26] but the Princeton Radio Project itself was part of a broad movement in communications research to examine radio for its uses as propaganda. Directed by Hadley Cantril (a psychologist at Princeton), Frank Stanton (a former research director for Columbia Broadcasting Systems), and Paul Lazarsfeld (a sociologist at Columbia University), the Project's goal was, in Cantril's words, "to try to determine . . . the value of radio to people psychologically, and the various reasons why they like it."[27] As Paul Lazarsfeld wrote, the project intended to investigate "psychological and social factors which determine the trend and limitations of radio's influence."[28]

The Project received its financial support from the Rockefeller Foundation, which viewed radio as an immensely powerful medium that could be
exploited to influence political opinion in the United States and in Latin
America, where the Rockefellers had numerous financial and political
interests. As Christopher Simpson has argued in *Science of Coercion*, the
Rockefellers were interested in communication research to safeguard the
United States from the influence of subversive ideas like communism and
fascism.[29] In 1939 the Rockefeller Foundation organized a series of secret
seminars whose aim was to build public support for the war effort against
Germany.[30]

The Princeton Project was thus part of the effort not only to analyze,
survey, and manipulate the opinions of audiences, but also to develop radio
for the purposes of propaganda. In one study, entitled "The Psychological
Analysis of Propaganda," the Princeton Project made a case for the development of what it called "technological propaganda." Rather than issuing
abstract pronouncements about the value of "freedom" and "democracy,"
technological propaganda was more effective, the study urged, if it issued specific concrete "facts" that were conducive to producing the desired ideological effect. "Technological propaganda," they wrote, "doesn't try so hard to tell
people where to go, but rather shows them the path they should choose."[31]
"We should keep on remembering that propaganda is most successful when
it builds up and prepares attitudes prior to the time in which they are to be
effective," it said.[32] Indeed, at least one of the figures involved in the Project
would eventually be rewarded by Washington: in the 1950s the CIA funded
Hadley Cantril's Public Opinion Research project, largely as a result of his
work on radio and communication at Princeton.[33]

In the end, Adorno's Princeton work – "A Social Critique of Music," "On
Popular Music," and "The Radio Symphony" – did not meet the stipulations
of the Project.[34] John Marshall, the Rockefeller official responsible for the
Princeton Radio Research Project, wrote that Adorno seemed "psychologically engaged at the moment by his ability to recognize deficiencies in the
broadcasting of music to an extent that makes questionable his own drive to
find ways of remedying them."[35] Partly as a result of Adorno's unwillingness
to acquiesce to the project's assumptions, the Rockefellers cut the Project's
funding in the summer of 1940.

In many respects, Adorno and Horkheimer's *Dialectic of Enlightenment*
registers the specific institutional and political predicaments of the European
scholar confronted with instrumentalization of precisely the forms of knowledge that Adorno had produced for the Princeton Project. Indeed, Adorno
and Horkheimer's critique of Enlightenment was essentially articulated in
terms of a critique of American positivism. If reification was reflected as

instrumental reason in the field culture, as they argued, it also was apparent in the form of the positivist and empirical method itself. That the Enlightenment had lost its emancipating impulse was apparent because the Enlightenment had become expressed in the form and practice of American positivism, which held that nature could be measured, tamed, analyzed, and reduced to empirical observations. Horkheimer and Adorno's *Dialectic of Enlightenment* thus begins with a critique of Francis Bacon for his "substitution of knowledge for fancy."[36] They describe Bacon as the "father of experimental philosophy" who propounds "vain notions" and "blind experiments."[37] Modern science, they write, renounces any claim to "meaning" by substituting "formula" for "concepts," "rules" and "probability" for cause and motives.[38] They decry the "triumph of the factual mentality" in which "numbers become the canon of the Enlightenment."[39] Everything that cannot be quantified for the Enlightenment thinkers is, they argue, an "illusion" which modern positivism considered "literature." "Scientific calculation" and "equivalence" drive its method.[40]

Adorno and Horkheimer thus extended the Weberian basis of Lukács' "Reification and the Consciousness of the Proletariat" to the subject of positivism, but with none of the romantic anti-capitalism that Lukács had imputed to working-class consciousness. Horkheimer and Adorno were therefore not repudiating Enlightenment reason in general, but were displaying how a specific social scientific practice had emerged out of Enlightenment principles. American positivist sociology, the methods of Lazarsfeld, Cantril, and others, were the object of Adorno and Horkheimer's dystopic polemic expressed in Nietzschean overtones. The reification of life could be found in the very methods of positivist research itself. Indeed, the chapter on the concept of enlightenment ends with a footnote attacking the Rockefeller Foundation for its funding of projects that attempt to devise "formulas" for bringing "technology under control."[41] They criticize Rockefeller sociologists who adhere to its principles in "search of an antidote."[42] *Dialectic of Enlightenment* was thus a critique of the very the form of instrumental reason that Adorno encountered when he first arrived in the US.

For Adorno, empiricism amplified the dislocations he experienced as an exile in the America. "It is unmistakably clear to the intellectual from abroad that he will have to eradicate himself as an autonomous being if he hopes to achieve anything," Adorno later wrote in *Prisms*.[43] Positivism and empiricism had reduced reality to a prosaic and administered calculus, the effect of which was embodied in the fate of the exile. If Adorno was aware of the FBI's surveillance (he was interrogated as early as 1943),[44] in *Minima Moralia* he represented that surveillance and logic of migration in terms of a critique of American positivism and empiricism:

The past life of émigrés is, as we know, annulled. Earlier it was the warrant of arrest, today is intellectual experience that is declared non-transferable and unnaturalizable. Anything that is not reified, cannot be counted and measured, ceases to exist. . . . Reification spreads . . . to the life that cannot be directly actualized. For this a special rubric has been invented. It is called "background" and appears on questionnaires as an appendix, after sex, age and profession. To complete its violation, life is dragged along the triumphal automobile of united statisticians, and even the past is no longer safe from the present, whose remembrance of it consigns it a second time to oblivion.[45]

The administration of empiricism had compromised the very category of experience. The juridical logic of immigration forms and questionnaires was associated with the development of the automobile industry and of interstate highways. "It is as if no-one had ever passed their hand over the landscape's hair," he wrote in *Minima Moralia*. "It is uncomforted and comfortless. And it is perceived in a corresponding way. For what the hurrying eye has seen merely from the car it cannot retain, and the vanishing landscape leaves no more traces behind than it bears upon itself."[46] For Adorno, the terrain and even the geography of the US bore the marks of this damage. As he later wrote,

[In America] I had to recognize in the form empiricism took when translated into scientific praxis that the full unregulated scope of experience is more constricted by the empiricist ground rules than it is in the concept of experience itself. It would not be the most erroneous characterization to say that what I have in mind after all that is a kind a restitution of experience against its empiricist deformation. That was not the least important reason for returning to Germany along with the possibility of pursuing my own interests in Europe without hindrance for the moment and of contributing something toward political enlightenment.[47]

If Adorno saw the experience of exile in terms of the ideology of positivism that had damaged the very category of experience in general, in postwar Germany Adorno's critique of positivism would face new, mostly institutional, and even corporate challenges. Indeed, the postwar Institute of Social Research was substantially different from its predecessor in New York and prewar Frankfurt. "As early as 1951, members of the Institute who remained in America noted a subtle change in its orientation," writes Martin Jay.[48] Max Horkheimer secured agreements with the same German officials who had presided over the Institute's closure in 1930s.[49] Grants from the US High Commissioner John McCloy, who had taken a personal interest in the Institute, affected the Institute's tone and lead to a systemic self-censorship of its early Marxist politics. Horkheimer placed many of the Marxist volumes of the Institute's journal "in a crate in the Institute's cellar, nailed, and out of our grasp."[50] In the 1950s, Horkheimer even signed contracts to study the labor relations of Mannesmann, a company that had financed the Nazi party and founded the anti-Bolshevik League during the war.[51] Furthermore, Horkheimer cultivated friendships with a scholars such as Hadley Cantril, a CIA scholar whom Adorno had known from the former's direction of the Princeton Radio Project. As of 1963, even Horkheimer was formally associated with the Congress for Cultural Freedom, an organization that the CIA had used as a cover for American operations abroad.[52]

As a result of these ties, Adorno lost much of his ability to criticize the discourse of anti-communism as well as critically to investigate his own relationship to postwar German society and culture. He wrote a number of uncharacteristically candid political disclaimers that reiterated his and the Institute's anti-communism. "We reject as strongly as possible any interpretation of our work as being an apology for Russia," Adorno wrote in a memo that he considered publishing in Melvin Lasky's *Der Monat*, an influential Berlin magazine that was funded by the Congress for Cultural Freedom.[53] Even many of Adorno's musical writings of the 1950s and early 1960s were published in the Congress' Viennese journal *Forum*; and he had no apparent reservations writing for *Der Monat*.

Der Monat, like *Encounter*, *Forum*, *Preuves*, and *Cuadernos*, was part of a vast cultural network established by the CIA as a cover to promote the anti-communist aims of US foreign policy by presenting an image of a soft and culturally sophisticated empire that challenged the traditional European intellectuals' view of America as empty, commercial, and imperialistic. Of the many journals that the CIA funded in the 1950s, *Der Monat* had perhaps the best reputation for publishing major authors of the postwar period, though its association with the American High Commissioner alarmed the more skeptical. Nearly all of the writings in *Der Monat* were, to one degree or another, anti-communist; and those essays that did not present such a negative view of the alternatives to capitalism instead offered a benevolent image of US ambitions and intentions abroad. At times, however, *Der Monat's* politics were worn on its sleeve, a tendency its editors tried to avoid for fear of being perceived as the public-relations arm of the US State Department. Nevertheless, it did, for example, originally publish all but one of the essays that were gathered in *The God That Failed*, a collection of writing by Arthur Koestler, Ignazio Silone, André Gide, Richard Wright, Louis Fischer, and Stephen Spender, who all provided their own Augustinian narrative of spiritual conversion to anti-communism and free-market capitalism. As Frances Stonor Saunders has shown in *Who Paid the Piper?*, *The God That Failed* was distributed around the world by the Congress for Cultural Freedom to fight the Cold War by non-military means.[54]

Adorno had few qualms about writing for *Der Monat* and saw it as an opportunity to assert his anti-communist credentials. Throughout the 1950s he wrote several essays for it, including "Remarks on the Politics of Neurosis" (1953), a review of Arthur Koestler's essay on the pro-Soviet intelligentsia (*Kritik*); and most importantly, "Extorted Reconciliation" (1958), a polemical review of Georg Lukács' *Realism in Our Time*. The tone of Adorno's review was heavy-handed and conformed with *Der Monat's* political posture. He called Lukács a "dogmatic . . . commissar of culture," even though Lukács had expressed his growing disillusionment with the Soviet Union and supported the Nagy regime against the Soviet invasion of his native Hungary in 1956.[55] Ironically, Adorno reconciled Lukács' work to the political duress of anti-communism.

Adorno's anti-communism was not simply the product of the Cold War consensus that faced West Germany; it was reinforced by the Institute's ties to the American High Commissioner, John McCloy, who had an interest in assessing the opinions of West German society toward the American presence.[56] Upon returning to West Germany, Adorno's political engagement thus assumed the form of a sociological activism that relied on empirical methods that he brought back like souvenirs from America. In a conference sponsored by the American High Commission in 1951, Adorno delivered a talk in which he emphasized the importance of empirical methods in assessing the objective conditions of German society. "Empirical research in Germany must rigorously . . . bring to light the objectivity of what is socially the case, far beyond the individual or collective consciousness," he observed.[57] He suggested that the methods themselves had the aim of a critical and political activity:

> If we are confronted with the statement, based on some alleged authorities in humanist sociology, that the so-called rural population is resistant to technical and social innovations because of its essentially conservative spirit, we will not be satisfied with explanations of this sort. . . . We will for example send interviewers familiar with farmers into the country and encourage them to persist with further questions when farmers tell them that they stay on their farms out of love for their homeland and loyalty to the customs of their fathers.[58]

For Adorno, the sociological study of culture was thus not a neutral or objective scientific practice, but confronted and altered the realities that the researcher was attempting to grasp. After his return to Germany, he thought it was crucial to identify the residual and latent fascist and antisemitic elements that remained in postwar Germany culture. His major collaborative project of those years grew out of the *Authoritarian Personality* (1950).[59] Entitled *Group Experiment*, the study was a sociological examination of the attitudes of the German population toward the US government, the Third Reich, democracy, and the Holocaust. As he later wrote in "The Meaning of Working Through the Past," he found "the survival of National Socialism *within* democracy to be potentially more menacing than the survival of fascist tendencies *against* democracy."[60] According to the results of the *Group Experiment*, which attempted to gauge its subjects' predilections for authoritarianism along what was called the "A-Scale," Adorno's fears were well-founded. Antisemitism remained a widespread phenomenon after the war. Many in Konrad Adenauer's West Germany displayed a disturbing ignorance of the realities of the Holocaust, and a sizable minority continued to express positive opinions of Nazism.[61]

In 1957, however, Adorno would reverse his course yet again. After his promotion to full professor in 1957, he no longer needed to rely as an intellectual on the legitimacy of empirical research. In several essays – "Sociology and Empirical Research" (1957), "Teamwork in Social Research" (1957), and "Opinion Delusion Society" (1961) – he systematically articulated what he clearly always thought problematic about positivism. He declared, "culture is precisely the very condition that excludes a mentality that would wish to measure it."[62] Not only did his critique of positivism institute a major split within German sociology that achieved its fullest expression in his debate with Karl Popper in Tübingen in 1961; but it also seems to have coincided with his realization that anti-communism undermined the democratic institutions that he was attempting to strengthen through his lectures and radio addresses. In fact, after he renounced positivism, Adorno made a more discernible effort at pointing out the ways in which anti-communism sustained the residual fascism and anti-semitism in postwar German society. In "The Meaning of Working Through the Past," Adorno argued that "The resistance to the East contains its own dynamic that reawakens the German past. Not merely in terms of ideology, because the slogans of struggle against Bolshevism have always served to mask those who harbor no better intentions toward freedom than do the Bolsheviks themselves."[63] Rejecting positivism was thus not only a methodological turn, but, for Adorno, also a political turn. In "Sociology and Empirical Research" (1957), he repeated much of what he had already implicitly stated in *Dialectic of Enlightenment*, but introduced an emphasis on "theory," which he variously coded as either "philosophy" or "critique," as a way in which the object and categories of analysis were to be questioned.[64]

For Adorno, the study of culture and its ideology was the reified object of empirical sociology. "Nowadays," he wrote in 1957, "in the train of disappointment with both cultural-scientific [*Geisteswissenschaftlich*] and formal sociology, there is a predominant tendency to give primacy to empirical sociology. Its immediate practicable utilizability, and its affinity to every type of administration undoubtedly play a role here."[65] Adorno's argument rested on the premise that empiricism had a reified view of its object that had been temporally and spatially fixed by empirical analysis. With its origins in market analysis, empirical sociology was yet another form of instrumental reason and identitarian thought. It imputed a status to its object that was fetishistic and avoided a questioning of the categories constituted by its method. He again criticized the Princeton Project's methods, calling its research "atomistic" and "overphysical." Their interest in data was a "fetish" that concealed "from the investigator the irrelevance of his conclusions."[66]

Adorno's criticism of empiricism had the effect of emboldening his critique of instrumental reason, which he then extended to the political practices of the student movement in 1960s. Much of his refusal to support the student and anti-war movement was the consequence of his intervention against empirical sociology, among the more dominant of the postwar academic fields in Europe as well as the United States. Not that Adorno was insisting that the student movement was a group of empiricists seeking to overturn the structures of existing society through an analysis of data. Rather, what motivated the thrust of his comments was the students' conflation of praxis with theory. Just as the empiricists had privileged the object of analysis, so too did the student movement place an unreflected emphasis on "tactics" and "action." For Adorno, this kind of thinking and activity recalled the dangers of instrumental reason. In "Critique" (1969), Adorno wrote that: "the collective compulsion for positivity that allows its immediate translation into practice has in the meantime been gripped precisely by those people who believe they stand in the starkest opposition to society. This is not the least way in which actionism fits so smoothly into society's prevailing trend."[67] In "Marginalia to Theory and Practice," he concluded his attack on Weber's "de-ideologization of science" by criticizing the student movement's emphasis on priorities for action. "Actionism is regressive," he said, "under the spell of the positivity . . . it refuses to reflect upon its own impotence."[68] For Adorno, the students' emphasis on praxis was mostly identitarian in their assumptions and based upon what he and Horkheimer called "ratio." The "dogma of unity of theory and praxis . . . is undialectical," he argued, "it underhandedly appropriates simple identity where contradiction alone had the chance of becoming productive."[69] What Adorno found authoritarian and instrumental thus was no different from his excoriation of reason in *Dialectic of Enlightenment*, ironically the same text that had inspired and was widely distributed by the student movement.

What resisted instrumental reason for Adorno was precisely the kind of thought based upon its antithesis and the refusal of a forced and reconciled identity between "means" and "ends." On a panel at Cambridge University with Lukács' former student, Lucien Goldmann, Adorno observed that "method should be a function of the object, not the inverse. This notion . . . is one which has been all too simply repressed by the positivistic spirit."[70] For Adorno both "theory" and works of art were the two practices that held out against reification. "Works of art . . . are instructions for the praxis they refrain from: the production of life as it ought to be," he wrote.[71] Works of art, Adorno argued, expressed the antagonism inherent in society, yet were at the same time autonomous. Were a work of art to externalize these antagonisms, Adorno suggested, there would no longer be artworks at all.

For Adorno, the autonomy of artworks ultimately possessed a social quality in so far as the socially mediated antagonisms they represented *inhered* within the works themselves. These antagonisms were mediated by society, he argued, and it was the role of the critic to describe these conflicts by emphasizing the relationship between the form and internal tensions themselves. The higher the degree of antagonism within the art, the better the art. On the one hand, Adorno made a formalist argument, suggesting in *Aesthetic Theory* that: "The unsolved antagonisms of reality return in artworks as immanent problems of form."[72] On the other hand, Adorno deprived the autonomy of art in the very act of elevating it. It is this ambivalence of which Adorno was well aware: "The art work has a double character," he told Goldmann. "It is simultaneously a social fact and also – something else in relation to reality, something which is against it and somehow autonomous. This ambiguity of art, inasmuch as it belongs to society and inasmuch as it is different from society, leads to the fact that the highest level of art, its truth content and what finally gives it its quality as a work of art, cannot be a purely aesthetic matter."[73]

Adorno's theory of critique and aesthetics grounded his relentless and intransigent independence for which he was widely criticized by former students, who were disappointed that he was not the least bit enthusiastic about their protests, sits-in, and strikes. Adorno's own doctoral student, Hans-Jürgen Krahl, charged that "Adorno was not able to translate his private compassion for the wretched of this earth into a . . . theory for liberation of the oppressed."[74] The League of German Socialist Students (SDS) accused him of political quietism and declared that he was guilty of "sophisticated despair."[75] Yet Adorno's despair was not rooted in a blind devotion to the existing structures of society. He thought that the vision of praxis that the student movement had identified in, for example, the national liberation movements of the 1960s was simply the expression of instrumental reason.

Much of this critique of the movement appeared in the form of a hostility to the "Third World." While, like other members of the Frankfurt School, Adorno never developed a theory of imperialism or colonialism (Jürgen Habermas once expressed an active *disinterest* in the developing world),[76] Adorno's Eurocentrism and his dismissal of national liberation movements arose out of his critique of instrumental reason. What Adorno was critical of was not the anti-colonial struggles themselves, but the fact they had become unreflective calls for political action.[77] In "Marginalia to Theory and Praxis" Adorno wrote:

> Barricades are ridiculous against those who administer the bomb, that is why the barricades are a game, and the lords of the manor let the gamesters go on playing for the time being. Things might be different with the guerrilla tactics of the Third World; nothing in the administered world functions wholly without disruption. This is why actionists in advanced industrial countries choose the underdeveloped ones for their models. But they are as impotent as the personality cult of leaders who are helplessly and shamefully murdered. Models that do not prove themselves even in the Bolivian bush cannot be exported.[78]

Even in his negative comments about the importation of guerrilla tactics from the "Bolivian bush," his remarks were characterized by an unshakeable belief that reason should not be instrumentalized, that identitarian thought is administrative and reified. Ultimately for Adorno, any thinking that unreflectively unified praxis with theory was non-dialectical and compromised the substance of critique itself. What grounded Adorno's theory of critique was his relentless insistence on the autonomy of theory opposed to the instrumentalization of reason and the reification of thought.

What Adorno was interested in preserving in his writings on philosophy and modernist art was the irreconcilability of the relation between the subject and the object. In his review of Lukács' *Realism in Our Time*, Adorno argued that Lukács had "reconciled" the theory of realism to the duress of socialism. In Adorno's view, Lukács had expelled the antagonism and contradictions of art and subjected them to a rigid dogma that ignored the dynamic contradictions inherent in artworks. While Adorno's remarks were undoubtedly heavy-handed and not without their anti-communist bias, his argument recapitulated a current which underlies nearly all of his writing. In his review, Adorno wrote: "Lukács' postulate [of the reflection between subject and object], which is the supreme criterion of his aesthetics, implies that reconciliation has been achieved, that society has been set right, that the subject has come into its own and is at home in its world."[79]

It is precisely this notion of irreconcilability that has been appropriated by critics and intellectuals such as Edward Said. For Said, it is Adorno's emphasis on irreconcilability that defines the activity of the critic to establish the conditions for "non-dominative" and non-coercive knowledge.[80] In *Representations of the Intellectual*, Said argues that the power of Adorno's critique lies in the "exilic" conditions of his thought. Adorno is, Said writes, "a permanent exile."[81] "There is no real escape," he says, "even for the exile who tries to remain suspended, since the state of inbetweenness can itself become a rigid ideological position, a sort of dwelling whose falseness is covered over in time, and to which one can all too easily become accustomed."[82] Yet, as Said observes, Adorno goes on to suggest that "writing becomes a place to live," while it is also a place whose comforts Adorno refuses. For Said, as for Adorno, irreconcilability is a means through which the domestication of thought and theory can be vigorously resisted and worked through: "The point of theory is to travel, always to move beyond its confinements, to emigrate, to remain in a sense an exile," Said writes.[83] The conditions of migration, of displacement, of the dispossession of people by the forces of imperialism, colonialism, and globalization, are thus transposed onto the activity of the engaged critic. Exile's antithesis is domestication. The *lived* experience of irreconcilability, of the dispossession of the subject from the object, therefore finds an equivalent in Adorno's negative dialectics. If Said initially saw the movement of theory as necessarily a taming and dulling of political nerve (as he did in "Traveling Theory"),[84] in "Traveling Theory Reconsidered" Said shows that the affiliation with other theories can actually refuse the impulse of instrumentalism. If Said had first implied that affiliation with "theory" entailed its becoming dogma, he reinscribes the tension between domestication and theory in terms of exilic experience and irreconcilability.

Speaking in Cape Town, South Africa, in 1991 shortly before the end of apartheid, Said urged his audience not to use the classroom to settle old scores. He expressed his concern about the emergence of nativist politics that had necessarily betrayed the spirit of the anti-apartheid movement and academic freedom. In a related article that he wrote to address the situation of teaching literature in the United States, Said asked, "Would it be more appropriate to teach and read *The Tempest* as a play mainly about modern colonialism (using Memmi and Fanon) or as a late play of reconciliation and departure with Shakespeare's oeuvre?"[85] For Said, politics and literature were related through an Adornian paradox: "In itself, the investigation of literature will certainly neither determine an election nor end exploitation and cruelty. But it might encourage and deepen the tension and irreconcilability between the search for knowledge and political oppression and injustice. . . . The

paradox between the world and the teaching situation needs to be maintained, not resolved under duress of any sort."[86] What some might find unexpected about Said's affiliation with Adorno is that Said has emphasized
precisely those aspects of Adorno's writing that are in fact most critical of
certain forms of political commitment.

With the rise of multinational mergers and acquisitions, the alarming
industrialization of universities, where "excellence" is increasingly reified as
the promise of professional success,[87] the space of the critic has narrowed.
Federal laws, such as the University-Small Business Patent Act, for example,
have insured that the universities increasingly function in the service of corporate and commercial interests.[88] Even many of the originally insurrec-
tionary fields – like postcolonial and cultural studies – that arose in response
to the historical injustices and inequities of colonialism and capitalist exploitation have, in certain exceptional instances, contributed to and served the very
conditions they set out to criticize. At the University of North Carolina, for
example, one of the programs involved in border studies was commissioned
by the state to in effect administer and to stem the flow of migrant labor
from Mexico to North Carolina.[89] As Masao Miyoshi has observed, "There
is a large area of agreement between corporate needs (labor control, market
expansion, denationalization, privatization, entrepreneurism, and transnation-
alization) and cross border studies."[90]

In the context of this conjuncture of forces, the renewed interest in
Adorno's writings thus designates a crisis on the one hand, and offers the
conditions for a response to it on the other. Adorno's negative dialectics and
his critique of instrumental reason, however fraught, arose ultimately out of
a situation that resisted the pressures of dominative and coercive knowledge.
For this reason, the attention lavished on Adorno's critical model is utterly
symptomatic.[91] When the very conditions for even imagining alternatives are
themselves under threat, Adorno's critique holds out much like his aesthetic.
"Thinking is not the intellectual reproduction of what already exists anyway,"
Adorno wrote. "Its insatiable aspect, its aversion to being quickly and easily
satisfied, refuses the foolish wisdom of resignation. The utopian moment in
thinking is the stronger the less it . . . objectifies itself into utopia and hence
sabotages its realization."[92]

Notes

1   See, for example, Edward W. Said, *Representations of the Intellectual* (New York:
     Vintage, 1994); Edward W. Said, "Traveling Theory Reconsidered," *Critical Recon-
     structions: The Relationship of Fiction and Life*, ed. Robert M. Polhemus and Roger
     B. Henkle (Palo Alto, CA: Stanford University Press, 1994).

2   See, for example, Asha Varadharajan, *Exotic Parodies: Subjectivity in Adorno, Said, and Spivak* (Minneapolis: University of Minnesota Press, 1995).

3   Peter Uwe Hohendahl, *Prismatic Thought: Theodor W. Adorno* (Lincoln: University of Nebraska Press, 1995): 21.

4   Martin Jay, "Adorno in America," *New German Critique*, 31 (Winter 1984): 161.

5   Nico Israel, "Damage Control: Adorno, Los Angeles, and Dislocation of Culture," *Yale Journal of Criticism*, 10:1 (1997): 105.

6   Alexander Stephan, *Communazis: FBI Surveillance of German Émigré Writers*, trans. Jan van Heurck (New Haven: Yale University Press, 2000): 2. For his unabridged analysis of the FBI's surveillance campaign, see the German edition of Stephan's book. Alexander Stephan, *Im Visier des FBI: Deutsche Exilschriftsteller in den Akten amerikanischer Geheimdienste* (Stuttgart; Weimar: Metzler, 1995).

7   Alexander Stephan, *Communazis: FBI Surveillance of German Émigré Writers*, trans. Jan van Heurck (New Haven: Yale University Press, 2000): 2.

8   Stephan, 231.

9   Stephan, 50.

10 Letter from an unnamed official to J. Edgar Hoover, July 31, 1940. Federal Bureau of Investigation. Freedom of Information Act.

11 Undated and unsigned memo from the Los Angeles Bureau of the FBI. Federal Bureau of Investigation. Freedom of Information Act.

12 Rolf Wiggershaus, *The Frankfurt School: Its History, Theories, and Political Significance*, trans. Michael Robertson (Cambridge, MA: MIT Press, 1994): 401.

13 Wiggershaus, 401.

14 Wiggershaus, 401.

15 Wiggershaus, 401.

16 Wiggershaus, 401.

17 Wiggershaus, 401.

18 Wiggershaus, 401.

19 Memo from NY SAC to J. Edgar Hoover, May 20, 1955. Federal Bureau of Investigation. Freedom of Information Act.

20 Letter to Ladd from J. Edgar Hoover, July 18, 1941. Federal Bureau of Investigation. Freedom of Information Act.

21 Letter from J. Edgar Hoover to an unnamed Special Agent in El Paso, Texas, July 18, 1941. Federal Bureau of Investigation. Freedom of Information Act.

22 Censorship Daily Reports, vol. VI, July 22, 1942, Federal Bureau of Investigation. Freedom of Information Act.

23 Theodor W. Adorno, "Memorandum to Dr. Lazarsfeld," 1. Paul Lazarsfeld Collection, Butler Library, Columbia University, New York.

24 Adorno, "Memorandum to Dr. Lazarsfeld," 2.

25 Undated letter to Theodor Adorno from Paul Lazarsfeld. Paul Lazarsfeld Collection, Butler Library, Columbia University, New York.

26 Theodor W. Adorno, "Scientific Experiences of a European Scholar in America," *Critical Models: Interventions and Catchwords*, trans. Henry Pickford (New York: Columbia University Press, 1998): 222.

27 Wiggershaus, 239.

28 Memorandum to Dr. Cantril and Dr. Stanton from Paul Lazarsfeld, January 1, 1938. Paul Lazarsfeld Collection, Butler Library, Columbia University, New York.

29 Christopher Simpson, *Science of Coercion: Communication Research and Psychological Warfare* (New York: Oxford University Press, 1994): 22.

30 Simpson, 22.

31 "The Psychological Analysis of Propaganda," 16. Paul Lazarsfeld Collection, Butler Library, Columbia University, New York.

32 "The Psychological Analysis of Propaganda," 18.

33 John M. Crewdson and Joseph B. Treaster, "Worldwide Propaganda Network Built by the CIA," *New York Times* (December 26, 1977): 37.

34 "The Radio Symphony: an Experiment in Theory," *Radio Research* (New York: Harper, 1941): 110–39. "On Popular Music," *Studies in Philosophy and Social Science*, 9:1 (1941): 17–48. "A Social Critique of Radio Music," *Kenyon Review*, 8 (1945): 208–17.

35 Wiggershaus, 243.

36 Theodor W. Adorno and Max Horkheimer, *Dialectic of Enlightenment*, trans. John Cumming (New York: Continuum, 1988): 3.

37 Adorno, Horkheimer, *Dialectic of Enlightenment*, 3.

38 Adorno, Horkheimer, *Dialectic of Enlightenment*, 7.

39 Adorno, Horkheimer, *Dialectic of Enlightenment*, 4, 7.

40 Adorno, Horkheimer, *Dialectic of Enlightenment*, 8.

41 Adorno, Horkheimer, *Dialectic of Enlightenment*, 41.

42 Adorno, Horkheimer, *Dialectic of Enlightenment*, 41.

43 Theodor W. Adorno, *Prisms: Culture Criticism and Society*. trans. Samuel and Shierry Weber (London: Spearman, 1967): 98.

44 FBI Report, December 7, 1943. Federal Bureau of Investigation. Freedom of Information Act.

45 Theodor Adorno, *Minima Moralia: Reflections from a Damaged Life*, trans. E. F. N. Jephcott (London: Verso, 1978): 46–7.

46 Theodor W. Adorno, *Minima Moralia*, 48.

47 Theodor W. Adorno, "Scientific Experiences of a European Scholar in America," 242.

48 Martin Jay, *Adorno* (Cambridge, MA: Harvard University Press, 1984): 47.

49 Wiggershaus, 399.

50 Jay, *Adorno*, 48.

51 Wiggershaus, 479.

52 Pierre Grémion, *Intelligence de l'anticommunisme: Le Congrès pour la liberté de la culture à Paris (1950–1975)* (Paris: Fayard, 1995): 421.

53 Wiggershaus, 405.

54 Frances Stonor Saunders, *Who Paid the Piper? The CIA and the Cultural Cold War* (London: Granta, 1999).

55 Theodor W. Adorno, "Extorted Reconciliation," *Notes to Literature*, vol. I, trans. Shierry Weber Nicholsen, ed. Rolf Tiedemann (New York: Columbia University Press, 1991): 218.

56   Wiggershaus, 434.

57   Wiggershaus, 452.

58   Wiggershaus, 452.

59   Theodor W. Adorno et al., *The Authoritarian Personality* (New York: Harper, 1950).

60   Theodor W. Adorno, "The Meaning of Working Through the Past," *Critical Models: Interventions and Catchwords*, trans. Henry Pickford (New York: Columbia University Press, 1998): 90.

61   Theodor W. Adorno, "The Meaning of Working Through the Past," 100–3.

62   Theodor W. Adorno, "Opinion Delusion Society," *Critical Models: Interventions and Catchwords*, trans. Henry Pickford (New York: Columbia University Press, 1998): 121.

63   Theodor W. Adorno, "The Meaning of Working Through the Past," 94.

64   Theodor W. Adorno, "Sociology and Empirical Research," *The Positivist Dispute in German Sociology*, trans. Glyn Adey and David Frisby (London: Heinemann, 1976).

65   Theodor W. Adorno, "Sociology and Empirical Research," 70.

66   Theodor W. Adorno, *Sound Figures*, trans. Rodney Livingstone (Palo Alto, CA: Stanford University Press, 1999): 7.

67   Theodor W. Adorno, "Critique," *Critical Models: Interventions and Catchwords*, trans. Henry Pickford (New York: Columbia University Press, 1998): 288.

68   Theodor W. Adorno, "Critique," 273.

69   Theodor W. Adorno, "Marginalia to Theory and Praxis," *Critical Models: Interventions and Catchwords*, trans. Henry Pickford (New York: Columbia University Press, 1998): 277.

70   Lucien Goldmann, "Goldmann and Adorno: To Describe, Understand and Explain," *Cultural Creation in Modern Society* (Saint Louis, MO: Telos Press, 1976): 131.

71   Theodor W. Adorno, "Commitment," *Notes to Literature*. vol. II, trans. Shierry Weber Nicholsen, ed. Rolf Tiedemann (New York: Columbia University Press, 1991): 93.

72   Theodor W. Adorno, *Aesthetic Theory*, trans. Robert Hullot-Kentor (Minneapolis: University of Minnesota Press, 1997): 6.

73   Goldmann, 135–6.

74   Hans Jürgen Krahl, "The Political Contradictions of Adorno's Critical Theory," *Telos*, 21 (Fall 1974): 165.

75   Wiggershaus, 620.

76   Edward W. Said, *Culture and Imperialism* (New York: Vintage, 1994): 278.

77   It should be pointed out, however, that Adorno had different views of the situation in Palestine and Israel. When Adorno did speak out against the German police killing of a student protesting a visit to Berlin by the Shah of Iran, Adorno framed his remarks by condemning the Arab states for the 1967 Arab-Israeli war. The Arab states posed, Adorno declared, "a terrible threat to Israel." See Wolfgang Kraushaar (ed.), *Frankfurter Schule und Studentenbewegung. Von der Flaschen-*

post zum Molotowcocktail 1946 bis 1995, vol. II (Hamburg: Roger und Bernhard bei Zweitausendeins, 1998): 123.

78   Theodor W. Adorno, "Marginalia to Theory and Praxis," 269–70.
79   Theodor W. Adorno, "Extorted Reconciliation," *Notes to Literature*, vol. I, trans. Shierry Weber Nicholsen, ed. Rolf Tiedemann (New York: Columbia University Press, 1991): 240.
80   Edward W. Said, *Orientalism* (New York: Vintage, 1994): 336.
81   Edward W. Said, *Representations of the Intellectual* (New York: Vintage, 1994): 43.
82   Edward W. Said, *Representations of the Intellectual*, 43.
83   Edward W. Said, "Traveling Theory Reconsidered," *Critical Reconstructions: The Relationship of Fiction and Life*, ed. Robert M. Polhemus and Roger B. Henkle (Palo Alto, CA: Stanford University Press, 1994): 264.
84   Edward W. Said, "Traveling Theory," *The World, the Text, and the Critic* (Cambridge, MA: Harvard University Press, 1983).
85   Edward W. Said, "An Unresolved Paradox," *MLA Newsletter* (Summer 1999): 3.
86   Edward W. Said, "An Unresolved Paradox," 3.
87   Bill Readings, *The University in Ruins* (Cambridge, MA: Harvard University Press, 1994): 21–43.
88   The ramifications of the University-Small Business Patent Act are astonishing. The University of California at Berkeley recently signed a $25 million agreement with Novartis, a Swiss pharmaceutical company and the producer of genetically engineered crops. Under the agreement, Novartis plans to pay Berkeley $25 million to fund basic research in the Department of Plant and Microbiology. In exchange, Berkeley has granted Novartis exclusive rights to the department's discoveries, including the results of research funded by state and federal sources as well as by Novartis. It also affords the company unprecedented representation within the Department: two of five seats on the department's research committee are occupied by Novartis researchers. See Eyal Press and Jennifer Washburn, "The Kept University," *Atlantic Monthly*, 285:3 (March 1, 2000): 39–54.
89   "Officials Travel South of the Border to Study Border Influx," *Herald-Sun* (January 30, 2000): B1.
90   Masao Miyoshi, "'Globalization' and the University," *The Cultures of Globalization*, ed. Fredric Jameson and Masao Miyoshi (Durham, North Carolina: Duke University Press, 1998): 264.
91   For a discussion of Adorno's continued relevance in the context of globalization and the emergence of new media, see Andreas Huyssen, "Postscript 2000," pp. 51–4 of this book.
92   Theodor W. Adorno, "Resignation," *Critical Models: Interventions and Catchwords*, trans. Henry Pickford (New York: Columbia University Press, 1998): 292–3.

Part II

Aesthetics

8

Adorno as Lateness Itself

Edward W. Said

Beginnings of course stand at the first moment of any undertaking and in most cases express hopefulness and a sense of forward-looking expectation. Beginnings are usually associated with youth, not with age, although literature, music, and art are full of examples of renewal, beginning again, that are found in the work of older artists. Verdi, for instance, is justifiably described as having started again with *Othello* and *Falstaff*, both of them operas written when he was well into his late seventies, nearly eighty. Cyclical thinkers like Vico and Ibn Khaldun (and in our own time Northrop Frye) associate endings with beginnings. The decrepitude of a dynasty in Ibn Khaldun's *Muqaddimah*, the terminal despair and barbarism of reflection that Vico describes in his account of civil wars, these finally bury an old state of affairs in order that a new one might begin again. The cycles of autumn and winter that Northrop Frye talks about in *The Anatomy of Criticism* inevitably give rise to spring and summer, more or less unendingly.

In all these instances beginnings can either be recovered or somehow returned to. There is absolutely no finality implicit in the idea: hence its optimism and hopefulness which, to speak as someone whose feelings about mornings are much more enthusiastic than they are about evenings, is very much the same sort of rise in energy and expectation some of us feel at the dawning of a new day, its prospects seeming to raise one up from the darkness and gloom of even the unhappiest night.

As opposed to endings of that generally cyclical type, that is, endings that are part of a recurring pattern of birth, death, and rebirth, there are endings of an altogether, more or less terminal, finality. They too occur after some earlier beginning, obviously enough, but we sense in them much more of the conclusiveness of death, of an absolute and irrevocable cadence for which beginnings have at best only a very distant and even ironic appeal. It is these that I want to talk about here.

Few writers to my knowledge have focused so severely and unrelentingly on the difficulties of life at the ending than Swift. In Book III of *Gulliver's Travels*, the peculiar race of Struldbruggs at first opens up an extremely pleasing prospect for Gulliver, who believes that the immortality of these rare creatures guarantees them all sorts of privileges and insights; rather vainly he then proceeds to imagine how such miraculous beings will make it possible for him to derive many advantages. Together, he dreams, they will oppose the corruption of time and the "degeneracy of human nature" and, quite without any justification except his own gullibility and egotism, he also starts to imagine how well he would live if, like the Struldbruggs, he could be released from the threat of death. When at last he is told the truth about these miserable creatures he is sadly disillusioned. Far from immortality bringing salvation and insight it brings the Struldbruggs an apparently unending catalogue of woes. They lose their teeth and hair, as well as memory and desire. Past the age of ninety, because the language changes from generation to generation, they can no longer communicate with anyone. And all this is preceded by a disastrous process of physical, mental, and moral decrepitude that is awful to read about:

> they had not only all the Follies and Infirmities of other old Men, but many more, which arose from the dreadful Prospect of never dying. They were not only opinionative, peevish, covetous, morose, vain, talkative; but uncapable of Friendship, and dead to all natural affection, which never descended below their Grandchildren. Envy and impotent Desires, are their prevailing Passions. But those Objects against which their envy seems principally directed, are the Vices of the younger Sort, and the Deaths of the old. (p. 212)

One can easily imagine Swift, with his fierce conservatism and Christian fatalism, rather enjoying his quite horrendous demystification of age. But although both the Struldbruggs and Gulliver actually long for death as a result of these appalling circumstances, it is, I think, Swift's portrait of age itself that concentrates the modern secular reader's mind so acutely. When you are old there really is no escaping the fact that you are approaching the end, and at the end there is, properly speaking, nothing but the end, without in the end any real or alleged satisfactions. It is the quite peculiar power of that realization that is compressed in Swift's portrait of the dying Struldbruggs, who remain in the end without experiencing the conclusiveness of death. This terrifying but potentially comic situation is what appealed to one of Swift's modern disciples, Samuel Beckett, many of whose characters are in effect equivalents of the Struldbruggs. To be old in these circumstances is to lose contact with the beginning, to be left in a place and time without recourse either to hope or enthusiasm. Hence *Endgame*.

Swift's tactic is transparent. Endings are quite bad enough without trying to postpone them, he seems to be saying, and therefore the more readily we accept what is inevitable the less painful it will seem. Yet by giving the Struldbruggs too much life without any of the legendary attributes of immortality (eternal youth, for example) he also affords his readers, in a kind of sadistic slow-motion, a glimpse of what waiting for the end is like. The result, almost by inadvertence, is an unpleasant anatomy of ending, which is enacted for Gulliver in the reports he hears about the Struldbruggs and confirmed when he meets them. Beckett seems to have seized on this experience for his plays and novels, and extended it with quite remarkable ingenuity. Like Swift, Beckett is severe and minimalist: endings are comic because at such moments human struttings and posturings have a lucid futility to them that can be entertaining.

Besides Beckett there is a whole roster of modern writers who are fascinated by endings. This includes fin-de-siècle figures like Wilde and Huysmans, as well as writers like Mann, Eliot, Proust, Yeats, for whom mortality carries with it considerable sadness and nostalgia. Nevertheless these writers differ from Swift and Beckett in that *their* sense of an ending is mitigated by some glimmer of redemption, that in growing old one achieves insight, or some new and rounded sense of life's wholeness, or as in Proust's case, through art one can perhaps survive death. A book that deeply impressed me when I read it about twenty years ago – David Grene's *Reality and the Heroic Pattern: Last Plays of Ibsen, Shakespeare, and Sophocles* – puts forth a version of this argument very convincingly. Ibsen, Grene says, uses his last plays to understand the mistakes, failures, and wounds of a person's life, allowing backward vision to provide a new, integrative vision of the whole. In this Ibsen's *John Gabriel Borkman* and *When We Dead Awaken* recall *The Tempest*, *Cymbeline*, and *The Winter's Tale*, which in turn send us back to the *Ajax* and the *Philoctetes*. Drama, Grene says, is the vehicle enabling this final vision in ways that are not available intellectually but only aesthetically. Here too art is redemptive.

For Ibsen, as for the other modernist writers to whom I have referred, personal time corresponds to the general time. Personal exhaustion and failing health mirror the insufficiencies, dangers, threats, and debasements of modernity itself. A great deal (perhaps too much) of what has been written about the modernist movement has emphasized this traffic between the individual and the general. Modernism has therefore come to seem paradoxically not so much a movement of the new but rather a movement of aging and ending, a sort of "Age masquerading as Juvenility," to quote Hardy in *Jude the Obscure*. For indeed the figure in that novel of Jude's son, Little Father Time, does seem like an allegory of modernism with its sense of accelerated decline and its compensating gestures of recapitulation and inclusiveness. Yet for Hardy the little boy is hardly a symbol of redemption, any more than the darkling thrush is. This is quite evident in Little Father Time's first appearance riding the train to be met by Jude and Sue.

> He was Age masquerading as Juvenility, and doing it so badly that his real self showed through crevices. A ground swell from ancient years of night seemed now and then to lift the child in this his morning-life, when his face took a back view over some great Atlantic of Time, and appeared not to care about what it saw.
>
> When the other travellers closed their eyes, which they did one by one – even the kitten curling itself up in the basket, weary of its too circumscribed play – the play remained just as before. He then seemed to be doubly awake, like an enslaved and dwarfed Divinity, sitting passive and regarding his companions as if he saw their whole rounded lives rather than their immediate figures. (pp. 342–3)

Little Jude represents not so much a premature senescence but a montage of beginnings and endings, an unlikely jamming together of youth and age whose divinity – the word has a sinister sound to it here – consists in being able to pass judgment on himself and on others. Later, when he performs an act of judgment on himself and his little siblings, the result is collective suicide, which is to say, I think, that so scandalous a mixture of extreme youth with extreme age cannot survive for very long.

But there is ending *and* surviving together, and this is what I want to spend the rest of the time discussing here. For reasons that will become clear in a moment, I have given this rather peculiar modern aesthetic mode the name of *late style*, a phrase whose meaning was given a fascinating range of references by Theodor Adorno: he uses it most memorably and most powerfully in an essay fragment entitled "Spätstil Beethovens" dated 1937, but included in a 1964 collection of Adorno's musical essays, *Moments musicaux*. For Adorno, far more than for anyone who has ever spoken of Beethoven's last works, those compositions that belong to what is known as his third period (the last five piano sonatas, the Ninth Symphony, the *Missa Solemnis*, the last six string quartets, a handful of bagatelles for the piano), Beethoven's late-style works constitute an event in the history of modern culture: a moment when the artist who is fully in command of his medium nevertheless abandons communication with the bourgeois order of which he is a part and achieves a contradictory, alienated relationship with it. One of Adorno's most extraordinary essays, included in the same collection with the late-style fragment, is on the *Missa Solemnis*, which he calls an alienated masterpiece (*Verfremdetes Hauptwerke*) by virtue of its difficulty, its archaisms, and its strange subjective revaluation of the Mass.

What Adorno has to say about late Beethoven throughout his voluminous writings is clearly a construction by Adorno that serves him as a sort of beginning point for all his analyses of subsequent music. The American musicologist Rose Subotnik has done an extended analysis of this late Beethoven construction and shown its astonishing influence within Adorno's work, from beginning to end of his career. So convincing as cultural symbol to him was the figure of the aging, deaf, and isolated composer that it even turns up as part of Adorno's contribution to Thomas Mann's *Doctor Faustus* in which, early in the novel, young Adrian Leverkuhn is impressed by a lecture on Beethoven's final period given by Wendell Kretschmer:

> Beethoven's art had overgrown itself, risen out of the habitable regions of tradition, even before the startled gaze of human eyes, into spheres of the entirely and utterly and nothing but personal – an ego painfully isolated in the absolute, isolated too from sense by the loss of his hearing; lonely prince of a realm of spirits, from whom now only a chilling breath issued to terrify his most willing contemporaries, standing as they did aghast at these communications of which only at moments, only by exception, they could understand anything at all. (p. 52)

This is almost pure Adorno. There is heroism in it, but also intransigence. Nothing about the essence of the late Beethoven is reducible to the notion of art as a document, that is, to a reading of the music that stresses "reality breaking through" in the form of history or the composer's sense of his impending death. For "in this way," by stressing the works as an expression of Beethoven's personality, Adorno says "the late works are relegated to the outer reaches of art, in the vicinity of document. In fact, studies of the very late Beethoven seldom fail to make reference to biography and fate. It is as if, confronted by the dignity of human death, the theory of art were to divest itself of its rights and abdicate in favor of reality" (*Moments musicaux*, 13).

Impending death is there of course, and cannot be denied. But Adorno's stress is on the formal law of Beethoven's final compositional mode, by which he means to stress the rights of the aesthetic. This law reveals itself to be a queer amalgam of subjectivity and convention, evident in such devices as "decorative trill sequences, cadences and *fiorituras*." In an immensely powerful formulation of the relationship between convention and subjectivity Adorno says the following:

This law is revealed precisely in the thought of death . . . Death is imposed only on created beings, not on works of art, and thus it has appeared in art only in a refracted mode, as allegory . . . The power of subjectivity in the late works of art is the irascible gesture with which it takes leave of the works themselves. It breaks their bonds, not in order to express itself, but in order, expressionless, to cast off the appearance of art. Of the works themselves it leaves only fragments behind, and communicates itself, like a cipher, only through the blank spaces from which it has disengaged itself. Touched by death, the hand of the master sets free the masses of material that he used to form; its tears and fissures, witnesses to the powerlessness of the ego confronted with Being are its final work [*der endlichen Ohnmacht des Ichs vorm Seienden, sind ihr letztes Werk*]. (*Moments musicaux*, 17)

It is very easy to be impatient with this sort of writing but, as with nearly everything in Adorno, the dense and extremely involuted style are always based on a remarkably fresh and direct sensuous insight, and will usually yield up considerable interpretive capital if one is patient with them. What has gripped Adorno in Beethoven's late work is its episodic character, its apparent carelessness about its own continuity. Compare the development sections of such works as the *Eroica* or the third piano concerto on the one hand with, on the other, the opus 110 or the *Hammerklavier* and you will be struck with the totally cogent and integrative logic of the former and the somewhat distracted, often extremely slapdash-seeming character of the latter. The opening theme in the thirty-first sonata is spaced very awkwardly and when it gets going after the trill its accompaniment – a student-like, almost clumsy repetitive figure – is, Adorno correctly says, "unabashedly primitive." And so it goes in the late works, massive polyphonic writing of the most abstruse and difficult sort alternating with what Adorno calls "conventions," but which are often seemingly unmotivated rhetorical devices like trills, or appoggiaturas whose role in the work seems unintegrated into the structure. "His late work still remains process, but not as development; rather as a catching fire between extremes, which no longer allow for any secure middle ground or harmony of spontaneity" (*Moments musicaux*, 17). Thus, as Kretschmer says in Mann's *Doctor Faustus*, Beethoven's late works often communicate an impression of being unfinished, something that the energetic teacher of Adrian Leverkühn discusses at great and ingenious length in his disquisition about the two movements of opus 111.

Adorno's thesis is that all this is predicated upon two facts of mortality: first, that when he was a young composer Beethoven's work had been vigorous and *durchcomponiert*, whereas it has become more wayward and eccentric; and second, that as an older man facing death Beethoven realizes, as

Subotnik puts it, that his work cannot even achieve "a Kantian duality, for which no synthesis is conceivable, [but is in effect] the remains of a synthesis, the vestige of an individual human subject sorely aware of the wholeness, and consequently the survival, that has eluded it forever" (1976: 270). Beethoven's late works therefore communicate a tragic sense in spite of their irascibility; quoting Adorno on the *Missa* directly, Subotnik reminds us that "the sorrow he detects in Beethoven's last style, [is] where 'failure [becomes] in a supreme sense the measure of success'" (1976: 270). How exactly and poignantly Adorno discovers this is readily evident at the end of his fragment on Beethoven's late style. Noting that in Beethoven, as in Goethe, there is a plethora of "unmastered material," he goes on to observe that in the late sonatas conventions, for instance, are "splintered off," the main thrust of the composition left to stand, fallen away and abandoned, like the odd recitations that precede the fugues in opus 106 and 110. As for the great *unisons* (in the ninth symphony or the *Missa*), they stand next to huge polyphonic ensembles. Adorno then adds:

> It is subjectivity that forcibly brings the extremes together in the moment, fills the dense polyphony with its tensions, breaks it apart with the *unisons*, and disengages itself, leaving the naked tone behind; that sets the mere phrase as a monument to what has been, marking a subjectivity turned to stone. The cesuras, the sudden discontinuities that more than anything else characterize the very late Beethoven, are those moments of breaking away; the work is silent at the instant when it is left behind, and turns its emptiness outward. (*Moments musicaux*, 17)

What Adorno describes here is the way that Beethoven seems to inhabit the late works as a lamenting, or somehow feeling personality, and then seems to leave the work or phases in it incomplete, suddenly, abruptly left behind, as in the opening of the F Major Quartet, or the various pauses in the slow movement of opus 106. The sense of abandonment is peculiarly acute in comparison with the driven and relentless quality of second-period works such as the fifth symphony, where at moments like the ending of the fourth movement Beethoven can't seem to tear himself away from the piece. Thus, to conclude, Adorno says that the style of the late works is both objective and subjective:

> Objective is the fractured landscape, subjective the light in which – alone – it glows into life. He does not bring about their harmonious synthesis. As the power of dissociation, he tears them apart in time, in order perhaps, to pre-

serve them for the eternal. In the history of art late works are the catastrophe. (*Moments musicaux*, 17)

The crux of this, as always in Adorno, is the problem of trying to say what it is that holds the works together, makes them more than just a collection of fragments. Here he is at his most paradoxical: you cannot say what connects the parts together other than by invoking "the figure they create together." Neither can you minimize the differences between the parts, and, it would appear, you cannot actually *name* the unity, or give it a specific identity, which would then reduce its catastrophic force. Thus the power of Beethoven's late style is negative, or rather it *is* negativity: where one would expect serenity and maturity, one finds a bristling, difficult, and unyielding – perhaps even inhuman – challenge. "The maturity of the late works," Adorno says, "does not resemble the kind one finds in fruit. They are . . . not round, but furrowed, even ravaged. Devoid of sweetness, bitter and spiny, they do not surrender themselves to mere delectation" (*Moments musicaux*, 13). Beethoven's late works remain unco-opted: they do not fit any scheme, and they cannot be reconciled or resolved, since their irresolution and unsynthesized fragmentariness are not constitutive, nor ornamental or symbolic of something else. Beethoven's late compositions are about, are in fact "lost totality," and therefore catastrophic.

Here we must return to the notion of lateness. Late for what? we are inclined to ask. The American critic Harold Bloom has evolved an interesting theory about poetic creation which is based on what he calls belatedness. All poets, he says in *The Anxiety of Influence* (1973), are haunted by their great predecessors, as Wordsworth was by Milton, and Milton by Homer and Virgil. Poetry is therefore an antithetical art, since what poets do is to write against their antecedents: *The Prelude* is a rewriting and a distortion of *Paradise Lost*. By the same token criticism is misreading too, since critics come after poets. There is some similarity here between Bloom and Adorno, except that for Adorno *lateness* includes the idea of surviving beyond what is acceptable and normal; in addition lateness includes the idea that one cannot really go beyond lateness at all, not transcending or lifting oneself out of lateness but rather deepening the lateness, as in his book *The Philosophy of New Music*, where Adorno says Schönberg essentially prolonged the irreconcilabilities, negations, immobilities of the late Beethoven.

Two further points. The reason Beethoven's late style so gripped Adorno throughout his writing is that in a completely paradoxical way Beethoven's immobilized and socially resistant final works are at the core of what is new in modern music. In *Fidelio* – the quintessential middle-period work – the idea of humanity is manifest throughout, and with it an idea of a better world. Similarly for Hegel irreconcilable opposites were resolvable by means of the dialectic. Late-style Beethoven keeps the irreconcilable apart, and in so doing "music is transformed more and more from something significant into something obscure – even to itself" (*Philosophy of Modern Music*, 19). Thus late-style Beethoven presides over music's rejection of the new bourgeois order, and forecasts the totally authentic and *novel* art of Schönberg, whose "advanced music has no recourse but to insist on its own ossification without concession to that would-be humanitarianism which it sees through . . . Under the present circumstances [music] is restricted to definitive negation" (p. 20). Secondly, far from being simply an eccentric and irrelevant phenomenon, late-style Beethoven, remorselessly alienated and obscure, becomes the prototypical aesthetic form, and by virtue of its distance from and rejection of bourgeois society acquires an even greater significance for that very reason.

And in so many ways the concept of lateness, as well as what goes with it in these astonishingly bold and bleak ruminations on the position of an aging artist, comes for Adorno to seem *the* fundamental aspect of aesthetics, and of his own work as critical theorist and philosopher. One of the best recent books on Adorno – Fredric Jameson's *Late Marxism: Adorno, or, the Persistence of the Dialectic* (1990) – goes further than anyone in reclaiming Adorno for lateness, even though Jameson finally does situate (and to a certain degree instigate) the man's lateness within Marxist thought. My reading of Adorno, with his reflections about music at its center, sees him as injecting Marxism with a vaccine so powerful as to dissolve its agitational force almost completely. Not only does the notion of advance and culmination in Marxism crumble under his rigorous negative scorn, but so too does anything that suggests movement at all. With death and senescence before him, with a promising start years behind him, Adorno is, I think, prepared to endure ending in the form of *lateness* but *for itself*, its own sake, not as a preparation for or obliteration of something else. Lateness is being at the end, fully conscious, full of memory, and also very (even preternaturally) aware of the present. Adorno as lateness itself, not as a Swiftian Struldbrugg, but as a scandalous, even catastrophic, commentator on the present.

No one needs to be reminded that Adorno is exceptionally difficult to read, whether in his original German or in any number of translations. Jameson speaks very well about the sheer intelligence of his sentences, their incomparable refinement, their programmatically complex internal movement, the way they have of almost routinely foiling a first, or second, or third attempt at paraphrasing their content. Adorno's style violates various norms: he assumes little community of understanding between himself and his audience, he is slow, unjournalistic, unpackageable, unskimmable. Even an autobiographical text like *Minima Moralia* is an assault on biographical, narrative, or anecdotal continuity; its form exactly replicates its subtitle – *Reflections from Damaged Life* – a cascading series of discontinuous fragments, all of them in some way assaulting suspicious "wholes," fictitious unities presided over by Hegel, whose grand synthesis has derisive contempt for the individual. "The conception of a totality through all its antagonisms compels him to assign to individualism however much he may designate it a driving moment in the process, an inferior status in the construction of the whole," Adorno writes (*Minima Moralia*, 17).

Adorno's counter to false totalities is not just to say that they are inauthentic but in fact to write, to *be* an alternative through subjectivity, albeit subjectivity addressed to philosophic issues. Moreover he says, "Social analysis can learn incomparably more from individual experience than Hegel conceded, while conversely the large historical categories . . . are no longer above suspicion of fraud" (*Minima Moralia*, 17). In the performance of individual critical thinking there is "the force of protest." Indeed, such critical thought as Adorno's is very idiosyncratic and often very obscure, but, he wrote in "Resignation," his last essay, "the uncompromisingly critical thinker, who neither superscribes his conscience nor permits himself to be terrorized into action, is in truth the one who does not give in" (p. 292). To work through the silences and fissures is to avoid packaging and administration, and is in fact to accept and perform the *lateness* of his position. "Whatever was once thought however, can be suppressed, forgotten, can vanish. But it cannot be denied that something of it survives. For thinking has the element of the universal. What once was thought cogently must be thought elsewhere, by others: this confidence accompanies even the most solitary and powerless thought" ("Resignation," 293).

Lateness therefore is coming after, and surviving beyond what is generally acceptable. Hence Adorno's evaluation of the late Beethoven and his own lesson for his reader. The catastrophe represented by late style for Adorno is that in Beethoven's case the music is episodic, fragmentary, riven with the absences and silences that can neither be filled by supplying some general scheme for them, nor ignored and diminished by saying "poor Beethoven, he was deaf, he was approaching death, these are lapses we shall overlook." Years after the first Beethoven essay appeared, and in a sort of counterblast to his book on new music, Adorno published an essay called "Das Altern der neuen Musik," the aging of the new music. He spoke there of advanced music, which had inherited the discoveries of the second Viennese School and had gone on "to show symptoms of false satisfaction" by becoming collectivized, affirmative, safe. New music was negative, "the result of something distressing and confused": Adorno recalls how traumatic for their audiences were the first performances of Berg's *Altenberg Songs* or Stravinsky's *The Rite of Spring*. That was the true force of new music, fearlessly drawing out the consequences of Beethoven's late-style compositions. Today, however, so-called new music has simply aged beyond Beethoven: "where once an abyss yawned, a railroad bridge now stretches, from which the passengers can look comfortably down into the depths. The situation of [aged modern] music is no different" (p. 146).

Just as the negative power of late Beethoven derives from its dissonant relationship with the affirmative developmental thrust of his second-period music, so too the dissonances of Webern and Schönberg occur "surrounded by a shudder;" "they are felt as something uncanny and are introduced by their authors with fear and trembling" ("Das Altern der neuen Musik," 148). To reproduce the dissonances academically or institutionally a generation later without risks or stakes emotionally or in actuality, says Adorno, is completely to lose the shattering force of the new. If you just line up a bunch of tone rows happily, or if you hold festivals of advanced music you lose the core of, for instance, Webern's achievement, which was to juxtapose "twelve tone technique . . . [with] its antithesis, the explosive power of the musically individual"; now, an aging, as opposed to a late art, modern music amounts to little more than "an empty, high-spirited trip, through thinkably complex scores, in which nothing actually occurs" ("Das Altern," p. 151).

There is therefore an inherent tension in late style which abjures mere bourgeois aging, with its geriatric therapies, relatively comfortable circumstances, and well-funded programs. One has the impression, reading Adorno from the aphoristic essays on such things as punctuation marks and book covers collected in *Noten zur Literatur* to the grand theoretical works like *Negative Dialectics* and *Aesthetic Theory*, that what he looked for in style was the evidence he found in late Beethoven of sustained tension, unaccommodated stubbornness, lateness and newness next to each other by virtue of an "inexorable clamp that holds together what no less powerfully strives to break apart" ("Late Style," 100). Above all, late style as exemplified by Beethoven and Schönberg, the former in the past, the latter in the present, cannot be replicated by invitation, or lazy reproduction, or by mere dynastic or narrative reproduction. There is a paradox: how essentially unrepeatable, uniquely articulated aesthetic works written not at the beginning but at the end of a career can nevertheless have an influence on what comes after them. And how does that influence enter and inform the work of the critic whose whole enterprise stubbornly prizes its own intransigence and untimeliness?

Philosophically, Adorno is unthinkable without the majestic beacon provided by Lukács' *History and Class Consciousness* (1971), but also unthinkable

without his refusal of the earlier work's triumphalism and implied transcendence. If for Lukács the subject–object relationship and its antinomies,
the fragmentation and the lostness, the ironic perspectivism of modernity,
were supremely discerned, embodied, and consummated in narrative forms
such as the rewritten epics both of the novel and the proletariat's class consciousness, for Adorno that particular choice was, he said in a famous anti-
Lukács essay, a kind of false reconciliation under duress. Modernity was a
fallen, unredeemed reality, and new music, as much as Adorno's own philosophic practice, took its task to be a ceaselessly demonstrated reminder of
that reality.

Were this reminder to be simply a repeated *no* or, *this will not do*, late style
and philosophy would be totally uninteresting and repetitive. There must be
a *constructive* element above all, and this animates the procedure. What Adorno
finds so admirable about Schönberg is his severity as well as his invention of
a technique that provides music with an alternative to tonal harmony, and to
classical inflection, color, rhythm. Adorno describes the twelve-tone method
of Schönberg in terms taken almost verbatim from Lukács' drama of the
subject–object impasse, but each time there is an opportunity for synthesis
Adorno has Schönberg turn it down. What we see is Adorno constructing
a breathtakingly regressive sequence, an endgame procedure by which he
threads his way back along the route taken by Lukács; all the laboriously
devised solutions volunteered by Lukács for pulling himself out of the slough
of modern despair are just as laboriously dismantled and rendered useless
by Adorno's account of what Schönberg was really about. Fixated on the
new music's absolute rejection of the commercial sphere, Adorno's words cut
out the social ground from underneath art. For in fighting ornament, illusion, reconciliation, communication, humanism, and success, art becomes
untenable.

> Everything having no function in the work of art – and therefore everything
> transcending the law of mere existence – is withdrawn. The function of the
> work of art lies precisely in its transcendence beyond mere existence . . . Since
> the work of art, after all, cannot be reality, the elimination of all illusory fea-
> tures accentuates all the more glaringly the illusory character of its existence.
> This process is inescapable. (*Philosophy of Modern Music*, 70)

Are late-style Beethoven and Schönberg actually like this, we finally ask,
and is their music so isolated in its antithesis to society? Or is it the case that
Adorno's descriptions of them are models, paradigms, constructs intended
to highlight certain features and thereby give the two composers a certain

appearance, a certain profile in and for Adorno's own writing? What Adorno does is theoretical, that is, his construction isn't supposed to be a replica of the real thing, which had he attempted it would be little more than a packaged and domesticated copy. The location of Adorno's writing is theory, a space where he can construct his demystifying negative dialectics. Whether he writes about music or literature or abstract philosophy or society, Adorno's theoretical work is always in a strange way extremely concrete, that is, he writes from the perspective of long experience rather than revolutionary beginnings, and what he writes about is saturated in culture. Adorno's position as a theorist of late style and of endgames is an extraordinary *knowingness*, the polar opposite of Rousseau's. There is also the supposition (indeed the assumption) of wealth and privilege, what today we call elitism, and more recently, political incorrectness. Adorno's world is the world of Weimar, of high modernism, of luxury tastes, of an inspired if slightly sated amateurism. Never was he more autobiographical than in the first fragment entitled "For Marcel Proust" of *Minima Moralia*:

> The son of well-to-do parents, who whether from talent or weakness, engages in a so-called intellectual profession, as an artist or a scholar, will have a particularly difficult time with those bearing the distasteful title of colleagues. It is not merely that his independence is envied, the seriousness of his intentions mistrusted, and that he is suspected of being a secret envoy of the established powers. Such suspicions, though betraying a secret resentment, would usually prove well-founded. But the real resistances lie elsewhere. The occupation with things of the mind has by now itself become practical, a business with strict division of labour, departments and restricted entry. The man of independent means who chooses it out of repugnance for the ignominy of earning money will not be disposed to acknowledge the fact. For this he is punished. He is not a "professional," is ranked in the competitive hierarchy as a dilettante no matter how well he knows his subject, and must, if he wants a career, show himself even more resolutely blinkered than the most inveterate specialist. (p. 21)

The dynastic fact of importance here is that his parents were wealthy. No less important is the sentence where having described his colleagues as being envious as well as suspicious of his relationship with "the established powers" Adorno adds that these suspicions are well-founded. Which is to say that in a contest between the blandishments of an intellectual Faubourg St. Honoré and those afforded by the moral equivalent of a working-class association Adorno would end up with the former not the latter. On one level his elitist predilections are of course a function of his class background. But on another what he likes in it well after his defection from its ranks is its sense of ease and luxury; this, he implies in the *Minima Moralia*, allows him a continuous familiarity with great works, great masters, great ideas, not as subjects of professional discipline but rather as the practices indulged in by a well-frequented habitué at a club. Yet this is another reason why Adorno is impossible to assimilate to any system, even that of upper-class sensuousness: he literally defies predictability, turning his disaffected but rarely cynical eye on virtually everything within range.

Nevertheless Adorno, like Proust, lived and worked his entire life next to, and even as a part of, the great underlying continuities of Western society: families, intellectual associations, musical and concert life, philosophical traditions, as well as any number of academic institutions. But always to one side, never fully a part of any. He was a musician who never had a career as one, a philosopher whose main subject was music. And Adorno never pretended to an apolitical neutrality, unlike many of his academic or intellectual counterparts. His work is like a contrapuntal voice intertwined with fascism, bourgeois mass society, and communism, inexplicable without them, always critical and ironic about them.

I have spoken about Adorno in this way because around his quite amazingly peculiar and inimitable work a number of general characteristics of endings have coalesced. First of all, like some of the people he admired and knew – Horkheimer, Thomas Mann, Steuermann – Adorno was a worldly person, worldly in the French sense of *mondain*. Urban and urbane, deliberate, incredibly able to find interesting things to say about even so unassuming a thing as a semicolon or an exclamation mark. Along with this goes the late style – that of an aging but mentally agile European man of culture absolutely not given to ascetic serenity or mellow maturity: there isn't much fumbling for references, or footnotes, or pedantic citations, but always a very self-assured and well-brought-up ability to talk equally well about Bach as about his devotees, about society as about sociology.

Adorno is very much a late figure because so much of what he does militates ferociously against his own time. Although he wrote a great deal in many different fields he attacked the major advances in all of them, functioning instead like an enormous shower of sulfuric acid poured over the lot. He opposed the very notion of productivity by being himself the author of an over-abundance of material, none of it really compressible into an Adornian system or method. In an age of specialization he was catholic, writing on virtually everything that came before him. On his turf – music, philosophy, social tendencies, history, communication, semiotics – Adorno was unashamedly mandarin. There are no concessions to his readers, no summaries, small talk, helpful roadsigns, convenient simplifying. And never any kind of solace or false optimism. One of the impressions you get as you read Adorno is that he is a sort of furious machine decomposing itself into smaller and smaller parts. He had the miniaturist's penchant for pitiless detail: the last blemish is sought out and hung out to be looked at with a pedantic little chuckle.

It is the *Zeitgeist* that Adorno really loathed and that all his writing struggles mightily to insult. Everything about him to readers who came of age in the 1950s and 1960s is prewar, and therefore unfashionable, perhaps even embarrassing, like his opinions on jazz or on otherwise universally recognized composers like Stravinsky or Wagner. Lateness for him equals regression, from *now* to *back then*, when people discussed Kierkegaard, Hegel, and Kafka with direct knowledge of their work, not with plot summaries or handbooks. The things he writes about he seems to have known since childhood, and were not learned at university or by frequenting fashionable parties. As I said earlier, there is a practiced knowingness in Adorno that seems unfazed by the dizzying variety of subject matter and fields.

What is particularly interesting to me about Adorno is that he is a special twentieth-century type, the out-of-his-time late nineteenth-century disappointed or disillusioned romantic who exists almost ecstatically detached from, yet in a kind of complicity with, new and monstrous modern forms – fascism, antisemitism, totalitarianism, bureaucracy, or what Adorno called the administered society and the consciousness industry. Like the Leibnizian monad he often discussed with reference to the artwork, Adorno – and with him rough contemporaries like Richard Strauss, Lampedusa, Visconti – is unwaveringly Eurocentric, unfashionable, resistant to any assimilative scheme, and yet he oddly reflects the predicament of ending without illusory hope or manufactured resignation.

Perhaps in the end it is Adorno's unmatched technicality that is so significant. His analyses of Schönberg's method in *The Philosophy of New Music* give words and concepts to the inner workings of a formidably complex new outlook in another medium, and he does so with a prodigiously exact technical awareness of both mediums, word and tones. A better way of saying it is that Adorno never lets technical issues get in the way, never lets them awe him by their abstruseness or by the evident mastery they require. He can be more technical by elucidating technique from the perspective of lateness, seeing Stravinskian primitivism in the light of later fascist collectivization.

Late style is *in*, but oddly *apart* from, the present. Only certain artists and thinkers care enough about their métier to believe that it too ages, and it too must face death with failing senses and memory. As Adorno said about Beethoven, late style does not admit the definitive cadences of death; instead, death appears in a refracted mode, as irony. But with the kind of opulent, fractured, and somehow inconsistent solemnity of a work such as the *Missa Solemnis*, or in Adorno's own essays, the irony is how often lateness as theme and as style keeps reminding us of death.

9

Immanent Critique or Musical Stocktaking? Adorno and the Problem of Musical Analysis

Max Paddison

In an unpublished notebook entry from late 1944 Adorno wrote revealingly: "What remains to be written in what I write is beyond my knowledge and my power, but is something to which I lay claim: that I understand the language of music just as the heroes in fairy tales understand the language of the birds."[1] This aspiration indicates the extent to which Adorno considered musical works to be not only meaningful, but revelatory, in that they tell the truth about the world to those who, like Siegfried listening to the birds in Wagner's *Ring*, are able to understand what they are saying. Two important conditions can be seen to underlie Adorno's writings on music: (i) that musical works constitute a mode of conceptless cognition (*begriffslose Erkenntnis*), and can be understood, in that they are not only meaningful in terms of their inner relations, but also point beyond themselves to tell us something about the world and our relationship to it; and (ii) that particular forms of understanding (*Verstehen*) and experience (*Erfahrung*) are called for that are adequate to the demands of the music – that is to say, that some forms of listening are more valid than others, because music, too, has its requirements. Indeed, in his typology of listeners in *Einleitung in die Soziologie der Musik* (1962) Adorno insists that what he calls "the expert listener" manifests the only really adequate form of listening, something which in his essay "Anweisungen zum Hören neuer Musik" (1963) he describes as follows:

The type of listening which would do justice to the ideal of the integrated composition could best be labelled "structural." The advice, that listening should be multi-levelled – hearing the musical phenomenon not only in the present but also in its relationship to what has already passed and to what is to come within the same composition – has already identified an essential moment of this listening ideal.[2]

This emphasis on "structural listening" at the same time also indicates the centrality of musical analysis to his thinking, because Adorno regards autonomous artworks as themselves objectively structured and multilayered, with their own demands to which the listener must respond. Musical analysis places the individual musical work as objective technical structure and as dynamic form at the forefront of our consideration, unlike the aesthetics, sociology, or psychology of music, or indeed at times historical musicology, which may focus on values, ideology, perception, or social and historical context without necessarily addressing the specificity of the individual musical work. In view of this, a discussion of Adorno's thinking on music – his writings in this area take up half the twenty volumes of the *Gesammelte Schriften* – could do no better than to start here. However, in spite of attempts within academic musicology to utilize Adorno's work for analytical purposes, the nature of its application to music analysis as an independent discipline remains elusive, and Adorno's own attitude to it is distinctly ambivalent.[3] While he has written with great insight on analytical problems, and has argued for analysis to be regarded as an autonomous activity not necessarily bound by any usefulness it might have for performance or composition, Adorno at the same time inevitably understands it as part of his larger sociological and philosophical critique of music. He is not content that it should deal with the work as a self-contained and self-consistent, closed world. There are certainly contradictions and lacunae in his position, and in trying to discuss his views on analysis we are inevitably thrown back toward a consideration of his overall theoretical approach and the difficulties inherent in this. Carl Dahlhaus points to a familiar feature when he complains that "Adorno not infrequently displays a penchant for aphoristic allusions to socio-musical parallels and analogies, allusions which are by no means intended to be taken playfully, but the logical status of which is difficult to perceive or [is] even questionable."[4] This problem – the relation of inner to outer, of the hermetically sealed autonomous work to its social other, and the need for a particular kind of discourse which is able to identify the connections between the two – is the inescapable problem posed by Adorno's theoretical position. While it is a problem which has special resonance for technical analysis, it is also one which has great relevance for the understanding of music as a whole, particularly when viewed from the perspectives of aesthetics and sociology.

In the introduction to *Philosophie der neuen Musik* (1949) Adorno states categorically: "Technical analysis is presupposed at all times and often demonstrated, but it needs to be supplemented by detailed interpretation if it is to go beyond mere cultural-humanist stock-taking and to express the relationship of the object to truth."[5] For Adorno, the truth content of musical works is the hermeneutic goal: "No analysis is of any value if it does not terminate in the [question of the] truth content of the work," he said in a public lecture given in Frankfurt in 1969 and entitled "Zum Problem der musikalischen Analyse."[6] But at the same time, he also says that "naturally it is only critique that can discover the truth content,"[7] and in *Ästhetische Theorie* he makes it quite clear that critique goes beyond technical analysis, into territory where analysis cannot go, and involves sociological critique and philosophical interpretation.[8] It seems to me that there is an ambivalence in Adorno's attitude toward analysis which is not simply to be accounted for by accepting it as a typical manifestation of Adornian dialectics – although, of course, it is also that. It is this contradictory attitude that I wish to explore in this essay.

I shall first consider some features of the reception of Adorno within musicology (understood in its broadest sense), particularly in the English-speaking world, before going on to suggest that, if Adorno has something to say to technical musical analysis as a discipline, this lies not so much in his individual analyses as models,[9] nor even in his few writings on analysis as such, but rather in situating the activity of analysis within the context of his aesthetic theory. And to understand his ambivalence toward analysis, we need also to see it in the context of his philosophical and sociological concerns and in the context of the polemics against empiricism and positivism which characterized debates in the social sciences in Germany in the 1950s and 1960s. Finally, we need to consider what Adorno himself saw as the task facing analysis. I argue that underlying Adorno's thinking on music is a dialectical, self-reflective theory of form as mediation which is highly relevant to his conception of what an immanent analysis should be when understood within the context of his theory as a whole – that is, when taken as an integral part of a model which includes sociological critique and philosophical-historical interpretation.

Musicology, Adorno's Reception, and Analysis

The reception of Adorno's work within musicology (and not only in the Anglo-Saxon world) has been somewhat piecemeal and uneven. Initial interest tended to focus on what was seen as his role as a key historical figure in the music of the first half of the twentieth century, rather than on any specifically theoretical contribution he had made to musicology. Adorno was early on consigned to his twin historical roles as the philosophical protagonist of musical modernism and as the sociological scourge of mass culture. This is not to suggest that Adorno's theory of modernism and of the avant-garde has lacked influence: it has been assimilated and developed in illuminating ways, and has been seen to offer valuable approaches to contemporary music since Adorno,[10] and to the aesthetics of music, particularly as filtered through Carl Dahlhaus[11] and others like Peter Bürger.[12] Given the originality and importance of his philosophy of music history,[13] however, one might have expected historical musicology to have been the most obviously fruitful area for the reception of Adorno's thinking. Indeed, what has the potential to be his most valuable contribution to historical musicology – his use of Max Weber's concept of rationalization and his interpretation of music history as the development and objectification of bourgeois subjectivity in terms of the interaction with, and rationalization of, musical material – has so far had only limited impact.

In view of this, I find it interesting that two areas that have been the first to take Adorno's theories most seriously (that is, in Anglo-American musicology in the 1980s and 1990s) have been just those in which his contribution has been most difficult to apply: namely, popular music studies and music analysis. It is surely also significant that both these areas, as sub-disciplines, saw themselves as somewhat marginalized within academic musical life up to the late 1970s. Both took similar steps to counter this situation through the launch of new academic journals in the early 1980s. The first issues of the journals *Popular Music* and *Music Analysis* appeared in the same year, 1981, followed by the establishment of their associated learned societies. In both cases this process of legitimation drew on Adorno's thinking in these areas – work which, in both cases, arguably represents Adorno at his most problematic.

Adorno's prickly critique of mass culture was well known, and there was no question that it had a place in any serious academic study of popular music. The question was more, how to deal with this awkward body of work in the establishment of a fledgling sub-discipline, popular music studies, involving, in the early issues of the *Popular Music* yearbook, the need to deal with problems of definitions and of methodologies, and also to establish a body of knowledge.[14] The answer, of course, was to deal with Adorno's theory of mass culture critically: the blind spots and contradictions were evident enough, but at the same time there were important issues identified by Adorno that remained after such a critique, and which could not be ignored.[15] Popular music studies had had from the start a strong interdisciplinary flavor, and Adorno had long been part of the critical theoretical framework employed by sociologists and cultural theorists in their approach to popular culture. The fact that sociologists and cultural theorists of a particular generation (that is, those who were students in the 1960s) had a weakness both for rock music and for the Critical Theory of the Frankfurt School (particularly Adorno), in spite of the latter's aversion to the former, merely seemed to intensify the desire to incorporate Adorno and his barbed critique into the academic study of popular culture.[16] If there was a problem, it was how to bring a musicological perspective into popular music studies, dominated as it remains by sociological and cultural studies approaches.[17]

The case was rather different with technical musical analysis. And yet, there are some parallels with the situation in popular music studies. Before the publication of the English translation of his lecture "Zum Problem der musikalischen Analyse" (the German original had not been published at the time), it was not widely known that Adorno had written anything directly on technical analysis, on the activity of analysis as a discipline, apart from the brief "Berg und Analyse" section of his *Berg* book. There are a few points in *Philosophie der neuen Musik* where he discusses analysis in general terms. His analyses of individual works were to an extent also known, but in their mixture of philosophical-sociological interpretation and descriptive analytical detail, together with the hiatus which often appeared to exist between these two levels, they had remained relatively neglected – in part, of course, in English-speaking countries for want of translations. In Germany,[18] nevertheless, this neglect appeared to have been the case almost as much as in English-speaking countries, a situation further complicated by the historical division of labor in German higher education institutions, where analysis is located in the conservatoires rather than in university music departments.[19] This division, essentially one between *Musikwissenschaft* (exclusive to the universities, historiographical in orientation, and with little systematic emphasis on technical analysis) and a practical training in composition or performance (limited to the Musikhochschulen, and employing technical analysis as an auxiliary discipline), in part could explain why Adorno's 1969 lecture "Zum Problem der musikalischen Analyse" was delivered at the Frankfurter Musikhochschule rather than at the University. Nevertheless, although at certain points the lecture makes links between analysis, performance, and composition, its tone is primarily philosophical and critical. Musicologists (Dahlhaus and a few others excepted) tended to avoid Adorno's writings on music because of what they perceived as the philosophical difficulties, or, as was the case with Dahlhaus and Diether de la Motte,[20] they were critical of what were seen as analytical shortcomings in Adorno's approach. Philosophers and sociologists, on the other hand, avoided the musical writings because, as non-musicians or non-musicologists, they considered that they lacked the necessary musical know-how to deal with the writings. Unlike the situation in popular music studies, therefore, this would appear to be a classic case of the perils of inter-disciplinarity. If there was a problem here, it was how to bring philosophical and sociological perspectives into musicology and analysis.[21]

In the final decade of his life, in the 1960s, Adorno had been giving the activity of musical analysis renewed thought. This came about in particular as a result of his revisiting the analyses of Berg's music he had written in the 1930s for Willi Reich's book *Alban Berg*.[22] He wished to prepare a new book on Berg, incorporating his analyses from Reich's book together with new material, for a volume which was published in Vienna in 1968 as *Berg: Der Meister des kleinsten Übergangs*.[23] Among that new material was the section already mentioned which introduces the analyses in the 1968 Berg book: "Berg und Analyse." The issues raised in that brief introductory essay focus important concerns which were occupying Adorno at this time. But because these concerns arise particularly from his further thoughts on his earlier indi-vidual analyses of Berg's music, they need to be supplemented with com-ments on analysis which are to be found in the other big projects on which he was also working at this stage. These are, in particular, the unfinished pro-jects *Ästhetische Theorie*,[24] published posthumously in 1970, and the Beethoven fragments, published in 1993 as *Beethoven: Philosophie der Musik*.[25] And many of these concerns, although by no means all, are raised in "Zum Problem der musikalischen Analyse," the lecture he gave a few months before his death in 1969.[26] This lecture, delivered, probably in semi-improvised fashion, on Feb-ruary 24, 1969 at the Hochschule für Musik und darstellende Kunst in Frank-furt, was thus dealing with issues concerning analysis that Adorno had been thinking through simultaneously in a number of different projects.

The talk has understandably come to be seen as an endorsement of the activity of analysis, a justification of technical analysis in the face of the kinds of hostility and misunderstanding it continues to provoke in some circles. Adorno's opening comments reinforce this interpretation, when he observes that "One can well say that the general underlying feeling towards analysis is not exactly friendly," and then goes on to argue that "'To get to know something intimately' . . . means in reality 'to analyse.'"[27] To that extent, therefore, Adorno's talk could also be seen as part of the process of legiti-mation, a process which is important to the establishment of any discipline. Likewise, it could also be argued that Adorno's theory of mass culture served partly in the legitimation of popular music studies as a discipline, while also serving as a handy foil, in a double act with Walter Benjamin, to set off more affirmative theories of popular culture. In both cases, perhaps, it is better to have Adorno inside the discipline than outside it. But at the same time, Adorno's talk "Zum Problem der musikalischen Analyse" has also to be seen as a *critique* of analysis – a critique which can be understood in two different senses. First, it is undoubtedly a critique in the dialectical sense, whereby, through identifying its significant characteristics and its absences, its blind spots, analysis, seen as a purely formalist, immanent activity, is also located in relation to a "totality," to its social other – albeit on a rather abstract level. But second, I suggest there is another plot. While Adorno argues strongly for the autonomy of analysis as a discipline, in the sense that he claims not to see it as a mere auxiliary activity but one which is central to our understanding of musical works, there is also, it seems to me, much that is left unsaid in his talk, or at least is only hinted at. His claim for the autonomy of analysis raises issues within his larger methodology. When seen in conjunction with the discussions of analysis which occur scattered throughout *Ästhetische Theorie*, some of the ideas expressed in "Zum Problem der musikalischen Analyse" seem at odds with the perspective we get from his aesthetics, and also from his concerns in the social sciences at this time.

Adorno's Criticisms of Analysis and the Relation to Aesthetics

On the one hand, Adorno argues that analysis is necessary and indispensable; on the other hand, it is at the same time merely the empirical arm of his aesthetics of music, and is found lacking. Analysis alone is inadequate unless it leads to interpretation. In spite of his insistence in "Zum Problem der musikalischen Analyse" that analysis is no mere auxiliary discipline, acting as support for other more central musical activities like performance or composition, Adorno nevertheless constantly implies that, as an empirical, rock-face activity dealing in the nuts and bolts of musical structure, with what he calls the simple facts (*die einfachen Tatbestände*), it is merely one stage in the larger process of critique, interpretation, and understanding, as *Verstehen*. "Analysis is more than merely 'the facts,'" he emphasises, "but is so only and solely by virtue of *going beyond* the simple facts by absorbing itself into them."[28]

Traditional approaches to aesthetics also have severe limitations, he acknowledges, dealing as they do in generalities which cannot grasp the particularity of the individual artwork.[29] In *Ästhetische Theorie* he recognizes that aesthetics has to immerse itself in the particularity of individual works. "There is no denying the progress made even in academic art scholarship through the demand for immanent analysis," he writes, "and the renunciation of methods concerned with everything but the artwork."[30] But, at the opposite extreme, immanent analysis risks being stuck with the absolute particularity of the individual work, the self-deceptive facticity of which becomes itself so abstract as to blind us to its sociohistorical content, to that which links the work to what lies outside it.

For Adorno, understanding (that is, *Verstehen* as "interpretative understanding") operates on several levels. It demands simultaneously a form of experience (*Erfahrung*) which immerses itself in the work as object of experience, while at the same time going beyond it as mere moment-to-moment experience (i.e., as *Erlebnis*, fragmented "lived experience") to an understanding of the immanent logic of the work. It is more than (1) simply grasping the facts of a piece, but has to do with (2), a level of understanding addressing the question of the "idea" or problem of the work in relation to its repressed social content. Adorno also appears to make a distinction between understanding as *Verstehen*, in the sense in which I have attempted to formulate it here, and *Verständnis*, by which he seems to mean a more limited sense of understanding as "intelligibility" or "comprehensibility," based on an acceptance of received formal norms and conventions.[31] "Understanding" of musical works is problematical in itself, as Adorno emphasizes, because it is tied up with what he calls the "riddle character" (or, as Hullot-Kentor translates it, the "enigmaticalness") of art. This is not something extraneous to art, but is, rather, constitutive. To understand an individual piece of music, he maintains, is to be absorbed into it, subsumed, to experience it from the inside. But this understanding is not the same thing as a solution to the riddle or enigma of the work. In *Ästhetische Theorie* he writes:

> Understanding art's enigmaticalness [riddle-character] is not equivalent to understanding specific artworks, which requires an objective experiential reenactment from within in the same sense in which the interpretation of a musical work means its faithful performance. Understanding is itself a problematic category in the face of art's enigmaticalness.[32]

To immerse oneself in the musical work in this way means also, of course, to fall completely under the spell of the work, and this precludes interpretative understanding (*Verstehen*). As he puts it: "Whoever seeks to understand artworks exclusively through the immanence of consciousness within them by this very measure fails to understand them and as such understanding [*Verständnis*] grows, so does the feeling of its insufficiency caught blindly in the spell of art, to which art's own truth content is opposed."[33] Thus, interpretative understanding requires that we demystify the work of certain of its enigmatic features, he argues, while its constitutive enigma remains nevertheless intact and persists in its resistance to understanding and interpretation.

But understanding as *Verstehen*, so Adorno insists, is also to be distinguished from immanent analysis of works of art, because of its emphasis on an experience (as *Erfahrung*) which also goes beyond the narrow confines of the self-enclosed world of the work to connect with what lies outside it. He recognizes that immanent analysis is undoubtedly a most important development for musicology, but also perceives an increasing complicity of analysis with positivism:

> work-immanent analysis, which is self-evident to artistic experience and its hostility to philology, unquestionably marks decisive progress in scholarship. Various branches of art scholarship, such as the academic study of music, only awoke from their pharisaical lethargy when they caught up with this method rather than busying themselves with everything except what concerns the structure of artworks. But in its adaptation by scholarship work-immanent analysis, by virtue of which scholarship hoped to cure itself of its alienness to art, has in turn taken on a positivist character that it wants to go beyond.[34]

And here we come to the crux of Adorno's resistance to analysis (at least, to the direction in which he saw analysis going): the problem of positivism (under which he subsumes empiricism),[35] and the rejection of art's enigma, its riddle-character. He accuses technical analysis of a narrowness of focus which excludes that which is left over after analysis — what he calls the remainder, the "surplus" (*Rest*) — as irrational, because not susceptible to its methods. The following passage, again from *Ästhetische Theorie*, clearly illustrates this:

> The strictness with which it concentrates on its object facilitates the disowning of everything in the artwork that — a fact to the second power — is not present, not simply the given facts of the matter. Even motivic-thematic musical analyses, though an improvement on glib commentaries, often suffer from the superstition that analyzing the work into basic materials and their transformations leads to the understanding of what, uncomprehended and correlative to the asceticism of the method, is gladly chalked up to a faulty irrationality. The work-immanent approach is indeed not all that removed from mindless craft, although its diagnoses are for the most part immanently correctable because they suffer from insufficient technical insight. Philosophical aesthetics has its focal point where work-immanent analysis never arrives.[36]

The Positivist Dispute and the Ambivalence
toward Analysis

Adorno's ambivalence toward technical analysis lies in the conviction that, left to its own devices and without the perspectives provided by philosophical aesthetics and critical sociology, technical analysis is in essence tautological, a form of identity theory which attempts, through empirical methods, to demonstrate that A = A, that a work *is* its structure, with no remainder. While it is far from my intention here to maintain that Adorno's ambivalence is to be explained in purely biographical-contextual terms, I would argue that some historical context is essential in order to illuminate his attitude toward technical analysis. This is because, although not without its contradictions, Adorno's position is founded on a very important idea which, precisely because of its difficulty, is frequently overlooked, ignored, or misunderstood: the idea of mediation (*Vermittlung*).

The notion of analysis as mere positivist fact-collection and the examination of data comes about, I suggest, as an inevitable aspect of the hostility toward empiricism and positivism in all their forms which characterized much of Adorno's writing during and after World War II. As a social scientist he had had little choice but to engage with all-pervading American empirical approaches to sociological and psychological research during his period of exile in the United States in the 1930s and 1940s, if only in order to get employment. Indeed, for a period he had even appeared to embrace such approaches (for example, in his contributions to *The Authoritarian Personality* (1950)[37] and his research into radio listeners on the Princeton Radio Research Project with Paul Lazarsfeld).[38] In fact, shortly after the return of members of the Frankfurt School to Germany in the early 1950s, Adorno presented a report on empirical sociology to a meeting convened on empirical research in the social sciences at the Institut für Sozialforschung, where he spoke in approving terms of the potentially enriching effect that such approaches could have on the German speculative tradition of social science. Within five years, however, he had changed his view completely, and had become highly critical of empiricism. Adorno's erstwhile research collaborator in America, the sociologist Paul Lazarsfeld, writing in 1970, makes the following charged observations about this turn:

> Adorno embarked on an endless series of articles dealing with the theme of theory and empirical research. These became more and more strident, and the invectives multiplied. Stupid, blind, insensitive, sterile became homeric attributes whenever the empiricist was mentioned . . . one paper followed another,

each reiterating the new theme. All have two characteristics in common. First the empiricist is a generalized other – no examples of concrete studies are given . . . Second, the futility of empirical research is not demonstrated by its products, but derived from the conviction that specific studies cannot make a contribution to the great aim of social theory to grasp society in its totality. Empirical research had become another fetish concealing the true nature of the contemporary social system.[39]

Lazarsfeld's strong criticisms had their origins in the sense of frustration he had felt in the late 1930s and early 1940s at what he saw as Adorno's "unscientific" and inconsistent use of empirical methods in the course of their collaboration on the Princeton Radio Project, and the application of what appeared to be unfounded value judgments.[40] For his part – looking back on this period in a radio talk he gave in 1968 – Adorno recognized the gulf between critical theory and empirical scientific methods that he had encountered in America, but insisted that his objection was not against empiricism as such, but against an all-pervading and uncritical belief at that time in the value of data and the dismissal of interpretative theory:

> My own position in the controversy between empirical and theoretical sociology . . . may be summarized roughly by saying that empirical investigations, even in the domain of cultural phenomena, are not only legitimate but essential. But they should not be hypostatized and treated as a universal key. Above all, they themselves must terminate in theoretical knowledge. Theory is not merely a vehicle that becomes superfluous as soon as the data are available.[41]

Against this background, I would argue, Adorno's ambivalence toward musical analysis is thrown into relief, and shown to be an aspect of his broader criticism of positivism and empiricism in the social sciences and in philosophy on the grounds of the lack of any concept of mediation. As we have seen, his crusade against positivism began in earnest in the 1950s, and culminated in the so-called "Positivist Dispute in German Sociology" in the 1960s. The latter was a series of public debates between, on one side, the Critical Theorists, led by Adorno and Jürgen Habermas, and, on the other side, the scientific rationalists, represented by Karl Popper (who insisted throughout that he was not a positivist). The debates were chaired by Ralf Dahrendorf, and lasted right through the 1960s, beginning in Tübingen in 1961 and ending with the publication of the proceedings, in 1969.[42] It is also relevant to remind ourselves of the musical background to these concerns, which could hardly have been kept in watertight compartments in Adorno's thinking. From its beginnings in the late 1940s Adorno had been closely involved with the Darmstadt Summer School. For the first half of the 1950s he had followed, at first with interest and then with concern, the experiments with multiple serialism which finally led him to write his critique of the movement in the article "Das Altern der neuen Musik" (1955),[43] around the time of his first spate of writings against positivism in philosophy and the social sciences. There then followed at Darmstadt the experiments with aleatoric techniques, after Cage's visit in 1958. In particular the experience of multiple serialism clearly left its mark on Adorno, and he could hardly avoid drawing the parallel with positivism. The strength of feeling against note-counting still shows through in the 1969 talk on analysis, where the parallels are obvious (although the further point is also being made that, given their resistance to traditional motivic-thematic types of analysis, both serial and aleatoric music have tended to encourage the kind of analytical response which constitutes a descriptive, positivistic "mere recording of facts"):

> It is precisely . . . when faced with aleatory and serial music, that analysis is frequently confused with the mere recording of facts [bloße Tatbestandsaufnahme]. This then results in the kind of absurdity once reserved for me at Darmstadt, where a composer . . . showed me a composition which seemed to me to be the purest nonsense [Galimathias]. When I asked him what this or that meant, what meaning, what kind of musical sense this or that particular phrase or development had, he simply referred me to correspondences between dynamic markings and pitches and so on – things which have nothing whatever to do with the musical phenomenon as such. This kind of description of the compositional process, of what the composer has done in the composition, is totally unproductive, just as are all those kinds of aesthetic examination which are unable to extract from a work any more than what has been put into it, so to speak – what it says in the Baedeker guide. All such approaches are doomed from the outset as worthless and irrelevant.[44]

The terms of the rejection of positivism are in both cases – music and the social sciences – remarkably similar. I would formulate Adorno's main objections in the following terms:

1 Positivism assumes an objectivity of method, based on a false understanding of the methodology of the natural sciences;
2 It also assumes the static givenness of the object of investigation, as "facts" or data to be collected and studied;
3 The viewpoint and agenda of the investigating subject (or agent) are not taken into account;
4 That which is not understood, and which is left over after empirical examination, the "remainder," is dismissed as irrational and of no significance;

5 Awareness of the relationship to the larger social totality is repressed, with resulting abstraction;

6 Positivism and empiricism are not critical methodologies, in that they do not reflect upon and make conscious their own underlying value-systems;

7 There is a lack of any concept of mediation.

I would like to support this connection with a further reference to *Ästhetische Theorie*:

> Today it is already evident that immanent analysis, which was once a weapon of artistic experience against philistinism, is being misused as a slogan to hold social reflection at a distance from an absolutized art. Without social reflection, however, the artwork is not to be understood in relation to that of which it constitutes one element, nor is it to be deciphered in terms of its own content. The blindness of the artwork is not only a corrective of the nature-dominating universal, it is also its correlative; as always the blind and the empty belong together in their abstractness. No particular in the artwork is legitimate without also becoming universal through its particularization.[45]

I do not wish to examine here the extent to which Adorno may have chosen to confuse the technical analysis of music with mere note-counting (for example, in the discussion of serial music), nor the degree to which he may have misunderstood Heinrich Schenker's theories (we know, of course, that he was critical of aspects of Schenker's analytical approach).[46] What is certain is that analysis was a very different exercise prior to the reception of Schenker's work in the United States and Britain in the 1970s (in Germany Schenker never had the same degree of influence, possibly due to his association with National Socialism). While it is possible that Adorno might have been justified in dismissing much of what passed for analysis in the 1950s and 1960s as positivist stocktaking or mere fact-collecting (apart, that is, from Schenkerian analysis, which he also acknowledged was "distinguished . . . by its extraordinary precision, subtlety and insistence"),[47] I suggest, nevertheless, that the real motive for his pursuing the debates over positivism and empiricism into musical analysis was in order to draw a strong contrast between earlier forms of analysis (including his own earlier examples, of which he was also critical)[48] and his type of what could be called "hermeneutic" analysis. This had occupied him particularly in connection with his Mahler book[49] at the beginning of the 1960s, with the unfinished fragments, *Beethoven: Philosophie der Musik*, and especially with his *Ästhetische Theorie*. It leads, I suggest, to a dialectical theory of form which encapsulates his concept of the immanent mediation of musical works, and which therefore has implications for analysis within the larger context of his sociology and aesthetics of music.

The Larger Theoretical Context: Toward a Dialectical Theory of Form

So far I have emphasized the relationship between analysis and aesthetics in Adorno in order to point to what I see as a certain undialectical contradictoriness in evidence in his views on analysis. I will now bring the discussion round to consider the relationship of analysis to aesthetics and sociology within his approach in more truly dialectical terms. I argue that the hiatuses remain, but that it is necessary to be able to envisage the direction of Adorno's thinking here at a theoretical level, even if his actual analyses usually fail to live up to the model. Of particular importance is his concept of *second reflection* (*zweite Reflektion*). As we have seen, Adorno argues that while aesthetics must immerse itself in the particularity of individual works through analysis in order to overcome its ignorance of art, it is nevertheless a different kind of activity to analysis. The concerns of aesthetics, Adorno insists, are to uncover the truth content of the work: "Second reflection must push the complex of facts that work-immanent analysis establishes, and in which it has its limit, beyond itself and penetrate to the truth content by means of emphatic critique."[50]

The concept of "truth content" in Adorno is somewhat obscure and elusive, and I do not intend to discuss it directly here (having devoted considerable space to it elsewhere).[51] It is the notion of "second reflection" on which I wish to concentrate at this stage, as it is fundamental to Adorno's theoretical position and enables us then to view the idea of truth content from a different perspective. A first level of reflection would be one where material is uncovered, a content is analyzed, relations are identified, a factual account of a structure can be given. I suggest that the aim of such an analysis is to establish the technical *consistency* (*Stimmigkeit*) of a work, its correspondence to its dominating idea as unity of form and content (*Form/Inhalt*). A level of second reflection involves both critique and interpretation, not only in terms of the inner relations of the closed world of the musical work revealed through immanent analysis, which is an aspect of "first reflection," but in terms of the relations between the work and its social and historical context – a context which also constitutes, if I understand Adorno correctly, the work's structure, as socially and historically mediated *content* (*Gehalt*). At this level works become contradictory and, indeed, ideological in their rejection of the outside world and their retreat into their own sphere. It is the "correspondence" between the inner structural relations of the work and the outer social relations within which it functions which is the focus of Adorno's interpretative method, and which is, of course, the bone of contention. It is the sociohistorical content of the work mediated through its form which Adorno identifies, as far as one can understand him here, as the truth content of the work, and which is thus the *telos* of his hermeneutics. The truth content he sees as a kind of "unconscious writing of history," the repressed social content of the work, sedimented in its structure. It is the deciphering of this content that gives the work its meaning, through relating it to its social other. The work is not merely identical to itself, to its own inner structure, as the tautologous logic of identity theory (i.e., A = A) would require. Neither is it simplistically to be identified totally with what lies outside it, as its social context and social function. When he writes in *Ästhetische Theorie* that "[c]ontemplation that limits itself to the artwork fails it," and goes on to say: "[i]ts inner construction requires, in however mediated a fashion, what is itself not art,"[52] he is indicating a sedimentation of social content within the work which cannot be identified and deciphered by immanent analysis alone.

But how are we to understand the concept of *mediation* (*Vermittlung*) here, and how is it to be interpreted in the analysis of actual works? I have elsewhere characterized Adorno's theoretical method as incorporating three interacting levels: that is, immanent analysis, sociological critique, and philosophical-historical interpretation.[53] Most problematical within his approach remains, however, the relation between analysis and the other two levels of his dialectical method, the sociological and the philosophical. This hiatus, which is to be encountered also in Adorno's analyses of individual works, has given rise to frequent criticism. Again, as usual, Dahlhaus puts his finger on the problem. In his essay "The Musical Work of Art as a Subject of Sociology" he argues that:

> the blind spots are not simply an accidental defect. Rather, the contrast between the methods – between the formal-analytically individualising and the sociologically generalising procedure – returns as a flaw in the individual analyses, though Adorno was able at times, by dint of great effort, to reconcile the opposing views by force. And the verbal analogies perform the function of hiding a gap which the arguments could not close.[54]

The difficulty with Adorno's conception of mediation, and at the same time its subtlety, is that the externality to which he points, the heteronomous social other apparently excluded by the blind autonomy of the work, is conceived as simultaneously constituting the material structure of the work itself – the content of the work, as *Gehalt*, but in refracted, mediated form. As he puts it in "Thesen zur Kunstsoziologie" (1967): "according to Hegel, mediation is in the object itself, not a relation between the object and those to whom it is brought."[55] The implications of this are far-reaching, and lead to the most elegant and ingenious trope. It means that the second reflection of sociological critique and philosophical interpretation, which Adorno argues is both separate from and, at the same time, dependent upon the first reflection of immanent analysis, has its model *within* the process of mediation which constitutes the technical structure of the work itself. That is to say, what Adorno calls the authentic work contains this process of critical self-reflection within itself as an immanent, material process. I have tried to identify this process at a theoretical level as what I have called Adorno's dual-level concept of form. For Adorno, the theory of form is expressed as an immanent dialectic of musical material constituting the mediated structure of the individual musical work as a process of material self-reflection. This occurs on two interrelated levels: the normative and universal level; and secondly the critical and particular level. The normative, universal level sees form as preformed, historically mediated material. Norms like genres, formal types, tonal systems and schemata, tuning systems, style systems, compositional techniques are part of a historically mediated sedimentation of society. The critical, particular level considers form as a mediated structure of the individual musical work. The recontextualization of historical material as critical second reflection, through deviation from schemata and negation of historical norms, is all connected with the individual work as a form of cognition and a force field of tensions. This dialectical interaction between the two levels brings together a number of important concepts in Adorno's theory of form as a process of music-immanent self-reflection. Central among them are the concepts of musical material, mediation, and form, and their interaction is to be understood as constituting the work's compositional structure as a dynamic coherence or context of meaning (*dynamischer Sinnzusammenhang*). The work is seen as *authentic* to the degree that its structure is the outcome of this inner dialectic. In the case of the modernist work, this is a conflictual interaction as a force-field of tensions left unresolved by the work's form; however, the model also applies in retrospect to autonomous music since the beginning of what Adorno calls "the bourgeois period," and I see no reason why it should not also apply to popular music, particularly when the music adopts a critical and self-reflective stance toward the culture industry. The authentic work, for Adorno, forms a *critique*, and is thus a mode of cognition (*Erkenntnis*) because within itself it constitutes, in material terms, a form of critical self-reflection. That is to say, the particular level of the work's individual structure also contains an interaction with the general level of historically handed-down musical material – a kind of Saussurean *langue–parole* interrelationship between particular and universal (by this connection I do not intend to suggest that music is a language, but merely that it is language-like).[56] The material is itself socially and historically mediated, and is understood by Adorno as "an objectivity which has forgotten its previous origins in subjectivity." It is not the so-called "natural stuff" of sound, but is culturally preformed – that is, mediated – as, for example, schemata, formal types, and genres, and can also be understood to include tuning systems, tonal systems, idioms, style systems, and so on. To the extent that the structure of the individual work is a critical reflection upon the historically preformed material (which is not the same for all historical periods), the work may be considered to "contain its own analysis," to use Adorno's own phrase. I would suggest that it is this self-contained analysis that needs to be revealed by the process of immanent technical analysis. But to the extent that the handed-down material is simultaneously both historically/socially mediated *and* structurally mediated as the form of the work, it is also meaningful. That is to say, the correspondences between inner and outer are actually built in to the structure of the work itself, but are in need of the conceptual mediation of sociological critique and philosophical-historical interpretation for their elucidation. Critical interpretation in this sense would aim to recover the music's sociohistorical content through the markings of its second reflection as form – that is to say, the truth content of the work.

Contained here is a "theory of form," in the sense that it is generalizable. What differentiates it from versions of the traditional *Formenlehre*, occupied primarily with generalized static formal types, is that Adorno's critical theory of form deals in dynamic, dialectical categories and not in invariants. That is to say, apparently static formal norms are seen as part of a constantly shifting, historically changing musical material, and this (that is, the material) is to be found only in the dynamic context of the individual musical work, in the process of focusing, dissolution, and refocusing that constitutes the form of the work. The barest geometry of Adorno's theory of form is the dialectical interaction of universal and particular, mediated within the structure of the work – a relation which is in need of further mediation through concepts in order to be understood. Thus the second reflection which is the structure of the individual work calls for a corresponding second reflection in aesthetics. In this Adorno shows himself yet again to be a Hegelian:

> If anywhere, Hegel's theory of the movement of the concept has its legitimacy in aesthetics; it is concerned with the dynamic relation of the universal and the particular, which does not impute the universal to the particular externally but seeks it rather in the force fields of the particular itself . . . Whenever artworks on their way toward concretion polemically eliminate the universal,

whether as a genre, a type, an idiom, or a formula, the excluded is maintained in them through its negation; this state of affairs is constitutive of the modern.[57]

Thus, although generalizable and presentable in the kind of terms I have employed here, the theory constitutes what Adorno would call "a material theory of musical form" (*eine materiale Formenlehre der Musik*), in that its categories, while identifiable at an abstract level of universality for purposes of theoretical discussion, are only really present as mediated in concrete material terms within the particularity of the individual work. This is not to say, however, that these mediated, material categories do not also function as norms of compositional practice at any particular historical period, and thereby acquire a certain abstract currency (and indeed, the effect of academic compositional exercises and training in the process of ensuring that such norms are disseminated and internalized by composers should also not be underestimated). What it does imply, nevertheless, is that the manifestation of these norms as compositional material is in individual works, and that the authentic work (in Adorno's terms) engages with them critically as material categories in a state of flux and not as static, abstract norms to be accepted unquestioningly. That the immanent critique exercised by particular artworks is a critique of the unstable universality of the handed-down material as manifested in other works is emphasized by Adorno when he states categorically that "the most authentic works are critiques of past works."[58] And furthermore, if the task of analysis can be construed as the structural mapping of this inner critique which is the work itself, then the task of aesthetics is to interpret it by relating particular to universal, deviation to schema, and the unfamiliar to the familiar, through the identification of shifting norms and the extent of their negation. As he puts it: "Aesthetics becomes normative by articulating such a critique."[59]

Adorno writes in his draft of an introduction to *Ästhetische Theorie*: "Artworks derive from the world of things in their preformed material as in their techniques; there is nothing in them that did not also belong to this world and nothing that could be wrenched away from this world at less than the price of its death."[60] Indeed, it is precisely this transit of material derived from the outer world of things into the inner world of the hermetically sealed artwork, a movement from heteronomy to autonomy, that constitutes its mediation (and, in a sense, its death): a transformation, as a complete change of state from one sphere to another, where everything is different and yet residues of externality remain, as what Adorno calls "sedimented history and society." There is, however, no one-to-one correspondence to be identified between these two spheres, and the tenuous threads connecting outer to inner, and which allow concepts to ply between the two in the dialectics of

interpretation, easily disappear from view. The work then becomes the labyrinth within which we lose the thread which enables us to move back and forth between one world and the other. A complete rift between the work of art and the world outside results, allowing us to treat the work (and in particular the musical work) as an abstract, free-standing unity "in and for itself." This has its advantages – namely, that the work can be addressed as technical structure, as sets of internal relationships, and as data, without the distraction of externality. But the problem of musical analysis as Adorno sees it is, in essence, how to go beyond the immediate facticity of the individual work through critique and interpretation, while remaining in constant touch with it as empirical structure. The limits of analysis lie not in what analysis succeeds in doing well, its technical achievements and its detailed account of the work as structure, but in the questionable belief either that this is all there is, and that the rest is irrationality and superstition, or that the semiotics of music can be plotted with all the positivist precision and apparent directness of an Ordnance Survey map. What is generally lacking in musical analysis is a sufficiently complex and sophisticated concept of mediation. If such a concept of mediation is to be discovered anywhere, then I suggest it is through a systematic reading of Adorno's aesthetics as a material theory of musical form.

Notes

1 "Was von dem was ich schreibe übrigbleibt ist meinem Wissen wie meiner Macht entzogen, aber auf eines erhebe ich Anspruch: daß ich die Sprache der Musik so verstehe wie die Helden in Märchen die Sprache der Vögel verstehen." Adorno, unpublished note in the possession of the Theodor W. Adorno Archiv, Frankfurt am Main, cited in Henri Lonitz, "Nachbemerkung des Herausgebers," Theodor W. Adorno and Alban Berg, *Briefwechsel 1925–1935*, ed. Henri Lonitz (Frankfurt am Main: Suhrkamp, 1997): 364. I am indebted to Henri Lonitz for drawing my attention to this extract.

2 "Das Hören, das dem integralen Kompositionsideal gerecht würde, ließe am ehesten als strukturelles sich bezeichnen. Der Rat, mehrschichtig zu hören, das musikalisch Erscheinende nicht nur als Gegenwärtiges sondern auch in seinem Verhältnis zu Vergangenem und Kommendem der gleichen Komposition, hat bereits ein wesentliches Moment dieses Hörideals benannt." Adorno, "Anweisungen zum Hören neuer Musik," *Der getreue Korrepetitor* (1963), *Gesammelte Schriften*, 15, ed. Rolf Tiedemann (Frankfurt am Main: Suhrkamp, 1976): 245.

3 A shorter version of this essay was originally given as the keynote address for the conference *Adorno and Analysis* held at the University of Bristol on February 20, 1997.

4   Carl Dahlhaus, "The Musical Work of Art as a Subject of Sociology," *Schoenberg and the New Music*, trans. Derrick Puffett and Alfred Clayton (Cambridge: Cambridge University Press, 1987): 243.

5   "Technische Analyse ist allerorten vorausgesetzt und oft dargelegt, bedarf aber des Zusatzes der Deutung im Kleinsten, wenn sie über die geisteswissenschaftliche Bestandsaufnahme hinausgehen, das Verhältnis der Sache zur Wahrheit ausdrücken soll." Adorno, *Philosophie der neuen Musik, Gesammelte Schriften*, 12, ed. Rolf Tiedemann (Frankfurt am Main: Suhrkamp, 1975): 33 (my trans.). Compare *Philosophy of Modern Music*, trans. Anne G. Mitchell and Wesley V. Blomster (London: Sheed & Ward, 1973): 26.

6   "Keine Analyse taugt etwas, die nicht in der Frage nach dem Wahrheitsgehalt der Werke terminiert." Adorno, "Zum Problem der musikalischen Analyse" (Lecture given at the Hochschule für Musik und darstellende Kunst, Frankfurt am Main, 24 February 1969; the tape recording and my transcription of it are in the Adorno Archiv, Frankfurt am Main, and the text is to be published for the first time in German in the archive's journal, *Adornoblätter*, in 2001). I published a translation of this lecture in the journal *Music Analysis* in 1982: see Adorno, "On the Problem of Musical Analysis," trans. and introduced by Max Paddison, *Music Analysis*, 1/2 (1982): 177.

7   Ibid., "den Wahrheitsgehalt treffen kann natürlich nur Kritik"; see "On the Problem of Musical Analysis," 177.

8   See Max Paddison, "Adorno's *Aesthetic Theory*," *Music Analysis*, 6/3 (Oct. 1987): 355–77. Also, Max Paddison, *Adorno, Modernism and Mass Culture* (London: Kahn & Averill, 1996): 45–80.

9   Adorno wrote a considerable number of analyses of individual works, especially of pieces by Schönberg, Berg, and Webern. For a full list of these, see the bibliography in Max Paddison, *Adorno's Aesthetics of Music*, in particular pp. 333–51.

10 See particularly Alastair Williams, *New Music and the Claims of Modernity* (Aldershot: Ashgate, 1997).

11 See especially Carl Dahlhaus, *Schoenberg and the New Music*, trans. Derrick Puffett and Alfred Clayton (Cambridge: Cambridge University Press, 1987).

12 See Peter Bürger, *Theory of the Avant-garde*, trans. Michael Shaw (Manchester: Manchester University Press, 1984; original German edn. 1974).

13 See Max Paddison, *Adorno's Aesthetics of Music* (1993): 218–78, for an account of Adorno's philosophy of music history.

14 See, for example, *Popular Music 2: Theory and Method*, a yearbook edited by Richard Middleton and David Horn (Cambridge: Cambridge University Press, 1982).

15 See Max Paddison, "The Critique Criticized: Adorno and Popular Music," in Richard Middleton and David Horn (eds.), *Popular Music 2: Theory and Method* (Cambridge: Cambridge University Press, 1982): 200–18. Also Bernard Gendron, "Theodor Adorno meets the Cadillacs," in T. Modelski (ed.), *Studies in Entertainment: Critical Approaches to Mass Culture* (Bloomington: Indiana University Press, 1986): 18–36.

16 "Many of the present generation of culture theorists took part in the radical movements of the sixties, which turned to rock 'n roll as their primary means of cultural expression and turned to the Frankfurt School for their first lessons in cultural theory." Bernard Gendron, "Theodor Adorno meets the Cadillacs," 10.

17 See Richard Middleton, *Studying Popular Music* (Milton Keynes: Open University Press, 1990). As well as situating popular music studies in a sociological and cultural studies context, Middleton examines analytical approaches to popular music. He also offers a penetrating critique of Adorno's thinking on popular music and mass culture.

18 See Claus-Steffen Mahnkopf, "Adorno und die musikalische Analytik," in Richard Klein and Claus-Steffen Mahnkopf (eds.), *Mit den Ohren denken: Adornos Philosophie der Musik* (Frankfurt am Main: Suhrkamp, 1998): 240–7.

19 See Ludwig Holtmeier, "Nicht Kunst? Nicht Wissenschaft? Zur Lage der Musiktheorie," *Musik & Ästhetik* I, 1/2 (March 1997): 131 n. 24.

20 See Diether de la Motte, "Adornos musikalische Analysen," in Otto Kolleritsch (ed.), *Adorno und die Musik* (Graz: Universal Edition, 1979): 52–63.

21 See Ludwig Holtmeier, Richard Klein et al., "Editorial," *Musik & Ästhetik*, 1/2 (Mar. 1997): 5–12, for an attempt to influence this situation in German musicology.

22 Willi Reich, *Alban Berg: Mit Bergs eigenen Schriften und Beiträgen von Theodor Wiesengrund-Adorno und Ernst Krenek* (Vienna: Herbert Reichner, 1937).

23 T. W. Adorno, *Alban Berg: Der Meister des kleinsten Übergangs* (Vienna: Verlag Elisabeth Lafite/Österreichischer Bundesverlag, 1968). *Berg: Master of the Smallest Link*, trans. Juliane Brand and Christopher Hailey (Cambridge: Cambridge University Press, 1991).

24 T. W. Adorno, *Ästhetische Theorie, Gesammelte Schriften*, 7, ed. Rolf Tiedemann and Gretel Adorno (Frankfurt am Main: Suhrkamp, 1970). Translated as: (i) *Aesthetic Theory*, trans. Christian Lenhardt (London: Routledge, 1984); and (ii) *Aesthetic Theory*, trans. Robert Hullot-Kentor (London: Athlone Press, 1997). The latter translation is the one used in this essay.

25 T. W. Adorno, *Beethoven: Philosophie der Musik*, ed. Rolf Tiedemann (Frankfurt am Main: Suhrkamp Verlag, 1993). *Beethoven: The Philosophy of Music*, trans. Edmund Jephcott (Cambridge: Polity Press, 1998).

26 See note 4.

27 T. W. Adorno, "On the Problem of Musical Analysis," 171. ("Man kann sagen, daß der Untergrund der Stimmung musikalischer Analyse gegenüber nicht gerade freundlich ist . . . Etwas sich genau ansehen . . . heißt aber in Wirklichkeit soviel wie analysieren.")

28 Ibid., 177. ("Sie [Analyse] ist aber mehr als das, was bloß der Fall ist, nur und allein dadurch, daß sie über die einfachen Tatbestände, so wie sie vorliegen, hinausgeht, indem sie sich in sie versenkt.")

29 T. W. Adorno, *Aesthetic Theory*, trans. Robert Hullot-Kentor (London: Athlone Press, 1997): 180. See *Gesammelte Schriften*, 7: 268.

30 Ibid., 180. ("Der Fortschritt sogar der akademischen Kunstwissenschaft in der Forderung immanenter Analyse, der Lossage von einer Verfahrungsweise, die um alles an der Kunst sich kümmerte außer um diese, ist nicht zu bestreiten." *Gesammelte Schriften*, 7: 268.)

31 See Max Paddison, *Adorno's Aesthetics of Music*, 213–16, for a more detailed account of the concepts of *Verstehen, Verständnis, Erfahrung,* and *Erlebnis.*

32 Ibid., 121. ("Nicht ist der Rätselcharakter der Kunst dasselbe, wie ihre Gebilde zu verstehen, nämlich sie objektiv, in der Erfahrung von innen her, nochmals gleichsam hervorzubringen, so wie die musikalische Terminologie es anzeigt, der ein Stück interpretieren soviel heißt, wie es sinngemäß spielen. Verstehen selbst ist angesichts des Rätselcharakters eine problematische Kategorie." *Gesammelte Schriften*, 7: 184.)

33 Ibid., 121. ("Wer Kunstwerke durch Immanenz des Bewußtseins in ihnen versteht, versteht sie auch gerade nicht, und je mehr Verständnis anwächst, desto mehr auch das Gefühl seiner Unzulänglichkeit, blind in dem Bann der Kunst, dem ihr eigener Wahrheitsgehalt entgegen ist." *Gesammelte Schriften*, 7: 184.)

34 Ibid., 348. ("Diese [werkimmanente Analyse], der künstlerischen Erfahrung gegen die Philologie, selbstverständlich, markiert fraglos in der Wissenschaft einen entschiedenen Fortschritt. Zweige der Kunstwissenschaft, wie der mit Musik akademisch befaßte, erwachten erst dann aus ihrer pharisäischen Lethargie, wenn sie jene Methode nachholten, anstatt mit allem sich abzugeben außer mit Strukturfragen der Kunstwerke. Aber in ihrer Adaptation durch die Wissenschaft hat die werkimmanente Analyse, kraft deren jene von ihrer Kunstfremdheit sich kurieren wollte, ihrerseits Züge des Positivismus angenommen, über den sie hinausmöchte." *Gesammelte Schriften*, 7: 517.)

35 The term "positivism" calls for definition here, as it is often used loosely. It was originally employed by Auguste Comte (1798–1857), the founding father of the discipline of sociology, which he modelled on the empirical principles of the natural sciences of his day, in opposition to theology and metaphysics, as a rational science of society. His main works are *Cours de philosophie positive*, 6 vols. (Paris: 1830–42) and *Système de politique positive*, 4 vols. (Paris, 1848–54). His aim was what he called a "social physics." Comte writes: "the first characteristic of the positive philosophy is that it regards all phenomena as subjected to invariable natural *laws*. Our business is . . . to pursue an accurate discovery of these laws, with a view to reducing them to the smallest possible number." Comte, cited in Kenneth Thompson (ed.), *Auguste Comte: The Foundation of Sociology* (London: Nelson, 1976): 43.

36 T. W. Adorno, *Aesthetic Theory*, trans. Hullot-Kentor, 348. ("Die Strenge, mit der sie auf die Sache sich konzentriert, erleicht die Absage an all das im Kunstwerk, was darin nicht, Faktum zweiter Potenz, vorliegt, der Fall ist. Auch musikalisch kranken motivisch-thematische Analysen, heilsam gegen das Geschwafel, häufig an dem Aberglauben, sie hätten durch Zerlegung in Grundmaterialien und ihre Abwandlungen bereits begriffen, was dann, unbegriffen und korrelativ zu solcher Askese, gern der schlechten Irrationalität eingeräumt wird.

Werkimmanente Betrachtung ist nicht gar zu fern von sturer Handwerkerei, wenngleich deren Befunde meist immanent, als unzulängliche technische Einsicht, korrigibel wären. Philosophische Ästhetik, in enger Fühlung, mit der Idee werkimmanenter Analyse, hat doch ihre Stelle dort, wohin diese nicht gelangt." *Gesammelte Schriften*, 7: 517–18.)

37 T. W. Adorno, Else Frenkel-Brunswik, Daniel J. Levinson, and R. Nevitt Sanford, *The Authoritarian Personality* (New York: Harper, 1950).

38 T. W. Adorno, "A Social Critique of Radio Music," *Kenyon Review*, 7 (1945): 208–17 (original in English), omitted from *Gesammelte Schriften*. To be republished by the Theodor W. Adorno Archiv, Frankfurt, as part of the book planned by Adorno as *Current of Music: Elements of a Radio Theory*.

39 Paul Lazarsfeld, *Main Trends in Sociology* (London: Allen & Unwin, 1973; orig. edn. 1970): 60–1.

40 See also Martin Jay, *The Dialectical Imagination* (London: Heinemann, 1973): 223, for an account of the friction between Lazarsfeld and Adorno.

41 T. W. Adorno, "Scientific Experiences of a European Scholar in America," in *Critical Models*, trans. Henry W. Pickford (New York: Columbia University Press, 1998): 228. See "Wissenschaftliche Erfahrungen in Amerika" (1968), *Stichworte: Kritische Modelle 2* (1969), *Gesammelte Schriften*, 10.2 (1977): 702–40.

42 T. W. Adorno, Hans Albert, Ralf Dahrendorf, Jürgen Habermas, Harald Pilot, Karl R. Popper, *Der Positivismusstreit in der deutschen Soziologie* (Berlin: Hermann Luchterhand, 1969). Translated as *The Positivist Dispute in German Sociology*, trans. Glyn Adey and David Frisby (London: Heinemann, 1976).

43 T. W. Adorno, "Das Altern der neuen Musik," *Der Monat* (May 1955); an expanded version appeared in *Dissonanzen* (Göttingen: Vandenhoek & Ruprecht, 1956); *Gesammelte Schriften*, 14 (1973, 1980): 143–67. Translated as: (i) "Modern Music is Growing Old," trans. from a French version by Rollo Myers, *The Score* (Dec. 1956): 18–29; (ii) "The Aging of the New Music," trans. Robert Hullot-Kentor and Friedrich Will, *Telos*, 77 (1988): 95–116.

44 T. W. Adorno, "On the Problem of Musical Analysis," 180–1. ("Gerade hier der aleatorischen und seriellen Musik gegenüber wird Analyse vielfach mit bloßer Tatbestandsaufnahme verwechselt, und es kommt dann zu dem Unsinn, der mir einmal in Darmstadt reserviert wurde, als mir ein Komponist . . . eine Komposition zeigte, die mir der reinste Galimathias schien, und als ich ihn fragte, was denn also dies oder jenes solle, welchen Sinn – welchen musikalischen Sinn – diese oder jene Phrase oder Entwicklung hätte, wies er mich einfach auf Korrespondenzen zwischen Pausen und Noten, zwischen dynamischen Zeichen und Höhen und ähnliche Dingen hin, die in das musikalische Phänomen überhaupt nicht eingehen. Eine solche Beschreibung dessen, was der Komponist gemacht hat, ist völlig unfruchtbar, wie denn überhaupt alle Arten von ästhetischer Betrachtung, die nicht mehr an einem Werk ergeben als das, was sozusagen hereingesteckt worden ist, was im Baedecker steht, von vornherein zur Gleichgültigkeit und zur Irrelevanz vorurteilt sind." "Zum Problem der musikalischen Analyse.")

45   T. W. Adorno, *Aesthetic Theory*, trans. Hullot-Kentor, 180. ("Heute bereits ist erkennbar, daß die immanente Analyse, einmal Waffe künstlerische Erfahrung gegen die Banausie, als Parole mißbraucht wird, um von der verabsolutierten Kunst die gesellschaftliche Besinnung fernzuhalten. Ohne sie ist aber weder das Kunstwerk im Verhältnis zu dem zu begreifen, worin es selber ein Moment abgibt, noch dem eigenen Gehalt nach zu entziffern. Die Blindheit des Kunstwerks ist nicht nur Korrektiv des naturbeherrschend Allgemeinen sondern dessen Korrelat; wie allemal das Blinde und das Leere, abstrakt, zu einander gehören. Kein Besonderes im Kunstwerk ist legitim, das nicht durch seine Besonderung auch allgemein würde." *Gesammelte Schriften*, 7: 269.)

46   See T. W. Adorno, "On the Problem of Musical Analysis," 173–5, for Adorno's views of Schenkerian analysis.

47   Ibid., 174.

48   Ibid., 184: "what I say here as criticism of analysis in general also applies without reservation as a criticism of all the countless analyses that I myself have ever produced" ("was ich zur Kritik der Analyse hier sage, gilt vorbehaltlos auch als Kritik der schließlich ja sehr zahllosen-zahlreichen Analysen, die ich selbst vorgelegt habe." "Zum Problem der musikalischen Analyse.")

49   T. W. Adorno, *Mahler. Eine musikalische Physiognomik* (Frankfurt am Main: Suhrkamp, 1960); *Gesammelte Schriften*, 13 (1971): 149–319. *Mahler: A Musical Physiognomy*, trans. Edmund Jephcott (Chicago and London: University of Chicago Press, 1992).

50   T. W. Adorno, *Aesthetic Theory*, trans. Hullot-Kentor, 348. ("Ihre zweite Reflexion muß die Sachverhalte, auf die jene Analyse stößt, über sich hinaustreiben und durch emphatische Kritik zum Wahrheitsgehalt dringen." *Gesammelte Schriften*, 7: 518.)

51   For my attempts to give some account of Adorno's concept of "truth content," see "Adorno's *Aesthetic Theory*," *Music Analysis*, 6/3 (Oct. 1987): 355–77. This article put forward an interpretative model for Adorno's aesthetics which was expanded to provide the structure for my book, *Adorno's Aesthetics of Music* (1993), and which was revised as "Adorno's Aesthetics of Modernism" in *Adorno, Modernism and Mass Culture* (1996).

52   Ibid., 348. ("Verfehlt wird das Kunstwerk von der Betrachtung, die darauf sich beschränkt. Seine innere Zusammensetzung bedarf, wie sehr auch vermittelt, dessen, was nicht seinerseits Kunst ist." *Gesammelte Schriften*, 7: 518.)

53   Max Paddison, *Adorno's Aesthetics of Music*, 59–64; also *Adorno, Modernism and Mass Culture*, 68–80.

54   Carl Dahlhaus, "The Musical Work of Art as a Subject of Sociology," *Schoenberg and the New Music*, 244.

55   T. W. Adorno, "Theses on the Sociology of Art," trans. Brian Trench, *Birmingham Working Papers in Cultural Studies*, 2 (1972): 128 (trans. modified). ("Vermittlung ist ihm [Hegel] zufolge die in der Sache selbst, nicht eine zwischen der Sache und denen, an welche sie herangebracht wird." "Thesen zur

Kunstsoziologie" (1967), in *Ohne Leitbild: Parva Aesthetica* (1967–8), *Gesammelte Schriften*, 10.1: 374.)

56 Ibid., 89.

57 T. W. Adorno, *Aesthetic Theory*, trans. Hullot-Kentor, 351. ("Wenn irgendwo, hat die Hegelsche Lehre von der Bewegung des Begriffs in der Ästhetik ihr Recht; sie hat es zu tun mit einer Wechselwirkung des Allgemeinen und Besonderen, die das Allgemeine nicht dem Besonderen von außen imputiert sondern in dessen Kraftzentren aufsucht . . . Wo immer Kunstwerke, auf der Bahn ihrer Konkretion Allgemeines: eine Gattung, einen Typus, ein Idiom, eine Formel polemisch eliminieren, bleibt das Ausgeschiedene durch seine Negation in ihnen enthalten; dieser Sachverhalt ist konstitutiv für die Moderne." *Gesammelte Schriften*, 7: 521–2.)

58 T. W. Adorno, *Aesthetic Theory*, trans. Hullot-Kentor, 359. ("so sind die authentischen Werke Kritiken der vergangenen." *Gesammelte Schriften*, 7: 533.)

59 Ibid., 359 (trans. modified). ("Ästhetik wird normative, indem sie solche Kritik artikuliert," ibid., 533.)

60 T. W. Adorno, *Aesthetic Theory*, trans. Hullot-Kentor, 133–4. There is a typographical error in Hullot-Kentor's translation, where "preformed" is rendered "performed." ("Kunstwerke stammen aus der Dingwelt durch ihr präformiertes Material wie durch ihre Verfahrungsweisen; nichts in ihnen, was ihr nichts auch angehörte, und nichts, was nicht um den Preis seines Todes der Dingwelt entrissen würde." *Gesammelte Schriften*, 7: 201–2.)

10

Adorno and the New Musicology

Rose Rosengard
Subotnik

[I]t is not just the disciplinary integrity of musicology that has become problematic; it is, to put it bluntly, the relationship between musicology and the rest of the universe.

Nicholas Cook and Mark Everist, *Rethinking Music*, p. vii.

American musicologists should have found Adorno sooner. Although numerous experts on non-musical topics have written on music in the twentieth century – works by Langer, Lévi-Strauss, Barthes, Said, Attali, Žižek, and Kittler come to mind – Adorno started earlier[1] and wrote incomparably more. Yet in the English-speaking countries, Adorno's writings on music languished for decades on library shelves with seemingly no borrowers and virtually no translators. My own first full-length article on Adorno's musical writings, which appeared in 1976, had only a handful of antecedents, and equally few immediate successors in English.

Nor, for that matter, did American musicology seem open at that time to large-scale redefinitions of any kind. Despite an increase in the number of non-traditional musical studies published from the mid-1970s on, some drawing upon Adorno,[2] despite percolating pockets of dissatisfaction during the 1980s,[3] and despite high-placed expressions of hope in 1985 that musicology was "on the move" (Kerman 1985: 229), the ground rules of English-language musicology in the 1980s were not fundamentally different from those of the 1960s.

Then, as if out of nowhere, came disconcerting changes. At the fall 1990 Annual Meeting of the American Musicological Society, in Oakland, California, scholars of all leanings were hit by an unprecedently strong blast of the critical theory that had been altering the study of literature at American universities for more than two decades.[4] A year later appeared the work that probably more than any other has come to epitomize the movement now known as the New Musicology: Susan McClary's *Feminine Endings* (currently in its fifth printing). More than any other, this book acted as the lodestone that pulled numerous others into the start of a perceptible new movement: books by Kramer (1990), Abbate (1991), Shepherd (1991), myself (1991), the philosopher Goehr (1992), Tomlinson (1993), and Leppert (1995); collections such as those edited by Bergeron and Bohlman (1992), Solie (1993), and Brett, Wood, and Thomas (1994); and articles in new journals such as the *Cambridge Opera Journal* and *repercussions*. The same year, Joseph Kerman singled out five rising scholars – Susan McClary, Richard Taruskin,[5] Carolyn Abbate, Gary Tomlinson, and Lawrence Kramer – as representatives of "a discipline undergoing a classic paradigm shift" (Kerman 1991: 142).

Of course, the changes did not come out of nowhere. Even before the 1980s, well before the scholars associated with the new paradigm gained prominence, wide recognition had been accorded major scholars, such as Leonard Meyer, Joseph Kerman, Charles Rosen, Edward Cone, Maynard Solomon, and Leo Treitler, whose work had altered, broadened, or challenged various expectations of their field from within.

Adorno's impact, by comparison, was late and uneven. Although a number of American and British scholars (outside music as well as within) would take varying degrees of interest in Adorno's work on music during the 1990s,[6] for many more, his effect was unprivileged or indirect. Kerman makes no more than passing reference to Adorno in "American Musicology in the 1990s." *Rethinking Music*, an imposing record of English-language musicology in the 1990s, includes Adorno in a group of musical scholars whom the field now treats as "authorities" beyond the need (and possibly reach) of "question or challenge" (Cook and Everist 1999: v). Yet of the twenty-four scholars represented in this book, only five make even fleeting mention of Adorno; and of those only one draws in a substantive way on his ideas (Samson 1999: 47, 51).[7] Max Paddison emphasizes the limits of Adorno's direct effect on British and American musicologists. Up to the mid-1990s, he argues, Adorno has

> had an incomplete reception by Anglo-American musicology. The engagement with French structuralist and post-structuralist theory which characterized the late 1970s and the 1980s, and which was fuelled by availability of translations, somewhat eclipsed the work of Adorno and German Critical Theory. (Paddison 1996: 6)[8]

On the same page he goes on to suggest that "the critical engagement with Adorno and Critical Theory is [only] now underway." Even Stephen Miles, who in two important accounts of recent Anglo-American musicology takes Adorno's influence for granted, cites few specific scholars as examples. In the present essay I shall not attempt to track down lines of filiation between Adorno and recent English-language musicology. Rather, I wish to pause and reconsider a few of the larger ways in which Adorno's work had relevance for the New Musicology as it crystallized in the early 1990s, and in which it may still have relevance to English-language musicology as the decade comes to a close. To keep my argument focused, I shall restrict my discussion of Adorno to ideas drawn from his *Introduction to the Sociology of Music*;[9] and I shall confine my musicological observations largely to the years leading up to the first flowering of the New Musicology, beginning with a once famous critique of American musicology.

On December 27, 1964, at a plenary session of the thirtieth Annual Meeting of the American Musicological Society, in Washington, DC, Joseph Kerman, on the rise as a professor of music at Berkeley, issued a provocative call for an overhaul of American musicology (published as "A Profile for American Musicology," 1965, the version to which all page references in my description of this speech refer). Urging his colleagues to move beyond the "scientific" priorities (pp. 64, 66) set by scholars trained in "the Great German tradition" (p. 67), Kerman proposed redefining American musicology in a way that would "[catch] something of the resonance of the American personality" by rebuilding the field upon "a native point of view" (p. 68).

Kerman's model was the New Criticism (p. 64), at the time still the dominant method of studying English literature at American universities. Praising the shift in English departments away from "older commitments to philology and literary history" (p. 64), Kerman advocated turning musicology into a field where history and sociology were valued not as ends but as means (p. 62); where music was not studied as a "means of furthering 'the study of men in society'" (p. 62, quoting Frank Ll. Harrison); but rather where "men in society [were] studied as a means of furthering the comprehension of works of art" (p. 62). In the new (though not yet New) musicology described by Kerman, all of its components – including paleography, sociology, performance practice, and analysis, among others – would become steps on a ladder (pp. 62–3). On the highest rung, "afford[ing] a platform of insight into individual works of art" (p. 63), would stand a discipline that provided "critical insight" into the "immanent" capacity of certain compositions from the past to create "meaning," "pleasure," and "value" in the present, and thereby engender a "[unique] intellectual, emotional, and physical experience" (p. 63) – which is to say, "our essential musical experience" (p. 66).[10]

The discipline Kerman had in mind was criticism. Although he did not define this term fully in his speech, his account did point toward a kind of reading that was at once formally grounded and intellectually broadening, i.e., aesthetic. Though centered on the formal relationships within an individual piece, criticism, unlike a narrowly technical analysis, would not be "too fascinated by its own 'logic,' and too sorely tempted by its own private pedantries, to confront the work of art in its proper aesthetic terms" (p. 65). The works of art Kerman had in mind were compositions by the "great masters," by which he meant great European masters (pp. 66, 68).[11] (He did not specify genres. Despite his own successful book about opera, he did not challenge the long-standing scholarly idealization of post-Renaissance instrumental music.) By developing critical insight into masterworks, scholars would gain the ability to make critical judgments of art, a process Kerman considered morally imperative (p. 69). And although Kerman admitted that criticism at its worst was nothing more than "one man's impressionism" (p. 63) – no more than the musings of a contingent subject – he also implied that criticism could get at something like "musical essences" (p. 67). So important did Kerman consider the development of criticism in musicology that he wanted the field to change at once: there should be no more "collecting all kinds of information in the vague expectation that someone – someone else – will find it useful in [some] great undertaking" (p. 62).

One strong reaction did come instantly, from the scheduled respondent to Kerman's speech, Edward Lowinsky, a renowned and controversial University of Chicago musicologist, who had been forced to leave Germany in 1933. As Kerman recalled the occasion thirty-five years later, Lowinsky's impassioned response took so much time that the other speeches on the panel had to be canceled; its tone took Kerman himself completely by surprise.[12] A few months after Kerman published his speech in the *Journal of the American Musicological Society*, Lowinsky published his response in the same journal.

Stung by what he heard as nativist overtones in Kerman's manifesto, Lowinsky (1965) argued for the universality of the (more or less scientific) principles required by "scholarly method" (pp. 229, 233). Lowinsky rejected the notion of scholarship as a pyramid or hierarchy (pp. 224–5, 233–4); instead, a multiplicity of musicological specialties – the very ones named by Kerman – should, in Lowinsky's judgment, coexist as equally valued contributors to musical knowledge (pp. 233–4). Furthermore, criticism seemed to Lowinsky particularly ill-equipped to constitute the goal of other musicological studies because it had a lateral rather than consequent relationship to those studies. In his view, criticism required "develop[ing] an entirely new set of questions [. . . and] methods and criteria of answering them . . . questions and criteria . . . much closer to [those used by] criticism in litera- ture or the visual arts than . . . to [those used by] a whole number of musical sciences" (p. 224). Where Kerman (1965: 67) envisioned a subordination of history and sociology to criticism motivated ultimately by "commitment to music as aesthetic experience," Lowinsky sought scholars who were "doubly motivated, by the passion for music and by the fascination of its history" (p. 230).

And yet, Lowinsky called attention to his own 1961 assertion that "the beginning and the end of musicological studies lie in sympathetic and critical examination and evaluation of the individual work of art" (p. 226); by "individual work[s] of art," Lowinsky at bottom meant the same works by great European masters as Kerman idealized. Lowinsky further showed his high regard for criticism by stressing the "huge" extent of "virgin territory" still to be explored and the number of problems to be solved before musi- cologists were in a position to take up criticism (p. 226). In effect, under- neath all his counter-arguments, Lowinsky seemed to agree with Kerman that musicological investigations should end by bringing critical insight into the great works of the Western art canon.

When the excitement of the Thirtieth Annual Meeting subsided, move- ment within American musicology seemed to set its pace by Lowinsky's caution rather than by Kerman's urgency: over the next two decades not much changed. Kerman himself marvels today at the contrast between what he sees as his lack of impact in 1964 and the effect of his book *Contemplat- ing Music*. Written in 1983,[13] this critique of musical scholarship in the early 1980s caused a sensation when it appeared in 1985. Everyone in the field (even the unemployed) read it, if only to see whose work got mentioned; many went on to attack it. This time, as Kerman now sees things, the field was ready to listen to him; he takes for granted a causal connection between the appearance of his book and the eruption of the New Musicology a handful of years later.

Kerman's assessment of his own impact seems to me not fully right at either end. I suspect that the effect of Kerman's 1964 speech on American musicology, reinforced by an accumulation of other dissents (including some influenced by Adorno), over time became corrosive. Although Susan McClary's name did not appear in Kerman's index, by 1985 McClary was tenured at the University of Minnesota, organizing conferences and finding or creating venues that were willing, unlike those of established musicology, to publish her work. By 1985, traditional musicology was probably living on borrowed time. Six years later, Kerman's book seemed less a challenge than an elegy: the field it described no longer existed.

But this is not to deny the power, for a time, of *Contemplating Music* (1985; the source of all quotations in this and the next paragraph) as a catalyst. Expanding considerably on his earlier conception of criticism, and implying a shift in his own orientation from (the formalism of) New Criticism to (the structuralism of) Northrop Frye (p. 122), Kerman made a clearer distinction between narrowly "formalistic criticism" (p. 67) – veering at its worst toward "myopi[c]" analysis (p. 73) – and broader kinds "of historically oriented criticism . . . oriented towards musicology" taking shape in America (p. 112).[14] Critical evaluation, Kerman further admitted, was by then "distinctly under a cloud" (p. 132).

I would argue, however, that Kerman's broadened conception of criticism in *Contemplating Music* signified more an adjustment to trends he saw on the horizon than a fundamental change of concept. The formalistic boundaries of Kerman's own most extended work of criticism, *The Beethoven Quartets* (1967), support my view.[15] Tellingly, Kerman's paragon of criticism in *Contemplating Music* (pp. 146–7, 150–4) was Charles Rosen's *The Classical Style* (1972), a book in which "[t]he master principle that keeps everything on the track is Rosen's commitment to musical analysis" (p. 151). And a book, one might add, in which the conception of criticism was normative, focusing on "the music . . . Rosen judges to be the best," especially instrumental works (p. 154). Kerman explicitly linked Rosen's achievement to the language of Kerman's 1964 speech, congratulating *The Classical Style* for providing "(as I have urged) 'a platform of insight into individual works of art'" (p. 154, quoting "Profile," 63). Indeed, Kerman explicitly admitted in *Contemplating Music* that his 1964 priorities still seemed right to him (p. 124).

Kerman's shift from a critique of "scientific" priorities to an attack on "positivism"[16] (pp. 12, 37–59) raised hackles among traditional musicologists, as exemplified by Margaret Bent, in her speech as departing president, at the 1985 Annual Meeting of the American Musicological Society in Vancouver (published as "Fact and Value," 1986). But even Bent couldn't resist appropriating the term "criticism" to defend the making of critical editions (pp. 87–9). Whether, to use Cook and Everist's terms (1999: viii), one believes the "myth" of the "before Kerman/after Kerman paradigm" – whether one believes that *Contemplating Music* "open[ed] Pandora's box" or merely made a "public announcement that it was being opened" – by the late 1980s, Kerman's twenty-year-old advocacy of criticism as the chief function of musical scholarship seemed to be gaining ground.

In 1962, two years before the famous exchange between Kerman and Lowinsky, Theodor W. Adorno, a scholar mentioned by neither, published the German edition of his *Introduction to the Sociology of Music* (1976), based on a series of lectures given in 1961–2 at Frankfurt University. These lectures shared notable features with Kerman's speech. Like Kerman's speech, Adorno's lectures analyzed deficiencies in the current academic study of music. Kerman's frustration with "scientific" musicology had a compelling counterpart in Adorno's objection to empiricist "proceedings in which general demonstrability of results matters more than their use to get to the heart of the matter" (1976: 195). (Kerman's critique was obviously compatible with Adorno's characterization of America as "the land of not just a positivistic mentality but of real positivism" [p. 139; see also p. 182]). For Adorno, as for Kerman, the epistemological remedy for empiricist (and other) inadequacies of musical study lay in a study that would focus primarily on "important works of [Western] art" (p. 201), each in its specificity (e.g., p. 150: "[T]he critic's task would . . . begin . . . with a demonstration of what is specific and new in the . . . score"). And Adorno shared Kerman's impatience for change: he would not put off essential inquiries into music "*ad kalendas Graecas*, feigning humility" until he had collected all the facts demanded by empiricism (p. 197).[17]

Now it is true that Adorno defined his ideas of musical scholarship in terms of a discipline quite different from the one with which Kerman claimed criticism "work[ed] best in alliance" ("Communications," 1965: 427). Adorno's concern was with "music sociology" (*Musiksoziologie*), whereas Kerman's was with "musicology." This distinction was no mere function of a difference between German and English. Kerman disliked the term "musicology" – "who ever heard of 'artology' or 'literology'?" ("Profile," 1965: 66). He seemed willing to abandon it altogether for the German term *Musikwissenschaft*, which is ordinarily translated as "musicology," but which Kerman associated with "musical scholarship" ("Profile," 1965: 66). Under the "ample canopy" of this term he was ready to include "ethnomusicology, historical scholarship, theory, analysis and . . . criticism" (p. 66). The sociology of music, which elsewhere Kerman either accepted as an unprivileged branch of musical scholarship (pp. 62–3) or explicitly relegated to secondary status (p. 62), did not even make it into this spacious enclosure.

Adorno, by contrast, had no particular interest in *Musikwissenschaft* or any other term that could be translated into English as "musicology."[18] It is not as if Adorno elsewhere gave (or contemplated) lectures that would serve as an "Introduction to Musicology." On the contrary, Adorno resisted any detachment from music sociology of a strictly musical discipline. From his perspective, such a "scientific division of labor into pigeonholes [would lead to] reification, confusing methodical arrangements with the thing itself" (1976: 197) – in effect, to an illusory discipline offering methodological comfort but no cognitive value.

Adorno did grant the power of the impression, dismissed by Germans such as Walter Benjamin but unchallenged by most Americans until the advent of the New Musicology, that (Western art) music has had an autonomous history, unfolding over time in accordance with its own laws (p. 206). "[W]e cannot overlook the fact," he conceded, "that art, rather like philosophy, knows a logic of progress, albeit a precarious one" (p. 206). But for Adorno this show of separateness constituted only an aspect of a larger historical "confluence," within which "the immanent logic of the problem context" – call this the evolution of musical style – remained dialectically inextricable from the "external determinants" – call these the social forces that act upon music, even to the point of shaping it (p. 207). "Esthetic and sociological questions about music," asserted Adorno, "are indissolubly, constitutively interwoven" (p. 197). For Adorno, in short, music sociology was not one of many disciplines through which scholars could go about "contemplating music." Rather it seems to have been the only musicological discipline, in the sense of constituting the entirety of the scholarly disciplines capable of yielding musical knowledge.

All the more noteworthy, then, is the importance Adorno attached to criticism, an enterprise Kerman valued for the aesthetic insights it offered. (Noteworthy also is Adorno's explicit preference for instrumental works, which unlike vocal ones, offered a semiotic autonomy open to self-contained structural analysis [see e.g., pp. 202–4 and 215 on "autonomous" music]). If anything, Adorno seemed to attach even greater significance to criticism than Kerman did. Adorno not only observed that "the genuine experience of music, like that of all art, is as one with criticism" (p. 152). He also went on to associate and explicitly identify musical knowledge with criticism. "Knowledge and the capacity to discriminate," Adorno declared, "are directly one" (p. 152). At the same time, Adorno's conception of criticism as the locus of knowledge was centrally concerned with the formal analysis and judgment of "important works of art" (p. 201). "Criticism," he insisted, "is immanent to music itself" (p. 149); and "the crux" of criticism was "a knowledge of composing, an ability to understand and judge the inner forms of structures" (p. 151). Indeed, "music criticism is required by music's own formal law: the historical unfoldment of works and of their truth content occurs in the critical medium" (p. 149).

Adorno shared Kerman's conviction that criticism entailed judgment as well as scrutiny. And while acknowledging "the spot of relativity that stains all judgments about art" (p. 148), Adorno did not question the epistemological possibility of objective judgment. On the contrary, he defined criticism so as to locate objectivity (like knowledge) at its very center. Objectivity, by Adorno's account, was not a function of empirical observations: the music critic who restricted himself to reporting facts actually "miss[es] the objectivity to which he would seem to submit" (p. 152). Rather, objectivity, for Adorno, "rests upon the adequacy or inadequacy of the act of listening to that which is heard" (p. 3). Early in the *Introduction to Sociology*, Adorno offered the "premise . . . that works are objectively structured things and meaningful in themselves, things that invite analysis and can be perceived and experienced with different degrees of accuracy" (p. 3). By "constant confrontation with the phenomenon" – i.e., the individual composition – the critic could come to grasp the specific structural relationships between the parts of a work and thereby "raise his impression to the rank of objectivity" (p. 148).

What the critic would gain in hearing those structural relationships was not (just) the aesthetic sort of "critical insight" available to Kerman's critic but rather "insight into [the] essential relation [of musical phenomena] to the real society" (p. 194), above all, into the situation of the individual in the society where a piece originated. Through the structuring of its internal relationships, a piece could either expose or attempt to conceal the social "fissures and fractures" (p. 63) that conditioned the individual's possibilities, while also admitting or denying the absence of a Utopian reconciliation (see e.g., pp. 68–9, 70, and 224) between individual and society.

This is not to say that Adorno envisioned music as a transparent vessel for social critique. His explicitly stated view was that "musical sociology is forbidden [*verwehrt*] to interpret music as if it were nothing but a continuation of society by other means" (p. 205; German edition, p. 219). The basis for Adorno's refusal to recognize a separation between musicology and music sociology lay in the indivisibility he perceived between the artistic and the social parameters of musical structure. "No music has the slightest esthetic worth," Adorno asserted memorably, "if it is not socially true . . . no social content of music is valid without an esthetic objectification" (p. 197). Though the "esthetic rank" of compositions and their "structures' own social truth" were "not directly identical," they were "essentially related" (p. 197) because they both had the same fundamental character: a critical character. To Adorno's way of thinking, the capacity of music to criticize society was inextricable from a high degree of intrinsic or autonomous artistic worth;[19] identifying either parameter – the social or the aesthetic – required subjecting the other to evaluation. This is what Adorno had in mind when he argued that the "social critique of music . . . presupposes an insight into its specific esthetic content" (p. 215).

It was this need of music for simultaneous social and critical evaluation that allowed Adorno to designate "the proper object" of music sociology both as "the antagonisms which today are really crucial for the relationships of music and society" and as "the great compositions" (pp. 84, 204). "The common ether of esthetics and sociology," according to Adorno, "is critique" p. 216; see also p. 63). For Adorno, unlike Kerman, evaluating the musical structure of a particular work could not be separated from evaluating the social situation of the individual in a particular society. Nevertheless, for Adorno, as for Kerman, it can fairly be said that at the heart of musical scholarship lay criticism.

Difficult as it may now be to remember, both of these visions of criticism stemming from the 1960s seemed liberating to disaffected musicologists as late as the 1980s. Notwithstanding Abbate's subsequent wholesale dismissal (1991: 24–6) of what I think of as nuanced criticism – attempts to capture the unfolding dynamic of a musical work through abstract (rather than concrete) metaphors – Kerman had good reason for the hopes he pinned on such writing. While teachers of New Criticism had thrilled literature students for years with provocative ideas drawn from poetic structures, scholarly writings on music from mid-century until well into the 1980s were typically heavier on data than ideas. Too often they lacked intellectual excitement. Nor was there a concerted interest, especially in the United States, in developing styles of writing about music that were literate and engaging. A mark of this stylistic aridity, and the thirst it engendered, was the splash made by Charles Rosen's readably technical analyses in *The Classical Style*, which won the National Book Award in 1972 for Arts and Letters – a prize also won by Norman Mailer (as well as Lillian Hellman, Roger Shattuck, Lewis Thomas, and Paul Fussell) before the category was discontinued. For Kerman, more than a decade later, this book still showed what musicologists could accomplish if, in the words of Cook and Everist, they "elevate[d] their gaze from the positivist purview of dusty texts to a humane, critically informed musicology" (1999: viii). To the extent that the New Musicology involved taking up criticism in either Kerman's or Adorno's sense, the need of restless scholars for intellectual excitement unquestionably provided strong motivation.

And a case can be made that the New Musicology did take shape by way of criticism. Looking back in 1999, Cook and Everist, scholars not especially sympathetic to Kerman, observed that "under the slogan of 'criticism', Kerman created the vacuum that was filled by what came to be called the 'New Musicology'" – a vacuum that "resulted in a dramatic expansion of the musicological agenda in the decade after 1985" (p. viii). The New Musicology began in no small measure with experiments in interpreting individual art compositions, by no means exclusively, to be sure, and not without some sharp dissent (most notably perhaps in Tomlinson's "Musical Pasts," 1993). Much of this interpretation, indeed, continued the traditional analytical focus on instrumental music, although with the arrival of the New Musicology, a tilt in scholarship toward texted music became noticeable.

But the kinds of excitement that arose in Kerman's aftermath were not the same as those that arose in Adorno's. The distinction did involve differences between American and German modes of thinking, though by 1990, discontented American musicologists tended to see more vitality in recent European scholarly developments than in the American traditions Kerman had advocated. This geographical reorientation, however, did not preclude some continuing affinities in new musical scholarship with Kerman and the New Criticism. Cook and Everist note that the narrow formalism and the positivism attacked by Kerman had a quality in common that made both vulnerable to attack: "[E]ach embodie[d] a stance of unproblematical authority" (1999: vi). But one could argue that Kerman's critical ideal itself had much of the same quality; in a sense it partook of the qualities it criticized. Cook and Everist may imply as much in their assertion that "*Kerman's* formalism and positivism" (italics mine) evoke in the late 1990s "the same kind of nostalgic aura as the tail-fins of American cars in the Fifties" (p. vii). Whatever adjustments Kerman incorporated into *Contemplating Music* (see especially pp. 123–5), certainly his original conception of criticism, like formalism and positivism, projected confidence in the self-sufficiency of its own enterprise. And the isolation underlying that attitude points to a weakness in the kind of intellectual excitement that could be generated by criticism as envisioned by Kerman, and as practiced by later scholars who were in some ways his spiritual heirs.

Lowinsky pointed early toward this weakness. Whereas Kerman had found in "commitment to music as aesthetic experience" a sufficient basis for undertaking criticism ("Profile," 1965: 67), Lowinsky had insisted that scholars need to be doubly motivated, "by the passion for music and by the fascination of its history" (1965: 230). Shaped by the New Criticism, Kerman's original critic stood on his love of music. Lowinsky's critic, by contrast, looked from the start to other disciplines, such as literary criticism (p. 224): his critics could be thinkers as well as concert pianists *manqués*. Though Kerman later insisted on his interaction with literary scholarship (1985: 122), his critical model, the broadly erudite Charles Rosen, seemed to let slip the real priorities of the Kerman–Rosen position decades later in his assertion of an agreement among "almost everyone" that "performing and listening to music are primary activities: writing about music is secondary, parasitical" (1994: 55). Perhaps, though, it would be more accurate to say that in his assertion, Rosen, a pianist anything but *manqué*, attacked both positions: Lowinsky's on the critic's need for any interest beyond a love of music; Kerman's on the value of writing about music at all.

But in fact the lines of opposition among these three positions are blurred. Obviously Rosen did write about music; and he was Kerman's model critic because his writing provided intellectual excitement. The danger in the Kerman–Rosen critical model was not the specter of dullness; it was the possibility that the excitements of this model would prove clever but trivial, feeding what Leonard Meyer has called the human "need for varied experience" (1967: 127), but functioning, finally, as a virtuosic defense against boredom. Note how, in *Contemplating Music*, forgiving Rosen "a certain self-indulgent sprawl" (p. 150), Kerman admires Rosen's "cheeky" tone (p. 147), his ability to "move around easily . . . vary his approach . . . [and] slip in . . . digressions" (p. 150) . . . "slip[ping] in affective words almost reluctantly, wary lest they reach past a decorous minimum" (p. 151), his "hit-and-run tactics" (p. 152). Kerman could almost be describing a tennis pro. The danger in Kerman's ideal of criticism was that it could turn into a mere game, played for the critic's enjoyment rather than for stakes of importance to anyone else.

Virtually all those involved in the New Musicology used Lowinsky's suggested strategy for staving off such narrowness: they looked beyond musical structures to other disciplines and theories, French poststructuralism prominent among them, that could lend their investigations substance. But the strategy was not foolproof. In the New Musicology, as in other humanistic disciplines of the 1990s, manipulations of elements from various fields brought vulnerability to charges of shallowness (see Miles, "Critical Musicology," 1997: 749). "Where does all of this lead?" asked a scholar who was no foe of the New Musicology; "post-structuralist analysis," he went on, "can become a quagmire, an academic game" (Miles, "Critics of Disenchantment," 1995: 33). To the extent that Kerman's advocacy of criticism helped fuel a quest for intellectual stimulation among the New Musicologists, it may well have perpetuated a game-playing mentality associated with an American style of the early 1960s, when Kerman presented his speech: pragmatic cool. The scholarly games of the 1990s may have been more complicated, sophisticated, or esoteric than the New Criticism; they were not always so different in spirit.

To be sure, any theory, Adorno's negative dialectics as well as deconstruction, can be used in a way that turns it into a "nihilistic exercise" (Miles, 1995: 36). And by the late 1990s, something close to a dialectical sensibility, once unthinkable in English-language musicology, had clearly taken up residence in a field where

> many [writers] . . . assume neither music's self-sufficiency (as early proponents of formalism did) nor its lack thereof (in the manner of much of the New Musicology). . . . [but rather] attempt to formulate the ways in which music

operates autonomously, and to establish limits beyond which the concept of musical autonomy ceases to be viable, or at any rate, useful . . . in a word . . . problematiz[ing] the issue of musical autonomy. (Cook and Everist, 1999: xii)

One can imagine manipulating such a dialectical sensibility through a series of clever moves or "swerves" (Abbate 1991: 26). Adorno himself, however, strenuously discouraged an ethos of game-playing, especially the kind of game-playing through which poststructuralism, and eventually postmodernism, would seek an end-run around antinomies that Adorno considered insoluble. One need not deny the clear affinities between Adorno's negative dialectic and, say, the infinite regress of poststructuralism, or turn away from useful attempts to reconcile Adorno's modernism with postmodernism, to acknowledge Adorno's resistance to criticism as a game.[20]

Though ultimately grounded on Adorno's refusal to relinquish his commitment to an Enlightenment ideal of the individual subject, this resistance can in part be explained by the dead seriousness with which Adorno viewed the act of composition itself. Looking back at the situation of art before World War I, Adorno recalled how

[t]he generation of Schönberg and his disciples felt carried by a boundless need to express themselves . . . [T]hey knew that what was in them, striving to see the light of day, was one with the world spirit. This concordance with the historic trend . . . helped artists to bear subjective isolation, poverty, slander, and ridicule. (1976: 186)

By mid-century this sense of possibility was, from Adorno's perspective, over. Composers, as he saw things, found themselves reduced to solving problems – not the serious problems of pursuing "[c]ontradictions that appear as resistance of the material . . . to the point of reconcilement" (p. 213), but the narrower sorts of problems involved in the fulfilling of commissions.[21] In current times, he noted with sympathy, composers labored under "the shadow of futility, of the disproportion between the decision to do the thing [i.e., write the piece] and its conceivable relevance" (p. 187). And yet such difficulties did not license composers to content themselves with producing works marked by "loss of tension, nugatory, trifling, [or] a parody of playful bliss" (p. 181). Just as he had little use for the "hard and brittle counterpoint of . . . montage" (p. 193),[22] so, too, Adorno rejected essentially postmodernist conceptions of composition as a game that one played from the position of a detached outsider. For Adorno, the only acceptable stance for a composer was inside the arena of composition, in direct confrontation with the materials, and thereby the problems, of his or her time. For Adorno, art had a "seriousness . . . [that] require[d] an unquestioned conviction of its relevance" (p. 186).

Adorno made comparable demands on the critic, beginning with an insistence that "it . . . takes someone seriously involved in [the] production [of music] to make distinctions in it"; it is in this context that Adorno asserts, "[I]mmanent critique alone will bear fruit" (p. 152). And here it is useful to recall that Adorno defined "the crux" of criticism as "a knowledge of composing, an ability to understand and judge the inner forms of structures" (p. 151). Though Adorno did not present composition and criticism as literally analogous activities, he believed both required their practitioners to engage directly with the central issue of their time. In bourgeois society, since well back in the nineteenth century, that issue was the ongoing impotence of the individual in relation to Western society (see especially p. 186, on the impotence of the individual).

If Adorno's mode of criticism, like his conception of art, had a "seriousness . . . [that] require[d] an unquestioned conviction of its relevance" (p. 186), what, then, was the source of its excitement? In a word, the possibility of engaging in *Praxis*, that is, in simplified terms, the ability to contribute in some way to a better life (Adorno would say of the individual) in society.[23]

A bit of fresh perspective on what Adorno's notion of *Praxis* might mean for musicology may perhaps emerge from a brief consideration of the relationship between signifier (*signifiant*, hereafter *sa*) and signified (*signifié*, hereafter *sé*). This relationship, drawn as it is from linguistics, plays no explicit role in Adorno's *Introduction*. Yet one might argue that Adorno's constant intertwining of two dialectically related terms on a clearly post-Kantian, non-noumenal basis establishes a kind of analogue to the *sa–sé* relationship.

The two terms are, of course, "music" and "society." Ideally, for Adorno, musical scholarship would allow "the social deciphering of musical phenomena as such" (p. 194); not "content to state some structural congruence . . . it [would have] to show how social circumstances are concretely expressed in types of music, how they determine music" (p. 223). Adorno's consistent references to music and society as realms that are irreparably distinct and yet cannot "be separated by scientific lines of demarcation" (p. 215) suggest a strong commitment on Adorno's part to knowledge as a connective process, one that moves between evaluating music and judging the condition of society. It is at this juncture that Adorno offers an exciting promise to musical scholars: that they can earn their living by exercising their minds while also doing social good.

This is not to say that Adorno establishes a simple sort of *sa–sé* correspondence in either his theory or his practice of criticism. Looking at the latter, for example, Miles, in his thoughtful essay "Critical Musicology" (1997), details extensive discrepancies and imbalances in Adorno's actual analysis of music and society. Adorno asserts that "[m]usical sociology is social critique accomplished through that of art" (p. 63); but Miles exposes the thinness of the connection, and hence the huge disparity between the two domains of criticism in Adorno's own writings. To connect these domains properly, Miles asserts, Adorno would need both to establish the complex "concrete links between music and society on the levels of production and reception" (1997: 723) and to offer a "theory of mediation" between the two (p. 727). But Adorno does neither, he argues; asserting that "Adorno can never bring himself to pay close attention to the object of his critique," Miles goes so far as to conclude that "Adorno's sociology of music is . . . remarkably free-floating. Though it is undertaken in a critical spirit, it rarely becomes self-critical" (p. 727) – at least, I would add, in this respect. Nor do Adorno's shortcomings end with his own work. Adorno's flawed example, argues Miles, encourages "a troubling feature of critical musicology . . . that many of its proponents posit a relation between music and society, yet develop only the former in detail" (p. 728). Miles' examples here are Susan McClary and John Shepherd; he could as well cite many other works of the New Musicology, including my own.

At the level of theory, too, the relationship Adorno delineates between *sa* and *sé* is not a simple one. Adorno emphatically denies a one-to-one corre-spondence between musical and social events,[24] thereby in effect taking the poststructuralist rather than structuralist view of the *sa–sé* relationship. Thomas Levin has stressed how Adorno's conception of the phonograph record as a signifier, shaped by the Jewish taboo against uttering the name of God, required potential rather than explicit meanings (1990: 39–41, 25). And, of course, Adorno's dialectic entails self-reflexiveness. No signifier functions transparently in Adorno's theory of criticism: just as the "authentic" compo-sition (see e.g., pp. 68, 85, and 224) criticizes society by calling attention to itself, so too, the critic works with a constant awareness of his or her own role as signifier in the dialectical process of producing knowledge.

But however much Adorno's music criticism exceeds his social criticism in richness of detail, and however forcefully he calls attention to the dialec-tical reciprocity of signification, Adorno's criticism does not condone, either in theory or in practice, any absolutizing of the concept, drawn from post-structuralist linguistics, that Leppert calls the "floating signifier" (1995: 153). Because it is attached to no particular *sé*, the floating signifier causes various kinds of instability in the discursive process, taking on shifting meanings and creating unease. Especially noteworthy is the tendency of such signifiers to call attention away from the realm of signified, back to themselves, to the acts or sounds of signifying, and in some instances, to the producers of those acts and sounds.

Floating signifiers played prominent roles, on one level or another, in most of the early works of the New Musicology. Leppert himself used the device to characterize the kinds of threat that music came to pose for various European cultures, especially cultures of masculinity (e.g., in connection with the clavichord, "Sounds without consequence are suspect sounds, in that 'free-floating' sonorities may transcend established boundaries. These boundaries differ for men and for women" [1995: 127]). Susan McClary evoked it in her characterization of Don José's Flower Song, in Bizet's *Carmen*, as a song more about its singer's frustration than about his love for the supposed object of his song (1991: 59). Abbate focused on it in narrowing the definition of musical narration to rare moments when "music . . . speak[s] (sing[s]) *in a narrative mode*, but we do not know *what* it narrates" (1991: 27). Quoting Adorno on Mahler she added, " 'music performs itself, has itself as its content . . . *dass Musik . . . ohne Erzähltes erzähle* [that music might *narrate*, without narrative *content*]" (p. 27, all italics hers). Kramer put it in a related context when he defined "structural tropes" in terms of "their illocutionary force, as units of doing rather than units of saying" (1990: 10). Tomlinson proposes shifting from analysis of forms created by jazz to a "search for jazz meanings *behind* the music" (1992: 77, italics his). I myself invoke it in a reading of a Chopin prelude that shifts attention from consequents to antecedents (1996: 113–45).

Taken to an extreme level of development, floating signifiers are incompatible with Adorno's concept of criticism. Yes, Adorno himself did use the floating signifier in his compositional imagery, as in Abbate's quotation, or in his definition of Mozart's "social aspect" as "the force with which his music returns to itself, the detachment from empiricism. . . . [whereby] the form keeps the degraded life at arm's length" (p. 69). But note in the latter instance how the image snags a connection with society even as it heads back to Mozart's composition.[25] Although compositional choices in "authentic" works are autonomous, they incorporate a social meaning (see especially p. 68), and thereby have a chance, if understood critically, of moving toward some change in society.

Floating signifiers can play a similar role within the critic's own arguments. Depending on how they are used, floating signifiers can illuminate connections between music and its social history, or music and social ideology; and they can force reconsideration by the reader of such things as what it means to know, and how language exercises power. In such potentially connective roles, the floating signifier can be absorbed into the spirit of Adorno's criticism. But critics, even when they pass outside the analysis of instrumental music to less "autonomous" mediums, can also use the floating signifier to "keep the degraded life at arm's length" in a more selfish sense than Adorno's: they can draw on such signifiers in a way that gives them intellectual excitement but refuses a connection between themselves and society. In doing this, they undermine the very possibility of *praxis*. It is when things get to this point that musicology, like other postmodernist disciplines, is accused of esotericism, and its practitioners charged with opportunism, self-indulgence, or even narcissism. It is at this point that the weaknesses of musical scholarship derived from Continental models of theory converge on the weaknesses latent in Kerman's model of criticism. And it is at this point that Adorno's version of criticism, whatever his own blind spots, offers a salutary function, even in a rapidly changing discipline. When the pleasure of manipulating tropes, allusions, and "moves" become self-referential to the point of solipsism, Adorno's chary stance toward the floating signifier recalls forcibly the epistemological, and finally the moral, limitations of scholarship as a game.

The shift from "Old" to "New" paradigms in musicology involved trade-offs that I have analyzed elsewhere.[26] Positivistic traditions, in particular, made large bodies of information about history and society widely available. Although writing styles could have been more inviting, "positivist minutiae, after all," as Ralph Locke has perceptively observed, "are often far less arcane to the general reader than certain forms of philosophical speculation and theoretical generalization, e.g., Lacanian analysis" (1999: 519, n. 71). What the older paradigms lacked in critical self-consciousness they may have made up for in encouraging an ideal of objectivity. Even the delays that so frustrated Kerman and Adorno offered the virtues of a cumulatively acquired expertise. With all their limitations, paradigms of this sort still connected scholarship, or hoped to connect it, to a *signifié*.

The New Musicology, by contrast, often set out – though by no means in all its works, and virtually never, I would argue, in those of McClary or Leppert – on a path toward the floating signifier: turning from art, history, and society to an examination of its own methods; tinkering with its own rules to make new games; offering readers fewer windows on other times and places than on the ways in which its own authors were thinking. Where unchecked, this tendency would make the Adorno of the *Introduction* uneasy. And yet Adorno, far more than Kerman or any other Anglo-American musicologist, helped launch the problem: in the last analysis, one reads Adorno's musical writings less to find out about Beethoven or even Schönberg than to get inside the mind of Adorno himself.

But also to find strategies of connection; and that is why Adorno's dialectical vision of criticism remains an important resource for musical scholarship, a discipline already quite different from the New Musicology of the early 1990s. With the growing demystification of the Western art canon, both in musical life and in musical scholarship, a focus on the criticism of individual works is becoming as problematical as normative aesthetic judgments already are. To the extent that scholars go on studying the canon, Adorno's general idea of linking structural merit with social authenticity seems more likely than any other remnant of twentieth-century criticism to keep alive an articulable sense of the hopes and values once invested in the notion of great art. But Adorno's insistence on the importance to musical scholarship of social critique is most readily honored in the study of the critic's own culture. Thus, ironically, his musical writings in their specificity may enjoy their longest legacy not in canonical research but in the study of contemporaneous American and British popular music – if only as an occasion for disagreement. Still, for the foreseeable future, Adorno's refusal to grant the signifier unconditional release from the signified will continue to exert pressure on all musical scholars touched directly, or even indirectly, by the ideas and by the example of the *Introduction*. That refusal reminds scholars to ask questions about connections: Where are my studies taking me? Whom will they reach?

Notes

1   Paddison starts his chronological bibliography of Adorno's works in 1921 (*Adorno's Aesthetics of Music* [1993]: 333). The following essay concerns itself only with English-language musicology. Adorno's long-standing impact on German (and other continental European) musicology is not at issue.

2   In addition to Shepherd et al., works by David B. Greene, John Deathridge, and Laurence Dreyfus, among others, were noteworthy in this context.

3   See, e.g., Leppert and McClary; and Kerman, "American Musicology in the 1990s," which is based on a speech Kerman gave in Italy in 1990.

4   On a possible connection between the Oakland conference and the origins of the term "New Musicology," see Cook and Everist, *Rethinking Music* (1999): viii–ix. Footnote 6 in this preface provides a useful overview of the texts that initially defined the New Musicology.

5   Taruskin, regarded by many as the most brilliant scholar of his generation, has not been widely associated with the New Musicology.

6   Aside from the New Musicologists already named (and excluding most specialists on Adorno and popular music and jazz), I would include here, among others, Paddison, Miles, Johnson, Barone, Lippman, and Witkin (a sociologist).

7   Samson in Cook and Everist, 47 and 51. In fairness, McClary's *Feminine Endings* also makes few explicit references to Adorno. Yet McClary traces directly to Adorno (by way of my own 1976 article and her participation in a seminar I

gave on Adorno at the University of Chicago) the orientation that led to her first book. In a private conversation at the Annual Meeting of the American Musicological Society, Kansas City, on November 5, 1999, she linked this orientation with her "interest in musical process as a register of social ideology."

8   Paddison implies a considerably greater presence of critical theory in musical publications of the late 1970s and 1980s than was actually the case, however.

9   All page references to Adorno are to the *Introduction* unless "German edition" is specified. I have checked my reading of the English translation carefully against the German original. Although definitely superior as a translation to the translation by Anne G. Mitchell and Wesley V. Blomster of Adorno's *Philosophy of Modern Music* (New York: Seabury [Continuum] 1973), Ashton's translation is not ideal. At times it gives the sense of English rendered by a German speaker who has picked the wrong equivalent out of an English dictionary. For example, Ashton renders Adorno's reference to Chopin's *"wählerische Scheu vorm Banalen"* (German edn. p. 71) as Chopin's "eclectic dread of banality" (*Introduction*, 61), when surely what Adorno meant by *"wählerische"* was "fastidious." At other times, one questions whether Ashton understood what he was translating. The term "discontinuous work" on pp. 85 and 107 of the *Introduction* refers to the term *"durchbrochene Stil"* (German edn. pp. 96 and 118), a term well known in the original German to traditionally trained musicologists. Unaccountably, Ashton later uses the more familiar "filigree" (*Introduction*, 160) for *"durchbrochene"* (German edn. p. 172). Similarly, "genteel style" (*Introduction*, 158) refers to *"galanten Stil"* – i.e., *style galant* – in the German edn. p. 171.

10   A few of the these terms appear in passages quoted approvingly by Kerman. Although Kerman does not explicitly exclude music of the present from his critical canon, his orientation toward the past is clear both from his choice of musical examples and from his notion (1965: 68) that "the critical attitude is exactly that which takes the past up *into the present*" (italics his).

11   In "Communications" (1965), replying to Lowinsky, Kerman did subsequently broaden his repertory to include *"the main line . . .* of American art-music – Ives, the generation of Sessions and Copland, and beyond" (p. 427).

12   I am grateful to Professor Kerman for taking time, on November 7, at the 1999 Annual Meeting of the American Musicological Society, in Kansas City, to share with me his recollections and appraisal of this event, and of his book *Contemplating Music.*

13   On date of writing see Kerman, "American Musicology in the 1990s" (1991: 131).

14   See Cook and Everist, *Rethinking Music*, x–xi; Maus, pp. 173–4; and Cook, pp. 253–5, on an analogous distinction by Treitler; also Miles, "Critics of Disenchantment," 13, on Kerman's support for "emerging sociological criticism" in *Contemplating Music.*

15   And so in a sense does Kerman himself when he links himself (though with "some reservations") to Edward Cone, Charles Rosen, and Leonard Meyer as evidence that critics are "in fact, *too* fascinated by analysis" (*Contemplating Music*, 72–3, italics his).

16 I have long suspected that my own use of the term "positivism" may have influenced Kerman's. I first focused on this term in "Musicology and Criticism," a speech I gave at the Annual Meeting of the American Musicological Society in Boston, November 13, 1981 (see *Developing Variations*, 90). Kerman essentially commissioned this speech; and he quoted from it in *Contemplating Music* (147–8). My critique of positivism was heavily indebted to Adorno's (see, e.g., his *Introduction*, 139 and 182). Thus, if my hunch is right, I may have served at this point as a conduit between Adorno and Kerman.

17 Adorno uses the word "essence" here. The term "*ad kalendas Graecas*" denotes debts that need never be paid. See also the critique on p. 195 of calls for "incontrovertible proof"; and Miles, "Critical Musicology," 725 and 750.

18 Readers of the English translation of Adorno's *Introduction* should be wary of taking the term "musicology" at face value. On p. 196, for example, Adorno appears to contrast it with sociology; in the German original, however, his term is "*Musiktheorie*" (German edn., p. 210), which probably has no exact counterpart in English. Or again, the students who in the English version say they are not musicians but rather "in musicology" (p. 135) identify themselves in the German edition (p. 147) as "*Schulmusiker*" (music educators) in the "*musikpädagogische Bereich*" (the realm of music pedagogy).

19 See p. 63, where Adorno excludes from consideration aesthetic flaws "attributable merely to the subjective inadequacy of an individual composer."

20 For analyses of Adorno's relation to poststructuralism or postmodernism in the context of music see, e.g., Paddison, *Adorno, Modernism and Mass Culture*, 40–4, 117, 132–3; Witkin, *Adorno on Music*, 181–200; Miles, "Critics of Enchantment," 35; and Subotnik, *Deconstructive Variations*, 43–55. Witkin also discusses this issue in "Why Did Adorno 'Hate' Jazz?". (2000).

21 "All compositions come close to composing to order; at best, the composer gets the assignment from himself" (p. 186). In the German edition (p. 199), the original of "composing to order" is "*Auftragskomposition*" (commissioned composition), and "assignment" is "*Auftrag*" (commission).

22 For qualifications of Adorno's attitude toward montage see Paddison, *Adorno, Modernism and Mass Culture*, 98–100 (especially on Mahler), Witkin, *Adorno on Music*, 178–9; and Levin (1990: 46).

23 For a useful analysis of the limits within Adorno's notion of music as praxis, see Witkin, *Adorno on Music*, 159.

24 See, e.g., p. 197 (the aesthetic and the social "are essentially related even though not directly identical"); p. 211 ("It is as a dynamic totality, not as a series of pictures, that great music comes to be an internal world theater"); and p. 215 ("[S]ociology and esthetics . . . are not immediately one: no work of art can vault the chasm to existence.")

25 Levin's account, 44–7 vs. 34–5, of Adorno's gradual acceptance of "gramophone-specific music" may describe an exception to this dynamic.

26 "Foundationalist vs. Aesthetic: A Cost-Benefit Analysis of the Changing Musicological Paradigm," closing keynote address at "Rethinking Interpretive Traditions in Musicology," Tel Aviv University (June 6–10, 1999), to be

published in the series *Orbis Musicae*. I would like to thank my Brown colleagues David Josephson and Marc Perlman, two of my Brown graduate students, Markus Mantere (music) and Christopher Lee (English), and Carol Tatian and Sheila Hogg of the Brown Music Library for their help with aspects of the present essay.

Part III

Critical Theory and After

11

Rethinking an Old Saw: Dialectical Negativity, Utopia, and *Negative Dialectic* in Adorno's Hegelian Marxism

Nigel Gibson

The absolute philosophy has not been read speculatively, because the reality of unfreedom has determined its reading. It has been read as the negative absolute which it sought to undermine.

Gillian Rose

They are most accurately called systems which apprehend the Absolute only as substance . . . they represent the Absolute as the utterly universal genus which dwells in the species or existences, but dwells so potently that these existences have no actual reality. The fault of all these modes of thought and systems is that they stop short of defining substance as subject and as mind.

G. W. F. Hegel

The Late Late Show

The proletariat has become invisible.

Adorno

Over the last decade, the popular idea of Adorno as a Hegelian-Marxist (e.g., Jay 1984a:[1] 105f, Jameson 1971; Jameson 1990: 229f)[2] has increasingly been abandoned under the weight of the philosophic influences of Heidegger,

Husserl, Kierkegaard, and Nietzsche. With the decline of the new left, the study of Adorno – shorn of a simplistic identification with Marxism – has undergone a transformation. While in the 1960s Adorno felt constrained to defend himself from charges of political conservativism and academic elitism, his political "moderation" is often perceived today as an advantageous adjunct to the permanent ideological critique with which his name is associated.

If this essay charts a perilous course, critical of Fredric Jameson's voluntarist attempts to make Adorno the basis of a Marxism for the 1990s, it is also wary of those who happily celebrate the gulf between Adorno and Marxism, dismissing the latter as "dogma" (Hohendahl 1995: 16). Indeed, Adorno agrees with Marx that the task is to "actualize philosophy" (cf. Adorno 1977), but what Adorno means by philosophy, even in his most "Marxist" moments, is quite distinct from Marx's idea. The difference between them – the problem of Adorno's understanding of *Capital* and Marx's dialectic – is rooted in Adorno's critique of Hegel.[3] To evaluate Adorno's relationship to Marxism, it is thus important to examine to what extent and in what ways Adorno's thought is based on his questionable interpretation of Marx's economic/philosophical categories.

While at first glance the globalization of late twentieth-century capitalism seems to fit with the Frankfurt School thesis of total commodification, Adorno's analysis of *Capital* provides a scant basis to evaluate the crisis of capitalism at the close of the twentieth century. One reason for this failure lies in Adorno's critical engagement with Georg Lukács.[4] Adorno's reaction to Lukács' formulation of a subject/object identity, and Lukács' subsequent over-reliance on consciousness, limits Adorno's treatment of Marxian categories. *Negative Dialectic* is in many ways a fundamental response to Lukács' conception of totality in which Adorno construes Lukács' thought as paradigmatically Hegelian (Lukácsian) Marxism. Adorno's reaction to Lukács becomes fundamental to Adorno's notion of the Hegelian dialectic "after Auschwitz."[5]

While Adorno grapples more rigorously with Hegel than do many other self-proclaimed Hegelian Marxists, he views the Hegelian dialectic as a process of progress and synthesis where the moment of negativity serves almost exclusively for the purposes of annexation and subsumption. However, a different view of Hegel can also be teased out of Adorno's writings. For example, in his essay "Aspects of Hegel's Philosophy," Adorno separates himself from simplistic evaluations of Hegel and castigates those who see Hegel's philosophy as an accommodation with the status quo. Adorno not only challenges the "lumping" of "Hegel together with German imperialism and Fascism" (i.e., Popper and the Hegel and Fascism school) but argues that Hegel's is a philosophy of freedom and genuine self-determination: "The real can be considered rational," he argues, "only insofar as the idea of freedom, that is, human being's genuine self-determination, shines through it" (Adorno 1993: 44).

Nevertheless, even one of Adorno's most acute critics, Susan Buck-Morss, who argues that Adorno was never much of an Hegelian Marxist (1977: xiii f.), makes the mistake of reducing Hegel's idea of reality to the present. In the name of non-identity, the logic of Adorno's negative dialectic flattens and politicizes Hegel's dialectic. In "Aspects of Hegel's Philosophy," Adorno claims that, for Hegel, Reason and freedom are interpenetrated and "nonsense without one another," but he adds in *Negative Dialectics* that the subject is so much detached from live human beings (a problem Marx had identified in Hegel in his *1844 Manuscripts*) that "its freedom in necessity can no longer profit them." He finds the clearest expression of this separation in Hegel's popularized *Reason in History*, which Adorno quotes in *Negative Dialectics*, where Hegel speaks of the dialectic of freedom and necessity as "submitting" to the state's laws. Apparently, it is not the separation of the subject from live human beings that finally interests Adorno, but Hegel's use of the term submission. "No amount of interpretive skill," Adorno proclaims, "would let us dispute away the fact that the word 'submission' means the opposite of freedom" (1973a: 350). Thinking he had trumped Hegel's idea of freedom, we are left with nothing more than this hollowed expression.

Rightly suspicious of "totality" in the age of totalitarianism, Adorno too quickly equates the Hegelian dialectic with totality, and views the Hegelian Absolute as simply an expression of totalization. First, Adorno maintains that the dialectic dissolves anything not proper to consciousness by reducing all existence to the self-movement of absolute subject. He finds it analogous to capitalist accumulation. Second, he explicitly rejects Hegel's absolute negativity – the negation of the negation (a category most "Hegelian Marxists" assume means a return to the beginning; for a contrasting view see Dunayevskaya 1989) – identifying it with an integration and such an integration with Auschwitz: He writes: "Genocide is the absolute integration . . . Auschwitz confirmed the philosopheme of pure identity as death . . . Absolute negativity is in plain sight and has ceased to surprise anyone" (1973a: 362).

The totalizing subject of Hegel's Absolute colonizes the actual and, in Adorno's view, bears a striking resemblance to what Marx conceptualized as capital. Just as Reason in Hegel subsumes all otherness into the self-movement of the concept, so too does the process of capitalist accumulation subsume all human and natural contingency into the movement of mechanized, abstract labor. While Adorno deploys Marxian language to criticize capitalism and remains within a broadly defined Marxian tradition, to a large degree his approach to Marx's *Capital* remains a neo-Ricardian one, namely a labor theory of value rather than its non-reified articulation as a value theory of labor. Additionally, the centrality of the terms "exchange value" and "the law of value" to the conception of identity is more akin to Ricardo than Marx (contrast Jameson 1990: 230).[6]

Third, rejecting all notions of universal history, Adorno nonetheless almost embraces a technicist development (and one that perhaps Engels would find congenial), proclaiming in *Negative Dialectics* that "No universal history leads from savagery to humanitarianism, but there is one leading from the slingshot to the bomb" – a dialectic of horror and "total menace which organized mankind poses to organized man" (Adorno 1973a: 320). Its apogee is found in the Nazi death camps. It is within such a technological determinism that Adorno takes Hegel to be verified. Given this attitude, it is no wonder that he slips into the common-language meaning of "negative."

Such claims – Hegel as a philosopher of progress, of the state, and of empire, based on a conception of Hegel as the philosopher of identity – might seem "obvious" to postmodern sensibilities. Yet these claims depend on a "barbaric" (in the sense of a non-reflective) view of Hegel, a caricature which, as stated earlier, Adorno slights, even if at the same time Adorno betrays his own dismissive attitude by declaring Hegel's dialectic in toto to be conceptual "straitjacket" (Adorno 1993: 10).

As a critic of Hegel, Adorno wrote some very important essays, but in the final analysis, despite brilliant insights, his treatment of Hegel's conception of negativity undermines the cogency of his critique. Adorno reads Hegel's Absolute as a neo-Kantian, that is to say, he "falls back" on viewing the Absolute as a reflection of the antinomy of bourgeois society. In doing so Adorno, like Lukács, views Hegel's dialectic as a reconciliation with reality rather than, as in Marx's conception, dialectic as motioning to a transcendence of reality. Transcendence becomes impossible and unknowable. If, as Gillian Rose observes, Adorno's critique of Lukács' remains within its "Fichtean assumptions," to what extent does his critique of Hegel?

Fichte's Police State and Imperial Annexation

No one must remain unknown to the police.

J. G. Fichte

There is something reminiscent of Fichte in Adorno's description of Hegel's dialectic as a "philosophical imperialism of annexing the alien" (1973a: 191). Like Rousseau's famous quip that one has to be forced to be free, or like Hobbes' Leviathan state, Fichte builds the realization of freedom and recognition in his *Grundlage des Naturrechts* upon a foundation of coercion. One freely embraces the laws of the state and is restricted by force, argues Fichte. Instead of the possibility of mutual recognition with an internal mediation of the self to itself by the other, for Fichte the potential negation of otherness remains an external negation which leaves the subject unaffected. With the replacement of reciprocity by coercion, it is quite easy to imagine why "no one must remain unknown to the police." The importance of reciprocity evaporates. The Other is simply annexed; coercion is needed to enforce the subject/object identity. Reciprocity is replaced by the all-seeing police state.

This is certainly the sense one gets from Adorno's reading of Hegel when he argues that the problem of the separation of subject (freedom) and "live human beings" is resolved for Hegel by man's "submission to laws." Adorno simply pronounces such submission as the "opposite to freedom," and rests his case. Yet Hegel clearly sought to avoid endorsing Fichte's "state as the world of galley slaves" as he put it in *Grundlage des Naturrechts* (quoted in Williams 1998: 288). Hastily equating submission with the lack of freedom, Adorno ironically almost embraces the bourgeois "freedom" of the market. For Hegel such unmediated marketplace freedom blocks the development of reciprocity. His solution is reluctantly to authorize supervision by a "rational" and "moral" public authority to ensure the freedom of public life and the development of a genuine reciprocity. Hegel rejects Fichte's argument that community be based on security and coercion, arguing instead that mutual reciprocity forms the basis of community. Nevertheless Adorno places Hegel inside the Fichtean problematic.

Twenty years ago, the Adorno scholar Gillian Rose wrote that while Adorno rightly criticized Lukács' theory of reification for remaining within Fichtean assumptions (cf. Adorno 1973a: 190), Adorno "accepted largely Lukács' generalization" and, in an almost Fichtean vein, understood capitalist social forms not historically but as "determinants of the contradictions of consciousness" (Rose 1981: 32). In his 1957 "Aspects of the Hegelian Dialectic" (Adorno 1993), which he called preparation for a "revised conception of the dialectic," Adorno argues against equating the subject/object dialectic with the speculative idealism of Fichte, and even goes so far as to call it more than "mere subjectivity" and "speculative idealism." Adorno concludes that if cognition is authentic, it is "more than simple duplication of the subjective; [it] must be the subject's objectivity" (translation altered, p. 6). Such a "revised conception of the dialectic," distinct from Lukács', could have produced a different conclusion than the thrust of Adorno's *Negative Dialectics*, which closes off such possibilities. In fact, the problematic of the subject's objectivity is partly reformulated in *Aesthetic Theory* as the self-mediation of an authentic piece of artwork. He states that the authentic artwork is "an objectivity that has forgotten its previous origins in subjectivity," in other words a subject that becomes objective. In *Aesthetic Theory* he continues:

> If anywhere, Hegel's theory of the movement of the concept has its legitimacy in aesthetics; it is concerned with the dynamic relation of universal and particular, which does not impute the universal to the particular externally but seeks it rather in the force fields of the particular itself. (1997: 351)

Adorno refuses Lukács' imputing "universality" to the proletariat. He challenges Lukács to seek that in the particular itself, and to show how the particular becomes the concrete universal. Yet Adorno fails to develop this point in *Negative Dialectics*. While music might have provided Adorno with inspiration for his philosophy, he was not able to translate the subject's objectivity beyond this form. Aesthetics became the best expression of Adorno's Hegelian Marxism.

However, in his philosophical readings Adorno's own "rescue" of Hegel is problematic. For example, his defense of Hegel against the conservative argument that the "real is rational," namely, that "the real can only be considered rational insofar as the idea of freedom, that is, human beings' genuine self-determination shines through it" (p. 44), is belied by his idea of the subject's drive for domination and the philosophical charge that absolute negativity finds its apogee in Auschwitz. Despite Adorno's own maxim that "intolerance of ambiguity is the mark of an authoritarian personality," Adorno seemingly could not hold on to the ambiguity, instead becoming intolerant of the seemingly endless stages of negation.

At stake in Adorno's revised conception of the dialectic is his approach to reciprocity and difference. In contrast to Fichte's conception of reciprocity where the Other is reduced to the same, a conception often taken as Hegel's own, Hegel actually argues in *The Phenomenology* for a somewhat different separation of the subject's objectivity from a passive subjectivity:

> Since the Notion is the object's own self, which presents itself as the *coming to be of the object*, it is not a *passive Subject* inertly supporting the Accidents; it is

on the contrary, the self-moving Notion which takes its determinations back into itself. In this movement the passive Subject itself perishes; it enters into the differences and the content, and constitutes the determinateness, i.e., the differentiated content and its movement, instead of remaining inertly over it. The solid ground which argumentation has in the passive Subject is therefore shaken, and only this movement itself becomes the object. (Hegel 1977: 37, my emphasis)

Hegel's language of shaking all that is solid has a resonance with the master/slave dialectic where the dependent consciousness, namely the "passive subject" of self-certainty, experiences the shaking of its foundations and thus moves forward in its comprehension of differentiated content. However, though this famous dialectic is central to understanding Hegel's conception of reciprocity, it would be wrong to think that the reciprocity in the master/slave dialectic is anything other than a *moment* in the process where the "I becomes a we," where the solipsistic passive subject perishes and enters into difference and movement. One must attend to the whole process of grasping the self-movement of the subject of which the master/slave dialectic is but an early moment.[7]

While the abstract undifferentiated identity – the type of Fichtean self-certainty and Schellingian absolute that Hegel labels as "the night in which all cows are black" – is in fact taken by Adorno to be Hegel's conception, nothing could be further from the truth. But it is just such a mistreatment that informs Adorno's *Negative Dialectics*. In his essay "Skoteinos or How to Read Hegel" (Adorno 1993), Adorno claims that Hegel can only be understood in respect to the "whole" and that nothing can be understood in isolation. On its own, Adorno's view of Hegel is one-sided. Just as for Hegel the Absolute is the beginning point of his philosophy, one finds that the "ultimate turns out to be not the Absolute . . . but a new beginning, a new point of departure" (Dunayevskaya 1989: 18).

Adorno understood the inner connection between Hegel's method and his speculative moment, yet he accused Hegel of simply narrowing absolute negativity into positivism. To him the dialectic is "cut short by Hegel" (Adorno 1973a: 334). Equating the rational positive with the state, Adorno argues that Hegel's "philosophy of the state . . . suspends the dialectic" because Hegel realizes that the contradictions in "civil society" cannot be resolved though its self-movement.

Though "the State," in terms of Hegel's *Philosophy of Mind*, occupies a position in "Objective" rather than "Absolute" Mind, Adorno nevertheless extends the "suspended dialectic" into Absolute Mind (we shall see that Adorno makes a similar extension with regard to the Absolute in *The Phenomenology*).[8] We should remember that this is not Marx's position. When

Marx extends his criticism of Hegel's *Philosophy of Right* to the "lie of the principle," he criticizes Feuerbach for dismissing both idealism and Hegel's absolute negation. In contrast to Marx, Adorno insists that "*in the last analysis* even in Hegel the quiescence of movement, the absolute, means simply the reconciled life" (Adorno 1993: 32, my emphasis). Thus, just as Hegel appealed to the state almost as a Fichtean external unifier to remove the contradictions in civil society, Adorno contends that the "contradiction [becomes] *alleviated* in the absolute" (Adorno 1993: 31, italics mine). It is this "alleviation" which leads to an imperialism of the concept, a drowning of the Other and difference into submission. Consumed by absolute identity, Hegel's dialectic undergoes only a "semblance of the negative." From there it is a logical step to equate Hegel's Absolute with Auschwitz.

Adorno's adieu to Hegel is based on two related claims. To proceed dialectically is to think in contradictions (1973a: 145), but such a dialectic is *not reconcilable* (or identifiable) with Hegel because Hegel is the philosopher of identity – of the identity of identity and non-identity. In contrast, negative dialectics is "a sense of nonidentity through identity." Thus Adorno privileges contradiction over negation of the negation in the dialectic, which he treats as identity. "Dialectics," Adorno adds, "is not only an advancing process but a retrograde one at the same time" (p. 157). Though evidence of any "process" is problematic for Adorno, the idea of the negative in the positive as well as the possibility of a retrogression in the dialectic is not unfamiliar to Hegel scholars. For example, H. S. Harris concludes his monograph on *The Phenomenology* by arguing that "there is nothing in his logical theory to warrant the belief that the motion of consciousness must always progress . . . regression is just as possible as progress" (Harris 1995: 107). From a Hegelian Marxist perspective, Raya Dunayevskaya argues that the Hegelian dialectic is not simply a sequence of never-ending progression, but "lets retrogression appear as translucent as progression and indeed makes it very nearly inevitable if one ever tries to escape regression by mere faith" (1989: xlii–xliii). This idea is found at the level of the Absolute. For example, Hegel writes in the *Science of Logic* of the "*unresolved* contradiction" at the threshold of the Absolute Idea, which interrupts the "advancing process" and warns that the Absolute Idea "contains the highest opposition within itself" (Hegel trans. Miller 1977: 824). Yet Adorno's Hegel, always marching roughshod over such problematics and such weighty contradictions at the level of the Absolute, is always already "in the final analysis" a conservative.

A more radical reading emphasizes the creativity of Hegel's dialectic of negativity at the heart of the Absolute. Adorno resists such a reading which, with its emphasis on movement and on *development through contradiction*, gives an impression that the contradictions never end, even in the Absolute. Instead,

Adorno proposes that the philosophical critique of identity be suspicious of all identity and entails a "logic of disintegration" of Subject. The critical thinker is aware of his own subject position which is always already disintegrating (see Buck-Morss 1977: 82–95).[9]

Rather than dialectical negativity, Adorno's *Negative Dialectics* concentrates not on a moment of negativity but on the logic of disintegration, a logic that demands intransigence and resistance to anything that smacks of identity. Whereas suspicion implies working through the skeptical moment and perhaps raising the suspicion to another level of contradiction, for Adorno (in our totally reified society) truth can only be the non-identity of the concept. Sounding like a deconstructionist, he insists that "ideas live in the cavities between what things claim to be and what they are." Unlike the positivists, who are the butt of much of Adorno's criticism, things are certainly not what they claim to be. Yet Adorno is making larger claims than a critique of ideology. Negative dialectics criticizes all systems *qua* ideologies. Yet as a total program, negative dialectics offers nothing in its place. That would be simply another ideology. The critique of ideology cannot provide a method to help liberate us from the capitalist reified reality we all inhabit.

What Adorno is asserting, however, through all the clamor about identity, is the logical impossibility of any theory about reality[10] – that is, if we take theory to mean the conceptualization of its object or simply theory as category building. The resistance to conceptualization leaves us with a sum of particulars not identifiable with any other sum. In Adorno's view, the "whole" is not only less than the parts but it destroys their specificity. The "whole" is totalitarian, because, by subsuming particulars, it denies their specificity. The "whole" erases the distinct particular, thereby abolishing the right of the self to determine its freedom as an aspect of the "whole."

Adorno's Utopia

Doesn't this [Schönberg's] music (I want to express myself carefully) have something to do with what in Marx is called the "association of free men"?

Adorno to Krenek

Of particular note in the context of Adorno's unwillingness to offer a positive in the negative is Adorno's creation of a positive utopia ungoverned by any dialectical development. Apart from being free of dialectic, little can be said of Adorno's utopia. It has often been argued that Adorno's unwillingness to spell out a utopian alternative was a result of the Jewish *Bilderverbot*, the prohibition on picturing God (Jay 1984: 20). Philosophically, Adorno's reference to "staring the Absolute in the face" would make such claims problematic. For Adorno, utopia is a place of transparency between cognition and reality, a place which "transcends philosophy," transcends contradiction and defies identity.[11] Adorno's utopia is important as the Other of his negative dialectic. It is free of dialectic: "neither system nor a contradiction," above identity and contradiction (1973a: 150): "Regarding the concrete utopian possibility, dialectic is the ontology of the wrong state of things. The right state of things would be free of it" (p. 11). In this right state what things are and how they appear would no longer be contradictory. In this place beyond ideology, of transparency, one witnesses the return of the repressed, reconciliation without duress – an anarchist regurgitation of Lukács' subject/object identity.

Adorno criticizes Hegel for suspending the dialectic and thus falling into a type of positivism. But does not Adorno's anarchist utopia represent a "return" to the pure subjectivism about which Hegel warned in his "Three Attitudes to Objectivity," where, weary of the dialectic, the endless contradictions, one would instead seek something ineffable, some nameless thing which transcends dialectic?[12] How else might one understand the "ineffable part of the utopia" (p. 11) than what Hegel calls a "fact of our consciousness . . . passed off for the very nature of mind" (Hegel 1968: 105)? Is its ineffability simply the pure subjectivism of the intuitionists?

Adorno's utopia realizes the subject/object identity. Observation and meaning converge; dialectic comes to an end. Adorno characterizes his utopia as a "togetherness of diversity." Even if we allow for some measure of identity to achieve diversity, the togetherness is isolated. The negative dialectic of togetherness and diversity is an "elective affinity." As the dialectic falls apart, nothing remains. Out of these ashes Adorno fashions a utopia. In other words, utopia is needed to ward off despair.

Why does Adorno assume that the subject/object dialectic is exhausted in identity? He argues against the limitation of such an approach in "Aspects," writing that, "cognition if it is genuine, and more than simple duplication of the subjective, must be the subject's objectivity" (p. 6). And even in *Negative Dialectics*, he contends that Hegel still has "an insight into the subject as a self-manifesting objectivity" (p. 350). So what has happened to the subject's objectivity?

The secret telos of identification, he states, is non–identity – this is philosophy's self-criticism. Though he wants to hold on to this unity of opposites, the methodology of negative dialectics disallows it. Can he have both things? One problem with his concept of identity is its *reduction* to equivalence (thinking of Adorno's appropriation of economic categories of exchange), or simply put as a predicate: Identity *equals* the conceptualization of all predication. He argues that identity thinking subsumes the thing while non-identity thinking "seeks to say what something is" (Adorno 1973a: 149). But surely by articulating what something is one identifies its genre. Is this not an identity? Non-identity thinking has an identifying drive; in fact, Adorno goes as far as to proclaim that non-identity is the "truth" of identity.[13] What he gives us is the identifying drive of non-identity thinking, or perhaps its self-manifesting objectivity. In other words, Adorno is claiming that non-identity thinking is a truer, more real, form of identity. It makes for a better identification of the thing: "it identifies to a greater extent, and in other ways, than identitarian thinking." There is what Buck-Morss calls the "hidden, positive moment of Adorno's 'negative dialectics' . . . [P]recisely because of its unrelenting negativity [there is] a utopian emblem, a secret affirmation" (1977: 131). Adorno does not follow this through; there is always another moment, almost only purely skeptical, that insists that all predication is identification.[14]

Following Marx, Adorno argues that Hegel's attempt to transcend the dichotomy of transcendental subject and empirical individual founders on the detachment of "live human beings" from the subject, "spirit" (Adorno 1973a: 350). Yet where Marx discerns in Hegel an alienated insight into the "actual objectification of man," Adorno finds nothing but the identity thesis. Although Marx criticizes the lack of concrete definition in the concept of subjectivity, what he calls the separation of thought from the *subject*, and although he calls absolute negativity an abstraction, he still emphasizes the "objectivity" of transcendence. Adorno, like Feuerbach, emphasizes only one side, namely the "false positivism" and "apparently critical position" of the Hegelian dialectic. Even if one could put this down to a skepticism about the possibility of historical development (in any case, a simplification of both Hegel's and Marx's conception of dialectic), Adorno reads Hegel as *a priori* a philosopher of identity: "Despite everything," he writes, despite all the insights Adorno gives us into the rich and multilayered character of Hegel's philosophy, despite all Adorno's arguments with other thinkers' attitudes to Hegel, despite ambiguity and Hegel's own goal, "Hegel ultimately remains tied to the identity thesis and therefore to idealism" (1958: 40). Adorno's earlier claim that Hegel's dialectic "finds its ultimate truth . . . in its unresolved and vulnerable quality" is subsumed under the will to identity. Adorno's insight into an open-ended dialectic in Hegel is muted. For Adorno, Hegel's thought remains tied to Fichte; as he puts it in the same essay, "Hegel literally outdid Fichtean idealism," reducing the other to itself. It is in contrast to this conception of Hegel that negative dialectic is performed.

Absolute Freedom and Terror

*The man who managed to recall what used to strike him in the words "dung hill" and
"pig sty" might be closer to Absolute Knowledge than in Hegel's chapter.*

Adorno

*Kant's results are made immediate beginnings of these philosophies, so that the preced-
ing exposition, from which these results are derived, and which is philosophic cognition,
is cut away beforehand. Thus the Kantian philosophy becomes a pillow for intellectual
sloth, which soothes itself with the idea that everything has already been proved and
done with.*

Hegel

In fact, Adorno's treatment of Absolute Negativity in terms of the dominance
of integration over difference does have an echo in Hegel's work, but not in
the way Adorno thinks. Hegel's critique of the Enlightenment, specifically in
the section on the French Revolution in *The Phenomenology*, provides us with
an opportunity to reread Adorno's critique of Hegelian negativity. Hegel's
"Absolute Freedom and Terror" in *The Phenomenology* (Hegel 1977: 355–63)
provides an interesting example of Hegel's own critique of the type of conceptualization of negation and absolute with which he is often associated. In
other words, Hegel anticipated Adorno's type of critique and had seen this
kind of ontological pessimism as a logical outgrowth of certain actions in
and attitudes toward the French Revolution.

Locked into a conceptualization of Absolute as totalitarian and confronted
with the visage of Nazism, Adorno laments the impossibility of freedom and
sees only terror. Adorno stops dead; it becomes impossible for him to transcend this standpoint. Hegel's understanding of the pitfalls of the French Revolution, with its important rearticulation of his earlier critique of Fichte and
Rousseau, is a useful gauge to readdress Adorno's critique of Hegel's "absolute
negativity" and its identification with Auschwitz.

For Hegel, "Absolute Freedom" equals the state that allows "nothing
individual but carrying out the laws and the functions of the state." It is
essentially totalitarian. Hegel does not support it and argues that the purely
destructive character of Absolute Freedom "cannot achieve anything positive."
In contrast to Adorno's critique of the positive in the negative, it is the negative without a positive that betokens meaningless destruction: "[T]here is left
for it only *negative* action; it is merely the *fury* of destruction . . . it is one of
wholly unmediated pure negation, a negation, moreover, of the individual
as a being *existing* in the universal" (Hegel 1977: 359). Absolute Freedom

with its utilitarian cold calculations equals death. Hegel has in mind the meaningless deaths occasioned by the French Revolution's terror, but after Auschwitz we might think that the "coldest and meanest of all deaths," the deaths "with no significance," without meaning, these deaths, this "cold, matter of fact annihilation," as Hegel puts it, find expression in genocide. The suggestive affinity of modernity with Hegel's description of the French Revolution's Absolute Freedom and Terror begs the question, why didn't Adorno make anything of it?[15]

By associating Hegel's absolute negativity with Auschwitz Adorno missed Hegel's critique of this vision of the negative.[16] In "Absolute Freedom and Terror," Hegel appears to repeat the stage before reason, namely, the dialectic of dependence and independence at the level of self-consciousness: The "individuals who have felt the fear of death, of their absolute master," Hegel writes, reminiscent of the master/slave dialectic, "submit to negation." Considering Hegel's dialectic, we should not be surprised by such repetition, yet where previously the dialectic of self-consciousness resulted in mutual though unequal reciprocity (that found its further expression in Stoicism, Skepticism and the Unhappy Consciousness), in "Absolute Freedom and Terror" Hegel proclaims there is "no reciprocal action." The negation is both more absolute and more abstract. In fact, he calls it a pure abstraction and "empty nothingness." Hegel sees nothing, not only in death, but also in the Utility of the Enlightenment where "all determinations vanish in the loss suffered by the self in Absolute Freedom; its negation is the death that is without meaning, the sheer terror of the negative that contains nothing positive, nothing that fills it with content . . . the meaningless death" (Hegel 1977: 359–60).

Adorno's description of Hegel's absolute negativity as an "absolute integration" reduces the Absolute to Rousseau's General Will, precisely the subsumption of the individual by the universal that Hegel criticizes. It is an abstraction that can "return nothing in return for the sacrifice." The result of Hegel's critique of Rousseau could well be Adorno's critique of Hegel. Absolute negation is not merely an abstraction, "dictated by the universal" (Adorno 1993: 6); it swallows up difference and previous negative moments. The positive in the negative is reduced to ideology and in this case the positivism that underpins Auschwitz.[17]

With the Enlightenment, Hegel argues, consciousness finds its notion in Utility. In that shopkeeper mentality everything, all social relations, are judged by their exchange value. This is not the consciousness of the individual self, but the "pure Notion, the gazing of the self into the self"; it is Rousseau's general will where "the certainty of itself is the universal Subject, and its conscious Notion is the essence of all actuality." Such a dominating universal that brooks no difference is the world of "absolute integration" where the General Will suffocates opposition. One could deduce the logic of the marketplace of labor, of labor's use value – labor power as a commodity and the reduction of all labor to simple labor – in Hegel's description of a being for itself which is "essentially a being for another" and "devoid of self." This "passive self," reminiscent of the "passive Subject" discussed earlier, is not simply a repetition of lordship and bondage but the domination by capital, if we can think of capital as the General Will dominating everything, reducing the specificity of the individual's labor to that of the whole, i.e., a commodity. Absolute Freedom of capital, the reduction of everything to its Utility, is the cause of what Hegel calls the "doing away with" the individual (p. 587). Has not Hegel intimated the process of alienation in capitalism with its reduction of individual labor to abstract homogenous labor?

Describing the process of universalization indifferent to its content, a purely abstract freedom, suggests the conception of alienated labor that Marx defines in his *1844 Manuscripts*, "a special form of work indifferent to its content, of complete being for itself, i.e., the abstraction from all other being." Marx's category of capital is a reinscription of Absolute Freedom as pure self-identity of the universal will that Hegel describes in *The Phenomenology*.

Barriers to Adorno's Marxism

If "Hegel" were just some kind of subjective idealist who reduces "life" to "consciousness" – all sensuous otherness to sublatable moments in the progress of self-consciousness to absolute knowing, to an utterly transparent self-consciousness of self-consciousness – then it would be hard to understand not only how much such a Hegel could be Hegel (rather than say a relatively simple-minded Fichte) but also how Marx could ever have become Marx by critiquing (however "deconstructively") such a Hegel.

Andrzej Warminski

Value, therefore, does not have its description branded on its forehead; it rather transforms every product of labor into a hieroglyphic. Later on, men try to decipher the hieroglyphic, to get behind the secret of their own social product.

Marx, *Capital*

In our totally administered and reified society, identity is something we always seem to want. We want to fit in. Being "different" and being "yourself" are simply other modes of "fitting in." It is "the *primal form* of ideology," opines Adorno, that finds its perfect expression in capitalism, where social relations become identified as relations among things. Even Adorno, known for rigorously pursuing non-identity, insists that the ideal of identity, even if it is a "bourgeois egalitarian ideal" that brooks no qualitative difference, "must not be discarded."

For Marx this bourgeois concept of equality is alienated labor, what he calls "abstract labor," which reduces "human labor to an abstract equivalence, the abstract universal concept of average working hours." For Adorno this was "fundamentally akin to the principle of identification" (1973a: 146). Yet there is also an ideal identity, the logical conclusion of the bourgeois ideal, which is realized in terms of exchange. In *The Critique of the Gotha Program*, Marx calls it "equal right," a stage of communist society as it emerges from capitalism:

> A given amount of labor in one form is exchanged for an equal amount of labor in another form . . . In spite of this advance, this equal right is still constantly stigmatized by a bourgeois limitation . . . This equal right is an unequal right for unequal labor . . . It is therefore, a right of inequality, in its content, like every right. (Marx 1978: 530)

Marx had written in his *1844 Manuscripts* of "vulgar communism" which, remaining within the sphere of property, levels everything to its lowest common denominator and makes alienated labor the standpoint of society. In *The Critique of the Gotha Program* (1875), he argues that in the "first phase of communist society," unequal individuals are regarded simply as workers and "nothing more is seen in them" because "everything else is ignored." This conception, which pushes the identity of exchange to its logical conclusion, is at the bottom of Adorno's admonition that "when we criticize the barter principle of thought, we want to realize the ideal of free and just barter." Like Marx, who sees bourgeois right as the "first stage" of communism[18] needing transcendence, Adorno argues that "its [barter's] realization alone would transcend barter." Adorno contextualizes this within political economy, adding that "if no man had part of his labor withheld from him any more, rational identity would be a fact, and society would have transcended the identifying mode of thinking. This comes close enough to Hegel" (1973a: 147). Yet Adorno leaves it there. Unlike Marx, he never returns to the problematic of transcendence of this alienated standpoint even though he called this transcendence "a rational identity."

Adorno's remark that this "comes close" to Hegel is significant in that Adorno claims that *transcending* the identity mode of thinking comes close to Hegel. But at the same time he consistently positions and limits Hegel within bourgeois political economy. For Adorno, though Hegel had limited the dialectic of labor to consciousness, Hegel still "comes close to the mystery behind synthetic apperception." The "mystery," Adorno discloses, is "none other than social labor." Adorno notes that such a conception was discovered by Marx and reiterates Marx's comment that "Hegel's standpoint is that of modern political economy" (p. 112). But Adorno assumes that this exhausts Marx's critique of Hegel. Thus while praising Marx, he limits Marx's critique of Hegel to the question of labor: "The outstanding achievement of Hegel's *Phenomenology* [Adorno quotes Marx] – the dialectic of negativity as the moving and creating principle – is . . . that he . . . grasps the nature and conceives man (true, because real man) as the result of his own labor" (Marx quoted in Adorno 1993: 18). In his reading of Marx, Adorno recognizes that translating Hegel's concept of spirit into "social labor . . . elicits the reproach of sociologism" (p. 18) and rejects a simple productionist conception of labor. He notes that the exertion needed for thought, what Hegel calls the "labor of the negative," has more than a metaphorical connection to the toil of labor, adding that the "labor of the concept" has the "strains and toils of the concept." Yet Adorno finds all ideas of labor and creativity distasteful for his utopia. Second, Adorno's conceptualization of Hegel's absolute subject is akin to Marx's conceptualization of capital. Just as Reason in Hegel subsumes all otherness in the self-movement of the concept, so capital is the "moving contradiction" (Marx 1973: 706) which subsumes all human and natural contingency into the movement of mechanized, abstract labor. Again, Adorno views Hegel as describing the world as it really is: "In Hegel, abstract labor takes on a magical form . . . The self-forgetfulness of production, the insatiable and destructive expansive principle of the exchange society, is reflected in Hegelian metaphysics. It describes the way the world actually is" (Adorno 1993: 44). Hegel's Absolute simply provides a philosophic gloss for the self-expansive power of the capitalist production process. This is a one-sided reading of Marx's "Critique of the Hegelian Dialectic" which is aided by tendentious quoting. Marx found more in Hegel's dialectic, as the entire quotation from Marx attests (the italicized sentences are removed by Adorno):

> The outstanding achievement of Hegel's Phenomenology – the dialectic of negativity as the moving and creating principle – *is thus first that Hegel conceives the self genesis of man as a process, conceives objectification as loss of object, as alienation and as transcendence of this alienation*; that he grasps the nature and conceives man (true, because real man) as the result of his own labor.

Despite Adorno's agreement with Marx that Hegel's is the standpoint of bourgeois political economy, Adorno makes little of Marx's critique of alienated labor as the basis of Hegel's alienated conception, and moreover makes little of Marx's praise of Hegel's dialectic as providing an insight into the transcendence of this alienation. In other words, Marx sees embedded in Hegel's dialectic the movement of history, i.e., the struggle for freedom. Again we read the positive in Marx's criticism: "Because Hegel has conceived the negation of the negation from the point of view of the positive relation inherent in it as the true act and self-realizing act of all being, he has only found the abstract, logical, speculative expression of the movement of history" (p. 110). Marx's appreciation of Hegel's negation of the negation clearly runs counter to the project of *Negative Dialectics*. More than describing the fate of labor under capitalism, it is the process of history that Marx claims Hegel has discovered, albeit abstractly, but still discovered through pushing the conception of the negation of the negation into the realm of the Absolute itself. Adorno ignores this and fails to appreciate the critical drive (transcending Hegel's own standpoint, as Marx put it) that is embedded in Hegel's dialectic and which is made explicit by Marx in the *1844 Manuscripts*. The *Phenomenology*, writes Marx, contains "all the elements of criticism . . . beyond Hegelian standpoint" in as much as it holds to "man's estrangement" and "transcendence as an objective movement" (Marx 1978: 111).

In fact, Adorno's claim that the mystery of social labor is uncovered by Marx recapitulates the standpoint of classical political economy (represented by Smith and Ricardo) that Marx is criticizing. The insight into social labor, its social character, in other words, is indebted to political economy, not to Marxian critique.[19] Marx instead focuses on alienated labor as the cause, not the consequence, of the exchange of equivalents – a mode of thinking which itself is a result of reification[20] – and that while capital might be considered the "automatic subject" and labor power simply a commodity, it is the laborers who are the "living subject," and who revolt in myriad ways against the condition of alienated labor. Consequently, with Adorno's reduction of the problematic of alienated labor to its social character, there is no need to speak of the transcendence of alienation, nor the "positive" aspect of the Hegelian dialectic. Instead, Adorno equates the idea of the social character with reification and contrasts it to the isolated and individual resistance of Schönberg, for example. Abstractly, Adorno does not disagree with the concept of a negating force. Schönberg takes the place of Marx's concept of the proletariat. It is not Schönberg's class position, his audience, nor the music's conscious intent but its composition that fulfills a "social function" as a dialectical negation. For Adorno there was only "one" proletariat and that was the German. Happier with citing Lenin's Lassalleanism[21] in 1936 to support his idea of the desultory consciousness of the "actual proletariat" (against Brecht, see Buck-Morss 1977: 30), Adorno was uninterested in its dialectical "others" (the "lower and deeper" strata, as Marx put it, whether outside or even inside

Western Europe) that underlay Marx's aphorism, "the proletariat is revolutionary or it is nothing."

Adorno's "Regression of Hearing" (1938), directed toward Benjamin, could hardly more appropriately describe his inattention to the Spanish revolution (1936–9) which under the whip of the Stalinist counter-revolution established workers' and peasants' collectives. It could be considered the first revolt against "state capitalism," but it played no part in Pollock's thesis. Additionally, Benjamin's death colored Adorno and Horkheimer's *Dialectic of Enlightenment*, but it is often forgotten that it was the Spanish counter-revolution that ultimately led to Benjamin's suicide; General Franco's border prevented him from staying in Spain after he had crossed the Pyrenees in September 1940.

Privileging individual virtuosity, based upon a "lonely subjectivity which draws into itself," as he characterizes Schönberg (1973b: 142),[22] Adorno identifies *social* labor as reified. The critique correctly identifies the violence of being "walled into the social," as Karel Kosik once put it, but in Manichean fashion Adorno equates the social with totalitarianism. There is something almost existentialist in Adorno's privileging individual virtuosity as the authentic expression of freedom. In this binary of individual versus social, he dismisses the social individual. It is Adorno's aphorism that best expresses, what is in a sense, the undialectical character of his thinking: "Solidarity," he claims in *Minima Moralia*, "is sick . . . all collaboration, all the human worth of social mixing and participation, merely masks a tacit acceptance of inhumanity" (Adorno 1974: 51, 26). The "identity" of totality and the social on one side, and anti-totality and the individual/monadic on the other, is at the core of negative dialectics. Methodologically, its justification is found in isolated, monadic experimental dissection, and thus the closest expression of freedom is the lonely subjectivity of Schönberg's "liberated music." Adorno's Manichean opposition of the "authentic" individual versus the social leads him to dismiss all human social productivity, decontextualizing alienated labor from its capitalistic context: "Only by virtue of opposition to production . . . can men bring about another more worthy of human beings" (1974: 15). Rather than offering a critique of alienated labor, "humanism" is here abstracted from human life. It is a one-dimensional, decorporealized human being which finds expression in the "great refusal" of Adorno's negative dialectic.

Adorno ignores the important distinction Marx draws between alienated labor – the historically specific labor under capitalism – and labor considered as "a conscious, purposeful activity."[23] Adorno thus repeats a problem posed in Lukács' *History and Class Consciousness*: the identity of labor (externalization) with the alienated and forced labor of capitalism. It is for this very reason that Adorno misses the point and originality in Marx's conceptualization of fetishism as a product of capitalism, slighting it as "truly a piece from the heritages of classic German philosophy" (pp. 189–90).

Marx's analysis of commodity fetishism is based on the discrepancy between appearance and reality, that what appears as equal exchange in the marketplace is in reality unequal. The core of this unreality and the appearance of its "magic and necromancy" (Marx 1976: 169) is that "the phantom-like objectivity" of products of labor are merely "congealed quantities of homogenous human labor," measured by time. Central to Marx's analysis is the dual character of labor. It is not labor itself that is the source of value, but the commodification of labor, namely labor power. Because labor power cannot be split from the human being, it is the abstract commodity labor power that takes on the quality of special powers, while the concrete laborer is reduced to a vessel that houses such powers. Marx wonders about the provenance of the fetishism of commodities, the transformation of "social relations between men" into the "phantasmagoric form of a relations between things?" He concludes that "clearly, it arises, from the form itself" (Marx 1976: 164). This emphasis on the form, that is, the commodification of labor, as a necessity implies a new concept of ideology. Marx's concept of commodity fetishism is ideology *par excellence* subjected to critique. Commodity fetishism is no longer mere illusion but rather a necessary and accurate expression of a false reality. The shift of emphasis from the "fantastic form" to the necessity of that form, leads to a recognition of the truth of the way things really are.

Adorno's theory of reification follows Marx's idea of fetishism as "the exchange principle, the reduction of human labor to its abstract average labor time" (1973a: 146). He appreciates Marx's categorization of abstract generalized labor measured by socially necessary labor time, which is essential to the idea of fetishism of commodities and central to its form. Following Lukács' generalization of commodity fetishism, he believes that all social relations are reduced to relations among things, but in contrast to Lukács, who over-emphasized the "consciousness" of the proletariat surmounting the fetish, and closer to Marx, Adorno argues that "the fetish character of commodities is not a fact of consciousness" (letter to Walter Benjamin quoted in Rose 1981: 47). While Adorno critically addresses an idealistic aspect of Lukács' conceptualization of reification, arguing that the fetish is not a result of "a subjectively errant consciousness, but objectively deduced," he adds that "the social *a priori*" is "the exchange process." The fixation on exchange (even if Adorno is not speaking of the marketplace) tends to overlook how the commodity form emerges in production (and how labor takes the form of a social relation between things).

Gillian Rose correctly points out that Adorno generalizes the theory of commodity fetishism as reification, but she assumes that the problem is Adorno's failure neither to take up "the theory of surplus value or any class formation" nor to develop "the theory of power and the state" (p. 47). Marx does not develop these concepts in chapter 1 of *Capital*, where he takes up fetishism (even if surplus value is implicit). Adorno's failure is far simpler. In his essay "Marginalia to Theory and Praxis" he argues that "the theory of surplus value does not tell one should start a revolution" (1998: 227), adding that Marx "hardly moves beyond the philosopheme that only the proletariat can be the cause of its own emancipation."[24] Like Lukács, Adorno ignores Marx's division of labor as "abstract" and "concrete," a distinction central to understanding Marx's critique of political economy and alienated labor. The dual character of labor *develops* the dual character of the commodity (use and exchange value) that so appeals to Adorno. Thus one limitation of Adorno's theory of reification with its emphasis on exchange value is that capitalism, rather than intensifying contradictions and bringing new elements forward, is able to assimilate them. The capitalist's problem of valorization is solved. Total rationalization does away with the "revolt" that Marx argued was central to capitalist reproduction. Rather than simply a "philosopheme," labor is the human dimension that is central to the dialectic of capital.

What is crucial to Marx's idea of reification is labor power, and he calls the dual category of labor the basis of "all understanding" and his original contribution (1976a: 132). This dual category is expressed as concrete and abstract labor: concrete individual labor with specific skills (use) is reduced to abstract labor (exchange), "a special sort of work indifferent to its content, of complete being for itself, i.e., the abstraction from all other being." Rather than adopting "conscious, purposeful activity" as an ethical imperative, the humanism of the laborer, the revolt of the laborer against alienation is immanent to the dialectic of capital (Marx 1976a: 929). Indeed, it is the idea of "freely associated labor" – conscious, purposeful, activity – in contradistinction to alienated labor, and the commodification of labor power – that reappears in *Capital* as the concrete, i.e., *human*, activity. The great struggle over the working day is one expression of capital's attempt to squeeze out the maximum of labor time from the worker while the worker continues to struggle in myriad ways against it. The decline of leisure time and increasing overtime in the US over the past twenty years is one expression of capital's logic. In *Capital* Marx finds this struggle over the working day not an additional story to capital's "werewolf hunger" for value but central to it. Indeed, "the theory of surplus value" might not "tell how one should start a revolution" but the reduction of labor time, based on the shortening of the working day, is a prerequisite, argues Marx, for the leap from necessity to freedom.

The Specter of Lukács

One could say that if Lukács re-Hegelianized Marx, then Adorno re-Kantianized Lukács.

Buck-Morss

It has already been intimated that many of Adorno's shortcomings vis-à-vis Marx arise because Adorno's analysis does not go beyond the appearance of the commodity. As Marx put it to Wagner, "this obscurantist has overlooked the fact that even in the analysis of the commodity my work does not stop with the dual modality in which it manifests itself, but rather there is an immediate progress on to the fact that within this duality of the commodity what is manifested is a double character of labor, the product of which is the commodity" (Marx 1976b: 216). Moreover, despite Adorno's many criticisms of Lukács' conception of reification – for example, that it is "inspired by the wishful image of unbroken subjective immediacy" (1973a: 374) and loses all power and dialectical drive in a "tireless charge" – it remains a central aspect of Adorno's philosophy. Adorno is aware of the uncritical use of the term "reification," which like any category is not immune to the very regression and transformation that it purportedly explains, and does not privilege reification as the methodology above dialectic. In fact, he argues in *Negative Dialectics* that to base critical theory on reification is to make it susceptible to reified thinking – where it offers only a mirror of the here and now. Without the dialectic, it would be uncritical. However, what is at issue is Adorno's relation to Lukács' original conceptualization. Of the major Frankfurt School theorists it was Adorno who remained profoundly touched by Lukács. Perhaps this is due to his age. As Siegfried Kracauer said of an eighteen-year-old Adorno in 1921: "At the moment he consists entirely of Lukács and myself." Even after the powerful influence of Benjamin and his "program" of presenting Benjamin to the academic world, Adorno remained wedded to, as Wiggershaus put it, "the same Hegelian-Marxist position which Lukács had developed in *History and Class Consciousness* – but he supported it independent of class considerations" (1994: 95).[25]

Gillian Rose argues that Adorno sought to develop a concept of reification that avoids the theoretical problems in Lukács' work by rejecting the idealist assertion of subject/object identity with the proletariat, but it is not clear to me that Adorno does avoid Lukács' problems. Certainly, he does not return to Marx's concept. Unlike Lenin, who, under the impact of the collapse of Marxism in the holocaust of World War I and his reading of Hegel's *Science of Logic* (see Anderson 1996), criticized the embourgeoisement of part of the European working class and emphasized the national liberation movements as part of the "dialectic of history," and unlike Marx, who spoke more abstractly in *Capital* of "new passions and new forces" – new subjectivities of revolution – which arose as part of the process of global capitalist accumulation, Lukács' undialectical solution to the subject/object problematic did not disclose new subjective impulses within the objective situation (thus while he became a "Leninist" on organization, he remained Luxemburgian on the national questions). In contrast, Adorno simply disorganizes the problem, taking recourse in another abstraction, a critique of the social: "Despite all the experience of reification . . . Critical Theory is oriented towards the idea of society as subject" (quoted by Jay 1984b: 268).[26]

Contrary to what is generally assumed, Lukács gives short shrift to the proletarian's real everyday experience. He believes that reification can be transcended through an imputed (rather than dialectical) change in consciousness. Thus the fully conscious subject is reduced to an act of *knowledge*: It is "knowledge [that] brings about an objective structural change in the object of knowledge" (1971: 169). It is the very act of consciousness, in other words, an enlightenment imparted from outside, that overthrows the objective form, the capitalist structure (1971: 178). Activity becomes an act of intellectual will, divorced from the conditions, the social relations and social existence, that are entered into and with which the struggle for freedom is dialectically entangled. In contrast to Marx, who remarks that the knowledge of the fetish does not pierce through or overthrow reified society because it is a reflection of real social relations that have to be overturned, Lukács simply asserts that proletarian victory is accomplished in consciousness.

Adorno's pessimism toward the working class finds its genealogy in Lukács' 1923 essay, "Reification and the Consciousness of the Proletariat," which, despite its critique, takes as a given the backwardness of workers' consciousness;[27] he stresses ideological critique (1971: 262), ignoring "objective factors" and also separating them from the task of raising consciousness.[28] Lukács' subject/object identity and his privileging of consciousness, in contrast to dialectics, means that he also dismisses the subjective inner core of objective developments. The disembodied proletariat is spirited away from its place in production where it confronts capital head-on, because, according to Lukács, "the ideological crisis of the proletariat must be solved *before* a practical solution to the world's economic crisis can be found" (my italics; cf. Mészáros 1995: 321). It can only be solved by the intellectual. Adorno agrees with

Lukács that the individual proletarian is constrained by false consciousness, but that is not his concern. He refuses Lukács' turn to an ethical imperative as "enlightener" of the proletariat, and abandons the project of proletarian emancipation. It is simply a throwback to "meaningful times for whose return the young Lukács yearned" (p. 191), he says, but still maintains that the only hope is the intellectual, though no longer as enlightener of a proletariat that he considers beyond hope. For Adorno "exchange had maimed everything" (cf. "On Subject and Object" in Adorno 1998: 253), even the intellectual "exchange," raising his suspicions of radical organizations.[29] Indeed Adorno does not rethink the dialectics of organization, but, accepting Lukács' Leninism, opts for its opposite. Adorno sees the non-collaborating, estranged, and isolated (antisocial) intellectual as the only possible resistance: "For the intellectual, inviolable isolation is now the only way of showing some measure of solidarity" (Adorno 1974: 26). The retrogressive period becomes an "age of subjective impotence" and with it Adorno retreats to an immanent critique external to the human subject which has become consumed by false consciousness (1998: 252). Adorno rejected the equation of the ethical imperative with the "revolutionary organization," but he did not reject the idea of an ethical imperative.

Weber's Lasting Imprint

The kind of enlightenment that does not carry out the self-reflection that forms the content of the Hegelian system, naming the relationship of the matter at hand to the idea – would end up in madness – thought that removes all participation on the subject's part and all anthropomorphism from the object, is the consciousness of the schizophrenic.

Adorno

The importance of Marx's dual character of labor is evident in Lukács' misunderstanding of Marx's categorization of capitalism as a process where dead labor dominates living labor. Lukács reduces the specific capitalistic form of dead labor (machines) over living labor (human beings) to a temporal problem of "past over present," completely missing the point of the social relations embedded in the organic composition of labor, manifested in the way the laborer becomes an appendage to the machine. Additionally, the "real life" struggles are missing. Technological developments are partly a result of the struggle to shorten the working day as capital looks for greater surplus value within the same time frame. The domination of dead over living labor is central to capitalist expansion and its crises are crucial expressions of labor's reification. The reduction of the living laborer to an appendage of a machine is its concrete expression. Rationalization, Taylorism, flexitime, workteams, etc., are all attempts to control and increase relative surplus value.

Lukács' generalizing of "reification" downplays the specificity of the proletarian's experience, and his conflating the idea of externalization with alienation glosses over the specificity of the capitalist process. Despite Lukács' own pronouncements about the centrality of chapter 1 of *Capital* to Marxism (for example, see 1971: 170), his understanding of Marx's critique of political economy and its category of labor is never fully developed. In its place appears the Weberian idea of rationalization which Adorno takes to its logical conclusion.

Both rationalization and the moral imperative associated with an intellectual "standpoint of the proletariat" (a vanguard of enlighteners)[30] have a philosophic pedigree in neo-Kantianism. Adorno rejects the philosophical idealism of the moral imperative, and instead espouses the Lukácsian generalization of fetishism as "the necessary immediate reality of every person in capitalist society" and its equation with rationalization. The logical conclusion of such reification, of total rationalization and administration, has its roots in Weber.[31]

Unlike Marx, Lukács reduces the historical specificities of modern capitalism to what Istvan Mészáros calls a "heap of superficial functional characteristics," claiming that Lukács (and Adorno) endorse Weber's view of the centrality of rational calculation to modern capitalism. Weber inverts the traditional Marxist determinism, making the superstructure the basis for the structure. It is the "rational" administration of law, politics, and "everyday life," that lies behind the capitalist economy. "The bloody legislation against the expropriated," the laws to lengthen the working day, and the power of the state to "hasten in hothouse fashion, the transformation of the feudal mode of production into the capitalist mode," all of which characterized the "primitive accumulation of capital" (Marx 1976: 896), are subsumed under the class-neutral "rational administration." Mészáros adds that

> while on the one hand the Weberian concept of capitalism is ahistorically extended to embrace, in a generic sense, a thousand years of socioeconomic and cultural development, at the same time, on the other hand, the materially grounded specificity of capitalism as an historically circumscribed antagonistic socioeconomic system, with its contending classes, and with the in :ur-able irrationality of its crisis-prone structure, is transformed into a fictitious entity: a social order characterized by the "strictly rational organization of work," coupled with a "rational technology" as well as with the corresponding "rational system of laws" and befitting "rational administration." (1995: 333)

In place of the centrality of a "free" proletariat to the development of capitalism, Lukács uncritically places Weber's conflation of the modern proletarian with the "independence" of the artisan, the landowning peasant, and cottage craftsman (see Lukács 1971: 95). Far from Lukács identifying capitalism's real historical specificities and thus its transitional character, Lukács, like Weber, emphasizes its rationalizing, calculating principles (p. 96). Lukács' Weberianism, especially the embrace of the myth of rationality, takes as its point of departure the "logical" and "rational" systematization of regulating life rather than an analysis of and an engagement with the class character of such "rationalism" built on the capitalistic division of labor (for example, cf. Lukács 1971: 96). Adorno's own move away from the "idealistic" "standpoint of the proletariat" to an analysis of the "social" character of reification does no better in getting back to these Marxian concerns.

In his *Time, Labor and Social Domination* (1993), Moishe Postone also shows that critical theory was in many ways an amalgam of a "pre-Marxian" understanding of labor and Weber's notion of rationalization. The two strands, he adds, "have one-dimensionality in common":

> The ambiguous legacy of Weber in strains of Western Marxism, as mediated by Lukács, involves the "horizontal" broadening of the scope of Marxian categories to include dimensions of social life ignored in more narrowly orthodox interpretations and, at the same time, their "vertical" flattening. In *Capital*, the categories are expressions of a contradictory social totality; they are two-dimensional. The notion of reification in Western Marxism, however, implies one-dimensionality; hence the possible determinant negation of the existent order cannot be rooted in the categories that purportedly grasp it. (p. 116)

Relying on Weber's notion of rationalization instead of Marx's analysis of the dual character of labor, Adorno treats reification not as a condition specific to capitalism but to all Western culture since Homer. It is not, for example, the teachings of Marx but the lesson of the *Odyssey* which inspires *Dialectic of Enlightenment's* dehistoricization. Reification is not specific to capitalism but a fact of Western civilization. Because the binary of use and exchange dominates Adorno's conception of Marxism, the specific trajectory of Marx's analysis of labor eludes him and, thus equated with exchange, reification can have a long history. Additionally, in place of what Postone calls negations of the existing social order in the categories that understand it, the shadow of Weber's "iron cage" – of modern "man" heading inevitably toward destruction – looms large. The objectivity of reification, however, even when Adorno becomes more critical of its conceptual status as a "philosopher's stone" and its "regress[ion] to the subjectivism of the pure act" (1973a: 374), remains

Adorno's central and conceptual noose. Though Adorno, like Marx, considered Hegel's philosophy objective, he reduces the Hegelian dialectic to the systematic expression of this drive of reification. The self-developing subject in Hegel is either the objectivity of all consuming capital or literally "nothing," as he puts it in the essay "Subject and Object." In other words, the subject is consumed by reification.

The separation of the subject from human beings reflects the objectivity of capital. The generalization of reification to all social relations reflects the utter reification of "living" labor. Had Adorno any key to offer to get out of this conceptual iron cage?

Flattened Dialectic

Care must be taken to distinguish between the first negation as negation in general, and the second negation of the negation: the latter is concrete, absolute negativity, just as the former is only abstract negativity.

Hegel

The problem is not that Adorno makes Auschwitz into a philosophic category but that he makes it synonymous with absolute negativity, thus the long march of the dialectic of enlightenment toward horror. There is no contradiction. Adorno has equated this with Hegel. Yet at the same time, Adorno wants to hang on to a dialectic and "rescue" Hegel from the pitfalls of the "subject." At the conclusion of Hegel's *Science of Logic* in the section "Absolute Idea," Hegel had spoken of subjectivity as a "negative self-relation" which he argued is the "innermost source of activity, of living and spiritual self-movement." It was this "living element" that Adorno found problematic, but embedded there was the kind of "utopia" for which he yearned. The negation of the negation, rather than a return to the past, is described as "the innermost and most objective moment of Life and Spirit, by virtue of which a subject is personal and free" (Hegel 1989: 836). Rather than "Absolute Terror," here we find Hegel speaking of "an absolute liberation" where there is "no transition in this freedom" (p. 843).

Despite all qualifications to the contrary, Adorno's negative dialectic is a flattening, all-consuming one that allows no place for an alternative to emerge. Certainly Adorno does allow for "liberating" moments in his description of Schönberg's music, but these moments are isolated, alone and temporary. Indeed, Adorno celebrates this monadism in the face of totalitarianism. Marx too emphasizes the freedom of the individual against vulgar communism. But whereas Marx speaks of the "individual as the social entity," always viewing the relational and historical process of individualization, in short, the social individual, Adorno reacts against the "social," which he identifies with "exchange" and the cause of reification. "After Auschwitz" Adorno remains locked within the binary of Absolute Freedom and Terror that Hegel speaks of, where the Absolute is equated with the subsumption of the individual by the social. The only hope is individual resistance against the juggernaut of "the social" with its pseudo-individualism and pseudo-resistance. And what of Adorno's individual? Is the isolated individual simply Fichte's solipsistic self-certain ego? In fact, the notion of human autonomy is a Kantian one: "The only true force against the principle of Auschwitz would be human autonomy, if I may use a Kantian term: that is, the force of reflection and of self-determination, the will to refuse participation" (quoted in Hohendahl 1995: 58).

Adorno borrows from Freudian psychoanalysis as a means to confront the stasis of the dialectic, yet with Freudian analysis are we not back again to the problem of the social in two ways? First, that analysis will have an impact on the social situation, and second, that the analysis of individual pathology and neurosis is itself constructed within a particular historical and social situation which is in need of analysis and change. In the end, Hohendahl is right; Adorno's thought is "predicated on his concept of a totally administered society, which leaves its members with the futile choice between a revolution that would not change the structure of domination, on one hand, and individual passivity, on the other" (p. 17). This is one reason why his idea of utopia is somewhat flaccid.

Adorno responds to charges of passivity in his essay "Resignation" written in 1969, posing an interesting contrast with the 1931 lecture "Actuality of Philosophy" (see note 26). In "Resignation," Adorno argues that when it came to praxis his situation was quite the opposite of Marx's. Today, he says, one clings to action because of its impossibility, praxis is simply "pseudo-activity" which is "allied with pseudoreality in the design of a subjective position." Losing any chance of reflexivity, praxis is simply an immediacy, a do-it-yourselfism, highlighted by Daniel Cohn-Bendit's quip in 1968 that theory could be "picked up en route." Yet at the end of the short essay he leaves us with a notion of an "uncompromising critical thinker" who does not give up. He defines praxis as "open thinking" which "points beyond itself." Open thinking, he says, is "more closely related to a praxis *truly involved in change* than in a position of mere obedience for the sake of praxis" (1978: 168; my emphasis). For critical thinking to be uncompromising, however, there must be a complete rift between its autonomy and the social world outside. Thus the problem is not with open thinking per se but in the belief that it alone is related to a praxis of true change. Adorno's position, his contemplative philosophy, becomes similar to that of the left Hegelians, though in his case, as a "materialist," the work of a critical thinker is also mediated and structured by the social and historical context. For Adorno, dialectical thinking is autonomous from the social world though also "structured" by it. The social world can be analyzed directly but is also sealed off from immanent critique. A critique is only available from a second order, namely the critical thinker, or more correctly, any authentic critique is made impossible. The circle cannot be broken; all praxis, which is not simply practice for Marx, cannot by definition be the subject's objectivity but only the pseudo-action of a subject position.

So Adorno reinstates a Kantian antinomy, substituting "permanent critique not alone for absolute negativity but also of 'permanent revolution itself,'" as Raya Dunayevskaya put it (1980: 173). Adorno is not simply in the bind between futile activity or passivity but that even the idea of open thinking is not receptive to new elements outside of thought because the world outside it is totally administered.

Despite Adorno's insight into the labor of the concept, the concept of labor always equals "work" and work is always forced labor. Thus Marx's call for the "abolition" of labor in the *Grundrisse* is significantly more attractive than his idea of labor as humanly creative. Reacting against the concept of "production," for example, Adorno also discards what Marx, also in the *Grundrisse*, calls the full development of a rich individuality whose labor is "the full development of activity itself" (p. 325). Where for Adorno reification was a closed ontology, Marx, following Hegel, located alienation phenomenologically. Thus it was lived experience that could be transcended by the revolt of laborers. This phenomenology of liberation is expressed by Marx in the struggle over the eight-hour day. Though Marx would not say how or the ways in which such struggles would unfold, the idea of their development through constant criticism became a signature theme. Nothing could be clearer than the gulf between Marx and Adorno in their contrasting visions of a liberated society. First Adorno:

> Perhaps the true society will grow tired of development and, out of freedom, leave possibilities unused . . . lying on the water and looking at the sky, being, nothing else without any further definition and fulfillment . . . none of these abstract concepts comes closer to fulfilled utopia than that of perpetual peace. (1974: 156–7)

Adorno again borrows from Kant (perpetual peace) to describe his utopia. In contrast to Adorno's account of the terror of the Absolute, consider Marx's, expressed in the *Grundrisse*, as a new society, an "absolute movement of becoming" where development is humanized:

When the bourgeois form is stripped away, what is wealth other than the universality of individual needs, capacities, pleasures, productive forces, etc., created through universal exchange? What, if not the full development of human control over the forces of nature – those of his own nature as well as those of so-called "nature"? What, if not the absolute elaboration of his creative disposition, without any preconditions other than antecedent historical evolution which makes the totality of this evolution – i.e., the evolution of all human powers as such, unmeasured by any *previously established yardstick* – an end in itself. What is this, if not a situation where man does not reproduce himself in any predetermined form, but produces his totality? Where he does not seek to remain something formed by the past, but is the absolute movement of becoming. (p. 488)[32]

Yet for Adorno, there is no answer to the "problem of practice." Praxis was vigilance, and the specter of Auschwitz, as both an event and a condition, colored his thinking. "Debarbarization of humanity is the immediate prerequisite for survival," Adorno argued (1998: 190). But how is that achieved? It is clear from "Education after Auschwitz" that Adorno assumes nothing other than a radical reform of society, and that, he argues, could begin through the transformation of education into a system of sociological critique. This kind of critical education, though nowhere in sight, might not stop the "desktop murderer" but might manage to do something to reform those "down below."

Having an effect on those "down below" is of a different order to the idea of critical thinking, which could deserve its name only if it were not sullied by practice. Nevertheless, without a subjective element that would resist such barbarism "down below," would Adorno's "practice" of an intransigence be much in advance of the debate? All he was left with was an unhappy hope, but are we left with anything other than hand-wringing and an unarticulated utopia? Aware of the rotten compromises with the state that Adorno was willing to entertain in 1968, is there is no reason to think that Adorno offers us any new perspectives for our post-Cold-War world?

In the spirit of *Negative Dialectics* we might say Adorno's thought, which once seemed obsolete, lives on because the moment to realize it was missed. While Fredric Jameson claims that Adorno is a model for the 1990s (Jameson 1990: 5), it may turn out at the *fin de millénaire* that the range of Adorno studies, new translations, and critical commentaries indicate Adorno's final commoditization. Has Adorno finally been tamed because he has been thought out of his own time and thus hypostatized precisely in the way that he warned against?

Notes

1 In *Marxism and Totality* (1984a), Jay argues that "for all of Adorno's interest in Lukács and Hegelian Marxism, for all his fascination with the concepts of reification, mediation, and second nature, for all his attraction to the totalizing methodology of Horkheimer's Institute, he stubbornly maintained that under present circumstances, the anti-holistic lessons he learned from Kracauer, Benjamin, and Schoenberg were of equal, if not greater, value" (p. 255). For an overview of debates about Adorno, "Western Marxism," and "Critical Theory," see chapter 1 of Lambert Zuidervaart's *Adorno's Aesthetic Theory: The Redemption of Illusion* (1994).

2 Tracing a lineage quite different from the determinist Marxism of the Second International, Hegelian Marxism (also often associated with "Western Marxism" (Jay 1984b: 1–3) re-emphasizes the centrality of dialectic and praxis within Marxism.

  In his essay "The Dialectic Today," Lucien Goldmann provides us with a definition of Hegelian Marxism as well as its lineage: "Hegelian categories are all recovered in Marxism; and it is no accident that they were reactualized in Europe around, say, the years 1917–23: first by Lenin in the *Philosophical Notebooks*, second by Lukács in *History and Class Consciousness*, and thirdly, I believe, somewhat later in Gramsci's concretely philosophical analyses" (1970: 112–13).

  One could quibble that each "reactualization" had its own intellectual heritage: i.e., Lukács to neo-Kantianism, and Gramsci's to Croce. The philosophic pedigree of each claim to Hegelian Marxism would thus have to be judged, but this is not my goal. My measure of a Hegelian Marxist is Goldmann's in that one is a Marxist who both emphasizes the Hegel–Marx relationship and uses Hegelian categories to creatively reactualize Marxism within their own context. Thus one would not have to be hampered by periodization (i.e., 1917–23), nor follow Hegel's *Philosophy of History* (as Jay argues) nor be "Western." Using this definition I would not include the Frankfurt School in toto, but I would include Marcuse (from 1932 until the new introduction to *Reason and Revolution* in 1960) because of his essay on Marx's *1844 Manuscripts* (1932) and his *Reason and Revolution* (1940), but I would not include Adorno's *Negative Dialectics*. An argument could be made for Karl Korsch's *Marxism and Philosophy*, though finally I would agree with Douglas Kellner and Mihály Vajda that he is not a Hegelian because he does not develop Hegelian categories, even if he claims that an understanding of Marxism depends on grasping its Hegelian roots.

3 Adorno's challenge to Hegel is framed in terms of Hegel's own philosophic goal. A quote from the preface of Hegel's *Phenomenology* in *Minima Moralia* captures this point: "The life of the mind only attains its truth when discovering itself in absolute desolation. The mind is not this power as a positive which turns away from the negative, as when we say of something that it is null, or false, so much for that and now for something else; it is this power only when looking

the negative in the face and dwelling upon it" (quoted in Adorno 1974: 16). The idea of absolute negativity is central to this paper. In other words, even when Hegel got to the Absolute Idea in the *Science of Logic*, we do not find that it contains the highest opposition within itself.

4   One does not have to be a Lukácsian to be a Hegelian Marxist (see note 2), yet scholars on both sides of the Marxist/poststructuralist divide tend to collapse the two. Even if Adorno created such an identity, it is another thing for scholars of the twenty-first century to continue such a mistake.

For different attitudes toward the Lukács–Adorno relationship, see Buck-Morss (1977) and Rose (1981). Martin Jay also provides an interesting summary in his essay "Adorno and the Lukácsian Concept of Totality" (1984) where he views Lukács as a paradigmatic Hegelian Marxist and Marxist humanist. However, his point that Lukács' neo-Kantian notion of "second nature" is Hegel's undermines Jay's categorization.

5   While Adorno's philosophic critique can be traced to the 1930s, for him "Auschwitz" is the concrete expression of Lukácsian totality.

6   If there are "class conditions" (Jameson 1990: 7) to Adorno, they are the division between political economy and Marx's critique.

Jameson slips between calling Frederic Pollock's theory "late capitalism" (pp. 31, 255) and "state capitalism" (p. 257). Though he mentions James Burnham, Jameson ignores the debates in the 1940s about Russia as a state capitalist society of which Pollock's was a part. "Late capitalism," perhaps exemplified in Ernest Mandel's book, has its genealogy in another tendency, namely that Russia and East Europe are, following Trotsky, not capitalistic but some kind of "degenerated workers states" etc. Though Adorno used the term "late capitalism" as part of a title in the 1967 ("Spätkapitalismus oder Industriegesellschaft") Jameson is clear that Adorno's attitude toward Russia bothers him: "Readers of *Marxism and Form*, however, will have sensed my increasing distance, by 1971, when the book was finally published, from what I took to be Adorno's hostility toward the Soviet Union" (1990: 4). Inexplicably, Jameson adds that Adorno's attitude was "class conditioned" (p. 7), which limits the problematic of his *Late Marxism*. To think that the proletariat are quite happy under a regime of forced labor betrays a class attitude on Jameson's part.

One might wonder why Jameson still chose to polemicize against Adorno in such a way in 1990. Wouldn't Adorno's "dilemma" as a left intellectual (to use Jameson's terms) be how one can remain critical toward the Soviet Union and his own social democracy? On this question we would do well to compare Mandel and Pollock to Raya Dunayevskaya and C. L. R. James's theory, which was also developed in the 1940s and led them to a rediscovery of Marx's *1844 Manuscripts*. See Dunayevskaya, *The Marxist-Humanist Theory of State Capitalism* (Chicago: News and Letters 1992).

7   This is central to understanding the difference between Hegel and much of the contemporary (poststructuralist and deconstructive) understanding of Hegel, indebted to Alexander Kojève.

8 For a view of the openness of Hegel's "Absolute Mind," see Dunayevskaya (1989).

9 Buck-Morss (1977) argues that for Adorno the "task of philosophy was to undermine the already tottering frame of bourgeois idealism by exposing the contradictions which riddled its categories and, following their inherent logic, push them to the point where made to self-destruct" (p. 64).

10 In a sense, the *Dialectic of Enlightenment* (written in 1944), in contrast to Marcuse's 1940 *Reason and Revolution*, marked a change from the Frankfurt School's earlier philosophic purpose (which had something of a high point as it embraced, even if ambivalently, a Nietzschean critique of the Enlightenment's identification with domination). Adorno's rejection of Hegel's Absolute, as an imperialism that subsumes the other, almost necessitated he embrace a Nietzschean perspectivism. Enlightenment's duality of freedom and subjugation is expressed through a progressive appreciation of Nietzsche: "Nietzsche was one of the few after Hegel who recognized the dialectic of enlightenment," opines Adorno who progressively takes over Nietzsche's position to point out the universality of domination (cf. Habermas 1987). By *Negative Dialectics* Adorno was willing to pay that price, as he became preoccupied with its own methodology which, Rose later argued, "remains in a realm of infinite striving or task, a morality in the limited sense which Hegel criticized: a general prescription not located in the social relations which underlie it, and hence incapable of providing any sustained and rigorous analysis of those relations" (1981: 33).

11 Adorno calls it "use value" (1973b: 11).

12 Lukács had named this ineffable thing as the party, beyond contradiction. Unwilling to deal concretely with the endless series of negations that Marx had characterized as the difference between proletarian and bourgeois revolutions in *The Eighteenth Brumaire*, Lukács idealistically posits the party as both subject/object mediation and as subject/object identity. Adorno's utopia recasts Lukács' idealism without the party.

13 Akin to Gramsci's understanding of historical materialism, critical philosophy rejects all competing philosophies by exposing them as ideologies. Gramsci's historicizing of philosophy includes the historicity of the "philosophy of praxis." He argues that each philosophy thinks of itself as the philosophy of the age, but what separates the philosophy of praxis from other philosophies is that it "thinks of itself in a historicist manner." "[I]t is made quite explicit in the well-known thesis that historical development will at a certain point be characterized by the passage from the reign of necessity to the reign of freedom" (1971: 404).

14 Patricia Mills' citation of Adorno in *Feminist Interpretations of Hegel* (1996) is in this spirit. She sees Adorno as providing a basis on which to "reconceive dialectical thinking" and prevent "the closure of identity logic" she finds in Hegel. She also claims that by doing so one can realize the goal of Hegel's philosophy: "an inter-subjective recognition without recourse to domination" (p. 85). However, such a vision of mutual reciprocity has to be conceived from outside Hegel's dialectic, and thus we are surely back to Kant.

15 In *Dialectic of Enlightenment* there is a passing reference to the preceding section in *The Phenomenology*, on Utility. The reduction of Hegel's Absolute to integration, even if it is accompanied by qualifications is precisely a vulgar reduction. How far away is it from the positivism and vulgarism of Karl Popper and his "Hegel and Fascism" faction?

16 For Derrida, Hegel doesn't tarry with the negative, namely death, long enough. Derrida is concerned with Hegel's discussion of the risk of life in the master/slave dialectic. In Derrida's reading of the master/slave dialectic Hegel backs away from negativity, which in truth Derrida celebrates as nihilistic and meaningless.

17 Rather than something new, the Hegel of *Negative Dialectics* replays Adorno and Horkheimer's earlier *Dialectic of Enlightenment*. Hegel's actual critique of the Enlightenment is left unengaged. Rousseau's General Will could be read differently as an articulation of a community originating in the explicit wills of particular citizens who form a common good. The common good is a rearticulation of particular goods prior to the construction of community. On this, see Teodros Kiros, *Self-Construction and the Formation of Human Values* (Greenwood Press, 1998).

18 Sometimes Adorno separates Marxism from "Communism" sometimes he slips into a Cold-War "anti-Marxism." One of the best expressions of his understanding of Russia as a state capitalist society can be found in passing in "Resignation" (1969) where he argues, "In Russia . . . the only meaning that praxis retained was this: increased production of the means of production. The only criticism still tolerated was that people still were not working hard enough" (p. 166). For Adorno, however, the problem was simply an example of how the subordination of theory to praxis results in repression.

19 What Marx called his unique contribution – not social labor nor the "labor theory of value," but the split in the category of labor – is completely ignored by Adorno, whose analysis remains pre-Marxian. (The most extensive criticism of the Frankfurt School on this point is found in Moishe Postone's *Time, Labor and Social Domination* [1993]).

20 It is not the labor theory of value, but the value theory of labor.

21 Ferninand Lassalle was a leader of the German Workers' Association, a precursor of German Social Democracy. Lassalle conceived his duty to "bridge the gulf between thinkers and the masses." His thinking permeated German Social Democracy and was echoed in Lenin's *What Is To Be Done*, where Lenin argued that socialist consciousness had to be brought to the working class by intellectuals. Marx wrote that Lassalle's "attitude is that of a future worker's dictator."

22 Interestingly, Lukács had criticized individual perception because it could only comprehend "minute fragments" (1971: 165). For Adorno, it was precisely the comprehension of minute fragments that could reveal a truth, a truth unable to be found in the totality. However, Critical Theory is a totalizing process, everything has to be reduced to it, even Schönberg's music. In Schönberg, like the

great writers of modernist literature, everything is based upon "lonely subjectivity which draws into itself" (1971: 142).

23   Like Lukács, who identified objectification and reification (Lukács correctly reappraises this in his 1967 introduction, but even then he makes no reassessment of Marx's *1844 Manuscripts*). Adorno sees little in Marx's early writings but reduces them by association with postwar radical theologians and existentialists (cf. 1973a: 190).

24   The Adorno of "Actuality of Philosophy" (1931) gives a much more "authentic" and "dialectical" view of praxis, arguing that "mere thought" cannot accomplish an authentic answer to the problem of philosophy:

> When Marx reproached the philosophers, saying that they had not variously interpreted the world, and counterposed to them that the point was to change it, then the sentence receives its legitimacy not only from political praxis but also from philosophic theory. Only in the annihilation of the question is the authenticity of philosophic interpretation first successfully proven, and mere thought by itself cannot accomplish this [authenticity]: therefore the annihilation of the question compels praxis. It is superfluous to separate out explicitly a conception of pragmatism, in which theory and praxis entwine with each other as they do in the dialectic. (p. 129)

25   In Lukács' *History and Class Consciousness*, Wiggershaus adds, Adorno found a "form of philosophical thinking about history which in the late 1920s was an inspiration for his ideas on the philosophy of music and musical development" (1994: 81).

26   Adorno, who was a generation younger than Lukács and Horkheimer, never became as disillusioned with the proletariat as they did, because he never placed his hopes so fully on it. During the 1940s Adorno, as he viewed its embourgeoisement (mistaking an elite section for the whole class), articulated more skepticism about the proletariat. With "shorter working hours, better nutrition, housing and clothing there can be no longer any talk of hunger necessarily bringing them together and driving them to revolution" (quoted in Kellner 1989: 106).

27   Like Luxemburg and Lukács, Adorno was never interested in any other potentially revolutionary subjectivities such as national liberation movements. The date of Lukács' "Reification and the Consciousness of the Proletariat" essay (1923) after the "defeat" of the "German revolution" is significant and quite different in tone than his 1919 essay "What Is Orthodox Marxism?" Because of the importance of Lukács' "Reification and the Consciousness of the Proletariat" essay on critical theory and Adorno, I have limited myself to it. My critical comments on Lukács should be understood in light of my interest in the importance of the reification essay on Adorno. A good discussion of this essay can be found in Andrew Arato and Paul Breines, *The Young Lukács and the Origins of Western Marxism* (London: Pluto Press, 1979).

28 The action needed to overcome the ideological crisis was simply a "struggle to acquire the correct proletarian class consciousness" (1971: 330). "The individual worker, because his own consciousness is reified," had to be subsumed by a type of "general will" – namely, the unified will of the proletariat, the party (Lukács 1972: 36).

29 Such statements should be put in the context of Adorno's own position within a "school" and collaborations with a number of its leading figures, especially Horkheimer.

30 "The party is moral," Lukács claims, the "embodiment" of class consciousness (1973: 42). Even during the period of high revolutionary activity of 1918–19 Lukács' notion of the party is essentially Kantian, a moral agency corresponding to the "ethics of the fighting proletariat."

31 Fredric Jameson perceives that Weber is more relevant to *Dialectic of Enlightenment* than is usually acknowledged (1990: 39), but fails to recognize the consequences for Adorno's "Marxism."

32 For another version of a liberated society, see John Rawls' idea of the "union of socialism unionism" in *A Theory of Justice*.

12

Hegel on Trial: Adorno's Critique of Philosophical Systems

Mauro Bozzetti

Even a cursory reading of Adorno's writings makes us accept that his position can only be viewed correctly as one of renewed conflict between Hegel's all-encompassing power of thought, on the one hand, and an opposing subjective perspective, on the other. Hegel's system influenced Adorno's *oeuvre* like no other philosophical work. Indeed, Adorno often argues as if no other philosopher had existed between Hegel and himself. Thus no one who seeks to understand Adorno can afford to overlook his Hegelianism, which so often switches over into anti-Hegelianism.

Adorno repeatedly emphasized the importance of Hegel's work for the study of philosophy in general, and especially for its terminology. In the *Three Studies on Hegel* he explicitly states: "These days it is hardly possible for a theoretical idea of any scope to do justice to the experience of consciousness, and in fact not only the experience of consciousness but the embodied experience of human beings, without having incorporated something of Hegel's philosophy" (1993: 2).

Although Adorno opposed the absolutization of rationality, we must situate his argumentation entirely within philosophical tradition, and in Hegel's idealism in particular. Although *Negative Dialectics*, his chief theoretical work, claims to illuminate philosophy from a wholly new angle, it continues to give structural recognition to the self-contradictory philosophical categories that Hegel considered decisive for philosophical thought. It is for this reason that negativity plays a central role in Adorno's thought. For in order to be anti-systematic, he must also maintain systematic claims, as Bubner (among others) has pointed out.[1] Indeed despite its unusual nature, Adorno's philosophy can be seen as an uninterrupted dialogue with Hegel. Kant, Husserl, Benjamin, and the thinkers of antiquity of course also enjoy an immense influence on his work – not to mention his favorite opponent Heidegger – but Hegel's resistance to facticity and the deficiencies of reason, when judged against a teleological standard of historical development, retains special primacy for Adorno.

Several critics have sought to interpret Adorno's epistemology, metaphysics, and practical reflections in terms of a "metacritique" of Kant's critical philosophy. This strikes me as unconvincing. Adorno's method does not consist in an "actualisation" of the Kantian model of knowledge but rather, evidently enough, in a revision of Hegelian logic. Kant is often employed by Adorno for the purposes of criticizing Hegel, but Adorno's perspective remains fundamentally dialectical, and this crucially distances him from Kant's method. Adorno's "negative metaphysics" does not relate primarily to Kant's "thing in itself"; rather, it is aimed at the problems of Hegel's conceptual subjectivity insofar as this fulfills the ideal goal of objectivity at the concluding point of Hegel's logic. Likewise, Adorno's theory of history does not take its point of departure from Kant's space-time speculations; instead, it is directed expressly toward criticizing Hegel's doctrine of the world-spirit and its command over world-history.[2]

Identity and Difference in *Negative Dialectics*

Hegel's attempt to derive claims to identity from a very close relationship of the logical and ontological levels of human thought represents a considerable problem for Adorno. In *Negative Dialectics*, Adorno appears to accept that thought and being issue in non-identity only by means of identity. Yet Hegel's second step, which definitively reconciles these moments, Adorno considers illusory and arbitrary.

For Adorno, synthesis creates involutions in thinking. "The tendency of synthesizing acts is reversible by reflection upon what they do to the Many" (1973: 158). Only "affinity" has a right to be, because Hegel's unity always destroys an irreducible element of otherness.

Where Hegel seeks to solve the problem of identity and difference anew, so that the idea of the absolute accords with the enlightened claims of science without neglecting the gradual, historical character of this relationship, Adorno fundamentally questions this solution in order to elicit a radical difference. Only through difference, he maintains, can there be any talk of unity: "The utmost distance alone would be proximity" (1973: 57), he writes.

Nonetheless, Adorno warns that the ideal of identity, the reconciliation of reason and reality, should not be discarded: "Living in the rebuke that the thing is not identical with the concept is the concept's longing to become identical with the thing" (1973: 149). Thus non-identity, Adorno's key objection to Hegel's idealism, must also be dialectical, though of a different nature: "Dialectically, cognition of nonidentity lies also in the fact that this very cognition identifies – that it identifies to a greater extent, and in other ways, than identitarian thinking . . . The more relentlessly our identitarian thinking besets its object, the farther will it take us from the identity of the object. Under its critique, identity does not vanish but undergoes a qualitative change. Elements of affinity – of the object itself to the thought of it – come to live in identity" (1973: 149). Adorno sees identity not as a logical means or regulative device to be exploited as part of the framework of dialectical procedure, but rather as an ideal that gains its power from its unattainability and thereby constantly sets new impulses for philosophy. If identity is imposed, philosophy loses the quality that resides also in its difference. From this it follows that dialectics must express the "consistent consciousness" of non-identity – no less, but no more, than of identity. Where it is less, there the green fields of positive theology take over at the level of the existential, and typically remain unproblematically affirmative. Where it is more, there our intellectual-political reflection descends into a "vulgar materialism" no longer even capable of appreciating the yearning for reconciliation. Both lie far removed from Adorno's speculative theoretical project.

So, we have now specified the first categories of Adorno's dialectic. The idea of dialectics, Adorno writes, "names the difference from Hegel. In Hegel there was coincidence of identity and positivity" (1973: 141). Against identity and positivity, Adorno posits non-identity and negativity. Yet there can be no rigid concept of non-identity for Adorno, not only because it hinges on identity but because it can only be pursued within a dialectical movement. It must therefore be critical of itself as well – which precludes a purely dualistic perspective.

It should, however, be clear at this point that Adorno's thesis cannot be thought of as purely immanent to Hegel. Rather, his reflections seek to combine metaphysical with materialist considerations. Adorno certainly wishes to think in a manner as consistent and complete as possible – something (and this is his great claim) that has not yet actually been achieved.[3] Nonetheless, as Beierwaltes points out, Adorno remains attached to what is a quite distinct framework: "Taking his point of departure from Hegel, Adorno's discussion of the word [identity] in modern philosophy and the history of concepts is restricted to Kant. This bold desire to pronounce a universal verdict on so-called metaphysical identity, without explicit or even implicitly recognizable reflection on the concept of identity in previous philosophical thought, is hard to understand" (Beierwaltes 1980: 280). Beierwaltes, author of one of the most important articles on Adorno, rightly has Neo-Platonism in mind here. However, I can only partially agree with his assertion that Adorno "mistreated" Plato and Hegel – for Adorno's exegesis of both these authors reaches to the deepest level.[4] The problem is that Adorno characteristically proceeds in a non-academic manner, both in his terminology and method.

Let us now consider Adorno's critique of Hegel's view of the beginning of philosophy; for it is here that the problems for Adorno with Hegel's procedure can best be glimpsed. For Adorno, Hegel, in his critique of immediacy, destroys the "mythology of the first" and the last principle of ontology.[5] Hegel argues that the word "being" remains "meaningless" because "being" stands beyond itself for "something" and thereby senses the "objectivity" of "indeterminacy." As Adorno sees it, however, this indeterminacy disappears as soon as it is considered dialectically as a concept and determined as "nothing." "Tacitly, indefiniteness is used as a synonym for the undefined. Vanishing in the concept of indefiniteness is what it [this 'indefiniteness'] is the concept of; the concept is equated with the undefined as its definition, and this permits the undefined to be identified with nothingness" (1973: 120). Adorno argues that it would have been better to begin with Something, not being. In comparison with being, the Something means "more tolerance" of the non-identical, insofar as, unlike being or nothing, it cannot be used as a pre-given term that already conforms to the dialectic: this makes objectivity more secure from intellectual manipulations. However, the dialectic should not cease with this concept of the Something. Rather, it must move further toward the "non-conceptual." Adorno here often cites Hegel's category of the "concept" with deliberate provocation: "The concept is an element in dialectical logic, like any other" (1973: 12). Adorno could be seen here as saying that the original movement of the first elements of thought ought not to appear as though preconceived by our supposedly "limited" cognitive capacities. Indeed he states that there can be no definitive answer to the dialectical conceptuality of concepts such as being, nothingness, and especially becoming: "The substance of concepts is to them both immanent, as far as the mind is concerned, and transcendent as far as being is concerned" (1973: 12). Neither of these two aspects can be lost. This is the problem Adorno identifies, and this is why he says not only that "ontological need" is fundamentally "false," but also that reason's dialectical procedure will not suffice as a basic structure for philosophy. Heidegger's "regression" of this ontological need in particular is even more serious, in comparison with Hegel's.[6] For, as Adorno stresses, being does not hold to what it promises: it stands for something else that cannot yet be said.

My thesis here is that despite Adorno's idiosyncratic departure from Hegel regarding identity, Hegel's primary identity of logic and metaphysics continues in Adorno's thought. Adorno upbraids Hegel's logic in the name of a "self-consistent" negative dialectic, and strenuously taxes Hegel's ontology in the name of a "radicalized" metaphysics. But he does not thereby destroy thought's structural relationship to the absolute. In a recently edited letter to Scholem from the *Frankfurter Adorno Blätter* on the subject of Benjamin's intentions in the *Passagenwerk*, Adorno emphasizes: "I remain true to *The Phenomenology of Spirit* in my view that the movement of the concept, of the matter at hand, is simultaneously the explicitly thinking movement of the reflecting subject" (1998: 158). Absolute conceptuality and subjective thought point to the same movement, that of philosophy itself. *Philosophische Terminologie* underscores the importance of these Hegelian claims: "If I focus exclusively on the laws of the movement of thought itself as they appear in the categories of logic, I not only have rules for correct thinking – this was how the logic of the Rationalists operated; I also have, in the form of logic, rules that relate to the absolute, because the absolute is nothing other than that spirit of which logic formulates the laws" (1974: II, 91). Adorno's recognition of this is entirely indebted to Hegel – even as he sought to remain faithful to it without leaving the last word to positivity. It is precisely from this that his philosophy derives its strength and retains its importance for today. Thus Adorno's Critical Theory follows a unique metaphysical code.

Explicating a category as central to Adorno's philosophy as non-identity forbids us from cutting corners. Non-identity cannot be interpreted primarily as some aporetic, enigmatic, "magical" word.[7] At the beginning of *Negative Dialectics*, Adorno presents non-identity as the "hinge" of the entire work, which means that it too represents a possible connecting thread of reason. In non-identity lies both a positive and a negative meaning. Adorno's dialectical critique of subjectivity represents the negative aspect: "What is true in the subject unfolds in relation to that which it is not, by no means in a boastful affirmation of the way it is. Hegel knew this" (1973: 127). This means that the thinking subject can find the meaning of truth only in objectivity. Hegel's synthetic solution of this negative meaning of non-identity is criticized because Hegel's theory of knowledge remains restricted to a subjective viewpoint: the object for Hegel is "spiritualized" and thereby "reduced." No solution yet results from this opposition of pure object and subject, only the object's subjectivization. Only "viewed from the outside" (1973: 193), Adorno argues, may the object become the "positive expression of non-identity"

(1973: 192). Philosophy, Adorno seems to be saying, ought not to treat the object as an ultimate logical foundation, but rather as an Archimedean point for its non-speculative perspective.

In the positive sense, the object is a "terminological mask" (1973: 192) that conceals the material unity of the new thinking. Like many passages in his text, this part of Adorno's work is somewhat opaque, and it is particularly this "view from outside" that generates most of the difficulties. Before we bring in the dogmatic tradition here to illuminate matters, it suffices to stress that Adorno holds Hegel not to have solved the dialectic of identity and difference between the thinking subject and the absolute object. Adorno declares that Hegel's "own concept of nonidentity – to him a vehicle for turning it into identity, into equality with itself – inevitably has its opposite for its content; this he brushes aside in a hurry" (1973: 120).

Adorno nonetheless holds fast to dialectics because he can declare himself in agreement with Hegel's "non-ontological, non-methodical" principle.[8] The fundamental structure of Hegel's procedure, that every category be inwardly mediated with its opposite, remains for Adorno the "strongest argument" in favor of dialectics.[9] Adorno's reservations begin where Hegel claims his dialectical procedure to have solved immediacy and secured difference, since Adorno maintains that no concordance can be discerned in reality: reconciliation must be opposed because reality itself is not reconciled.[10]

Dialectics, according to Adorno, "unfolds the difference between the particular and the universal, dictated by the universal" (1973: 6). The singular and particular must not be already presupposed as logical categories to be conceptually exploited as dialectical components. To be sure, Adorno's goal is to resume the dialectical process, and he writes that for good reasons, "through Hegel, philosophy . . . regained the right and the capacity to think substantively" (1973: 7). However, in Hegel's case, this renewal remained hampered by a standpoint of the subject. To say that Hegel gave back a content to philosophy, and that this content can only be defined through the inner work of the categories, entails that only the *negated* part of Hegel's dialectic holds true. Its constructive aspects and implications, on the other hand, remained false. Thus Adorno insists that the contradiction between particular and general can only be resolved from the position of the object, not the subject – for the ideal human being has yet to exist. "As the subject–object dichotomy is brought to mind, it [dialectics] becomes inescapable for the subject, furrowing whatever the subject thinks, even objectively – but it would come to an end in reconcilement. Reconcilement would release the nonidentical, would rid it of coercion, including spiritualised coercion; it would open the road to the multiplicity of different things and strip dialectics of its power over them" (1973: 6). Translated into logical categories, this means that Hegelian synthesis plays no role in Adorno's dialectic and is viewed only as "the return of what has been negated" (1973: 333). Synthesis resounds with ideological overtones for Adorno, for it already presupposes in the subject the point toward which the dialectic is to move. In truth, subject and object are never entirely what corresponds to their concept; yet neither ever transcend into a Third.

Adorno often uses the term "ideology" to characterize Hegel's category of identity, deploying it as a "warning signal" against all positive discursive regimes. Ideology for Adorno is synonomous with prejudice; although, importantly, he adds that "in the critique of idealism we do not dismiss any insight once acquired from the concept by its construction, nor any energy once obtained from the method under the concept's guidance" (1973: 145). Adorno's move beyond Hegel's system must be situated not outside of but *within* its logical-metaphysical structure. In short, Adorno's resistance to reconciliation, synthesis, the positive, and totality is always carried out in such a way that his procedure remains in dialectical contradiction.[11] He should be understood here as offering "anti-mythologizing" recognition of the unavailability of any absolute dialectical solution for us, recognition that contradiction cannot be solved through a priority of logic over the "meta-logical." The negativity of the world itself makes Hegel's logic unacceptable: "What is negated is negative until it has passed. This is the decisive break with Hegel. To use identity as a palliative for dialectical contradiction, for the expression of the insolubly nonidentical, is to ignore what the contradiction means. It is a return to purely consequential thinking" (1973: 160). Adorno sees contradiction at a practical level as insuperable, and this practical level stands connected to the theoretical.

With the slogan that thought can think against itself without abandoning itself, Adorno probably means that a new, nonpartisan logic that always keeps in view its practical effects and historical consequences must assume the role of antidote to the old logic.[12] But thinking against oneself here means too that our received way of thinking, conditioned as it is by social and cultural factors and by always repressive-ideological education, can be re-created through a revolution of thought.

Adorno's "other" view of logic in *Negative Dialectics* relates to the "preponderance of the object." Adorno sees the philosophical movement of epistemological reflection, also stemming from Hegel, as a process in which ever more objectivity is won back for the subject. "This very tendency needs to be reversed" (1973: 176), he declares. The object has preponderance because, in the object's otherness, as something absolute, the subject cannot think itself without it. The object can, of course, only be thought by the subject. However, the object "always remains something other than the subject"

(1973: 183). "To be an object also is part of the meaning of subjectivity"; whereas, dialectically speaking, in defining oneself, "it is not equally part of the meaning of objectivity to be a subject" (1973: 183).[13] Here Adorno seems to be saying that Hegel's dialectic can be valid only at a subjective level and only by sacrificing the object's transcendence. The logic of the object is never entirely within reach. Even so, despite the object's difference, Adorno retains the object as a moment of the dialectic: "To grant precedence to the object means to make progressive qualitative distinctions between things which in themselves are indirect; it means a moment in dialectics – not beyond dialectics, but articulated in dialectics" (1973: 184). In the Hegelian, anti-Kierkegaardian sense, these distinctions are not "infinite" but "progressive." But in the Kierkegaardian, anti-Hegelian sense, mediation of objects remains under the aspect of distinctions which cannot be sublated by Hegel's identity. Adorno here sums up his principal thesis in the following words: "Contradiction is nonidentity under the aspect of identity" (1973: 5).

Metaphysics and Materialism

To establish the correct interpretation of the preponderance of the object, Adorno's vision of metaphysics must be considered. In normal language use, this vision might seem unusual. "It is by passing to the object's preponderance that dialectics is rendered materialistic" (1973: 192). Here "materiality" is to be understood as the object of the phenomenological theory of knowledge that has repressed metaphysical hope and the "corporeal." Like Benjamin's, Adorno's materialism is closer to metaphysics than vulgar materialism. "It was Marx who drew the line between historic materialism and the popular-metaphysical kind. He thus involved the former in the problematics of philosophy, leaving popular materialism to cut its dogmatic capers this side of philosophy. Since then, materialism is no longer a counter-position one may resolve to take; it is the critique of idealism in its entirety, and of the reality for which idealism opts by distorting it" (1973: 197). My thesis here is that materialism is utilized by Adorno as a corrective to idealism in such a way that advances in the logical process – philosophy's advance – will simultaneously effect a recognizably better world. To complete Hegel's idealism, Adorno suggests the idea of a materialism that remains faithful to humanity's time-honored dream of immortality – though without conceding to theology the metaphysical last word.[14] "Metaphysics posits in principle something other than the collections of facts that concern us in science, yet without asserting that this other behaves as theology would have its godheads behave" (1974: II, 44).

For Adorno, the task is to understand how the object can be conceived without the filter of our subjective logical structures. The object must therefore show itself, "materialize" itself, as present being. For the only knowledge valid for philosophy is "that of redemption," the "messianic light" expressed in the last aphorism of *Minima Moralia* (1974: 247). I take it that what Adorno means here is that the object must give itself to be known as a being in command of language. Only beings endowed with language compel us to compare ourselves with their otherness and at the same time retain a certain immunity from our subjective perception. Adorno evidently thinks of the God of the Torah here, the speaking God. Adorno's letter to Scholem cited above, on the same movement of thought and the absolute, continues this idea in a paradigmatic manner: "Only the authority of sacred texts would be held out to this conception" (1998: 158). The objective in the object is thus perhaps to be understood as the language of God. In this sense, what Adorno accords to metaphysics, once it has been purified of blasphemous positivity, is the capacity for the prophetic word, understood as the attempt to appropriate the view "from outside" on the circle of one's existence.

This project of Adorno's contrasts with Hegel's vision, in which the object, as something which is both infinite and already bound up with finitude, becomes a moment of the subjectivity that stands in relation to objectivity dialectically. Hegel describes the object in terms of "immanent contradiction"; truth consists in the unity of the subjective with the objective. "The true is the concrete, the unity of the objective and subjective" (1892: III, 453). This identity is also understood in the *Encyclopaedia* as "absolute negativity" (1971: 8): subject and object remain for Hegel at once distinct and inseparable.

I am persuaded at this juncture that the various political and religious traditions of our authors and their life-histories have a role to play. For instance, Adorno's philosophical category of Auschwitz refers not only to the quantative extremity of brutality but also to the Jewish people's historical impossibility of fighting evil. This impossibility resounds like an undertone throughout Adorno's work, including his work on logic. Every logical-metaphysical project, he seems to be saying, must fall silent before history's bankruptcy.

Adorno's thinking does indeed bear a close kinship to the speculations of modern Hebrew philosophy. If we compare his position to Franz Rosenzweig's in *The Star of Redemption*, we find some remarkable commonalities that help explain his ideas better. In the introduction to the Italian edition of *Jargon of Authenticity*, Adorno's polemic against Heidegger, R. Bodei (1989: XV) speaks of Adorno's "partial debt of thought" to Rosenzweig. At issue is the category of redemption mentioned in the last aphorism of *Minima*

Moralia. Yet this "debt" seems to me much greater and more pervasive than this. For example, referring to the thematic of which category philosophy should begin with, Rosenzweig writes: "This path leads from an existing Aught to Nought; at its end atheism and mysticism can shake hands. We do not take this path, but rather the opposite from Nought to Aught" (1970: 23). Already in Rosenzweig we find the Something in place of being, just as in Adorno. The same holds for the critique of the identity of thought and being. Rosenzweig writes: "Thus the identity of reasoning and being presupposes an inner non-identity" (1970: 13). The category of the particular Rosenzweig also describes as the "dead stop" of philosophical systems (1970: 46). Even more surprising are Rosenzweig's reflections on aphoristic language: "In order to rid itself of clichés [*Aphorismus*], indeed for the sake of its very status as science, philosophy today requires 'theologians' to philosophize" (1970: 106); as also is his critique of logocentrism: "The logos is not creator of the world, as it was from Parmenides to Hegel" (1970: 51). And the emphasis of *Negative Dialectics* on justifying what makes dialectics possible negatively, by questioning the logical role of synthesis – this too Rosenzweig had already formulated: "Thus the conception of synthesis necessarily implies the reduction of the antithesis to mediation; the antithesis becomes a mere transition from thesis to synthesis, and is not itself original" (1970: 229). Out of honesty, Adorno ought at least to have acknowledged this "debt."[15] Admittedly, though, in contrast to Adorno (and Scholem), Rosenzweig's objections must be situated in a mystical framework that had completely dissociated itself from philosophy in its idealist form (although in the early 1920s some of Hermann Cohen's pupils, including Rosenzweig, Buber, and Rosenstock-Huessey, did make some attempt to combine the Jewish and German traditions).

Adorno sees the progress of Hegel's logic as having belittled the concept of the deity. Hegel's concept of God in fact no longer corresponded to the religious concept. Adorno rejects this reduction of logos to reason, to a rational possibility of mastering transcendence, suggesting that from the standpoint of the critique of metaphysics, Hegel's category of possibility does not necessarily step beyond Kant's limit of reality. Nevertheless, even from this minimally dialectical standpoint, the dialectic of possibility and reality must still be maintained: "The concept is not real, as the ontological argument would have it, but there would be no conceiving it if we were not urged to conceive by something in the matter" (1973: 404). This sentence makes clear Adorno's whole position. The concept is not yet truth, but metaphysics itself enables this conceiving. In this respect too, then, Adorno's position is not far removed from Hegel's. For if the concept can be thought, if the subject can thematize it through ideas, then the dispute over the existence or nonexistence of God becomes superfluous; for the most important element has already been thought. What Adorno seems not to underline sufficiently, however, is that for Hegel it is not our thoughts that ground the absolute but the absolute itself that grounds thinking.

Hegel's theoretical metaphysics is at once too strong and too impoverished for Adorno: too strong in its rationality and too impoverished in human experience. Yet although we sometimes find passages in Adorno's text where praxis, understood as resistance to "normality," takes on the moment of truth, more often the dialectic of theory and practice is upheld, so that his endless dialogue with Hegel continues. It is this that gives Adorno and Critical Theory a special place in the tradition of western Marxism. For the eastern Marxists this reflective tradition was always too unorthodox. For Adorno, by contrast, theory included not simply Marx's inverted Hegel but more essentially Hegel's original system. Under Horkheimer's direction, the Frankfurt School made sure to avoid any Marxian short-cut and, as far as was feasible, remained faithful to the Hegelian text.

As we have seen, Hegel secularized transcendence and retained theology merely as something insubstantial. Indeed Adorno's principal thesis here is that Hegel abolished transcendence: "In spite of and, so to speak, absorbing the Kantian critique, the ontological argument for the existence of God was resurrected in Hegelian dialectics. In vain, however. In Hegel's consistent resolution of nonidentity into pure identity, the concept comes to be the guarantor of the nonconceptual. Transcendence, captured by the immanence of the human spirit, is at the same time turned into the totality of the spirit and abolished altogether" (1973: 402). Kant's project, on the other hand, still draws no advantage from this. For just as Hegel's philosophy is criticized for secularism, so Kant too is criticized with similar arguments – albeit from a different angle, that of anthropomorphism: "Kant on his part, in defining the thing-in-itself as the intelligible being, had indeed conceived transcendence as non-identical, but in equating it with the absolute subject he had bowed to the identity principle after all . . . The identifications of the absolute transpose it upon man, the source of the identity principle. As they will admit now and then, and as enlightenment can strikingly point out to them every time, they are anthropomorphisms" (1973: 407). If traces of the religious tradition are still to be found in secularism, these traces are completely covered over in the subjective willfulness of anthropomorphism.

As is well-known, Adorno seeks to return in his texts to the dogmatic tradition in various ways. He says explicitly that Christian dogmatics was metaphysically more coherent than its idealist translation. "Christian dogmatics, in which the souls were conceived as awakening simultaneously with the resurrection of the flesh, was metaphysically more consistent – more enlightened, if you will – than speculative metaphysics, just as hope means a physical resurrection and feels defrauded of the best part by its spiritualization" (1973: 401). Yet he understands as well that these dogmatic metaphysical claims are still not "tenable" for philosophy, and also that an aesthetic outlook cannot occupy religion's place.

Philosophy must think further; it cannot rest content with dogmatic propositions. So the problem confronting Adorno is: How can we think the absolute further, how can we regenerate the language of philosophy without meeting Hegel's aporia, knowing at the same time that the path back to Kant is closed? Adorno's reflections remain caught in this dilemma. Adorno proposed no philosophical solution, for the only solution would have been the correspondence of concept and reality which Hegel had adopted as his criterion of truth. But if reality does not correspond to the concept – because social and economic interests and the anthropological and psychological distortions of socialization prevent the realization of this criterion – then metaphysics is condemned to an unbearable fate: "The resurrection of the dead would have to take place in the auto graveyards" (1981: 271), i.e., at the place where our principles and theories have lost their utility, where finally every moral theory, every categorical imperative, and every philosophical conviction is liable to become superfluous. Neither positive nor nihilistic discourse can legitimately have the last word.

"Idealism is not simply untruth. It is truth in its untruth" (1982: 234), states Adorno. As knowledge of the absolute, metaphysics is inconceivable without idealist claims, although thought itself cannot be described as the absolute without its forfeiting the principle of negativity. Yet Adorno also writes: "Vis-à-vis theology, metaphysics is not just a historically later stage, as it is according to positivistic doctrine. It preserves theology in its critique, by uncovering the possibility of what theology may force upon men and thus desecrate" (1973: 397). Here again, then, Adorno becomes very Hegelian: secularization is not the last objection to idealism; the category of possibility comes into play once more. Adorno's every attempt to define metaphysics remains unsuccessful because he eschews the very form of ultimate definitions. It is for this reason that interpreting *Negative Dialectics* as negative theology, as Theunissen (1983) and Thyen (1989) have attempted, seems to me fundamentally questionable. For even "what God is not" cannot definitively be said. When in *Philosophische Terminologie* Adorno speaks of "negative metaphysics," he has in mind not the negative theology of his friend Paul Tillich but the "positive" metaphysics of Hegel, to whose metaphysical problematic he wants to stay true.

What form of metaphysics *is*, then, still to be rescued for Adorno? Classical Neo-Scholastic metaphysics was too dependent on theology and therefore was unfree; Kantian critique fundamentally lacked hope, and was an insult to thought; Hegel's theodicy was too rationalist and at odds with reality; Kierkegaard's philosophy lacked logic; and negative theology remains insufficiently negative. The truth is that Adorno takes the category of "materialism" as a limitation on Hegel's logocentrism and, with this limitation, then returns to the idealist perspective. "Hence rescuing Hegel — and only rescue, not revival, is appropriate for him — means facing up to his philosophy where it is most painful and wresting truth from it where its untruth is obvious" (1993: 83).

The Powerlessness of the Political God

In Hegel, the difficult problem of correlation between the theoretical and practical levels of philosophy becomes especially recognizable in the development of his philosophy of history. If the philosophy of history must correspond to the logic of the development of philosophy itself, how can Hegel's naturalized fourfold evolution of world-history (the "four empires") be characterized as dialectical?[16] If the stages of the history of philosophy must present a certain "parallel" (1892: III, 410) to those of the philosophy of history, in which the goal of history, the political state, stands on the ground of the absolute,[17] how can world-history produce this outcome without the dialectical structure otherwise so essential to Hegel's entire system? Some writers distinguish between a linear progressive development of world-history for Hegel and a dialectical development in the history of philosophy.[18] This, however, appears to contradict Hegel's systematic claims, since the dialectic of form and content seems no longer sustained.

In my view, Hegel was himself conscious of this problem and only sees parallels and affinities between the two structures, rather than any strict methodological agreement. The meaning of history remains strongly idealized for him, and the recovery of causes otherwise so important for historical explanation plays no role in his philosophy of history. Yet if the central events of world-history are rational and necessary on account of their inner purposiveness, while the historical subject cannot influence this development, the absoluteness of the dialectical method is clearly put in question.

The history of philosophy is in fact for Hegel not only the "inside" of world-history but its very essence, yet Hegel as philosopher and philosophy itself fundamentally belong to a special separate world: "Philosophy forms in this connection a sanctuary apart, and those who serve in it constitute an isolated order of priests, who must not mix with the world, and whose work is to protect the possessions of Truth. How the actual present-day world is to find its way out of this state of disruption, and what form it is to take, are questions which must be left to itself to settle, and to deal with them is not the immediate practical business and concern of philosophy" (1962: III, 151). For this reason, Hegel did not see the undialectical four-part development of world-history as a methodological error, for only one of the two operators of his system – world-spirit – is conscious and effective as the object. Only in this way can we explain the historical asymmetry of Hegel's philosophical system.

History cannot be considered dialectical because historical subjects and social movements and the multitude (whom Hegel describes as superfluous) can only become conscious of a "limited" national spirit (1971: 282).[19] So these members are not yet free. However, even if we accept that freedom is only secured in the political state through rights and duties, it is hard to see why the world-spirit should not stand in relation to historical subjects from the very beginning, so that they share in and act upon historical development in full consciousness. For Hegel, only the "thinking spirit of world-history," world-spirit, ordered above the national spirit, "raises itself" to knowledge of absolute spirit. Hegel's reading of history thereby takes for granted and overvalues the objective spirit.

The idea of the good plays no corrective role in world-history for Hegel because it has found no rational soil on which to realize positivity. Only the Protestant state can be called good in itself, but there history comes to an end: "For the Christian world is the world of completion; the grand principle of being is realized, consequently the end of days is fully come. The Idea can discover in Christianity no point in the aspirations of Spirit that is not satisfied" (1956: 342). Politics and religion actually lie on the higher level of philosophical reason. On the other hand, Hegel defends no eschatology: the kingdom of God must be realized in this world, and the present age was sufficiently ripe for this. America was the "country of the future" (1956: 86), though only in a political sense: America's religion and basic structures were the same as those already realized in the Germanic empire.

From his standpoint in the twentieth century, Adorno does not look back on Hegel's interpretation of history and its logical-systematic structure of identity as utopian dreaming. This view of Hegel Adorno sees as resting on a misconception of Hegel's general systematic claim. Although Adorno does not thematize the problem of naturalized world-historical development in Hegel and its theological motives, he criticized the idea that historical development in Hegel is not governed dialectically and lacks a practical basis to its theory of progress. Adorno seems to me to some extent correct in this. Nevertheless, it must not be forgotten that world-history belongs only secondarily to Hegel's system, certainly not to its inner core. But of course Adorno does not try to read history in a way that would have been more consonant with Hegel's system: his primary interest was the search for aporetic motives.

Adorno's critique of the dominance of "objective spirit" in Hegel is certainly persuasive. Subjective spirit for Adorno is a historical category too: "In all of this, the subjective spirit also remains a historical category, a thing that has evolved, a changing, virtually transient thing. The still unindividuated tribal spirit of primitive societies, pressed by the civilized ones to reproduce itself in them, is planned and released by postindividual collectivism; the objective spirit is overpowering, then, as well as a barefaced swindle" (1973: 307). According to Adorno, Hegel ought to have construed the relation between general and particular differently, without needing to fear that history might not concord with the plan of Providence, and without reducing the general to ideology.

It is true that historical subjects for Hegel cannot transcend their time and national spirit. Adorno cites the following passage from *Reason in History*: "This universal substance is not the mundane; the mundane impotently strives against it. No individual can get beyond this substance; he can differ from other individuals, but not from the popular spirit" (cited in Adorno 1973: 323). Yet this sounds not very different from Adorno's conviction that "society precedes the subject" (1973: 126). Adorno too sensed something of this: "There is a grain of truth even to such ideology: the critic of his own popular spirit is also chained to what is commensurable to him, as long as mankind is splintered into nations" (1973: 323).

I believe that this historical context is the only aspect of Hegel's writing in which he merely takes advantage of religion without properly engaging with it. Protestantism is here chosen as the basic factor for the attainment of the goal of history because it is the religion most capable of dialogue and least susceptible to conflict with the state. Clearly, Hegel's intention is to resolve the antithesis of state and religion inasmuch as they represent a source of latent tensions and conflicts. Clear too is his conviction that the faith of the citizens creates problems for political interests, as we know today. But history has shown that this dual aspect of citizenship must also be understood and preserved as a positive factor, though sometimes a crucial one (as in the case of totalitarianism). Religion does not become more rational in the course of time, like philosophy; it remains by nature unmanipulable and autonomous. When Adorno blames idealism for the horrifying, he has in mind this attempt of Hegel's to resolve the dual aspect of citizenship.

Adorno's view that society maintains itself thanks to historical discontinuity and social antagonism, in opposition to the repressive principle of world-spirit, stands at the antipodes of Hegel's position. Adorno sees socially

dangerous antitheses as positive principles of vitality for communal life –
though he does not explain what grounds and strategies might permit social
consensus. His materialist reflections here find their justification – and yet
simultaneously make known their weaknesses. For social antagonism is transposed in Adorno to the logical level as well and read as antagonism within
reason itself. "It is not only now that compared with potential reason, with
the total interest of the associating individual subjects it differs from, the
reason of the world spirit is unreason. Like all his disciples, Hegel has been
chided for equating logical categories with social ones and some from the
philosophy of history; this was chalked up as a μετάβασις εἰς ἄλλο γένος, as
that point of speculative idealism which had to break off in the face of the
unconstruability of experience" (1973: 317). The problem for Adorno lies not
in the necessary concordance of theoretical and practical categories – "this
very construction was doing justice to reality" (1973: 317) – but in the radicalization and de-ideologization of the dialectical method. Rationality itself
for Adorno is "antagonistic," i.e., in itself also irrational: "The irrationality of
the particularly realized *ratio* within the social totality is not extraneous to
the *ratio*, not solely due to its application. Rather, it is immanent to it" (1973:
317). Adorno goes as far as to say: "*Ratio* is no more to be hypostatised than
any other category" (1973: 317). Yet ratio is not a category but a presupposition of thought: if the unity of ratio is questioned, if no distinction is drawn
between the irrationality of historical phenomena and the contradictoriness
of thought, we no longer have any categories at all, no philosophical language, no philosophy. This is indeed Adorno's greatest provocation and hard
to accept.

The removal of historical injustice characterizes the existential concern of
Critical Theory. This must always be understood in terms of the materialist
content of idealist conceptuality. In Horkheimer's words: "For all its insight
into the individual steps in social change and for all the agreement of its elements with the most advanced traditional theories, the critical theory has no
specific influence on its side, except concern for the abolition of social
injustice. This negative formulation, if we wish to express it abstractly, is the
materialist content of the idealist concept of reason" (1992: 242).[20] Yet we
must ask whether a philosophical perspective that justifies itself through the
antithesis of another system of thought does not also inherit that system's
problems. Adorno does not in fact resolve Hegel's weak spots, morality and
history. Rather, he problematizes them in a more thoroughgoing way. His
negative moral philosophy[21] and apocalyptic view of history are clearly no
attempt to solve the practical moral problems of philosophy, and his sociological critique takes insufficient account of the category of intersubjectivity,
as Habermas, Apel, and Hösle have sought to demonstrate in relation to

Hegel. Adorno's logical arsenal is consciously too weak. He remains fragmentary in form, yet he was both systematic and anti-systematic in content. He was understandably fascinated by Hegel's all-encompassing logic and could not release himself from its spell. And he also saw himself as a member of a school that upheld general "systematic" claims: the economic, psychological, sociological, political, philosophical, and aesthetic specialties of the school all shared in this and form the background and context of his work.

Formulated positively, then, my concluding remarks are as follows. The greatest synthetic and objective philosophy which we have inherited from tradition and the most absolutely negativist form of thought arising in response to the worst experiences of our century can come to fruitful mediation without diminishing the substance of their respective convictions. The problem confronting our authors lies in how intellectually to reconcile subject and object. I believe the "pure personality" that appears at the end of Hegel's logic as the absolute idea, as objective self-identity, and the light of knowledge in Adorno's *Minima Moralia* that is "shed on the world by redemption," refer fundamentally to the same problematic.

In keeping with the Aristotelian tradition, the geometrical figure Hegel chose for the interpretation of his system was that of the circle, at the center of which lay logical-metaphysical identity, the dialectical structure of the concept of the deity. More precisely, all spheres of his system – those of logic, nature, and spirit – are to be seen as a circle of circles. Most of the problems Adorno identified and criticized in Hegel result from this attempted symmetry. Thus there are at least three points on which our authors find no agreement: (1) in the interpretation of history as theodicy (Hegel) or as permanent catastrophe (Adorno); (2) in the evaluation of unreason and irrationality, to which Hegel accords no real philosophical status, and where Adorno sees a symbol for the impossibility of positively closing the philosophical system, at both the logical and moral-philosophical levels; and (3) in the definition of the significance of religious categories as rational phenomena (Hegel's speculative Good Friday, proof of the existence of God, and interpretation of the Holy Ghost), as against Adorno's readoption of dogmatic motives in materialist language. Yet the elements of kinship between Hegel and Adorno are greater, indeed thematically and methodologically inseparable from one another.

There is, then, no structural difficulty in comparing Hegel and Adorno. Dialectics, the thematics of identity, the claims of metaphysics and the role of logic, the basic operators of subject and object, the categories (contingency, possibility, necessity), negativity, and the criterion of truth (correspondence of concept and reality) – all possess the same matrix for both authors.

Adorno in my view has rightly criticized Hegel's theoretical tendencies, but in few parts of his struggle is he able to present alternative perspectives. As soon as he prosecutes this struggle at the logical level, he runs the danger of lapsing into the irrational, where the fascinations of aphorism come to his assistance. Despite Adorno's relentless critique, we cannot do without a form of systematic construction in philosophy, which, with Hegel, would be capable of both doing justice to the theoretical and practical demands of knowledge in philosophy and presenting a recognizable criterion of truth consonant with the principles of religion – yet, as Adorno shows, which also does not fall into ideology. As Adorno concludes: "[T]he need in thinking is what makes us think. It asks to be negated by thinking; it must disappear in thought if it is to be really satisfied; and in this negation it survives. Represented in the inmost cell of thought is that which is unlike thought" (1973: 408). Hegel would have agreed.

Notes

I am grateful to Austin Harrington for translating this chapter.

 1 Cf. Bubner (1983: 35): "Beyond stylistic quirks, the difficulties of [Adorno's] discussion stem clearly from the tremendous undertaking of writing a system against all systems."

 2 Adorno is sharply critical of Kant's philosophy: the doctrine of antinomies is exposed as logically incoherent and ideological, whilst that of freedom is shown to be limited by certain underlying imperatives and as leading to repression. Adorno sees Kant's concept of causality as ungrounded and regards earlier versions of the ontological proof of God's existence as more rationally formulated than Kant's.

 3 Note, however, the following remark from one of Adorno's letters to Benjamin: "I am convinced that our best thoughts are every time those which we cannot think completely" (Adorno–Benjamin 1994: 418).

 4 Cf. Krämer (1989: 277, 326–7): "Heidegger non tiene conto non solo della filosofia ellenistica e del neoplatonismo, ma per quanto concerne Platone stesso egli si fonda esclusivamente sull'immagine coniata dallo Schleiermacher basata sui dialoghi, senza prendere in considerazione la tradizione indiretta. Al contrario T. W. Adorno, nella metafisica del numero della tradizione indiretta, riconosce, a ragione, la tendenza a raggiungere la 'completezza', e la 'continuità' del sistema e la 'disponibilita' del mondo per l'uomo" (*Zur Metakritik der Erkenntnistheorie*, in *Gesammelte Schriften*, Bd. 5, 304).

 5 Adorno cites Hegel in the *Lectures on the History of Philosophy*, vol. I (Hegel 1892: I, 40): "That which first commences is implicit, immediate, abstract, general – it is what has not yet advanced; the more concrete and richer comes later, and the first is poor in determinations."

6   The whole thrust of the chapter on "The Ontological Need" in *Negative Dialectics* is directed against Heidegger. Adorno's principal thesis here is that "The attributes of Being do indeed, like those of the absolute idea of old, resemble the traditional attributes of the deity; but the philosophy of Being bewares of divine existence" (1973: 77). It is astonishing that contemporary political-philosophical critiques of Heidegger have still not engaged with the critique Adorno already laid out in *The Jargon of Authenticity*.

7   See in this connection Schmucker (1977: 143).

8   Cf. Adorno (1993: 8): "Hence the dialectic, the epitome of Hegel's philosophy, cannot be likened to a methodological or ontological principle that would characterize his philosophy the way the doctrine of ideas characterizes Plato in his middle period or the monadology characterizes Leibniz."

9   Cf. *Philosophische Terminologie*, vol. I, 222: "Precisely this, that not only is each one moment the problem of the other moment but each moment necessarily requires the other moment in order to be thought at all – this inner mediation, not simply mediation between moments, seems to me the strongest argument in favour of dialectical philosophy."

10 Beierwaltes (1980: 274) writes of a "strictly upheld, biblically resonant 'ban on images.'"

11 Cf. Adorno (1973: 147): "Totality is to be opposed by convincing it of nonidentity with itself – of the nonidentity it denies, according to its own concept." Totality in Adorno's work is at once rejected and rescued. He uses the term "social totality," for instance, as a critical category. Cf. Adorno 1976.

12 Cf. Adorno (1973: 141): "Thought need not be content with its own legality; without abandoning it, we can think against our thought, and if it were possible to define dialectics, this would be a definition worth suggesting." *Negative Dialectics* constantly returns to this point.

13 This statement could be compared with the idea of "absolute being" (*Sein schlechthin*) developed by Hegel and Hölderlin during their Frankfurt period.

14 Cf. Adorno (1973: 399) and also the following little-known passage from *Philosophische Terminologie* (1974: II, 186–7):

> I have spoken of quite notable connections between materialism and that type of theology in the great religions which for good reasons tends towards a doctrine of the resurrection of the flesh. These connections have in fact only been concealed by the official Platonic-Aristotelian metaphysics. On reading the Proverbs of Solomon, for instance, one encounters, without any sense of an immediate relation to hope, formulations that bear on the corporeal, material essence of man – the idea that we are all of dust – formulations which are also such an essential basis of materialism. I have of course sketched here a very particular, tendentious picture of materialism. It goes without saying that there other, completely different forms of materialism, such as repressive materialism.

15 Thanks to the *Frankfurter Adorno Blätter* edited by the Adorno Archive, we now
    know from a student's notes that during a seminar on Benjamin's *The Origin of
    German Tragedy* in the summer semester of 1932, Adorno discussed and criticized
    Rosenzweig's position. See Adorno (1995: 75).

16 As is well-known, Hegel divides world-history into four empires, which also
    represent four stages of development: the oriental empire, corresponding to the
    infancy of history, in which human subjects are mere "accidents"; the Greek
    empire, which manifests beautiful ethical individuality but no mature freedom;
    the Roman empire, in which the subject is "reborn" but universality remains
    still abstract; and finally the Germanic empire, in which Christianity and espe-
    cially the Reformation have reconciled the individual to the state and freedom
    has been realized.

17 In the *Lectures on the Philosophy of History* (1956: 76), Hegel writes of the god
    Jupiter: "He is the Political god, who produced a moral work – the State."

18 Even Hösle (1988: 149), who has justified the role of tetradic structures in Hegel,
    sees this four-staged development of world-history as "exceptional": "Tetra-
    chotomies actually have their rightful place for Hegel in the sphere of nature,
    while trichotomies predominate in the realm of spirit"; in a footnote he con-
    tinues: "The most important exception to this is the division of world-history
    into four empires."

19 Cf. Hegel (1971: 282): "The national spirit contains nature-necessity, and stands
    in external existence: the ethical substance, potentially infinite, is actually a par-
    ticular and limited substance; on its subjective side it labours under contingency,
    in the shape of its unreflective natural usages, and its content is presented to it
    as something *existing* in time and tied to an external nature and external world."

20 Two pages before this Horkheimer states outright: "In any event the critical
    theory is indeed incompatible with . . . idealist belief" (1992: 240).

21 The theme of "negative moral philosophy" cannot unfortunately be addressed
    here. See, however, Schweppenhäuser (1993), who discusses sections of Adorno's
    lectures on moral philosophy.

13

The Dialectic of Theory and Praxis: On Late Adorno[1]

Henry W. Pickford

If philosophy is still necessary, then solely in the way it has been since time immemorial: as critique.

Theodor W. Adorno, "Why Still Philosophy"

When Theodor W. Adorno, Max Horkheimer, and Friedrich Pollock returned from their American exile to Frankfurt in 1949 they were consciously bringing the Institute for Social Research back with them. The building that originally housed the Institute had suffered severe bomb damage during the war, but was repaired in a relatively short span of time with assistance from the American occupying forces, who felt that empirically oriented social research would promote democracy. It is perhaps safe to assume that the patrons got more than they bargained for. When the Institute officially reopened on November 14, 1951, its members were already close to concluding their first major research study, which would also mark the end of Adorno's direct participation in opinion surveys. In many ways the *Gruppenexperiment*[2] was a continuation of the depth-psychological content analysis he had pursued at Berkeley and presented in *The Authoritarian Personality*,[3] but now the research was adapted to the postwar (West) German context. The F-scale was modified into the A-scale (fascism to authoritarianism), though the purpose remained that of detecting latent anti-democratic attitudes in test subjects. Inspired by Horkheimer's observation that self-censorship tends to decrease when people find themselves in a casual group setting, the project's greatest methodological novelty lay in its being organized around interviews of pre-selected, sociologically or ideologically homogenous groups, designed to gain greater access to the pre-conscious structure and dynamics of attitudes toward delicate political topics. The interpretative study of attitudes regarding democracy, the Third Reich, Jews, Western Europe, Eastern Europe, and Germans themselves, produced a large-scale scandal: according to its conclusions, two-thirds of the 1,800 people interviewed expressed profound ambivalence about democracy and half rejected the notion of any guilt about the Third Reich, while antisemitism was as virulent as ever.[4] The authoritarian personality, the "anthropological conditions" of collective irrationalism that Adorno had philosophically conceptualized and empirically investigated during his American years, was alive and well in the postwar "German ideology":

> National Socialism lives on today less in the doctrines that are still given credence – and it remains questionable whether its doctrines were ever believed – than in certain formal features of thought. These features include the eager adjustment to the reigning values of the moment; a two-tiered classification dividing the sheep from the goats; the lack of immediate, spontaneous relations to people, things, ideas; a compulsive conventionalism; and a faith in the established order no matter what the cost. Structures of thought and syndromes such as these are, strictly speaking, apolitical in their content, but their survival has political implications. ("Philosophy and Teachers," *Critical Models*, 27)

Those political implications were succinctly stated by Adorno in another essay reflecting on the situation in postwar West Germany: "I consider the survival of National Socialism *within* democracy to be potentially more menacing than the survival of fascistic tendencies *against* democracy" ("The Meaning of Working Through the Past," *Critical Models*, 90). In a wide variety of scholarly and cultural practices, as well as his own experience in the United States, Adorno could detect the same underlying tendency: rather than actualizing its own potential for autonomy, mind [*Geist*] was becoming reified or "modeled" by the heteronomy confronting it. Adorno's strategic response was the construction of negative-dialectical "models," a method to loosen reified thought that underlies virtually all of his writings of philosophical and cultural critcism, from the notion's introduction in his Frankfurt inaugural lecture (1931) to its later elaboration in *Negative Dialectics* (1966)[5] and its tactical deployment in essays from the last decade of his life collected in *Interventions* (1963) and *Catchwords* (1969), both bearing the subtitle *Critical Models*. Here perhaps more than anywhere else in his compendious *oeuvre* are the practical and political aspects of Adorno's theoretical efforts most visibly at work.

Reification and Autonomy

In characterizing contemporary consciousness as reified, Adorno was critically developing Marxist theory in light of recent history. In *History and Class Consciousness* (1922) Georg Lukács had coined the term "reification" with reference to Marx's analysis of commodity fetishism, according to which "the social character of men's labor appears to them as an objective character stamped upon the product of that labor." Traditional economists had succumbed to the "second nature" of this "phantasmagoric objectivity" by assuming the abstract exchange-value of a commodity to be an inherent and immutable property of the object, whereas in fact it is a fetishistic projection of the mode of production and of the social form specific to capitalism. Psychologizing Marx's insight, Lukács maintained that the "commodity structure" was "the model of the objective forms of bourgeois society, together with all the subjective forms corresponding to them," so that "a relation between people takes on the character of a thing." Far more suggestive for Adorno was Lukács' critique of bourgeois ideology, in which he showed that the unresolvable antinomies of modern epistemology (such as the abstract separation of subject and object and the division between form and content in Kantian philosophy) spring "from the reified structure of consciousness," the same structure as the objective contradictions of the capitalist relations of production (Lukács 1971: 86).[6]

Adorno adopted Lukács' historical-materialist practice of ideology critique to produce the "self-revelation of the capitalist society founded upon the production and exchange of commodities" while rejecting his Hegelian historico-philosophical assumption that the worker's recognition of himself as fungible labor necessarily entails the emergence of the proletarian class as the subject–object of history. Lukács' theory relies on a non-mediated substantive reserve of "human nature" in the proletariat by which it can abide and ultimately transcend its reified consciousness and, as the "self-consciousness of capital," become the agent of social transformation. This teleology in which subject and object are ultimately reconciled accords with Lukács' nostalgia for a pre-capitalist age when the world was supposedly suffused with metaphysical meaning. Thus, for Adorno, Lukács' project is ultimately idealist, collapsing theory into praxis – because "only class can relate to the whole of reality in a practical revolutionary way" – and thereby renouncing the individual as well as the materialist mediations of society for the sake of immediate engagement (pp. 168–71).

Besides these theoretical reservations, Adorno held that on empirical grounds this Hegelian teleology was disproven. In two articles published in the Institute's journal, Friedrich Pollock argued that democratic liberalism and class antagonism belonged to an earlier phase of capitalism, and had now been superseded by state or monopoly capitalism. Regardless of whether in a democratic or authoritarian mode, the consolidation of economic processes prevents class antagonisms from reaching the self-transparency and intensity required for social change in Lukács' model. While Pollock's studies are open to trenchant criticisms, texts from the early forties onwards demonstrate Adorno's unwavering acceptance of their conclusions:[7]

> Material production, distribution, consumption are administered together . . . A societal meta-subject does not exist. The semblance could be expressed in the remark that everything existing in the society today is so completely mediated that precisely the element of mediation is obscured by the totality. There is no longer any standpoint outside the apparatus which one could take up in order to call the spectre by its real name; one can tackle it only where it is inconsistent with itself. ("Spätkapitalismus oder Industriegesellschaft," *Gesammelte Schriften*, 8: 369)[8]

Against a Lukácsian ontological refuge of immediate human needs, Adorno argues that it is impossible to separate human nature from the historical social forms with which it is entwined: "Needs were always mediated by society; nowadays they are completely external to their bearers, and their satisfaction means heeding the rules of the advertising game" ("Zum Verhältnis von Soziologie und Psychologie," *GS* 8: 56). The colonization of human needs by cultural commodities represents a new, interiorized form of domination which forecloses Lukács' story of revolutionary progress: "the danger of domination infiltrating into people through their monopolized needs . . . is an actual tendency of late capitalism. It relates not to the possibility of barbarism after the revolution, but to the prevention of revolution by the societal totality" ("Thesen über Bedürfnis," *GS* 8: 393).[9]

The strategic manipulation of needs motivates Adorno's critique of the culture industry, in which authentic (for him, modernist) art, whose use-value previously lay in its uselessness and which therefore functioned as a cipher of the continued possibility of non-reified experience,[10] is replaced by the increasingly indistinguishable mélange of entertainment and advertising, with the result that the cultural superstructure affirmatively reproduces the economic base to such a degree that its consumers no longer recognize themselves or their own suffering: "the most intimate reactions of human beings are so completely reified even to themselves that the idea of anything specifically characteristic of them now persists only in uttermost abstraction" (*Dialectic*, 167, translation modified). The political consequences are considerable, for the culture industry "becomes the means of shackling consciousness. It prevents the formation of autonomous, independent individuals who consciously make judgments and reach decisions. And such individuals are the prerequisite for a democratic society, which can survive and develop only in people who are politically mature [*mündig*]" ("Résumé über Kulturindustrie," *GS* 10.1: 345).[11]

With the new objective conditions attending late capitalism comes also a new mode of subjectification: the more administration, economy, and culture form a totality and liquidate the nineteenth-century notion of market entrepreneurialism and the cultural avant-garde, the more vulnerable becomes the individual autonomy characteristic of that now bygone liberal era. Adorno emphasizes the historical specificity of the autonomy which liberal market capitalism had enabled for the individual, identifies its homologous psychic counterpart in Freudian psychoanalysis based on the dynamic interplay between drives, super-ego, and mediating ego, and concludes that "the individual no longer has to decide what he himself is to do in a painful inner dialectic of conscience, self-preservation, and instinctual drives. Decisions for men as active workers are taken by the hierarchy, ranging from the trade associations to the national administration, and in the private sphere by the system of mass culture which takes over the last inward impulses of individuals" (*Dialectic*, 203). Drawing on Kant and Freud, Adorno theorizes this inversion by which the individual psyche – which was, during the liberal era, the irreducible economic and democratic determinant of society – now becomes secondary to and dependent upon the societal processes, that is, becomes superstructure itself. Adorno's attempts to think through the epistemological consequences of the unconscious date back to his first *Habilitationsschrift*, in which he used Freudian theory to interpret Kant's model of synthetic apperception, through which the individual organizes and recognizes perceptual impressions,[12] and in his later writings on social psychology and prejudice he continues this impulse. At the epistemological level, Kant's theory of the schematism, which constructs a complex and fluid interaction between the reception of sense impressions and their spontaneous synthesis under concepts by the perceiver, provides the framework for diagnosing social perception and prejudice:

> Kant said that there was a secret mechanism in the soul which prepared direct intuitions in such a way that they could be fitted into the system of pure reason. But today that secret has been deciphered. While the mechanism is to all appearances planned by those who serve up the data of experience, that is, by the culture industry, it is in fact forced upon the latter by the power of society, which remains irrational, however we may try to rationalize it. (*Dialectic*, 124–5)

Kant and Husserl had shown that "every perception contains unconsciously conceptual elements . . . every judgment contains unclarified phenomenalist components" and that "all perception involves subjective projection" (*Dialectic*, 188);[13] however, for that very reason the perceiver "must learn at one and the same time to refine and inhibit" that projection. Otherwise, the schema mediating knowledge of the world may become inseparable from what Adorno calls the "false," "pathic," or "morbid projection" underlying prejudice: that is, the id's aggressive wishes are projected onto the outside world by means of societally pre-established and affectively charged "deeply implanted schemata" which, by denying the particular specificity of experience, "commit the mental act of violence which is later put into practice" (*Dialectic*, 192–3). Stereotype usurps the delicate and demanding interaction between subject and object: the perceiver "no longer uses the active passivity of cognition in which the categorial components can be appropriately formed from a conventionally pre-shaped 'given,' and the 'given' formed anew from these elements, so that justice is done to the perceived object . . . [I]n the world of individual experience, blind observation and empty categories are grouped together rigidly and without mediation. In the age of three hundred key words, the ability to make the effort required by judgment disappears, and the distinction between truth and falsehood disappears" (*Dialectic*, 201–2).

The subject's ability to interrogate and acquire reflective distance from the pre-judgments and cognitions which inhere within perception, in effect to perform ideology critique, relies in turn upon the strength of the ego. In his social-psychological writings, especially *Group Psychology and the Analysis of the Ego* and *Civilization and its Discontents*, Freud, who "clearly foresaw the rise and nature of fascist mass movements in purely psychological categories,"[14] provided Adorno with the vocabulary for describing the evanescence of liberal individualism and the rise of irrational mass movements: on the one hand the "bourgeois chill" of increasingly reified and autarkic social structures prevents the ego from finding a conducive environment in which to develop and cohere, and on the other hand the culture industry's manipulation of fabricated needs weakens the individual's ability to choose its objects of affective investment and to form an ego-ideal – as Freud says, a "conscience." The ego's functions as "the coordinator of psychic impulses" and reality-tester are usurped by identification, idealization, and introjection, all psychic mechanisms through which the ego loses its anchor in consciousness (and hence rationality) and narcissistically makes the "beloved object part of itself," becoming "suggestible" to forming libidinous bonds with collectives which liquidate the possibility of individual autonomy. Powerful instinctual drives can be mobilized by the narcissistic identification of the authoritarian leader in "postindividual collectivism" (*GS* 6: 302; *Negative Dialectics*, 307). Ego-weakness is not only vulnerable to taboo and prejudice at the cost of individual experience, but the narcissistic identification creates a politically tractable mass subject. Much of Adorno's contributions to the empirical investigation of prejudice were interpretative "content analyses" of the schemata operative in "pathic projection," the rhetorical propaganda "devices" by which they were psychologically reinforced, and the concomitant psychological traits which made particular people susceptible to their irrationality.[15]

Ego-weakness and narcissistic projection; the usurpation of the subject's participation in perception and cognition by heteronomous "pathic projection"; the formation of the mass subject and postindividual collectivism; these are the social-psychological factors which for Adorno indicate that "the fundamental conditions that favored the relapse continue unchanged. That is the whole horror . . . barbarism itself is inscribed within the principle of civilization" ("Education after Auschwitz," *Critical Models*, 191). These factors constitute the precondition for authoritarian personalities and the social structures that cultivate them; the personality structure is *not* specific to a given political system such as fascism;[16] quite the contrary, "this type has become much more prevalent today . . . I would call it the type of *reified consciousness*. People of such a nature have, as it were, assimilated themselves to things. And then, when possible, they assimilate others to things" ("Education after Auschwitz," *Critical Models*, 199). In his investigations of this personality structure Adorno developed a set of terms to describe its behavior patterns: pseudo-individuality, pseudo-activity, pseudo-realism, and bi-phasic belief are the ideological shadows of their namesakes, caricatures of their original significances. Pseudo-individuality closely parallels the inversion of the Kantian concept of "personality" as the perspective of universal humanity in the individual's moral self into the culture industry's practice of self-advertisement:[17] one's "individuality" is constructed more or less ad hoc from the palette of mass cultural prosthetics on offer, which themselves are only "pseudo-individuated," differing merely in terms of inessential emphases added for marketing reasons.[18] Pseudo-activity, a term Adorno adopted from Erich Fromm,[19] denotes the irrational and inconsequential "self-willed" actions which in fact are pre-ordained by their socio-cultural contexts and which actually reflect the individual's lack of will and lack of real influence on his environment. Adorno explicates the concept in his critique of astrology columns: "What is thus emphasized is not so much the addressee's real ego power as his intellectual identification with some socialized ego ideal. He is led to interpret his actions as though he were strong and as though his activity would amount to something. The phoniness of this concept is indicated by the spuriousness of most of the activities encouraged by the column" (*Stars Down to Earth*, 63). Pseudo-realism banishes imagination in order to conform to a reality made even more reified than it already is: "Nothing remains then of ideology but that which exists itself, the models of behavior which submit to the overwhelming power of existing conditions" (*Aspects of Sociology*, 202). Finally, bi-phasic belief explains the phenomenon of people recognizing the irrationality of their actions and yet nonetheless carrying on out of a psychological self-interest. For example, on the level of discursive reason people will admit that astrology is senseless, yet in an environment which they perceive as irrational and beyond their control, they irrationally prefer the solace of there being an imaginary sense to it all.[20] Similarly, Adorno notes the apparent distinction test subjects drew between their immediate, absorptive viewing of mass cultural events on television and their subsequent sober evaluation of what they had viewed, thus suggesting the possibility that bi-phasic belief once made conscious might work against the effect of pseudo-realism ("Free Time," *Critical Models*, 174–5). For the behavior patterns which reproduce the status quo without mediation indicate the menacing collapse of the space between reality and its justification from which critical reflection can be practiced,[21] and for Adorno this is above all a "failure of culture":

> If culture is understood emphatically enough as the debarbarization of human beings, which elevates them from their raw conditions, and certainly without perpetuating those conditions through violent oppression, then culture has failed entirely. It was not able to migrate into people as long as they lack the preconditions for a humane existence: not by coincidence are they still prone to barbaric outbursts, out of repressed ressentiment about their fate, their deeply felt unfreedom. That they run to the culture industry's rubbish, which they partly realize is rubbish, is another aspect of the same state of affairs, probably harmless only on the surface. Culture has long become its own contradiction, the congealed contents of a privileged education; that is why culture now inserts itself into the material process of production as its administered appendage. ("Kultur und Verwaltung," GS 8: 140)[22]

Debarbarization [*Entbarbarisierung*], Adorno's coinage and presumably indicating his diagnostic and prescriptive corrective to a politically expedient "denazification" [*Entnazifizierung*], is "the immediate prerequisite for survival." It would be no exaggeration to say that Adorno's postwar intellectual activities upon his return to Germany center upon cultivating "the single genuine power standing against the principle of Auschwitz . . . autonomy, if I might use the Kantian expression: the power of reflection, self-determination, not cooperating" ("Education After Auschwitz," *Critical Models*, 195).

The goal of education and culture is for Adorno nothing less than the "production of a correct consciousness" that is "politically necessary": "a democracy that not only should function, but should work in accordance with its own concept, requires politically mature people. An actual working democracy can only be conceived as a society of politically mature people" ("Erziehung – wozu?" *Erziehung zur Mündigkeit*, 107).[23] The task then is to maintain the possibility of autonomy and political maturity under conditions of a nearly total identity of ideology and reality.

Theory: Critical Models

In contrast to Lukács, Adorno refuses to reduce reification to a subjective "fact of consciousness" because "the trouble is with the conditions that condemn mankind to impotence and apathy and would yet be changeable by human action; it is not primarily with people and with the way conditions appear to people": the "fetish character" of reified thought "is not laid to a subjectively errant consciousness, but objectively deduced from the social a priori, the exchange process" (*GS* 6: 190–1; *Negative Dialectics*, 189–90, translation modified). In analogy with Marx's insight that "value" does not inhere in objects but is a mystification practiced by the exchange economy, Adorno locates "conceptual fetishism" in identity thinking, the coercive subsumption of the particular under the universal: "The exchange principle, the reduction of human labor to its abstract universal concept of average labor time, has the same origin as the principles of identification. It has its social model in exchange and exchange would be nothing without identification . . . The spread of the principle imposes on the whole world an obligation to become identical, to become total" (*GS* 6: 152; *Negative Dialectics*, 146, translation modified). That is, identity thinking in philosophical theory and the exchange-principle in socio-economic praxis are isomorphic in their exercise of domination through the imposition of abstract equivalence. For example, Adorno and Horkheimer had located the "dialectic of enlightenment" in the doubled concept of Kantian reason:

> As the transcendental, superindividual self, reason comprises the idea of a free human social life in which people organize themselves as the universal subject and overcome the conflict between pure and empirical reason in the conscious solidarity of the whole. This represents the idea of true universality: utopia. At the same time, however, reason constitutes the tribunal of calculation, which adjusts the world for the ends of self-preservation and recognizes no function other than the preparation of the object from mere sensory

material in order to make it the material of subjugation. (*Dialectic* 83–4, translation modified)[24]

Thus the full idea of reason comprises both the idea of transcendent reason (*Vernunft*) and the subordinate practice of identity thinking (*ratio*) as the means for progressively realizing those ends through the technical subjugation of nature; yet a dialectical reversal occurs when the instrumental *ratio* becomes its own end and hence betrays the true idea of enlightenment. Identity thinking and the exchange-principle characteristic of capitalism have repressed the utopian dimension of reason: just as exchange-value, the abstraction of labor time invested in the production of a commodity, is not an inherent property of a thing but rather the necessary form in which objects appear under capitalism, so too identity thinking imputes the identity between the particular and the concept under which it is subsumed. And just as, according to Marx, a thing has a use-value – its inherent properties that satisfy human needs – so too a concept has its intrinsic or "emphatic idea": the set of properties, the situation, the object that would ideally fulfill the concept. This fulfillment Adorno calls "rational identity." And as use-value is repressed under capitalism by the supposition that the exchange-value captures the "essence" of the commodity, so too identity thinking imputes that a present instantiation fulfills its concept, e.g., that *ratio* is equivalent to reason, that individual freedom can exist in a society founded on unfreedom, or that exchange founded on profit is the "ideal of free and just exchange . . . whose realization would transcend exchange." By taking the emphatic idea of a concept not only as ideology but also as a proleptic "promise" of "what the concept would like to be," Adorno performs *negative dialectics*: a two-way differential critique in which present conditions are shown to contradict the reigning ideology, and – rather than being discarded for not representing reality – the ideology is taken "at its word," as the as yet unfulfilled promise of its realization:

> The supposition of identity is indeed the ideological element of pure thought, all the way down to formal logic; but hidden in it is also the truth moment of ideology, the pledge that there should be no contradiction, no antagonism. In the simple identifying judgment, the pragmatist, nature-controlling element already joins with a utopian moment. "A" is to be what it is not yet. Such hope is contradictorily tied to the breaks in the form of predicative identity. The philosophical tradition had a word for these breaks: "ideas". They are neither *choris* nor an empty sound; they are negative signs. The untruth of any identity that has been attained is the obverse of truth. The ideas live in the cavities between what things claim to be and what they are. Utopia would be above identity and above contradiction; it would be a togetherness in diversity. (*GS* 6: 154; *Negative Dialectics*, 150–1)

"Idea" as the truth moment of ideology represents Adorno's noetic Platonism, the ideal of the full identity of a concept and its fulfillment which he calls the "hope of the name" which "wants to say what something is, not under what concept it falls" (GS 6: 62, 152; Negative Dialectics, 53, 146).[25] Likewise a Platonic topos, "all reification is a forgetting" (Dialectic, 230), for reified consciousness conforms itself to second nature and represses the "idea" of concepts. Negative dialectics works to regain the consciousness of non-identity between present society and the concepts with which it understands and justifies itself, such as "opinion," "freedom," or "progress." The utopian "rational identity" provides the implicit normative standard against which the historical formation and deformation of concepts can be apprised and the possibility of ideology critique, and ex hypothesi the possibility of change, prised open.

Such a differential critique cannot avail itself of the modes of presentation relying on identity thinking such as deductive syllogism, inductive generalization, or example and systematic context. As early as 1931, in his inaugural lecture in Frankfurt, Adorno introduced his alternative mode of presentation, that of "models" [Modelle], invoking Marx's interpretation of the commodity form as an example ("Die Aktualität der Philosophie," GS 1: 325–44). Critical models in fact operate throughout his oeuvre, and received sustained description in Negative Dialectics. "The demand for binding cogency without system is the demand for thought models [Denkmodelle] . . . Philosophical thinking means as much as thinking in models, and negative dialectics an ensemble of paradigmatic analyses [Modellanalysen] . . . They elucidate key concepts of philosophical disciplines, in order to intervene radically in them" (GS 6: 39, 10; Negative Dialectics, 29, translation modified). As with several of his philosophemes, "critical model" is Adorno's "corrected" development of an impetus from Walter Benjamin, in this case, his notion of "dialectical image," the cognitive armature of the studies that compose his unfinished Passagenwerk. Benjamin, whom Adorno felt was too much under the sway of the Surrealists, had suggested that juxtapositions of historical material in "constellations" would release archaic dream and wish images lodged in the collective unconscious at the threshold to modernity.[26] In a now renowned exchange of letters, Adorno rejected the theory's implicit idealism: "If you transpose the dialectical image into consciousness as a 'dream', then not only has the concept been disenchanted and made more tractable, it has also thereby forfeited precisely that objective interpretive power which could legitimate it in materialistic terms. The fetish character of the commodity is not a fact of consciousness but rather dialectical, in the eminent sense that it produces consciousness" (Briefwechsel, 139).[27] Later in the same letter Adorno specifies, "accordingly, the dialectical image should not be transposed into consciousness as a dream but rather through the dialectical construction the dream should be externalized; the immanence of consciousness itself should be understood as a constellation of the real," and refers approvingly to Benjamin's earlier "concept of *model*" (pp. 140–1).[28] In Adorno's view, Benjamin had resurrected the Lukácsian collective subject as bearer of utopian dreams, and thereby lost the historical-materialist objectivity of the earlier plan: the juxtaposition of the nineteenth century's utopian vision of unlimited technical progress in the forces of production with the twentieth century's melancholic gaze backward at what was in fact the merciless consolidation of the relations of production and the resultant barbarism ("Progress," *Critical Models*, 143–60). Models thus are the instruments for producing "critical social consciousness" (*GS* 6: 317; *Negative Dialectics*, 323) because their negativity, though experienced by the subject, is the failed promise of objectivity, the organization of society. The exposure of the dialectical relationship, the objective interdependency between a reified phenomenon and its supposed contrary (e.g., free time and labor time in the essay "Free Time" [*Critical Models*, 167–75]), without hypostatizing any pole or principle, makes legible the immanent or "inner history" of the phenomenon, whose "fetish of irrevocability" falls away:

> What dissolves the fetish is the insight that things are not simply so and not otherwise, that they have come to be under certain conditions. Their becoming vanishes and dwells within the things; it can no more be stabilized [*stillstellen*] in their concept than it can be split off from its results and forgotten. Similar to this becoming is temporal experience. It is when things in being are read as a text of their becoming that idealistic and materialistic dialectics intersect. But while idealism sees in the inner history of immediacy its vindication as a stage of the concept, materialism makes that inner history the measure, not just of the untruth of concepts, but even more of the untruth of what is immediately existent. (*GS* 6: 62; *Negative Dialectics*, 52, translation modified)

The first dimension, preeminently *immanent*, could be called conceptual ideology critique: "Ideology lies in the substitution of something primary, the content of which hardly matters; it lies in the implicit identity of concept and thing" (*GS* 6: 50; *Negative Dialectics*, 40). Just as Marx showed how the sociohistorical formation of the commodity form relies on the capitalist production of value in exchange and the division of labor, so too Adorno, here taking up Nietzsche's genealogical method, traces the formation of concepts such that they lose their semblance of self-evidence and reveal their necessary conceptual and sociohistorical mediations.

The second dimension is *transcendent*, for what the immanent analysis also shows is that the concept under analysis is not *yet* true in its emphatic or

utopian sense. A concept is true only when it wholly fulfills its own requirements of realization, and in this case functions analogously to the Kantian
"regulative" idea of reason: although never fulfilled by empirical experience,
the emphatic meaning nonetheless offers a standard against which candidates
for the concept can be evaluated. Hegel in turn explicitly distinguishes the
descriptive dimension of the meaning of "true," signifying correspondence
between a judgment and an empirical state of affairs (*adequatio rei ad intellec-
tus*, what he calls "mere accuracy"), from the *normative* sense of "true" in
which "objectivity corresponds to its concept":

> Truth usually is intended to mean that I *know* how something *is*. But this is
> truth only in relation to consciousness or formal truth, mere accuracy
> [*Richtigkeit*]. In contradistinction to this, truth in the deeper sense means
> that objectivity is identical with its concept. This deeper sense of truth is what
> is involved when, for instance, one speaks of a *true* state or a *true* artwork.
> These objects are *true* when they are what they *should* be, that is, when their
> reality corresponds to their concept. Understood in this way, the untrue is the
> same as what otherwise is called the bad. (Hegel 1970: 368–9 [§ 213 and
> Zusatz])

As Wittgenstein had shown and some recent moral philosophy develops,
because one can be wrong about one's use of a word or concept, there is an
implicit normativity in our shared language and inherited tradition.[29] Making
that normativity explicit can amount to a critique of our shared life, society;
until society fulfills its concept through the realization of humanity and
reason, its totality remains "untrue."[30] It is illuminating to compare this idea
of social criticism with what might be called its centripetal contrary: John
Rawls' notion of "reflective equilibrium," which in the interest of establishing a "reasonable" description of society as an initial position for discussion,
strives to mitigate the very disjunction between situation and principles of
judgment Adorno prises apart: "By going back and forth, sometimes altering
the conditions of the contractual circumstances, at others withdrawing our
judgments and conforming them to principle, I assume that eventually we
shall find a description of the initial situation that both expresses reasonable
conditions and yields principles which match our considered judgments duly
pruned and adjusted" (Rawls 1971: 20). By contrast, Adorno's technique of
dialectically freeing up the immanent concepts with which society understands itself and holding society accountable for its failure to embody those
concepts is rather more akin in structure to Michael Walzer's notion of
"interpretive" social criticism that, as exemplified in his reading of the Old
Testament prophet Amos, "challenges the leaders, the conventions, the ritual
practices of a particular society and . . . does so in the name of the values

recognized and shared in that same society" (Walzer 1987: 63).[31] As Adorno claims, a critical model is indeed the point of intersection between materialist and idealist dialectics: a materialist critique of concepts in that they are shown to be the result of historical and social conditions, an idealist critique of those conditions because they are shown not to fulfill the normative meaning of their concepts. Or, to turn a Hegelian phrase on its head: the rational is faulted for not being real, and the real is faulted for not being rational.

The form in which critical models are presented is that of "constellation." While Benjamin seems to have used the term to denote the montage presentation of citations, illustrations, and minimal commentary in order to elicit the spontaneous recognition of archaic wish images, Adorno lends it a discursive use. He patiently tacks back and forth, following the interrelationships by which a supposedly self-evident and self-sufficient phenomenon such as "opinion" is revealed to partake dynamically of both delusion and truth and, moreover, to require both for its critical potential;[32] or he demonstrates how the apparent epistemological divide between subject and object is belied by the presence of subjectivity in the object (the idealist insight into the subject's active participation in the perception of the object) and the presence of objectivity within the subject (the materialist insight that the subject's schemata of perception are co-constituted by society) to arrive at a description not far from Durkheim's notion of "formative constituents."[33] While this analytical technique has been compared to Heidegger's destruction of metaphysics and its linguistic deconstructive variation in Derrida,[34] Adorno's analyses demonstrate how these mediations are always concrete, particular, and historically situated in the organization of society and its members: as he wrote to Benjamin, "dialectical images as models are not societal products, rather they are objective constellations, in which the conditions of society present themselves" (*Briefwechsel*, 140). Thus while "the inside of non-identity is its relation to that which it is not, and which its managed, frozen self-identity withholds from it, . . . the *chorismos* of without and within is historically qualified in turn. The history locked in the object can only be delivered by a knowledge mindful of the historic positional value of the object in its relation to other objects" (GS 6: 165; *Negative Dialectics*, 163).[35] The dialectical critic traces out both the synchronic conceptual supplementarity and diachronic inner history of phenomena, reconstructing the web of mediations that both "disenchants" the concept and gestures toward its emphatic fulfillment: "the substance of concepts is to them both immanent, as far as the mind is concerned, and transcendent, as far as being is concerned. To be aware of this is to be able to get rid of concept fetishism" (GS 6: 23; *Negative Dialectics*, 11).

This procedure has consequences for the style and validity claims of Adorno's analyses. First, as an interpretive construction, constellation would appear to run the risk of subjectivism and relativism. In his essays on method Adorno concedes that there is ultimately no absolute justification, but that the objectivity of the construct increases to the extent that it "suffuses itself" with the object it interprets: "The open thought has no protection against the risk of decline into randomness; nothing assures it of a saturation with the matter that will suffice to surmount that risk. But the consistency of the performance, the density of its texture, helps the thought to hit the mark" (GS 6: 45; Negative Dialectics, 35).[36] In this way the constellation exhibits what Adorno calls its "resemblance to writing," its necessity to be read and hermeneutically interpreted. The subjectively composed constellation "becomes legible as a sign of objectivity" by unfolding the phenomenon's inner non-identity, its "relationship to that which it itself is not, and which its orchestrated, frozen self-identity withholds from it," i.e., its historical and conceptual mediation (GS 6: 164–7; Negative Dialectics, 162–5, translation modified). Critical models thus are the means of performing the doubled critique of negative dialectics that was announced as early as the introduction to Dialectic of Enlightenment: "Dialectical thought interprets every image as writing. It teaches how to read in its own features the admission of falsity so as to deprive it of its power and appropriate it for truth" (Dialectic, 24).[37] Second, the "saturation of the object" in thought is to be achieved not through moderation, but by exaggeration, or "over-interpretation" ("Essay as Form," Notes, 4); by portraying the extremes of a given phenomenon, justice is done to its present untruth in light of its potential truth. Under the reified conditions of society and mind, "only exaggeration is true"(Dialectic, 126) since those conditions have already witnessed their extreme: "If thought is not measured by the extremity that eludes the concept, it is from the outset in the nature of the musical accompaniment with which the SS liked to drown out the screams of its victims" (GS 6: 358; Negative Dialectics, 365).[38] Third, critical models as constellations are non-systematic, non-totalizing, because they are "always a conflict brought to a standstill" ("Essay as Form," Notes, 16). As genealogical and societal mediations of the concept under analysis unfold, the web of the concept's history and its mutual interdependence with what it pretends to exclude reopens the contingency of the conflict and leads thought "beyond the concept by means of the concept" (GS 6: 27; Negative Dialectics, 15, translation modified). If, as Nelson Goodman has persuasively argued, our inductive understanding of the world's regularities and our categorial system for organizing them are ultimately anchored not in their truth-realism but in their efficacy within our conventional linguistic practices, then Adorno's technique brings those habitual background linguistic practices and their historical genesis momentarily into a double focus and their efficacy into question.[39] Finally, constellations that succeed in rendering the mediations of a phenomenon legible produce what Adorno calls "genuine" or "metaphysical experience," which consists in the awareness of the negativity between the emphatic concept and its present unfulfillment. But the experience of this negativity entails the recognition of one's own reified consciousness, which is the prerequisite for being able to conceive of change, for "a false consciousness must inevitably move beyond itself, it cannot have the last word" (*GS* 6: 339; *Negative Dialectics*, 346). The production of that experience through *theory* is Adorno's *praxis*.

Praxis: Media, Politics

This section will recount some of the various venues in which Adorno during the postwar years practiced cultural criticism through the construction of critical models, and will argue against his caricature as a mandarin theoretician who scorned praxis, politics, and the mass media.[40] Besides demanding teaching commitments[41] he published prodigiously, including several technical philosophical works, monographs of musical, musico–sociological, literary, and cultural criticism; however, with the publication of *Minima Moralia* (1951), Adorno became a popular author. In a letter to his friend and early mentor, Siegfried Kracauer, he ascribed his surprising success to a fortunate conjunction of a general cultural vacuum and the waning interest in Heideggerian themes, and reveled in the freedom his fame afforded him.[42] And in 1963 he wrote with a mixture of pride and astonishment to his old friend in New York that a paperback edition of *Prisms* (1955) had appeared with a print run of 25,000 copies, while *Interventions* started with an initial run of 18,000 copies.[43] And although at times he seemed to dismiss his essays as modest bagatelles and quickly dispatched occasional pieces,[44] Adorno nevertheless conscientiously reworked and published them primarily in popular journals such as *Der Monat*, *Frankfurter Hefte*, *Merkur*, and *Neue Sammlung*, which were read by well-educated citizens and those in cultural and political positions of authority. And whereas he was certainly once again taking up the intellectual and polemical journalism he had practiced so robustly in the twenties and thirties,[45] Adorno's postwar politics of publication represents one aspect of his "intervention" in the bourgeois public sphere in which "the cultural climate" undergoes formation and possibly self-reflection. When he remonstrates that "the element of the *homme de lettres*, disparaged by a petty bourgeois scientific ethos, is indispensable to thought" he is joining a German tradition in intellectual essayism that effloresced in the Weimar Republic with such skilled practitioners as Georg Simmel, Siegfried Kracauer, and Walter Benjamin, and that reaches back via Friedrich Nietzsche to the figure of the French Enlightenment moralist and the discursive form of the non-systematic critique, as in Voltaire's *Philosophical Dictionary*. In an analogy he repeats in his introduction to *Catchwords*, Adorno says of negative dialectics that "thinking as an encyclopedia, rationally organized and nonetheless discontinuous, unsystematic, loose, expresses the self-critical spirit of reason" (*GS* 6: 40; *Negative Dialectics*, 29).[46]

Besides his essayism Adorno attacked the culture industry in its own preeminent media: radio and later, television. Whereas he had averred that radio "turns all participants into listeners and authoritatively subjects them to broadcast programs which are all exactly the same" (*Dialectic*, 122–3),[47] incomplete documentation indicates that during the period between 1950 and 1969 alone Adorno participated in more than 180 radio programs, not including broadcast performances of his own musical compositions. In fact, Adorno's radio broadcasts date back at least to the early thirties, and in letters from that time he expresses his enjoyment and success with the medium.[48] While his work in musical and musico-sociological criticism found a natural medium in radio, more than two-thirds of the postwar programs were devoted to non-musical topics, including issues in the critical theory of society, education, and contemporary politics. Most of his essays on literature, music, and culture were first given as radio lectures as well, and published later in the interests of furthering debate. Likewise the thinker who wrote that "in essence I consider the usual television dramas to be politically far more dangerous than any political program ever was" ("Fernsehen und Bildung," *Erziehung*, 56) also cautioned that "contrary to what is repeatedly said about me, I am not an opponent of television per se . . . I would be the last to deny that the medium of television has an incredible potential for education in the sense of disseminating enlightening information" (pp. 51–2) and participated in at least thirteen television programs, several of which were devoted to criticizing the medium and championing its most advanced techniques, such as montage and alienation.[49] Just how seriously he took his "media work" can be gleaned from the reminiscences of one of his editors at Hessischer Rundfunk in Frankfurt: Adorno, who left the United States in part over issues of language and editorial autonomy,[50] even allowed his mannered style to be corrected to conform to standard German syntax:

"I want to be understood by my listeners," was his answer. He thought that I, as "an expert," knew better how to achieve that. It was, surprisingly, of the utmost importance that he be understood even and especially in a medium of the "culture industry." The sound technicians who were responsible for recording him afterwards had to repeat spontaneously and in their own words what he had said, and often there ensued a discussion that was much better and more comprehensible than the lecture he had just read into the microphone. We had to take care that when he came to the radio station there were appropriate sound technicians who were able to justify their answers to him. It was preferable to postpone a session rather than Adorno having to forgo the important discussion afterward with our assistant. Once we recorded one such discussion between Adorno and his sound technician without him or her noticing, and then played it back to them. He found himself "surprisingly good," which meant a great deal in consideration of his demanding conceit, his pronounced skepticism toward the mass media and his general aversion for organizations and institutions that shape opinion. (Kadelbach 1990: 51–2)

With almost Leninist acumen Adorno recognized a moment of vulnerability within the "apparatus": "Precisely the relative fixity of the bureaucracies within certain institutions of the culture industry paradoxically permit these institutions to behave with less conformity than if they stood under apparently direct democratic control" ("Fernsehen und Bildung," *Erziehung*, 56–7).

Adorno's engagement with the mass media was motivated, of course, by his critique of the *use* to which the culture industry's organs of dissemination were put. Thus his initial studies of radio in the Princeton Radio Research Project[51] and television while working at the Hacker Foundation[52] were developed into a prolonged polemic against conventional television's "ideologization of life" that reinforces pseudo-realism and other behavioral patterns thwarting reflection. "I think that exactly where even the faintest tendency towards this harmonization of the world is encountered is where the most severe attack must be launched, and that the intellectuals, notorious for being subversive, would be doing a service to humanity if they would uncover this swindle" (p. 52). Adorno did not shy away from drawing very concrete recommendations, advocating a kind of media "inoculation" in the schools. The uncharacteristic detail and wry pragmatism of his proposals warrant an extended quotation from an as yet untranslated radio talk:

I could imagine that in the upper classes of high schools, but also probably in primary schools, commercial films could be viewed together and the pupils simply shown what a swindle it is, how mendacious it is. In a similar way they could be immunized against certain morning programs, such as still exist in radio, in which on early Sunday mornings cheerful music is played as though we lived in a "perfect world" ["*heile Welt*"] as people say, by the way a truly terrifying thought. Or that they once would read together an illustrated weekly and be shown how they are run roughshod over by the exploitation of their own instinctual needs. Or that a music teacher, who for once doesn't come from the musical Youth Movement, would analyze hits and show them why a hit song is so incomparably worse than a movement of a quartet by Mozart or Beethoven or a really authentic work of modern music . . . Although I can very well imagine, for instance, that as soon as someone tried something like this, the film industry lobby would immediately lodge a protest in Bonn and declare on the one hand, that one-sided ideological propaganda was being propagated and, on the other, that the economic interests of the film industry, which are so important for the financial well-being of Germany, are being injured. All these things must be included in the actual process towards promoting political maturity [*Mündigkeit*]. ("Erziehung zur Mündigkeit," *Erziehung*, 145–6)[53]

Such direct recommendations may come as a surprise to English readers of Adorno who are more familiar with his rigorously theoretical writings. Yet it is precisely his radio broadcasts and essayistic work that attest to his impassioned participation as a public intellectual in the "culture wars" of his day. Essays such as "Working through the Past," "Education after Auschwitz," "Taboos on the Teacher's Vocation," and "Sexual Taboos and Law Today" underscore the therapeutic importance Adorno ascribed to psychoanalysis for the critical understanding and practical enlightenment of society, and these essays include extremely tactical "interventions": recommendations for reform in primary and higher education; practical suggestions for raising awareness about the psychological dispositions and "propaganda tricks" that exploit prejudice and chauvinism; proposals for psychoanalytically oriented empirical studies of the judicial and penal procedures relating to sexual offenses. Indeed, in 1969 Adorno was asked, along with many other leading cultural figures, for his views on the continued illegality and persecution of homosexuality in West Germany. His response, included in the published collection, was this paragraph followed by an extended excerpt from his essay "Sexual Taboos and Law Today" decrying the law against homosexuality which "managed to find safe passage into postwar liberated Germany" (*Critical Models*, 79f.):

Kindest thanks for your lovely letter. What I have to say on the topic of sexual morality, in the most diverse spheres of the harm that it wreaks, can be found in the essay "Sexual Taboos and Law Today" in *Interventions*, and in "Morals and Criminality" in the third volume of *Notes to Literature*. Both works I sent immediately to Dr. Heinemann as soon as he took over the Ministry of Justice, asking him to read them in the context of plans to reform the penal law, and I received an extremely friendly response. At the moment I wouldn't know what to add to what I have written there. That I most fiercely oppose every kind of sexual repression should in the meantime be more or less common knowledge, which I gladly confirm explicitly to you. (Italiaander 1969: 227–8)

Clearly the image of Adorno as a disdainful aesthete and incorrigible opponent of mass media per se warrants reconsideration in light of these late
essays; as their many references to contemporary events demonstrate, even
minor scandals were subjected to micrological analysis. Far from lounging on
the porch of the "Grand Hotel Abyss" and bemoaning the failure of culture
(Lukács' quip), Adorno energetically endeavored to raise it to its emphatic
idea.

German political culture went through a sea-change in the mid-sixties. By
incorporating the three principal parties in the grand coalition in December
1966, the German federal government had virtually eliminated effective
opposition in its parliament, the Bundestag. The emergence of non-
parliamentary opposition groups entailed an increasingly antagonistic polarization between the political establishment and the politically disenfranchised.
On the right, the National Democratic Party attracted former Nazis and new
converts, won 7–10 percent of the vote in regional elections, and proved to
be a continual source of anxiety to the government.[54] On the left, student
activists, particularly the SDS (League of German Socialist Students), turned
to the critical theorists expecting leadership. On several occasions Adorno
had spoken quite approvingly of the students' demands and demonstrations[55]
and in April 1968 he openly protested the Bundestag's deliberations toward
amending the constitution so as to give the government emergency powers,
including the authority to suspend civil rights, concluding that "with the
greatest possible publicity the emergency powers laws must be opposed,
because of the suspicion that those who would pass the laws delight at the
crisis. That they would do so is no coincidence, but rather the expression of
a powerful societal tendency, and should increase rather than decrease the
opposition" ("Gegen die Notstandsgesetze, GS 20.1: 396–7). Despite these
judgments and displays of solidarity with the student activists, Adorno was
accused of quietism. Perhaps the sharpest accusation came from one of his
former doctoral students, Hans-Jürgen Krahl, who interpreted his mentor's
refusal to participate in protest actions as the "monadological fate of the individual isolated by the laws of production" characteristic of the ideological
contradictions of bourgeois individuality; his passive intellectual subjectivity
is "why Adorno was not able to translate his private compassion for the
wretched of this earth into an integral partisanship of his theory for the liberation of the oppressed" (Krahl 1974: 165). As the SDS movement grew
more militant, Adorno's reluctance intensified and other critical theorists who
were initially far more receptive to the student actions, such as Herbert
Marcuse and Jürgen Habermas (who finally coined the term "left fascism"
after one particularly savage encounter), also sought to distance themselves.
Just before the student strike and first occupation of university buildings on

May 27, 1968, by Krahl and the SDS, Adorno on April 8 spoke approvingly of student protests as an effective "counter-tendency" against blind conformism in his opening lecture of the sixteenth German Sociology Conference ("Spätkapitalismus oder Industriegesellschaft." *GS* 8: 368). However, on January 31, 1969, Adorno and other Institute members summoned the police to clear out several dozen students who had apparently occupied rooms in the building (the students maintained they were only looking for an available classroom), and Krahl was charged with breaking and entering. In April 1969 Adorno's philosophy lecture course entitled "An Introduction to Dialectical Thinking" was disrupted when three shirtless women members of the SDS accosted him at the lectern.[56]

These events have reinforced the opinion that Adorno was apolitical, even reactionary, but beyond the enumeration of his practical interventions in the public sphere, his critical model of the relationship between theory and praxis and his advocacy of theory *as* praxis represents the strongest rejection of that view. In this sense, "Marginalia to Theory and Praxis" (*Critical Models*, 259–78) and other late essays[57] should be considered Adorno's rejoinder to the criticisms of the student activists. The controversy was paradigmatic for Adorno: he approved of political action, including student protests, when the ends were reasonable in the emphatic sense of *Vernunft* (*Erziehung*, 123–8). When, however, activism attacks theory for not being "partisan," that is, when it maintains that theory should be subservient to concrete praxis (just as Lukács had argued in the twenties), then, as it were in the form of an epicycle of the dialectic of enlightenment, praxis as *ratio* has prescinded precisely the organon that reflects on ends and has become its own end, pseudo-praxis, characterized by instrumental "tactics." The divergence between praxis and theory, born of the division of labor,[58] cannot be revoked by nostalgic fiat; it can only be intensified to the point of open contradiction and "qualitative reversal" – until the concept of praxis is brought to its own idea, namely that labor should be the conscious production of the conditions of humane life and not the reproduction of society's antagonisms. Therefore what is required is not the collapse of theory and praxis or the subordination of the former to the latter, but rather the *further* alienation of theory as an autonomous "force of production." Adorno's allusion to Marx is unmistakable: bourgeois autonomy is taken as an emphatic concept by which present autonomy is immanently shown to be an ideological semblance and transcendentally driven forward toward the idea of a society freely and consciously organized along reasonable ends rather than by instrumental *ratio*: "the goal of a just praxis would be its own abolition" (*Critical Models*, 267).

Theory thus, for Adorno, *is* the foremost instance of uncompromised praxis, what he calls the "morality of thinking" (*Minima Moralia*, 73). In a transformative return to the Greek notion of *theoria*, Adorno emphasizes the moment of contemplation as the possibility of change at *this* historical period: "the recovery of theory's independence lies in the interest of practice itself. The interrelation of both moments is not settled once and for all but fluctuates historically. Today, with theory paralyzed and disparaged by the all-governing bustle, its mere existence, however impotent, bears witness against the bustle" (*GS* 6: 147; *Negative Dialectics*, 143).[59] Thinking the totality in its untruth, where it is inconsistent with itself,[60] and bringing about the experience of negativity and contradiction is thus a thoroughly political undertaking. This political role of theory might be called, with a nod to Foucault, intervention by *problematization*: theoretical analysis contributes to a more self-conscious "cultural climate" by first conceptualizing culture's failure *as* a problem: "If in education . . . the problem of barbarism is posed in its urgency and with every rigor, then I would think that simply the fact that the question of barbarism becomes a focus of awareness already effects a change" ("Erziehung zur Entbarbarisierung," *Erziehung*, 122). In the final year of his life, enmeshed in controversy and disbelief that "people would want to realize my theoretical model with Molotov cocktails" (*GS* 20.1: 400), Adorno defined "the emphatic concept of thinking" as "prior to any particular content of the force of resistance" ("Resignation," *Critical Models*, 293) and upheld critique as a "human right" and the "human duty" of every citizen of democracy ("Critique," *Critical Models*, 284).

While the second generation of Critical Theory, in its propria persona of Jürgen Habermas, has rejected Adorno's reliance on a "philosophy of consciousness,"[61] it could be argued that his late essays and their social-psychological insights remain all too contemporary. Following fatal neo-fascist arson attacks on Turkish families in 1993, the weekly *Die Zeit* republished "Education after Auschwitz." Radio lecture versions of several of the late essays are periodically rebroadcast. In his travels in Bosnia-Herzegovina, Northern Ireland, the reunified Germany, and the Ukraine, the BBC reporter Michael Ignatieff drew thematically on Adorno to help explain the phenomenon of a new nationalism that "no longer quite believes in itself" and recognized precisely the schematic function of prejudice and chauvinism, the impoverishment of experience and autonomy, the bi-phasic belief and collective delusion that Adorno diagnosed more than twenty-five years ago; Ignatieff concludes, "In this divided consciousness, the plane of abstract fantasy and the plane of direct experience were never allowed to intersect. Nationalism's chief function as a system of moral rhetoric is to ensure this compartmentalization and in so doing to deaden the conscience . . . The authority of nationalist rhetoric is such that most people actively censor the testimony of their own experience" (Ignatieff 1993: 244–5). The analytical tools of

Adorno's theory still demonstrate their practical relevance for diagnosing and confronting the ongoing threats *to* and *within* the project of enlightenment.

Notes

1 This article was originally intended to be the introduction to the English publication of Adorno's last two essay collections, *Eingriffe* and *Stichworte*, entitled *Critical Models*. My thanks to the DAAD and the Deutsches Literaturarchiv in Marbach for an idyllic research sojourn, and to Sonja Asal, Thomas Levin, Christoph Menke, Ruth Sonderegger, and Emily Sun for helpful comments.

2 Adorno's contribution, "Schuld und Abwehr," a qualitative interpretation of the defence mechanisms with which test subjects denied the Nazi past, is reprinted in *GS* 9.2: 121–326.

3 Chapters 1, 7, 16, 17, 18, and 19 of *Authoritarian Personality*, considered to be at least in part Adorno's work, appear in *GS* 9.1: 143–509 under the title *Studies in the Authoritarian Personality*.

4 Although this was the last large-scale empirical research project to which Adorno contributed substantively, the A-scale was used and modified in a number of smaller studies by the Institute throughout the fifties and sixties, on attitudes toward employment, rearmament, foreigners, and "guest-workers," etc. On Adorno and the activities of the Institute up to his return to Germany, see Jay 1984.

5 In setting off his strategy from that of conventional dianoetic argumentation, Adorno writes: "While the argument pretends to be democratic, it ignores what the administered world makes of its compulsory members. Only a mind which it has not entirely moulded [*gemodelt*] can withstand it" (*GS* 6: 51; *Negative Dialectics*, 41 [translation modified]). In the Institute's introductory exposition of the concept of ideology, contemporary consciousness is defined as "the totality of what is manufactured in order to hook the masses as consumers and if possible to model and fix [*modellieren und fixieren*] the state of their consciousness" (*Soziologische Exkurse*, 176).

6 On Adorno's relationship to Lukács and the theory of reification see Buck-Morss 1977: 24–42 and Grenz 1974: 35–42. On Adorno and ideology critique see Geuss 1981.

7 See Pollock 1941. Pollock unfortunately does not indicate in any detail how state intervention qualifiably changes underlying modes of production, nor does he explain in detail sufficient to be persuasive how class antagonism as such is eclipsed by the economic planning of the state. For more on Adorno's relationship to Pollock and economic theory in general, see Johannes 1995.

8 Cf. also: "the most recent phase of class society is dominated by the monopolies; it surges toward fascism, the form of political organization worthy of it. While it vindicates the doctrine of class struggle with concentration and centralization, extreme power and extreme impotence unmediated, opposed to each

other in complete contradiction, it lets the existence of antagonistic classes slip into oblivion," from the 1942 "Reflexionen zur Klassentheorie" (*GS* 8: 376).

9   These moves are quickly recapitulated in the Introduction to *Dialectic of Enlightenment*: "Under existing conditions the gifts of fortune themselves become elements of misfortune. Their quantity, in default of a social subject, operated during the internal economic crises of times past as so-called 'surplus production'; today, because of the enthronement of power-groups as that social subject, it produces the international threat of Fascism: progress becomes regression" (*Dialectic*, xv).

10   "With the progress of enlightenment, only authentic works of art were able to avoid the mere imitation of that which already is" (*Dialectic*, 18); "The work of art, by completely assimilating itself to need, deceitfully deprives men of precisely that liberation from the principle of utility which it should inaugurate. What might be called use-value in the reception of cultural commodities is replaced by exchange-value" (*Dialectic*, 158).

11   Cf. also the introduction to *Dialectic of Enlightenment*: "Spirit's true concern is the negation of reification; it cannot survive where it is fixed as a cultural commodity and doled out to satisfy consumer needs. The flood of detailed information and candy-floss entertainment simultaneously instructs and stultifies mankind" (*Dialectic*, xv).

12   *Der Begriff des Unbewußten in der transcendentalen Seelenlehre* in *GS* 1: 79–322. Adorno withdrew the work, presumably at his advisor Hans Cornelius' suggestion.

13   For a contemporary related argument, see John McDowell, *Mind and World* (1994).

14   "Freudian Theory and the Pattern of Fascist Propaganda" (*GS* 8: 410). On the relationship between ego formation and society, cf. also "Zum Verhältnis von Soziologie und Psychologie" (*GS* 8: 42–85).

15   For instance, Adorno's contributions to *The Authoritarian Personality*, and the essays now collected in *The Stars Down to Earth*. The relation betweeen thought and narcissism is theoretically elaborated in "Opinion Delusion Society" (*Critical Models*, 105–22) and undergirds several other late essays in *Critical Models* in which Adorno examines the irrational force of taboos in law and pedagogy and the role of collective narcissism in recrudescent nationalism.

16   Indeed, Adorno and Horkheimer purged the original (1944) version of the *Dialectic of Enlightenment* of its Marxist attacks on Fordist capitalism and pseudo-democracy, which are now available in volume 5 of Max Horkheimer's *Gesammelte Schriften*. For a discussion of some of the authorial, bibliographical, and political issues raised by the republication of the original version, see Hullot-Kentor 1989.

17   Cf. "Gloss on Personality" (*Critical Models*, 161–6).

18   Adorno in "On Popular Music" actually provides two types, both correlates of standardization in the culture industry: (1) standardization of a product and even of its possible superficial varieties gives semblance of individualization where

there is none: "Thus, standardization of the norm enhances in a purely technical way standardization of its own deviation – pseudo-individualization" (p.
25); (2) labelling technique of styles and name-brands of products which in
fact only negligibly differ provides the illusion of consumer choice: "It provides
trade-marks of identification for differentiating between the actually undifferentiated . . . Popular music becomes a multiple choice questionnaire" (p. 26).

19 Erich Fromm, "Zum Gefühl der Ohnmacht."

20 Another example of bi-phasic belief is the conclusion of the "Culture Industry"
chapter of *Dialectic of Enlightenment*: "This is the triumph of advertising in the
culture industry, the compulsive mimesis of consumers towards the cultural commodities which they at the same time see through" (*Dialectic*, 167, translation
modified). For a useful discussion of "seeing through and obeying" see J. M.
Bernstein's introduction to *The Culture Industry*.

21 "There are no more ideologies in the authentic sense of false consciousness, only
advertisements for the world through its duplication and the provocative lie
which does not seek belief but commands silence . . . The more total society
becomes, the greater the reification of the mind and the more paradoxical its
effort to escape reification on its own" ("Cultural Criticism and Society," *Prisms*,
34). Cf. also *GS* 8: 8, 115, 477. And compare, from this side of the Atlantic,
Daniel Boorstin's contemporary observation that the "American citizen thus lives
in a world where fantasy is more real than reality, where the image has more
dignity than its original" (1987: 37).

22 Cf. also *GS* 7: 200, 361 on the failure of culture, and *Dialectic*, 131f. on the
"aesthetic barbarism" of the industrial organization and manipulation through
classification of culture as total ideology.

23 This collection of radio lectures and conversations, which shows Adorno at his
interventionist best, contains several initial radio versions of essays included in
Interventions and *Catchwords* ("Working through the Past," "Philosophy and Teachers," "Taboos on the Teacher's Vocation," and "Education after Auschwitz").

24 This is of course a reformulation of Max Weber's thesis of the rise of purpo-
sive over value rationality in occidental modernity.

25 Adorno's "Platonism" is indebted to Benjamin's notion of "idea" in the
"Epistemological-critical prologue" to his *Origin of German Tragic Drama*. On
Adorno as a "platonist of the non-identical" cf. Schnädelbach 1983 and Tiede-
mann 1992.

26 Of course, what Benjamin precisely meant by "dialectical image" remains a question of interpretation; my characterization relies on the work of Susan Buck-
Morss (*Origin* and *Dialectics of Seeing*) and Jennings (*Dialectical Images*).

27 Possibly also motivating Adorno's critique was his displeasure with Benjamin's
recent friendship with Bertolt Brecht, which led him to suspect the proletariat
as the implied bearer of Benjamin's "collective unconscious."

28 In personal correspondence Henri Lonitz, editor of the correspondence, sur-
mises that Adorno is almost certainly referring to conversations with
Horkheimer and Benjamin in 1929 at Königstein, when Benjamin was first

developing the idea of what would become the *Passagenarbeit*. I have not been able to find mention of "*Modell*" in any of Benjamin's published notes from that time.

29 See the discussion of Wittgenstein's private language argument and its consequences for moral theory in Korsgaard (1996: 136–8).

30 This would be one interpretation of Adorno's notorious "The whole is the untrue" ("Das Ganze ist das Unwahre") in *Minima Moralia*, 50.

31 My thanks to Christoph Menke for suggesting this parallel.

32 "Opinion Delusion Society," *Critical Models*, 105–22.

33 "On Subject Object," *Critical Models*, 245–58. See Martin Jay's very useful explication of this text in his *Adorno*, 56–81.

34 Cf. Alexander García Düttmann's and my discussion of this and other recent work on Adorno in "Under the Sign."

35 This quote might suggest Quine's "web of beliefs"; I have explored how Adorno might look in the context of contemporary debates in "Bedeutung, Wahrheit, Kritik: Davidson, Rorty und Adorno."

36 Cf. similar remarks from Adorno's programmatic "Essay as Form": "The criteria for such interpretation are its compatibility with the object and with itself, and its power to give voice to the elements of the object in conjunction with one another"; "Thought's depth depends on how deeply it penetrates its object, not on the extent to which it reduces it to something else" (*Notes to Literature*, 4–5, 11).

37 In an insightful article Miriam Hansen (see pp. 57–84) has traced out Adorno's twofold notion of writing: "In the context of the culture industry, writing apparently means script in the sense of *Vorschrift*, or prescription, a discourse that masks itself in iconic images and familiar sounds. In the context of aesthetic theory, however, writing becomes *écriture*, the non-subjective, indirect language of modern music and abstract painting. In its renunciation of traditional imitational and even expressive elements, this *écriture* is profoundly historical." In the passage from *Negative Dialectics*, Adorno explicitly likens constellations to musical compositions, as he does in a passage from the *Philosophy of New Music*, discussed by Jameson (1972: 61).

38 Cf. "Education after Auschwitz": "One speaks of the threat of a relapse into barbarism. But it is not a threat – Auschwitz *was* this relapse, and barbarism continues as long as the fundamental conditions that favored that relapse continue largely unchanged" (*Critical Models*, 191).

39 Cf. Goodman's *Ways* (1978); his underlying argument, that the predictive regularity comprising inductive validity is a function of habitual linguistic practices, can be found in chapter "IV" of his *Fact, Fiction, and Forecast* (1965).

40 For a representative example of this all too typical topos in the reception of Adorno, particularly in certain directions within media studies, cf. Collins 1987.

41 Adorno typically taught an introductory sociological Proseminar, an advanced philosophical Hauptseminar, often together with Horkheimer and devoted to Kant and/or Hegel, and a lecture course (topics included aesthetics, dialectics,

Kantian epistemology, and moral philosophy, and are currently under preparation for eventual publication). Adorno took only one sabbatical leave during this time in order to complete *Negative Dialectics*.

42 Letter from Adorno to Kracauer, 19 July 1951, from the Adorno–Kracauer correspondence located in the Deutsches Literaturarchiv, Marbach am Neckar (hereafter abbreviated DLA).

43 Letter of Adorno to Kracauer, 14 Nov. 1963 (DLA). Suhrkamp Verlag cannot confirm these figures because of incomplete records.

44 Letter of Adorno to Kracauer, 17 Dec. 1963 (DLA). Adorno's modus operandi since the late thirties was to collect copious notes, then dictate and repeatedly edit the typescripts. For many of the essays there are between three and seven typescript versions.

45 For instance, between 1928 and 1932 Adorno published in and edited the musical journal *Anbruch* while in Vienna. The dates and Adorno's exact duties are somewhat controversial. Cf. Steinert 1993: 152–76. During the early thirties Adorno published under Siegfried Kracauer's editorship in the *Frankfurter Zeitung*, and as his correspondence with Kracauer indicates, entertained the idea of becoming a journalist like Kracauer and Georg Simmel rather than an academic.

46 The form also describes *Dialectic of Enlightenment*, in whose opening page Voltaire is cited and which contains a section "For Voltaire" (mistranslated as "In Praise of Voltaire"). Adorno praises Proust for similar reasons in "The Essay as Form" (*Notes*, 8) and the opening of *Minima Moralia* (21). Kracauer too recognized the affinity and praised the author of *Jargon of Authenticity* for being a real "moraliste" (Kracauer to Adorno, 22 Nov. 1963, in DLA).

47 Cf. also *Dialectic* (159f.) on the radio as a "universal mouthpiece": "The inherent tendency of radio is to make the speaker's word, the false commandment, absolute. A recommendation becomes an order."

48 Letter from Adorno to Hannes Küpper, 22 April 1931. In a letter of 25 July 1930 to Kracauer, Adorno proudly reports of a well-received radio broadcast of his "Lesestücke," and in a letter of 27 September 1930 he reports to Kracauer that the Frankfurt Radio has invited him to give a large number of lectures on modern music. All letters from Adorno's correspondence in the DLA.

49 Adorno poses as a task for television "to find contents, programmes, which by their own content are adequate to this medium, instead of contents being borrowed externally from somewhere else," and he offers as examples "the informational and documentary element," "montage and alienation of realism," "the mutual influence between research and production," "breaking through the so-called intimate sphere of the school," and "the interaction between specialized and general programmes" (ibid., 68–9). Cf. the transcript of a television discussion devoted to the work of Beckett in which Adorno participated: "'Optimistisch zu denken ist kriminell'. Eine Fernsehdiskussion über Samuel Beckett." Neither radio broadcasts nor television appearances have yet been centrally archivized.

50 "On the Question: 'What is German?'" (*Critical Models*, 205–14).

51   The studies will eventually be published as *Current of Music. Elements of a Radio Theory* from Adorno's *Nachlaß*. One study has been published separately, "Analytical Study of the NBC Music Appreciation Hour," with an informative introduction by Thomas Y. Levin and Michael von der Linn, "Elements of a Radio Theory: Adorno and the Princeton Radio Research Project."

52   The Hacker Foundation studies were later reworked for German publication and included in *Interventions* as "Prologue to Television" and "Television and Ideology" (*Critical Models*, 49–58, 59–70).

53   Similar recommendations can be found in "Fernsehen und Bildung" (*Erziehung*, 54, 62).

54   The breakdown of the NPD's popularity as indicated in regional elections is as follows: 7.9% in Hessen (Nov. 1966); 7.4% in Bavaria (Nov. 1966); 8.8% in Bremen (Oct. 1967); and 9.8% in Baden-Württemburg (April 1968).

55   For example, in a "Radio Discussion about 'the Unrest of the Students'" with Peter Szondi on October 30, 1967, Adorno asserted that "it must be said, first of all that the students' criticism of our form of university contains very serious aspects of truth, and that it is part of their rights, unquestionably anchored in our general democracy, without any inhibition whatsoever to exercise criticism upon these institutions, which they know from their most intimate and most aggravated experience" (Szondi 1973: 91–2). On another occasion Adorno lauded one student demonstration, saying, "If the behavior of the high school students in Bremen proves anything, then it proves that precisely for them the civics class was not as unsuccessful as it is always claimed to be." And he defended student demonstrations: "If one has some familiarity, at close hand, with the events that are taking place nowadays with the rebellious students, then one realizes that the situation is by no means one of primitive outbursts of violence; rather in general they are politically reflected modes of behavior" ("Erziehung zur Entbarbarisierung," *Erziehung*, 123–4). On several occasions Adorno commended the combined protests of professors and students in Göttingen that brought about the resignation of the cultural minister of Lower Saxony, e.g., "Kritik," (*GS* 10.2: 792). On a more anecdotal note, Ulrich Sonnemann recalls "how [Adorno] was pleased as Punch at every successful rebellious palpitation of his 'children,' the oppositional students, every stirring of spirit, imaginative polemic, of wit, which usually was rewarded with the occasional success" (Sonnemann 1971: 158). Even after the SDS women disrupted his lecture course, Adorno in an interview with *Der Spiegel* maintained that the student strikes aimed to prevent delivery of the reactionary Springer press newspapers was "legitimate" ("Keine Angst vor dem Elfenbeinturm," reprinted in *GS* 20.1: 402–9; here p. 406).

56   For a more detailed and more critical overview of the SDS and the criticial theorists see Wiggershaus 1994: 609–35. The relationship between the Frankfurt School and the Student Movement has now been exhaustively chronicled on a day-by-day basis in a three-volume work undertaken by the Hamburg Institut für Sozialforschung; see Kraushaar 1998.

57 These include "Critique" and "Resignation" (*Critical Models*, 281–93), and the two interviews Adorno gave in the midst of the student unrest, now collected in *GS* 20.2: 398–409. For a history of the conceptual pair, see Lobkowicz 1967.

58 Adorno draws on the early, at the time unpublished, work of his friend Alfred Sohn-Rethel, *A Sociological Theory of Knowledge*; cf. *GS* 6: 178, *Negative Dialectics*, 177, and *Dialectic*, 243–4.

59 On Critical Theory's revalorization of Greek contemplative "theory," see Theunissen 1981: 51f.

60 See "Why Still Philosophy?" (*Critical Models*, 5–18).

61 See especially Habermas, *Theory of Communicative Action*, vol. 1: 339–402 and *Philosophical Discourse*, 106–30. While it is beyond the scope of this article to consider Habermas' paradigm shift in Critical Theory, it should be noted that his recent work on democracy theory has renewed the importance of a liberal public sphere and politically mature citizens and hence has also renewed the relevance of many of Adorno's criticisms outlined in this article.

14

Radical Art: Reflections after Adorno and Heidegger

Krzysztof Ziarek

In the twentieth century, the labels "radical art" or "radical aesthetics" have been used to refer not only to various avant-garde movements of the 1910s and 1920s but also to leftist art, the so-called second avant-garde, and pop art, and more recently, to politically charged art representative of cultural, racial, or ethnic differences. In fact, it seems that twentieth-century art has exchanged adherence to rules, schools, and aesthetic ideals for preference for a continuous radicalization, which has turned innovation into the "standard" for the assessment of modern art. Adorno sounds a clear note of caution in his writings about the proliferation of this idea of novelty, and insists on making a distinction between radical art and the aesthetic of the new, which, instead of producing a transformation in the social, merely masks the repetition of the same. At the same time that Adorno underscores the importance, even critical necessity of radical art, he also makes clear that such radicality cannot be identified simply with new or different forms of representation.[1] Although Heidegger became interested in more radical modern aesthetics only late in his life,[2] his thought too proclaims the necessity of a decisive transformation in art, which Heidegger links to a change in our relation to language, at the same time that he remains reluctant to identify this transformation with the invention of "new" representational and linguistic forms: "In order to think back to the occurrence of language, in order to reiterate what is its own, we need a transformation of language, a transformation we can neither compel nor concoct. The transformation does not result from the fabrication of neologisms and novel phrases. The transformation touches on our relation to language" ("Way," 1993: 424–5). Heidegger seems to caution here against exaggerated enthusiasm about avant-garde linguistic innovations, as he nonetheless presses for continued work on transforming our relation to language, poetry, and art. For Heidegger, the radicality of art would lie then in the ability to transform our relation to language, and thus to the world, beyond the invention of new linguistic and representational paradigms.

For both Heidegger and Adorno, such a transformation cannot be reduced to the celebration of the new and the different, so "familiar" and ordinary in contemporary culture; in other words, radical art exceeds the question of a new aesthetic style and cannot be sufficiently explained as rejection of existing artistic conventions. As important and interesting, both aesthetically and historically, as the succession of artistic orientations may be, especially in the context of the ruptures of modernism, both Adorno's and Heidegger's reflections on art indicate the necessity of remaking this modern optics within which we encounter art. They both see art in terms of history: not as containing universal or unchangeable truth but as figuring a happening of historical truth. Such historical truth is not merely represented in art; it is enacted, critiqued, and thus opened up in its very historicity. In art, the futural force of experience is brought to bear on the historical forms of truth, not only to displace or question them, but to bring into the open the transformative dimension of futurity, which makes it possible to mark within the representation of the present what escapes and alters it. This may well be the temporal and historical significance of Adorno's negative considered as the futural (rather than utopic) force that eludes the modern administration of experience. In their different ways, Adorno and Heidegger explore how art gathers this force into itself, figures it into its *poiēsis*, and, by virtue of its existence as an artwork, keeps releasing this force into the world around it. Art does more than inscribe itself into the world within which it originates and exists; it opens up this world differently, transforms it by redisposing relations within it, by changing the very valency of relating which constitutes art's source.

The questions of temporality and transformation are some of the most important parameters of Adornian and Heideggerian revisions of aesthetics, pointing to the level on which the radicality of art has to be addressed: namely, in terms of the historical "roots" of modern experience. The meaning of the word *radical* comes from the Latin *radix*, which refers to root, fundament, basis, origin, or source. The *Oxford English Dictionary* defines radical as "1. Of and pertaining to a root or to roots 2. Forming the root, basis, or foundation; original, primary 3. Going to the root or origin; touching or acting upon what is essential or fundamental; thorough; esp. *radical change, cure*."

Thus, radicality refers specifically to going to the root or origin of something. For art to be radical, then, it has to address the very roots of experience in the midst of the modern techno-rationality, to touch upon what is fundamental to it and act upon it in a way that may bespeak change or transformation. The historical "roots" of modern experience in both Heidegger and Adorno have to do with technicity or the techno-administered world, on the one hand, and with the originary temporality, that is, with the force of the possible which temporality releases into existence with each unfolding moment, on the other. Remarking in *Aesthetic Theory* that "[t]he artwork is at once process and instant" ("Prozess und Augenblick in eins," 100, 154), Adorno indicates the double temporal vector of art: its inscription *in* and *of* the process of historical change, on the one hand, and its momentary explosion of the very framework of such a history, on the other. What becomes released in this rupture is the futural force through which art "negates the categorial determinations stamped on the empirical world and yet harbors what is empirically existing in its own substance" (p. 5). In *Being and Time*, Heidegger argues that history should not be just a matter of the knowledge of the past but that it should, first and foremost, touch upon the historicity of existence. In other words, historical thought should first consider historicity's source in the temporal projection of being, and, thus, to continuously question and open up, through the force of futurity, the historical articulations of being. Heidegger describes temporality as originary to underscore the fact that existence comes to be "rooted" in each of its moments in temporality, that is, not just in the past but in the futural direction and opening of the present beyond itself. To say that temporality is originary means to point to how being is, in each "now," always already released into its futurity, opened up beyond what obtains in the present. As a retrieval of the past, history happens for the sake of the future, but such future is not conceived as a future moment that will one day become "present"; rather, Heidegger understands it as the futurity intrinsic to each moment, which lets the present unfold as always already projecting itself into the future. Heidegger calls such transformativity at heart of history, the "silent force of the possible."[3]

For modern art to be radical, it needs to both confront and refigure the "rooting" of modern experience in terms of the relation between technicity and originary temporality. Enlisting the help of Adorno and Heidegger, I propose to consider art's radicality in terms of a certain redisposition of relations constitutive of being in modernity which art performs by virtue of bringing into the foreground the historicity of being. Gathering into its work the silent force of the possible, art transforms the power orientation of forces in modernity, their instrumentalizing predisposition, so to speak, toward technicity and power. This revision of the aesthetic should be explored in terms of art's relation to modern forms of power (*Macht*) and mastery (*Herrschaft*).[4] Radicality in art can be thought of as a specific aesthetic force irreducible, strictly speaking, to the ideas of either complicity or resistance with the powers that be. This force of art is radical in the sense that, instead of participating in the power relations in which it originates, either by replicating them or resisting them as a counter*power*, it has the valency of calling into question the very formation of relations into power. The negative imprint of the social reality Adorno discusses in Beckett or Kafka, i.e., what is negatively marked as absent in the modern society, is a kind of power-free relatedness. Since modern reality is characterized by overinstrumentalized rationality (Adorno) or by technicity understood as the mode of relationality which governs and forms all relations (Heidegger), art's radicality lies in unfolding a world that no longer operates in the mode of technicity and its specifically modern forms of techno-scientific rationality. This kind of relatedness beyond power and powerlessness is what art registers in its enigmatic figure.

In contemporary discussions, the idea of radical art refers to two closely related, though distinct, domains, which are often kept strictly apart or even opposed: on the one hand, the sphere of formal radicality – for instance, in the revolutionary formal and linguistic innovations of the avant-garde – and, on the other, political radicalism of socially critical or revolutionary art; an example here could be the theater of Bertolt Brecht. Obviously, those two spheres often intersect, as is the case in the "formal" innovations of Brechtian plays or, in Adorno's estimation, in the social critique at work in the serial music of Schönberg and Webern. One could easily multiply here such examples or cite the continuing debates about the aesthetic and political significance of modernist avant-gardes, where at issue still remains the extent to which avant-garde art is or was radical: can the importance of the avant-garde breakthrough be circumscribed simply within aesthetic terms or is it also radically political? If that is the case, is all avant-garde "political," or do we need to make distinctions between, for example, explicitly leftist and political Berlin Dada and its apparently less overtly political Zürich antecedent or its progeny, Surrealism? If Dadaism or Constructivism is political, are they more so than, say, Cubism or Orphism? And what would decide this issue of radicalism: explicit engagement with political themes, espousal of leftist or Marxist ideas, social critique?[5]

The prevalent terms of contemporary debates about radicalism in art frequently force the issue into the all too easily established polarization between the politicization of art and the aestheticization of politics. As a result, the issue of art's radicalism gets confined to the terms of the socio-cultural context of art, and addressed mostly through historicist, cultural, and discursive analyses. Responding in *Aesthetic Theory* to the polemics about the social significance of art, Adorno indicates, however, that tilting the understanding of art toward its historical-cultural context may not be the answer, as it quickly establishes the primacy of the cultural/theoretical discourse over the aesthetic "language" of art and, thus, denies a priori any force intrinsic to art:

> Once art has been recognized as a social fact, the sociological definition of its context considers itself superior to it and disposes over it. Often the assumption is that the objectivity of value-free positivistic knowledge is superior to supposedly subjective aesthetic standpoints. Such endeavors themselves call for social criticism. They tacitly seek the primacy of administration, of the administered world even over what refuses to be grasped by total socialization or at any rate struggles against it. (*Aesthetic Theory*, 250)

Adorno's warning about the dominance of this "socio-discursive" approach to art, articulated long before the current prevalence of cultural studies, is well worth examining. It points out the main philosophical assumption structuring this "cultural" approach to art: the equivalence between art and the social, historical, and political forces animating the context of its production and reception. This equivalence relies on the translatability between the social forces and the forces at work in art. Hence, the explanation of how forces operate within the historical and cultural context of art and the demonstration of their reflection or the revision they undergo within the artwork, is assumed to be enough to account for how art works. To Adorno, however, it is precisely this explanation that muffles the radicality of art; circumscribing art without remainder into the cultural and the social, it denies art the possibility to be radical, as it were, on its own terms, the possibility that hinges on art's carefully understood autonomy. Such an approach does not see art as having any "real" force of its own; rather, art's force is always merely reflected or borrowed, it is an "aesthetic," and therefore illusory force, a mere shadow of "real" political, psychological, and economic forces. For Adorno, this perspective is problematic because it does not allow art to speak its "aesthetic" language but forces it into the categories that culture, including even the most radically critical discourses in it, has constructed for art. In a way, the true radicalism of *Aesthetic Theory* is its insistence that even the most radical discourse gets called into question in "radical" art, and that it is precisely this aesthetic force that constitutes art's precarious autonomy as a constant "threat" to culture and its parameters. Such autonomy remains emphatically distinguished from social isolationism or indifference; instead, it marks a critical margin within art, a sphere of art's force, irreducible to social forces and, as such, capable of their radical critique.

Expounding this idea of paradoxical autonomy, Adorno's *Aesthetic Theory* is the strongest, theoretically and philosophically most complex rejoinder to any superficial politicization of art, especially to the claims that thematics itself is enough to make art radical. Adorno's insistence on the priority of radical form over any thematic content or contextual material is well known: "Real denunciation is probably only a capacity of form, which is overlooked by social aesthetic that believes in themes" (*Aesthetic Theory*, 230). *Aesthetic Theory* demands that we rethink radicalism in art apart from the terms dictated by discourses external to art: "Art is the social antithesis of society, not directly deducible from it" (*Aesthetic Theory*, 8). It is what cannot be deduced or explicated in terms of external forces — cultural, discursive, historical — that constitutes art's critical force. We need to look into art itself, into its redisposition of forces, for terms that would precisely call into question the prevalent discourses that surround and intersect with art, trying to contain it discursively and institutionally. While obviously such discourses can be hegemonic and politically conservative, on the one hand, or radically critical and progressive, on the other, for Adorno, the fact that they operate as "external" to art, as forceful by virtue of constituting art as their object and, thus, denying art any autonomous aesthetic force, requires their critique. Moreover, this critique should develop its terms precisely from art and the force that marks its autonomy. For Adorno, modern art is "true" art, that is, radical art, only when it has the force, a specifically artistic force, to negate and maybe even transform, the social matrix of forces.

This is why I would insist on the importance in this context of Heidegger's and post-Heideggerian critiques of aesthetics, which get their momentum from reflection on the place of art in modernity. Adorno was certainly reluctant to acknowledge this impetus in Heidegger's thought, downplaying Heidegger's transformative conception of art, especially its critical relation to modern rationality and technicity, which Adorno, on his own part, vigorously called into question as well. Despite all the conceptual, aesthetic, and political differences between Adorno and Heidegger, even the misrepresentations of Heidegger common in Adorno's texts, this insistence on the autonomous force of art brings them together; that is, on the aesthetic or, for Heidegger, specifically poietic, force,[6] which is not isolated from or indifferent to the social order but, instead, different and strong enough to work a rupture and transformation within it. What is important to Heidegger and to poststructuralist discourses that rethink and appropriate his work, is not only the central place of aesthetic reflection but, more significantly, the insistence on problematizing philosophical, political, or cultural discourses, including aesthetics itself, *from within* the "aesthetic." This critique combines the questioning of aesthetics and of the aestheticization of experience with seeking in art "after aesthetics" the sites of both transformation and radical rupture in relation to society and the discourses it produces about art. In a way, these approaches elaborate the two-pronged critical force of art that Adorno was after: the force at once critical of both the social order and of those aesthetic accounts that neutralize art's force. This is why this critique in either Heidegger, Derrida, Lyotard, Foucault, or Irigaray cannot be mistaken under any circumstances for aestheticization: it does not aestheticize the political, but, I would say, it releases the radicality of art into the domain of other discourses, into the political and the cultural. To declare such approaches as somehow formalistic or aestheticized and, therefore, divorced from the substantial social and political issues, is to make categorial mistakes about the level on which poststructuralist thought engages aesthetics.

It is only when we examine how Heidegger's critique of aesthetics and technology attempts to uncover the radicality of art in order to call into question modern instantiations of power relations that we will be able to see how the role that art comes to play in Heidegger and post-Heideggerian thought can help us encounter and develop Adorno's idea of the socially critical force intrinsic to art – the force that remains irreducible either to the social sources of artworks or the cultural significations of art. Such a meeting between Adorno and Heidegger calls for a reformulation of current approaches that seek to explain art primarily through its context, that is, as a reflection or a revision of culture which remains explicable *within* the terms produced and available in that culture. By contrast, Adorno and Heidegger solicit art itself in order to bring into the open art's force, which needs the social context not to reflect it or provide a new vision of the social but to forcefully register its difference; that is, to imprint the difference of the aesthetic on the social and, thus, mark the radical incomprehensibility of art's figure and its "political" relevance within the critical paradigms used to explicate it.

It is evident that such a notion of art's radicality requires a rethinking of both the aesthetic and the social. And it is through this two-pronged revision that art may exhibit a certain political force. In revising the relation between the aesthetic and the political, however, the very meaning of the political is at issue; certainly, it becomes problematized beyond the notion of aesthetic ideology. Adorno's long-standing polemic with Lukács takes issue not only with the idea of realist aesthetics as the best vehicle for social and political critique but also concerns the level on which art can be thought of as radical.[7] Criticisms of Lukácsean and Brechtian approaches in *Aesthetic Theory* call into question the idea that art's social significance can be explained to our satisfaction in terms of the ideology of the aesthetic. It does not mean that art is not implicated within aesthetic and even political ideology or that it does not participate in producing the ideology of the aesthetic. Rather,

Adorno's remarks suggest that this is not where art's radicality lies. What is singularly important about this strand in Adorno's thinking is its search for understanding art's radicality beyond the terms of either critique or opposition. To that extent, for Adorno art is not political in any immediate or easy sense. To suggest that art is oppositional, and therefore ("correctly") political, because it endorses a leftist ideology, undertakes an explicit critique of existent social relations, or paints a utopian alternative, simplifies and distorts art's radicality. As Adorno's polemic against social realism makes clear, art can and does address social reality on this representational level, but in the process it betrays and loses its autonomous aesthetic force. And it is this autonomous force which allows art to throw into question the historical and social reality beyond the terms – political, cultural, or aesthetic – existing in it. This does not mean that art cannot be ideological, that it does not reflect political relations or cannot be brought to bear on political matters. Adorno's remarks speak specifically to the fact that the radical moment in art should not be confused with art's political/ideological function.

Adorno's examples, Schönberg, Webern, Kafka, or Beckett, all build their works as a second or different language, whether musical or literary, that both courses through the "ordinary" discourses in which the sociopolitical reality constitutes and experiences itself and undermines, almost cancels, those dominant languages. Minuscule Webernian compositions not only rewrite the tone language into serial constructions but also invert and evacuate into silence the grandiose sonic world of symphonic music and its synthesizing ambitions. Webern's music, though, is more than the terrain of the non-identical since, in foregrounding silence as the musical "element" par excellence, that is, as the element in which the organized sound, or music in the "narrow" sense, exists, it breaks open a different disposition of (musical) relations. The force of Webern's music lies in initiating a new, "silent" tuning or pitch as the modality of relation in the aftermath of the "conquering" reason. Paradoxically, this force of silence forgoes power; it refuses the power to form relations and underscores the futural character of temporality. This Webernian pitch of silence can be seen as registering, in Heidegger's terms, the silent force of the possible, namely historicity and the futural dimensionality of experience. In *Being and Time*, Heidegger rethinks history in terms of futurity, underscoring the fact that history, before it concerns itself with the past, needs to attend to its own futural dimension. The historical character of existence lies not just in the passage of time but in the "quiet force of the possible" within reality which is, therefore, by force of historicity, never fully present. Webern's Sechs Bagatellen, opus 9, steeping sound in silence, trailing or abruptly transforming notes into absence, foreground and revise the very relation between sound and silence, pointing to a silence beyond

sound and its absence. It is in this new register of silence beyond the presence and/or absence of sound, that Webern's music forgoes the power of
sound, the power to organize it, to compose relations into a fully "sounded"
or articulated image. In this register, Webern's compositions for the string
quartet instantiate this other dimension of silence as the force "proper" to
art: not the force of mastery, expression, or representation but the futural
force of temporality. The silence in Webern's music rekeys or retunes relations with a view to the force of the possible as the force with which unfolds
being as power-free, beyond its articulations into forms of power. It is this
ability of art to key us into a relationality beyond power and powerlessness,
in which the historial character of existence erupts with the power-free force
of the possible, that constitutes the radical force of art. And this force remains
beyond critique and resistance, which both claim power and "play" its game.

What for Adorno makes art radical does not enter the domain of politics
but, instead, calls this very domain into question, it interrogates the very idea
of politics. Art is political only when it refuses to be ideological: not rejecting this or that ideology but the very force with which modern being
becomes formed into ideology. Art's political relevance lies in its refusal to
be political: "This is not a time for political works of art, but politics has
migrated into autonomous works, and nowhere more so than where these
seem politically dead" ("Commitment," 318). Such art is neither political nor
apolitcal but, rather, *political otherwise*, otherwise than what society would like
to define and "preserve" as the meaning of the political. In this phrase, "political otherwise," I want to capture the force with which art can capsize in its
aesthetic space not just this or that political order but, rather, the very order
of politics, i.e., the instrumentalization of being into politics. Within its poietic
figure irreducible to what society can signify or understand of art (as political), art releases experience from its regulation by modern rationality. The
political relevance of art is of the order of the aesthetic, whose force, when
released or opened up within an artwork, transforms the social context in
which it appears. In Beckett's play, *Waiting for Godot*, the idea of "nothing happening" keeps pointing to its negative: the collapse of the futural force of the
possible. The destitution which pervades the play appears to comes about as a
result of the dominance of "waiting": the characters do not live, they wait, as
their entire existence is structured around a desire which they themselves
cannot quite name, and which they channel into the mysterious figure of
Godot. What is key in Beckett's play is the collapse of temporality, the disappearance of its space of possibilities into the single line of waiting for what will
not happen. In a way, Godot blinds Vladimir and Estragon to the temporality
of their existence, which disappears and loses meaning. The paralysis of being
comes about through the institution of goals (the coming of Godot) which, as

Nietzsche's philosophy continuously points out, freezes being by evacuating its event temporality – temporality irreducible to aims, objectives, or their desired fulfillment. Thus, what insistently forces itself into Beckett's play, even though only as absence, is temporality, which keeps calling into question the very order of "reality" in which the play is situated.

For Heidegger too art's transformative force cannot be located simply within the realm of aesthetics. Even though art's force is obviously contained in the artwork, in the work's figure,[8] as Heidegger calls it, art always opens up or projects an entire world, a whole complex of relations, whose mode of relationality depends precisely on how the figure works in its differential event. Coming from the world of its origin, the work of art transforms this world in such a way that with it history begins again: "Whenever art happens – that is, whenever there is a beginning – a thrust enters history; history either begins or starts over again" ("Origin," 201). Because it sets open a world in a way that draws into the open being's historicity, art calls into question the very world in which we encounter it; it takes our existential, conceptual, and representational footing away from us, not only undermining the political and social articulations of being within which we exist but also calling into question the very formation of being *as* social or political. The work of art does "transport us into this openness and thus at the same time transport us out of the realm of the ordinary. To submit to this displacement means to transform our accustomed ties to the world and earth and henceforth to restrain all usual doing and prizing, knowing and looking, in order to stay within the truth that is happening in the work" ("Origin," 191). The truth happening in the work is the play of concealment and unconcealment in which the historicity of being comes to the fore, and in which human existence becomes released into its originary futural temporality.

Heidegger sees the radical thrust (*Stoss*) of art in the spatio-temporal dimensionality characteristic of human being, this most "familiar" dimensionality which becomes foreclosed and evacuated within the techno-calculative regimen of modernity. While Adorno describes modernity in terms of the domination of the overinstrumentalized rationality, Heidegger associates the modern with what he calls *Technik*, technics or technicity. Technicity defines the prevalent mode of revealing, i.e., the manner in which beings historically come to be what they are. Heidegger suggests that in modernity beings occur as what they are when they manifest themselves as intrinsically calculable and manipulable. At issue is not just the leading role of science and technology but the understanding of how beings and relations among them are disposed: "The revealing that rules in modern technicity [*Technik*] is a challenging [*Herausfordern*], which puts to nature the unreasonable demand that it supply energy which can be extracted and stored as such"

("Question," 320). Technicity refers to a revealing that forces out, that disposes and discloses everything, including human beings, into a giant, global resource of forces and energy. Such a revealing that forces out constitutes being into a relationality of power. In Heidegger's understanding, technicity is what courses through and disposes all relations, in a manner similar to Foucault's conception of capillary power.

In this context, we can understand art's role in specifically modern terms: art becomes a sphere where technicity comes to understand and maybe even transform itself. To be radical, art cannot therefore close its eyes to technicity or try to escape the modern reality of everyday life. On the contrary, art has to become more "technical" than technicity itself, precisely in order to bring out into the open the very character of technicity, the fact that technicity is not just a tool in human hands, (a) technology, but an overpowering disposition of modern relations into a global resource (*Bestand*). In some ways, modern art can only be radical if it provides a mirror to technicity, a mirror that would allow technicity to both see itself for what it is and to discover its own limit, and, thus, perhaps, become able to face its otherwise:

> Because the essence of technology is nothing technological [i.e., it is not a technological object but, rather, a mode of revealing], essential reflection upon technology and decisive confrontation with it must happen in a realm that is, on the one hand, akin to the essence of technology and, on the other, fundamentally different from it.
>
> Such a realm is art. But certainly only if reflection upon art, for its part, does not shut its eyes to the constellation of truth, concerning which we are *questioning*. ("Question," 340)

Art is akin to the essence of technicity because it too is a mode of revealing, but, by contrast with technics, a poietic modality of revealing. If technicity reveals in a manner that forces out, disciplines, calculates, and organizes, the poietic revealing lets be, it brings beings into the open in a way that allows them to be as what they are, in their otherness. Art, then, is radical only when it *questions* toward this other mode of revealing in which relations would be disposed otherwise than through technicity. It is easy to see that at stake in Heidegger's reflection on art is freedom; this freedom, however, is not conceived in terms of rights belonging to human beings but as a relationality in which what is becomes brought forth into the free dimension of its historical being.

In this context, the radicality of art can be reformulated as its ability to recognize and instantiate this connection between technicity and art, and thus to open a rift within the modern reality that manifests itself as technological through and through. Opening up this rift, art begins to draw technicity into a self-questioning, to possibly initiate a transformation in the univocally technical being characteristic of modernity. Art releases the silent force of the possible on the level that begins to redispose relation, to rewrite technicity. In Adorno's terms, we could say that art is radical when it realizes its own relation to the modern techno-rationality at the same time that it lays bare its non-identity, its difference from technicity. In the same gesture, art infuses the non-identical into technicity itself, the non-identical beyond the idea of the other of the same, a radical difference that cannot be sublated back into technicity. The fold within technicity becomes the negative beyond negation, the other not only marked in the same, i.e., technicity, but also remarking it, redrawing the very dynamic of relations that form the world as technical.

Adorno's idea of the non-identical in art, of art as the negative imprint of social reality, and Heidegger's conception of art as a poietic fold within modern technicity, indicate the level on which to consider the idea of radical art: on the "elemental" level of force relations. By the "elemental" I mean not the rudimentary but the element, the dimension, or the disposition, within which forces come to be regulated and formed in their relations. Reflecting on Beckett's aesthetic, Adorno indicates that Beckett's plays assimilate themselves to the claim of reality around them but also unfold a matrix of forces that undermines the administered world:

> New art is as abstract as social relations have in truth become. In like manner, the concepts of the realistic and the symbolic are put out of service. Because the spell of external reality over its subjects and their reactions has become absolute, the artwork can only oppose this spell by assimilating itself to it. At ground zero, however, where Beckett's plays unfold like forces in infinitesimal physics, a second world of images springs forth, both sad and rich, the concentrate of historical experiences that otherwise, in their immediacy, fail to articulate the essential: the evisceration of subject and reality. This shabby, damaged world of images is the negative imprint of the administered world. To this extent Beckett is realistic. (*Aesthetic Theory*, 31)

As in Heidegger's distinction between *technē* and *poiēsis*, in this remark too Adorno differentiates between the abstract sphere of social relations, in which forces are disposed in a manner that increases the administrability of the world but also eviscerates reality, and "ground zero," where Beckett's texts unfold like a play of forces that produces the negative of the modern world. It seems that "ground zero" refers to an invisible layer of force relations which operate underneath the visible social reality. Adorno indicates that, beyond the thematic and the formal in art, Beckett's works redispose the field of forces that regulate everyday life.

The approach to art in terms of a play of forces becomes necessary in view of the absolute hold that modern reality exercises over its subjects. This hold makes the traditional artistic orientations, whether realistic or symbolic, no longer adequate for engaging modern reality, because the symbolic has no meaning within a reality uniformly organized around its techno-rationalistic matrix while the realistic merely replicates the status quo. In "The Question Concerning Technology," Heidegger wonders whether a poietic revealing of reality is at all possible in the face of the domination of the technic revealing. Adorno's remark on Beckett and his overall engagement with avant-garde art, absent in Heidegger, suggests that it is the radical modernist art that, at least in a few cases, may bring into view the limit of the techno-administered world. But to make this limit visible, to turn it into an issue and a question, or even to bring home the idea that there is a limit to the technic, we need to rethink art beyond the thematic, the formal, and the cultural, in terms of its ability to redispose forces which produce art and which become gathered into art's poietic space. Art's radicality comes to be located, then, in reference to but also beyond art's inscription within its historical context; it concerns art's ability to unfold force relations otherwise than the relational patterns prescribed within the instrumental rationality of the modern world. Like Heidegger, Adorno associates this radical rupture in art with the force of historicity: it redisposes and stamps reality in the manner of a proto-history or historicity, which "recommences in every moment of history" (*Aesthetic Theory*, 113). The "second world of images" that springs forth as the world opened up by art enacts a certain recommencement of history: the world presented and made "present" in art has the force that lets the reality around art begin again. As in "The Origin of the Work of Art," history starts over in art, it begins in a different key – a key that is non-calculative and non-administered but opens relations in terms of the force of the possible. It renders relations historical "in essence."

It is in the context of Heidegger's critique of Nietzsche in the late 1930s, especially of the conception of the Will to Power, that I propose to examine this possibility of transformation in force relations that both Adorno and Heidegger associate with art. Heidegger's writings on Nietzsche, but especially two recently published texts which Heidegger wrote around the beginning of World War II and put into his drawer, *Besinnung* (1938–9, published in 1997) and *Die Geschichte des Seyns* (1938–40, published in 1998), develop this question of transformation in terms of a radical critique of power. In *Besinnung*, Heidegger describes metaphysics as an unfolding of reality in which being becomes synonymous with power. His remarks on the fluidity of power, its flows through all types of relations, its inseparability from the orders of experience, knowledge, and culture, its lack of a central point, anticipate Foucault's conception of power articulated in *History of Sexuality*.[9] Such a fluid coursing of power determines the very valency of relation; it gives its stamp to the modern relationality, which explains itself as power and has its historical direction in what Heidegger refers to as the self-overpowering of power (*Geschichte*, 62–71). In the midst of this increasing of power, which eviscerates the historico-temporal character of human existence, Heidegger examines the possibility of a different disposition of being, one that would not transpire in terms of power. In *Besinnung*, he explicitly states that being occurs beyond power and powerlessness: "ausserhalb von Macht und Ohnmacht west das Seyn"(p. 84); and, at another point, he articulates being that is beyond the opposition between power and powerlessness as *das Machtlose*: "Seyn – das *Machtlose, jenseits von Macht und Unmacht*, besser ausserseits von Macht und Unmacht, wesenhaft unbezogen auf Solches." "Being – the *power-free, beyond power and unpower*, better yet, outside of power and unpower, essentially unrelated to them," that is, unrelated to the opposites of power and its absence (*Unmacht*)" (pp. 187–8).

I venture the translation of *das Machtlose* as "the power-free," which I hope reflects Heidegger's emphatic assertions that *das Machtlose* is not to be confused with powerlessness (*Ohnmacht* or *Unmacht*). While *machtlos* does literally mean powerless (*macht-los*), Heidegger clearly distinguishes it from the idea of powerlessness (*Ohnmacht*), of being without power. The suffix *los* indicates instead a certain forgoing or letting go of power, a release from the power formation of being into a relationality that is powerfree. Heidegger associates the power-free with a non-metaphysical disposition of being, which he differentiates from *Sein* (the metaphysical idea of being) and calls *das Seyn*. This non-metaphysical, power-free being is associated in *Besinnung* with the idea of freedom, which Heidegger conceives of as the spatiotemporal dimensionality of being, as the play of time-space (*Zeit-Raum*). This dimensionality works in such a way that it is pervaded by refusal (*Verweigerung*); it retains the non-identical, it refuses full articulation and formation of forces. Marking an otherwise to the order of visibility and representation, this dimensionality of being refuses its own formation into power. What is crucially important here is the idea that this refusal – the refusal to unfold in terms of the self-overpowering of power – resists "more" than resistance itself. For resistance always operates within the sway of power, it resists power by means of claiming its own power; resistance resists by virtue of being a counterpower. *Das Machtlose* "resists" by altering the very terms of relating, by operating otherwise than power. It is the difference of *das Machtlose*, which does not explain itself in terms of differentiation *within* the operations of power, its startling and freeing otherwise, that gives its specific force. This force is very hard to conceive of, since it is a force that releases or lets free instead of compelling, disciplining, or forming into power. It is "forceful" by virtue of refusing to be either strong or weak, active or passive, powerful or powerless.

What *das Machtlose* frees are the "roots" of being in originary temporality, that is, in the futural projection of the historical unfolding which is animated by the silent force of the possible. This silent force discussed in *Being and Time*, which in the light of *Besinnung* has to be dissociated from power, is the force of releasing existence from the grasp of representation and administration into its historicity, that is, into the futurity of its possible becomings. Such temporality is originary in the sense that it functions as the index of the non-identical or of difference, which are here understood as markers of futurity. It is the oblivion of the futurity intrinsic to the historicity of being, that produces being in terms of power relations. Heidegger suggests that we measure time but we do not experience temporality: we do not experience our own being in its temporal dimensionality. When this dimensionality, and thus also futurity, become covered over, then being manifests itself as power, it can only transpire in terms of this self-intensifying power, without any possible alternative. The power-free thus refers to the futural dimensionality of experience, which has the force of foregoing power. The release of the silent force of this dimensionality transforms the very valency of relating, rendering the site of all relationality power-free in the sense described above. It describes the very moment of transformation (into freedom) which Heidegger and Adorno seek in art.

It is precisely in terms of such a release and freeing that Heidegger redefines radicalism in *Besinnung*. He describes radicalism as "*Bewahrung des Ursprungs*"or the "keeping of the origin," that is, of the originary futural "leap" of temporality, which releases forces in the rupture of the event.[10] In other words, radicalism consists in letting being unfold in its specifically futural dimensionality, with the "originary" force of the possible in play. This radicalism is decisively opposed to the idea of conserving an origin or essence, for the occurrence of being "essences" precisely as the freeing opening of futurity within the present. More important for our argument here, this radicalism comes to be defined beyond the scope of power relations, that is, in terms other than counterpower. In a way, the idea of counterpower is not "radical" enough, since it still explains being metaphysically, i.e., in terms of power and resistance to it, which have their place within the history unfolding as the intensification of power. The radicalism Heidegger proposes is a precarious and difficult one, since it has no "power" and refuses itself *to* power. It is a radicalism in a constant tension with power, threatened with collapsing into "truths" or values. Yet, there is also an undeniable force to this radicalism of the originary disposition which, as Heidegger writes, translates "[t]he word of the truth of being, the saying of the science-free knowing, which is never a command and which does not know powerlessness."[11]

Although in *Besinnung* Heidegger is very critical of modern art, his later texts describe this alternative relationality in terms of *poiēsis*, which ruptures and releases being in modernity from its regulating technicity. It seems, therefore, legitimate to link this later rethinking of *poiēsis* with *Besinnung*'s redefinition of radicalism, and to think radicalism in art not just as opposition or resistance but as a "more" radical redisposing of relations that lets them free of power. This is also the sense of radicality in Adorno's negative, which extends beyond critique or opposition, beyond the idea of the possibility of reconciliation implied in the critique of the unreconciled world. Throughout *Aesthetic Theory* Adorno keeps redescribing the negative in art, so that it does not refer to a future possibility or moment of reconciliation but to art's force of transforming the reality beyond the very terms which this reality permits. Although he uses a different term from Heidegger, *Veränderung* rather than *Verwandlung*, Adorno extends at that moment the import of the negative beyond negation, toward an otherwise of the positive and the negative: "By emphatically separating themselves from the empirical world, their other, [artworks] bear witness that that world should be other than it is; they are the unconscious schemata of that world's transformation [*Veränderung*]" (pp. 177, 264). This "otherwise" implied in the transformation is a non-coercive,[12] or power-free, relationality of forces.

Such radicalism beyond resistance or negation can also be articulated, for example, in the work of Baraka, in particular, in his most recent collection, *Funk Lore*. Baraka's poetry is undeniably contestatory and defiant, often iconoclastic, even deliberately insulting. All those aspects are present in abundance in *Funk Lore*, for example, in "Sin Soars" (pp. 27–36), where Baraka complains that in the midst of the world completely controlled by corporations that "The American Peoples' Voice / is never heard," and "Incriminating Negrographs" (pp. 65–70) where he turns his critique also against members of African-American community. Some would say that Baraka is truly radical when he satirizes and violently rejects global capitalism and its cultural incarnations in "Sin Soars!" when he "denounces" Spike Lee, or maybe when he counters Adorno by showing how jazz remains radical for contemporary aesthetics (in "JA ZZ [The 'Say What?'] IS IS JA LIVES"). What adds another layer to these moments of contestation and resistance, when Baraka evidently uses poetry as a cultural and political "counterpower," is the aesthetic of the freeing and enabling force of being, of a funky jazz rhythm, which courses through the poems of *Funk Lore* (pp. 9, 60–1). In "Art Against Art Not" and "JA ZZ . . . ," Baraka links this rhythm force with the rhythm and sound of jazz. While Adorno dismisses jazz as part of the culture industry, Baraka sees in it the realization of the radical potential of art, which he assimilates into his poetry, (re)writing the syncopated rhythms of jazz music into new language forms. Adorno associates the radical social art with new classical music, in particular the second Viennese school of Schönberg and Webern, forms of music based on a series of notes rather than rhythm. Baraka, on the other hand, emphasizes precisely the rhythm of jazz as the structuring principle, the weaving force behind relationality and connectedness. In a way, Baraka attempts to produce a jazz writing, to inflect poetic language into a kind of jazz rhythm and relationality.

It is this connecting, relating rhythm that unfolds and weaves the strands of *Funk Lore*. The source of this alternative "jazz" rhythm within Baraka's work is the African culture. Baraka, therefore, registers in the same gesture the specificity of African art and "force" and generalizes its underlying rhythms into the non-appropriative relationality, a mode of force relations coursing underneath the power formations and representational order: "The Universe / is the rhythm / there is no on looker, no outside / no other than real, the universe / is rhythm, and whatever is is only is as / swinging" (p. 9). European music, then, becomes subsumed as part of this relational rhythm. Playing with this rhythm to revise the cultural figurations of blackness in "Art Against Art Not," Baraka produces an oppositional aesthetic of blackness, revaluing the cultural differences constitutive to the project of modernity. However, Baraka describes this rhythm also as a cosmic force, as a relationality of a general scope, running hidden through the techno-capitalist culture of the present day: "The snake was music the visible thought / the answer, as the Sea crawls in waves / the waves of is' story the shared center" (p. 60). This rhythm has to do with producing a pattern of relations between forces that manifests an alternative to domination, inequality, racial prejudice, etc. More important, the force relations which Baraka weaves into the poetic jazz rhythm at the core of his poetry eschew power; they are set both against the present power relations and inequalities – thus registering a voice of resistance – but they also develop an alternative relationality whose force lies precisely in forgoing power.

Art's is the peculiar radicalism of the power-free (*das Machtlose*); that is, modern art is radical not by virtue of political opposition or contestation but when the relationality of the world it opens up is instantiated in a power-free disposition. Taking further Heidegger's comments on technicity, we could say that such aesthetic radicalism turns technicity and its manipulative flows of power inside out, and discloses the internal outside of technicity as the power-free *poiēsis*. It is a minimal, difficult, but also radical turn within being as power and mastery. It is the radicalism that exists as the negative, in a

somewhat modified Adornian sense, of the social and political radicalisms –
not as their negation but as their otherwise. While such radicalisms operate
within the dialectic of power and powerlessness, their negative reflects the
obverse side of this dialectic, the power-free. This link between art and the
turning in being into *das Machtlose* outlines my interpretation of Adorno's
idea of the autonomy in modern art. It shows art's inscription within and
determination by the social, at the same time that it opens up a margin of
a power-free force intrinsic to art. But this force, specific as it is to art is the
force of turning within power-oriented relations of forces. It is a refigura-
tion of the very valency of relations within this world and as such, reaches
into or reverberates within the social reality into which art becomes inscribed
through creation. Art's autonomy is thus a complex process, an event, one
might say, which marks art's dependence on the social but also frees art's force
and describes the thrust with which such force revises the categorial determinations of modern being, to paraphrase at once Adorno and Heidegger.

Notes

1 Adorno's favorite examples include Schönberg, Webern, Kafka, and Beckett,
   whose work he associates with the necessity of continuous change in the direction of artistic invention in contemporary art. He warns, however, that invention can all to easily become a repetition of the same: "If a possibility for
   innovation is exhausted, if innovation is mechanically pursued in a direction that
   has already been tried, the direction of innovation must be changed and sought
   in another dimension. The abstractly new can stagnate and fall back into the
   ever-same" (*Aesthetic Theory*, 22).
2 Although Heidegger's discussions of art are largely limited to Greek art, Hölderlin, and the modernist poetry of Rilke, George, or Trakl, in the 1960s Heidegger was increasingly drawn to the paintings of Cézanne and Klee, and discussed
   the sculpture of Chilida. Heidegger's texts evidence his notion that there has
   been very little important art, art that could speak to and transform the metaphysical foundations of modern being. Still, the small openings his later thought
   makes toward contemporary art make it possible to rethink his critique of aesthetics in a context broader than the one indicated by his writings. In particular, it would be important to address Heidegger's idea of the critical role,
   suggested in "The Question Concerning Technology," that art understood as
   poiēsis plays in questioning modern technicity.
3 "Because in each case existence is only as factically thrown, historiology will
   disclose the silent force of the possible (*die stille Kraft des Möglichen*) with greater
   penetration the more simply and the more concretely having-been-in-the-world
   is understood in terms of its possibility, and 'only' presented as such" (*Being and
   Time*, 446/*Sein und Zeit*, 394).

4   Extensive discussion of the proximities and differences between Adorno and Heidegger in relation to the questions of power and mastery can be found in Mörchen's *Macht und Herrschaft im Denken von Heidegger und Adorno* (1980). His second book on this topic, *Adorno und Heidegger* (1981), painstakingly chronicles all the instances where Heidegger's thought is present in Adorno, and argues for the possibility of constructive critique and dialogue between the two orientations.

5   There is also the thorny problem of Italian Futurism, both of the seminal importance of its radical manifestos and art for twentieth-century aesthetics and of the conservative turn toward Mussolini's fascism proclaimed by Marinetti. It is far from easy to determine where the aesthetic, and even political, radicalism of Futurism ends and the fascist sympathies begin. Similar questions could be raised with respect to Russian Cubo-Futurism, especially Mayakovsky, who after the 1917 revolution aligned Futurism not only with the revolutionary movement but, in the end, also with the repressive regime of Stalin.

6   I discuss this idea of a poietic force in art in "Powers to Be: Art and Technology in Heidegger and Foucault," *Research in Phenomenology*, XXVIII (1998), where I argue that the poietic as Heidegger describes it is not limited to art but refers to a certain disposition of forces, which Heidegger distinguishes from the dominant technic forms of relations in modernity.

7   Zuidervaart (1991) provides a concise and illuminating discussion of Adorno's differences from Benjamin, Brecht, and Lukács, and points out Adorno's insistence on linking the political import of art with both the autonomous status of artworks and the modernist aesthetic (pp. 28–43).

8   In "The Origin of the Work of Art," Heidegger formulates his conception of art in terms of the figure (*Gestalt*) as the differential relation between the open context of historical relations (world) and the moment of withdrawal and refusal (earth). See "The Origin of the Work of Art," 188–90.

9   See *Besinnung*, and Foucault, *History of Sexuality*, vol. I, 93–4. For Heidegger, power pervades being at any moment, since power and its increase becomes the very meaning of being, which gives relations their historical shape. The modern version of such relationality is what Heidegger calls *Technik*, technology or technics. *Technik* means that manipulability (*Machenschaft*) becomes the essence of being, that all forces become compelled (*erzwingen*) to participate in the "self-superpowering of power" (*das Sichübermächtigen der Macht*) (*Besinnung*, 17–18). Within such modern techno-metaphysics of power, culture is of the same essence as *Technik*, i.e., it is technological: "Culture is the technics of history, the manner in which historical calculation of values and making of goods organize themselves and expand the forgetting of being." Modern culture renders history (*Geschichte*) manipulable, it changes the non-ground of historial unfolding into *Historie*, i.e., into the object of historicism, thus obscuring the radical historiality of being. Culture covers over the radical temporality of being with the idea of values and turns historial occurrence into historical facts and situations, available as pieces of knowledge or manifestations of ideology. Culture as technics

of history (i.e., historicism) uproots the human mode of being because it severs it from the originary non-ground of history, from the historiality of being. Another instance of such manipulability of being is the modern nation, in which, Heidegger remarks, the idea of the subject, of humanity conceived as subjectivity, achieves its most pure form: "the subjectivity of the humankind reaches its most pure form in the nation; the community of a nation drives to the extreme the isolation of man into the subjectivity." Culture, historicism, and the nation are all forms of the metaphysics of power, versions of the technics of history, which manipulate and master the forces of being. Parallels between Heidegger's understanding of *Technik* as manipulability for the sake of power and Foucault's historically more specific analyses of the disciplining of forces are obvious.

10 See Heidegger's discussion of nihilism and radicalism (*Besinnung*, 67).

11 "Das Wort der Wahrheit des Seyns, den Spruch des wissenschaftslosen Wissens, der nie Machtspruch ist und die Ohnmacht nicht kennt" (*Besinnung*, 52).

12 In his discussion of Adorno's approach to aesthetics, Jarvis (1998) looks at Adorno's attempts to think of the negativity in art in terms of non-coercive relations (pp. 140–4). Even though Adorno argues that poetry is always a certain form of the domination of language, he explores the possibility that this domination happens in the service of non-coercive relating.

15

Queerly Amiss: Sexuality and the Logic of Adorno's Dialectics

Jennifer Rycenga

"An idea whose time has come has no time to waste" (Adorno 1973: 96). With this maxim from Adorno in mind, queer revolutionaries might urgently inquire into the relevance of revolutionary philosophic methods and insights developed before the emergence of mass movements for sexual freedom. Given the overt heterosexism of the Left, there is much from the past that needs to be strongly critiqued, and even discarded.[1] The legacy of Adorno on questions of homosexuality is a particularly thorny case, fraught with contradictions created by his historic epoch and by his approach to dialectics. The same thinker who equated "characterological" homosexuality with fascism (Horkheimer and Adorno 1972: 192–3, Adorno 1974: 46) also maintained that Germany's homophobic laws tended "toward the destruction of intellectual powers" (Adorno 1998: 80). Despite his vaunted detachment from political engagement, Adorno here lent his intellectual reputation to a practical fight. But even in his article condemning the laws, the best hope he has for homosexuals is that in less restrictive societies they could become "less neurotic" than in Germany (Adorno 1998: 80)!

Adorno's status as an intransigent critic of modernity and "the fallacy of constitutive subjectivity" (Adorno 1973: xx) render him an important figure for contemporary theorists. His valorization of the aesthetic realm lends support to a cultural turn in radical thought (despite the fact that most cultural studies perspectives enthusiastically embrace the popular arts that Adorno despised). But his psychoanalytic framework, where he tries to meld the insights of Freud about individuals with the social realm, are glaringly essentialist and embarrassingly heteronormative. Randall Halle's 1995 article, "Between Marxism and Psychoanalysis: Antifacism and Antihomosexuality in the Frankfurt School," does a fine job of tracing Adorno's explicit references to homosexuality. These fall into two distinct periods: the works of the 1940s, especially the studies in *The Authoritarian Personality* and the analysis of anti-semitism in *Dialectics of Enlightenment*, and essays from the 1960s, most notably the two articles "Sexual Taboos and Law Today" and "Morals and Criminal-ity: On the Eleventh Volume of the Works of Karl Kraus." Halle concludes that despite an apparently tolerant acceptance of overt homosexuality in these later essays, Adorno never broke with his psychologistic understanding of homosexuality as "inherently pathological" (Halle 1995: 306), a perspective which equated the homosexual personality with that of the antisemite (Halle 1995: 303; cf. Adorno 1974: 46).[2]

The literal evidence does not make a strong case for Adorno's relevance to queer theory. But how fair is it to judge any pre-1969 figure by the yard-stick of their explicit references to homosexuality? There are a few excep-tions who stand out, of course – Charles Fourier, Edward Carpenter, Harry Hay, Herbert Marcuse – but, for the most part, even theorists and philoso-phers who are central to queer theory have to be "queered" to be applica-ble. As reprehensible as his pejorative use of "homosexuality" as a category is, it is not the only (or even the most important) place for a queer critique of Adorno to dwell. One reason is that the homogenic/homophile move-ments, from the turn of the twentieth century until the late 1960s, had them-selves adopted the language of the sexologists and psychologists; the fact that a heterosexual theorist would use the same language, albeit with less sympa-thy, is hardly surprising: it reflects a specific social-historical context. Fur-thermore, Adorno is consistently critical of bourgeois moralism; in all his work he decries capitulation to the leveled-out society that presents itself as normal.[3] This, and Adorno's passionate stance against all oppression, provide ample openings to rescue what is liberatory from his thought, and to over-look or minimize his heterosexism.

While I am not attempting to excuse Adorno – his scientifically in-flected use of homosexuality is reprehensible and could well be deployed against queers at some point – the tendencies that led to Adorno's mis-characterizations of homosexuality are part and parcel of larger philosophic problems that affect the revolutionary dimensions of his thought. Specifically, having decisively rejected the category of subject, he does not search for, let alone perceive, a possible revolutionary subject emerging from the realm of sexuality. He thus falls into the error of privatizing sexuality rather than seeing it as bearing transformative social potential. Not surprisingly, his brief against sexual taboos has the quality of reformism – as he himself admits – rather than being revolutionary (Adorno 1998: 4, 71–2, 268). He abandons the transformation of reality because, quite literally, there is no one to carry out such a project in the absence of the subject. The very idea of a gay, lesbian, or queer liberation movement could not appear on his horizon, even as a hoped-for utopic possibility.

Gay liberation movements needed to explicitly break through the silencing mechanisms of the closet, and to articulate a position beyond mere tolerance and medicalization: this required live subjects.[4] In a correspondence with lesbian-feminist writer Adrienne Rich, the Marxist-Humanist philosopher Raya Dunayevskaya put this revolutionary principle quite simply: "Each revolutionary force does have to concretize the question for what it considers, holds, as proof that freedom is here and does relate to them. No one can do it for (the) Other" (Dunayevskaya 1986–7: 11302–11303). The emergence of lesbian-feminism in the late 1960s and early seventies and the Gay Liberation Fronts in 1969–70 marked a turning point in which the doors of the closet were burst open,[5] and, as with the Women's Liberation Movement, the shortcomings of both the bourgeoisie *and* the Left were targeted. The demands of the movement resonated with the roots of Marx's philosophy of revolution: the need for a total uprooting of the current society, and for totally new human relations, including those relations which had been previously considered "personal."[6]

While the movements of the 1960s failed to achieve such a total transformation, they raised important new questions and new perspectives at their high points. The realms of thought which queer movements brought to the fore of liberatory discourse include examination and destabilization of categories such as body, gender, and other false naturalisms, placing stress on the constructed categories of "normal" in human relations, the roles of pleasure and desire in liberation, and the demand that queer lives and liberation not be postponed until "after the revolution" (again, a characteristic shared with many New Left social movements).[7] All of these categories and emphases ultimately have a dialectical nature: they have internal contradictions which can lead to a transcendence of current conditions, or fall back into the parameters set by the existing society, and fail to create a transformed world. The question of how and why this occurs elucidates the role of theory in relation to practice.

Adorno's practice of dialectics offers very little for queer revolutionary perspectives (aside from vigilantly alerting us to the risks of co-optation and commodification). Drawing on three of his writings from the 1960s – "Sexual Taboos and Law Today," "Morals and Criminality: On the Eleventh Volume of the Works of Karl Kraus," and *Negative Dialectics* – I will illustrate how Adorno's rejection of the negation of the negation, his disdain for subject, and his post-Marx Marxist view of philosophy create his own philosophic limitations and social determinism.[8] The Marxist-Humanist thought of Raya Dunayevskaya, and the multiple manifestations of what I call "the queer left legacy" – thinkers such as Audre Lorde, Edward Carpenter, Harry Hay, and Mario Mieli – have vitally informed the direction of my critique.

What is the role of philosophy in relation to revolution, according to Adorno? The last of Marx's 1845 "Theses on Feuerbach" reads "The philosophers have only *interpreted* the world in various ways; the point is, to *change* it" (Marx 1967: 402). While generations of Marxists have argued over the meaning of this potent aphorism, Adorno launches *Negative Dialectics* with a rather unimaginative reading of it, fastening onto philosophy itself, rather than philosophers:

> Philosophy, which once seemed obsolete, lives on because the moment to realize it was missed. The summary judgment that it had merely interpreted the world, that resignation in the face of reality had crippled it in itself, becomes a defeatism of reason after the attempt to change the world miscarried. (Adorno 1973: 3)

Now Marx says nothing about philosophy being resigned; on the contrary, he is focused on showing the symmetrical inadequacies of materialism and idealism by themselves, and arguing for a unity of theory and practice. The note of resignation here is self-reflexive on Adorno's part. Marx's thesis, far from an attack on philosophy, seeks to broaden philosophy's scope to integrally include "revolutionary practice" (Marx 1967: 401). Adorno caught a whiff of this when, complaining against the actionists of the late 1960s, he harrumphed against the "banishment (of theory) by an impatience that wants to change the world without having to interpret it while so far it has been chapter and verse that philosophers have *merely* interpreted" (Adorno 1998: 265). But his usual attitude is to follow those who read the final thesis as a rejection of philosophy:

> Anyone who still philosophizes can do so only by denying the Marxist thesis that reflection has become obsolete. Marx believed that the possibility of changing the world from top to bottom was immediately present, here and now. But only stubbornness could still maintain this thesis as Marx formulated it. (Adorno 1998: 14)

While there is no textual evidence in any of the "Theses on Feuerbach" that Marx said reflection was obsolete,[9] what Adorno speaks to in his own thought here is more crucial to explicate. He is arguing for a reflection that *does not feel compelled* to change the world, because he fears that any praxis "at this historical moment would inevitably eternalize precisely the present state of the world, the very critique of which is the concern of philosophy" (Adorno 1998: 14).[10] In suggesting this praxis-less perspective for philosophy, Adorno has retreated to merely interpreting the world, and has removed philosophy from preparation for revolution. To adopt this misreading of Marx would have a devastating effect on any queer philosophy of revolution, because it pulls asunder not only reflection and action, but also expels the sensuousness with which Marx wishes to infuse both materialism and idealism. In contrast, Adorno's philosophy can only deliver a theory of retrogression and decay.

It is with a heavy heart that Adorno views the retrogression of society at the opening of "Sexual Taboos and Law Today," remarking that "society itself . . . seems to be regressing to earlier stages," and "(e)ven critical thought risks becoming infected by what it criticizes" (Adorno 1998: 71). This becomes a self-fulfilling prophecy when the article ends with a series of practical, even positivistic, proposals for "objective" psychological testing, presumably in search of more just laws;[11] but whatever the case, the stench of reformism here prefigures the infamous call to the police that Adorno made against the students who occupied the Institute for Social Research (Rubin 1998: 29).

Even more damning, to my philosophic ear, is his attempt to reconcile "tolerance" for homosexuals while retaining the objectifying psychoanalytic opprobrium heaped on the term "homosexuality" in *The Authoritarian Personality*, whose studies he still cites approvingly in "Sexual Taboos and Law Today."[12] Thus, he accurately names the repressive force of what we would now call "the closet" when he says "Even if homosexuals were finally left more or less in peace, the atmosphere of persistent legal discrimination would necessarily subject them to unremitting anxiety" (Adorno 1998: 80). But he then follows this up with reductive theories:

> If one accepts the psychoanalytic theory that claims that homosexuality in many cases is neurotic, a manner of resolving childhood conflicts that prevents the so-called normal resolution of the Oedipal complex, then the social and legal pressure, even if indirectly, will perpetuate and reinforce the neuroses, according to the psychological law of anaclisis. (Adorno 1998: 80)

Confirming that he *does* believe that homosexuality is neurotic (this might appear uncertain in the above quote), he also invokes class-based stereotypes against gay men: "Where at least the social taboo against homosexuality is more modest, for instance in many aristocratic, closed societies, homosexuals appear to be less neurotic, in terms of characterology less deformed than in

Germany" (Adorno 1998: 80). If this were not enough, he proceeds to a discussion of youth sexuality and the fears around it, by claiming that "in the
twentieth century, possibly due to an unconscious homosexualization of
society, the erotic ideal has become infantalized" (Adorno 1998: 80–1). In
addition to reinscribing (possibly unconsciously) another familiar trope against
homosexuals (pedophilia),[13] his sleight of hand moves seamlessly from actual
incarnate homosexuals to the use of the word "homosexual" to express an
idea (and a pejorative one at that). The sensuousness of sexuality – what he
calls elsewhere in the article (presumably with a heterosexual referent in
mind) "the actual spiciness of sex" (p. 73) – is nowhere present when homosexuality is discussed: the corporeal homosexual is neurotic, and the abstract
psychoanalytically inflected category of "the homosexual" has not been
cleared of its association with violence and totalitarianism.

As Halle notes, Adorno "had found no way out of the impasse of
Frankfurt School social psychology" (Halle 1995: 308), but the argument
can be extended: the impasse is a philosophic shortcoming. While there may
be individuals who correspond to "that type of homosexual whose admira-
tion of virility is coupled with an enthusiasm for order and discipline and
who, with the ideology of the noble body, is ready to set upon other
minorities – intellectuals, for instance" (Adorno 1998: 79), such a passage can
only come across as hateful in the absence of its opposite: a liberatory homosexual consciousness. There are, in essence, two kinds of homosexuals in
Adorno's essay: the ones imbued with totalitarian ideologies, and the ones
who aren't. This latter category is blank, an empty slate, with no positive character or potential; such "not-bad" homosexuals should be tolerated (they
might even be smart), and the law should not intrude in their private lives.[14]
But Adorno's tolerance emerges only from good will (in the Kantian sense),
not politics.

There are three opportunities in the articles on sexuality where Adorno
could have corrected this, and didn't. The first instance occurs when, in the
case of heterosexual women prostitutes, he glimpses a potential: "the whores
. . . should be defended against the ignominy of morality as unsuspecting representatives of an alternative sexuality" (Adorno 1998: 78; cf. Adorno 1974:
174). But not only does he not credit the women as conscious subjects of
their own creativity, his only description of male prostitutes is as blackmail-
ers (pp. 79–80, 82). Even when an alternative opens up, there is no conscious
subject to embody it; therefore it falls back to being a mere blink of the eye
of the theorist.[15]

The second opportunity occurs as Adorno describes the alleged loosen-
ing of mores in the time since World War II. While his statement that "sexual
liberation in contemporary society is mere illusion. . . . (i)n an unfree society,

sexual freedom is hardly any more conceivable than any other form of freedom" rings true, he fails to investigate the dialectically dual nature of these tendencies (pp. 72–3). Where he anticipates, by negation, all that can go wrong, he forecloses on possibility (ironically because it can't be total). This becomes clear when he discusses the new vocabulary of "partner," while invoking yet another trope which has been used against homosexuality, narcissism:

> What is merely identical with itself is without happiness. Genital sexuality's concentration on the ego and its likewise self-centered Other – and it is not by chance that the designation "partner" has come into fashion – harbors narcissism. (p. 75)

Apparently he hears only the instrumentality of the word "partner," and not its simultaneous resistance to heterosexual norms, or its rejection of hierarchy in intimate relations.

But the most egregious missed opportunity comes in the article on Karl Kraus' work, where Adorno appears ready to critique the category of privacy:

> The concept of privacy, which Kraus honors without criticism, is fetishized by the bourgeoisie and becomes "my home is my castle." Nothing, on the other hand, neither what is most holy nor what is most private, is safe from the exchange principle. Once concealed delight in the forbidden provides capital with new opportunities for investment in the media, society never hesitates to put on the market the secrets in whose irrationality its own irrationality is entrenched. (Adorno 1992: 43)

Once again we have a moment which, if it is to have liberatory content, must be seen in its dialectic duality. But this Adorno refuses to do. Instead he gives all power to the culture industry, and seems to lament the constant erosion of a bourgeois notion of privacy under the onslaught of the market, rather than critiquing this kind of "privacy" as a way of masking that same market ideology and social repression (i.e., the oppression of women and children in "private" homes, and the silencing chill of the closet).

I am not asking Adorno to speak with the foresight of the late twentieth century's movements. Nor am I disputing the presence of some truth in what he says here; he does anticipate problems which have emerged in the gay and lesbian movements, such as lesbian chic, ghettoized commodification, sexual fetishization (as in sexual tourism) and reformist "right-to-privacy" campaigns (whose ultimate results logically include the farcical "don't-ask-don't-tell" policies of states and churches, about which, I feel certain, Adorno would have had some sardonic things to say). But his dialectic is incomplete,

charting only retrogression. His inadequacies, if embraced, render revolutionary transformation impossible.

This is a philosophic flaw or, more accurately, a series of philosophic
missteps. Crucial categories for a Marxist philosophy of revolution – subjects
of revolution, revolution in permanence, negation of the negation, and
Dunayevskaya's contribution of Absolute negativity as new beginning – are
the very tendencies of thought which Adorno singled out for definitive
attack. To critique Adorno as elitist, or as lacking subject in his thought, is
hardly original to my analysis; for instance, Martin Jay opines that

> There are no specific social forces or structures that embody resistance to the
> totalizing power of the administered world, nor is there an irreducible psy-
> chological substratum that can hold out forever against the increasing inter-
> ventions of the external society. And, of course, politics, as Adorno saw it, is
> utterly bereft of any genuinely subversive energies that are not immediately
> turned into instrumentalized mechanisms for preserving the status quo. (Jay
> 1984: 110)

Why these problems are particularly deadly to any liberatory philosophy
focused on sexuality is what concerns me. Because even currents which are
usable in Adorno on the hold of the commodity fetish, and his personal
outrage over the brute facts of oppression change: they are dead ends.

Negative Dialectics, Adorno's capstone philosophic work, is remarkably free
of the psychologizing that marked the immediate postwar years, and even
the essays of the early sixties.[16] There are almost no references to sexuality
or gender, although there is a brief passionate protest against the false moralism of sexual repression for its masking of the real moral imperatives: "No
man should be tortured; there should be no concentration camps" (Adorno
1973: 285). He also has a series of important reflections on the role of the
body – what he calls "the somatic moment" – where the link between sensation and thought is considered, resulting in one of the few places where
he speaks of dialectic movement: "It is the somatic element's survival, in
knowledge, as the unrest that makes knowledge move, the unassuaged unrest
that reproduces itself in the advancement of knowledge . . . The physical
moment tells our knowledge that suffering ought not to be, that things should
be different" (Adorno 1973: 203).[17] In sum, it would appear that, at least at
the most literal level, *Negative Dialectics* poses the fewest problems, and provides some promising avenues for queer revolutionaries to consider.

But that would not be a philosophically sound deduction. If we begin at
the beginning of any serious grappling with Marx, chapter 1 of *Capital*,
and the fetish of the commodity, we could hardly find a more rigorous de-
tector of the fetish's omnipresence than Theodor Adorno. He even has

the bravery to declare himself – and theory – part of the commodity fetish's contradictions:

> No theory today escapes the marketplace. Each one is offered as a possibility among competing opinions; all are put up for choice; all are swallowed. There are no blinders for thought to don against this, and the self-righteous conviction that my own theory is spared that fate will surely deteriorate into self-advertising. (Adorno 1973: 4)

Aside from the tone of intellectual despair here – that particular despair that infects any intellect living under capitalism who is not a relativist – one begins to detect the ensuing problem: for Adorno, railing against the commodity fetish, and dreaming of the new society, shares the quality of a fish railing against water and pining for the forest – no solution can be imagined.[18] This reaches a climax when he is critiquing Heideggerian ontology:

> Society's own concept says that men want their relations to be freely established; but no freedom has been realized in their relations to this day, and society remains as rigid as it is defective. All qualitative moments whose totality might be something like a structure are flattened in the universal barter relationship. The more immense the power of the institutional forms, the more chaotic the life they hem in and deform in their image. The production and reproduction of life, along with whatever the name superstructure covers, are not transparencies of reason – of that reason whose reconciled realization alone would be as one with a nonviolent order, an order worthy of men . . . That freedom has largely remained an ideology; that men are powerless against the system, cannot rationally determine their lives and the life of the whole, cannot even think of such a determination without adding to their torment – this is what forces their rebellion into the wrong, invidious form of preferring the bad to a semblance of the better. (Adorno 1973: 88–9)

The stakes of Adorno's leading gambit in *Negative Dialectics* is now clear. The book opens with the declaration that it will "free dialectics from such affirmative traits" as the negation of the negation "without reducing its determinacy" (Adorno 1973: xix). A strict interpretation of this charge would mean that the commodity fetish's reign is dialectically unbreakable: it is rigidly deterministic. Despite his philosophic uneasiness with the Absolute, Adorno uses a great deal of absolute language: "no freedom has been realized," "all qualitative moments . . . are flattened," and "men are powerless against the system." This means that the any action people do take is likely to rebound upon themselves, forcing "their rebellion into the wrong, invidious" forms of retrogression.[19]

If that is the case, a queer liberation movement, which hopes to create new human relationships, is at best a desperate, doomed attempt to outrun the monster of the exchange culture. At worst, it is an easily assimilated energy which creates new markets for capitalism, and whose best moments slide into commodified chic: "Buy your Freedom Rings from Company Q!" These are, of course, genuine dialectic concerns. But to Adorno, they are not *living* moments: they unfold like Calvinistic predestination. Free will is an illusion, subjectivity is an illusion, the taste of freedom (even the hope of it is a torment) is an illusion; the only thing that is not an illusion is the crushing determinism of the commodity fetish in its gargantuan totalizing.

This, however, is not Marx's Marxism. While Marx was certainly attempting to be scientific in his dialectics, he was never looking for a rigid determinism. At the climax of chapter 1 of *Capital*, he introduces those who can "remove the veil" from the fetish: freely associated people, "expending their many different forms of labour-power in full self-awareness" (Marx 1977: 171; cf. 173).[20] Subjectivity ("full self-awareness") for the social individual ("freely associated" with differing skills and talents) is alive in Marx. Adorno's predilection for overwhelmingly totalizing the fetish, at the expense of the subject, effectively drains the humanism out of both Hegel and Marx, defying a most direct sentence in Hegel's *Phenomenology:* "everything depends on grasping and expressing the ultimate truth not as Substance but as Subject as well" (Hegel 1967: 80).

In his rage to undermine all constituent subjectivity, Adorno douses the flame of any subject of revolution who could oppose the system *despite, even because, they are part of the contradictions in that system.* For a dialectician to declare that "(s)chizophrenia is the truth about the subject, from the viewpoint of the philosophy of history" would be comical if it weren't tragic; even more poignantly tragic when he elaborates that the "subject's dissolution" through its schizophrenia, presents "the ephemeral and condemned picture of a possible subject" (p. 281). The psychoanalytic categories stall oppositional movement in their medicalizing rigidity; but nothing is even capable of stopping the totalizing evil of the fetish.

While Adorno never lets his cosmic pessimism drown his compassion for the suffering (pp. 17–18), he lives in dread of making any positive statement. Philosophically the question pivots on the negation of the negation. Apparently concerned that the negation of the negation supplied a humming resolution and bland synthesis, he rejects it utterly. "To equate the negation of the negation with positivity" disgusts him as simplistic, as unserious, so he declares that "(t)o negate a negation . . . proves . . . that the negation was not negative enough . . . What is negated is negative until it has passed. This is the decisive break with Hegel" (pp. 158–160; cf. 393).

The problem is that a decisive break with the negation of the negation leaves not only Hegel in the dust, but Marx, too, who invokes the negation of the negation most crucially in chapter 32 of *Capital* (Marx 1977: 929). In her essay, "Hegel's Absolute as New Beginning," Dunayevskaya lays the stress on negativity as a *moving* force, as a creative power. With Adorno in mind, she notes that "it is the power of the negative which is the creative element. It is not the synthesis, but the absolute negativity which assures the advance movement" (Dunayevskaya 1974: 5). She too rejects any harmonized view of Hegel's system as a series of syntheses, and accepts no easy positives. A revolutionary dialectic calls for "the seriousness, the suffering, the patience, and the labour of the negative" (Hegel 1967: 81), and no one viewing the carnage of the twentieth century – including Adorno and Dunayevskaya – could hold any naive hopes of the inevitability of successful revolutions. But the difference between them is about reality, not hope: negativity creates moving forces, moments of transition, turning points. The world-weariness of Adorno – who sees nothing new under the sun but the blotting out of its light by the barter society – contrasts with Dunayevskaya's eager yet rigorous search for the new in the social movements of the mid-twentieth century.

Here is how she analyzed *Negative Dialectics'* claim that "Auschwitz confirmed the philosopheme of pure identity as death . . . Absolute negativity is in plain sight and has ceased to surprise anyone" (Adorno 1973: 362; Dunayevskaya 1974: 10–11). Dunayevskaya is shaken by the enormity of his error, and at such a key point in both world history and for a philosophic understanding of the dialectic. She marvels that someone who had "devoted an adult lifetime to fighting fascist ideology as the very opposite of Hegelian dialectics" could confuse fascism's most horrifying reality with the moving force of a liberatory dialectic. Adorno had confused the philosophic meaning of "negativity" and "positivity" with their common language equivalents, a move which she says is not only wrong, but must bear "Adorno's own curse word 'naive'" (Dunayevskaya 1974: 11).

But the question remains, what could have caused such a disorientation? Rather than blaming Auschwitz itself, Dunayevskaya pinpoints the absence of subject and the subsequent abandonment of any overtly revolutionary project:

Why, then, such a vulgar reduction of absolute negativity? Therein is the real tragedy of Adorno (and the Frankfurt School). It is the tragedy of a one-dimensionality of thought which results when you give up Subject, when one does not listen to the voices from below – and they were loud, clear, and demanding between the mid-fifties and mid-sixties. It is a tragedy once one returns to the ivory tower and reduces his purpose to "the purpose of discussing key concepts of philosophic disciplines and centrally intervening in

those disciplines." The next step was irresistible, the substitution of a permanent critique not alone for absolute negativity, but also of "permanent revolution itself." (Dunayevskaya 1974: 11)[21]

Adorno's permanent critique is static; it does not promote the transformation of reality. Interventions are the only safe route open to him in his
isolation. Criticizing Adorno's elitism is too simple; what is crucial is how
that elitism is rooted in the rejection of revolution in permanence and
subject. Adorno posits that individuals – artists and intellectuals most often –
can most effectively hide out (though always, finally, to no avail)[22] from the
leveling effects of exchange, by bring something unwanted or incomprehensible to market (i.e., Schönberg's music). What is revealed when Adorno
reaches his nadir is that the only subject he did retain resembles himself, an
isolated and alienated intellectual who knows his own alienation:

> "What does it really matter?" is a line we like to associate with bourgeois cal-
> lousness, but it is the line most likely to make the individual aware, without
> dread, of the insignificance of his existence. The inhuman part of it, the ability
> to keep one's distance as a spectator and to rise above things, is in the final
> analysis the human part, the very part resisted by its ideologists. (Adorno 1973:
> 363)

The only thing he can recover from the wreckage is the perspective of alienation that he knows needs to be overcome. But such a stance is deadly for
any queer revolutionary philosophy. Watching the world in lone isolation, as
an alienated spectator, is the closeted fate that les-bi-gay movements wish to
eradicate. Queer self-development is stifled by the isolation of individuals.
When it is revolutionary, when it is resisting the pull of the commodity
exchange, any movement about sexuality has, at its center, new visions and
transformations of human relations. And it was exactly such a revolutionary
subject – one based in a collective social movement – that Adorno eschewed
most vigorously.[23]

Thus, the philosophic categories which need to be richly developed for
the queer dimension, such as passion, love, happiness, diversity, are philosophically underdefined, even subjective, individualized, privatized, and
nostalgic in Adorno. To take the category of "passion" as an example, he
removes it from what he sees as its Hegelian pedestal, where it served as "the
motor of individuality." Describing Hitler's idiosyncrasies as a parody of
passion (which has about as much to do with the category as it exists in
Hegel and Marx as absolute negativity does with Auschwitz), Adorno declares
that for "the powerless, who find more and more narrowly prescribed

what they can and cannot attain, passion becomes an anachronism." He then describes, with some nostalgia, the loss of passion even in "the private realm;" lamenting, Nestor-like, how youth "no longer musters the strength for passion." And passion is dissipated "because the integrating social organization sees to the removal of the patent obstacles that used to kindle passion and makes up for them by placing the controls into the individual, in the form of adjustment at any price" (Adorno 1973: 343). Adorno has confined the category of passion – central to liberatory moments in both Hegel and Marx[24] – to old-fashioned structures of heterosexual romance, of all things! Likewise, Adorno disparages the possibility of love, remarking that "(p)eople, of course, are spellbound without exception, and none of them are capable of love, which is why everyone feels loved too little" (Adorno 1973: 363).[25]

Passion is messy, and movements that were unruly, "untidy affirmations" to use Fanon's famous phrase, were especially difficult for Adorno. As Dunayevskaya mentioned, Adorno substituted permanent critique for Marx's dialectic category of revolution in permanence (Dunayevskaya 1974: 11). Given the determinism of the oppressive forces, and the lack of any revolutionary subject who can effectively oppose it, even getting one successful revolution is an unlikely outcome from Adorno's dialectics, let alone the unceasing movement of revolution in permanence. The fact is that he feared the "unleashing of productive forces," even when he recognized its creative power, for its "affinity to the violent domination of nature . . . The very word 'unleashed' has undertones of menace" (Adorno 1973: 306–7). This is more than equivocating about the effectiveness of intervention: it is genuine terror of revolution.[26] It then becomes more than ironic that a theatrical political disruption of Adorno's April 1969 lecture by three women socialist students in leather jackets who exposed their breasts to him – the *Busenaktion* – had a fatal effect, albeit a slightly delayed one (Adorno 1998: 347, n. 5; Isenberg 1998: 19).

In light of the shaping factors of his philosophic pessimism – the defeat of German revolutionary movements, Auschwitz, and fascism – can we be charitable toward Adorno's philosophic errors? He even speaks, with agonizing self-reference, of survivor's guilt, a guilt which "calls for the coldness, the basic principle of bourgeois subjectivity, without which there could have been no Auschwitz; this is the drastic guilt of him who was spared" (Adorno 1973: 363). Dunayevskaya implies (and she's not gentle about it) that Auschwitz disoriented Adorno's grasp on basic revolutionary categories. From a queer perspective, the fact that he regularly placed homosexuals among the perpetrators, and not among the victims, is a repetition of his errors, which makes it even harder to excuse his failings (Halle 1995: 305; Oosterhuis 1995: 245).

The seriousness of Auschwitz cannot be doubted; perhaps Adorno is right when he opines that "(i)f thought is not measured by the extremity that eludes the concept, it is from the outset in the nature of the musical accompaniment with which the SS liked to drown out the screams of its victims" (Adorno 1973: 365). It was, in fact, the very impossibility of living up to this self-assignment that led him to fear the positive, to renounce the moving shuttle of the negation of the negation. Terrified that Marx's very few positive pronouncements seemed to him to have been proven false by history, Adorno was unwilling to risk any. It was easier, as Dunayevskaya says, to retreat to the academy and make strategic interventions than to undertake the tremendous responsibility for revolutionary theory.[27] But I think Adorno went even further than that: by asserting that Marx had (incorrectly) assumed the revolution would happen almost immediately, he legitimated an institutional continuity of Marx's thought separated from any movement from practice. Like the Fathers of the Church – faced with the need to redact the New Testament texts, and aware of the contradiction that the Second Coming was already past its estimated time of arrival – Adorno saw the evils of the world closing in on truth: "Subalternity increases, once the revolution has suffered the same fate as the Second Coming" (Adorno 1973: 205). With the eschaton infinitely delayed, intervention replaces expectation, strategies of retreat take precedence over "hopeless" causes, and the building of Institutes has more objectivity than revolutionary urgency.

On his deathbed, as Hippo lay under siege, and his institution-building work in Africa was destroyed, Augustine took more solace in the stoic resignation of Plotinus than from the grandiose architectures of his own City of God. A parallel leaps to mind from Adorno's deathbed concession to the movement of the 1960s, when he wrote to Marcuse " 'I am the last to underestimate the merits of the student movement,' he insisted. 'It has disrupted the smooth transition to a totally administered world' " (Isenberg 1998: 22). But even then his bitterness oozes out: he cannot acknowledge the students as potential subjects of revolution, only as irritants to the system, who will merely delay the inevitable. While Adorno's writings won't wreak the same damage to sexuality that Augustine's shame over his own libido did, I doubt Adorno could have recognized today's queer revolutionaries as engaging in what he called the subjective side of dialectics – "thinking so that the thought form will no longer turn its objects into immutable ones, into objects that remain the same" (Adorno 1973: 154) – because he had built the impossibility of revolution into an immutable object.[28]

Notes

1 See Edge, Weeks, Oosterhuis, Blasius and Phelan, Studinski, Rycenga 1998, all passim.

2 Adorno also always seems to have male homosexuality in mind; his psycho-analytic thought is tainted by masculinist presumptions; he seems (blissfully?) unaware of lesbian possibilities. When submitting his 1963 article "Sexual Taboos and Law Today" to a 1969 collection, he writes to the editor on why he isn't revising the piece: "At the moment I wouldn't know what to add to what I have written there" (Adorno 1998: ix). The fact that in the intervening six years there had been a worldwide women's liberation movement had not made enough of an impact for him to even add a footnote.

3 Adorno's critiques of society are often very arrogantly expressed, and contribute to the denigration of the possibility of subjects: "The pressure exerted by the prevailing universal upon everything particular, upon the individual people and the individual institutions, has a tendency to destroy the particular and the indi-vidual together with their power of resistance. With the loss of their identity and power of resistance, people also forfeit those qualities by virtue of which they are able to pit themselves against what at some moment might lure them again to commit atrocity" (Adorno 1998: 193).

4 The need for live subjects should not be construed as an endorsement of a sim-plistic identity politics or biologistic essentialism on my part: I am referring to human beings as active shapers of history and creators of meaning. Dunayevskaya critiques Rosa Luxemburg for railing against the evils of imperialism without looking to the colonized as a source of revolutionary opposition: a failing that Adorno is infinitely more culpable of than even Luxemburg (see Dunayevskaya 1991, passim). The emergence of subjects of revolution is understood philo-sophically as "new appearances surface as so profound a philosophy of revolu-tion that what inheres in it is a living Subject that will resolve the great contradiction . . . because it is no abstraction, but a live Subject, it unites rather than divides theory and reality" (Dunayevskaya 1996: 269–70).

5 See Blasius and Phelan 1997, Part IV "Gay Liberation and Lesbian-Feminism," 377–559.

6 See Marx 1977, esp. 927–30; Marx 1967: 303–14; and Dunayevskaya 1991, esp. 99–101. Monique Wittig, Mario Mieli, Guy Hocquenghem, David Fernbach, Harry Hay, and Audre Lorde are among the lesbian and gay theorists from the 1970s who grappled explicitly with Marxist categories; see Blasius and Phelan 1997: 377–559.

7 Gays and lesbians also bring and sustain elements of theatricality within protest movements, which simultaneously critique and utilize the channels of the culture industry (e.g., Radical Faeries, Lesbian Avengers, ACT-UP), an area of interest, vis-à-vis Adorno.

8 Dunayevskaya developed the category of "Post-Marx Marxist as pejorative, beginning with Engels," specifically to challenge all revolutionaries to self-

critically examine the totality of the transformation in thought wrought by Marx; see Dunayevskaya 1991: xxiii–xxiv.

9   A tortured reading of Marx's second thesis, "In practice man must prove the truth, that is, actuality and power, this-sidedness of his thinking," could see it as an erasure of reflection. But, like the entire short document, it appears to be more about the unity of theory and practice than about jettisoning one for the other (Marx 1967: 401).

10   These two quotes are from a 1962 talk, "Why Still Philosophy?"

11   Here is one example: "3. A representative sample of prisoners incarcerated for having committed sexual offenses or sexual crimes should undergo psychoanalytical study for the duration of their sentence. The analyses should then be compared with the judicial opinions for the purpose of examining their soundness" (Adorno 1998: 86).

12   The most explicit characterological materials against homosexuality in *The Authoritarian Personality* were authored by Else Frenkel-Brunswik, not Adorno. But he uses the material she has assembled in other areas rather uncritically, and his own comments on the "Tough Guy" persona in *The Authoritarian Personality* need to be compared with his comments in *Minima Moralia* on the same phenomenon, where he says that "repressed homosexuality present[ed] itself as the only approved form of heterosexuality . . . Totalitarianism and homosexuality belong together" (Adorno 1974: 46; cf. Adorno et al. 1950: 762–5).

13   Adorno also invokes decadence, dandyism, and the perception of male artists and intellectuals as sexually effete in relation to homosexuality at various points in the essays from the 1960s (Adorno 1998: 151–2, 184, 64, respectively; see also Adorno 1974: 167–9).

14   For Adorno, sexuality of all types is without liberatory content since it "has become the delusion that was earlier comprised by abnegation" (Adorno 1974: 168–9).

15   See Margo St. James and Gail Pheterson, *A Vindication of the Rights of Whores* (Seattle: Seal Press, 1989) for material that reflects the subjectivity and resistance of sex workers.

16   *Negative Dialectics* has a few echoes of the psychologizing, as in this quote about the realm of death: "The unconscious power of that realm may be as great as that of infantile sexuality; the two intermingle in the anal fixation, but they are scarcely the same. An unconscious knowledge whispers to the child what is repressed by civilized education; this is what matters, says the whispering voice . . . The man who managed to recall what used to strike him in the words 'dung hill' and 'pig sty' might be closer to absolute knowledge than Hegel's chapter in which readers are promised such knowledge only to have it withheld with a superior mien" (Adorno 1973: 366).

17   The entire discussion of the somatic moment ranges over pp. 192–207; it is interesting to compare what Adorno says here to a passage from Marx's *1844 Manuscripts* (which Adorno disparages; see Adorno 1973: 190) which is central to

the dialectics of queer liberation: "As an objective sentient being man is there-fore a *suffering* being, and since he feels his suffering, he is a *passionate* being. Passion is man's essential capacity energetically bent on its object" (Marx 1967: 326).

18 In fact, it is practically equivalent to certain traditional philosophic interpreta-tions of the Buddhist nirvana, which cannot be imagined from our present perspective as a positive, but rather as the negation of any positing that can be made of it. But at least Adorno has the Stoic honesty not to follow Heidegger who, as he says, creates systems which pretend "to crush fetishes" while actually "crushing nothing but the conditions of their recognition as fetishes" (Adorno 1973: 85). Eventually, Adorno even has Marx subsumed under the fetish (Adorno 1973: 189–92; cf. Dunayevskaya 1974: 15, n. 11); this is wholly consistent with the logical outcome of Adorno's dialectic: "Negative philosophy, dissolving everything, dissolves even the dissolvent . . . As long as domination reproduces itself, the old quality reappears unrefined in the dissolving of the dissolvent: in a radical sense no leap is made at all" (Adorno 1974: 245).

19 Sometimes the whole thing feels like one of the genre of Star Trek episodes where an amorphous energy cloud is going to absorb the ship; the ship fires at it, but it simply gains strength, until the crew figures out to stop firing, turn off all power, and thus not feed it. This is a technological version of quietism, which corresponds all too well to Adorno's passivity.

20 It is significant that, by contrast, Adorno has the fetish unveiled solely by indi-vidual insights: "What dissolves the fetish is the insight that things are not simply so and not otherwise, that they have come to be under certain conditions" (Adorno 1973: 52). The individuals who have these insights are not necessarily associated with other human beings in any way.

21 The internal quote from *Negative Dialectics* is from the preface (Adorno 1973: xx). The essay on "Sexual Taboos and Law Today" came from a collection orig-inally entitled *Interventions*. Dunayevskaya's reference to "one-dimensionality" is a clear invocation of her disappointment in Marcuse's *One-Dimensional Man*, which shares many deterministic failings with Adorno; prior to that book, Dunayevskaya and Marcuse had maintained a rich correspondence. Marcuse's much more intriguing relationship to queer revolutionary movements is one that I do not take up here; see Weeks 1985 and Halle 1995.

22 "If man is in harmony with the world spirit precisely because he is ahead of his time, his very ruin as an individual is sometimes linked with a sense of not being in vain. Irresistible in the young Beethoven's music is the expression of the possibility that all might be well" (Adorno 1973: 306). Adorno's aestheti-cism, though not my topic here, reaches a logical end when he declares that "Taste is the most accurate seismograph of historical experience" (Adorno 1974: 145)

23 Marxist musicologist Bill Martin noted a similar lack in Adorno's aesthetics; dis-cussing progressive rock of the 1970s, he notes "there was the possibility of a 'popular' avant-garde . . . this was not a time of cultural or political 'business as

usual.' I worry that formulations such as Adorno's are not sufficiently attuned to the possibility that such a moment may erupt" (1996: 248, n. 52).

24   This category of passion is developed by Hegel, most explicitly in the section of *Philosophy of Mind* that deals with "Impulses, Inclinations and Choices" (¶473–8). Hegel clarifies the concept of impulse as "a form of *volitional consciousness*," not "mere appetite." The "rationality of impulse" comes from its drive "to get realized, overcoming the subjectivity by the subject's own agency" (¶474, p. 235, emphasis mine). Passion emerges as a category when "*the whole subjectivity of the individual is merged . . . to one special mode of volition*" (¶474, p. 235, emphasis mine), adding that "Nothing great has been and nothing great can be accomplished without passion" (¶474, p. 235). Hegel shows that "impulse and passion are *the very life-blood of all action*" (¶475, p. 236, emphasis mine). So while a goal might be universal, it remains "an inactive thing," needing a subject to actualize it, to internalize it (Hegel uses the phrase "immanent in the agent") – a subject who holds this universal as its own "interest and – should it claim to engross his whole efficient subjectivity – his passion" (¶475, p. 237). In a line which is crucial to a Marxist-Humanist queer dialectic, Hegel writes that the "will to liberty" develops, such that it "is no longer an *impulse* which demands satisfaction, but the permanent character" of people – "the spiritual consciousness grown into a non-impulsive manner" (¶482, p. 240, Hegel's emphasis).

25   He has some more promising reflections on love in the 1967 essay "Education after Auschwitz," which resonate with Adrienne Rich's category of "compulsory heterosexuality": "Love is something immediate and in essence contradicts mediated relationships. The exhortation to love – even in its imperative form, that one *should* do it – is itself part of the ideology coldness perpetuates. It bears the compulsive, oppressive quality that counteracts the ability to love" (Adorno 1998: 202).

26   Dunayevskaya submits that "philosophers who stand only in terror before revolution not only" miss the category of revolution in permanence, but "cannot comprehend the revolution *in thought*" wrought by Hegel and Marx (1974: 13, emphasis hers).

27   Adorno's railing against activity that jettisons theory is important, especially in the context of why the movements of the 1960s and 1970s failed; but he has slipped into the opposite extreme (Adorno 1998: 259–78).

28   I want to thank the following people for inspiration, conversation, goading, and assistance on this project: Nigel Gibson, Andrew Rubin, Lou Turner, Michelle Gubbay, Louis Mazza, Karen Barad, Ruth Charloff, Laurie Green, and Paul Attinello.

16

"As though the end of the world had come and gone" or *Allemal ist nicht immergleich* – Critical Theory and the Task of Reading

Samuel Weber

I

As a kind of frontispiece to my remarks, I want to cite a passage, or rather a scene, from one of Kierkegaard's writings, usually translated in English as *Repetition*. I cite it, among other reasons, because it suggests a framework within which to approach the writings of Adorno today. The passage I am about to quote is fairly long, but it was considered by Adorno to be one of the most important that Kierkegaard wrote. This, then, is the passage from Kierkegaard, which in a certain sense goes nowhere, neither from, nor to, and yet, doesn't simply stand still either:

So I arrived in Berlin. I hurried at once to my old lodgings . . . one of the most pleasant apartments in Berlin . . . Gensd'arme Square is certainly the most beautiful in Berlin; *das Schauspielhaus* and the two churches are superb, especially when viewed from a window by moonlight. The recollection of these things was an important factor in my taking the journey. One climbs the stairs to the first floor in a gas-illuminated building, opens a little door, and stands in the entry. To the left is a glass door leading to a room. Straight ahead is an anteroom. Beyond are two entirely identical rooms, identically furnished, so

that one sees the room double in the mirror. The inner room is tastefully illu-
minated. A candelabra stands on a writing table; a gracefully designed armchair
upholstered in red velvet stands before the desk. The first room is not illumi-
nated. Here the pale light of the moon blends with the strong light from
the inner room. Sitting in a chair by the window, one looks out on the great
square, sees the shadows of passersby hurrying along the walls; everything is
transformed into a stage setting. A dream world glimmers in the background
of the soul. One feels a desire to toss on a cape, to steal softly along the wall
with a searching gaze, aware of every sound. One does not do this but merely
sees a rejuvenated self doing it. Having smoked a cigar, one goes back to the
inner room and begins to work. It is past midnight. One extinguishes the
candles and lights a little night candle. Unmingled, the light of the moon is
victorious. A single shadow appears even blacker; a single footstep takes a long
time to disappear. The cloudless arch of heaven has a sad and pensive look as
if the end of the world had already come and heaven, unperturbed, was occupied with itself. Once again one goes out into the hallway, into the entry, into
that little room, and – if one is among the fortunate who are able to sleep –
goes to sleep.[1]

This passage, which Adorno cites as evidence of the retreat into the inner
sanctum of private space, that *intérieur* which, he argues, is the nucleus of
Kierkegaard's work – this passage is inscribed in a problematic but decisive
movement of repetition. Constantin Constantius returns to Berlin because, as
he announces at the very outset of the work, at home has he found himself
totally blocked by the question of *repetition*: is there such a thing, and if there
is, what does it mean? The simplest way to find out, he decides, is for him
to go back to Berlin, where he once studied, to see if repetition exists or
not. All of this sounds absurd if retold thus out of context and at least part
of that absurdity plays an important role in the text as a self-ironizing
moment. We will have occasion later to come back to some of this context.
Despite the many and important differences in the various positions that
Constantin, fictional author and narrator of this text, asserts and assumes, one
at least anticipates the positions which Adorno himself will adopt and this
perhaps explains why Adorno was drawn to write on Kierkegaard, however
critically. Adorno critiques the subsumptive tendencies of the Hegelian
system, and through it, of a certain philosophical rationalism itself. To be sure,
what Adorno will sharply criticize is what he takes to be the fundamental
subjectivism of this critique, which as such in his eyes falls behind that which
it is criticizing. For both, however, for Constantin Constantius as for Theodor
Adorno, the Hegelian notion of universal "mediation" has to be critically
examined. For Constantin, indeed, the German *Vermittlung* must be replaced
by "the good Danish word" that is translated as "Repetition," but that is

actually far closer to the literal meaning of the German, *Wiederholen*. The Danish word is *Gjentagelse*, which literally means to "take again." And indeed, much of Kierkegaard's text remains incomprehensible if one does not refer to this literal meaning. Despite his methodological call for attention to the *Wörtlichkeit* of the text, Adorno shows no concern for this "good Danish word," quite different from his own interpretation of "repetition" as the return of what is eternally the same: *das Immergleiche*. Rather, confronted with what he takes to be Kierkegaard's subjectivist move away from the Hegelian dialectic, Adorno defends the trajectory that leads "from Kant to Hegel," as the following passage demonstrates:

> If however, the Kantian conception of philosophy as science was first comprehensively formulated by Hegel in the following proposition, "that the time has come for philosophy to be raised to the level of science," his demand for scientific conceptualization does not coincide with the unambiguous givenness of concepts [construed] as bundles of traits [*Merkmaleinheiten*]. The dialectical method, to which, all opposition to Hegel notwithstanding, Kierkegaard's work entirely belongs [*gänzlich zugehört*], has its essence rather in the fact that the elucidation of individual concepts, in the sense of their complete definition, can only be accomplished through the totality of the elaborated system and not in the analysis of the isolated individual concept.[2]

The dialectic thus involves not just an appeal to the whole, to "the totality of the elaborated system," but in fact presupposes in a certain sense its virtual presence, its constant and ubiquitous accessibility. As Hegel himself puts it, in a celebrated passage from the Introduction to the *Phenomenology of Spirit*:

> If the Absolute could be brought closer to us simply by means of a device [*Werkzeug*], without anything in it being altered, the way a bird is attracted by a decoy, it would – were it not in and of itself with us and did it not wish to be – (it would) scorn this trick . . . Or if the examining of knowledge, which we imagine as a (kind of) *medium*, teaches us the law of its refraction [*Strahlenbrechung*], it serves no purpose to (try to) subtract it from the result; for it is not the *breaking* of the ray, refraction, but the ray itself [*der Strahl selbst*] that constitutes knowledge and to subtract it would leave us nothing but the designation of a mere direction or of an empty place.[3]

"Mere direction . . . empty place": the epitome of Abstraction, from a Hegelian point of view at least. Conversely, concreteness – a key word in the writings of Adorno – concreteness consists essentially in the *growing together* of thought through which knowledge is constituted. Such concretion involves the move beyond the conception of knowledge as passive *medium* to a conception of knowledge as an active *process of self-constituting*. That the medium itself, for instance, language, could be that active process, is a position that the Hegelian tradition tends to reject and to supplant by the notion of mediation. We will have occasion to return to this critique of the "medium" later: suffice it to say that it contrasts radically with the emphasis to be found in the writings of Walter Benjamin, from the earliest texts on language on, upon the question of Medium and Mediality. From a Hegelian point of view, however, this rejection of the medium by the notion of mediation is perhaps the most decisive gain in the move from static Kantian epistemology to the speculative dialectic. And this perspective is still dominant in Adorno's study of Kierkegaard.

And yet if "concreteness" is the result of *mediation*, then it is no longer a property of simple sense-perception, is never *immediately* given or present *as such*, but must be constructed, configured, construed – through a process that necessarily involves *reading* as much as it involves *interpretation*. Although Adorno tended to keep his distance from the venerable German tradition of "hermeneutics," nevertheless he often found himself obliged to address hermeneutic issues such as the relation of reading and interpretation. For instance – and it is not just any instance – in the third of his *Studies on Hegel*, entitled, significantly, *Skoteinos or How to Read* (*Skoteinos oder Wie zu lesen sei*), he attempts to outline a strategy of reading Hegel and in the process arrives at a series of familiar problems – or are they paradoxes?

> In the realm of great philosophy Hegel is surely the only instance where upon occasion one literally does not know and cannot decide what is going on [*wovon überhaupt geredet wird*] and where the very possibility of such a decision is not guaranteed.[4] [. . . Individual passages] are interpretable through knowledge of the overall Hegelian thrust [*des Hegelschen Gesamtzuges*] . . . not however from the words of the paragraphs themselves . . . Nothing can be understood in isolation, everything only with respect to the whole, with the embarrassing difficulty – *mit dem Peinlichen* – that the whole, in its turn, lives only from and in the singular moments (that compose it) . . . One must, however provisionally, have present to mind in each case what Hegel is after [*worauf Hegel jeweils hinaus will*], elucidating him, as it were, retrospectively [*von rückwärts aufhellen*].

Embarrassing, *peinlich*, is the necessary supposition of a pre-given Whole in order for individual words, sentences, propositions, and passages to be comprehensible. And yet, the embarrassment cuts both ways. For the whole "is" nothing if separated from the movement of the individual "moments." The Whole, or Totality is thus called upon to direct and orient the movement of that which constitutes it. If, as Adorno repeatedly insists, in a quotation that he ascribed to Aby Warburg — if "God is to be found in details" — *Der liebe Gott steckt im Detail* — then the problem is to demonstrate "concretely" just how God can be both "in the detail" and at the same time identical to the Whole, to the Absolute, which by definition cannot be reduced to any single "detail" but which is everywhere and at all times, *an und für sich schon bei uns*. Or, as Hegel does not say but Adorno writes, in a very different context to be true: *allemal*.

It is here that the problem of *reading* rears its ugly head. Ugly, because, in the eyes of Adorno at least, it cannot solve the problem but at best act it out. Reading acts out the problem, at least in the case of reading Hegel, by trying to get at the quintessence of that proper name: One has to know, however provisionally, just what Hegel is *after, worauf er hinaus will*, what Hegel *wants* and *wills*, in order to be able to read his individual words, sentences, and paragraphs. But such knowledge of the Whole, of the Governing Intention or Design, depends in turn upon the way one reads those individual words and sentences. There is no simple answer to this hermeneutic dilemma. On the one hand, Hegel "requires repeated reading [*mehrfache Lektüre*]" objectively, and not just in order to habituate the reader. On the other hand,

> if one relies entirely on this procedure, one can easily falsify him. One can easily produce that which up to now has been most harmful to interpretation: an empty consciousness of the system, incompatible with the fact that the latter is not supposed to form an abstract and superior concept [*abstrakten Oberbegriff*] but rather to acquire its truth through its concrete moments. (p. 328)

Hegel's text itself, Adorno makes clear, cannot be taken as a model for resolving this problem since its "concreteness" is often achieved by sleight of hand: "The isolated moments go beyond themselves only by virtue of the fact that the identity of subject and object has already been preconceived [*vorgedacht*]. The relevance of individual analyses is again and again broken by the abstract primacy of the Whole" (p. 330).

Such primacy of a Whole which as such remains abstract, should not, however, Adorno insists, serve as a pretext for simply dismissing Hegel, as has been done by contemporary Anglo-American philosophy. Rather, the problematic relation of whole and part must provoke a new and different kind of reading: one that does not invoke the inevitability of a general understanding in order either to confirm or to disqualify the dialectical movement. This other kind of reading Adorno calls — with a word he surely does not invoke lightly — an *art*: "The art of reading Hegel would have to discern where something new, where content sets in [*wo Neues, Inhaltliches einsetzt*] (as opposed to) as distinct from those places where the machine keeps on running, even though it should not be able to continue" (p. 330). The fact that Adorno construes of the "New" here in terms of "content," as *Inhaltliches*, a term that is rarely discussed, is however the sign of a further problem. For how will the borders be determined, without which nothing can be "held-in"? To discriminate between "content" and non-content requires the same sort of "knowledge" that is here in question. And is the "new" necessarily to be determined as "content"? Does the onset of the New exclude repetition, for instance? Or can repetition be a mode through which the New manifests and articulates itself? I will return to these questions a bit further on.

For now, let us simply note that Adorno describes two conditions that are necessary, although in tension with one another, for a reading to discern the "new" in Hegel. The first is a certain "immersion" (*Versenkung*) in the text's most minute details; the second is the ability to retain one's freedom and "distance" from them, despite such "immersion."

But how does one get absorbed into such "minute" details while at the same time keeping a safe and "free" distance from them? How is such reading possible – if indeed it is possible at all?

II

In order to gather elements in the work of Adorno that might help to respond to this question, it will be helpful to make a detour via another, earlier text, which in a certain sense constitutes a significant "moment" in Adorno's reflections on the question of reading. This text, although only published posthumously, was completed in 1942 as the projected continuation of the chapter in *Dialectic of Enlightenment* on the "Culture Industry." In certain respects, the analyses of the "Culture Industry" can be seen as a sociological anticipation of the later critique of the Hegelian dialectic. In both instances, a general "system" or "scheme" subjugates and subordinates its individual components. To be sure, this analogy, like all analogies, has its limits. Adorno insisted that the Culture Industry could never operate dialectically. Nevertheless, Adorno's critique of the Culture Industry reposed on its *systematic* and *totalizing* character. The question that has been raised since, as a critique of Critical Theory, questions the extent to which critical theory itself, as a systematization of the System of the Culture Industry, necessarily falls prey to the same tendencies it claims to criticize: the subsumptive tendency of the system. The same question could also be raised with respect to the critique of the Hegelian dialectic, and perhaps with respect to criticism as such. To the extent, at least, that critique is always critique of a system, it always runs the risk of becoming systematic in its critique and hence, of being "overtaken" – in German, Adorno would have written *übereilt*, a favorite expression – of being "overtaken" or contaminated by what it is criticizing. Which, perhaps, is why the fascination with being *overtaken: übereilt*, is so pervasive in his writings. No simple appeal to the dialectic can serve to "ban" – another favorite word and concept of Critical Theory – this danger, if it turns out to be coextensive with the very notion of Critique itself.

Be that as it may, from its opening words, the analysis of the Culture Industry is concerned with revealing the system dissimulated behind what appears as the anarchy of liberal social relations, including cultural activities. The first sentence of the chapter announces that, contrary to received sociological opinion, the development of modern capitalism does not bring with it "cultural chaos" but rather a highly coordinated and unified system: "Culture today stamps everything with the seal of similitude. Film, radio, magazines – all constitute one system. Each segment coheres within itself and with all others" (p. 141). Of course, to be critical, the theoretical analysis of such a system had to demonstrate how its unity was anything but simply natural, given, self-identical: how it was a product of historical, conflictual forces and how its operation dissimulated the alternatives upon whose suppression its survival depends. In *Dialectic of Enlightenment*, the word that sums up these suppressed alternatives is *subjectivity*:

> It is only insofar as they are subjects that people themselves constitute the limit of reification; hence mass culture must reestablish its control over them again and again [*immer aufs Neue wieder sie erfassen*]: the hopeless effort of this repetition is the only trace of hope, that this repetition is in vain, that in spite of everything, people are not controllable. (p. 331)

It is precisely this motif of repetition, in all of its ambivalence, its despair and hope, a motif that forms the negative backbone of the critique of the Culture Industry. Let us take a closer look at one such instance.

The contribution of mass culture to the Sisyphean task of monopoly capitalism consists above all in "the fabrication of archetypes" of "archaic symbols" (*urzeitliche Symbole*). Immediately following the text just quoted, we come upon this rather remarkable passage, remarkable not least of all in appearing to blend the very different scenarios of monopoly capitalism, Nazism, and fascism into a single ritual of reading and writing:

> The dream factory does not so much fabricate the dreams of its customers as disseminate those of its suppliers . . . In the dream of those who steer the mummification of the world, mass culture is the priestly hieroglyphics [*Hieroglyphenschrift*] that provides the subjugated with images not to enjoy but to read. The authentic (images) of film, but also the inauthentic[5] ones of hit songs and

texts, appear so rigid that they are often not even perceived as such, but only as repetitions whose perennial selfsameness [*Immergleichheit*] expresses an identical meaning. The looser the connections of plot and progression [*Handlung und Verlauf*], the more the isolated image [*das abgesprengte Bild*] becomes an allegorical seal [*allegorisches Sigel*]. Optically the flashing, passing images in the movie theater become increasingly like writing. They are grasped, not observed . . . Thus, the transition from image to writing brought about by the technique of mass artworks consummates the absorption of art through monopolistic practice. (p. 332)

Writing absorbs "authentic" imagery, Adorno argues, the same way "monopolistic practice" absorbs authentic art, in a triumph of self-identical repetition, in *Wiederholungen* as *Immergleichheit*. Despite the terminological borrowings from Benjamin, nothing could be further from the analyses of the *Trauerspielbuch* than this equation of "archetype," "archaic symbol," and "allegorical seal" (*allegorisches Sigel*).[6]

Whereas Benjamin's elaboration of allegory was presented as an *alternative* to the predominant theory of the symbol as unity of image and meaning, Adorno here collapses the difference into a unity that consummates his critique of the Culture Industry. The dissolution of narrative-historical continuities is marked by a scripturalization of imagery that Adorno interprets strictly in terms of reification and ritualization. Reading, in this context, is presented as a "deciphering" of a fixed code of isolated, abstract "graphic signs" (*Schriftzeichen*), as a more or less mechanical effort to reduce the strange and alien to the known and familiar.

Now it is undeniable that all reading must include an element of decoding: all reading presupposes reference to a known code, to a relatively closed system; if one doesn't have some knowledge of the system prior to encountering a text, one cannot read, not at least as reading is commonly understood. However, and this was precisely the point of Benjamin's discussion of allegory, the German Baroque allegory with which he was concerned no longer involved a "conventional expression," but an "expression of convention." Which is to say, an expression of the *problematic* status of all such *coming-together*, of all *convenus*, however indispensable such convergence is to all language and culture. And as a result, allegory in the German Baroque, and perhaps in general, was fundamentally *theatrical*: it involved representations whose referent was necessarily problematic, open, heterogeneous. And theatricality, as I understand it at least, entails first and foremost: representation for the Other. We will come back to this later.

In Adorno's analysis of mass culture, by contrast, the transformation of imagery into allegorical inscription and the ensuing replacement of observation by reading is portrayed as the sign and symptom of the concealed, traumatic core of the Culture Industry and of the society it helps to reproduce. The breaking of narrative continuity does not merely "isolate . . . individual allegorical gestures," as in film, Adorno argues: it transforms human faces into "culture masks," whose rigid, death-like traits mark the limits of the unified individual and perhaps the limits of subjectivity itself. Such graphic inscriptions encourage both flight into Dionysian self-abandonment (Adorno's example is "dancing to jazz") as well as its ostensible (but dialectical) opposite, the no less exuberant effort to conform with established social norms.

Adorno concludes his description of the death of imagery at the hands of reading and writing, with the following image:

> The streamers that cross high above the cities and whose light obscures the natural night light announce, like comets, the natural catastrophe of society, its death by freezing [*Kältetod*]. But they do not come from heaven. They are guided from the earth. It's up to human beings to decide if they want to put them out [*sie auslöschen wollen*] and awake from the nightmare, which only threatens to become reality as long as people believe in it. (p. 335)

To be sure, this passage, whose voluntaristic tone − it's up to you! − gives this text as Hollywoodian an ending as could be imagined − to be sure, this passage occurs in a text that Adorno himself did not publish and perhaps would never have published in such a form. However, these words were obviously not written casually: they were written to conclude. And the critical perspective they announce seems to consist in the slim hope that "people" − *die Menschen* − may one day finally decide to put an end to the nightmare of reading and writing in order finally to awaken, to open their eyes and see! America, awake out of your bad dream . . . See, and live!

But if this is the last word of the supplementary text on the Culture Industry, other passages in the same text are less "conclusive" and suggest that the nightmare of reading is at any rate more complex than appears here at the end. The following observation is one such:

> The more the viewer of a film, the listener of a pop song, the reader of detective or magazine stories anticipates the conclusion, the result, the more his attention shifts to the How, from the worthless result to the rebus-like detail, and in the process of this shifting search, the hieroglyphic meaning appears to him in a flash. It articulates all phenomena down to their most subtle nuances according to the simple binary logic of do and don't, and through its consequent reduction of the foreign and the incomprehensible, it catches up with the consumers. (p. 333)

What Adorno is describing here is both impressive and puzzling. Impressive, inasmuch as it highlights a tendency that if anything has increased in the half-century since he wrote: the way interest in the making of the films, for instance, their cost, their techniques, etc., accompanies the interest in "content" and theme. What is curious, however, is the tendency to condemn critically the shift of interest from theme and content to "rebus-like detail." For precise attention to detail is what Adorno, as we have seen, would later defend against the Hegelian – and not just Hegelian – tendency to subsume the singular under the general, the non-identical under the identical. To be sure, not all details are equal and the "rebus-like detail" referred to here is one that leads to that baleful flash of "hieroglyphic meaning." But why such flashes of hieroglyphic meaning should then be so rapidly identified with a "binary logic of do and don't," especially when the hieroglyph involves an enigma, is a question that is hardly discussed in this text. No room is left for the allegorical resources of writing and inscription which would question the priestly authority ascribed to "hieroglyphics." Hence, it is only consistent that the dream, which as Adorno well knew was a writing system, would also be assimilated to the sacerdotal tendencies of the system. And consequently, that his essay would envisage a resolution of the problem by proposing what can only be described as an extremely binary alternative: either continuing to dream the nightmare of reading or finally deciding to *awake*.[7] It is as though the Critical Theory of the Culture Industry were here *ereilt* – overtaken – by the reductive binarism of the system it seeks to criticize.

III

To find an alternative not just to this nightmare, but to the alternative dream or awakening in which it is inscribed, let us return to Adorno's earlier study of Kierkegaard, where he already found himself obliged to address the question of reading, albeit in a somewhat different "light." In the process he demonstrates that whatever his ambivalence toward reading may be, he is still far more attentive to its complexities and resources than one might expect, especially in view of passages such as the one we have just discussed. Indeed, his book on Kierkegaard begins with a determination of how the latter is to be read: not as poetry, Adorno insists, but as philosophy. Why is this distinction necessary? Among other reasons, because of the peculiar and highly distinctive style of writing that characterizes Kierkegaard's texts:

> To the claim of being poetry, Kierkegaard's work assumes an ambiguous stance. With cunning it is laid out to anticipate every misunderstanding that inaugurates in the reader the process of appropriating its tenor [*Gehalte*]. The

dialectic in the issues [*Sachen*] is for it at the same time a dialectic of communication. (1962: S. 12/p. 5)

The encounter with the writings of Kierkegaard raises two issues that will turn out to be decisive for all of Adorno's work. The first is the question of *Gehalt* or, less emphatically, of *Inhalt*: the question of *content* or as I have just translated it, using a word once popularized by I. A. Richards, of *tenor* (as opposed to "vehicle"). The German word should not be forgotten, however, for it recalls connotations all too easily effaced in English. The root of the words *Inhalt* and *Gehalt* is, of course, the verb *halten*, to hold, but also to stop, to halt, to arrest. The action that constitutes "contents" is a *holding action*, an act of *containment*.[8] Given Adorno's constant insistence on the importance of *Inhalt* and *Gehalt* as opposed to mere *form* – and the notion of *Gehalt* emerges in his work to designate the dialectical synthesis of form and content – the following question must be addressed: What are the conditions under which the *holding action* required to constitute a *Ge-halt* can be effective? To be *held* the passage of time must be interrupted and suspended. Only by arresting the passage of time can a *Gehalt* be constituted. And since we have seen that the Hegelian notion of determinate negation is not sufficient to legitimate the stoppages that give rise to *Gehalte*, another category must be found to account for what Adorno, in "How to Read Hegel," describes as "the principle of fixation, without which nothing linguistic can be at all" (*ohne die kein Sprachliches überhaupt ist*).[9] Although Hegel's writing is seen by Adorno as deliberately offering a "provocative challenge" to this "principle of fixation," and hence to language itself, the Hegelian dialectic cannot, as we have seen, be considered as a satisfactory resolution of the problem. Perhaps because a holding action is not the same as seizing or grasping, *Halten* is not *Greifen*, *Gehalt* not merely a synonym for *Begriff*. Against the tendency toward dialectical *Aufhebung*, Adorno insists on the necessity of immersing oneself "in details" that precisely are not "resolved" or transcended through "universal mediation," but rather resist, persist, and insist as *"das Moment des Nichtaufgehenden,"* the moment of that which resists absorption by the mediating movement of conceptualization. To be sure, this does not justify the pure and simple dismissing of conceptual content: rather it calls for its reconfiguration. And that reconfiguration can take place only in and through a reading process that orients itself not simply on the concept, however dialectical, but on what Adorno, once again doubtless indebted to Benjamin, calls the *name*: "The better procedure would be one that, carefully avoiding verbal definitions as mere constative determinations [*Feststellungen*], shapes [*anbildet*] its concepts to conform as faithfully as possible with what they say in language: virtually as *names*" (1993: 340).

The problem, of course, is that the "pure language" of authentic names, in which language does not merely designate general meanings but creates or re-creates that which it singularly distinguishes – this language, as Benjamin had argued in his 1916 text on language, disappeared at the very latest with the desire of man to use language as a means, an instrument of knowledge, and, above all, of critical judgment. To *know the difference* between Good and Evil, and perhaps, even more simply, to *know* the *difference*, is to construe it as an object of knowledge. To know the difference, even in order to criticize it, can mean to subordinate its alterity, its non-identity, to the assimilative acid-bath of the familiar, even if the latter is elaborated with the dialectical rigor of fully determined conceptuality. It is characteristic that for Adorno this danger appeared above all as that of being trapped in language, as a kind of terminological rigor mortis.

> Whoever makes himself the slave of his own words, takes the easy way out by shoving them in front of the issues [*vor die Sachen*] . . . Nevertheless such a procedure is insufficient. For in empirical languages words are not pure names but always also θεσει, products of subjective consciousness and insofar themselves also similar to definitions. (pp. 340–1)

How then can one hope to arrive at a configuration of concepts that is oriented upon a purity of proper names that is irrevocably gone? By a practice, which, it turns out, is not foreign to reading, albeit of the right kind:

> A proper linguistic procedure could be compared to the way an emigrant learns a foreign language [It should be noted that Adorno writes of an *emigrant*, and not an *immigrant* – SW]. He may, impatient and under pressure, operate less with the dictionary than by reading as much as he possibly can. Numerous words will, of course, open up through their context, but remaining for a long time surrounded by a halo of indeterminacy, and even subject to ridiculous confusions, until finally, through the plenitude of combinations in which they appear, they unravel entirely [*sich ganz enträtseln*] and better than the dictionary would have permitted. (p. 341)

A difficulty in translating the above passage points us directly to the key problem: Adorno's appeal to the practical linguistic experience of the *émigré*, rather than of the *immigrant*, an experience involving above all *reading*, culminates in what appears to be the full resolution of the enigma, the puzzle, the *Rätsel* of the foreign word, disclosed through the plenitude, *die Fülle*, of its uses. This pragmatic optimism, however, is called into question by the pragmatic difficulty of idiomatically translating into English the German word used by Adorno to designate this Happy End, the word *enträtseln*: literally, "un-riddle" or "un-puzzle." I prefer to render it as *unravel*, however, in order to emphasize the paradox that this Pragmatist Happy End does its best to conceal. For the "plenitude of combinations" in which a word is used does not merely fix the meaning of a word, it also opens it to constant transformation. Usage may well provide a more reliable way to arrive at the prevailing meaning of words than the dictionary: it still does not resolve the question of reading and interpretation – except insofar as one's object is primarily to avoid being the object of "ridicule." What the appeal to linguistic usage underscores is that the experience of language cannot be confined to grammatical and lexical categories, to definitions, because such experience is intrinsically open. But such openness is not without consequences for the Name itself: how "proper" or transparent can a Name be that is subject to the unlimitable combinatorics that constitute the experience of language? Is there such a thing as a Proper Name? This question permits us to return, finally, to Adorno's study of that other émigré, Søren Kierkegaard.

Adorno begins his study of Kierkegaard – his second and decisive attempt to acquire the *Habilitation*, without which no academic career would have been possible – by seeking to establish, beyond the shadow of a doubt, that Kierkegaard's text was not *poetical*, but *philosophical*, and as such, amenable to a philosophical *critique*. To establish the philosophical nature of the text, however, Adorno has first to deal with the ostensibly literary device of the *pseudonyms*, which, *qua pseudo*, tend to undercut the power of the proper name to put a *definitive* and *authoritative* halt to the dynamics of language, of reading, and of writing. The task and its resolution Adorno describes as follows:

> Every observation that unqualifiedly accepts the claims of the pseudonyms and takes them as the decisive measure, goes astray. They are not figures [*Gestalten*], in whose incomparable being [*Dasein*] intention is densely enclosed. They are entirely abstract-representative figures. This does not mean that criticism could ever neglect their function, taking their opinions to be those of Kierkegaard. Rather, criticism must confront the abstract unities of the pseudonyms with the concrete motifs that are embedded (*eingefaßt*) in the framework of pseudonymity, and then measure the cogency (*Stimmigkeit*) of the context . . . Critique must first understand the assertions of the pseudonyms in accordance with their philosophical construction, which can be shown at every moment to function as a dominant scheme. What the pseudonyms then say that exceeds the philosophical scheme: their secret and concrete core, falls to interpretation in the literalness [*Wörtlichkeit*] of the communication. No writer uses words more cunningly than Kierkegaard. (S. 23–4, p. 11)

The pseudonyms are on the one hand governed by schematic philosophical categories, of which, Adorno writes elsewhere, they are the "illustration" (S. 24, p. 7); but at the same time, what they say and do is both more and other than what the philosophical scheme prescribes or comprehends, and it is here, in this divergence, that "critique" finds its Archimedean point: the point where conceptual-thematic content overflows in and into literal language itself. But if this is the general scheme of how the schematism of the text is to be outwitted, the text itself has, as Adorno knows all too well, already prepared a response: for "no writer uses words more cunningly than Kierkegaard" and thus to trust or take those words at face value, or at any value, is still to run the risk of falling prey to the cunning strategem of the text:

> In the labyrinthine lair [*Fuchsbau*: "fox kennel" translates Hullot-Kentor] of infinitely reflected inwardness, there is no means of cornering [Kierkegaard] [*ihn zu stellen*] other than taking him at his word, which, planned as traps, ultimately snare him himself. The choice of words, their stereotypical, not always planned recurrence, points towards a tenor [*Gehalte*] that even the most profound of dialectical procedures would rather conceal than reveal. (S. 24, pp. 11–12)

Taking Adorno at his word here, one would have to wonder about a fox, clever and hunted, laying traps for the hunter and then being caught in them himself. A consoling scenario, for the hunter at least. But what does it mean to take a text at its word, or rather, at its words? If those words, as the Emigrant was to discover, are accessible only through the configurations in which they are used, and if those configurations are *in principle infinite* – each new combination opening possibilities for further use and recombination – then where is the position from which one might *take* the text at its word and thereby *wrest* it away from the "pseudonyms" to whom those words are ascribed? And the question grows even more complicated when, as Adorno insists, the very name of the author himself, "Kierkegaard," must also be read as a "pseudonym": "The interpretation of the pseudonym Kierkegaard has to dissect the simulated poetic unity into the polarity of its own speculative intention and that of the literalness that betrays it" (S. 24, p. 12). But how is the literalness, the *Wörtlichkeit* of the words to be determined, to be read, if those words all are spoken or written by fictional characters, by persona, by pseudonyms whose authority is always relative to their position with respect to other textual elements?

In a short text to which Adorno refers and quotes, "A First and Last Explication," "Kierkegaard," apparently finally speaking in his own name, defines his own authorial position precisely in relation to those of his fictional pseudonyms (polyphonic long before Bakhtin introduced the term). He makes two statements that are relevant here:

As a result, I express the desire and the prayer that, should anyone have the idea of citing one of the pseudonymic books, that he should be so kind and do me the favor of citing the name of the pseudonymic author in question and not mine, which is to say, to distribute things among us so that the statements belong in feminine fashion to the pseudonym and the responsibility, civilly, to me.[10]

What I know about about the pseudonyms naturally does not give me the right to affirm or to doubt their reaction, since their significance (whatever it might be in *reality*) absolutely does not consist in making any new propositions, any unheard-of discoveries or in founding a new party and wishing to "go further," but precisely, on the contrary, in not wanting to have any significance, in wanting only to read, at a distance from the remove of double reflection [i.e., that on the object and on the "author" – SW] that singular, originary and human writing of existence, the ancient text known and transmitted by our fathers, rereading it one more time, if possible in a more interior manner. (p. 426)

The statement of the "author," "Kierkegaard," can of course claim no greater authority than those of the "pseudonyms." But it nevertheless opens a perspective for further consideration: if the significance of the words spoken and written in a text is not reducible to the intention of the speaker or writer; if the latter is itself part of a larger signifying process, then the process of reading, writing, and interpreting will never be simply distinguishable from the text the way a "subject" seems to be distinguishable from an "object." And then, it will not be enough to speak, as Adorno does, of *Wörtlichkeit*; rather, the notion will have to supplemented, as Benjamin does in "The Task of the Translator," when he writes of "*Wörtlichkeit der Syntax*": literalness of *syntax* as the principle guiding the task of the translator. Syntax here stands for the spatial relations that go beyond the rule-governed system of grammar and semantics.

There is no time left today to speak of such syntactical space. Suffice it to say that it will never be reducible to the kind of subjective Inwardness in which Adorno seeks to trap his prey, "Kierkegaard." We can demonstrate that briefly by returning to the scene from which we set out, in which Constantin Constantius – not "Kierkegaard" – describes the apartment to which he returns after arriving in Berlin. This is the conclusion of Adorno's rather brief commentary to the long scene he quotes, and which he considers to be "the most thought-provoking (*denkwürdigste*) passage that Kierkegaard devoted to the Interior" (S. 84, p. 45):

Out of the half-light of such melancholy emerge the contours of "domestic-
ity", which for Kierkegaard constitutes the arena of existence. It therefore
constitutes the contours of his doctrine of existence itself . . . In the interior,
historical dialectics and the eternal power of nature compose their strangely
enigmatic image [*ihr wunderliches Rätselbild*]. It must be unraveled [*aufgelöst*] by
philosophical criticism, which seeks to attain the real ground of his idealistic
inwardness in the Historical as well as in the archaic [*Vorzeitlichen*]. (S. 86,
p. 46)

Adorno's claim to take Kierkegaard's text at its word seems here to founder
on the *parti pris* of the general interpretive argument. What he ignores, in
any case, is precisely that *literalness of syntax* which would require one to take
into account the context and relations in which this scene is inscribed. To
see it as a direct expression of "Kierkegaard's" "doctrine of existence itself,"
is not just to ignore the wish or "prayer" of that "First and Last Explication,"
but far more problematic, to ignore the surface facts of the text: the "fact"
that the description is that of a pseudonym, a fictional figure, Constantin
Constantius, whose return to Berlin and to these lodgings has a very distinct
and precise history. It is to ignore that the "interior" being described is not
simply "domestic," as Adorno calls it, but that of a rented apartment in a
pension, and no less important, a place to which Constantin *returns*. And what
is fully ignored by Adorno is the incidence of "repetition" in the description, which structurally doubles and breaks open the closed space of any
Interior, including this one. To see this room as a site of "historical dialectics
and the eternal power of nature" is hardly a response to the literalness of the
text, much less to its syntax.

To be sure, there can be no reading that is entirely "literal," or even *wörtlich*
in the sense Adorno envisages. Every reading must be selective and hence
must respond, more or less, to preconceived intentions. This one no less than
any other. But the selections and exclusions that underlie all reading must be
justifiable in terms of the relations they thereby remark. In this particular
passage, the phrase to which *I* would want to call attention, in the context
of such relations, is one in which Adorno seems uninterested. And yet it sums
up the atmosphere of repetition and of doubling, of shadows and echoes and
at the same time designates a very important quality of that *intérieur* with
which Adorno is so concerned. It is the phrase, "Sitting in a chair by the
window, one looks out on the great square, sees the shadows of passersby
hurrying along the walls: everything is transformed into scenic decor" (S. 85,
p. 45).

This gives the "interior" a very different aspect from that which Adorno
seeks to assign to it: namely, that of a theological cipher or "allegory." For
what is truly *denkwürdig* about this scene is that it is the position of the spec-

tator, looking out, is described as situated in a kind of *theater*. And the "interiority" of a theater is very different from that of a private home or a domestic house (a fact that worried Plato no end).[11] In a theater, on a stage, as part of a scene, subjects are no longer authentic, no longer at home, no longer fully in control. Inside and outside are no longer simply binary opposites. The space of the theatrical scene, which is not necessarily that of traditional drama, is no longer simply an interior space, since it is always directed outward, away, toward others. As already mentioned, theatricality can even be defined as *representation for others*. In this case, however, dramatic conflict and plot are not its constitutive ingredients.

But if the "interior" is a theater, this endows the description of the night scene outside with a very different resonance from that which Adorno describes. It is not simply the projection of eternal nature upon transient history. Remember the key phrase: "The cloudless vault of heaven looks so melancholy, so dreamlike and so thoughtful as though the end of the world had *come and gone*, had already passed, and heaven, undisturbed, was occupied with itself." In the German translation cited by Adorno, this phrase reads: "*Als ob der Untergang der Welt vorüber . . . wäre*" (note the formulation, which literally renders Kierkegaard's Danish [*som var Verdens Undergang forbi . . .*]). Remembering Adorno's concluding image to the appendix on the Culture Industry: it is as though the streamers had finally passed, taking with them the "world" and leaving in its wake not the alternative of nightmare, on the one hand, and waking reality on the other, but something very different: a moonlit stage, a "glimmering dreamworld," and at the center of the stage, a small, candle-lit table, upon which one can write if one cannot sleep.

It would, I belive, be extremely illuminating to explore further the implications of this theatrical dimension in the encounter of Adorno with Kierkegaard and in the confrontation of their respective texts. Since that cannot be done here, however, I will conclude instead with two brief remarks.

First, Adorno in his study of Kierkegaard is surely one of the few readers to have remarked the importance of Kierkegaard's theory of the *Posse*, the theatrical, popular farce, mass culture if there ever was one, but also very different from that criticized by Adorno. What is characteristic of that theater, which is essentially non-dramatical, non-conflictual, and non-narrative, is that it is scenic in the sense described quite precisely in the passage we are discussing: the "actors" in this theater are important not for what they represent, but for how they *move* on the stage. The greatest of them, like Beckmann of the Königstädter Theater, are distinguished first and foremost by the way they move. In the case of Beckmann, this is quite specific. It has to do with his manner of *coming and going*. What is absolutely singular, defying the rules of a certain logic, is that Beckmann's *coming* is at the same time inseparable from his *going*.[12] His movement is described, by Constantin, not as a movement *from* one place *to* another: from Kant to Hegel, Hegel to Nietzsche, or even from Enlightenment to Dialectics; rather, Beckmann, literally, *comes going*: in Danish, *komme gaaende*, whereby *gaaende*, like the German *gehend*, can mean both *walking* and *going* or *leaving*. In this coming-going, a very different kind of apparition emerges from the "concrete universal" of Hegelian aesthetics. In *Gjentagelse*, Constantin calls it "accidental concretion," a theatrical growing together in which the universal and particular do not simply converge and blend, but also diverge, leaving room for the aleatory, and hence for the singular. This is ultimately why theater, as exemplified in the *Posse*, is neither poetical nor "aesthetic." The *Posse* has nothing to do with the traditional aesthetic-dramatic genres, *tragedy* and *comedy*. In this coming that is simultaneously a going, Beckmann effaces himself as individual figure and instead, through his movement that in a certain sense – a narrative sense – is going nowhere, makes way for a world of *relations*, a village peopled with places and ways and things as much as with persons.

This brings me to my second, and final, point. One of the many fascinating discussions in the annex to the Culture Industry, concerns the status of the variété, the variety show. In this connection, Adorno describes, but also criticizes, certain features of this eminently theatrical phenomenon that seem profoundly related to aspects of the media today: the interruption of narrative structure, the implication of the audience in the spectacle, and perhaps above all, a certain suspension of the linear-teleological movement that Adorno identifies, however dialectically, with historical progress. Adorno himself considers this suspension to reveal the cardinal sin of the Culture Industry:

> What constitutes the variety act, what impresses the child at its first visit to such a show, is the fact that *at one and the same time, both something and nothing happens* [*daß allemal zugleich etwas und nichts geschieht*]. Every variety act is actually a waiting. Subsequently it turns out that the waiting for something . . . was actually the things itself. Applause always [*allemal*] comes a split second too late, when the spectator notices that what he at first took to be preparation was already the event [*das Ereignis*], of which he has been, as it were, deprived. In this temporal swindle, [*In diesem Betrug um die Zeitordnung*], bringing the instant to a halt comprises the trick of the variety show . . . the symbolic suspension of the process [*des Verlaufs*]. This is why the spectator who always comes late can never be too late: he jumps on as though it were a carrousel . . . The joke is not on the spectator, but on time itself. (p. 308)

No matter if Adorno himself concludes this account by assimilating it to a certain domination of nature, which functions through a "technical disposition over time." The "event" of an instant that suddenly breaks the continuum of progress, and of the kind of history that depends upon such continuity – the event, in which something *happens* without anything *taking place*, stops short and opens out onto a very different dynamic of space and place, time and instant, concretion and abstraction, from that in which critical theory is at home. It is the *uncanny, iterative* space-time of an irreducible theatricality that is elusive but that, *nevertheless and at the same time – allemal* – must not just be seen but also *read*. In this *allemal* is congealed not merely the reification, hypostasis, and levelling that Adorno saw as the essence of the Culture Industry, but also, at the same time, *allemal*, a movement of repetition as alteration and transformation that cannot be reduced to the *Immergleichen*. *Allemal* is not *immergleich*. But it also leaves no room for that Past or Future Perfect of a dialectic which will always have been the other of what it was.

What Adorno construed univocally as an object of critique, the "ghostly" (*gespenstisch*) spectacle of "the unremitting repetition of the unrepeatable" (p. 317), *can also* operate as the mode in which singularity is articulated. This possibility must be kept open, even if in reality repetition is most often far closer to the Selfsameness with which Adorno was obsessed. What Adorno refused to grant to the variety show, although he nevertheless described it, he did accord to the *Posse* in *Repetition*. In a chapter of his study of Kierkegaard entitled "The Passing of Existence" he noted the following:

> The spontaneous intervention of the spectator in the work, which accordingly defines the form of the *Posse*, only apparently derives from the principle of self-centered subjectivism. For it turns against the unity of the work [*des Gebildes*], which bears witness to the unity of the subjective synthesis, and plays itself out in momentary impulses that remain as incommensurable with respect to each other as do laughing and melancholy confronted with the *Posse*: responses to the change of images – "situations" – in which "in general" the existence of the *dramatis personae* like that of the existing person disappears. What Kierkegaard took license to say about the anarchy of the *Posse* could come to endanger the "hierarchy of the spheres." (S. 232, pp. 129–30)

The inscription of theater as *Posse*, in the text on *Repetition*, does indeed undermine any positive "theory," "philosophy," or even religious "dogma" that might otherwise be ascribed to Kierkegaard's texts. But these texts, in their pseudonymic character at least, were never designed to comprise a "critical theory" but at most, a critical *theater*. Or at least not one that could be separated from an experience of reading and of repetition.

It was the opening to this experience that the notion of the *Immergleich* has served to block. This cursory attempt to reread Adorno on Kierkegaard, but also Adorno *through* Kierkegaard, suggests that it may be high time to distinguish the pseudo-simultaneity of repetition, as reading, theater, and staging, from the monolithic quality of the *Immergleichen* as the return of the Same. What Adorno saw as a ghostly spectacle in which the unrepeatable is incessantly repeated might then turn out to have been nothing more or less than a particularly powerful *pseudonym* for the "non-identical." Or vice versa.

Notes

1　S. Kierkegaard, *Repetition*, edited and translated by Edward V. Hong and Edna Hong (Princeton: Princeton University Press, 1983): 151–2.

2　Theodor W. Adorno, *Kierkegaard: Konstruktion des Ästhetischen* (Frankfurt am Main: Suhrkamp, 1962), S. 12. English, translated by Robert Hullot-Kentor (Minneapolis: University of Minnesota Press, 1989): 3–4. Translations here as elsewhere modified.

3　G. W. F. Hegel, *Phänomenologie des Geistes*, Einleitung, XXX (my translation – SW). Cited in M. Heidegger, *Hegels Begriff der Erfahrung*, in *Holzwege* (Frankfurt am Main: Klostermann, 1963): 106.

4　The example Adorno gives is the following, from the Second Book of the Greater Logic: *"Das Werden im Wesen, seine reflektirende Bewegung, ist daher die Bewegung von Nichts zu Nichts, und dadurch zu sich selbst zurück. Das Übergehen oder Werden hebt in seinem Übergehen sich auf; das Andere, das in diesem Übergehen wird, ist nicht das Nichtseyn eines Seyns, sondern das Nichts eines Nichts, und dieß, die Negation eines Nichts zu seyn, macht das Seyn aus. – Das Seyn ist nur als die Bewegung des Nichts zu Nichts, so ist es das Wesen; und dieses hat nicht diese Bewegung in sich, sondern ist sie als der absolute Schein selbst, die reine Negativität, die nichts außer ihr hat, das sie negirte, sondern die nur ihr Negatives selbst negirt, das nur in diesem Negiren ist."*

5　This was obviously long before Adorno discovered the Jargon of Authenticity.

6　For a similar, but more interesting and more productive sleight of hand with the same Benjaminian categories, see Adorno's *Essay on Wagner*, where the notion of "allegory" is transformed into a *critical* and *geschichtphilosophisches* tool.

7　Given the insistent pathos of such admonitions to "awake" in the writings of *both* Adorno *and* Benjamin, it should be remembered that the first line of the Horst Wessel Lied *also* demands that "Germany awake . . . out of your bad dream!"

8　According to *Duden: Das Herkunftswörterbuch* (Mannheim-Vienna-Zurich: 1989), "viewed etymologically" *Gehalt* is "the same word" as *Behälter, Behältnis, Aufbewahrungsraum*: that is, as "container," a place in which things are conserved and saved (S. 224).

9　*Drei Studien zu Hegel*, 351.

10　Søren Kierkegaard, "Une première et dernière explication," from *Post-Scriptum aux miettes philosophiques*, translated by Paul Petit (Paris: Gallimard, 1949): 425.

11   See Plato's remarks on the corruption of the home by theatrical mimesis in the *Nomoi*. See also my discussion of these passages in "The Canon: Music and the Law," *Angelaki*, vol. 3 no. 1 (Oxford, 1996).

12   This is also a characteristic assigned in Kierkegaard's texts to music. In a passage quoted by Adorno we read: "Music has time as its element, but it gains no permanent place in it; as notes are struck they dissipate" (p. 19). But the consequences that are drawn from this temporal interpretation of music are utterly unacceptable to Adorno: "His assertion that music '*is* merely because it is constantly repeated, existing merely in the instant of performance,' is completely absurd. In the musical text, readable just like a literary work, music has an existence independent from its punctual performance." (p. 19)

Bibliography

Adorno in English

"The Actuality of Philosophy," *Telos*, 31 (1977): 120–32.

The Adorno Reader, ed. Brian O'Connor. Malden, MA: Blackwell, 2000.

Aesthetic Theory, trans. Christian Lenhardt. London: Routledge and Kegan Paul, 1984.

Aesthetic Theory, trans. Robert Hullot-Kentor. Minneapolis: University of Minnesota Press, and London: Athlone Press, 1997.

Against Epistemology: A Metacritique. Studies in Husserl and the Phenomenological Antinomies, trans. W. Domingo. Oxford: Blackwell, 1982; Cambridge, MA: MIT Press, 1983.

"The Aging of the New Music," trans. Robert Hullot-Kentor and Friedrich Will, *Telos*, 77 (1988): 95–116.

"Alienated Masterpiece: The *Missa Solemnis*," *Telos*, 28 (1976): 113–24.

"Analytical Study of the NBC Music Appreciation Hour," *Musical Quarterly*, 78 (1994): 325–77.

Beethoven: The Philosophy of Music, trans. Edmund Jephcott. Stanford, CA: Stanford University Press, and Cambridge: Polity Press, 1998.

Berg: Master of the Smallest Link, trans. Juliane Brand and Christopher Hailey. New York: Cambridge University Press, 1991.

"Bourgeois Opera," in *Opera through Other Eyes*, ed. David Levin. Stanford, CA: Stanford University Press, 1993: 25–43.

"Commitment," in *Aesthetics and Politics*, ed. Ronald Taylor London: New Left Books, 1977; reprinted in *The Essential Frankfurt School Reader*, ed. Andrew Arato and Eike Gebhardt. New York: Urizen, 1978.

Critical Models: Interventions and Catchwords, ed. and trans. Henry W. Pickford. New York: Columbia University Press, 1998.

"Cultural Criticism and Society," in *Prisms*. London: Neville Spearman, 1967.

The Culture Industry: Selected Essays on Mass Culture, ed. J. M. Bernstein. London and New York: Routledge, 1991.

"The Culture Industry Reconsidered," in *Critical Theory and Society: A Reader*, ed. Stephen Eric Bronner and Douglas Kellner. New York: Routledge, 1989: 128–35.

"The Culture Industry Revisited," *New German Critique*, 6 (Fall 1975): 12–19.

"The Curves of the Needle," trans. Thomas Y. Levin, *October*, 55 (1990): 49–55.

"The Form of the Phonograph Record," trans. Thomas Y. Levin, *October*, 55 (1990): 56–61.

"Freudian Theory and the Pattern of Fascist Propaganda," in *The Essential Frankfurt School Reader*, ed. Andrew Arato and Eike Gebhardt. Oxford: Blackwell, 1978.

Hegel: Three Studies, trans. Shierry Weber Nicholsen. Cambridge, MA: MIT Press, 1993.

"How to Look at Television," *Quarterly of Film, Radio, and Television*, 7 (Spring 1957): 213–35.

In Search of Wagner, trans. Rodney Livingstone. London: New Left Books, 1981.

Introduction to Sociology. Stanford, CA: Stanford University Press, 2000.

Introduction to the Sociology of Music, trans. E. B. Ashton. New York: Seabury, 1976; Continuum, 1989.

"Is Marx Obsolete?" trans. Nicholas Slater, *Diogenes*, 64 (Winter 1968): 1–16.

The Jargon of Authenticity. Evanston, IL: Northwestern University Press, 1973.

Kierkegaard: Construction of the Aesthetic, trans. Robert Hullot-Kentor. Minneapolis: University of Minnesota Press, 1989.

"Late Style in Beethoven," *Raritan*, 13 (1993): 102–7.

Mahler: A Musical Physiognomy, trans. Edmund Jephcott. Chicago: University of Chicago Press, 1992.

Minima Moralia: Reflections from Damaged Life, trans. E. F. N. Jephcott. London: New Left Books, 1974.

"Music, Language, and Composition," *Musical Quarterly*, 77 (1993): 401–14.

Negative Dialectics, trans. E. B. Ashton. New York: Seabury Press, 1973; Continuum, 1990.

Notes to Literature, trans. Shierry Weber Nicholsen, ed. Rolf Tiedemann. 2 vols. New York: Columbia University Press, 1991–2.

"On Popular Music" (with the assistance of George Simpson), *Studies in Philosophy and Social Science*, 9 (1941): 17–48.

"On the Fetish Character in Music and the Regression of Listening," *The Culture Industry*, 1995. Also printed in *The Essential Frankfurt School Reader*, ed. Andrew Arato and Eike Gebhardt. Oxford: Blackwell, 1978, pp. 270–99.

"On the Problem of Musical Analysis," trans. Max Paddison, *Music Analysis*, 1 (1982): 169–87.

"On the Social Situation of Music," *Telos*, 35 (Spring 1978): 128–64.

"Opera and the Long-Playing Record," trans. Thomas Y. Levin, *October*, 55 (1990): 62–6.

Philosophy of Modern Music, trans. Anne G. Mitchell and Wesley V. Blomster. New York: Continuum, 1973, 1994.

Prisms, trans. Samuel and Shierry Weber. Cambridge, MA: MIT Press, 1967, 1981.

Quasi una fantasia: Essays on Modern Music, trans. Ridney Livingstone. London: Verso, 1992.

"Resignation," trans. Wes Blomster, *Telos*, 35 (1978): 165–9; also in *Critical Models*, trans. Henry Pickford. New York: Columbia University Press, 1998.

"Scientific Experiences of a European Scholar in America," in *The European Migration*, ed. Donald Fleming and Bernard Bailyn. Cambridge, MA: Harvard University Press, 1969; also in *Critical Models*, trans. Henry W. Pickford. New York: Columbia University Press, 1998: 215–42.

"A Social Critique of Radio Music," *Kenyon Review*, 8 (1945): 208–17.

Sound Figures, trans. Rodney Livingstone. Stanford, CA: Stanford University Press, 1999.

The Stars Look Down to Earth and Other Essays on the Irrational in Culture, ed. Stephen Crook. London and New York: Routledge, 1994.

"Television and the Patterns of Mass Culture," in *Mass Culture*, ed. Bernard Rosenberg and David Manning White. Glencoe, IL: Free Press, 1957.

"Theses on the Sociology of Art," trans. Brian Trench, *Birmingham Working Papers in Cultural Studies*, 2 (1972): 121–8.

"Transparencies on Film," *New German Critique*, 24–25 (1981): 186–205.

"Vers une musique informelle," in *Quasi una fantasia*, trans. Rodney Livingstone. London: Verso, 1992 pp. 269–322.

Adorno, Theodor W. (ed.), *The Positivist Dispute in German Sociology*, trans. Glyn Adey and David Frisby. London: Heinemann, 1976.

Adorno, Theodor W., Albert, Hans, Dahrendorf, Ralf, Habermas, Jürgen, Pilot, Harald, Popper, and Karl R., *The Positivist Dispute in German Sociology*, trans. Glyn Adey and David Frisby. London: Heinemann, 1976.

Adorno, Theodor W., and Benjamin, Walter, *The Complete Correspondence, 1928–1940*. Cambridge, MA: Harvard University Press, 1999.

Adorno, Theodor W., and Eisler, Hans, *Composing for the Films*. London: Heinemann, 1994.

Adorno, Theodor W., Frenkel-Brunswik, Else, Levinson, Daniel J., and Sanford R. Nevitt (in association with Betty Aron, Maria Hertz-Levinson, and William Morrow), *The Authoritarian Personality*. Studies in Personality, ed. Max Horkheimer and Samuel H. Flowerman. New York: Harper, 1950; abridged edn. 1982.

Adorno, Theodor W., and Horkheimer, Max, *Dialectic of Enlightenment*, trans. John Cumming. New York: Continuum, 1972, 1988, 1999.

——"Odysseus or Myth and Enlightenment," *New German Critique*, 56 (Spring–Summer 1992).

Adorno, Theodor W., and Marcuse, Herbert, "Correspondence on the German Student Movement," *New Left Review*, 233 (1999): 118–36.

Adorno in German

Alban Berg: Der meister des kleinsten Übergangs (1968), in *Gesammelte Schriften* 13, ed. Rolf Tiedemann. Frankfurt am Main: Suhrkamp, 1971: 321–494.

"Antwortschreiben an Claus Chr. Schroeter," in Kraushaar, *Frankfurter Schule und Studentenbewegung*, vol. 2, 1998.

"Anweisungen zum Hören neuer Musik," *Der getreue Korrepeetitor* (1963), in *Gesammelte Schriften* 15, ed. Rolf Tiedemann. Frankfurt am Main: Suhrkamp, 1976: 188–248.

Ästhetische Theorie, in *Gesammelte Schriften* 7, ed. Rolf Tiedemann. Frankfurt am Main: Suhrkamp, 1970.

Beethoven: Philosophie der Musik, ed. Rolf Tiedemann. Frankfurt am Main: Suhrkamp, 1993.

"Bemerkungen über Politik und Neurose," *Kritik*. Frankfurt am Main: Suhrkamp, 1971.

"Das Altern der neuen Musik," *Der Monat* (May 1955); expanded version in *Dissonanzen*, Göttingen: Vandenhoek and Ruprecht, 1956; in *Gesammelte Schriften* 14, ed. Rolf Tiedemann. Frankfurt am Main: Suhrkamp, 1973.

"Denken Sie etwa an die Vorgänge, die sich in Berlin abgespielt haben . . . Gedanken über die Verfolgung Berliner Studenten in der Vorlesung 'Einleitung in die Soziologie,'" in Kraushaar, *Frankfurter Schule und Studentenbewegung*, vol. 2, 1998: 375–7.

"Engagement," *Noten zur Literatur*, 1974, and in *Gesammelte Schriften* 11, ed. Rolf Tiedemann. Frankfurt am Main: Suhrkamp, 1974: 409–30.

Einleitung in die Musiksoziologie: Zwölf theoretische Vorlesungen. Reinbek bei Hamburg: Rowohlt, 1962, and in *Gesammelte Schriften* 14, ed. Rolf Tiedemann (Frankfurt am Main: Suhrkamp, 1973: 169–433.

"Erpresste Versöhnung," *Noten zur Literatur*, 1974, and in *Gesammelte Schriften* 11, ed. Rolf Tiedemann. Frankfurt am Main: Suhrkamp, 1974: 251–80.

"Erziehung nach Auschwitz," in *Kultur und Gesellschaft II*, and in *Gesammelte Schriften* 10.2, ed. Rolf Tiedemann, 1977, 674–90.

Erziehung zur Mündigkeit. Vorträge und Gespräche mit Hellmut Becker 1959–1969, ed. Gerd Kadelbach. Frankfurt am Main: Suhrkamp, 1970.

"Es ist mir micht möglich, die Vorlesung heute zu beginnen . . . Aufforderung zu einer Gedenkminute für Benno Ohnesorg in der Vorlesung über Aesthetik," in Kraushaar, *Frankfurter Schule und Studentenbewegung*, vol. 2, 1998: 241.

Frankfurter Adorno Blätter, IV and V. Munich: text + kritik, 1995–8.

"Gegen die Notstandgesetze," in Kraushaar, *Frankfurter Schule und Studentenbewegung*, vol. 2, 1998: 392.

Gesammelte Schriften, ed. Rolf Tiedemann et al. 20 vols. Frankfurt am Main: Suhrkamp, 1973–86.

Kierkegaard: Konstruktion des Ästhetischen. Frankfurt am Main: Suhrkamp, 1962.

Mahler. Eine musikalische Physiognomie. Frankfurt am Main: Suhrkamp, 1960, and in *Gesammelte Schriften* 13, ed. Rolf Tiedemann. Frankfurt am Main: Suhrkamp, 1971.

Moments musicaux. New edn. Frankfurt am Main: Suhrkamp, 1964.

"Musik und Sprache," *Forum*, 33 (Sept. 1956).

"'Optimische zu denken ist kriminell.' Eine Fernsehdiskussion über Samuel Beckett," *Frankfurter Adorno Blätter*, III (1994): 78–122.

Philosophie der neuen Musik, Gesammelte Schriften 12, ed. Rolf Tiedemann. Frankfurt am Main: Suhrkamp, 1975.

Philosophische Terminologie. 2 vols. Frankfurt am Main: Suhrkamp, 1974.

"Spätkapitalismus oder Industriegesellschaft," 1968.

"Thesen zur Kunstsoziologie," *Ohne Leitbild: Parva Aesthetics* (1967, 1968), and in *Gesammelte Schriften* 10.1, ed. Rolf Tiedemann. Frankfurt am Main: Suhrkamp, 1977: 367–74.

"Was bedeutet Aufarbeitung der Vergangenheit," in *Kulturkritik und Gesellschaft II*, and also in *Gesammelte Schriften* 10.2, ed. Rolf Tiedemann. Frankfurt am Main: Suhrkamp, 1977: 555–72.

"Wien und die Neue Musik," *Forum*, 73 (Jan. 1960): 27–30.

"Wissenschaftliche Erfahrung in Amerika," *Stichworte: Kritische Modelle 2*. Frankfurt am Main: Suhrkamp, 1969, and in *Gesammelte Schriften* 10.2, ed. Rolf Tiedemann. Frankfurt am Main: Suhrkamp, 1977: 702–40.

"Zum Kurras-Prozess," in Kraushaar, *Frankfurter Schule und Studentenbewegung*, vol. 2, 323–4.

"Zum Problem der musikalischen Analyse," lecture delivered on February 24, 1969, at the Hochschule für Musik und darstellende Kunst, Frankfurt am Main (tape recording and transcript in the Theodor W. Adorno Archive, Frankfurt am Main).

Adorno, Theodor W., Albert, Hans, Dahrendorf, Ralf, Habermas, Jürgen, Pilot, Harald, and Popper, Karl R., *Der Positivmusstreit in der deutschen Soziologie*. Berlin: Hermann Luchterhand, 1969.

Adorno, Theodor W., and Benjamin, Walter, *Theodor Adorno–Walter Benjamin: Briefwechsel 1928–1940*, ed. Henry Lonitz. Frankfurt am Main: Suhrkamp, 1994.

Adorno, Theodor W., and Dirks, Walter (eds.), *Gruppenexperiment. Ein Studienbericht (Frankfurter Beiträge zur Soziologie*, vol. 2). Frankfurt am Main: Europäische Verlagsanstalt, 1955.

Adorno, Theodor W., Friedeburg, Ludwig von, and Habermas, Jürgen, "Wir unterstützen den Protest unserer Studenten . . ." in Kraushaar, *Frankfurter Schule und Studentenbewegung*, vol. 2, 1998: 502–3.

Adorno, Theodor W., and Horkheimer, Max, "Die UdSSR und der Frieden," in Kraushaar, *Frankfurter Schule und Studentenbewegung*, vol. 2, 1998: K51–2.

Secondary Work Cited

Abbate, Carolyn, *Unsung Voices: Opera and Musical Narrative in the Nineteenth Century*. Princeton, NJ: Princeton University Press, 1991.

Agger, Ben, *The Discourse of Domination from the Frankfurt School to Postmodernism*. Northwestern University Studies in Phenomenology and Existential Philosophy. Evanston, IL: Northwestern University Press, 1992.

Alford, C. Fred, *Narcissism: Socrates, the Frankfurt School, and Psychoanalytic Theory*. New Haven: Yale University Press, 1988.

Alway, Joan, *Critical Theory and Political Possibilities: Conceptions of Emancipatory Politics in the Works of Horkheimer, Adorno, Marcuse, and Habermas*. Westport, CN: Greenwood Press, 1995.

Anderson, Kevin, *Lenin, Hegel, and Western Marxism*. Urbana: University of Illinois Press, 1996.

Arato, Andrew, *From Neo-Marxism to Democratic Theory: Essays on the Critical Theory of Soviet-type Societies*. Armonk, NY: M. E. Sharpe, 1993.

Arato, Andrew, and Gebhardt, Eike (eds.), *The Frankfurt School Reader*. New York: Urizen, 1979.

—— *The Essential Frankfurt School Reader*. Oxford: Blackwell, 1978; New York: Seabury, 1982.

Arendt, Hannah, *The Origins of Totalitarianism*. New York: Meridian, 1958.

Bahr, Ehrhard, and Schneider, Helmut J., "Art Desires Non-Art: The Dialectics of Art in Thomas Mann's *Doctor Faustus* in the Light of Theodor W. Adorno's Aesthetic Theory," in *Thomas Mann's Doctor Faustus: A Novel at the Margin of Modernism*, ed. Herbert Lehnert and C. Pfeiffer Peter. Columbus, SC: Camden House, 1991: 145–66.

Baker, Robert, "Crossings of Levinas, Derrida, and Adorno: Horizons of Nonviolence," *Diacritics: A Review of Contemporary Criticism*, 23/4 (1993): 12–41.

Baldacchino, John, *Post-Marxist Marxism*. Brookfield, VT: Avebury, 1996.

Baraka, Amiri, *Funk Lore*. Los Angeles: Littoral Books, 1996.

Barnouw, Dagmar, "Modernity and Enlightenment Thought," in *The Enlightenment and its Legacy: Studies in German Literature in Honor of Helga Slessarev*, ed. Sara Friedrichsmeyer and Barbara Becker Cantarino. Bonn: Bouvier, 1991: 1–14.

Barone, Anthony, "Wagner's *Parsifal* and the Theory of Late Style," *Cambridge Opera Journal*, 7 (1995): 37–54.

Barry, Davis, " 'Ist uns nichts ubrig?': The Residue of Resistance in Goethe's *Iphigenie auf Tauris*," *German Life and Letters*, 49 (1996): 283–96.

Bauer, Karin, *Adorno's Nietzschean Narratives: Critiques of Ideology, Readings of Wagner*. Albany: State University of New York Press, 1999.

Baugh, Bruce, "Left-Wing Elitism: Adorno on Popular Culture," *Philosophy and Literature*, 14 (1990): 65–78.

Beierwaltes W., *Identität und Dialektik*. Frankfurt am Main: Suhrkamp, 1980.

Benhabib, Seyla, Butler, Judith, Cornell, Drucilla, and Fraser, Nancy, *Feminist Contentions: A Philosophical Exchange*. London: Routledge, 1995.

Benjamin, Andrew, "Tradition and Experience: Walter Benjamin's 'Some Motifs in Baudelaire,'" in *The Problems of Modernity: Adorno and Benjamin*, ed. Andrew Benjamin. London and New York: Routledge, 1988 (1989): 122–40.

Benjamin, Andrew (ed.), *The Problems of Modernity: Adorno and Benjamin*. London and New York: Routledge, 1988 (1989).

Benjamin, Walter, *Illuminations*, trans. Harry Zohn. New York: Schocken, 1969; London: Fontana, 1973.

—— *The Origin of German Tragic Drama*, trans. J. Osborne. London: New Left Books, 1977; Verso, 1985.

—— *Theodor Adorno and Walter Benjamin: The Complete Correspondence, 1928–1940*. Cambridge, MA: Harvard University Press, 1999.

—— "The Work of Art in the Age of Mechanical Reproduction," in *Illuminations*, 1969.

Bent, Margaret, "Fact and Value in Contemporary Scholarship," *Musical Times*, 127 (1986): 85–9.

Bergeron, Katherine, and Bohlman, Philip V. (eds.), *Disciplining Music: Musicology and its Canons*. Chicago: University of Chicago Press, 1992.

Berman, Russell A., "The Peace Movement Debate," *Telos*, 57 (1983): 129–44.

Bernasconi, Robert, *Heidegger in Question: The Art of Existing*. Atlantic Highlands, NJ: Humanities Press, 1993.

Bernstein, Jay, "Aesthetic Alienation: Heidegger, Adorno, and Truth at the End of Art," in *Life after Postmodernism: Essays on Value and Culture*, ed. John Fekete. New York: St. Martin's Press, 1987: 86–119.

—— "Art against Enlightenment: Adorno's Critique of Habermas," in *The Problems of Modernity: Adorno and Benjamin*, ed. Andrew Benjamin. London and New York: Routledge, 1988 (1989): 49–66.

—— *The Fate of Art: Aesthetic Alienation from Kant to Derrida and Adorno*. University Park: Pennsylvania State University Press, 1992.

—— *The Frankfurt School: Critical Assessments*. London and New York: Routledge, 1994.

—— "Grand Narratives," in *On Paul Ricoeur: Narrative and Interpretation*, ed. David Wood. London: Routledge, 1991: 102–23.

—— "Introduction," to T. W. Adorno, *The Culture Industry*. London: Routledge, 1995.

—— "Philosophy's Refuge: Adorno in Beckett," in *Philosophers' Poets*, ed. David Wood. London: Routledge, 1990: 177–91.

—— "The Rage against Reason," *Philosophy and Literature*, 10 (1986): 186–210.

Bernstein, Susan, "Journalism and German Identity: Communiqués from Heine, Wagner, and Adorno," *New German Critique*, 66 (1955): 65–93.

Beverley, John, "The Ideology of Postmodern Music and Left Politics," *Postmodern Culture: An Electronic Journal of Interdisciplinary Criticism*, 1/1 (1990): 37 paragraphs.

Biskind, Peter, *Seeing is Believing: How I Stopped Worrying and Came to Love the Fifties*. New York: Pantheon, 1983.

Blasius, Mark, and Phelan, Shane (eds.), *We Are Everywhere: A Historical Sourcebook of Gay and Lesbian Politics*. New York: Routledge, 1997.

Bloom, Harold, *The Anxiety of Influence*. New York: Norton, 1973.

Bodei R., "introduzione: Segni di distinzione," in *T. W. Adorno: Il gergo dell'autenticità*. Turin, 1989.

Boggs, Carl, *The Two Revolutions*. Boston: South End Press, 1984.

Boorstin, Daniel, *The Image: A Guide to Pseudo-Events in America*. New York: Atheneum, 1987. [First published in 1961.]

Born, Georgina, "Against Negation, for a Politics of Cultural Production: Adorno, Aesthetics, the Social," *Screen*, 34 (1993): 223–42.

Bottomore T. B., *The Frankfurt School*. Chichester: Tavistock, 1984.

Bowie, Andrew, "Music, Language and Modernity," in *The Problems of Modernity: Adorno and Benjamin*, ed. Andrew Benjamin. London and New York: Routledge, 1988 (1989): 67–85.

Brecht, Bertolt, "Radio as a Means of Communication," *Screen*, 20/3–4 (1979): 24–8.

Brett, Philip, Wood, Elizabeth, and Thomas, Gary C. (eds.), *Queering the Pitch: The New Gay and Lesbian Musicology*. New York: Routledge, 1994.

Bronner, Stephen Eric, and Kellner, Douglas (eds.), *Critical Theory and Society: A Reader*. New York: Routledge, 1989.

Brosio, Richard A., *The Frankfurt School: An Analysis of the Contradictions and Crises of Liberal Capitalist Societies*. Muncie, in Ball State University, 1980.

Brunkhorst, Hauke, *Adorno and Critical Theory*. Cardiff: University of Wales Press.

Brunkhorst, Hauke, and Daniel, Jamie Owen, "The Tenacity of Utopia: The Role of Intellectuals in Cultural Shifts within the Federal Republic of Germany," *New German Critique*, 55 (1992): 127–38.

Bubner R., "Adornos negative Dialektik," in *Adorno-Konferenz 1983*. Frankfurt am Main: Suhrkamp, 1983.

Buck-Morss, Susan, *The Dialectics of Seeing: Walter Benjamin and the Arcades Project*. Cambridge, MA: MIT Press, 1989.

—— *The Origins of Negative Dialectics: Theodor W. Adorno. Walter Benjamin and the Frankfurt Institute*. New York: Free Press, and Brighton: Harvester, 1977.

Burger, Christa, "Mimesis and Modernity," *Stanford Literature Review*, 3 (1986): 63–73.

Bürger, Peter, *Theory of the Avant-Garde*, trans. Michael Shaw. Manchester: Manchester University Press, 1984. [German edition published in 1974.]

—— "Theory of the Avant-garde and Critical Literary Science (1974)," in *Contemporary Marxist Literary Criticism*, ed. Francis Mulhern. London: Longman, 1992: 146–67.

Butler, Judith, "A 'Bad Writer' Bites Back," *New York Times* (Mar. 20, 1999): A15.

Butterfield, Bradley, "Enlightenment's Other in Patrick Suskind's *Das Parfum*: Adorno and the Ineffable Utopia of Modern Art," *Comparative Literature Studies*, 32 (1995): 401–18.

Cahn, Michael, "Subversive Mimesis: Theodor W. Adorno and the Modern Impasse of Critique," in *Mimesis in Contemporary Theory: An Interdisciplinary Approach*, vol. I: *The Literary and Philosophical Debate*, ed. Mihai Spariosu. Philadelphia: Benjamins, 1984: 27–64.

Caughie, John, "Adorno's Reproach: Repetition, Difference and Television Genre," *Screen*, 32 (1991): 127–53.

Champion, James W., "Tillich and the Frankfurt School: Parallels and Differences in Prophetic Criticism," *Soundings: An Interdisciplinary Journal*, 69 (1986): 512–30.

Collins, Jim, *Uncommon Cultures: Popular Culture and Post-Modernism*. New York: Routledge, 1987.

Connerton, Paul, *The Tragedy of Enlightenment: An Essay on the Frankfurt School*. Cambridge Studies in the History and Theory of Politics. Cambridge and New York: Cambridge University Press, 1980.

Connerton, Paul (ed.), *Critical Sociology: Selected Readings*. Harmondsworth, New York, etc.: Penguin, 1976.

Cook, Deborah, *The Culture Industry Revisited: Theodor W. Adorno on Mass Culture*. Lanham, MD: Rowman and Littlefield, 1996.

Cook, Nicholas, and Everist, Mark, "Analysing Performance and Performing Analysis," *Rethinking Music*, 239–61.

Cook, Nicholas, and Everist, Mark (eds.), *Rethinking Music*. Oxford: Oxford University Press, 1999.

Cooper, Harry, "On Uber Jazz: Replaying Adorno with the Grain," *October*, 75 (1996): 99–133.

Cornell, Drucilla, *Philosophy of the Limit*. London: Routledge, 1992.

Cramer, Erich, *Hitlers Antisemitismus und die Frankfurter Schule*. Düsseldorf: Droste, 1979.

Culver, Stuart, "What Manikins Want: The Wonderful Wizard of Oz and the Art of Decorating Dry Goods Windows," *Representations*, 21 (1988): 97–116.

Dahlhaus, Carl, *Schoenberg and the New Music*, trans. Derek Puffett and Alfred Clayton. Cambridge: Cambridge University Press, 1987.

Dallmayr, Fred, "Adorno and Heidegger," *Diacritics: A Review of Contemporary Criticism*, 19/3–4 (1989): 82–100.

Dallmayr, Fred R., *Between Freiburg and Frankfurt: Toward a Critical Ontology*. Amherst: University of Massachusetts Press, 1991.

Daniel, Jamie Owen, "'On Jazz!'" *Discourse: Journal for Theoretical Studies in Media and Culture*, 12 (1989): 36–69.

Dennis, Christopher J., *Adorno's Philosophy of Modern Music*. Lewiston, NY: Edwin Mellen, 1997.

Derrida, Jacques, "Ulysses Gramophone: Hear Say Yes in Joyce," in *Acts of Literature*, ed. Derek Attridge. New York: Routledge, 1995: 253–310.

Dews, Peter, "Adorno, Poststructuralism, and the Critique of Identity," in *The Problems of Modernity: Adorno and Benjamin*, ed. Andrew Benjamin. London and New York: Routledge, 1988 (1989): 1–22.

—— *Logics of Disintegration: Post-Structuralist Thought and the Claims of Critical Theory*. London: Verso, 1987.

Diner, Dan, "Reason and the 'Other': Horkheimer's Reflection on Anti-Semitism and Mass Annihilation," in *On Max Horkheimer*, ed. Seyla Benhabib, Wolfgang Bonss, and John McCole. Cambridge, MA: MIT Press, 1993; 346–60.

Donovan, Josephine, "Everyday Use and Moments of Being: Toward a Nondominative Aesthetic," in *Aesthetics in Feminist Perspective*, ed. Hilde Hein. Bloomington: Indiana University Press, 1993: 53–67.

Dubiel, Helmut, *Theory and Politics*. Cambridge, MA: MIT Press, 1985.

Dumm, Thomas L., "The Politics of Post-Modern Aesthetics: Habermas Contra Foucault," in *The Aesthetics of the Critical Theorists: Studies on Benjamin, Adorno,*

Marcuse, and Habermas, ed. Ronald Roblin. Lewiston, NY: Edwin Mellen, 1990: 476–510.

Dunayevskaya, Raya, "Absolute Negativity as New Beginning," in *Art and Logic in Hegel's Philosophy*, ed. Warren E. Steinkraus and Kenneth L. Schmitz. Atlantic Highlands, NJ: Humanities Press, 1980. [First published, Chicago: News and Letters Committees, 1974.]

—— *The Marxist-Humanist Theory of State Capitalism*. Chicago: News and Letters, 1992.

—— *Philosophy and Revolution: From Hegel to Sartre, and From Marx to Mao*. New York: Columbia University Press, 1989.

—— *The Raya Dunayevskaka Collection – Marxist-Humanism: A Half Century of its World Development*. Detroit: Wayne State University Archives of Labor and Urban Affairs.

—— *Rosa Luxemburg: Women's Liberation, and Marx's Philosophy of Revolution*. 2nd edn. Urbana, IL: University of Illinois Press, 1991.

—— *Women's Liberation and the Dialectics of Revolution: Reaching for the Future*. 2nd edn. Detroit: Wayne State University Press, 1995.

During, Simon, "Postmodernism or Post-Colonialism Today," *Textual Practice*, 1 (1987): 32–47.

Düttmann, Alexander Garcia, *Gedächtnis des Denkens. Versuch über Heidegger und Adorno*. Frankfurt am Main: Suhrkamp, 1991.

Eagleton, Terry, *The Ideology of the Aesthetic*. Ozford: Blackwell, 1990.

Edgar, Andrew, "An Introduction to Adorno's Aesthetics," *British Journal of Aesthetics*, 30 (1990): 46–56.

Edgar, Andrew, and Sedwick, Peter, "Adorno, Oakeshott, and the Voice of Poetry," in *Theorizing Culture: An Interdisciplinary Critique after Postmodernism*, ed. Barbara Adam and Stuart Allan. New York: New York University Press, 1995: 100–12.

Edge, Simon, *With Friends Like These . . . Marxism and Gay Politics*. London: Cassell.

Fanon, Frantz, *Black Skin, White Masks*, trans. Charles Lam Markmann. New York: Grove Press, 1967.

—— "Racism and Culture," *Toward the African Revolution*, trans. Haakon Chevalier. New York: Grove Press, 1968.

—— "This is the Voice of Algeria," *Studies in a Dying Colonialism*, trans. Haakon Chevalier. New York: Grove Press, 1967.

Feenberg, Andrew, *Lukács, Marx, and the Sources of Critical Theory*. Totowa, NJ: Rowman and Littlefield, 1981.

Fenves, Peter, "Image and Chatter: Adorno's Construction of Kierkegaard," *Diacritics: A Review of Contemporary Criticism*, 22 (1992): 100–14.

Floyd, Wayne W., *Theology and the Dialectics of Otherness: On Reading Bonhoeffer and Adorno*. Lanham, MD: University Press of America, 1988.

Fluxman, Tony, "Bob Dylan and the Dialectic of Enlightenment: Critical Lyricist in the Age of High Capitalism," *Theoria*, 77 (1991): 91–111.

Forgacs, David, "Marxist Literary Theories," in *Modern Literary Theory: A Comparative Introduction*, ed. Ann Jefferson. Totowa, NJ: Barnes and Noble, 1982: 134–69.

Foucault, Michel, "Critical Theory/Intellectual History," in *Politics, Philosophy, Culture: Interviews and Other Writings, 1977–1984*. New York: Routledge, 1988.

——*History of Sexuality*, vol. 1. New York: Random House, 1978.

Freud, Sigmund, *Moses and Monotheism*, trans. James Strachey. London: Hogarth Press, 1939.

——*Totem and Taboo*, trans. James Strachey. New York: W. W. Norton, 1950.

Friedman, George, *The Political Philosophy of the Frankfurt School*. Ithaca, NY: Cornell University Press, 1981.

Fromm, Erich, "Zum Gefühl der Ohnmacht," *Zeitschrift für Sozialforschung*, 4 (1937): 95–118.

Gendron, Bernard, "Theodor Adorno Meets the Cadillacs," in *Studies in Entertainment: Critical Approaches to Mass Culture*, ed. Tania Modleski. Bloomington: Indiana University Press, 1986: 18–36.

Geuss, Raymond, "Art and Criticism in Adorno's Aesthetics," *European Journal of Philosophy*, 6 (1998): 297–317.

——*The Idea of a Critical Theory: Habermas and the Frankfurt School*. Cambridge and New York: Cambridge University Press, 1981.

——*Morality, Culture and History: Essays in German Philosophy*. Cambridge: Cambridge University Press, 1999.

Gibson, Nigel, "Jammin' the Airwaves and Tuning into the Revolution: The Dialectics of the Radia in *L'An de la révolution algérienne*," in *Fanon: A Critical Reader*, ed. Lewis R. Gordon, T. Denean Sharpley-Whiting, and Renee T. White. Oxford: Blackwell, 1996: 272–82.

Gillespie, Susan, "Translating Adorno: Language, Music, and Performance," *Musical Quarterly*, 79 (1995): 55–79.

Giordano, John Thomas, "The Destinies of the Work of Art: Aesthetic Theories in Hölderlin and Adorno." Dissertation, Duquesne University, 1996.

Goehr, Lydia, *The Imaginary Museum of Musical Works: An Essay on the Philosophy of Music*. Oxford: Oxford University Press, 1992.

Goldhagen, Daniel Jonah, *Hitler's Willing Executioners: Ordinary Germans and the Holocaust*. New York: Knopf, 1996.

Goldmann, Lucien, *Cultural Creation*. St. Louis: Telos Press, 1970.

Gomez Mariano, Antonio, "The (Relative) Autonomy of Artistic Expression: Bakhtin and Adorno," *Critical Studies: A Journal of Critical Theory, Literature and Culture*, 1 (1989): 95–105.

Goodman, Nelson, *Fact, Fiction, and Forecast*. Indianapolis: Bobbs-Merrill, 1965. [See chapter IV for his underlying argument that the predictive regularity comprising inductive validity is a function of habitual linguistic practices.]

——*Ways of Wordmaking*. Indianapolis: Hackett, 1978.

Gramsci, Antonio, *Prison Notebooks*. London: Lawrence and Wishart, and New York: International Publishers, 1971.

Grene, David, *Reality and the Heroic Pattern: Last Plays of Ibsen, Shakespeare, and Sophocles*. Chicago: University of Chicago Press, 1967.

Grenz, Friedemann, *Adornos Philosophie in Grundbegriffen*, Frankfurt am Main: Suhrkamp, 1974.

Grünenberg, Antonia, *Antifascismus: ein deutscher Mythos.* Reinbek bei Hamburg: Rowohlt, 1993.

Habermas, Jürgen, *A Berlin Republic: Writings on Germany,* trans. Steven Rendall. Lincoln: University of Nebraska Press, 1997.

—— "The Entwinement of Myth and Enlightenment: Re-reading *Dialectic of Enlightenment,*" *New German Critique,* 26 (1982): 13–30.

—— *The Philosophical Discourse of Modernity: Twelve Lectures,* trans. Frederick G. Lawrence. Cambridge, MA: MIT Press, 1987.

—— *Theory of Communicative Action,* trans. Thomas McCarthy. 2 vols. Boston: Beacon Press, 1984.

Halle, Randall, "Between Marxism and Psychoanalysis: Antifascism and Antihomosexuality in the Frankfurt School," *Journal of Homosexuality,* 29 (1995): 295–317.

Hamilton, Carol V., "All That Jazz Again: Adorno's Sociology of Music," *Popular Music and Society,* 15/3 (1991): 31–40.

Hanisch, Ernst, "The Politics of Wagner," in *Wagner Handbook,* ed. Ulrich Müller. Cambridge, MA: Harvard University Press, 1992.

Hannush, Mufid J., "Adorno and Sartre: A Convergence of Two Methodological Approaches," *Journal of Phenomenological Psychology,* 4 (1973): 297–313.

Hansen, Miriam, "Mass Culture as Hieroglyphic Writing: Adorno, Derrida, Kracauer," *New German Critique,* 56 (1992): 43–73.

—— "Of Mice and Ducks: Benjamin and Adorno on Disney," *South Atlantic Quarterly,* 92 (1993): 27–61.

Harding, James Martin, *Adorno and "A writing of the ruins."* Albany: State University of New York Press, 1997.

—— "Adorno, Ellison, and the Critique of Jazz," *Cultural Critique,* 31 (1995): 129–58.

—— "Historical Dialectics and the Autonomy of Art in Adorno's *Aesthetics Theorie,*" *Journal of Aesthetics and Art Criticism,* 50 (1992): 183–95.

—— "Integrating Atomization: Adorno Reading Berg Reading Buchner," *Theatre Journal,* 44 (1992): 1–13.

—— "The Resurgence of Negated Origins: A Configuration of Adorno, Falstaff and Woyzeck." Dissertation, University of Maryland, 1991.

—— "Trying to Understand Godot: Adorno, Beckett, and the Senility of Historical Dialectics," *CLIO: A Journal of Literature, History, and the Philosophy of History,* 23 (1993): 1–22.

Hardy, Thomas, *Jude the Obscure.* New York: Penguin, 1954. [First published in 1896.]

Harris H. S., *Hegel: Phenomenology and System.* Indianapolis: Hackett, 1995.

Hegel G. W. F., *Enzyklopädie der philosophischen Wissenschaften I. Werke 8.* Frankfurt am Main: Suhrkamp, 1970: 368–9.

—— *Lectures on the History of Philosophy,* trans. E. S. Haldane. 4 vols. London: Routledge, 1892.

—— *Lectures on the Philosophy of Religion,* trans. E. B. Speirs and J. Burdon Sanderson. 3 vols. London: Routledge, 1962.

—— *Phänomenologie des Geistes.* Berlin: Akademie Verlag, 1998. [First published in 1807.]

—— *The Phenomenology of Mind*, trans. J. B. Baillie. New York: Harper and Row, 1967.

—— *The Phenomenology of Spirit*, trans. A. V. Miller. Oxford: Oxford University Press, 1977.

—— *The Philosophy of History*, trans. J. Sibree. New York: Dover, 1956.

—— *The Philosophy of Mind*, trans. W. Wallace. Part III of *The Encyclopaedia of the Philosophical Sciences*. Oxford: Oxford University Press, 1971.

—— *Reason in History*, trans. R. S. Hartman. Indianapolis: Bobbs-Merrill, 1953.

—— *The Science of Logic*, trans. A. V. Miller. Atlantic Highlands, NJ: Humanities Press, 1989.

—— *Smaller Logic*, trans. William Wallace. Oxford: Oxford University Press, 1975.

Heidegger, Martin, *Basic Writings*, ed. David Farrell Krell. San Francisco: Harper-Collins, 1993.

—— *Being and Time*, trans. John Macquarrie and Edward Robinson. New York: Harper and Row, 1962.

—— *Besinnung, Gesamtausgabe*, vol. 66. Frankfurt am Main: Klostermann, 1997.

—— *Die Geschichte des Seyns, Gesamtausgabe*, vol. 69. Frankfurt am Main: Klostermann, 1998.

—— *Hegels Begriff der Erfahrung*. Frankfurt am Main: Klostermann, 1963.

—— "The Origin of the Work of Art," in *Basic Writings*, ed. David Farrell Krell. San Francisco: HarperCollins, 1993.

—— *Sein und Zeit*. Tübingen: Max Niemeyer, 1986.

—— "The Way to Language," in *Basic Writings*, ed. David Farrell Krell. San Francisco: HarperCollins, 1993.

Held, David, *Introduction to Critical Theory: Horkheimer to Habermas*. Berkeley: University of California Press, 1980.

Hewitt, Andrew, "A Feminine Dialectic of Enlightenment? Horkheimer and Adorno Revisited," *New German Critique*, 56 (1992): 143–70.

Hohendahl, Peter Uwe, "Adorno Criticism Today," *New German Critique*, 56 (1992): 3–15.

—— "Autonomy of Art: Looking Back at Adorno's *Aesthetische Theorie*," *German Quarterly*, 54 (1981): 133–48.

—— "The Displaced Intellectual? Adorno's American Years Revisited," *New German Critique*, 56 (1992): 76–100.

—— *Prismatic Thought: Theodor W. Adorno*. Modern German Culture and Literature. Lincoln: University of Nebraska Press, 1995.

Holtmeier, Ludwig, "Nicht Kunst? Nicht Wissenschaft? Zur Lage der Musiktheorie," *Musik & Ästhetik*, 1 (1997): 119–36.

Holtmeier, Ludwig, Klein, Richard, et al., "Editorial," *Musik & Ästhetik*, 1 (1997): 5–12.

Horkheimer, Max, *Critical Theory*. New York: Seabury Press, 1972.

—— "Die Juden und Europa," *Gesammelte Schriften*, vol. 4. Frankfurt am Main: Fischer, 1988.

—— *Gesammelte Schriften*, ed. Alfred Schmidt and Gunzelin Schmid Noerr. Frankfurt am Main: Fischer 1987, 1999.

—— "Nachgelassene Schriften 1931–1949," *Gesammelte Schriften*, vol. 12, ed. Alfred Schmidt and Gunzelin Schmid Noerr. Frankfurt am Main: Fischer, 1985.

—— "Sociological Background of the Psychoanalytical Approach," in *Anti-Semitism: A Social Disease*, ed. Ernst Simmel. New York: International Universities Press, 1946.

—— "Traditional and Critical Theory," in *Max Horkheimer: Critical Theory, Selected Essays*, trans. M. J. O'Connell. New York: Continuum, 1992.

Horkheimer, Max, and Adorno, Theodor W., *Dialectic of Enlightenment*, trans. John Cumming. New York: Continuum, 1973, 1989.

Hösle, V., *Hegels System*. 2 vols. Hamburg, 1988.

Huhn, Thomas, "The Sublimation of Culture in Adorno's Aesthetics," in *The Aesthetics of the Critical Theorists: Studies on Benjamin, Adorno, Marcuse, and Habermas*, ed. Ronald Roblin. Lewiston, NY: Edwin Mellen, 1990: 291–307.

Huhn, Thomas, and Zuidervaart, Lambert, *The Semblance of Subjectivity: Essays in Adorno's Aesthetic Theory*. Cambridge, MA: MIT Press, 1997.

Hullot-Kentor, Robert, "Back to Adorno," *Telos*, 81 (1989): 5–29.

—— "Notes on *Dialectic of Enlightenment*: Translating the Odysseus Essay," *New German Critique*, 56 (1992): 101–8.

—— "Odysseus or Myth and Enlightenment," *New Geman Critique*, 56 (1992): 109–41.

Huyssen, Andreas, "Adorno in Reverse: From Hollywood to Richard Wagner," *New German Critique*, 29 (1983): 8–38.

—— *After the Great Divide: Modernism, Mass Culture, Postmodernism*. Bloomington: Indiana University Press, 1986.

—— "Introduction to Adorno," *New German Critique*, 6 (Fall 1975).

Ignatieff, Michael, *Blood and Belonging: Journeys into the New Nationalism*. New York: Farrar, Straus, and Giroux, 1993.

Ingram, David, "Completing the Project of Enlightenment: Habermas on Aesthetic Rationality," in *The Aesthetics of the Critical Theorists: Studies on Benjamin, Adorno, Marcuse, and Habermas*, ed. Ronald Roblin. Lewiston, NY: Edwin Mellen, 1990: 359–421.

—— *Critical Theory and Philosophy*. New York: Paragon.

Institut für Sozialforschung, *Aspects of Sociology* (by the Frankfurt Institute of Social Research), trans. John Viertel. Boston: Beacon Press, 1972.

—— *Soziologische Exkurse*. Frankfurter Beiträge zur Philosophie, vol. 4. Frankfurt am Main: EuropUaische Verlagsanstalt, 1955.

Isenberg, Noah, "Critical Theory at the Barricades," *Lingua Franca*, 8 (1998): 19–22.

Israel, Nico. *Outlandish: Writing between Exile and Diaspora*. Palo Alto, CA: Stanford University Press, 2000.

Italiaander, Rolf (ed.), *Weder Krankheit noch Verbrechen. Plädoyer für eine Minderheit*. Hamburg: Gala Verlag, 1969.

Jackson, George, *Blood in My Eye*. Baltimore, MD: Black Classic Press, 1990.

Jameson, Fredric, *Late Marxism: Adorno, or, The Persistence of the Dialectic*. London and New York: Verso, 1990.

—— *Marxism and Form*. Princeton, NJ: Princeton University Press, 1971.

——"Reification and Utopia in Mass Culture," *Social Text*, 1 (1979): 130–48.

——"T. W. Adorno, or, Historical Tropes," *Salmagundi*, 2 (1967): 3–43.

Jameson, Fredric (ed.), *Aesthetics and Politics*. London: Verso, 1980.

Jarvis, Simon, *Adorno: A Critical Introduction*. New York: Routledge, 1998.

Jay, Martin, *Adorno*. Cambridge, MA: Harvard University Press, 1984.

——"Adorno and Kracauer: Notes on a Troubled Friendship," in *Permanent Exiles: Essays on the Intellectual Migration from Germany to America*. New York: Columbia University Press, 1986, pp. 217–36.

——"Adorno in America," *New German Critique*, 31 (1984): 157–82.

——*The Dialectical Imagination: A History of the Frankfurt School and the Institute of Social Research, 1923–1950*. Boston: Little, Brown; London: Heinemann, 1973.

——"The Jews and the Frankfurt School: Critical Theory's Analysis of Anti-Semitism," in *Permanent Exiles: Essays on the Intellectual Migration from Germany to America*. New York: Columbia University Press, 1986: 90–100.

——*Marxism and Totality*. Berkeley: University of California Press, 1984.

Jennings, Michael, *Dialectical Images: Walter Benjamin's Theory of Literary Criticism*. Ithaca, NY: Cornell University Press, 1987.

Johannes, Rolf, "Das ausgesparte Zentrum. Adornos Verhältnis zur Ökonomie," in *Soziologue in Spätkapitalismus. Zur Gesellschaftstheorie Theodor W. Adornos*, ed. Gerhard Schweppenhäuser. Darmstadt: Wissenschaftliche Buchgesellschaft, 1995.

Johnson, Janet, "Review of *Antonin Dvorák: Symphony from the New World*, CD-ROM Companion Series, by Robert Winter," *Journal of the American Musicological Society*, 49 (1996): 114–26.

Kadelbach, Gerd, "Persönliche Begegnungen mit Theodor W. Adorno im Frankfurter Funkhaus," in *Politische Pädagogik. Beiträge zur Humanisierung der Gesellschaft*, ed. Friedhelm Zubke. Frankfurt am Main: Deutscher Studien Verlag, 1990: 51–2.

Kaufman, Robert, "Legislators of the Post-Everything World: Shelley's Defence of Adorno," *ELH*, 63 (1996): 707–33.

Kellner, Douglas, "Critical Theory and British Cultural Studies: The Missed Articulation," in *Cultural Methodologies*, ed. Jim McGuigan. London: Sage, 1997: 12–41.

——"Critical Theory and Ideology Critique," in *The Aesthetics of the Critical Theorists: Studies on Benjamin, Adorno, Marcuse, and Habermas*, ed. Ronald Roblin. Lewiston, NY: Edwin Mellen, 1990: 85–123.

——*Critical Theory, Marxism, and Modernity*. Baltimore, MD: Johns Hopkins University Press, 1989.

——"Critical Theory, Mass Communications, and Popular Culture," *Telos*, 62 (1984): 196–206.

——*Karl Korsch: Revolutionary Theory*. Austin: Texas University Press, 1979.

——"Kulturindustrie und Massenkommunikation. Die Kritische Theorie und ihre Folgen," in *Sozialforschung als Kritik*, ed. Wolfgang Bonss and Axel Honneth. Frankfurt am Main: Suhrkamp, 1982: 482–514.

——*Media Culture: Cultural Studies, Identity and Politics between the Modern and the Postmodern*. London: Routledge, 1995.

—— "Political Economy and Cultural Studies: Overcoming the Divide," in *Cultural Studies in Question*, ed. Marjorie Ferguson and Peter Golding. London: Sage, 1997: 102–20.

Kellner, Douglas, and Ryan, Michael, *Camera Politica: Politics and Ideology in Contemporary Hollywood Cinema*. Bloomington: University of Indiana Press, 1988.

Kerman, Joseph, "American Musicology in the 1990s," *Journal of Musicology*, 9 (1991): 131–44.

—— *The Beethoven Quartets*. New York: Knopf, 1967; reprint, Norton, 1979.

—— "Communications," *Journal of the American Musicological Society*, 18 (1965): 426–7.

—— *Contemplating Music: Challenges to Musicology*. Cambridge, MA: Harvard University Press, 1985.

—— *Opera as Drama*. Rev edn. Berkeley: University of California Press, 1988.

—— "A Profile for American Musicology," *Journal of the American Musicological Society*, 18 (1965): 61–9.

Kierkegaard, Søren, *Repetition*, ed. and trans. Edward V. Hong and Edna Hong. Princeton, NJ: Princeton University Press, 1983.

—— "Une première et dernière explication," in *Post-Scriptum aux miettes philosophiques*, trans. Paul Petit. Paris: Gallimard, 1949.

Kistner, Ulrike, "Writing 'After Auschwitz': On the Impossibility of a Postscript," *Acta Germanica: Jahrbuch des Germanistenverbandes im Sudlichen Afrika*, 21 (1992): 171–83.

Korsgaard, Christine M., *The Sources of Normativity*. Cambridge: Cambridge University Press, 1996.

Koval, Howard, "Homogenization of Culture in Capitalist Society," *Popular Music and Society*, 12 (1988): 1–16.

Krahl, Hans-Jürgen, "The Political Contradictions in Adorno's Critical Theory," *Telos*, 21 (1974): 164–7. [Originally published as "Der politische Widerspruch in der kritischen Theorie Adornos," *Frankfurter Rundschau,* Aug. 13, 1969; reprinted in Krahl, *Konstitution und Klassenkampf*, Frankfurt am Main: Verlag Neue Kritik, 1971; in Kraushaar, *Frankfurter Schule und Studentenbewegung*, vol. 2, 1998: 673–5; and in *Foundations of the Frankfurt School of Social Research*, ed. Judith Markus and Zoltán Tar. New Brunswick, NJ: Humanities Press, 1984: 307–10.]

Krakauer, Eric L., *The Disposition of the Subject: Reading Adorno's Dialectic of Technology*. Evanston, IL: Northwestern University Press, 1998.

Krämer, H., *Platone e i fondameni della metafisica*. Milan, 1989.

Kramer, Laurence, *Music as Cultural Practice, 1800–1900*. Berkeley: University of California Press, 1990.

Kraushaar, Wolfgang (ed.), *Frankfurter Schule und Studentenbewegung. Von der Flaschenpost zum Molotowcocktail 1946 bis 1995*. 3 vols. Hamburg: Rogner and Bernhard, 1998.

Krukowski, Lucian, "Form and Protest in Atonal Music: A Meditation on Adorno." *Bucknell Review*, 29 (1984): 105–24.

La Motte, Diether de, "Adornos musikalische Analysen," in *Adorno und die Musik*, ed. Otto Kollerisch. Graz: Universal Edition, 1979: 52–63.

Lacoue-Labarthe, Philippe, and Bresnick, Adam, "The Caesura of Religion," in *Opera through Other Eyes*, ed. J. Levin David. Palo Alto, CA: Stanford University Press, 1993: 45–77.

Larsen, Neil, Concha, Jaime, and Millet, Kitty, *Modernism and Hegemony: A Materialist Critique of Aesthetic Agencies*. Minneapolis: University of Minnesota Press, 1990.

Lazarsfeld, Paul, "An Episode in the History of Social Research: A Memoir," in *The European Migration*, ed. Donald Fleming and Bernard Bailyn. Cambridge, MA: Harvard University Press, 1969.

—— *Main Trends in Sociology*. London: Allen and Unwin, 1973. [First published in 1970.]

Lazarus, Neil, *Nationalism and Cultural Practice in the Postcolonial World*. Cambridge: Cambridge University Press,

Leppert, Richard, *The Sight of Sound: Music, Representation, and the History of the Body*. Berkeley: University of California Press, 1995.

Leppert, Richard, and McClary, Susan (eds.), *Music and Society: The Politics of Composition, Performance and Reception*. Cambridge: Cambridge University Press, 1987.

Levin, Thomas Y., "For the Record: Adorno on Music in the Age of its Technological Reproducibility," *October*, 55 (1990): 23–47.

—— "Nationalities of Language: Adorno's Fremdwörter: An Introduction to 'On the Question: What is German?'," *New German Critique*, 36 (1985): 111–19.

Levin, Thomas Y., and von der Linn, Michael, "Elements of a Radio Theory: Adorno and the Princeton Radio Research Project," *Musical Quarterly*, 78 (1994): 316–24.

Lewis, Pericles, "The 'True' Homer: Myth and Enlightenment in Vico, Horkheimer, and Adorno," *New Vico Studies*, 10 (1992): 24–35.

Lippman, Edward, *A History of Western Musical Aesthetics*. Lincoln: University of Nebraska Press, 1992.

Lobkowitz, Nicholas, *Theory and Practice: History of a Concept from Aristotle to Marx*. Notre Dame, IN: University of Notre Dame Press, 1967.

Locke, Ralph, "Musicology and/as Social Concern: Imagining the Relevant Musicologist," in *Rethinking Music*, ed. Nicholas Cook and Mark Everist. Oxford: Oxford University Press, 1999: 499–530.

Löwenthal, Leo, "On Sociology of Literature," in *Literature and Mass Culture*. New Brunswick: Transaction Books, 1984.

—— "Recollections of Theodor W. Adorno," *Telos*, 61 (Fall 1984): 257–73.

Lowinsky, Edward E., "Character and Purposes of American Musicology: A Reply to Joseph Kerman," *Journal of the American Musicological Society*, 18 (1965): 222–34.

Lukács, Georg, *History and Class Consciousness*, trans. Rodney Livingstone. Cambridge, MA: MIT Press, 1971.

—— *Political Writings*. London: New Left Books, 1972.

—— *Theory of the Novel*, trans. Anna Bostock. Cambridge, MA: MIT Press, 1971.

Lunn, Eugene, The Frankfurt School in the Development of the Mass Culture Debate," in *The Aesthetics of the Critical Theorists: Studies on Benjamin, Adorno, Marcuse, and Habermas*, ed. Ronald Roblin. Lewiston, NY: Edwin Mellen, 1990: 26–84.

Lyotard, Jean-François, "Adorno as Devil," *Telos*, 19 (1974): 127–37.

Mahnkopf, Claus-Steffen, "Adorno und die musikalische Analytik," in *Mit den Ohren denken: Adornos Philosophie der Musik*, ed. Richard Klein and Claus-Steffen Mahnkopf. Frankfurt am Main: Suhrkamp, 1998: 240–7.

Mann, Thomas, *Doctor Faustus: The Life of the German Composer Adrian Leverkuhn*, trans. H. T. Lowe-Porter. New York: Vintage, 1948.

Mannheim, Karl, *Ideology and Utopia: An Introduction to the Sociology of Knowledge*, trans. Louis Wirth and Edward Shils. New York: Harcourt, 1960.

Marcuse, Herbert, "The Foundations of Historical Materialism," *Studies in Critical Philosophy*. Boston: Beacon Press, 1973: 1–48.

——*Reason and Revolution*. Boston: Beacon Press, 1960.

Marsh, James L., "Adorno's Critique of Stravinsky," *New German Critique*, 28 (1983): 147–69.

Martin, Bill, *Music of Yes: Structure and Vision in Progressive Rock*. Chicago: Open Court, 1996.

Marx, Karl, *Capital: A Critique of Political Economy*, vol. 1, trans. Ben Fowkes. London: Penguin, and New York: Vintage, 1976, 1977. [German edition first published in 1867.]

——*Grundrisse*. London: Penguin, 1973.

——*Value Studies*, trans. Albert Dragstedt. London: New Park, 1976.

——*Writings of the Young Marx on Philosophy and Society*, ed. and trans. Loyd D. Easton and Kurt H. Guddat. Garden City, NY: Doubleday, 1967.

Marx, Karl, and Engels, Frederick, *A Marx–Engels Reader*, ed. Robert Tucker. New York: Norton, 1978.

Matthews, John, "Faulkner and the Culture Industry," in *The Cambridge Companion to William Faulkner*, ed. Philip Weinstein. New York: Cambridge University Press, 1995: 51–74.

Maus, Fred Everett, "Concepts of Musical Unity," in *Rethinking Music*, ed. Nicholas Cook and Mark Everist. Oxford: Oxford University Press, 1999: 171–92.

McCallum, Patricia, "Michelet's Narrative Practice: Naturality, Populism, and the Intellectual." Dissertation, 1985.

McClary, Susan, *Feminine Endings: Music, Gender, and Sexuality*. Minneapolis: University of Minnesota Press, 1991.

McCormack, W. J., "Seeing Darkly: Notes on T. W. Adorno and Samuel Beckett," *Hermathena: A Trinity College Dublin Review*, 141 (1986): 22–44.

McDowell, John, *Mind and World*. Cambridge, MA: Harvard University Press, 1994.

McLaughlin, Kenneth, *Writing in Parts: Imitation and Exchange in Nineteenth-Century Literature*. Palo Alto, CA: Stanford University Press, 1995.

Menke-Eggars, Christoph, *The Sovereignty of Art: Aesthetic Negativity in Adorno and Derrida*. Cambridge, MA: MIT Press, 1998.

Mészáros, István, *Beyond Capital*. London: Merlin, 1995.

Meyer, Leonard B., *Music, the Arts, and Ideas: Patterns and Predictions in Twentieth-Century Music*. Chicago: University of Chicago Press, 1967.

Michel, Andrea, "Formalism in Psychoanalysis: On the Politics of Primitivism in Carl Einstein," in *The Imperialist Imagination: German Colonialism and its Legacy*, ed. Sara

Friedrichsmeyer, Sara Lennox, and Suzanne Zantop. Ann Arbor: University of Michigan Press, 1998.

Middleton, Richard, *Studying Popular Music*. Milton Keynes: Open University Press, 1990.

Miles, Stephen, "Critical Musicology and the Problem of Mediation," *Notes*, 53 (1997): 722–50.

——"Critics of Disenchantment," *Notes*, 52 (1995): 11–38.

Mills, Patricia, *Feminist Interpretations of Hegel*. University Park: Pennsylvania State University Press, 1996.

Mills, Patricia Jagentowicz, *Woman, Nature, and Psyche*. New Haven: Yale University Press, 1987.

Miyoshi, Masao, "'Globalization,' Culture, and the University," in *The Cultures of Globalization*, ed. Fredric Jameson and Masao Miyoshi. Durham, NC: Duke University Press, 1998: 247–72.

Mörchen, Hermann, *Adorno und Heidegger: Untersuchungen einer philosophischen Kommunikationsverqeigerung*. Stuttgart: Klett-Cotta, 1981.

——*Macht und Herrschaft im Denken von Heidegger und Adorno*. Stuttgart: Klett-Cotta, 1980.

Morrison, David E., "Kultur and Culture: The Case of Theodor W. Adorno and Paul F. Lazarsfeld," *Social Research*, 45/2 (Summer 1978).

Mundhenk, Michael, "Appropriating (Life-)History through Autobiographical Writing: André Gorz's *The Traitor, a Dialectical Inquiry into the Self*," *Prose Studies*, 8 (1985): 81–96.

Nagele, Rainer, "The Scene of the Other. Theodor W. Adorno's Negative Dialectic in the Context of Poststructuralism," *Boundary 2: A Journal of Postmodern Literature and Culture*, 11 (1982): 59–79.

Navasky, Victor, *Naming Names*. New York: Viking, 1980.

Nicholsen, Shierry Weber, "The Curious Realist: On Siegfried Kracauer," *New German Critique*, 54 (1991): 159–77.

——*Exact Imagination, Late Work: On Adorno's Aesthetics*. Cambridge, MA: MIT Press, 1997.

——"Toward a More Adequate Reception of Adorno's Aesthetic Theory: Configurational Form in Adorno's Aesthetic Writings," *Cultural Critique*, 18 (1991): 31–54.

Nye, William P., "Theodor Adorno on Jazz: A Critique of Critical Theory," *Popular Music and Society*, 12/4 (1988): 69–73.

Ogden, Thomas H., *The Matrix of the Mind: Object Relations and the Psychoanalytic Dialogue*. Northvale, NJ: Jason Aronson, 1986.

O'Neill, John, *On Critical Theory*. New York: Seabury Press, 1976.

Oosterhuis, Harry, "The 'Jews' of the Antifascist Left: Homosexuality and Socialist Resistance to Nazism," *Journal of Homosexuality*, 29 (1995): 227–57.

Osborne, Peter, "Adorno and the Metaphysics of Modernism: The Problem of a 'Postmodern' Art," in *The Problems of Modernity: Adorno and Benjamin*, ed. Andrew Benjamin. London and New York: Routledge, 1988 (1989): 23–48.

——"A Marxism for the Postmodern? Jameson's Adorno," *New German Critique*, 56 (1992): 171–92.

Paddison, Max, *Adorno, Modernism and Mass Culture: Essays on Critical Theory and Music*. London: Kahn and Averill, 1996.

——"Adorno's Aesthetic Theory," *Music Analysis*, 6 (1987): 355–77.

——*Adorno's Aesthetics of Music*. Cambridge and New York: Cambridge University Press, 1993.

——"The Critique Criticized: Adorno and Popular Music," in *Popular Music 2: Theory and Method*, ed. Richard Middleton and David Horn. Cambridge: Cambridge University Press, 1982: 200–18.

——"The Language Character of Music," revised version in *Mit den Ohren denken: Adornos Philosophie der Musik*, ed. Richard Klein and Claus-Steffen Mahnkopf. Frankfurt am Main: Suhrkamp, 1998: 71–91.

Pecora, Vincent P., "Nietzsche, Genealogy, Critical Theory," *New German Critique*, 53 (1991): 104–30.

Pensky, Max, *The Actuality of Adorno: Critical Essays on Adorno and the Postmodern*. Albany: State University of New York Press, 1997.

Pepper, Thomas, "Guilt by (Un)free Association: Adorno on Romance et al.," *MLN*, 109 (1994): 913–37.

Piccone, Paul, "From the New Left to the New Populism," *Telos*, 101 (1994): 173–208.

——"Introduction," in *The Frankfurt School Reader*, ed. Andrew Arato and Eike Gebhardt. New York: Urizen, 1978.

Pickford, Henry, "Bedeutung, Wahrheit, Kritik: Davidson, Rorty und Adorno," in *Philosophische Diskurse. Grenzen der Ästhetik*, ed. Jörg H. Gleiter and Gerhard Schweppenhäuser. Weimar: Universitätsverlag Bauhaus-Universität Weimar, 2000.

——"Critical Models: Adorno's Theory and Practice of Cultural Criticism," *Yale Journal of Criticism*, 10 (1997): 247–70.

——"Under the Sign of Adorno," *MLN*, 108 (1993): 564–83.

Pollock, Della, "Aesthetic Negation after World War II: Mediating Bertolt Brecht and Theodor Adorno," *Literature in Performance: A Journal of Literary and Performing Art*, 8 (1988): 12–20.

Pollock, Friedrich, "Is National Socialism a New Order?" *Studies in Philosophy and Social Science*, 9 (1941): 440–55.

——"State Capitalism: Its Possibilities and Limitations," *Studies in Philosophy and Social Science*, 9 (1941): 200–25.

Posnock, Ross, "Henry James, Veblen, and Adorno: The Crisis of the Modern Self," *Journal of American Studies*, 21 (1987): 31–54.

——"The Politics of Nonidentity: A Genealogy," *Boundary 2: An International Journal of Literature and Culture*, 19 (1992): 34–68.

Postone, Moishe, *Time, Labor, and Social Domination: A Reinterpretation of Marx's Critical Theory*. Cambridge and New York: Cambridge University Press, 1993.

Rawls, John, *A Theory of Justice*. Cambridge, MA: Harvard University Press, 1971.

Reich, Willi, *Alban Berg: Mit Bergs eigenen Schriften und Beiträgen von Theodor Wiesengrund-Sdorno und Ernst Krenek*. Vienna: Herbert Reichner Verlag, 1937.

Reinelt, Janelle, "Approaching the Postmodernist Threshold: Samuel Beckett and Bertolt Brecht," in *The Aesthetics of the Critical Theorists: Studies on Benjamin, Adorno, Marcuse, and Habermas*, ed. Ronald Roblin. Lewiston, NY: Edwin Mellen, 1990, pp. 337–58.

Roberts, David, *Art and Enlightenment: Aesthetic Theory after Adorno*. Lincoln: University of Nebraska Press, 1991.

Roblin, Ronald, "Collingwood and Adorno on the Popular Arts," in *The Aesthetics of the Critical Theorists*, ed. Ronald Roblin. Lewiston, NY: Edwin Mellen, 1990: 308–36.

Roderick, Rick, *Habermas and the Foundations of Critical Theory*. New York: St. Martin's Press, 1986.

Rohrwasser, Michael, *Der Stalinismus und die Renegaten. Die Literatur der Exkommunisten*. Stuttgart: J. B. Metzler, 1991.

Rose, Gillian, *Hegel Contra Sociology*. London: Athlone Press, 1981.

——— *The Melancholy Science: An Introduction to the Thought of Theodor W. Adorno*. European Perspectives. New York: Columbia University Press, 1978.

Rosen, Charles, *The Classical Style: Haydn, Mozart, Beethoven*. New York: Norton, 1972.

——— "Music à la Mode," *New York Review of Books*, 41 (23 June 1994): 55–62.

Rosenzweig, F., *The Star of Redemption*, trans. William W. Hallo. Notre Dame, IN: University of Notre Dame Press, 1970.

Rubin, Andrew, "Grand Hotel Abyss: Review of *Critical Models: Interventions and Catchwords*, by Theodor W. Adorno," *Nation*, 25 May 1998: 28–30.

Ryan, Michael, *Marxism and Deconstruction*. Baltimore, MD: John Hopkins University Press, 1982.

Rycenga, Jennifer, "Review of *We Are Everywhere*, edited by Shane Phelan and Mark Blasius," *Lesbian Review of Books*, 4 (Summer 1998): 33–4.

Said, Edward W., "Adorno as Lateness Itself," in *Apocalypse Theory and the Ends of the World*, ed. Malcolm Bull. Cambridge, MA: Blackwell, 1995: 264–81.

——— *Representations of the Intellectual*. New York: Vintage, 1994.

——— "Traveling Theory Reconsidered," in *Critical Reconstructions: The Relationship of Fiction and Life*, ed. Robert M. Polhemus and Roger B. Henkle. Palo Alto, CA: Stanford University Press, 1994: 251–65.

Samelson, Franz, "Authoritarianism from Berlin to Berkeley: On Social Psychology and History," *Journal of Social Issues*, 42 (1986): 191–208.

Sample, Colin, "Adorno on the Musical Language of Beethoven," *Musical Quarterly*, 78 (1994): 378–93.

Samson, Jim, "Analysis in Context," in *Rethinking Music*, ed. Nicholas Cook and Mark Everist. Oxford: Oxford University Press, 1999: 35–54.

Saunders, Frances Stonor, *Who Paid the Piper? The CIA and the Cultural Cold War*. London: Granta, 1999.

Schnadelbach, Herbert, "Dialektik als Vernunftkritik. Zur Konstruktion des Rationalen bei Adorno," in *Adorno-Konferenz 1983*, ed. L. von Friedeburg and Jürgen Habermas. Frankfurt am Main: Suhrkamp, 1983: 66–94.

Scheuerman, William, *Between the Norm and the Exception: The Frankfurt School and the Rule of Law*. Cambridge, MA: MIT Press, 1994.

Schindler, Ronald Jeremiah, *The Frankfurt School Critique of Capitalist Culture*. Brookfield, MA: Avebury, 1996.

Schmucker, J. F., *Adorno: Logik des Zerfalls*. Stuttgart, 1977.

Schonherr, Ulrich, and Daniel, Jamie Owen, "Adorno, Ritter Gluck, and the Tradition of the Postmodern," *New German Critique*, 48 (1989): 135–54.

Schultz, Karla L., *Mimesis on the Move: Theodor Adorno's Concept of Imitation*. New York: New York University Press, 1990.

Schweppenhauser, G., *Ethik nach Auschwitz. Adornos negative Moralphilosophie*. Hamburg, 1993.

Sharpley-Whiting, T. Denean, "The Dawning of Racial-Sexual Science: A One Woman Showing, a One Man Telling, Sarah and Cuvier," *FLS*, 23 (1996): 115–28.

Shepherd, John, *Music as Social Text*. Cambridge: Polity Press, 1991.

Shepher, John, Virden, Phil, Vulliamy, Graham, and Wishart, Trevor, *Whose Music? A Sociology of Musical Languages*. New Brunswick, NJ: Transaction Books, 1997.

Siebert, Rudolf J., *The Critical Theory of Religion, the Frankfurt School: From the Universal Pragmatic to Political Theology*. Religion and Reason 29. Berlin and New York: Mouton, 1985.

Simon, Richard Keller, "Between Capra and Adorno: West's *Day of the Locust* and the Movies of the 1930s," *Modern Language Quarterly*, 54 (1993): 513–34.

Simpson, Christopher, *Science of Coercion: Communication Research and Psychological Warfare*. New York: Oxford University Press, 1994.

Singer, Alan, "The Ventriloquism of History: Voice, Parody, Dialogue," in *Intertextuality and Contemporary American Fiction*, ed. Patrick O'Donnell and Con Davis Robert. Baltimore, MD: Johns Hopkins University Press, 1989: 72–99.

Slater, Phil, *Origin and Significance of the Frankfurt School: A Marxist Perspective*. London and Boston: Routledge and Kegan Paul, 1977.

Sohn-Rethel, Alfred, *Intellectual and Manual Labor: A Critique Epistemology*. Atlantic Highlands, NJ: Humanities Press, 1983.

—— *Soziologische Theorie der Erkenntniss*. Frankfurt am Main: Suhrkamp, 1985.

Solie, Ruth (ed.), *Musicology and Difference: Gender and Sexuality in Music Scholarship*. Berkeley: University of California Press, 1993.

Söllner, Alfons, *Geschichte und Herrschaft: Studien zur materialistische Sozialwissenschaft, 1929–1942*. Frankfurt am Main: Suhrkamp, 1979.

Sonnemann, Ulrich, "Erkenntniss als Widerstand. Adornos Abusage an Aktionsgebärden und ihr Ertrag für die Kritieren von Praxis," in *Theodor W. Adorno zum Gedächtnis*, ed. H. Schweppenhauser. Frankfurt am Main: Suhrkamp, 1975: 152–76.

Spivak, Gayatri, *A Critique of Postcolonial Reason: Toward a History of the Vanishing Present*. Cambridge, MA: Harvard University Press, 1999.

Sprinker, Michael, "The Grand Hotel Abyss," *New Left Review*, 237 (Sept.–Oct. 1999).

Stamps, Judith, *Unthinking Modernity: Innis, McLuhan, and the Frankfurt School*. Montreal: McGill–Queen's University Press, 1995.

Steinberg, Michael P., "The Musical Absolute," *New German Critique*, 56 (1992): 17–42.

Steinert, Heinz, *Adorno in Wien. Über die (Un-)Moglichkeit von Kunst, Kultur und Befreiung*. Frankfurt am Main: Fischer, 1993.

Studies in Philosophy and Social Science, 9/1 (1941).

Studinski, Kristina, *Lesbians Talk Left Politics*. London: Scarlet Press, 1994.

Subotnik, Rose Rosengard, "Adorno's Diagnosis of Beethoven's Late Style: Early Symptom of a Fatal Condition," *Journal of the American Musicological Society*, 29 (1976): 242–75.

——*Deconstructive Variations: Music and Reason in Western Society*. Minneapolis: University of Minnesota Press, 1996.

——*Developing Variations: Style and Ideology in Western Music*. Minneapolis: University of Minnesota Press, 1991.

Suchoff, David, *Critical Theory and the Novel: Mass Society and Cultural Criticism in Dickens, Melville, and Kafka*. Madison: University of Wisconsin Press, 1994.

Sullivan Michael, and Lysaker, John T., "Between Impotence and Illusion: Adorno's Art of Theory and Practice," *New German Critique*, 57 (1992): 87–122.

Swift, Jonathan, *Gulliver's Travels*. New York: Oxford, 1971. [First published in 1726.]

Szondi, Peter, *Über eine "Freie (d.h. freie) Universität." Stellungnahmen eines Philologen*. Frankfurt am Main: Suhrkamp, 1973.

Tar, Zoltán, *The Frankfurt School: The Critical Theories of Max Horkheimer and Theodor W. Adorno*. New York: John Wiley, 1977.

Theunissen, Michael, *Kritische Theorie des Gesellschaft*. Berlin and New York: De Gruyter, 1981.

——"Negativität bei Adorno," in *Adorno-Konferenz 1983*. Frankfurt am Main: Suhrkamp, 1983.

Thompson, Kenneth (ed.), *Auguste Comte: The Foundation of Sociology*. London: Nelson, 1976.

Thyen, A., *Negative Dialektik und Erfahrung*. Frankfurt am Main: Suhrkamp, 1989.

Tiedemann, Rolf, "Begriff, Bild, Name. Über Adornos Utopie der Erkenntniss," *Frankfurter Adorno Blätter II*. Munich: text + kritik, 1992: 92–111.

Tomlinson, Gary, "Cultural Dialogues and Jazz: A White Historian Signifies," in *Disciplining Music*, ed. Katherine Bergeron and Philip V. Bohlman. Chicago: University of Chicago Press, 1992: 64–94.

——*Music and Renaissance Magic: Toward a Historiography of Others*. Chicago: University of Chicago Press, 1993.

——"Musical Pasts and Postmodern Musicologies: A Response to Lawrence Kramer," *Current Musicology*, 53 (1993): 18–24.

Townsend, Peter, "Adorno on Jazz: Vienna versus the Vernacular," *Prose Studies*, 11 (1988): 69–88.

Turner, Lou, "The Young Marx's Critique of Civil Society, and the Self-Limiting Emancipation of Black Folk: A Post-Los Angeles Reconstruction," *Humanity & Society*, 19 (1995): 91–107.

Varadharajan, Asha, *Exotic Parodies: Subjectivity in Adorno, Said, and Spivak*. Minneapolis: University of Minnesota Press, 1995.

Volosinov, V. N., *Marxism and the Philosophy of Language*. Cambridge, MA: Harvard University Press, 1986.

Wald, Alan, *The New Intellectuals: The Rise of the Anti-Stalinist Left*. Chapel Hill, NC: University of North Carolina Press, 1987.

Walsh, Michael, "A(dorno) to Ž(ižek): From the Culture Industry to the Joyce Industry, and Beyond," in *Joyce and Popular Culture*, ed. R. B. Kershner. Gainesville: University Press of Florida, 1996: 39–46.

Walther, Bo, "One God among the Gods: Traces of Hölderlin in Adorno and de Man," *Orbis Litterarum: International Review of Literary Studies*, 51 (1996): 1–10.

Walzer, Michael, *Interpretation and Social Criticism*. Cambridge, MA: Harvard University Press, 1987.

Warminski, Andrzej, "Hegel/Marx: Consciousness and Life," in *Hegel After Derrida*, ed. Stuart Barnett. London: Routledge, 1999: 171–93.

Weber, Max, "Science as a Vocation," in *From Max Weber: Essays in Sociology*, ed. H. H. Gerth and C. Wright Mills. New York: Oxford University Press, 1958: 124–56.

Weeks, Jeffrey, *Sexuality and its Discontents: Meanings, Myths and Modern Sexualities*. London: Routledge and Kegan Paul, 1985.

Weissberg, Lilian, "Myth, History, Enlightenment: 'The Silence of the Sirens,'" *Journal of the Kafka Society of America*, 9 (1985): 131–48.

Weissenborn, Ulrike, *"Just Making Pictures": Hollywood Writers, the Frankfurt School, and Film Theory*. Tübingen, 1998.

Wellmer, Albrecht, "Metaphysics at the Moment of its Fall," in *Literary Theory Today*, ed. Peter Collier and Helga Geyer Ryan. Ithaca, NY: Cornell University Press, 1990: 35–49.

White, Stephen K., "Foucault's Challenge to Critical Theory," in *The Aesthetics of the Critical Theorists: Studies on Benjamin, Adorno, Marcuse, and Habermas*, ed. Ronald Roblin. Lewiston, NY: Edwin Mellen, 1990: 440–75.

—— *The Recent Work of Jürgen Habermas: Reason, Justice, and Modernity*. Cambridge and New York: Cambridge University Press, 1988.

White, Stephen K., and Dumm, Thomas L., "Postmodern Aesthetics and Political Thinking," in *The Aesthetics of the Critical Theorists: Studies on Benjamin, Adorno, Marcuse, and Habermas*, ed. Ronald Roblin. Lewiston, NY: Edwin Mellen, 1990: 511–26.

Whitebook, Joel, *Perversion and Utopia: A Study in Psychoanalysis and Critical Theory*. Cambridge, MA: MIT Press, 1994.

Wiggershaus, Rolf, *Die Frankfurter Schule: Geschichte, theoretische Entwicklung, politische Bedeutung*. Munich: Carl Hanser, 1986.

—— *The Frankfurt School: Its History, Theories, and Political Significance*, trans. Michael Robertson. Cambridge, MA: MIT Press, 1994.

Wilke, Sabine, "The Role of Art in a Dialectic of Modernism and Postmodernism: The Theatre of Heiner Muller," *Paragraph: A Journal of Modern Critical Theory*, 14 (1991): 276–89.

—— "'Torn Halves of an Integral Freedom': Adorno's and Benjamin's Readings of Mass Culture," *Journal of Comparative Literature and Aesthetics*, 11 (1988): 39–56.

Williams, Alastair, *New Music and the Claims of Modernity*. Aldershot and Brookfield, VT: Ashgate, 1997.

Williams, Raymond, *Politics and Letters: Interviews with the New Left Review*. London: New Left Books, 1979.

Williams, Robert, *Hegel's Ethics of Recognition*. Berkeley: University of California Press, 1998.

Williams, Simon, "The Director in the German Theater: Harmony, Spectacle, and Ensemble," *New German Critique*, 29 (1983): 107–31.

Williamson, Ian Brian, "Adorno: The Conscience of Thinking: An Interpretation and Critique." Dissertation, University of Essex, 1992.

Witkin, Robert W., *Adorno on Music*. New York: Routledge, 1998.

—— "Why Did Adorno 'Hate' Jazz?" *Sociological Theory*, 18/1 (Mar. 2000): 145–70.

Wolin, Richard, "Benjamin, Adorno, Surrealism," *Journal of Comparative Literature and Aesthetics*, 11 (1988): 124–56.

—— "Utopia, Mimesis, and Reconciliation: A Redemptive Critique of Adorno's Aesthetic Theory," *Representations*, 32 (1990): 33–49.

Wurzer, Wilhelm S., "The Critical Difference: Adorno's Aesthetic Alternative," in *The Textual Sublime: Deconstruction and Its Differences*, ed. Hugh J. Silverman and Gary E. Aylesworth. Albany: State University of New York Press, 1990: 213–21.

—— *Filming and Judgment: Between Heidegger and Adorno*. Atlantic Highlands, NJ: Humanities Press, 1990.

Yerushalmi, Yosef, *Freud's Moses: Judaism Terminable and Interminable*. New Haven: Yale University Press, 1991.

Žižek, Slavoj, *For They Know Not What They Do: Enjoyment as a Political Factor*. London: Verso, 1994.

—— "George Lukács as the Philosopher of Leninism," *A Defence of History and Class Consciousness*. New York: Verso, 2000.

—— "Is There a Cause of the Subject?" in *Supposing the Subject*, ed. Joan Copjec. New York: Verso, 1994.

Zuidervaart, Lambert, *Adorno's Aesthetic Theory: The Redemption of Illusion*. Studies in Contemporary German Thought. Cambridge, MA: MIT Press, 1991.

—— "Methodological Shadowboxing in Marxist Aesthetics: Lukács and Adorno," *Journal of Comparative Literature and Aesthetics*, 11 (1988): 85–113.

Index

Abbate, Carolyn 235, 243, 249
absolute: freedom 268–70; Hegel 20, 23, 158–9, 171n3, 257, 263–4, 272, 288n10, 302–3, 381; language 369; negativity 171n3, 259, 268, 269–70, 282, 300, 368, 371; totalitarianism 259, 268–9
abstract art 49
Adorno, Theodor W. 1–2; cultural studies 86–7, 99–106; in Frankfurt 4; as Hegelian-Marxist 257–8; as influence 1–2, 14–15, 51; Marxism 17–18, 150–1, 159–60, 201–2; music studies 2–3, 4; obituaries 111–12; in Oxford 6–7; philosophical studies 3; politics 17–19, 110–11; return to Germany 10–11, 312; in United States 7–10, 174; in Vienna 4; writing for journals 327; see also Frankfurt School; Institute for Social Research
Adorno, Theodor W. (works): "The Actuality of Philosophy" 5, 283, 290n24; Aesthetic Theory 32, 64, 203, 262, 343, 344–5, 346, 356; "Das Altern der neuen Musik" 202–3, 220; "Anweisungen zum Hören

neuer Musik" 209–10; "Art and the Arts" 85n51; "Aspects of Hegel's Philosophy" 258–9; Aspects of Sociology 319; "Aspects of the Hegelian Dialectics" 261; Ästhetische Theorie 41–2, 211, 214, 215–16, 217, 221, 223, 226–7; Beethoven: Philosophie der Musik 214, 221; Berg: Der Meister des kleinsten Übergangs 214; "Berg und Analyse" 213; Catchwords 313; Composing for Films 9, 52, 58; Critical Models 159, 322–3; "Critique" 182; "Cultural Criticisms and Society" 22–3; "The Culture Industry Reconsidered" 51; "The Curves of the Needle" 4; Dialectic of Enlightenment 8, 9, 15, 25, 40, 58, 66–7, 116–17, 125, 139–41, 176–7, 281, 326, 385; Dissonances 12; "Education after Auschwitz" 121, 125–6, 129, 130, 283, 285, 318, 319–20, 330, 333, 378n25; "Engagement" 120; "Extorted Reconciliation" 120, 122–3, 180; "How to Look at Television" 94; "How to read Hegel" 389; Interventions 12, 313, 327; "An

Hohendahl, Peter 17, 120, 172, 258, 283
Hollywood 42, 45, 103, 118
Holocaust 19–20, 119
Homer 200
homosexuality 362; *The Authoritarian Personality* 362, 376n12; class-based stereotypes 365–6; *Dialectic of Enlightenment* 362; fascism 361; perpetrator/victim 373–4; psychoanalytic view 376n11; Rycenga 24; totalitarianism 366
Hoover, J. Edgar 174
Horkheimer, Max 3, 312; and Adorno 5, 111; Adorno as student 5; anti-positivism 176–8; antisemitism 135, 137–8; authoritarianism 115; Benjamin 274; culture industry 32, 87, 88, 93–9; *Dialectic of Enlightenment* 8, 9, 15, 25, 66–7, 116–17, 125, 139–41, 176–7, 281, 326, 385; dismissed from teaching 6; *The Eclipse of Reason* 150; Federal Bureau of Investigation 174; film 91; Institute for Social Research 5, 178–9; Judaism 19; "Die Juden in Europa" 132–3, 135; Marxism 150–1; Princeton Radio Project 8; "Schema der Massenkultur" 64, 65–6; social justice 307; student movement 163; *Studies in Prejudice* 159
Hullot-Kentor, Robert 138, 216, 392
Husserl, Edmund 3, 6, 317
Huysmans, J. K. 195
Huyssen, Andreas 16, 25

Ibn Khaldun 193
Ibsen, Henrik 41, 195
iconicity 58, 62–3
idealism 303–4
identity: capitalism 270–1; difference 79–80, 293–4; Hegel 260, 264, 267, 271–2, 296–7; hieroglyphic

imperative 63; ideology 270–1, 298, 321; Kant 294–5; positivism 294; subjectivity 25, 266; transcendent 271–2; *see also* non-identity
identity logic 119, 271–2
identity politics 161
identity thinking 320, 321
ideology: *The Authoritarian Personality* 153–4; capitalism 171n6; conceptual 322–3; critique 265; culture 181–2; entertainment 98; fetishism 162; Hollywood 103; identity 270–1, 298, 321; Marxism 88; mass culture 63–4, 101; personality types 153–4; racism 157; synthesis 298
image 60, 66–7, 75, 385–7
immanence, concept 323, 324–5
immediacy: Hegel 295, 297
immortality 194
inauthenticity 142
individual: capitalism 96; culture industry 87; freedom 274; Hegel 202; Odysseus 139; society 167, 316
industrialization 46, 118–19, 186, 190n88
ineffability 266, 288n12
ingroup personality 156
Institute for Social Research 5–6, 10–11, 312; Adorno 86–7; antisemitism 132–3; empirical sociology 218–19; Federal Bureau of Investigation 173; Horkheimer 5, 178–9; Marxian ideology critique 5–6, 88; mass culture 107n10; media research 94; Nazism 115; postwar 178–9; reification 88; student occupation 130, 165, 331–2; *see also* Frankfurt School
instrumentality 15, 176, 182–3, 349
intellectuals 1, 68, 75–6, 153, 166
interdisciplinarity 214
interiority 394–5
interpretation 72, 225, 243–4, 382, 391